NOLO Products & Services

→ Books & Software

Get in-depth information. Nolo publishes hundreds of great books and software programs for consumers and business owners. Order a copy—or download an ebook version instantly—at Nolo.com.

→ Legal Encyclopedia

Free at Nolo.com. Here are more than 1,400 free articles and answers to common questions about everyday legal issues including wills, bankruptcy, small business formation, divorce, patents, employment and much more.

→ Plain-English Legal Dictionary

Free at Nolo.com. Stumped by jargon? Look it up in America's most up-to-date source for definitions of legal terms.

→ Online Legal Documents

Create documents at your computer. Go to Nolo.com to make a will or living trust, form an LLC or corporation or obtain a trademark or provisional patent. For simpler matters, download one of our hundreds of high-quality legal forms, including bills of sale, promissory notes, nondisclosure agreements and many more.

→ Lawyer Directory

Find an attorney at Nolo.com. Nolo's consumer-friendly lawyer directory provides in-depth profiles of lawyers all over America. From fees and experience to legal philosophy, education and special expertise, you'll find all the information you need to pick the right lawyer. Every lawyer listed has pledged to work diligently and respectfully with clients.

→ Free Legal Updates

Keep up to date. Check for free updates at Nolo.com. Under "Products," find this book and click "Legal Updates." You can also sign up for our free e-newsletters at Nolo.com/newsletters.

21st edition

How to Probate an Estate

in California

Julia Nissley

NOLO
LAW for ALL

Twenty-first Edition	MARCH 2011
Editor	BETSY SIMMONS HANNIBAL
Cover Design	SUSAN PUTNEY
Production	MARGARET LIVINGSTON
Proofreading	CATHERINE CAPUTO
Index	ELLEN SHERRON
Printing	DELTA PRINTING SOLUTIONS, INC.

International Standard Serial Number (ISSN): 1940-6282

ISBN-13: 978-1-4133-1315-4

ISBN-10: 1-4133-1315-9

Please note

We believe accurate, plain-English legal information should help you solve many of your own legal problems. But this text is not a substitute for personalized advice from a knowledgeable lawyer. If you want the help of a trained professional—and we'll always point out situations in which we think that's a good idea—consult an attorney licensed to practice in your state.

Acknowledgments

This book was made possible through the efforts of many people. I would especially like to thank Mary Randolph and Shae Irving, two splendid editors, who reviewed the text and made numerous suggestions for improvement. Others who made valuable contributions are Jake Warner, Steve Elias, Mari Stein, Margaret Livingston, Robert Wells, and Betsy Simmons Hannibal. My gratitude also to the many readers who have taken the time to write and offer comments and suggestions. Finally, a special thank you to my former boss Alan Watenmaker, a probate and estate planning attorney in West Los Angeles, for giving me the opportunity to learn so much about the subject, my children for their patience, and especially my husband, Ron, for always being there with encouragement and support.

> **CAUTION**
>
> **The procedures in this book are for California estates only.** You cannot transfer real estate located in other states using the instructions in this book. To transfer property located outside of California, you must either learn that state's rules or consult a lawyer in the state where the property is located.

Table of Contents

15 Handling Property That Passes Outright to the Surviving Spouse or Domestic Partner

16 If You Need Expert Help

Glossary

Appendixes

DE-111   Petition for Probate

DE-120   Notice of Hearing

DE-121   Notice of Petition to Administer Estate

DE-121(MA)   Attachment to Notice of Petition to Administer Estate

DE-131   Proof of Subscribing Witness

DE-135   Proof of Holographic Instrument

DE-140   Order for Probate

Your Legal Companion for Probate

The loss of a close family member or friend can bring feelings of anxiety and uncertainty, as well as grief. While you're trying to cope and adapt to major changes, taking on the added burden of settling the deceased person's affairs may seem like too much to deal with.

This book can help.

How to Probate an Estate in California explains the major steps required to settle a simple California estate. It makes the law as easy to understand as possible, in plain English. The early chapters explain how probate works and discuss what you'll need to do first. The second half of the book guides you through the estate administration process. You'll get clear instructions for how to complete a formal probate court proceeding, how to deal with community property, how to bypass the probate court when transferring a small estate, how to handle joint tenancies, and much more.

Not all estates need a formal probate court proceeding. California law contains many shortcuts —methods for transferring property after a death without probate court proceedings, most of which can be completed in a matter of weeks.

Only when there is no other way to transfer title from the deceased person to the new rightful owner is a formal probate proceeding necessary. Even then, court involvement has been reduced to a minimum. Probate is mostly paperwork—and you can use printed, fill-in-the-blanks forms provided by the court. This book contains all the forms you'll need, and we'll show you how to fill them in and file them. Patience and the willingness to take time to carefully follow directions is all it takes. As long as the estate is without unusual problems, you can wind up the deceased person's affairs quickly and easily with the instructions in this book.

There may be times, however, when you need some expert help. This may mean hiring an attorney to advise you on one or more specific points, or it may require turning over the entire probate proceeding to an attorney. Throughout the book we alert you about possible problems that may warrant consulting a lawyer.

Please note that this book explains how to handle the estate of someone who was a resident of California at death and who owned property in this state. If the deceased person lived elsewhere or owned real estate in another state, this book is not for you.

If you're in the midst of grieving, you may wonder whether you can cope with the details and possible complexities of settling a loved one's affairs. We can only suggest that you give it a try. You don't have to do everything at once; we'll let you know what can wait until you're ready. And sometimes the concentration needed to do bureaucratic work can even be a form of therapy, especially when you realize that your efforts will help preserve the estate and distribute it as your loved one intended. Good luck.

An Overview

What Is Probate?

Many people aren't sure what the term "probate" really means. They think of it only as some long, drawn out, and costly legal formality surrounding a deceased person's affairs. Technically, probate means "proving the will" through a probate court proceeding. A generation ago, virtually every estate had to be reviewed by a judge before it could pass to those who would inherit it. Today there are several ways to transfer property at death, some of which don't require formal court proceedings, so the term is now often used broadly to describe the entire process by which an estate is settled and distributed.

For example, a surviving spouse or domestic partner may receive property outright from the deceased spouse or partner without any probate proceedings at all. Joint tenancy property also escapes the need for formal probate, as does property left in a living (inter vivos) trust and property in a pay-on-death bank account (Totten trust). If an estate consists of property worth less than $100,000, it, too, can be transferred outside of formal probate. Fortunately, the paperwork necessary to actually transfer property to its new owners in the foregoing situations is neither time-consuming nor difficult. We discuss all of these procedures, as well as how to do a formal probate court proceeding.

There is one thing you should understand at the outset: The person who settles an estate usually doesn't have much choice as to which property transfer method to use. That is, whether you are required to use a formal probate or a simpler method to transfer property at death depends on how much (or little) planning the decedent (deceased person) did before death to avoid probate. This is discussed in detail as we go along.

Both formal probate and some of the other nonprobate procedures involve filing papers at a court clerk's office, usually in the county where the decedent resided at the time of death. In larger counties, going to the main courthouse and other government offices in person can be an ordeal. To avoid this, you may settle most simple estates entirely by mail, even if a formal probate court proceeding is required. In other words, most probate matters don't require that you appear in court before a judge. In fact, settling an estate by mail is now the norm in many law offices. We will show you how to do this as we go along.

What Is Involved in Settling an Estate?

Generally, settling an estate is a continuing process which:

- determines what property is owned by the decedent
- pays the decedent's debts and taxes, if any, and
- distributes all property that is left to the appropriate beneficiaries.

When a person dies, she may own several categories of assets. Among these might be household belongings, bank and money market accounts, vehicles, mutual funds, stocks, business interests, and insurance policies, as well as real property. All property owned by the decedent at the time of his or her death, no matter what kind, is called his or her "estate."

To get this property out of the name of the decedent and into the names of the people who inherit it requires a legal bridge. There are several types of legal procedures or bridges to move different kinds of property to their new owners. Some of these are the equivalent of large suspension bridges that will carry a lot of property while others are of much less use and might be more analogous to a footbridge. Lawyers often use the word "administrate" and call this process "administering an estate." In this book we refer to these procedures collectively as "settling an estate."

Most of the decedent's estate will be passed to the persons named in his or her will, or, if there is no will, to certain close relatives according to priorities established by state law (called "intestate succession"). However, to repeat, no matter how property is held, it must cross an estate settlement bridge before those entitled to inherit may legally take possession. The formal probate process is but one of these bridges. Some of the other bridges involve community property transfers, clearing title to joint tenancy property, winding up living trusts, and settling very small estates that are exempt from probate. Again, we discuss all of these in detail.

How Long Does It Take to Settle an Estate?

If a formal probate court procedure is required, it usually takes from seven to nine months to complete all the necessary steps, unless you are dealing with a very complicated estate. On the other hand, if the decedent planned his or her estate to avoid probate, or the estate is small, or everything goes to a surviving spouse or domestic partner, then the estate may be settled in a matter of weeks by using some easier nonprobate procedures.

 CAUTION
The procedures in this book are only for California estates. Real property and tangible personal property (see Chapter 4 for definitions) located outside of California are not part of a California estate and cannot be transferred following the instructions in this book. To transfer property located outside of California, you will either have to familiarize yourself with that state's rules (these will be similar, but by no means identical to those in effect in California) or hire a lawyer in the state where the property is located.

What This Book Covers

Not all estates can be settled entirely by using a self-help manual. Although most California estates can be settled easily with the procedures described in the following chapters, some will require at least some formal legal assistance. Therefore, it's important to know if the one you are dealing with is beyond the scope of this book.

First, an estate that can be settled using this book (a "simple estate," for lack of a better term) is one that consists of the common types of assets, such as houses, land, a mobile home, bank accounts, household goods, automobiles, collectibles, stocks, money market funds, promissory notes, etc. More complicated assets, such as complex investments, business or partnership interests, or royalties from copyrights or patents, are often not as easy to deal with because they involve additional factors, such as determining the extent of the decedent's interest in the property and how that interest is transferred to the new owner. However, it may be possible to include unusual assets in a simple estate if the person settling the estate is experienced in such matters or has help from an accountant or attorney along the way. When questions arise as to ownership of an asset, or when third parties (anyone not named in the will or by intestacy statutes) make claims against the estate (as would be the case if someone threatened to sue over a disputed claim), you have a complicated situation that will require help beyond this book.

Second, for an estate to be "simple" there should be no disagreements among the beneficiaries, especially as to the distribution of the property. There is no question that dividing up a decedent's property can sometimes bring out the worst in human nature. If you face a situation where family members are angry and lawsuits are threatened, it is not a simple estate. To settle an estate without unnecessary delays or complications and without a lawyer, you need the cooperation of everyone involved. If you don't have it (for example, a disappointed beneficiary or family member plans to contest the will or otherwise engage in obstructionist behavior), you will have to try to arrange a compromise with that person by using formal mediation techniques or the help of a person respected by all disputants. If this fails, you will need professional help. (See Chapter 16.)

Third, and contrary to what you might think, a simple estate does not have to be small. The only additional concern with a large estate is federal estate taxes, which affect estates of at least $5 million for deaths in 2011 and 2012. Estate income tax returns may also be required. You can hire an accountant who is familiar with estate taxes to prepare the necessary tax returns for you, leaving you free to handle the rest of the settlement procedures yourself. We provide an overview of estate taxation in Chapter 7.

Simple Estate Checklist

The checklist below shows all the basic steps in settling a simple estate in California. Each step is thoroughly explained later in the book.

This list may appear a bit intimidating at first, but don't let it discourage you. Not all of these steps are required in every situation, and even then you won't find them difficult. As with so many other things in life, probating a simple estate is much like putting one foot in front of the other (or one finger after another on your keyboard). If you take it step by step, paying close attention to the instructions, you should have little difficulty. Remember, if you get stuck, you can get expert help to solve a particular problem and then continue with the rest.

Important Terms in Probate

As you read through this material, you will be introduced to a number of technical words and phrases used by lawyers and court personnel. We define these as we go along, with occasional reminders. If you become momentarily confused, refer to the glossary, which follows Chapter 16.

The Gross Estate and the Net Estate

You will encounter the terms "gross estate" and "net estate" while settling any estate. The distinction between the two is simple as well as important. The decedent's gross estate is the fair market value at date of death of all property that he owned. It includes everything in which the decedent had any financial interest—houses, insurance, personal effects, automobiles, bank accounts, unimproved land, etc.—regardless of any debts the decedent owed and regardless of how title to the property was held (for example, in a living trust, in joint tenancy, or as community property). The net estate, on the other hand, is the value of what is left after subtracting the total amount of any mortgages, liens, or other debts owed by the decedent at the time of death from the gross estate.

EXAMPLE: Suppose Harry died, leaving a home, car, stocks, and some cash in the bank. To arrive at his gross estate you would add the value of all his property without looking to see if Harry owed any money on any of it. Let's assume that Harry's gross estate was $500,000. Now, assume when we check to see if Harry owed money, we discover that he had a mortgage of $150,000 against the house. This means his net estate (the value of all of his property less what he owed on it) would be worth $350,000.

EXAMPLE: If Bill and Lorie, husband and wife, together own as community property a house, car, and savings account having a total gross value of $800,000, and owe $300,000 in debts, the net value of their community property would be $500,000. However, if Lorie died, only one-half of their property would be included in her estate because under California community property rules, discussed in detail in Chapter 4, the other half is Bill's. Thus, Lorie's gross estate would be $400,000 and her net estate $250,000.

The Probate Estate

The "probate estate," quite simply, is all of the decedent's property that must go through probate. This is very likely to be less than the total amount of property the decedent owned, because if an asset already has a named beneficiary, or if title is held in a way that avoids probate, then it isn't part of the probate estate. To return to the bridge analogy we discussed earlier, this means that property which is held in one of these ways can be transferred to the proper beneficiary using one of the alternate (nonprobate) bridges.

As a general rule, the following types of property need not be probated:

- joint tenancy property
- life insurance with a named beneficiary other than the decedent's estate
- pension plan distributions
- property in living (inter vivos) trusts

Checklist for Settling a Simple Estate

☐ **1.** Locate the will, if any, and make copies.

☐ **2.** Order certified copies of the death certificate.

☐ **3.** Determine who will be the estate representative.

☐ **4.** Determine the heirs and beneficiaries and get their names, ages, and addresses.

☐ **5.** Determine the decedent's legal residence.

☐ **6.** Collect insurance proceeds, Social Security benefits, and other death benefits.

☐ **7.** Arrange for final income tax returns and estate fiduciary income tax returns, if required.

☐ **8.** Assemble and list assets such as:

- Bank accounts
- Cash and cash receivables, uncashed checks, money market funds
- Promissory notes and other debts owing to decedent
- Stocks and bonds (including mutual funds)
- Business interests, copyrights, patents, etc.
- Real property
- Antiques and collectibles, motor vehicles (including motor homes)
- Miscellaneous assets including household goods and clothing, and
- Insurance.

☐ **9.** Determine whether each item of property is community or separate property and how title is held (for example, in the decedent's name alone, in joint tenancy, etc.).

☐ **10.** Estimate the value of each asset and, if the decedent was a co-owner, the value of his or her share.

☐ **11.** List debts and obligations of decedent unpaid at date of death, including:

- Funeral and last illness expenses
- Income taxes
- Real property taxes
- Encumbrances or liens on real or personal property
- Debts outstanding, and
- Approximate expenses of administering the estate, such as court filing fees, certification fees, appraisal fees, etc. (These fees usually total less than $800, unless the estate is large.)

☐ **12.** Determine priority of debts.

☐ **13.** Pay debts having priority, as soon as estate funds are available.

☐ **14.** Prepare and file U.S. estate tax return, if required.

☐ **15.** Determine method of transferring assets:

- Terminate joint tenancy title to property; transfer bank trust accounts to beneficiaries.
- Transfer estates under $100,000 without formal probate administration.
- Transfer property going outright to surviving spouse or domestic partner without formal probate.
- If property is in a living trust, the trustee named in the trust document may transfer (or administer) the trust property in accordance with the trust's provisions.
- Begin simple probate court proceedings if necessary to transfer other property. (A detailed checklist of the steps in the actual probate court process is in Chapter 13.)

How to Settle an Estate

Preliminary Steps: Examine decedent's files, records, and safe-deposit box for will and burial instructions; collect asset information; determine estate representative; obtain certified copies of death certificate; notify government agencies; ascertain heirs and beneficiaries; and collect insurance proceeds and death benefits payable to named beneficiaries (Chapters 2, 3, 4).

List assets, determine date-of-death values, and figure out how title is held. (See Chapters 5 and 6.) Does the gross value of the estate exceed the estate tax exemption? (See Chapter 7.)

No | **Yes**

File a federal estate tax return (Form 706) within nine months of date of death (Chapter 7).

Do any assets pass outright to a surviving spouse or domestic partner, either under a will or by intestate successsion?

No | **Yes**

Title may be confirmed in name of surviving spouse or partner with Spousal or Domestic Partner Property Petition (Chapter 15).

Are any assets held in joint tenancy?

No | **Yes**

Are any joint tenancy assets the community property of decedent and his or her surviving spouse or domestic partner?

No | **Yes**

Clear joint tenancy title in names of survivors (Chapter 10).

Did decedent have a living trust?

No | **Yes**

Are the trust assets registered in the name of the trust?

No | **Yes**

Is the gross value of the estate $100,000 or less (excluding joint tenancy or properly registered trust assets or assets that pass to a surviving spouse or domestic partner)?

No | **Yes**

Transfer trust property to trust beneficiaries (Chapter 12).

Transfer assets using summary probate procedures (Chapter 11).

Commence probate court procedures to transfer assets to beneficiaries (Chapters 13 and 14).

No formal probate required.

- money in a bank account that has a named beneficiary who is to be paid on death (this is sometimes called a "Totten trust")
- individual retirement accounts (IRAs) or other retirement plans that have named beneficiaries, and
- community property or separate property that passes outright to a surviving spouse or domestic partner (this sometimes requires an abbreviated court procedure).

Put another way, the probate estate (property that must cross the formal probate bridge) consists of all property except the property that falls into the above categories. Where there has been predeath planning to avoid probate, little or no property will have to be transferred over the probate court bridge. To repeat, whether or not probate is needed is not in your hands. The decedent either planned to avoid probate, or didn't—there is nothing you can do once death has occurred.

CAUTION

You can simplify the settlement of your own estate, however. The best resources covering this subject are *Plan Your Estate*, by Denis Clifford (Nolo), and *8 Ways to Avoid Probate*, by Mary Randolph (Nolo). You can also find lots of good information at Nolo's Wills, Trusts & Estates Center at www.nolo.com.

The Taxable Estate

Although this book is primarily about settling an estate, we include some mention of taxes because estates over a certain value are required to file a federal estate tax return. Therefore, you should know how to compute the value of the decedent's estate for tax purposes, which—not surprisingly—is called the "taxable estate." Keep in mind that the property that must go through probate (probate estate) is not necessarily the same as the taxable estate. Not all assets are subject to probate, but they are all counted when determining whether estate taxes must be paid. In other words, the taxable estate includes all assets subject to formal probate, plus joint tenancy property, life insurance proceeds (if the decedent was the owner of the policy), death benefits, property in a living trust, and property in any other probate avoidance device. However, if any of the assets are community property (discussed in Chapter 4), only the decedent's one-half interest is included in his or her taxable estate.

If the estate is large enough to require a federal estate tax return, any tax is computed on the net value of the decedent's property (net estate). That is, the tax is determined by the value of all property, less any debts owed by the decedent and certain other allowable deductions.

Insolvent Estates

An "insolvent estate" is one that does not have enough assets to pay creditors in full. Insolvent estates are subject to special rules and we do not include specific details here. Usually you must consult an attorney.

In general, however, creditors are divided into classes according to their respective priorities. (Probate Code § 11420.) First priority is given to debts owed to the United States or to the State of California, such as various taxes. Those debts must be paid before other debts or claims. (Probate Code § 11421.) Next in priority are administration expenses (attorneys' fees, court costs, etc.) and, after that, funeral expenses, last illness expenses, judgment claims, and general creditors are paid, in that order. Each class is paid in full before going to the next class.

When you come to a class that cannot be paid in full, the payments are prorated. For example, if Creditor One is owed $5,000 and Creditor Two is owed $10,000 and only $1,000 is left, Creditor One gets one-third of the $1,000 and Creditor Two gets two-thirds. An accounting must be presented for insolvent estates in a formal probate court proceeding. In summary proceedings (Chapter 11), the successors are responsible for paying the decedent's unsecured debts out of the property they receive. The debts are paid in the same order, and the successors are not personally liable for debts that exceed the value of the estate property.

Estate Taxes

Not every estate will owe estate taxes. A person who dies in 2011 or 2012 may own up to $5 million in property without having to pay any estate taxes. Estates having a gross value over the exemption must file a federal estate tax return. The tax is computed on the net estate after certain allowable deductions have been taken.

If the net estate is under the exempt amount, a return must still be filed if the estate has a gross value over the exemption amount, although no tax will be owed. For example, if someone who dies in 2011 has a gross estate of $5.2 million and debts of $400,000, a federal estate tax return must be filed, although no tax will be due because the debts reduce the net value of the estate to less than the $5 million exempt amount. We discuss federal estate tax in more detail in Chapter 7.

California does not impose its own inheritance tax or estate tax.

> **⊙ CAUTION**
>
> **Pay taxes first.** Although most estates don't have to worry about federal estate taxes, if yours is a large estate for which federal estate taxes are due, the taxes should be paid before property is transferred to the people who inherit it. Many wills set aside money for the payment of taxes, so this isn't a problem.

Federal and state income tax returns for the decedent's last year and sometimes for the estate (if there is a formal probate) must also be filed. (See Chapter 7.)

Do You Need an Attorney?

The law does not require you to hire an attorney to settle an estate. The average simple estate can be settled with the guidelines and background information in this book. Nevertheless, some complications that require special knowledge or handling may crop up even in an otherwise simple estate. Some examples are:

- Ambiguities in the will. For example: "I give $50,000 to the poor children in the County Hospital." This would raise several problems. Does "poor" mean low income or just unfortunate enough to be in the hospital? And what did the decedent intend when it came to dividing the money? Is it to be divided among all the children in the hospital, or did the decedent intend to set up a central fund to be used to make life a little easier for all kids in the hospital?
- Contested claims against the estate (for example, a surviving spouse or domestic partner who claims a community property interest in property left by will to someone else);
- The decedent's unfinished contracts (for example, a sale of real property begun but not completed prior to death);
- Insolvent estates (more debts than assets);
- Claims against the estate by people who were left out or think they were given too little; or
- Substantial property given to a minor, unless legal provisions to handle this are made in the will.

Besides the satisfaction of doing the estate work yourself, another advantage is not having to pay attorneys' fees. In a probate court proceeding, standard attorneys' fees have been set by law and are based on a percentage of the gross estate (the gross value of the assets that are subjected to probate). It's important to understand, however, that even though allowed fees are set out in the statute, you have the right to negotiate a lower fee with your lawyer. In other words, think of these statutory fees as the *maximum* the attorney is allowed to charge, and negotiate downward from there.

"Gross value" refers to the total value of the property before subtracting any encumbrances or debts owed by the decedent. Computing attorney's fees based on the gross estate, of course, means lawyers do very well, since the gross value of the property is often higher than the value of what the decedent actually owned after the debts and encumbrances are subtracted. For instance, the gross value of your house may be $350,000, but after you subtract your mortgage, you may actually own only a portion of this (say $50,000). Yet the attorney's fees are based on the $350,000 gross value figure.

The formula for computing attorneys' fees in a formal probate court proceeding is found in California's Probate Code §§ 10810 and 10811. An attorney may collect:

- 4% of the first $100,000 of the gross value of the probate estate
- 3% of the next $100,000
- 2% of the next $800,000
- 1% of the next $9,000,000
- 0.5% of the next $15,000,000, and
- a "reasonable amount" (determined by the court) for everything above $25,000,000.

For example, in a probate estate with a gross value of $100,000 the attorney is allowed $4,000; in an estate with a gross value of $200,000 the attorney may collect $7,000, and so on. If, for example, a probate estate contains only one piece of real property, perhaps an apartment building worth $600,000, the attorney could collect $15,000 to transfer title in a probate proceeding, even if the building might have a substantial mortgage that reduces the decedent's equity to only $150,000.

If an estate doesn't require formal probate because it can be settled in another way, such as a community property transfer to a surviving spouse or domestic partner or a joint tenancy termination, then an attorney is not entitled to receive a statutory fee. In these situations, an attorney will bill for his or her time at an hourly rate, which commonly varies from $200 to $400 an hour.

Executor's Fees

In a probate court proceeding, the court appoints a personal representative to handle the estate, called either an "executor" (if there is a will) or an "administrator" (if the decedent died without a will or without naming an executor in his or her will). This person is entitled to fees, called the estate representative's "commission." These fees are set in the Probate Code, and are listed in this book in Chapter 13. Because the commission is subject to income tax and most probates are family situations where the executor or administrator is a close relative or friend who will inherit from the decedent anyway, the executor's or administrator's fee is often waived.

EXAMPLE: Returning to Harry's estate for a moment (discussed above), if a lawyer were hired to probate Harry's estate, the attorney's fee could be as high as $13,000, computed on a gross estate of $500,000. Let's assume that Harry's will left all of his property to his daughter, Millicent, and son, Michael, and one of them, acting as executor, probated Harry's estate without an attorney and also waived the executor's fee. The entire job could be accomplished through the mail for the cost of adminstration expenses only, which would amount to about $1,500 (including filing, publication, certification, and appraisal fees).

California is one of only a few states with this kind of fee system. The California Law Revision Commission has recommended that statutory fees be abolished, but the legislature hasn't acted.

Some people hire attorneys to settle even simple estates for much the same reason they order over-fancy funerals. When a friend or loved one dies, everyone close to the decedent is naturally upset. It often seems easier to hire an expert to take over, even one who charges high fees, than to deal with troublesome details during a time of bereavement. Obviously, there is nothing we can do to assuage your grief. We would like to suggest, however, that expending the time and effort necessary to keep fees to a minimum and preserve as much of the decedent's estate as possible for the objects of his or her affection is a worthy and honorable endeavor, and may even constitute a practical form of grief therapy.

Just because you do not wish to hire an attorney to probate an entire estate, however, does not mean you should never consult one as part of the estate settlement process. As we discuss in detail in Chapter 16, there are at least three times we believe a consultation with a lawyer is wise:

- **Complicated estates.** As noted above, not all estates are relatively simple. If the estate you are dealing with is likely to be contested, or has complicated assets, such as a going business owned by the decedent or substantial income from royalties, copyrights, trusts, etc., see a lawyer.

- **Questions.** If, after reading this book, you are unsure of how to proceed in any area, get some help. You should be able to consult an attorney at an hourly rate, clear up the problem area, and then finish the estate settlement job on your own.

- **Checking your work.** If you face a fairly involved estate, you may want to do all the actual work yourself and then have it checked by a lawyer before distributing the estate. This will be much less expensive than paying the attorney to handle the whole job and, at the same time, it will make you feel more secure. ⬤

First Steps in Settling an Estate

When someone dies, everything stops in connection with the decedent's affairs, and someone must step in and take charge of things until the estate is settled and the property transferred to its new owners. This person is usually called the "estate representative," or sometimes the "decedent's personal representative."

You may already know that you are going to be the estate representative, either because you were named in the will as executor, because you are the closest living relative in a position to handle things, or because you inherit the bulk of the decedent's estate. If that's the case, you can safely skip or skim the first section of this chapter, which explains how the estate representative is normally chosen. But carefully read the second and third sections, which set out your responsibilities and duties as representative.

Who Should Act as the Estate Representative?

Who will serve as estate representative depends on a number of factors: whether or not the decedent left a will, whether the will named someone to be executor, whether that person is willing or able to serve, and so on. About the only definite legal requirement is that the estate representative, whether formally appointed or acting informally, must be over 18 years of age, of good moral character, and competent. Normally, the representative must first be formally appointed by the court before having authority to act on behalf of the estate.

If There Is a Will That Appoints an Executor

If the decedent left a will naming an executor, normally this is who will be the estate representative unless the executor named in the will is unwilling or unable to serve. In that case, the alternate executor named in the will is next in line to be the estate representative. If a formal probate court proceeding is necessary (discussed in Chapter 6), the executor named in the will is appointed by the court and issued a formal badge of office, called "Letters Testamentary." If no formal probate is necessary because you are dealing with a small estate (one that goes to a surviving spouse or domestic partner, or one that for one of the reasons discussed in Chapter 6 qualifies as a small estate), then the executor named in the will (or the alternate, if the first choice can't serve) normally serves as the informal estate representative.

If There Is No Will

If there is no will, a court appoints an "administrator" as estate representative if a formal probate proceeding is necessary. If no formal probate is necessary because an estate is small, or the decedent planned his or her estate using probate avoidance devices such as joint tenancy, or because the estate goes mostly to the surviving spouse or domestic partner, then no administrator is formally appointed. In this situation, a close relative, often the person who inherits the bulk of the estate, serves as an informal estate representative.

Assuming probate is necessary, the administrator is appointed by the probate court according to a certain order of priority, with a surviving spouse or domestic partner, or a child of the decedent usually handling the job. The administrator must be a United States resident. If a person having priority to be administrator does not want to serve, he or she may sign a document stating that although he or she is entitled to be administrator, he or she does not wish to assume the responsibility and wishes to nominate someone to act in his or her place. If the person making the nomination is a surviving spouse or domestic partner, child, grandchild, parent, brother, sister, or grandparent of the decedent, this nominee has priority after those in the same class as the person making the request. For example, if a decedent's son does not wish to be the administrator and nominates someone to serve in his place, his nominee does not have priority over the decedent's daughter, but would have priority over more distant relatives.

> **EXAMPLE:** Andy died a resident of California, leaving no will. His surviving relatives are four children. He leaves no surviving spouse or domestic partner. Any or all of his children are

entitled to priority as administrators of his estate; if none wishes to serve as administrator, any one of them may nominate someone else—not necessarily a relative of the decedent.

The logic behind the priority system is simple. Relatives who are entitled to inherit part or all of the estate under intestate succession laws (we discuss these in Chapter 3) are entitled to priority, because lawmakers feel that a person who is entitled to receive property from the estate is the person most likely to manage it to the best advantage of all the heirs. Below is the priority list for appointing an administrator, which is contained in Section 8461 of the Probate Code.

If the Will Appoints No Executor or an Executor Who Can't or Won't Serve

Sometimes a will does not name an executor, or names a person who has since died, or names someone who for some reason does not want to act as the estate representative.

CAUTION

Former spouses. If a former spouse is named as executor and the marriage was dissolved or annulled after January 1, 1985, the former spouse is prevented from serving as executor, unless the will provides otherwise. (Prob. Code § 6122.) This law also applies to domestic partners.

If there is a will, but no coexecutor or alternate executor is named, and formal probate is necessary, the court will appoint an "administrator with will annexed" (sometimes called an "administrator C.T.A.") to act as representative. An administrator with will annexed is appointed in the same order of priority as a regular administrator, except that any person who receives property under the will has priority over those who don't. (Prob. Code § 8441.) Any person, regardless of his or her relationship to the decedent, who takes over 50% of the value of the estate under the will and is a resident of the United States has first priority to serve as administrator or to appoint any competent person to act as administrator with will annexed.

Priority List for Appointing an Administrator When Someone Dies Without a Will

a. Surviving spouse/domestic partner*
b. Children**
c. Grandchildren
d. Other issue (great-grandchildren, etc.)
e. Parents
f. Brothers and sisters
g. Issue of brothers and sisters
h. Grandparents
i. Issue of grandparents (uncles, aunts, first cousins, etc.)
j. Children of a predeceased spouse or domestic partner
k. Other issue of a predeceased spouse or domestic partner
l. Other next of kin
m. Parents of a predeceased spouse or domestic partner
n. Issue of parents of a predeceased spouse or domestic partner
o. Conservator or guardian of the estate of the decedent acting in that capacity at the time of death
p. Public administrator
q. Creditors
r. Any other person.

* For purposes of these provisions, persons qualify as domestic partners only if they have filed a Declaration of Domestic Partnership with the California Secretary of State. (Prob. Code §§ 8461 and 8462.)

** Normally, one child, selected informally within the family, will serve. However, two or more children may petition to be coadministrators.

EXAMPLE: Sally died a resident of California, leaving a will giving all of her property to her boyfriend, Mort. Sally's will does not name an executor. Mort is entitled to priority as administrator with will annexed because he receives all property under Sally's will, even though Sally may have surviving relatives. If Mort does not wish to serve as administrator, he may appoint anyone of his choosing to be administrator with will annexed of Sally's estate, because he is entitled to inherit over 50% of the estate.

If Formal Probate Isn't Necessary

As you now know, many estates do not require a formal probate court proceeding. (If you are in doubt as to whether or not probate will be required, read Chapter 6.) More and more estates avoid probate because many people now carefully plan their estates. Formal probate isn't necessary if most of the decedent's assets were held in joint tenancy or in a trust, as community or separate property that passes outright to a surviving spouse or domestic partner, or in small estates containing property valued under $100,000. (See Chapter 11.)

If a formal probate court proceeding is not necessary, there is no court-appointed representative for the estate. This, of course, raises the question of who informally acts as the estate representative. Sometimes, where through extensive planning a decedent has left most property outside of the will, there will also be a will naming an executor. In this instance, the executor named in the will usually takes over informally, and does whatever is necessary to help settle the estate and transfer the property. If there is no will naming an executor, a close relative or trusted friend is a logical choice—preferably one who will inherit most, or at least part, of the estate. Normally, families and friends decide this among themselves, and it is not uncommon for several people to share the responsibility. If there is a major dispute as to who this should be, you should see a lawyer.

Responsibilities of the Estate Representative

Acting as an estate representative can be a tedious job, but in most cases it doesn't require any special knowledge or training. Your main responsibilities are to be trustworthy and reasonably organized.

Organize Your Material

Organization is the best tool of anyone who wants to wind up the affairs of a deceased person efficiently and without frustrating delay. As you go along, the information and material you collect should be arranged in an orderly manner.

A good way to do this is to have a separate legal-sized file folder (available at office supply stores) for each category of information. For instance, one folder may hold unpaid bills, another may hold copies of income tax returns, another could be for official documents like the will and death certificate, and still others may be reserved for information on specific assets, such as insurance, real property, stocks, or bank accounts. Then, when you get involved in one or another of the actual steps to transfer assets described in this book, you can set up an additional folder for each (for example, formal probate or community property transfers). The folders should be kept together in one expansion file or file drawer. If you have a lot of material to organize, you might find it helpful to arrange it in the same order as the checklist in Chapter 1.

The Estate Representative's Fiduciary Duty

The principal duty of the representative, whether court appointed or acting informally, is to protect the estate and to see that it is transferred to the people who are entitled to it. In other words, the representative must manage the assets in the best interests of all persons involved in the estate (this includes creditors and taxing authorities) until the property is delivered to the beneficiaries.

The law does not require the representative to be an expert or to display more than reasonable prudence and judgment, but it does require the highest degree of honesty, impartiality, and diligence. This is called in law a "fiduciary duty"—the duty to act with scrupulous good faith and candor. As a fiduciary, the representative cannot speculate with estate assets and must keep all excess cash not needed to administer the estate in safe, interest-producing investments approved by the court. (These include bank accounts or insured savings and loans accounts or obligations of the U.S. maturing in one year or less.)

If you, as an estate representative, breach your fiduciary duty, you are personally liable for any damages. Specifically, if you commit a wrongful act that damages the estate, you are personally financially responsible; although, if you are without fault, you will be indemnified (paid back) by the estate. In addition, if you advance your own interests at the expense of the estate, the court can remove you as executor. Finally, if you improperly use estate money for your own needs, you will be cited to appear before the court and probably charged criminally.

In a formal probate court proceeding, the estate representative may have to post a bond (see Chapter 13) to guarantee he or she will carry out the fiduciary duties faithfully; however, the decedent's will or the beneficiaries acting together usually waive bond requirements, preferring to rely on the honesty of the representative. This makes sense, because normally the estate representative is a family member or close friend who stands to inherit a substantial part of the estate and who is highly unlikely to act improperly.

Note of Sanity: You may be reluctant to serve as a personal representative of an estate without a lawyer, fearing that even if you make an innocent mistake, you will be held personally liable. This is very unlikely in a simple estate where the assets and beneficiaries are clearly established. However, if you face an estate with a great many assets and a large number of beneficiaries, you may have a legitimate cause for concern. One way to feel secure that you have met your duty of care is to check all of your conclusions (and paperwork) with a lawyer before actually distributing assets. Since you will be doing all the actual work yourself, having a lawyer merely to check your work needn't be expensive. See Chapter 16.

Specific Duties of the Estate Representative

Whether acting formally or informally, your job as an estate representative is to take possession of the decedent's property and safeguard it until all obligations of the estate are met and the remaining assets are distributed to the proper persons. If the decedent lived alone, the residence should be made secure, and all valuables and important papers removed to a safe place. Here are some of your main responsibilities as representative.

Determine the Residence of the Decedent

In order for the estate to be settled under California law, the decedent must have been a resident of this state, or owned property in California, when he or she died. The principal factor that determines residence is the decedent's state of mind—whether at the time she died she considered California, and a particular place within this state, as her permanent residence. Usually, the decedent will have established some permanent ties to California, but sometimes it isn't absolutely clear what a decedent intended. Here are several factors important to making this determination:

- the length of time the decedent lived in the place
- where his or her driver's license was issued
- the location of the decedent's business assets and bank accounts, and
- the place where the decedent voted.

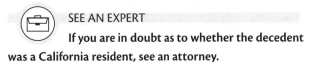

SEE AN EXPERT

If you are in doubt as to whether the decedent was a California resident, see an attorney.

If the decedent was a California resident, it is also necessary to determine the county of his or her residence, because this is where the court proceedings will be held, if any are required. Normally, where a person resides is clear enough, but occasionally, as would be the case if the decedent was ill or elderly and had moved to live with relatives or in a rest home, there may be a question as to whether he or she had changed his or her residence. If the decedent was temporarily staying in a hospital or care facility at the time of death, while intending to return to his or her usual residence, the permanent home ordinarily determines the county of residence.

Locate the Will

Make a thorough search for the most recent will and any codicils that may exist. If there is no will, the decedent is said to have died "intestate," and the persons who will inherit his or her property are determined under state law. (See "If There Is No Will," in Chapter 3.)

Wills may be either "formal" or "holographic." A formal will is one that is signed by witnesses. A holographic will is one that is written and signed in the handwriting of the person making the will. (A commercially printed form will that is completed in the testator's own handwriting is valid as a holographic will. Prob. Code § 6111 (c).) A holographic will need not be witnessed or dated. However, if it is undated and there is another will with inconsistent provisions, the holographic will is invalid to the extent of the inconsistency, unless the time it was signed can be established by other evidence. If you face this sort of highly unusual situation, see a lawyer.

A codicil is a later document that supplements or modifies a will. It may also be either formal or holographic. A formal, witnessed will can have a holographic codicil, although this is unusual. Normally, a codicil is used to make a relatively small addition, subtraction, or change in a will, as would be the case if the decedent bought or sold a piece of property that would alter the will. Sometimes, however, codicils make major changes in a will that conflict with or are inconsistent with the language of the original will so that it's difficult to understand what the decedent intended. In this situation, you would be wise to have the will and codicil interpreted by a lawyer before continuing the probate process on your own. We discuss how to consult a lawyer to get particular questions answered in Chapter 16.

Most people keep their wills in a fairly obvious place, such as a desk, file cabinet (often at the office), a safe-deposit box, closet, or shelf, or entrust it to their lawyer. Banks usually allow a member of the surviving family to open a safe-deposit box in the presence of a bank officer to search for a will or burial instructions. However, nothing else may be removed until the box is officially released. (See "Examine Safe-Deposit Boxes," below.)

When you find a will, make six photocopies, which you will need at various stages of the estate work. Be sure each page of the photocopy is complete and that the signatures are legible. You are under no obligation to provide copies of the will to anyone. After a will is admitted to probate, it becomes public record.

If Someone Else Has the Will: Probate Code § 8200 requires anyone in possession of a will to deliver it to the clerk of the Superior Court for safekeeping within 30 days after being informed of the death and to mail a copy to the named executor. The usual procedure followed by attorneys, however, is to file the original will at the same time a Petition for Probate is filed, if such a proceeding will be commenced. This avoids the possibility of the original will being misplaced by the court, which would delay the filing of the petition. In nonprobate matters, where the original will is not required by the court, it is a good idea for the named executor to keep the will in a safe place with other valuable papers. If someone delivers a will to you, it is appropriate to give him or her a receipt if he or she requests one.

Obtain Certified Copies of the Death Certificate

When a person dies in California, an official death certificate is filed in the county health department or vital statistics office of the county where the death occurred. The death certificate provides important personal information about the deceased person, including Social Security number, date of birth and death, occupation, and cause of death. You will need certified copies of the death certificate to carry out many of your tasks as estate representative—for example, collecting insurance proceeds and other death benefits, and transferring jointly owned property. You should order at least ten certified copies to save time and avoid arguments with petty bureaucrats about whether they will accept a photocopy.

The easiest and quickest way to obtain certified copies of the death certificate is to ask the mortuary you deal with to obtain them for you and add the cost to your bill. This is a common practice, and the mortuary will know how to make the arrangements.

If you need to order death certificates yourself, you can do so by contacting the vital records office in the county where the person died; this office is usually called the county recorder's office or the county clerk. Death certificates are normally available from the county a few weeks after the death. You can expect to pay between $10 and $15 per copy.

TIP

If an autopsy is required. If an autopsy is performed after the death, it may delay the final death certificate by several months. In this case, you will receive an interim death certificate that indicates the cause of death is "deferred." Financial institutions and government agencies will accept this certificate, but insurance companies will not. (They need to know the cause of death before processing claims.)

Because of concerns about identity theft, California allows only certain individuals to obtain certified copies of a death certificate. (Health & Safety Code § 103526.) If you are the executor or a close family member, however, you won't have a problem getting the documents you need.

To order, you must fill out the county's application form and submit it along with a "certificate of identity" that proves you are entitled to receive certified copies. You must sign the certificate of identity in front of a notary public. In most California counties, you can download a death certificate request form and a certificate of identity from the county website. You can find the website by visiting the California State Association of Counties website at www.csac.counties.org. Once there, select "California's Counties," and then choose "County Web Sites." Of course, you can also obtain the

necessary forms by visiting or calling the county recorder's office. Sample forms from Los Angeles County are shown below.

RESOURCE

Ordering from the state. If six months or more have passed since the death, you can order death certificates from the California Department of Health Services. It can take up to six weeks to process a request, however, so even the state office recommends that you get death certificates from the county, if you can. If, for some reason, you must order from the state, you can find information on the Department of Health Services website at www.dhs.ca.gov. Choose "Services" and look for the link about ordering death certificates.

Ascertain the Heirs and Beneficiaries

As we will discuss in more detail in Chapter 3, an heir is a person who inherits if there is no will or alternative estate plan, according to the laws of intestate succession. A beneficiary, on the other hand, is a person who inherits under the terms of a will. If the decedent left a will, you should determine the names, ages, and exact addresses of the beneficiaries named in the will. If any are deceased (or don't survive the decedent by any period of days specified in the will), you should carefully read the will to ascertain the names of alternate beneficiaries. We discuss how to do this in detail in Chapter 3. Occasionally, you will find that a beneficiary has predeceased a decedent and no alternate beneficiary is named, or that there are other problems in determining who inherits. Again, we discuss this in detail in Chapter 3.

Even if an estate must go through formal probate (we discuss this in detail in Chapter 6), you must determine the names, ages, and exact addresses of the decedent's heirs (the people who would inherit if there were no will). At first this may not make much sense; why do you need to figure out who would inherit in the absence of a will, if, in fact, there is one? The answer is simple. In a formal probate court proceeding (discussed in Chapter 14), the heirs must be listed on a Petition for Probate so they can be

Sample Request for Death Certificate: Los Angeles County

COUNTY OF LOS ANGELES • REGISTRAR-RECORDER/COUNTY CLERK, P.O. BOX 489, NORWALK, CA 90651-0489 (562) 462-2137

APPLICATION FOR DEATH RECORD

Pursuant to Health and Safety Code 103526, the following individuals are entitled to an AUTHORIZED Certified Copy of a death record.

- ◆ A member of a law enforcement agency or a representative of another governmental agency, as provided by law, who is conducting official business.
- ◆ A child, grandparent, grandchild, sibling, spouse or domestic partner of the registrant
- ◆ An attorney representing the registrant or the registrant's estate, or any person or agency empowered by statute or appointed by a court to act on behalf of the registrant or the registrant's estate.
- ◆ Any funeral director or agent/employee of a funeral establishment acting within the scope of their employment who orders certified copies of a death certificate on behalf of any individual specified in paragraphs (1) to (5), inclusive of subdivision (a) of Section 7100 of the Health and Safety Code.

If applying in person the application must be signed in the presence of the cashier.

Those who are not authorized may receive an INFORMATIONAL Certified Copy with the words "INFORMATIONAL, NOT A VALID DOCUMENT TO ESTABLISH IDENTITY" imprinted across the face of the copy.

MAIL REQUESTS <u>MUST</u> BE ACCOMPANIED BY A NOTARIZED CERTIFICATE OF IDENTITY

☐ I am requesting an AUTHORIZED copy ☐ I am requesting an INFORMATIONAL copy

	NUMBER OF COPIES / NUMERO DE COPIAS			FOR RECORDER USE ONLY
	Month/Mes	Day/Dia	Year/Año	————————
Date of Death – Fecha De Defuncion				

NAME OF DECEASED (first, middle , last) –NOMBRE DEL DIFUNTO (primero, segundo, apellido)

File Number

Searched ——————

CITY OF DEATH - CIUDAD DE DEFUNCION

Doubled ——————

RELATIONSHIP TO REGISTRANT (SEE ABOVE) - PARENTESCO CON LAS PERSONA REGISTRADA (VEÁSE ARRIBA)

I _____ certify (or declare) under penalty of perjury under the laws of the State of California that the foregoing is true and correct.

Date _____ Signature_____

Veterans-See reverse side
of first copy
Veteranos-Vean el dorso
de la segunda copia

DL/ID_____

NAME/NOMBRE		
STREET ADDRESS/NUMERO Y CALLE		
CITY /CIUDAD	STATE/ESTADO	ZIP/ZONA POSTAL

76A639D Rev. 12/09

Sample Certificate of Identity: Los Angeles County

COUNTY OF LOS ANGELES
REGISTRAR-RECORDER/COUNTY CLERK
P.O. BOX 489, NORWALK, CALIFORNIA 90651-0489 - www.lavote.net

"Enriching Lives"

DEAN C. LOGAN
Registrar-Recorder/County Clerk

CERTIFICATE OF IDENTITY/SWORN STATEMENT - BIRTH, DEATH & PUBLIC MARRIAGE

In accordance with California State Law, the following identifying information is required to obtain a certified copy of Birth, Death or Public Marriage Certificate. You must be one of the following to receive an authorized copy of a birth, death or public marriage record, individual named on certificate, parent, child, legal guardian/custodian, grandparents, grandchild, sibling, spouse/domestic partner, attorney for individual/estate of individual or representative of an adoption agency (birth only), funeral director or agent/employee (death only).

This certificate must be signed in the presence of a Notary.

Name(s) on Certificate	Relationship

I,_____, declare under penalty of perjury under the laws of the State of
       (Print Name)
California, that I am an authorized person, as defined in California Health and Safety Code Section 103526(c), and am eligible to receive a certified copy of the birth or death record for the individual(s) listed above.

Subscribed to the _____ day of_____ 20 _____, at _____ , _____ .
         (Day)   (Month)   (City)   (State)

_____
(Signature)

CERTIFICATE OF ACKNOWLEDGEMENT

STATE OF CALIFORNIA   )
) ss
County of   )

On_____, before me _____ personally appeared
                                     (Insert name and title of officer here)

_____, who proved to me on the basis of satisfactory evidence, to be the person

whose name is subscribed to the within instrument and acknowledged to me that he/she executed the same in his/her

authorized capacity, and that by his/her signature on the instrument the person, or the entity upon behalf of which the person

acted, executed the instrument.

I certify under PENALTY OF PERJURY under the laws of the State of California that the foregoing paragraph is true and

correct.

WITNESS my hand and official seal.

(NOTARY SEAL)

_____
     NOTARY SIGNATURE

R1995 Rev. 3/2010

notified, even if some or all of them inherit nothing under the terms of the will. The purpose is to let these people know that the decedent's affairs are being wound up so that they can object or otherwise participate if they wish. They rarely do.

In addition, if a decedent who died without a will was married or had a registered domestic partner and there will be a formal probate, you must list all heirs who might inherit something depending on whether the decedent's property is ultimately characterized as community or as separate property. Every person who could have an interest in the estate must be considered a possible heir. If there is no surviving spouse or domestic partner, there will be no community property, and you need list only the heirs of the separate property.

You are not required by law to make impractical and extended searches, but you must make reasonably diligent efforts to locate all heirs and beneficiaries. Often, questioning survivors is sufficient. You can obtain additional information from telephone directories and U.S. post office forwarding procedures, or try searching the Web.

Examine Safe-Deposit Boxes

Any safe-deposit boxes in the decedent's name should be examined for assets and important papers. Safe-deposit boxes are no longer "sealed" on the death of the box holder. In many instances, their contents can immediately be turned over to the person who inherits them. However, be sure to contact the bank before you visit, because each bank has its own procedures for opening and releasing boxes. A certified copy of the decedent's death certificate is usually required, and don't forget that you'll need the key. If you can't find it, you'll have to make an appointment to have the box drilled, with the expense charged to the estate. If you suspect a box may exist at some bank, but have no proof, write the bank or inquire in person. Most banks will tell you whether or not there is a box if you present a certified copy of the death certificate.

The procedures banks follow depend on how the box was owned and who inherits its contents.

Joint Tenancy

A joint tenancy safe-deposit box is generally released to the surviving joint tenant without delay. If the survivor wishes to have title to the box reregistered in his or her name alone, the bank will require a certified copy of the decedent's death certificate.

Surviving Spouse or Domestic Partner Inherits Everything

When property (either community or separate) goes outright to a surviving spouse or domestic partner under the decedent's will or by the law of intestate succession, it may be collected by the surviving spouse or partner without probate. (Prob. Code § 13500.) This means a surviving spouse or partner who, either by will or intestate succession, inherits all of the decedent's property can have the safe-deposit box released to him or her upon presenting to the bank a certified copy of the death certificate and a signed declaration in the form shown below, setting forth the facts that allow the box to be released to her. There is a blank sample of this form in Appendix C. The bank will also probably wish to see a copy of the decedent's will, if there is one.

Restrictions: This declaration is for personal property only, not real property. And if any of the decedent's separate property or his or her one-half interest in any community property goes to someone other than the surviving spouse or domestic partner, or if the surviving spouse or partner is given a qualified ownership in the property, the estate usually requires probate and this simple procedure can't be used. This is discussed in Chapter 15.

Safe-Deposit Box in Decedent's Name (Surviving Spouse or Domestic Partner Does Not Inherit Everything)

Probate is commonly, but not always, required when the box is in the decedent's name alone, and a surviving spouse or partner does not inherit all community and separate property. Probate is not required when the decedent leaves a small estate (broadly defined as having less than $100,000 of property, not counting property that passes outside probate). We discuss small estates and the procedures

Declaration Regarding Property Passing to Decedent's Surviving Spouse or Registered Domestic Partner Under Probate Code § 13500

The undersigned declares:

1. _____Mary Anna Jones_____

died on _____May 15_____, 20__XX__, and on the date of death was a resident of California.

2. On the date of death, decedent was married to or was a registered domestic partner of _____William F. Jones_____ , who survives the decedent.

3. Among the decedent's assets was _____safe-deposit box #41FOO, at Bank of the East, 411 Main St., San Francisco _____

_____ .

4. The decedent's interest in the described property passed to decedent's surviving spouse or partner upon decedent's death by the terms of decedent's will and any codicils to it.

or

4. The decedent died intestate and the above-described property is the community property of the decedent and the decedent's surviving spouse or partner, having been acquired during the parties' marriage or domestic partnership while domiciled in California, and not having been acquired by gift or inheritance, and passes to the decedent's surviving spouse or partner by the laws of inheritance governing passage of title from decedent in the absence of a will.

5. Decedent's surviving spouse or domestic partner therefore is entitled to have the described property delivered to that spouse or partner without probate administration, pursuant to California Probate Code § 13500.

The undersigned declares under penalty of perjury that the foregoing is true and correct and that this declaration was executed on _____July 1_____, 20__XX__, at _____San Francisco_____ , California.

William F. Jones
Signature

to deal with their assets without probate in Chapter 11. If probate is required, the bank requires a certified copy of the death certificate and a certified copy of the estate representative's letters issued by the probate court. We show you how to get these in Chapter 14. When there is no living co-owner of the box, Probate Code § 331 permits limited access by a person in possession of the key to remove wills, trusts, and burial instructions.

Small Estates

When no probate is required, as is the case with small estates (generally those with assets of $100,000 or less), the bank will usually release the box to the heirs or beneficiaries of the estate when they present a certified copy of the decedent's death certificate and sign a declaration provided by the bank. You should also present a copy of the decedent's will if there is one. This procedure, which you can use to bypass probate in a variety of small estate situations, is discussed in Chapter 11.

Collect the Decedent's Mail

If the decedent lived with relatives or friends, collecting his or her mail may not be a problem. If he or she lived alone, it is a good idea to notify the post office to have the mail forwarded to you so you may keep track of it. Assets, debts, or other important information may come to light from looking through the decedent's mail.

You should file the request in person at your local post office. The postmaster will honor forwarding instructions if provided with a certified copy of letters. If there is a delay in receiving letters, or if there is no court proceeding in which letters will be issued, the post office will usually accept a notarized statement from the individual expected to be the estate representative. For more information, call 800-ASK-USPS (800-275-8777).

Cancel Credit Cards and Subscriptions

To prevent unauthorized use, you should destroy or cut in half all credit cards in the decedent's name and return them to the company promptly with a statement that the decedent died, giving the date of death. Because many credit card companies will cancel the balance due when a cardholder is deceased if the amount owing is not substantial, it is worthwhile to inquire about this policy. You should send similar notices to businesses from which the decedent made purchases on credit. When you send the notices, it is a good idea to enclose an extra copy of the letter and ask that receipt of the notice be acknowledged by signing and returning the copy. A sample letter is shown below.

You should also cancel newspaper and magazine subscriptions. Ask for reimbursement of the unused portion of the subscription price if the amount is enough to be worth the trouble.

Letter to Credit Card Issuer

[Name of credit card company] _____
[Address] _____
[City, State, Zip] _____

Re: _____, deceased

Date of Death: _____

I am the representative of the estate of the above-named decedent.

Enclosed is the decedent's credit card,
No. _____, which has been cut in half and should be immediately canceled. Please acknowledge receipt of the card and this notice by signing the duplicate copy of this letter and returning it to me in the enclosed stamped, self-addressed envelope.

Very truly yours,

[Signature] _____
[Address] _____
[City, State, Zip] _____

Receipt acknowledged by:
_____
Name
_____
Title

Notify Government Agencies

Notice must be given to certain public entities notifying them of the decedent's death and advising them to file any claims they may have against the estate within the time allowed by law. (Probate Code §§ 215, 216, and 9200.) The estate representative, a beneficiary, or any person in possession of decedent's property is responsible for giving the notice.

Notice may be in letter form, as shown in the sample below. It should give the name, address, and telephone number of the personal representative, and it should include a copy of the decedent's death certificate. If a formal probate proceeding has been started, include the court title, case name, and number. The notice should be sent to any agency that might have a claim against the estate. Send two copies of the letter of notice, and ask the recipient to acknowledge receipt of the notice by signing the bottom and returning one copy to you. Enclose a self-addressed stamped envelope. If estate property is distributed before the time allowed for the public entity to file a claim, the distributee(s) are liable to the full extent of the claim. (Probate Code § 9203(b).)

Letter to Agency

[Name of agency] _____

[Address] _____

[City, State, Zip] _____

Re: _____, deceased

Superior Court of California, County of _____
    Case No. _____

NOTICE IS HEREBY GIVEN that the above-named decedent died on, _____, 20xx, and that letters (testamentary/of administration) were issued to _____ on _____, 20xx. Under Probate Code Section 9200, you are hereby requested to file any claim you may have against the decedent or the estate in the manner and within the time required by law. A copy of the decedent's death certificate is enclosed.

Date _____, 20xx

[Signature of Personal Representative] _____

[Name of Personal Representative] _____

[Phone Number of Personal Representative]

Receipt acknowledged by:

Name _____

Title _____

Agency _____

Franchise Tax Board

In probate proceedings with letters issued on or after July 1, 2008, the personal representative must give notice of the decedent's death to the Franchise Tax Board. If a probate proceeding is not required, the beneficiary or any person in possession of the decedent's property should give the notice. The Franchise Tax Board has four months after the notice is mailed to file a claim for any personal income taxes owed by the decedent. (Prob. Code § 9202(c).)

Mail the notice to :

    Franchise Tax Board
    Attention: Probate Unit
    P.O. Box 2952, Mail Stop A-454
    Sacramento, CA 95812

Social Security Administration

If the decedent was receiving monthly Social Security benefits, you should call Social Security at 800-772-1213 and notify them that the decedent has died. In addition, the check for the month in which the decedent died must be returned (even if he or she died on the last day of the month), along with any checks received for months after the decedent died. Checks issued at the beginning of a month (usually on the 3rd) are for the previous month. So if a recipient dies on April 28, the May 3 check must be returned. Take the check in person or mail it to your local Social Security office and get a receipt. It is illegal for anyone to cash the checks or deposit them to the decedent's account. If they are cashed, the government will require reimbursement from the estate account or the beneficiary receiving the property. If the decedent's Social Security checks were being deposited directly into his or her bank account, notify the bank to return the funds to Social Security. It may take several weeks to stop the direct deposit of checks to an account, and such monies should be kept separate and not used by the estate. You may use the sample letter below to return the checks. You can find out the address of your local office by checking the phone book or going to the agency's website at www.ssa.gov.

Director of Health Services

If an estate representative, beneficiary, or a person in possession of property of the decedent believes the decedent was receiving benefits under Medi-Cal, or was the surviving spouse or registered domestic partner of a person who received that health care, that person must notify the Director of Health Services of the death within 90 days. The Department of Health Services may file a claim against a decedent's estate to recover Medi-Cal expenditures for nursing home care for either the decedent or the decedent's predeceased spouse. In some cases, the Department may also impose a lien on a Medi-Cal beneficiary's home to recover expenses. (Prob. Code § 215, § 9202(a).)

Address the notice to:

Director of Health Services
Estate Recovery Section
MS 4720
P.O. Box 997425
Sacramento, CA 95899-7425

Victim Compensation Board

If an heir of the decedent is known to be or reasonably believed to be in a correctional facility, either the estate representative, beneficiary, or a person in possession of the decedent's property must notify the Director of the California Victim Compensation and Government Claims Board within 90 days of the decedent's death, including the name and location of the decedent's heir. The notice, with a copy of the decedent's death certificate, should be addressed to the director at his Sacramento office. The director has four months after the notice is received to pursue collection of any outstanding restitution fines or orders. (Prob. Code § 216 and § 9202(b).)

Letter to Social Security Administration

Social Security Administration
[Address of local office] _____

_____

Re: _____, deceased

Date of Death: _____

I am the representative of the estate of the above-named decedent.

Enclosed is the decedent's Social Security check for the month of _____, which is being returned as required. Please acknowledge receipt of the enclosed check by signing the duplicate copy of this letter and returning it to me in the enclosed stamped, self-addressed envelope. [*Add, if applicable:* Please stop the direct deposit of the decedent's checks immediately.]

Very truly yours,

[Signature] _____
[Address] _____
[City, State, Zip] _____

Receipt acknowledged by:

_____
Name

_____
Title

Obtain Basic Estate Information

You should learn as much about the decedent's business affairs as you can by examining all of his or her legal papers at the earliest possible time. If the decedent was not an organized person, it may take some detective work on your part to find out what his or her assets and liabilities are. Here are some suggestions:

- Examine bank books, canceled checks, notes, deeds, stock certificates, insurance policies, recent tax returns, and all other tangible evidence of property.
- Contact friends, relatives, and business associates who may have information on the decedent's assets and debts.
- Accountants and bookkeepers who prepared the decedent's tax returns may be helpful.
- County grantor-grantee indexes, assessor's records, and title companies may provide evidence of real property holdings.
- Confer with the decedent's broker or circulate an inquiry to stock companies for information on securities held by the decedent.
- Contact the decedent's employer and, if applicable, unions or professional groups, for information about life and health insurance policies or retirement plans the decedent may have had.

Keep what you find in organized files with other important estate information. Again, a convenient way to do this is to have a separate file folder for each category of information. If original documents are valuable, you may want to keep them in a secure place and make copies for day-to-day reference.

RESOURCE

Help with records. If you need help getting organized, try *Get It Together: Organize Your Records So Your Family Won't Have To,* by Melanie Cullen and Shae Irving (Nolo). It is designed primarily as a way for people to organize their own affairs so that they will not leave a mess when they die, but it is also a fine organizational tool for an estate representative. It provides a place to list the details concerning all major assets and investments.

Studying the decedent's income tax returns is a good way to discover assets. For instance, if it shows the decedent received stock dividends, you will know she owned stock. If the tax return reports interest earned, this is a clue there are savings accounts or promissory notes, or other kinds of interest-bearing assets.

Get Bank Accounts Released, If Possible

Sometimes, immediate cash may be needed to pay some obligations of the decedent, or the decedent's family may need funds for living expenses. Many people think that as soon as a person dies, all his or her cash is immediately frozen for some indefinite period. This is not true.

Obtaining the release of cash held in the name of the decedent in banks and savings and loan associations in California usually presents no substantial problems. The procedures for releasing bank accounts are similar to those required to release safe-deposit boxes:

- If the decedent held an account in joint tenancy with someone else, the bank will release the funds immediately to the surviving joint tenant.
- If the decedent held a bank account as trustee for another (called a Totten trust or a pay-on-death account), the bank will release the funds to the beneficiary if furnished with a certified copy of the decedent's death certificate.
- If the account is in the decedent's name alone, and the value of the estate is under $100,000, the bank should release the funds without the necessity of probate upon being presented with a certified copy of the death certificate and a form affidavit (usually provided by the bank) signed by the heirs or beneficiaries entitled to the account. There is a 40-day waiting period for this type of transfer, which is discussed in Chapter 11.
- If the account is held in the names of the decedent and the surviving spouse or domestic partner, or the decedent alone, and the decedent's will provides for such property to go to the surviving spouse or partner, or if the decedent didn't leave a will but the account is

community property (in which case it would go outright to the surviving spouse or partner by the law of intestate succession—see Chapter 3), then the bank may release the account to the surviving spouse or partner without probate under Probate Code § 13500. To accomplish this, the surviving spouse or partner should submit a certified copy of the decedent's death certificate to the bank, along with a copy of the will (if there is one), and an affidavit or declaration signed by the surviving spouse or partner setting forth the facts that allow her to receive the account without probate administration. A sample of this declaration is shown earlier in this chapter, and a blank sample appears in Appendix C. Alternatively, the surviving spouse or partner may obtain a Spousal or Domestic Partner Property Order from the probate court to obtain release of the account. The procedures for obtaining this order are given in Chapter 15.

- If the account is the separate property of the decedent and the estate is over $100,000 and will pass to someone other than a surviving spouse or partner, probate proceedings will ordinarily be required. Before releasing the account, the bank will need a certified copy of the letters (the formal authorization of the estate representative by the probate court) issued to an estate representative appointed in a formal probate court proceeding. The procedures for obtaining the letters are detailed in Chapter 14. It usually takes about four or five weeks to obtain the letters after the court proceeding has begun.

All funds released to an estate representative in a formal probate court proceeding should normally be placed in an estate account in the name of the representative as "Executor (or Administrator) of the Estate of _____." Obviously, if funds are released directly to a beneficiary under one of the procedures discussed just above, this isn't necessary.

Collect Life Insurance Proceeds

Life insurance claims are frequently handled directly by the beneficiary of the policy, and the proceeds are usually paid promptly. All that is usually required is a proof of death on the company's printed claim form signed by the beneficiary, a certified copy of the decedent's death certificate, and the policy itself. If you can't find the policy, ask the company for its form regarding lost policies. It's also a good idea to submit a formal request to the deceased's employer and any unions or professional groups the deceased belonged to for information about life and health insurance policies. You may discover additional policies that were in effect at the time of the decedent's death.

Always carefully examine the life insurance policy to make certain who the beneficiary is. Most policies name a primary beneficiary and a secondary beneficiary, meaning if the primary beneficiary predeceases the insured, the secondary beneficiary receives the proceeds. If the beneficiary is a secondary beneficiary, a certified copy of the death certificate of the primary beneficiary is also required.

How to Find Insurance Policies

If you haven't had any luck finding an insurance policy in the usual places (file cabinets, desk drawers, and so on), here are some other ways to track it down.

Look through cancelled checks. Even if you find a ten-year-old check to an insurance company, contact the company. The policy could still be in force.

Ask former employers and any union to which the person belonged. Some companies and unions provide free group life insurance coverage for employees and members; family members may not be aware of the policies.

Pay a service to look. For $75, you can use the policy locator service of MIB, a company that provides services to the insurance industry. It will search millions of records to see whether the deceased person owned any life insurance policies. You can get more information at www.mibsolutions.com/lost-life-insurance.

You must call or write the home or regional office of the life insurance company, inform it of the decedent's death, and request a claim form to be sent to the beneficiary. The company will want the decedent's name, the date of death, the number of the life insurance policy, and the name and address of the beneficiary.

Life insurance proceeds that are paid to a named beneficiary (other than the decedent's estate or personal representative) are not part of the decedent's probate estate and thus do not have to go before a probate court. The proceeds are payable under the life insurance contract, not by the terms of the decedent's will or the laws of intestate succession. However, the proceeds will be included in the decedent's taxable estate, if he or she was the owner of the policy. (We discuss ownership of life insurance in Chapter 7.) Many insurance policies do not indicate who the owner of the policy is, and you may have to ask the insurance company to verify this for you. It is a good idea to ask for this information when you return the claim form to the company. You should also ask the company for a copy of *Life Insurance Statement*, Form 712, which must be filed with the federal estate tax return, if one is required. A sample letter is shown below.

Collect Annuity Benefits

If the decedent had purchased annuities naming someone to receive the benefits on his or her death, the beneficiary may obtain the benefits by submitting a certified copy of the decedent's death certificate and a completed claim form to the insurance company issuing the annuity.

Collect Social Security Benefits

If the decedent was covered by Social Security, there may be lump sum death benefits and survivor's benefits payable to the surviving spouse or dependent children. Minor children or children in college may also be entitled to benefits. To determine the rights of the estate or the heirs to Social Security benefits, contact the Social Security office in person.

Letter to Insurance Company

[Name of Insurance Company]
[Address]
[City, State, Zip]
Attention: Death Claims Division

Re: _____, deceased

Date of Death: _____

Policy No.: _____

Enclosed is your claim form executed by the named beneficiary under the above policy, along with a certified copy of the decedent's death certificate and the original policy.

Please process this claim and forward the proceeds to the beneficiary at the address indicated on the claim form.

Also, please provide an original and one copy of *Life Insurance Statement*, Form 712.

Thank you for your cooperation.

Very truly yours,

[Signature]
[Address]
[City, State, Zip]

For more information, go to www.ssa.gov, where you can download booklets on survivors benefits.

The federal government does not recognize registered domestic partnerships; Social Security benefits are provided only to heterosexual spouses.

 RESOURCE

More on Social Security. To get a better idea of the rights of all family members, see *Social Security, Medicare & Government Pensions*, by Joseph Matthews with Dorothy Matthews Berman (Nolo).

Collect Veterans Benefits

Dependents of deceased veterans may be eligible for benefits. Information on veterans benefits may be obtained by phoning the Department of Veterans Affairs at 800-827-1000, or checking its website at www.va.gov. Also, you will want to see the government publication *Federal Benefits for Veterans, Dependents and Survivors*, which can be obtained in hard copy from the Government Printing Office, Washington, DC 20402 or online at www.va.gov.

Collect Railroad Retirement Benefits

Death benefits and survivors benefits may be available if the decedent was covered by the Railroad Retirement Act. If the decedent was employed by a railroad company, you should contact the nearest Railroad Retirement Board office for specific information and assistance. Or check out the board's website, at www.rrb.gov.

Prepare Decedent's Final Income Tax Returns

As another early step in settling the estate, you should also consider preparing the decedent's final state and federal individual income tax returns (Forms 1040– U.S. and 540–California) covering the period from the beginning of the decedent's tax year to the date of death. (We discuss this in detail in Chapter 7.) If the decedent is survived by a spouse, the final returns may be joint returns. (Domestic partners cannot file joint returns.) An accountant can advise you about this.

Collect Miscellaneous Death Benefits

Survivors are often faced with myriad forms, questionnaires, and regulations in the process of claiming certain disability and death benefits. These benefits are sometimes overlooked during mourning and then forgotten. Some examples are:

State Disability Income Payments: If the decedent was receiving state disability benefits at the time of death, make sure all benefits were paid through the date of death and notify the California Employment Development Department.

Workers' Compensation: If the decedent was receiving workers' compensation benefits at the time of death, notify the private insurance carrier who pays these benefits and make sure all benefits are paid.

Retirement or Disability Income From Federal Employment: If the decedent was a federal employee, the decedent's family or named beneficiaries may be entitled to benefits. Contact the agency the decedent worked for.

Benefits From Medical Insurance Through Decedent's Employment or an Association: Most employers and some unions provide group medical insurance which helps pay for medical expenses and, sometimes, funeral expenses. You should make claims to cover any expenses of a last illness, and you should ask about any additional lump sum death benefits.

Group Life and Disability Income Benefits: Life insurance or disability benefits may be payable through a group policy provided by the decedent's employer, union, or other organization. No one procedure to obtain the benefits will apply in all cases; you should contact the administrator of the plan under which death benefits are payable (or the organization obligated to pay the benefits) to ask about the procedure to follow. Usually a claim form must be signed and submitted with a certified copy of the decedent's death certificate. Death benefits are normally excluded from the decedent's probate estate if they are paid to a designated beneficiary (not the decedent's estate or personal representative), which means they can be collected without the approval of the probate court.

Who Are the Heirs and Beneficiaries?

Studies indicate that most people don't know who will inherit their property if they die without a will. In one recent survey, 55% of the people interviewed had not made a will, but 70% of them believed they knew who would inherit their property if they died without one. Then, when each was asked to name his or her heirs and how much each would receive, only 40% were correct.

This key chapter gives you, the estate representative, the information necessary to determine what is in the decedent's estate and to figure out who is legally entitled to it. Obviously, this is one of the central tasks involved in settling any estate.

Mercifully, it is usually easy to figure out which beneficiaries or heirs receive which property if the decedent did one or more of the following:

- left a simple will that effectively identified the beneficiaries (often a surviving spouse, partner, or children)
- died without a will in a situation where it is clear which relatives will inherit under state law (the law of intestate succession), or
- placed title to the bulk of his or her property in joint tenancy or a living trust.

Life is not always this easy, however. If a will is unclear, or if the decedent died without a will and left no close relatives, or in some circumstances, if the will accidentally left a child, spouse, or registered domestic partner out in the cold, it may be more difficult to decide who inherits the decedent's property.

If it is clear who inherits the property in the estate you are dealing with, skim the material in this chapter to be sure you haven't overlooked something, and then go on to the next. On the other hand, if you aren't sure who gets what property, study this chapter carefully. If it doesn't provide sufficient clarification, you will either need to do some additional research or see a lawyer.

 CAUTION
Rights for registered domestic partners. California law gives registered domestic partners most of the same rights, protections, and benefits as spouses. This chapter notes the circumstances under which a registered domestic partner is entitled to inherit a portion of a partner's estate.

Where to Start

A deceased person's property is divided (after expenses are paid) among the people who are legally entitled to inherit it. Who these people are (beneficiaries or heirs) is normally decided by:

- the terms of the decedent's will
- state law (the law of intestate succession) if there is no will
- estate planning devices such as life insurance, joint tenancy, or living trusts, which the decedent established while still living, or, more rarely,
- state law, if a will provision turns out to be ineffective or if a few types of beneficiaries are accidentally left out of the will.

Important Terms

There are two fundamental types of estates. The estate is "intestate" if there is no will and "testate" if there is a will.

Those who inherit when the estate is intestate are called "heirs." Those who inherit under wills are termed "beneficiaries" (or, more rarely, "devisees").

The identity of the heirs who stand to inherit from an intestate estate is determined by state laws, called the laws of "intestate succession." The identity of beneficiaries who stand to inherit from a testate estate is determined, as much as possible, according to the decedent's intent as reflected in the will.

The Will

If you are dealing with an estate where there is a will, the chances are good that the beneficiaries will be clearly defined and the property they are to receive will also be accurately specified. An obvious example would be a will that simply states, "I leave all my property to my husband, Aldo Anderson," or "I leave my real property located at 112 Visalia Street, Ukiah, CA, to my husband, Aldo Anderson, and all my personal property to my son, Alan Anderson, and my daughter, Anne Anderson-McGee, in equal shares."

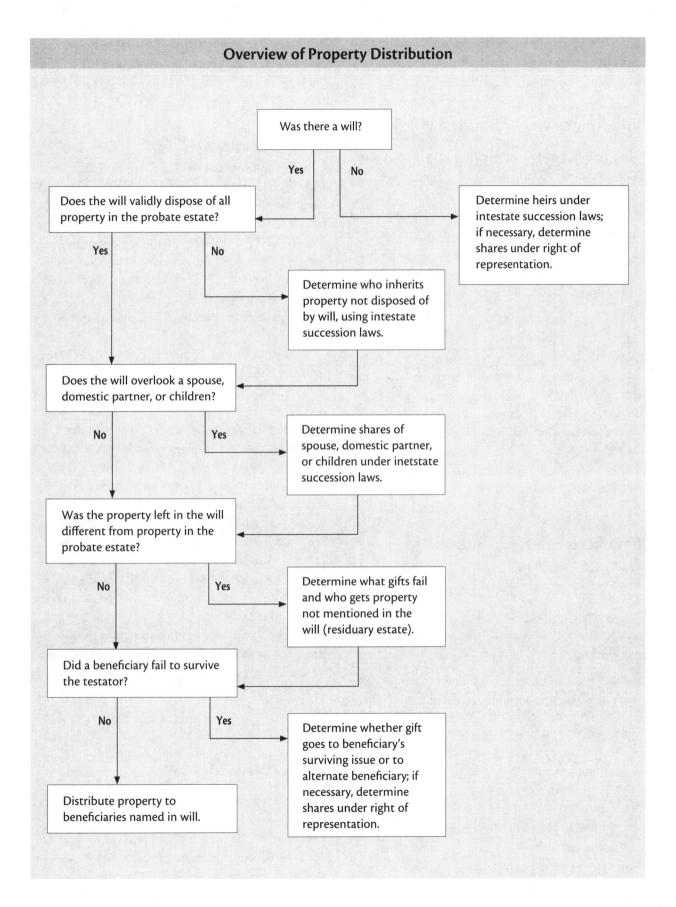

Overview of Property Distribution

Was there a will?

Yes | No

Does the will validly dispose of all property in the probate estate?

Determine heirs under intestate succession laws; if necessary, determine shares under right of representation.

Yes | No

Determine who inherits property not disposed of by will, using intestate succession laws.

Does the will overlook a spouse, domestic partner, or children?

No | Yes

Determine shares of spouse, domestic partner, or children under inetstate succession laws.

Was the property left in the will different from property in the probate estate?

No | Yes

Determine what gifts fail and who gets property not mentioned in the will (residuary estate).

Did a beneficiary fail to survive the testator?

No | Yes

Determine whether gift goes to beneficiary's surviving issue or to alternate beneficiary; if necessary, determine shares under right of representation.

Distribute property to beneficiaries named in will.

If the will you are concerned with reads like this, you can skim or skip this chapter. Otherwise, carefully read "How to Read a Will," below.

Inheritance Under State Law

More people die without a will than with one. If this is the situation you face, you obviously don't have to interpret the decedent's will. This means that, with the exception of real estate (and certain types of tangible personal property) located in another state, the decedent's property is divided according to California law. The rules are normally fairly simple; we explain them later in this chapter.

CAUTION

Out-of-state property is subject to different rules. Real estate or tangible personal property located out of state and not covered by a probate avoidance device is divided according to the intestate succession laws of the state in which it is located. Succession laws in other states are similar to, but not necessarily exactly the same as, those in California. To transfer this property, you must comply with the laws of the state where the property is located.

Beneficiary Designations Outside the Will

Various types of assets pass to beneficiaries more or less automatically, without probate. In such cases, the beneficiaries were selected by the decedent either in a contract or by some other probate avoidance arrangement. Such assets include:

- life insurance policies with a named beneficiary
- property covered by a living (inter vivos) trust
- joint tenancy property
- property held by spouses or domestic partners as community property with right of survivorship
- property in a pay-on-death account (Totten trust), and
- property placed in a life estate.

If the estate you are concerned with is entirely made up of these types of property, you can safely skip or skim this chapter because you already know who will take the property. In Chapter 6, you will find a summary of how these types of assets are transferred, with specific directions as to which of the "how to" chapters you should use to make the actual transfers.

CAUTION

Divorce can change everything. If a spouse or domestic partner was named as the beneficiary of nonprobate assets—for example, those held in a living trust, pay-on-death accounts, or by joint tenancy title—those transfers will fail if, at the time of the transferor's death, the person named as beneficiary is no longer the surviving spouse or domestic partner because the couple divorced or terminated the partnership. (Prob. Code §§ 5600–5604.) This law does not cover life insurance beneficiary designations.

To complicate matters, the U.S. Supreme Court has ruled that if the decedent named his or her former spouse as the beneficiary of an *employer-sponsored* 401(k) account, pension plan, or employer-provided life insurance policy and failed to change the beneficiary designation after the divorce, then the former spouse is entitled to the assets. (*Egelhoff v. Egelhoff*, 121 S.Ct. 1322 (2001).) The Court's decision was based on the fact that 401(k) and similar accounts, including severance plans and employee savings accounts, are governed by a federal law, the Employee Retirement Income Security Act (ERISA). That law, the Court ruled, requires the plan administrator to simply pay the proceeds to the beneficiary named by the plan participant—not to figure out who should get them under a particular state's law.

The bottom line is that where the former spouse or domestic partner is the designated beneficiary of an asset, you must take special care in determining whether he or she is entitled to receive it. Consult a lawyer if you're not sure how to proceed.

How to Read a Will

Most wills are easy to read and understand. However, at times what purports to be the "last will and testament" of the decedent may be filled with so much bewildering language that it is about as easy to decipher as the Rosetta stone. How do you, as a nonlawyer personal representative, unravel this sort of will to discover the identity of the intended beneficiaries and what they inherit? We include here several suggestions that may help. But if, after applying the suggestions you read here, you are still not absolutely sure of what the will says, you should definitely consult a lawyer. Put differently, if you aren't sure what the decedent intended, don't guess.

Some of the more common problems to watch out for are:

- attempts to dispose of property not part of the decedent's estate (for example, a house or vehicles that were sold years ago or property held in joint tenancy)
- attempts to leave property to people who have died before the decedent, where no alternate has been named
- attempts to dispose of a surviving spouse's or domestic partner's one-half of the community property, and
- omissions of a child, spouse, or domestic partner from the will.

Prepare a List of Beneficiaries

First, we suggest that you get a pencil and tear out the form entitled "Who Inherits Under the Will?" in Appendix C. After you read this section carefully and study the will, insert in the left-hand column the names of the people, institutions, and charities who might possibly inherit under it. These include named beneficiaries, unnamed beneficiaries, alternate beneficiaries, and contingent beneficiaries. Most wills don't have trust provisions, but if the one you are dealing with does, list the trust beneficiaries here. We discuss trust property below. Then, list in the right-hand column the property the will says they inherit.

In Chapter 5, you will be asked to prepare a list of all of the decedent's property. Because the property mentioned in the will might be different from the property actually existing when the decedent died, you may wish to wait and fill in the right-hand side of the chart after you have finished the detailed list in Chapter 5.

The next section contains some sample will provisions and information to assist you in solving the routine sorts of will interpretation problems you might encounter.

Common Clauses Used in Wills to Leave Property

Your first job is to read the will carefully. Most wills use several distinct types of clauses to pass property. Although the syntax and jargon in these clauses vary from will to will, they accomplish basically the same things.

Clauses That Leave Specific Property

One type of clause names beneficiaries of "specific" assets, such as a set amount of cash, certain defined securities, a particular parcel of real estate, or a particular motor vehicle. (In wills prepared prior to 1985, personal property gifts are generally termed "bequests" and gifts of real estate are called "devises." Since 1985, all gifts, whether real or personal property, are called devises.) Here are some examples:

> "I leave my house at 111 Apple Street, Anaheim, Orange County, to my son Keith." *(This is a specific devise of real property.)*

> "I give my 1995 green Chevrolet Camaro automobile to my nephew Michael." *(This is a specific bequest/devise of personal property.)*

As noted above, once you determine the people, institutions, and charities named to receive specific bequests or devises in the will, write their names on your list. Very simple, so far.

Residuary Clause

Wills also generally have what is termed a "residuary clause," which designates a beneficiary for the testator's residuary estate. This is all property not specifically disposed of by specific bequest or devise. The clause often refers to this remaining property as the "residue." Here are some examples:

> "I give, devise, and bequeath all other property, real, personal, or mixed, not previously disposed of by this will to my son, Jasper Phillips."

> "I give all the rest, residue, and remainder of my estate to the Sierra Club, San Francisco, California."

Here again, the people, institutions, or charities named to receive the residue of an estate are usually clearly stated. Add them to your list of beneficiaries. To determine exactly what they get, you will first have to go through the steps outlined in Chapter 5 to determine what the decedent owned at his or her death. Then, simply subtract the property left under the terms of the specific bequests and devises from the total estate. The residue is what's left.

> **EXAMPLE:** The decedent, Tammy Rucker, died owning $50,000 cash, a 2005 Oldsmobile, a residence in San Jose, household furniture and furnishings, and personal effects. Tammy's will disposed of her property as follows: "I give the sum of $10,000 to my son Richard. I give my 2005 Oldsmobile automobile to my nephew Reggie. I give all the rest, residue, and remainder of my estate to my husband, John." The residue of the estate going to John consists of the San Jose residence, the household furniture and furnishings, Tammy's personal effects, and the remaining cash ($40,000); that is, all property that was not otherwise specifically disposed of.

Trust Provisions

Especially where minor children are involved, it is common for a will to leave property in a simple trust for one or more beneficiaries until they reach a certain age. You will know when this is happening because the magic word "trust" is always used. It is also common for an elderly person to leave a spouse some property in a simple trust. In this way, the surviving spouse can use the income during life, with the principal going to the children (or other relatives or charities) when the surviving spouse dies. In larger estates, trusts are also used for a variety of tax planning purposes, many fairly complicated. If you are dealing with a large estate with a number of trust provisions, yours is not a simple estate, and you will need to get professional help.

Any property placed in trust goes to the person named as "trustee" (the person who cares for the property in the trust) to be held and used for the

designated beneficiaries, and turned over to them at the specified time. Here is an example:

> "I give 50 shares of IBM stock to my executor, as trustee, to be held for the benefit of my son Joseph until his twenty-first birthday. The trustee shall hold, administer, and distribute the trust as follows." *[Instructions would be spelled out here.]*

If you discover one of these provisions in the will, you should list it under the trust section in the left-hand column of the Schedule of Assets (Chapter 5) and list the designated beneficiaries, as well as the trustee, in your beneficiary chart.

Terminology Used in Wills to Denote Groups of People

Once you find the main clauses described above, you may be uncertain about who is included in them. For instance, it is common for wills to leave specific bequests and devises and residuary bequests to groups of people—for example, "my issue," "my children," or "my heirs."

If you encounter these types of group terms, proceed very carefully. Here are some definitions. Please pay close attention to them, since even the apparently simple term "children" does not necessarily mean what you might think.

Note: You may also run into the term "right of representation" (or "per stirpes"). We deal with this concept at the end of this chapter, and it is important for both interpreting wills and for figuring out who inherits if the decedent died intestate.

Issue

> "I give one-third of the residue of my estate to my sister Clara Peters. Should Clara predecease me, this gift shall go and be distributed by right of representation to her lawful issue."

"Issue" generally means all natural children and their children down through the generations. Thus, a person's issue includes his or her children, grandchildren, great-grandchildren, and so on. Adopted children are considered the issue of their adopting parents, and the children of the adopted children (and so on) are also considered issue. A term often used in place of issue is "lineal descendants."

Children

"I give the sum of $1,000 to each of the children of my two nephews, Edward Long and Charles Long, living at the date of my death."

Children include:
- biological offspring, unless they have been legally adopted by another (but see below)
- persons who were legally adopted
- children born outside of marriage, if the parent is the mother
- children born outside of marriage, if the parent is the father and he has acknowledged the child as his under California law (this can be done in writing or by the conduct of the father—for more information, see *Living Together: A Legal Guide for Unmarried Couples*, by Ralph Warner, Toni Ihara, and Fred Hertz (Nolo))
- children born to registered domestic partners (these children are legally considered to be the children of both partners), and
- stepchildren and other children if the relationship began during the child's minority, continued throughout both parties' lifetimes, and if it is established by clear and convincing evidence that the decedent would have adopted the person but for a legal barrier (if, for example, the child's biological parent would not consent).

The relationship that must have existed during the child's minority and continued throughout the parties' lifetimes is more than the mere stepchild-stepparent relationship that arises automatically upon the biological parent's remarriage. It must be a *family* relationship like that of a parent and child. Even in cases where a family relationship existed, there must still be clear and convincing evidence that the stepparent or foster parent would have adopted the stepchild or foster child but for a legal barrier. (Prob. Code § 6454.) A stepchild or foster child who is an adult but whom the decedent did not adopt will probably not qualify as an intestate heir.

Generally, adoption severs the legal relationship between biological parents and their children. However, children who have been adopted are still considered, for purposes of inheritance, children of their biological parents if both of the following exceptional circumstances apply:
- the biological parent and the child lived together at any time as parent and child, or the biological parent was married to or cohabiting with the other biological parent when the child was conceived but died before the child's birth, and
- the adoption was by the spouse of either biological parent or after the death of either biological parent. (Prob. Code § 6451.)

Parent and child relationships are covered by Probate Code §§ 6450–6455. If you have difficulty interpreting provisions that may apply to your situation, you should consult an attorney.

Heir

"I give $10,000 to my sister Julie Lee. Should Julie predecease me, this gift shall be divided among her heirs who survive me by 45 days."

An heir is any person who inherits in the absence of a will or who is entitled by law to inherit in the event an estate is not completely disposed of under a will.

Other Confusing Language

You are undoubtedly aware that the language used in wills can be extremely muddled. Lawyers tend to repeat everything several times and love to use "wherefores," "heretofores," and "parties of the third part." And even if the language in a will is relatively clear, you may encounter ambiguous statements. For instance, how would you interpret this provision: "I give $15,000 to my three sons, Tom, Dick, and Harry"? Does $15,000 or $5,000 go to each one?

Start by reading the will provision in question several times and see if it becomes clearer. Charting out the language can sometimes help. If you encounter strange words or suspect that several words mean the same thing, you can consult the glossary

Interpreting Wills

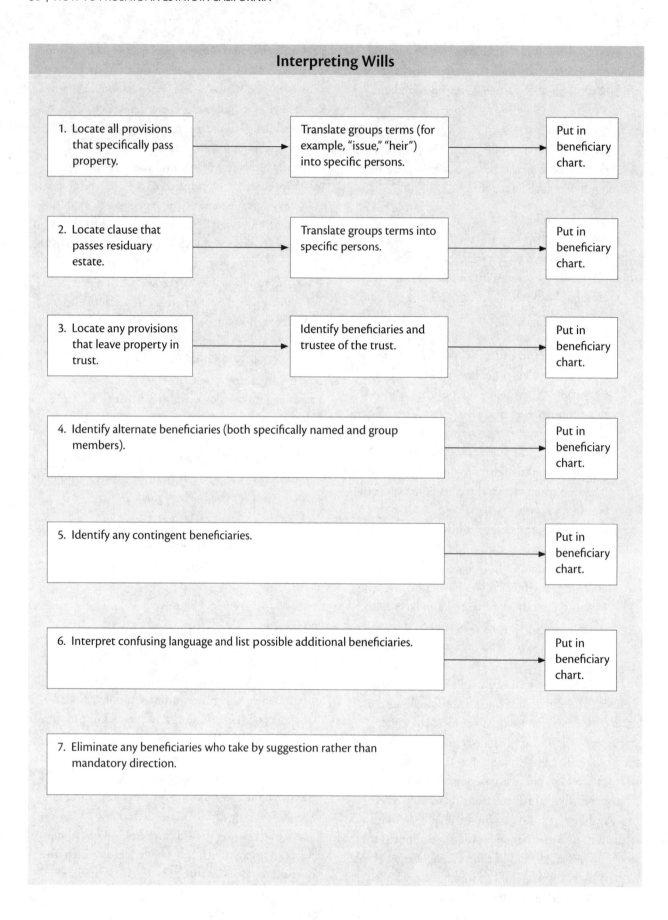

1. Locate all provisions that specifically pass property. → Translate groups terms (for example, "issue," "heir") into specific persons. → Put in beneficiary chart.

2. Locate clause that passes residuary estate. → Translate groups terms into specific persons. → Put in beneficiary chart.

3. Locate any provisions that leave property in trust. → Identify beneficiaries and trustee of the trust. → Put in beneficiary chart.

4. Identify alternate beneficiaries (both specifically named and group members). → Put in beneficiary chart.

5. Identify any contingent beneficiaries. → Put in beneficiary chart.

6. Interpret confusing language and list possible additional beneficiaries. → Put in beneficiary chart.

7. Eliminate any beneficiaries who take by suggestion rather than mandatory direction.

at the end of this book. Then see if the will provision makes sense. If it doesn't—which is very possible—consult an attorney.

Alternate Beneficiaries

Most wills specify who should get the property in the event a named beneficiary, or one or more of a group of beneficiaries, fails to survive the decedent. You should list these alternate beneficiaries in your chart. The language creating alternates is often quite straightforward:

> "If any of my children dies before I do, then that child's share shall pass equally to my surviving children."

> "I give to my wife, Jane, all of my clothing, jewelry, furniture, books, and all property of a personal nature. In the event she predeceases me, I leave all such personal property to my sister Ella."

> "I give to my son Richard my Porsche automobile, License No. _____, or, if I no longer own that automobile at my death, any automobile I own at the time of my death. Should my son predecease me, my automobile shall be left as part of my residuary estate."

Again, only you can judge whether the language is straightforward enough for you to understand it or you need the opinion of a lawyer.

Conditional Bequests

It's uncommon, but you may find bequests or devises in the will that are left to people upon one or more conditions and which will go to other people in the event the conditions are not met. In this situation, you will need to identify for your beneficiary chart both the main or primary beneficiaries and the beneficiaries who contingently stand to inherit. For example, you might find a clause leaving a house to "my three sons so long as they live in it, but if they move out, then to my sister Hannah."

Contingent and conditional gifts have long been responsible for many of the lawsuits that arise over

the interpretation of wills. (In our example, who inherits if one son moves out but the others continue to live there?) If you run into one of these clauses and are unsure of who is entitled to what, talk it over with the affected family members. If everyone is reasonable and arrives at a successful compromise, you can probably continue to handle the estate settlement work yourself. However, if a dispute festers or threatens to do so, you have to face the fact that you're not dealing with a simple estate and need professional help.

Unenforceable Will Provisions

Wills sometimes contain wishes, suggestions, or unenforceable demands. As the executor or administrator of the estate, you have no duty to comply with these, although you may wish to carry out the decedent's intentions to the greatest degree possible. For instance, suppose you encounter a will that says something like this:

> "I give to my sister Bertha all my clothing, jewelry, furniture, furnishings, books, and all other property of a personal nature with the request that she give to my children as they come of age such articles as they might desire or need."

Because the clause suggests rather than mandates, it cannot be enforced, and Bertha is legally entitled to keep all of the property.

Compare Schedule of Assets With Property Left in Will

Now that you have identified the beneficiaries of the will, your next job is to roughly compare the amount and character of the property the decedent actually left with the property mentioned in the will. To say this another way, you must ask whether the property listed in the will was still owned by the deceased person at death. We give you essential information about property in Chapter 4 and show you how to identify and list the decedent's property in Chapter 5.

Sometimes this task is easy because the will doesn't give away any specific assets but instead leaves everything to a spouse or children in clearly defined portions. For example:

> "I give, devise, and bequeath all of my estate, both real and personal, as follows: Two-thirds thereof to my wife, Mary, and one-third thereof to my son John."

However, if a decedent has left a long list of specific items to a long list of people, it can be a bit trickier. What happens, for example, if a decedent's will leaves his 2006 Dodge van to his son Herb, but the decedent sold it and used the money for a vacation? Does Herb get anything? Or, suppose the decedent leaves his share of his house to Herb, but later places the property in joint tenancy with his wife. Here are some general rules that apply if a person does not keep the will up to date and dies without owning certain assets listed in it.

Specific Gifts

A gift of a particular thing, specified and distinguished from all others of the same kind belonging to the decedent, is a specific gift. If the specific asset is not, in fact, owned by the decedent when he or she dies (or if it has been put into joint tenancy or a trust in the meantime), the gift simply fails. (The legal word for this is "lapses.") The beneficiary is not entitled to take another asset instead. Thus, in the example just above, if the decedent no longer has the 2006 van, Herb is not entitled to any other property. But if the will said, "I give any automobile I may own at the time of my death to my son Herb," and the decedent had sold the Dodge and bought a Jeep just prior to death, then Herb would inherit the Jeep.

In some circumstances, if a specific item has "merely changed form," the original beneficiary may still have a claim—if, for example, a testator leaves a promissory note due him or her to a friend, and the note is paid before his or her death, leaving easily traceable proceeds. In such a case, a court would look at the testator's intent to decide if the beneficiary should inherit from the estate.

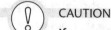

CAUTION

If you need to trace assets, you are not dealing with a simple estate. Normally, tracing involves looking at what was done with the proceeds of the sale of an asset to see if they are still identifiable. If the decedent sold a car and put the money in a new bank account, it's easy to trace. However, if the decedent put the money in an existing bank account with other funds, and lots of money flows in and out, tracing is generally not possible.

If you face a situation where some assets have been replaced by others between the time a will was drafted and when the decedent died, you should get professional help unless all people who stand to inherit agree to a sensible compromise. For instance, say the decedent left Herb a Dodge but sold it and bought a Jeep a few months before death. If everyone in the family agreed that the decedent wanted Herb to have the Jeep but simply hadn't updated his will, you would be safe in honoring this intent.

Gifts of Money

Gifts of money are called "general legacies" or "bequests" because they are not tied to specific items but rather can be satisfied by the payment of cash. If there is enough cash in the estate to satisfy the terms of the will, fine and good. However, it becomes more complicated if the will leaves a beneficiary money but insufficient cash is available when the testator dies. Suppose, for instance, that a decedent's will leaves $50,000 each to two different people (call them Herb and Cathy) and there is, in fact, only $60,000 in the decedent's estate. Here is what happens:

- If the decedent has other assets in his residuary estate (that is, they have not been left to specific beneficiaries), Herb and Cathy as "named" beneficiaries of general legacies first split what money the decedent did leave, and then take assets of sufficient value from the residuary estate to make up the difference. Typically, this involves selling residuary assets, thus decreasing the amount received by the beneficiaries of the residuary estate.
- If the decedent dies leaving only $60,000 in cash and no other assets, Herb and Cathy

would split the $60,000 in proportion to their original shares, assuming they were either both related or both unrelated to the decedent. In our example, Herb and Cathy were willed an equal amount, so they would divide the $60,000 in half. However, if Cathy was related to the decedent and Herb was not, Cathy could receive her entire bequest ($50,000) while Herb would receive only the balance. This is because the law gives preference to a spouse, domestic partner, or relative and would thus satisfy that person's legacy first, unless the will stated a different intention. If you face this situation, you may wish to consult a lawyer.

Property Left to Someone Who Doesn't Survive the Decedent

What happens if the decedent's will leaves property to someone and that person dies before the decedent? Obviously, the deceased beneficiary receives nothing. In the great majority of instances, wills provide for this by naming an alternate beneficiary. For example: "I leave $5,000 to Mary P. if she survives me. If she does not, I leave this money to Sally P." (Alternates are discussed above.)

If, however, the will does not specify an alternate beneficiary, the result will depend on the relationship of the original beneficiary and the decedent. We discuss the California laws that apply in these situations below.

Deceased Beneficiary Was a Relative

If the gift was made to any relative of the decedent, or to a relative of a surviving, deceased, or former spouse or domestic partner of the decedent, the property goes to the children, grandchildren, or great-grandchildren (termed issue) of the person named to receive it, by right of representation. "Relative" means relationship by blood or legal adoption—it doesn't include spouses. However, this doesn't apply if the beneficiary is required to survive for a specific period of time (30 days, for example). This law is called the "anti-lapse" statute, and is set forth in Probate Code § 21110. The term "right of representation" refers to how shares are

divided among the issue and is discussed in detail at the end of this chapter.

Deceased Beneficiary Was Not a Relative

If the beneficiary who does not survive the decedent was not a relative or a relative of a surviving or deceased spouse or domestic partner, and no alternate beneficiary was named, the gift simply lapses and is added to the residue of the estate. This means the relatives of the predeceased beneficiary inherit nothing, and the gift passes under the terms of the will's residuary clause. This is the clause that disposes of all property not covered by a specific devise or bequest. A residuary clause usually states something like this: "I give any and all property, real, personal, or mixed, not previously disposed of by this will, to my wife, Jane."

EXAMPLE 1: Bill, who has never married, says in his will: "I give $1,000 to my housekeeper Jennie." Jennie dies before Bill, who never changed his will. Jennie receives nothing, because she's deceased. Similarly, her children or grandchildren receive nothing (unless Jennie was a relative of Bill), because under California law, the gift lapses. The money becomes part of the residuary estate.

EXAMPLE 2: Andrew's will says, "I give $5,000 to my sister Claudia," and makes no provision for an alternative beneficiary. If Claudia dies before Andrew, Claudia's $5,000 will go to her issue (children, grandchildren, and so on) because Claudia is related to the decedent.

If Claudia left a will when she died, it would have no bearing on how the $5,000 would be distributed—the money would still go to Claudia's children. On the other hand, if Andrew's will says, "I give $5,000 to my sister Claudia, but if Claudia should fail to survive me, this gift shall go to Sally," then Claudia's issue receive nothing.

It may be easier to grasp how the antilapse laws work by studying the diagram below.

How Antilapse Laws Work

If the beneficiary of a specific bequest of devise fails to survive the testator

↓

Does the will state who should receive the property of the deceased beneficiary?

No → Was the deceased beneficiary a relative of the decedent—or of the decedent's surviving or deceased spouse or domestic partner?

Yes → The will controls whom the property should go to.

No → The gift passes through the residuary estate.

Yes → The property passes to the children, grandchildren, etc., of the deceased beneficiary by right of representation.

Property Left to Someone Who Dies Before Distribution

A beneficiary may survive the decedent—but die before the estate is closed and the property distributed. What happens then depends on what the will says.

If the will states that the beneficiary must survive a certain time or until the date of distribution, then the gift fails, and the property goes to the alternate beneficiary. If there's no alternate, it will go either to the residuary estate or to the beneficiary's children if the state antilapse law applies.

If the will doesn't have any survivorship requirement, the property is turned over to the representative of the deceased beneficiary's estate. It will go to the beneficiary's own heirs or beneficiaries. (Prob. Code §§ 11801–11802.)

Who Inherits When the Will Is Ineffective?

Wills sometimes don't have the effect that the testator may have intended. This primarily occurs in three situations:

- Spouses or domestic partners who are entitled to inherit are left out of the will.
- Children who are entitled to inherit are left out of the will.
- The will was not updated after a divorce or termination of a domestic partnership.

Let's consider these areas one at a time.

Spouse or Domestic Partner Left Out of the Will

If a person marries or enters into a domestic partnership after making a will and (a) doesn't provide for the new spouse or partner in the will or in a codicil (or by any other means), and (b) doesn't indicate an intention in the will to exclude the spouse or partner, and (c) dies first, then the surviving spouse or partner will be entitled to all the community and quasi-community property (the decedent's half and the one-half already owned by the surviving spouse or partner), plus up to one-half of the decedent's separate property. This is called the "statutory share" of the estate. (Prob. Code §§ 21600 through 21612.)

Looking at this rule from the opposite perspective, a person who married the decedent after he or she made a will and who is not provided for in the decedent's will may claim some of the estate unless:

- the decedent intentionally omitted the spouse or partner (by language such as, "I intentionally omit any future husband")
- the decedent provided for the spouse or partner by property transfers outside the will instead (such as in a marriage contract, joint tenancy transfers, or insurance proceeds), and it can be clearly shown by statements made by the decedent, by the amount of the transfer, or by other evidence that the decedent intended the transfer to be in lieu of a will provision, or
- the omitted person made a valid written agreement waiving the right to share in the decedent's estate.

 SEE AN EXPERT

Consult a lawyer if a spouse or domestic partner is left out of the will. In the unusual event that you must deal with this situation, check your conclusions with a lawyer.

Children Left Out of the Will

Here are the rules that apply if the decedent failed to provide for one or more of his or her children in the will (see Glossary for definition of children):

- If, at the time of writing a will, the decedent was unaware of the birth of a child, or mistakenly believed the child was dead, the omitted child will receive a share in the estate equal in value to that which the child would have received if the decedent had died without a will. Otherwise, the law assumes that the omission was intentional and the child inherits nothing.
- If the decedent fails to provide in the will for any of his or her children born or adopted after the execution of the will (and, thus, not foreseen at the time), the omitted child is entitled to receive a share in the estate equal in value to that which the child would have received had the decedent died without a will, unless one or more of the following conditions exists, in which case the omitted child does not receive a share of the estate:

    a. It appears from the will that the omission was intentional—for example, the will says, "I have intentionally omitted to provide in this will for my daughter Lynn," or, "I don't like my daughter Lynn and leave her nothing." Or, the will could simply name Lynn as a child and leave her nothing.

    b. When the will was signed, the decedent had one or more children and left substantially all the estate to the other parent of the omitted child.

    c. The decedent provided for the child by transfer outside the will (gifts during the decedent's lifetime, life insurance, joint accounts), and the intention that the transfer be in lieu of a will provision is shown by statements of the decedent (oral or written), and/or from the amount of the transfer or by other evidence.

Situations involving omitted children, covered by Probate Code §§ 21620 to 21623, can be intricate. If you face an estate where a child has not been mentioned in a will and has not otherwise been clearly and obviously provided for to that child's satisfaction, you have a problem. If it can't be resolved

Rights of Surviving Spouse or Domestic Partner

Did testator marry or enter into a domestic partnership after making out his or her will?

Yes / No

Did the will provide for the new spouse or partner?

No / Yes

Did the will expressly specify the testator's intent to exclude the new spouse or partner?

No / Yes

Did the testator transfer property to the spouse or partner outside of the will?

No / Yes

Is there evidence the transfer was intended to be in lieu of the will?

No / Yes

Did the omitted spouse or partner sign a written waiver of the right to share in the estate?

No / Yes

The spouse or partner is entitled to a statutory share of the estate under the intestate laws.

The spouse or partner is not entitled to a statutory share of the estate.

within the family, you should consult a lawyer before continuing.

Grandchildren: The law does not protect omitted grandchildren or more remote issue (great-grand-children) of the decedent who are living when the will is signed. If a decedent's child is deceased at the time the will was signed and the decedent failed to provide for children of that deceased child (grandchildren of the decedent), that omission is treated as intentional and the grandchildren receive nothing. However, if a child who was living when the will was made is named as a beneficiary under the will and that child dies before the decedent, leaving a child or children surviving (grandchildren of the decedent), then the grandchildren will divide the deceased child's share absent other direction in the will. We discuss how this works in "The Concept of Right of Representation," below.

Will Not Updated After Divorce

If a decedent's will gives property to his or her spouse, but the marriage to that spouse was dissolved or annulled after January 1, 1985, any gift of property made to the former spouse by the will is canceled unless the will specifically provides otherwise. The estate is then distributed as if the former spouse did not survive the decedent. However, if the divorce or annulment occurred before January 1, 1985, bequests to a former spouse stand, unless in the property settlement agreement, the parties waived their rights to inherit the estate of the other at the other's death. (Prob. Code § 6122.)

> **EXAMPLE:** Harold made a will while married to Sally that gave Sally $200,000 and the rest of his estate to his children in equal shares. The marriage was dissolved on July 1, 1986, but Harold never made a new will. Sally gets nothing on Harold's death. The $200,000 gift to her is added to the portion of the estate going to his children. However, if the divorce had occurred before January 1, 1985, Sally would get the $200,000.

Similarly, under California's domestic partnership law, if, after executing a will, the testator's (person making the will) domestic partnership is terminated, that termination revokes any gift of property to the former domestic partner. (Prob. Code § 6122.1.)

If There Is No Will

When a decedent dies without a will, you must determine the heirs of the estate under intestate succession laws. This should not be difficult if you refer to the Intestate Succession chart, below. California's intestate succession laws are set out in Probate Code §§ 6400 to 6414.

Note that the portion of the decedent's estate going to each relative first depends on whether or not the decedent was married or had a registered domestic partner when he or she died and whether the estate contains both community property and separate property, only community property, or only separate property. (We define and discuss community and separate property in Chapter 4.) Of course, if the decedent was not married, all of his or her property will be separate property.

By looking at the chart, you should get a good idea of what happens to property left by intestate succession. To summarize, if a person dies without a will:

- The surviving spouse or domestic partner inherits all community property.
- The surviving spouse or domestic partner inherits either one-third, one-half, or all of the separate property, depending on whether the decedent is survived by one or more children or other close relatives.
- Separate property not inherited by the surviving spouse or domestic partner is divided into fractional shares and distributed to the children, parents, grandparents, or brothers and sisters.

To inherit property from an intestate decedent, a prospective heir must survive the decedent for at least 120 hours. Otherwise, the prospective heir is deemed to have "predeceased" the decedent, and the heirs are determined accordingly. (Prob. Code § 6403.)

If a decedent dies intestate with no alternative estate plan—that is, a plan outside of a will for passing on his property—and leaves only more distant relatives (no spouse, domestic partner, children, grandchildren, great-grandchildren, parents or their issue, or grandparents or their issue), then the property goes to the next of kin. Deciding who will inherit involves understanding a concept called "degrees of kinship." Each generation is called a "degree." The degrees are determined by counting up to a common ancestor and then down to a decedent.

The Table of Consanguinity, below, shows the degree of different relatives. For instance, children are in the first degree, and nieces and nephews are in the third degree. Second cousins are in the sixth degree.

Terminology: In reading this chart and the ones that come later in this section, you will see that legal terminology is often used to specifically differentiate between certain persons or classes of persons. We provide simple definitions of the most important terms in the Glossary.

Although the definition of children discussed above applies when determining heirs under the intestate succession laws as well as identifying beneficiaries of a will, the statute contains some special rules for intestate succession situations. A child who has been adopted may still inherit from his or her biological parents:

- if the deceased parent was married to or cohabiting with the other biological parent at the time of the child's conception and died before the child was born, or
- if the adoption was by the spouse or domestic partner of either of the biological parents or took place after the death of either biological parent.

The Concept of Right of Representation

The concept of inheritance by right of representation (or per stirpes) can be very important in determining whether particular people will inherit property under a will (and, sometimes, by intestate succession in the absence of a will) and if so, how much.

Right of Representation Defined

Let's start with a simple definition. The right of representation means that the descendants of a deceased beneficiary take the same share collectively that the deceased beneficiary would have taken if living at the time of the decedent's death. For instance, assume John makes a bequest to his brother Tommy, and Tommy dies before John but leaves three children of his own. Unless the will provided otherwise, the children would take the bequest by right of representation—that is, the children would equally divide Tommy's bequest.

While this concept may seem straightforward, it often is not. And to confuse matters further, a statutory change has left us with two different definitions of the right of representation concept—each of which applies in certain specific situations. In other words, there is just no way to make the concept of right of representation as simple as we would wish.

When You Need to Understand Right of Representation

Fortunately, most people will not have to deal with this material at all. However, if you face one of the four situations set out just below, it is essential that you understand the concept of right of representation. Please read the following discussion carefully and see a lawyer to check your conclusions.

Situation 1: A will specifically leaves property to a group of beneficiaries using the words "by right of representation" or "per stirpes."

> **EXAMPLE:** Daisy leaves her house "to my children Myra and Andrew, but if either of them should not survive me, then to that child's children by right of representation."

Situation 2: The will provides that issue of a predeceased beneficiary should inherit their ancestor's share, but doesn't specify the method by which to determine their shares.

Intestate Succession (Who Inherits When There Is No Will?)		
Survivor(s)	**Community or Quasi-Community Property**	**Separate Property**
A spouse or domestic partner, but no issue, parent, brother, sister, or issue of deceased brother or sister	All to spouse or domestic partner	All to spouse or domestic partner
Spouse or domestic partner and one child, or issue of deceased child	All to spouse or domestic partner	½ to spouse or domestic partner ½ to only child
Spouse or domestic partner and more than one child, or one child plus issue of one or more deceased children	All to spouse or domestic partner	⅓ to spouse or domestic partner ⅔ to children*
Spouse or domestic partner, no children or their issue, but a parent or parents	All to spouse or domestic partner	½ to spouse or domestic partner ½ to parent or parents
Spouse or domestic partner, no children or their issue, no parent, but brothers or sisters or issue of deceased brothers or sisters	All to spouse or domestic partner	½ to spouse or domestic partner ½ to brothers and/or sisters or issue of deceased brothers or sisters*
No spouse or domestic partner, but issue	N/A	All to children*
No spouse or domestic partner, no surviving issue, but parent or parents	N/A	All to parent or parents‡
No spouse or domestic partner, no surviving issue, no parent, but issue of parents (brothers or sisters of decedent, or their issue if they are deceased)	N/A	All to brothers and/or sisters*‡
No spouse or domestic partner, no surviving issue, no parent, no brother or sister or their issue, but one or more grandparents or issue of grandparents	N/A	All to grandparents*‡
No spouse or domestic partner, no issue, no parent or issue of parent, no grandparent or issue of grandparent, but a predeceased spouse or domestic partner with issue surviving		Property goes to issue of predeceased spouse or domestic partner, issue taking equally if they are all the same degree of kinship to the predeceased spouse or domestic partner, but if of unequal degree, those of more remote degree take by right of representation. If decedent leaves no surviving spouse, domestic partner, issue, parents, grandparents, brothers or sisters or their issue, or issue of a predeceased spouse or domestic partner, all property goes to decedent's next of kin. If no next of kin, then all property goes to parents or issue of parents of predeceased spouse or domestic partner.

* Issue take equally if they are all the same degree of kinship to the decedent, but if of unequal degree, those of more remote degree take by right of representation in the manner provided in Probate Code § 240.

‡ If decedent leaves no spouse, domestic partner, or issue, but had a predeceased spouse or domestic partner who died within 15 years of the decedent, property in the decedent's estate attributable to the predeceased spouse or domestic partner goes to certain close relatives of the predeceased spouse or domestic partner. (Prob. Code § 6402.5.)

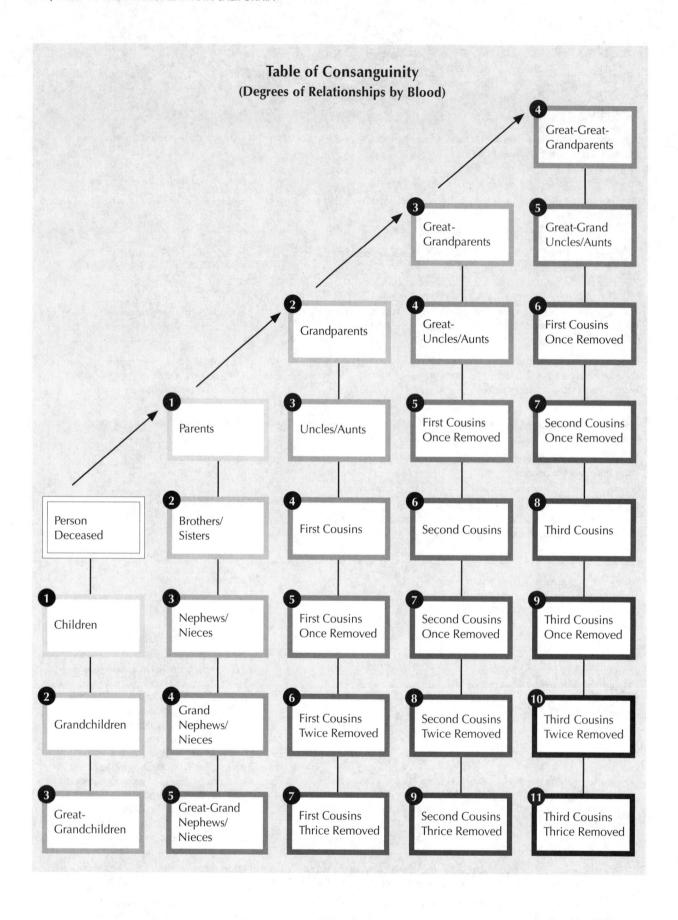

Table of Consanguinity
(Degrees of Relationships by Blood)

EXAMPLE: Daisy leaves her house "to my children Myra and Andrew, but if either of them should predecease me, then to their issue."

Situation 3: A will leaves property to a relative of the decedent and *both* of the following are true:

- The relative died before the decedent, or failed to survive the decedent by the time specified in the will (often 45–180 days).
- The will names no alternate beneficiary.

EXAMPLE: Albert left his sister Agnes $50,000 and made no provision for what would happen if Agnes died before he did, which she did. Who will inherit the money depends on how the right of representation is applied. If, however, Albert had left the same amount to his faithful, but not related, nurse, Phil, who didn't survive Albert, the gift to Phil would be wiped out. The money would pass under the residuary clause of Albert's will. Because it wouldn't go to Phil's descendants, you wouldn't need to worry about right of representation.

Situation 4: There is no will, and the intestacy laws call for succession (inheritance) by right of representation.

EXAMPLE: Jane dies without a will. Two of her three children survive her, as does a child of her predeceased child. The relevant intestate succession statute (Prob. Code § 6402) provides that Jane's issue (her children and grandchild) inherit her estate and that the grandchild takes by right of representation.

If you face one of these four situations, read on. If you don't, proceed to Chapter 4, where we discuss assessing different types of property.

The Two Meanings of Right of Representation

As we mentioned, there are currently two methods or formulas in use for determining who inherits in right of representation situations. It is essential that you

understand which one applies to the estate you are dealing with:

- Formula 1 (set out in Probate Code § 240) is used when a will provides that issue of a deceased beneficiary take but doesn't specify by what method, or when a kindred beneficiary dies before the testator, and whenever the intestate succession laws call for division by right of representation (Situations 2, 3, and 4). It is discussed in "Formula 1," below.
- Formula 2 (set out in Probate Code § 246) applies only when the will specifically calls for division by right of representation (Situation 1). It is discussed in "Formula 2," below.

Formula 1

When Formula 1 applies, you must first identify the closest generation of issue that has living members. The closest possible generation is that of the children. If there are no children living, go on to the grandchildren's generation, and so forth. The property is divided into as many shares as there are living members and deceased members who left issue living, of that generation. Each living member of the generation gets a share, and the issue of a deceased member take their ancestor's share.

EXAMPLE 1: Assume John died without a will and all three of his children, Bob, Bill, and Ben, survived him. The portion of his estate that would go to his children under the intestate laws would be divided equally among the children (the closest generation with a living member). It would look like this:

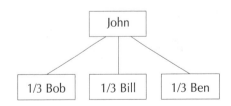

EXAMPLE 2: James makes a will and leaves his house to his three children. Two of his children, Jill and Jack, are alive when James dies. One daughter, Joyce, has died before James, but after the will was signed, leaving two surviving children, Janice and Jake (James's grandchildren). James' house would be inherited as follows: Each of his surviving children (Jill and Jack) would own one-third. The two grandchildren (Janice and Jake), inheriting their deceased parent's share equally, would each own one-sixth.

If Joyce had died before James made his will, Joyce's children (James's grandchildren) would receive nothing. They would be considered "intentionally omitted" under the law.

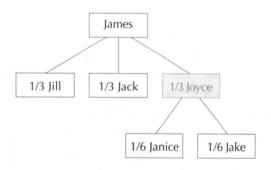

EXAMPLE 3: Jeffrey makes a will and leaves all of his property to his three children, Phil, Paul, and Peter. At Jeffrey's death, Phil survives, Paul is deceased, leaving two children of his own (Sarah and Sabrina), and Peter is deceased, leaving no children, but one surviving grandchild (Lew) of his own. Jeffrey's only surviving child, Phil, would receive one-third of the property. The two grandchildren, Sarah and Sabrina, would split their parent's share (one-sixth each), and the great-grandchild, Lew, would take his grandparent's share (one-third).

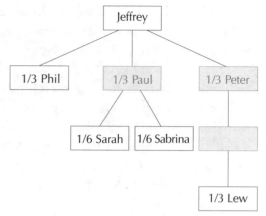

If all members in the closest degree of relationship are deceased, the property is equally divided at the next generation having a living member.

EXAMPLE 4: Angela leaves her property to her three children (Rosie, Marie, and Josefa) and none of them survives. However, Josefa leaves four children of her own, Rosie leaves two children, and Marie leaves one child. Because there are no living members in the next closest generation to Angela (that is, her children), each of the grandchildren takes an equal share (that is, one-seventh of the property).

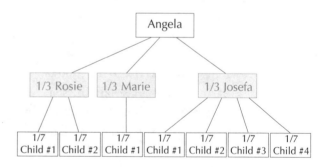

EXAMPLE 5: Suppose Rosie survived Angela. Then the other grandchildren would take only their parent's share. Thus the four grandchildren would have to split one-third of the property (one-twelfth each) while the single grandchild of the other deceased child would inherit one-third of the property.

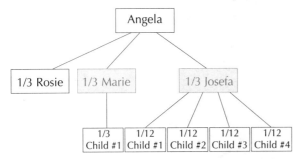

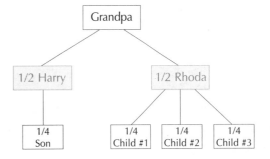

Here is a final example that demonstrates all these principles:

EXAMPLE 6: Grandpa dies without a will and leaves a childless son (Harry) and three children of a deceased daughter (Rhoda). In this situation, the estate is first divided at his children's level into two shares: one for the decedent's surviving son Harry and the other for the deceased daughter Rhoda. Harry would get half, and the three grandchildren would share the half that their mother would have had, or one-sixth each.

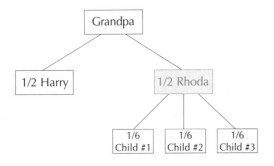

EXAMPLE 7: Suppose, however, the son also died before Grandpa and left a son. In this case, the four grandchildren would each get one-fourth. Why? Because Grandpa's property is divided first at the grandchildren's level (it being the generation closest to the decedent with a living member) instead of the children's level. Because the grandchildren are all in the same generation and are all living, they share equally.

EXAMPLE 8: If one of the grandchildren had also died and left surviving children (great-grandchildren of the decedent), then the deceased grandchild's children would share the one-fourth their parent would have received.

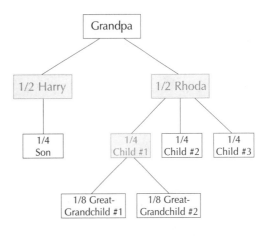

Formula 2

Formula 2 is used only if a will expressly directs that inheritance be by right of representation or per stirpes. Under this system, a generation that has no living members is not ignored; the estate is always divided first at the children's generation. This can make the distribution different than it would be under Formula 1.

For example, review the Right of Representation chart in Example 8, above. Under Formula 1, the estate is divided first at the closest generation with living members—here, the decedent's grandchildren. The three living grandchildren take one-fourth, and the fourth grandchild's share is split between his two children (the decedent's great-grandchildren).

If, however, Grandpa had left a will leaving his estate to his children or their issue by right of representation, the situation would be analyzed under Formula 2. The estate would be divided first at the children's level. Thus the estate would be divided in half, even though neither Harry nor Rhoda survived Grandpa. Harry's child would take his father's one-half share. Rhoda's two surviving children would take one-third of their mother's share (one-sixth each), and the great-grandchildren would split their parent's one-sixth share.

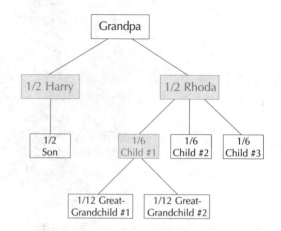

What Is the Decendent's Estate?

To settle an estate, you must first be able to identify the decedent's property. Everything the decedent owned—from real estate, bank accounts, securities, insurance, and antiques, to furniture, art, coin collections, copyrights, cars, campers, computers, collies, and canoes—collectively makes up his or her estate. We specifically instruct you on how to prepare an inventory of whatever the decedent owned in the next chapter. Our goal in this chapter is to introduce you to the basic property law concepts you must know to make sense of this inventory.

You will need to answer the following questions with respect to each item of the decedent's property:

- Is it real property (real estate) or personal property?
- Did the decedent hold title to the property in his or her own name or jointly with someone else (for example, community property, joint tenancy, or tenancy in common)?

The answers to these questions will have a direct bearing on two important points—who is entitled to the property, and what is the best method of transferring it to its new owner(s). While some very simple estates can be settled without mastering the information in this chapter, most require at least a passing knowledge of it. Start by reading this chapter carefully. We do our best to separate simple property ownership situations from those that are more complex. You may find that if your estate qualifies for the former category, you can safely leave this chapter and go on to Chapter 5 without digesting the whole thing.

TIP

Debts owed on property. For now, don't worry about whether the decedent owed money on a particular piece of property. Once ownership rules are firmly established, it will be easy to subtract debts as part of valuing the property. (See Chapter 5.)

Real Property

"Real property" is land and things permanently affixed to land, such as houses, trees, and growing crops. If a mobile home or other structure is permanently attached to the land, it is treated as part of the real property, the same as a house. However, if it is registered with the Department of Motor Vehicles or the Department of Housing and Community Development and can be taken from place to place, it is personal property. Real property also includes condominiums, leasehold interests in cooperatives, and underground utility installations. (Some life interests in condominiums and co-ops which do not survive the decedent are not considered real property.) A real estate lease with an unexpired term of ten years or longer, or a lease together with an option to purchase, or an oil or gas leasehold interest, is also treated as real property; any other leases are considered personal property. (Prob. Code §§ 10203, 10204.)

Real property is transferred to its new owners following the laws and procedures of the state in which it is located. This book covers only California real estate. To transfer real property located outside of California, you will need to find self-help information or a lawyer in that state. If the property was owned in joint tenancy with right of survivorship or title had been transferred to a living trust, you can probably handle it yourself. If formal probate is required on the out-of-state property, you will probably need a lawyer.

Real property is transferred from one person to another by a document. When both parties are living, this is usually done with a deed. Various kinds of deeds are used for this purpose, some of which you may have discovered among the decedent's papers. Most deeds are clearly labeled, but just in case you aren't sure whether a particular document is a deed, here are the basic elements. A deed must contain the name of the grantee (purchaser or person receiving title to the property), name of the grantor (seller or person conveying title to the property), a legal description of the property, a granting clause which says, "I hereby grant to …" (sometimes the words "transfer" or "convey" are used), and the signature(s) of the grantor(s). Below are some of the more common deeds and what they are used for.

Grant Deed

This is the most commonly used deed in California. The grantor (seller) conveys the property, and the grantee (buyer) receives it. The grantor in a grant deed makes certain implied guarantees that he or she owns the property and has not previously conveyed, mortgaged, or otherwise encumbered the property except as stated in the deed. A sample grant deed is shown below.

Quitclaim Deed

This type of deed is used when the grantor makes no warranties about title, saying in effect that whatever the grantor has, he or she is conveying. Assuming the grantor owns the property, this type of deed is just as effective to transfer ownership as is a grant deed. A sample quitclaim deed is shown in Chapter 12.

Joint Tenancy Grant Deed

Joint tenancy is one way two or more people may own property. A "joint tenancy grant deed" is merely any deed that is used to convey property to two or more people as joint tenants. Any grant deed or quitclaim deed can be a joint tenancy grant deed if it identifies the grantees (people who receive the property) as joint tenants. A sample joint tenancy grant deed is shown below.

Trust Deed

This type of deed is commonly used when real property is purchased and the buyer borrows part of the purchase price from a third party such as a bank or savings and loan association. In some states this document is called a "mortgage," but "deed of trust" is the term usually used in California. When a deed of trust is given, it is normally used with a grant deed, quitclaim deed, or joint tenancy grant deed as part of a single transaction.

It works like this. A grant deed is executed by the seller to convey title to the purchaser, who becomes the owner. If the purchaser needs additional money for the purchase price, he or she borrows it and executes a promissory note in favor of the lender. This involves the use of a second deed, in this case a trust deed. The trust deed, signed by the purchaser, is used to make the real estate security for money borrowed by the owner/purchaser from the bank, savings and loan, or other lender. The trust deed is actually transferred to a third-party (neutral) trustee to hold "in trust" until the lender is paid off. The trustee is normally a title insurance company. The trust deed becomes an encumbrance on the real property. Trust deeds and mortgages are recorded by their owner (usually, but not always, a financial institution) at the county recorder's office where the property is located, so they will have priority over any liens on the real property that may be recorded afterwards. When the buyer has paid in full, the trustee reconveys the title.

When someone dies and leaves real property subject to a mortgage or encumbrance, as a rule the real property passes to the new owner along with the encumbrance, unless the decedent's will provides otherwise. The new owner of the property then becomes responsible for making the payment on the mortgage, taxes, and so on. After the property is officially transferred, it is customary to notify the person or entity collecting the mortgage payments of the name and address of the new owner. No notice to the trustee is necessary.

> **EXAMPLE:** Bruce and June want to purchase a house from Sol for $170,000, but have only $70,000 in cash for the down payment. Bruce and June borrow the balance of the purchase price from a savings and loan that will accept the property as security for payment of the loan.
>
> Sol executes a grant deed transferring title to the residence to Bruce and June. At the same time, Bruce and June execute a promissory note payable to the savings and loan and execute a deed of trust transferring the residence to a trustee to hold as security for the loan. Bruce and June then take the $100,000 they have

Grant Deed

RECORDING REQUESTED BY:

Thomas B. Buyer and Helen A. Buyer

AND WHEN RECORDED MAIL TO:

Name: Thomas and Helen Buyer

Address: 35 Overview Lane

City & State: San Francisco, CA

Zip: 91378

ASSESSORS PARCEL NO.   SPACE ABOVE THIS LINE FOR RECORDER'S USE

GRANT DEED

The undersigned Grantor(s) declare(s) under penalty of perjury that the following is true and correct:

Documentary transfer tax is $ $70.65

    ❑ Computed on full value of property conveyed, or

    ☒ Computed on full value less value of liens and encumbrances remaining at time of sale.

    ❑ Unincorporated area: ❑ City of   , and

FOR A VALUABLE CONSIDERTION, receipt of which is hereby acknowledged,

George S. Seller and Mary M. Seller, his wife

hereby GRANT(S) to

Thomas B. Buyer and Helen A. Buyer, his wife

the following described real property in the City of San Francisco   , County of San Francisco State of California:

Lot 4 in Block 28, as designated on the map entitled "Twin Peaks Tract, City and County of San Francisco, State of California," filed in the Office of the Recoreder of the City and County of San Francisco, State of California, on August 5, 1909 in Volume 3 of Maps, at page 8.

Dated: __June 26, 1986__   *George S. Seller*

                         Mary M. Seller

ACKNOWLEDGEMENT

State of California   )

County of San Francisco   )

On _____June 26, 1986_____, before me, ___Nancy Notary___, personally appeared

__George S. Seller and Mary M. Seller__, who proved to me on the basis of satisfactory evidence to be the person(s) whose name(s) is/are subscribed to the within instrument and acknowledged to me that he/she/they executed the same in his/her/their authorized capacity(ies), and that by his/her/their signature(s) on the instrument the person(s), or entity upon behalf of which the person(s) acted, executed the instrument.

I certify under PENALTY OF PERJURY under the laws of the State of California that the foregoing paragraph is true and correct.

WITNESS my hand and official seal.

Signature ___*Nancy Notary*___   (SEAL)

Title Order No.   **Escrow, Loan, or Attorney File No.**

MAIL TAX STATEMENTS TO PARTY SHOWN ON FOLLOWING LINE; IF NO PARTY SHOWN, MAIL AS DIRECTED ABOVE

NAME   STREET ADDRESS   CITY & STATE

GRANT DEED

Joint Tenancy Grant Deed

RECORDING REQUESTED BY:

  Robert Doe and Mary Doe

AND WHEN RECORDED MAIL TO:

Name: Robert Doe and Mary Doe

Address: 567 First Street

City & State: Los Angeles, CA

Zip: 90017

ASSESSORS PARCEL NO.   2345   092   086   SPACE ABOVE THIS LINE FOR RECORDER'S USE

JOINT TENANCY GRANT DEED

The undersigned Grantor(s) declare(s) under penalty of perjury that the following is true and correct:

Documentary transfer tax is $ $70.40

  ☒ Computed on full value of property conveyed, or

  ❏ Computed on full value less value of liens and encumbrances remaining at time of sale.

  ❏ Uncorporated area: ❏ City of   , and

FOR A VALUABLE CONSIDERTION, receipt of which is hereby acknowledged,

  JOHN SMITH and MARY SMITH

hereby GRANT(S) to

  ROBERT DOE and MARY DOE, husband and wife

the following described real property in the City of   Los Angeles   , County of   Los Angeles   State of California:

  Lot 101 in Tract 26834, as per map recorded in Book 691, Pages 3 to 8 of Maps,
  in the Office of the County Recorder of said count.

Dated: ___June 20, 1995___   *John Smith* _____

                                             Mary Smith _____

                                             _____

                                             _____

ACKNOWLEDGEMENT

State of California   )

County of Los Angeles   )

On ___June 20, 1995___, before me, ___Nancy Notary___, personally appeared

 __John Smith and Mary Smith__, who proved to me on the basis of satisfactory evidence

to be the person(s) whose name(s) is/are subscribed to the within instrument and acknowledged to me that he/she/they

executed the same in his/her/their authorized capacity(ies), and that by his/her/their signature(s) on the instrument the

person(s), or entity upon behalf of which the person(s) acted, executed the instrument.

I certify under PENALTY OF PERJURY under the laws of the State of California that the foregoing paragraph is true and

correct.

WITNESS my hand and official seal.

Signature ___*Nancy Notary*___   (SEAL)

Title Order No.   Escrow, Loan, or Attorney File No.

MAIL TAX STATEMENTS TO PARTY SHOWN ON FOLLOWING LINE; IF NO PARTY SHOWN, MAIL AS DIRECTED ABOVE

NAME   STREET ADDRESS   CITY & STATE

JOINT TENANCY GRANT DEED

Short Form Deed of Trust and Assignment of Rents

RECORDING REQUESTED BY:

AND WHEN RECORDED MAIL THIS DEED AND,

UNLESS OTHERWISE SHOWN BELOW, MAIL TAX

STATEMENT TO:

Name:

Address:

City & State:

Zip:

Title Order No.   Escrow No.

ASSESSORS PARCEL NO.   SPACE ABOVE THIS LINE FOR RECORDER'S USE

SHORT FORM DEED OF TRUST AND ASSIGNMENTS OF RENTS

THIS DEED OF TRUST, made this _____ day of _____, between

   (Names of signer(s))   herein called TRUSTOR,

Whose address is   , a California corporation,   herein
   (Name of title insurer)

Called TRUSTEE, and   (Name(s) of beneficiary(ies))   , herein called BENEFICIARY,

Witnesseth: That Trustor IRREVOCABLY GRANTS, TRANSFERS AND ASSIGNS to TRUSTEE IN TRUST, WITH POWER OF SALE,

that property in   (City and County)   Coun ty, California, described as

   (Description of property)

TOGETHER WITH the rents, issues and profits thereof, SUBJECT, HOWEVER, to the right, power and authority given to and conferred upon Beneficiary by paragraph (10) of the provisions incorporated herein by reference to collect and apply such rents, issues and profits.

For the Purpose of Securing: 1. Performance of each agreement of Trustor incorporated by reference or contained here. 2. Payment of the indebtedness evidenced by one promissory note of even date herewith, and any extension or renewal thereof, in the principal sum of _(Amount)_ executed by Trustor in favor of Beneficiary or order. 3. Payment of such further sums as the then-record owner of said property hereafter may borrow from Beneficiary, which evidenced by another note (or notes) reciting it is so secured. To Protect the Security of This Deed of Trust, Trustor Agrees: By the execution and delivery of this Deed of Trust and the note secured hereby, that provisions (1) to (14), inclusive, of the fictitious deed of trust recorded in Santa Barbara County and Sonoma County October 18, 1961, and in all other counties October 23, 1961, in the book and at the page of Official Records in the office of the county recorder of the county where said property is located, noted below opposite the name of such county, viz.:

County	Book	Page	County	Book	Page	County	Book	Page	County	Book	Page
Alameda	435	684	Kings	792	833	Placer	895	301	Sierra	29	335
Alpine	1	250	Lake	362	39	Plumas	151	5	Siskiyou	468	181
Amador	104	348	Lassen	171	471	Riverside	3005	523	Solano	1105	182
Butte	1145	1	Los Angeles	T2055	899	Sacramento	4331	62	Sonoma	1851	689
Calaveras	145	152	Madera	810	170	San Benito	271	383	Stanislaus	1715	456
Colusa	296	617	Marin	1508	339	San Bernardino	5567	61	Sutter	572	297
Contra Costa	3978	47	Mariposa	77	292	San Francisco	A332	905	Tehama	401	289
Del Norte	78	414	Mendocino	579	530	San Joaquin	2470	311	Trinity	93	366
Eldorado	568	456	Merced	1547	538	San Luis Obispo	1151	12	Tulare	2294	275
Fresno	4626	572	Modoc	184	851	San Mateo	4078	420	Tuolumne	135	47
Glenn	422	184	Mono	52	429	Santa Barbara	1878	860	Ventura	2062	388
Humboldt	657	527	Monterey	2194	538	Santa Clara	5336	341	Yolo	653	245
Imperial	1091	501	Napa	639	86	Santa Cruz	1431	494	Yuba	334	486
Inyo	147	598	Nevada	305	320	Shasta	684	528			
Kern	3427	60	Orange	5889	611	San Diego	Series 2 Book 1961 Page 183887				

(which provisions identical in all counties, are printed on the attached page to this form) hereby are adopted and incorporated herein and made a part hereof as fully as though set forth herein at length; that said Trustor will observe and perform said provisions; and that the references to property, obligations, and parties in said provisions shall be construed to refer to the property, obligations, and parties set forth in this Deed of Trust. The Trustor requests that a copy of any Notice of Default and of any Notice of Sale hereunder be mailed to Trustor at the address hereinbefore set forth.

Dated: _____   (Signature)

    ACKNOWLEDGEMENT   (Typed name)

State of California   )   (Signature)

County of   )   (Typed name)

On _____, before me, _____, personally appeared _____, who proved to me on the basis of satisfactory evidence to be the person(s) whose name(s) is/are subscribed to the within instrument and acknowledged to me that he/she/they executed the same in his/her/their authorized capacity(ies), and that by his/her/their signature(s) on the instrument the person(s), or entity upon behalf of which the person(s) acted, executed the instrument. I certify under PENALTY OF PERJURY under the laws of the State of California that the foregoing paragraph is true and correct.

WITNESS my hand and official seal.

Signature   (Notary's signature)   (SEAL)

SHORT FORM DEED OF TRUST AND ASSIGNMENT OF RENTS

Note Secured by Deed of Trust

NOTE SECURED BY DEED OF TRUST
(INSTALLMENT INTEREST INCLUDED)

$ _____ _____ *(place of execution)* , California, _____ *(date)*

In installments as herein stated, for value received, I promise to pay to _____ *(names of payees)*

_____

_____ , or order,

at _____ *(place of payment)* _____

the sum of _____ DOLLARS,

with interest from _____ on unpaid principal at

the rate of _____ per cent per annum; principal and interest payable in installments

of _____ Dollars,

or more on the _____ day of each _____ month, beginning

on the _____ day of _____

and continuing until said principal and interest have been paid.

Each payment shall be credited first on interest then due and the remainder on principal; and interest shall thereupon cease upon the principal as credited. Should default be made in payment of any installment when due, the whole sum of principal and interest shall become immediately due at the option of the holder of this note. Principal and interest payable in lawful money of the United States. If action be instituted on this note, I promise to pay such sum as the court may fix as attorneys' fees. This note is secured by a Deed of Trust.

_____   _____
(Signature)   *(Signature)*

_____   _____
(Typed Name)   *(Typed Name)*

borrowed, plus the $70,000 cash they already had, and give it to Sol.

Bruce and June remain the owners of the property, subject to repayment of the $100,000 loan owed to the savings and loan, which is an encumbrance against the property. In legal jargon, Bruce and June are known as trustors. The third party who holds the property subject to the deed of trust is the trustee, and the financial institution that lends the money is the beneficiary.

Personal Property

All property that is not real property is "personal property." Personal property is divided into two broad categories, tangible and intangible.

Tangible Personal Property

Tangible personal property includes items you can touch, such as books, automobiles, boats, animals, clothing, household furniture, farm equipment, jewelry, machinery, motor homes, firearms, tools, antiques, and actual cash like coins or dollar bills. Like real property, tangible personal property is legally required to be transferred following the laws and procedures of the state in which it is located. However, in practice, many types of tangible personal property (for example, cars registered in California, jewelry, cash, etc.) are highly portable and often find their way back to the state of a person's residence at death. If this occurs in a small or medium-sized estate, there is, in practice, normally no objection to transferring the property using the simplified procedures discussed in Chapter 11.

Intangible Personal Property

Intangible personal property is abstract. It is a right to be paid money or to legally exercise some type of power (for example, stopping others from using your patented invention). It is usually represented by a paper or document that states the nature of the rights associated with it. Some examples are promissory notes, bank passbooks, court judgments giving a right to receive money, mortgages, deeds of trust establishing an interest in property as security for a debt, stock or bond certificates giving an ownership interest in a corporation, mutual fund certificates, money market fund certificates, copyrights, patents, and trademarks. Other examples of intangible personal property include contracts giving the right to future income, as would be the case with a publishing contract granting a royalty share of income derived from the sale of a book, or a film contract providing a share of the gross receipts of a movie.

Intangible personal property is transferred under the laws and procedures of the state in which its owner resides. In other words, if a California resident dies owning stocks and bonds located in a New York safe-deposit box, has $50,000 in an Illinois bank, and has $25,000 in a money market fund headquartered in Boston, ownership of all this property (no matter where the decedent lived when it was purchased) can be transferred in California using the instructions in this book.

RELATED TOPIC

More information for couples. We discuss intangible personal property acquired by California couples before they moved to California at the end of this chapter.

What Establishes Ownership of Property?

Most valuable assets have a title document that shows who owns the property (establishes title). For instance, a bank issues a passbook showing the name in which a savings account is held. Stock certificates establish title to the ownership of shares in a corporation. "Pink slips" serve as title documents for motor vehicles, motor homes, and boats. Some kinds of intangible personal property, like copyrights and patents, have documents issued by the federal government that to some extent act like certificates of title. If a decedent had executed a contract giving him or her a right to receive periodic payments in exchange for property or services, the contract itself shows ownership of the future income.

Title to real property, including condominiums and cooperatives, must always be in writing. It is usually represented by a deed containing a legal description of the property.

Some kinds of personal property don't have formal title slips. Nevertheless, there is usually little doubt who owns them. For instance, you can normally assume things such as clothing, books, furniture, and personal effects belonged to the decedent if they are in his or her possession at death and if no one steps forward to claim them. Valuable objects, such as jewelry, furs, or works of art don't come with a title document in the formal sense, but their purchase is normally accompanied by a receipt or bill of sale, which accomplishes a similar purpose. If not, questions of ownership can sometimes be resolved by reference to canceled checks or by contacting the seller.

As a rule, you will find it relatively easy to figure out what property the decedent at least claimed to own by checking in all the obvious places: desk drawers, safe-deposit boxes, file cabinets, and the like. If, as part of doing this, you find an unfamiliar document and don't know what it means, it is best to consult an expert to be sure you're not overlooking any assets (or liabilities, for that matter).

How Was the Decedent's Property Owned?

Property, both real and personal, may be owned either separately (the decedent owned it all) or concurrently with other persons.

Separate Property Ownership

Separate ownership simply means ownership by one person. The sole owner alone enjoys the benefits of the property, but is also responsible for its burdens, such as mortgages or taxes. He may dispose of his separate property by will to anyone he chooses, and if he dies without a will, the separate property goes to his heirs under intestate succession laws. All property owned by unmarried people, whether or not they were previously married, is separate property, except for property owned in joint tenancy (discussed below).

A married person can also own separate property. This is because all property acquired prior to marriage and property received by an individual by gift or inheritance, whether before, during or after a marriage, remains separate property. In addition, if a married couple separates, the earnings and accumulations of each after the date of permanent separation are also separate property. Finally, even during marriage, the earnings of a husband or wife can be separate property if they sign a written contract providing for this result and, in fact, keep the property separate. These rules apply to California domestic partners as well.

Concurrent Ownership

Concurrent ownership means ownership by two or more people at the same time. Some estates, especially those of single individuals, contain no property owned concurrently with another person. If this is your situation, you can skip this entire section.

In California, concurrent ownership normally takes one of the following legal classifications:

- tenancy in common
- joint tenancy
- community property
- community property with right of survivorship, or
- life tenancy (or life estate).

We discuss each of these forms of concurrent ownership just below. However, please note that the information on community property ownership applies only to decedents who were married or in a registered domestic partnership at the time of death; therefore, if you are settling the estate of a single person, you can skip the discussion of community property. You also do not need to worry as much about whether or not property is community property if the decedent willed all of his property to his surviving spouse or domestic partner. Since the surviving spouse or partner gets it all anyway, it's not necessary to understand technical rules as to who owned what portion. We discuss community property ownership last because it requires more extended coverage, not because it is less important. It isn't.

Tenancy in Common

This occurs when two or more people own an undivided interest in property, without an automatic right to inherit the property from each other if one owner dies. An undivided interest means a tenant in common does not own a particular portion of the property but rather a fractional share of the whole property. If you own a piece of land as a tenant in common with your sister, absent any agreement to divide it differently, you each own an undivided one-half interest in the whole property. However, cotenants can own unequal shares in a property if a written contract so provides. Thus, one cotenant may own one-tenth, another three-tenths, and a third may own the remaining six-tenths under the terms of a written agreement.

A tenancy in common is created when an ownership document states, for example, "Jill Evers and Finley Fox as Tenants in Common." In addition, whenever an ownership document does not specify that more than one owner acquires it in joint tenancy or as community property, it is presumed the owners hold the property as tenants in common. If any of the tenants in common dies, that person's interest is not acquired by the remaining tenants in common, but instead goes to the beneficiaries named in the deceased person's will or to the heirs if there is no will.

Joint Tenancy

For property to be held in joint tenancy, it must be expressly stated in the deed or ownership document that the owners own it "as joint tenants" or "with right of survivorship," or the abbreviations "JTRS" or "WROS" must be used. In addition, registration of a motor vehicle in the names of two people joined by "or" is treated as joint tenancy, as are certain bank accounts held in this way. U.S. savings bonds held in co-ownership form also have the same legal effect as if the words "joint tenancy" were used.

Owning property in joint tenancy means if one of the joint tenants dies, that person's interest immediately becomes the property of the remaining joint tenant(s) by operation of law. A will has no effect on joint tenancy property, nor do the laws of intestate succession have any control over who gets the property. People who own property as joint tenants always own an undivided equal interest, and all have the same rights to the use of the whole property.

Usually, only people with a very close personal or family relationship to each other hold property this way, such as husband and wife, parent and child, an unmarried couple, or brothers and sisters. It isn't normally practical for others, such as business associates, to be joint tenants, because the families and relatives of a joint tenant would inherit nothing in such a situation. More than two people may be joint tenants, but this is not common. If there are three or more joint tenants and one dies, the others acquire his or her interest and still remain joint tenants.

Joint tenancy property need not go through a formal probate proceeding, but there are several formalities necessary to clear the joint tenancy title to the property so that it appears in the name of the surviving tenant. We discuss how to do this in Chapter 10.

SEE AN EXPERT

Potential conflicts between joint tenancy and community property. If a spouse or domestic partner puts a piece of community property into joint tenancy with someone other than his or her spouse or partner, and the other did not agree to it at the time, and after death the surviving spouse or partner wishes to claim a one-half community property interest in the property, you have a problem and should see a lawyer.

Sometimes a person who owns real property will execute a deed transferring title to himself or herself and another person as joint tenants. That way, when the original owner dies, the property will be transferred to the surviving joint tenant with no need for probate. When this happens, the original owner has actually made a gift of one-half of the property to the other joint tenant, and he or she is responsible for federal gift taxes, which are levied on the giver, not the recipient. A gift tax return may be required when the transfer is made, but not always.

If the receiver does not exercise his or her rights as owner of a half interest (such as selling his or her interest or borrowing against it), the taxation can be put off until the death of the giver (original owner who put up all the money). Any taxes will be assessed as part of the death taxes of the giver's estate.

Life Tenancy (Life Estate)

A life tenancy (sometimes called "life estate") is used infrequently. It is ownership of property for the period of a lifetime only. Life tenancies are sometimes created to allow an elderly person (often a spouse) to use property for the rest of her life and then to give the property to a person in the next generation without the necessity of probate proceedings. Or, a life estate can be used by a living person to avoid probate at his death.

> **EXAMPLE:** Wanda is an elderly widow who owns a home, which she wishes to go to her son Steven upon her death. Wanda may deed the property to Steven during her lifetime, with the deed saying that "Grantor (Wanda) reserves to herself a life estate in said property." This will transfer the ownership to Steven, but subject to Wanda's life estate. It will accomplish Wanda's objective of avoiding probate of the home upon her death because she will die without ownership of the property. Her life estate will terminate at the moment of death, and the home will be owned by Steven.

RESOURCE

Reducing taxes with a life estate. This sort of transfer can also save on federal estate taxes in larger estates if the person who gets the life estate (as opposed to getting the property outright) already has considerable property of his or her own. Since the life estate terminates at death, the property covered by it isn't included in that person's estate and therefore is not taxed as part of it. For more details on this sort of estate planning (which must be done before death, of course), see *Plan Your Estate*, by Denis Clifford (Nolo).

Community Property

Married people and registered domestic partners present another subclassification as far as the concurrent ownership of property is concerned.

California has community property laws that apply to property acquired during marriage or domestic partnership. Briefly, these laws give spouses and domestic partners equal interest in property— including wages and other earned income and the property acquired with this income—they accumulate during the marriage or partnership. In other words, each spouse or domestic partner owns a one-half interest in the community property.

Any property owned before the marriage or partnership is not community property, but is the separate property of the owner, who can deal with it as he or she wishes. The same is true if either spouse or partner inherits or is given property during the marriage— such property remains the separate property of the person who receives it. Earnings from separate property are also separate property. Thus, if a spouse or partner owns an apartment house as separate property because he or she acquired it prior to marriage, or inherited it or received it as a gift during the marriage or partnership, the rents from it are also her separate property.

Certain events, however, can alter the character of property owned by spouses or partners. They can agree to change (transmute) community property into separate property, or vice versa. Or, they may combine their separate property and community property to such an extent that it all becomes community property. And commonly, an asset (such as a family business, house, or pension) will be part community property and part separate property.

Accurately drawing the line between community property and non-community property can be both difficult and tedious. Accordingly, before you struggle through the rest of this rather intricate material, stop and think whether you really need to know if the decedent owned any community property. For instance, do any of the following situations apply to your estate?

- Was the decedent neither married nor in a registered domestic partnership? If so, he did not own any community property.
- If the decedent was married or a domestic partner, did he leave a will that gives his entire estate to his surviving spouse or partner? In this case, it is not as important to know whether the

property is community or separate, since it all goes to the survivor anyway. The only reason you may want to clearly identify the community property in this situation is if the estate might be large enough to require a federal estate tax return. (A tax return may be due even though there will be no estate tax payments for married people, as property transferred to a surviving spouse is tax exempt. This exemption is not available for domestic partners.) You may also want to account for community property if you need a court order to transfer it to the surviving spouse or partner. (See Chapter 15.)

The main reasons you will probably want to know if the decedent owned any community property are:

- If a person dies without a will (intestate), the decedent's one-half of the community property goes to the surviving spouse or partner.
- If a decedent uses a will or other estate planning device to try to transfer more than his one-half of the community property to someone other than his spouse or partner,

   that spouse or partner can object and claim one-half.

Community Property With Right of Survivorship

If spouses or registered domestic partners held title to property as "community property with right of survivorship," the survivor inherits the deceased person's half-interest automatically, without probate. The property must be clearly identified, on the transfer document (a real estate deed, for example) as community property with the right of survivorship. (Civ. Code § 682.1.)

How to Determine Whether Property Is Community or Separate

Here is a step-by-step approach to determining whether any given property item is community property or separate property. Read it now for a general understanding of community property principles. Later on, when you are filling out your

Schedule of Assets in Chapter 5, you will want to return and use this information. Follow this analysis for each piece of property the decedent left, unless you can conclude that all property fits into the same basic category, in which case your task will be very easy.

Step 1: Is there an ownership document (deed, certificate of title, pink slip, or bank account card) that says something like "John and Mary Doe, husband and wife," or "John and Mary Doe, domestic partners as community property," or "Mr. and Mrs. John Doe"? If so, the property is presumed to be community property. Go to Step 10. If not, go to Step 2.

Step 2: If the decedent was married or partnered for a long time and began the marriage or partnership with little or nothing, you can usually assume at the outset that all property was community property. If so, go to Step 10. If not, go to Step 3.

Step 3: Was the property acquired during the marriage or partnership (after the wedding or registration but prior to a permanent dissolution)? If so, go to Step 4. If not, go to Step 8.

Step 4: Does the property consist of earnings (including employment fringe benefits such as insurance, pension plans, stock options, and so forth) of either spouse or partner during the marriage or partnership, gifts, or inheritances to the couple jointly or property purchased with such earnings, gifts, or inheritances? If so, go to Step 10. If not, go to Step 5.

Step 5: Was the property acquired during the marriage or partnership through a gift given to just one person as an individual? If not, go to Step 6. If yes, go to Step 8.

Strictly speaking, a gift is a transfer of property without anything being paid by the person receiving it. Commonly, gifts made during marriage or partnership by one spouse or partner to the other are considered the separate property of the person who receives them unless the spouses or partners agree differently. Sometimes these gifts can be quite valuable, such as furs, diamonds, and the like.

Step 6: Was the property acquired during the marriage or partnership by an inheritance of one of the spouses or partners as an individual? If not, go to Step 7. If yes, go to Step 8.

Step 7: Was the property acquired by one spouse or partner as an award in a personal injury action? If not, go to Step 10. If yes, go to Step 8.

Step 8: Did the spouse or domestic partner who owned the property agree orally or in writing prior to January 1, 1985, to put it into community property form? See "Actions That Change the Character of Property," below. If so, go to Step 13. If not, go to Step 9.

Step 9: Did the spouse or partner who owned the property agree in writing after January 1, 1985, to put it into community property form? See "Actions That Change the Character of Property," below. If so, go to Step 13. If not, go to Step 12.

Step 10: Did both spouses enter into an oral or written agreement prior to January 1, 1985, that the property be the separate property of one of them? See "Actions That Change the Character of Property," below. If so, go to Step 12. If not, go to Step 11.

Step 11: Did both spouses or partners agree in writing after January 1, 1985, that the property be the separate property of one of them? See "Actions That Change the Character of Property," below. If so, go to Step 12. If not, go to Step 13.

Step 12: Was separate property mixed with community property (lawyers call this "commingling") so that its separate nature can no longer be traced? If so, go to Step 14. If not, go to Step 15.

The most common example of commingling is when spouses or partners deposit both separate and community property in a joint bank account and make withdrawals over the years that make it impossible to characterize the funds left in the account. See "Actions That Change the Character of Property," below.

Step 13: Is the property a mix of community property and separate property such as a house, a contract for future payments, a family business, or a pension that was only partially earned during the marriage? See "Property That Is a Mixture of Community and Separate Property," below. If so, you might wish to obtain help from a lawyer or accountant in characterizing which portion of this asset is community property and which is separate property. If not, go to Step 14.

Step 14: The property should be treated as community property, which means the decedent owned only one-half of it.

Step 15: The property should be treated as separate property, owned by whichever spouse or partner acquired, inherited, or was given the property as his or her separate property.

Actions That Change the Character of Property

In the above step-by-step analysis, we indicated that certain acts by spouses or partners could change the nature of property from community to separate and vice versa. Here we take a closer look at how this can occur.

The general rule is that the community or separate nature of property is determined by its source. However, you should understand that no matter what its source, the community or separate nature of property can be changed by actions of the spouses or partners. This is more likely to result in separate property becoming community property than the reverse, but both types of changes occur fairly frequently. Let's look at some common examples.

Commingling Assets

In general, property can change its physical form without changing its community or separate character. For instance, if money kept in a husband's checking account before marriage (separate property) is used during marriage to buy stocks and bonds, and if the stocks and bonds are later sold and the proceeds used to buy a house, then the house remains the husband's separate property.

Many couples, however, change the separate or community nature of their property without realizing it. One common example of this phenomenon is what lawyers call "commingling." The basic commingling rule, subject to a number of technical subtleties which are beyond the scope of this book, is that if separate property assets are mixed together (commingled) with community funds so that it is impossible to trace them to their source, the formerly separate property becomes community property. If parties to an account are married or in a registered domestic partnership, contributions to the account are presumed to be community property. (Prob. Code § 5305.)

> **EXAMPLE:** A husband and wife open a savings account during the marriage in which they deposit money they have earned during their marriage. Assume the wife receives an inheritance of $3,000, which is separate property, and deposits it into the joint account. If no withdrawals are made from the account, she can trace her $3,000 to her inheritance. However, if a number of deposits and withdrawals are made by the parties over the years and the balance dips below $3,000, she will no longer be able to trace her money and it will be treated as having been given to the community.

SEE AN EXPERT

Tracing commingled property. This subject is so complicated and confusing that it is the subject of endless litigation. If you find yourself dealing with a commingling problem, check your conclusion with a lawyer.

Agreements Between Spouses or Partners

The separate property of either spouse or domestic partner may be "transmuted" (changed) into community property, and community property may be transmuted into separate property of a spouse or partner merely by an agreement between them. Prior to 1985, this could be accomplished by an informal oral agreement whereby one spouse indicated to the other that he or she wished the property to be community rather than separate, or if both simply agreed that a community asset would become the separate property of one. Since January 1, 1985, a change in the nature of property must be made in writing, signed by the person whose property is adversely affected. This law, however, does not apply to property whose character was changed by oral agreement prior to 1985.

The most important element of an agreement to change the status of property is the intention to do so. When there is no expressly stated intention, the courts will sometimes examine the actions and conduct of the parties. Up to 1985, the courts were quite liberal in inferring such agreements from rather skimpy facts. For instance, in one case the court considered a statement by a husband that "I wanted to do something for my wife," as sufficient evidence of his intention to make his property community rather than separate.

Sometimes a spouse or partner may also change the character of property owned by one of them by making a gift of it to the other. For example, when a single person who owns a house gets married or enters a domestic partnership, the house is not automatically converted into community property by that fact. The house remains the separate property of the owner. However, if the owner makes a deed after marriage or registration that puts the house in the names of both spouses or partners, thereby making a gift of it, it is converted into community property.

Property That Is a Mixture of Community and Separate Property

Sometimes when property is received over a period of time and a marriage or divorce—or registration and termination of a domestic partnership—takes place during that time, it can be difficult to determine how much of the property is community property and how much is separate. Let's look at some examples of this sort of situation.

Contract Rights

It is not uncommon for high-earning executives and entertainers to receive compensation payable over a period of several years. If the right to collect the money arises—that is, if the work is done—before the marriage or partnership registration date, then any money received under such a contract is separate property, even though the payments are made during the marriage or partnership. However, if the work isn't done until after the marriage or registration, as might be the case when a sports figure or entertainer gets a large up-front payment for work to be done over several years, the money would be community property to the extent that the work needed to earn the money was performed after the marriage or partnership registration date. In other words, the test of whether the property is community normally depends on the time when the right to payment arises and not on the time when payment is actually made. In another situation, a writer could do substantial work on, or even complete, a book during a marriage or partnership, and if the union is later dissolved, the right to future royalties would be split equally between the spouses or partners as community property, even though payment would be made after the dissolution.

> **SEE AN EXPERT**
>
> **Get help if you need it.** Sometimes it becomes extremely difficult to determine what is and isn't community property, so much so that thousands of court cases are litigated over this question every year. If you have difficulty determining which is which, see a lawyer.

Insurance Proceeds

The extent to which proceeds from life insurance on a spouse or partner are treated as community property depends on what proportion of the premiums paid for such insurance came from community funds, not on who is named as the beneficiary. In other words, the surviving spouse's or partner's community property interest in the insurance proceeds must be recognized regardless of who is named as beneficiary of the policy. For example, if a woman in a domestic partnership purchases insurance on her life, naming her brother as beneficiary, and one-half of the premiums are paid from community funds, when she dies, her partner is entitled to one-fourth of the proceeds of the policy (that is, one-half of the community half) and her brother is entitled to the rest. If all the premiums were paid with community

property funds, her partner would be entitled to one-half of the insurance policy proceeds.

Improvements to Property

What happens when improvements are made to one type of property (community or separate) using funds that are a different type of property? For example, if one person has a separate property cabin or boat, and community property funds are used to fix it up, what happens when the property is left to a third person? Does the surviving spouse or partner have a right to claim one-half of the value of the improvements? Similarly, if one partner uses his separate property to improve his spouse's or partner's separate property and feels unfairly treated by that person's will or alternative estate plan, what are his rights?

As you can probably gather, the law in this area can be complex. Put another way, you are dealing with an estate that isn't simple, and you need more information about the ins and outs of California marital or domestic partnership property law than we can give you here.

Pensions

A pension is regarded as compensation for services previously rendered, and a percentage of the pension right is deemed to have been earned during each year that the pensioner worked to qualify for the pension. Thus, if a pensioner worked for 15 years, then married and worked for another five years before qualifying for a pension on the basis of 20 years' service, three-fourths of the pension payments (and anything accumulated with them) would be separate property and one-fourth would be community property. If the pensioner was married for the entire time he or she had the job, pension payments are community property.

Rents and Profits

The rents and profits received on community property (interest, dividends, royalties, rents, capital gains, and so on) are community property. Rents and profits from separate property remain separate property.

Separate Property Businesses

It is often difficult to determine whether income from a separate property business in which one spouse or partner works during the marriage or partnership is community or separate property. The value of the business at the time of marriage or registration is clearly separate property. Wages paid to the person who owns the business during the marriage or partnership are clearly community property. But what about the increase in the value of the business itself? Is this just the natural growth of a separate property asset and, therefore, separate property, or is it the result of the continuing work of the spouse or partner and, therefore, community property? Often the answer to this question is some combination of the two. However, it is an area of particular difficulty, and in some situations you will need professional help in deciding what is separate and what is community property.

Examples of Property Ownership

Perhaps the best way to review the material we have covered in this chapter is to examine several examples of community and separate property ownership.

Brad

Brad is a bachelor who moved to California from Nevada in 1998. While living in Nevada he inherited $50,000 from his father's estate, which he invested in a motel in Las Vegas. While living in California from 1998 until his death, he acquired 300 shares of Marvelous Corporation stock in which he took title as a joint tenant with his mother. He also purchased a Porsche and a $10,000 life insurance policy, naming his mother as beneficiary.

Since Brad was never married, all of his property is his separate property in which he has a 100% interest. His interest in the Las Vegas motel, being real property, will be transferred according to Nevada law and excluded from his California estate. The 300 shares of Marvelous Corporation stock, being held in joint tenancy, is not subject to probate because it automatically became his

mother's property on his death by right of survivorship. However, title to this property must be cleared, a procedure we discuss in Chapter 10.

The $10,000 life insurance proceeds are not subject to probate either, because Brad's mother is the named beneficiary under the policy, and the proceeds will be paid under the insurance contract entered into between Brad and the insurance company. Brad's mother needs only to send a certified copy of the death certificate and a claim form to the insurance company to collect the proceeds. The remaining asset—his Porsche—can probably be transferred using the simple affidavit procedure available for small estates, which we discuss in Chapter 11. Who gets the Porsche will depend on whether Brad left a will or died without one (intestate).

Joe and Jack

Joe and Jack registered as domestic partners on March 18, 2002, and lived in California during their entire partnership. Prior to their registration, Jack owned some valuable antiques and a $10,000 bank account. Joe owned a $20,000 promissory note secured by a deed of trust on real property located in San Diego; a boat, which he kept at Marina del Rey (in Los Angeles County); and $5,000 in a California bank savings account. During their partnership, Jack inherited 50 shares of AT&T stock from his aunt's estate. During their partnership they opened a bank account at Culver City Bank in California as tenants in common. They deposited their excess earnings into this account, plus the proceeds of the two bank accounts they each owned individually before registration, periodically making withdrawals from, and deposits into, the account. They also acquired, with their combined earnings during the partnership, a condominium located in Culver City, California, and a BMW.

When Joe dies, his estate in California is determined as follows: The boat at Marina del Rey (tangible personal property) and the $20,000 trust deed note (intangible personal property) are Joe's separate property, having been acquired before registering his partnership with Jack. The two bank accounts that Joe and Jack owned prior to registration have been commingled and are both community property, as is the Culver City Bank account, which Joe and Jack established after registration. Therefore, Jack owns a one-half interest in each of these. The AT&T stock is Jack's separate property, since he acquired it by inheritance. The antiques that Jack owned prior to registration are also his separate property. The condominium and the BMW acquired with the couple's earnings during the partnership are California community property. Thus, Joe's estate in California consists of the following:

- A 100% separate property interest in:
  - the $20,000 trust deed note, and
  - the Marina del Rey boat.
- A one-half community property interest (Jack owns the other half) in:
  - the Culver City condominium
  - the BMW, and
  - the Culver City Bank account.

Beverly and Randolph

Beverly was a scriptwriter for a large motion picture studio in Los Angeles when she married Randolph, an aspiring actor, in 1970. At the time of their marriage, Beverly owned a home in Pacific Palisades, a 1969 Mercedes-Benz automobile, and a $10,000 bank account. Also, at the time of their marriage, Beverly had completed ten of the necessary 25 years of service required to qualify for a $50,000 pension from the studio on her retirement. Beverly's daughter by a prior marriage was named contingent beneficiary of the pension.

Randolph's property at the time of their marriage consisted of an interest in a motor home, worth about $15,000, and a $5,000 savings account. Randolph was also entitled to receive residual payments from several television commercials he completed prior to their marriage, which are still rolling in at an average of $500 per month. Shortly after their marriage, Randolph sold his interest in the motor home, and he and Beverly pooled their money and deposited all cash in joint bank accounts, paying their expenses from the accounts and also depositing their earnings during marriage into the accounts. In 1975, they improved the Pacific Palisades residence by building a lap pool and redwood deck, at a cost of about $20,000. Since the house was Beverly's separate property, Randolph generously agreed to treat the cost of the improvements as a gift to Beverly, and did not ask for reimbursement of his one-half interest in the community funds used for the improvements.

Beverly retired from the studio in 1985 and died in 2005, after she and Randolph had been married 35 years. Their combined assets at the time of Beverly's death consisted of:

- the Pacific Palisades home
- the 1969 Mercedes-Benz automobile
- the cash in joint bank accounts of approximately $15,000
- Beverly's vested interest in her pension, and
- Randolph's rights to future residual payments from his TV commercials.

How do we know which of these assets are included in Beverly's estate? First, we know the Pacific Palisades house and Mercedes are Beverly's separate property, because she owned them prior to her marriage to Randolph. Even though the improvements to the residence were made with community funds, they took on the same character as the house (because of Randolph's gift) and are, therefore, also her separate property, along with the house. Therefore, these two assets are 100% Beverly's separate property.

Beverly's vested interest in her $50,000 pension was earned two-fifths prior to marriage and three-fifths during marriage (that is, she was married 15 of the 25 working years required to qualify for the pension). This means two-fifths of the pension ($20,000) is separate property and three-fifths ($30,000) is community property, and Randolph owns a one-half interest in the community portion, or $15,000. Randolph would have to work out an arrangement with the pension plan administrators and Beverly's daughter to receive his share. If this can't be done, then Randolph would have to see an attorney. (Of course, Randolph might not choose to claim his share and let it all go to Beverly's daughter, but he is entitled to $15,000 if he wants it.)

Beverly's separate property portion ($20,000) of the pension, plus her one-half interest in the community portion ($15,000), will go to her daughter, as the contingent beneficiary. Since the pension has named beneficiaries, it will not be subject to probate. Randolph's residual payments are his separate property, since the right to payment was earned before marriage, and they are not included in Beverly's estate. Beverly also has a one-half interest in the $15,000 in the couple's joint bank accounts. Her half interest is part of her gross estate but will not be subject to probate because the accounts were held in joint tenancy. Therefore, Beverly's estate consists of the following assets:

- the Pacific Palisades home
- the 1969 Mercedes-Benz automobile
- a $35,000 interest in the pension, and
- a $7,500 interest in the bank accounts.

Unless Beverly has used an estate planning device, such as joint tenancy or a living trust, the home and automobile will be subject to probate in California.

Property Acquired by Couples Before They Moved to California

This section applies only if the decedent was a married Californian or registered domestic partner who acquired property during marriage or a domestic partnership prior to moving to California. To deal with this situation, lawyers invented the term "quasi-community property." Quasi-community property includes all real property situated in California and all personal property, wherever located, that would have been community property if the owner had been a resident of California at the time he or she acquired it. The label is generally applied to property owned by married couples or domestic partners at the time they move to California from a non-community property state. The only exception is real property located outside of California, which is not quasi-community property. Quasi-community property is treated the same way as community property in estates of persons who die while residents of California.

California also treats community property acquired by a married couple or domestic partners while living in another community property state as community property, even though such property would not be community property in California. For instance, some community property states classify income from separate property as community property when the income is received during marriage. Although such income would be treated as separate property in California, it is treated as community property when the owner who acquired the property in such other community property state dies a resident of California.

If you have difficulty in establishing any of the decedent's out-of-state property as community or separate, you should seek the advice of an attorney.

Harry and Marsha

Harry and Marsha had only a small amount of cash between them and a few personal belongings when they were married in New York City in 1983. During their marriage, while living in New York, they acquired with their earnings an apartment building and 200 shares of XYZ Corporation stock. They moved to California in 1990, where they lived as husband and wife until Marsha's death. No property was acquired by either of them by gift or inheritance at any time. At the time of Marsha's death, Harry and Marsha owned the following assets:

- the apartment house in New York City, held in both their names
- 200 shares of XYZ Corporation stock, in Harry's name
- a residence in Van Nuys, California, in both names as community property
- two automobiles, one in Marsha's name and one in Harry's name, and
- a joint tenancy bank account at Union Bank in Van Nuys.

What does Marsha's estate consist of for California purposes? First of all, it doesn't include the real property (apartment house) in New York City, which will have to be transferred independently under the laws of the state of New York. The XYZ Corporation stock is included in the California estate because it is intangible personal property. Since the stock was acquired with the combined earnings of Harry and Marsha during their marriage, it would be treated as community property in California even though the stock is in Harry's name alone and, therefore, is technically quasi-community property. The joint tenancy bank account (although obviously community property funds) is included in

Marsha's estate, although it is not subject to probate and becomes Harry's property by operation of law immediately on Marsha's death. Thus, Marsha's estate in California consists of her one-half interest in the following assets:

- the 200 shares of XYZ Corporation stock
- the Van Nuys residence
- the two automobiles, and
- the Union Bank account.

Preparing a Schedule of the Assets and Debts

By now you should have examined the necessary papers and documents and gathered sufficient information to prepare a schedule of all property owned by the decedent at the time of his or her death. The schedule, once it is completed, will be used as a worksheet in conjunction with the remaining steps required to transfer the assets and settle the estate.

To help you with this project, we have included a blank Schedule of Assets in Appendix C. Instructions for completing the schedule are contained in the following sections. Since this schedule will serve as your record of all property in which the decedent had any interest when he or she died—including assets that are subject to probate, as well as those that are not—you will refer to it often, and it should be as accurate as possible.

You should not only list the assets, but should also briefly and carefully describe them so you can easily identify each one. A more detailed description of some items may be required on later documents, but a brief listing will do now. In addition, you should indicate for each asset, in the column provided for this purpose:

- the value of the asset
- how the decedent owned it (for example, as separate property, as community property, in joint tenancy, etc. See list on next page.)
- the portion owned by the decedent and the value of the decedent's interest, and
- whether the asset is subject to formal probate or can be transferred in a simpler way. (If you are in doubt about whether a particular asset must be probated, leave this column blank until you read Chapter 6.)

The first sections of this chapter provide information and tools to assist in the process of preparing your Schedule of Assets. Then the final sections of the chapter show you how to complete the schedule, item by item. Thus, your best approach is not to try to fill in the schedule until you have read this entire chapter. Please understand, however, that this book is not designed to provide extensive coverage of California property ownership rules, a large and sometimes complex area of the law. If, after reading the previous chapter and what follows, you are still unsure about how to characterize a particular asset, see a lawyer.

Describe Each Asset

It is helpful to group assets, such as cash items, bank accounts, real property, securities, and so on, according to their general type as part of listing them on your schedule. Describe each asset briefly, including enough pertinent detail to identify it accurately. For example, a bank account might be described like this: "Personal checking account #57111; Bank of Occidental, Santa Rosa." At this point, don't worry about what percentage or type of ownership is involved, or how much the account is worth. Simply list every asset you are aware of that might be owned by the decedent. We provide more details on how to describe particular assets in "Checklist of Property to List on Schedule of Assets," below, so you may want to read this section as you make your list.

Value Each Asset (Column A)

As well as describing each item of property, you must also determine the total date-of-death value of each asset as accurately as possible and put this amount in Column A. Here are some guidelines to help you do this. If you desire more detail on evaluation, consult the extended discussion in "Checklist of Property to List on Schedule of Assets," below, for the type of asset in question, or see an accountant.

1. In placing a dollar value on an asset, the usual rule is to try to determine its "fair market value." The definition of fair market value is generally the price that a willing buyer would pay to a willing seller, both of them acting of their own free will and under no compulsion to buy or sell. Some assets have a definite record of value, such as stocks, bonds, and bank accounts, while others are valued by special rules, which we will discuss as we go along.

2. You should list the *gross* value of each asset in this column without regard to any liens or

encumbrances against the property. In other words, for our purposes right now, do not subtract amounts owed on the property.

3. All assets and their values should be listed as of the *date of the decedent's death*, not as of the date you complete the schedule. This means that if a security is involved, you need to do a little research.

How to Determine Ownership of Property (Columns B & C)

Now you must list the manner in which the decedent owned each asset. You should insert this information in Column B. To do this, use the following abbreviations:

- separate property (SP)
- community property (CP)
- joint tenancy (JT)
- tenancy in common (TIC)
- life tenancy (LT), and
- trustee of a trust (T).

For mixed property (items that are part one type of property and part another), put both designations indicating the percentage share of each (for example, "one-third CP, two-thirds SP").

We describe general California property ownership rules in Chapter 4. Also, consult the extended discussion in "Checklist of Property to List on Schedule of Assets," below.

If you have any doubt about the ownership of any item in the decedent's estate, or you want to check your conclusions, take the following steps:

Step 1: Was the decedent married or a registered domestic partner at time of death? If so, proceed to Step 2. If not, proceed to Step 3.

Step 2: Was the particular item community property or separate property? See "How to Determine Whether Property Is Community or Separate," in Chapter 4, to help you answer this question. If the asset is a house, family business, pension, contract for future payment, or some other form of property that might be a mixture of community and separate property, also see "Property That Is a Mixture of Community and Separate Property," in Chapter 4. As stated above, if the property was community property,

put "CP" in Column B and proceed to Step 6. If the property was a mixture of community property and separate property, put the respective portions in Column B (for example, "one-fourth CP, three-fourths SP") and proceed to Step 6. If not, proceed to Step 3.

Step 3: Was the property held in joint tenancy— that is, jointly held with others with right of survivorship? (See "How Was the Decedent's Property Owned?" in Chapter 4.) If so, put "JT" in Column B and proceed to Step 6. If not, go to Step 4.

Step 4: Was the property held in tenancy in common—that is, jointly held with others with no right of survivorship? If so, put "TIC" in Column B and proceed to Step 6. If not, go to Step 5.

Step 5: Was the item owned solely by the decedent as nearly as you can tell? If so, put "SP" in Column B. Otherwise, go to Step 6.

Step 6: Compute the share of the property owned by the decedent and put this fraction in Column C. For instance, if the decedent was married or a registered domestic partner when he or she died, you may find that he or she owned a one-half interest in many assets as community property. Sometimes, you may find that the decedent and his or her spouse or partner together owned (as community property or as joint tenants) a fractional interest in property with third parties. In this case, the decedent will have owned one-half of the couple's shared fractional interest. For example, if the decedent and his or her surviving spouse or partner owned a one-fourth community property interest in a commercial building with several other people, the decedent's interest would be one-eighth (that is, one-half of one-fourth).

We discuss shared ownership situations in detail in Chapter 4. In most estates, determining what the decedent owned should not be a problem after you read this material. However, if a decedent was married or a registered domestic partner and owned a number of pieces of property jointly with people other than his or her spouse or partner, the portion of the property he or she owned may be in doubt, or there may be a difference of opinion between the surviving spouse or partner and the third party. If you face this situation, see an expert. (For information on finding and compensating lawyers, see Chapter 16.)

List the Value of the Decedent's Interest (Column D)

Now that we have listed all the assets, evaluated them, and determined the type of interest the decedent had in the property, it is time to insert the value of the decedent's interest in Column D. Fortunately, this is normally easy. If the decedent owned the entire asset, the dollar figure you insert here is the same as listed in Column A. (Remember, the specifics of valuing assets are described later in this chapter.)

If the decedent owned less than a full interest in any property, such as an undivided one-half interest as a tenant in common or a one-half interest as community property, include only the value of the decedent's fractional interest in Column D. For example, if the decedent owned a one-half community property interest in a residence valued at $170,000, the value of the decedent's interest in Column D is $85,000.

The total of Column D will give you the value of the decedent's gross estate to help determine if a federal estate tax return will be required. (See "Federal Estate Tax Return," in Chapter 7.)

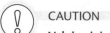

CAUTION

Valuing joint tenancy property. If the decedent owned joint tenancy property with anyone other than his or her spouse (federal tax laws don't apply to domestic partners), the IRS presumes (for estate tax purposes) that the decedent owned 100% of the property, so include 100% of the property's value in Column D. If the decedent, in fact, didn't contribute 100% of the purchase price of the property, you can rebut that presumption by showing that the surviving joint tenant contributed some of the purchase price.

Determine Whether Property Is Probate or Nonprobate Asset (Column E)

In Column E, indicate whether the asset must go through formal probate (P) or can be transferred outside of formal probate and is therefore a nonprobate asset (N/P). As you will remember from our discussion in Chapter 1, probate assets are handled differently from nonprobate assets in settling an estate, and even some assets that are theoretically subject to probate can be transferred with no need to go to court. These are primarily assets in small estates of $100,000 or less and property that passes to a surviving spouse or domestic partner.

Let's review the distinctions between the assets that do not have to go through probate.

- **Assets not subject to probate:** Generally, nonprobate assets are those for which the beneficiary has been predetermined by reason of a contract or by law, such as life insurance proceeds, death benefits, property held in trust (including living trusts and savings bank trusts), and joint tenancy property. The will doesn't affect disposition of the asset.
- **Assets subject to "summary" probate:** Property that passes outright to a surviving spouse or domestic partner and property in small estates ($100,000 or under) can be transferred by simple "summary" probate procedures without a formal probate court proceeding. These procedures are so simple that we classify these assets N/P. After you have completed your schedule and add up the total gross value of the assets, you will be able to determine whether any assets that would otherwise be subject to probate, in fact, fall in this category.
- **Assets subject to formal probate:** Everything not included in the above two categories requires formal probate court proceedings before the property can be transferred.

If any of this confuses you, leave this column blank until you read Chapter 6. Chapter 6 serves as a sort of road map to the rest of the book in that it directs you to the chapter containing instructions on which property transfer procedure to follow.

List All Debts

We have also included a separate section at the end of the Schedule of Assets for listing debts and obligations owed by the decedent at the time of his or her death. This information is not necessary for the purposes of this chapter. However, it will serve as a valuable record of these items for your future use. You'll need it to prepare the decedent's final income tax returns and, if necessary, estate income tax and federal estate tax returns.

Usually, the decedent's general debts as well as the expenses of administering the estate are paid from the general assets (residuary) of the estate, either during formal probate or a summary probate administration procedure. However, if specific assets carry with them their own obligations (such as property taxes, mortgage payments in the case of real property, or installment payments on "secured" items, such as motor vehicles, furniture, etc.), the beneficiaries who receive these assets ordinarily assume these obligations, unless the decedent's will provides otherwise. You can check this out by carefully reading the will provision that makes the specific devise.

Checklist of Property to List on Schedule of Assets

This section contains an extended discussion of how to describe, evaluate, and characterize the various kinds of assets commonly found in an estate. By this time, you should have a good start on your Schedule of Assets, and the material here is intended to fill in any gaps you might have.

Cash Items

List all cash, checks, money orders, traveler's checks, or other items that can be immediately converted to cash. The value of these items (Column A) is their face value, unless they are antique coins or something else of unusual value. These are normally community property assets if the decedent was married or a registered domestic partner, and separate property if he or she was single at the time of death. All items in this category are potentially subject to being transferred through a formal probate court proceeding unless they are (1) covered by a living trust or other probate avoidance device, (2) part of a small estate, or (3) to be transferred to a surviving spouse or partner.

EXAMPLE:

Cash in decedent's possession

Uncashed checks payable to decedent:

Three American Express traveler's checks

Refund check, Watco Corporation

Bank and Savings and Loan Accounts

Examine all bank books, statements, or other evidence as to accounts or amounts on deposit with any financial institution, such as banks, trust companies, savings and loan associations, or credit unions. Describe the type of account (checking account, savings account, savings certificate, money market account, or other), the number of the account or certificate, and the name and location of the institution where the account is held. You should always verify with the bank or institution how title to the account is held.

Banks often resist giving out information about a decedent's accounts to third parties without first seeing letters issued by the court in a formal probate proceeding. This can be a problem if the decedent did not leave detailed records and you do not know if a court proceeding will be required. In this case, we suggest you contact the banks nearest the decedent and present a certified copy of the death certificate. Most banks will provide information to beneficiaries if they sign a notarized affidavit 40 days after the decedent's death alleging that no probate proceeding is pending. That done, the bank will usually tell you if the decedent had bank accounts there and the size, and also if the decedent had a safe-deposit box at the bank.

The amount to put in Column A is the balance on the date of death. Savings accounts and certificates should include accrued interest to the date of death, even if not credited to the account until the end of the quarter following the date of death. The accrued interest can be added as a separate item. The exact balances, including accrued interest, may be obtained directly from the bank or from a recent bank statement. Remember, you are going to insert the full value in Column A, even if it is a joint account or community property account. Then, if the decedent owned only a part interest, you will insert the amount of the fraction or portion owned in Column C and the value of the fractional interest in Column D.

Under Probate Code § 5301, there is a presumption that a joint account is owned proportionately according to the net contributions made by each joint owner.

If the decedent was married or a registered domestic partner and owned a certificate of deposit as community property, you would describe it like this:

	A Total Value of Asset on Date/Death	B How Is Asset Owned?	C Portion Owned by Decedent	D Value of Decedent's Interest	E Probate or Non-probate
2. Bank and Savings & Loan Accounts					
Certificate of Deposit, No. 10235,					
Lighthouse Savings & Loan Assn.,					
Ventura, CA	20,000	CP	1/2	10,000	P*
accrued interest	150			75	

* As you will remember from our earlier discussion, if the decedent's estate is small ($100,000 or less) or if it all goes to a surviving spouse or domestic partner, no formal court proceeding is required and you can put N/P here.

If the decedent wasn't married or a registered domestic partner, or owned an account as his or her separate property, then you should list it like this:

	A Total Value of Asset on Date/Death	B How Is Asset Owned?	C Portion Owned by Decedent	D Value of Decedent's Interest	E Probate or Non-probate
2. Bank and Savings & Loan Accounts					
Interest-bearing checking account,					
Sun Bank, Malibu, CA	5,000	SP	all	5,000	P*

* See footnote above.

Pay-on-Death Accounts (Also Called Totten Trusts or Savings Bank Trusts)

Many people own what are called variously "Totten trust" accounts, "pay-on-death" accounts, or "savings bank trust" accounts. They all amount to the same thing. Title to this kind of bank account will be shown as "Mary Jones, Trustee for Harry Jones." This means the account is owned by Mary Jones, as trustee for the beneficiary, Harry Jones. On the death of the trustee (Mary Jones) the balance of the account automatically passes to the beneficiary, Harry Jones, and the funds are not subject to probate. The account can be held in the name of one or more parties as trustee(s) for one or more parties (Prob. Code § 80), and may be transferred by the same procedures used to terminate joint tenancy bank accounts. If the decedent owned a Totten trust account, you should make a notation in Column B that it is owned in trust (T) and in Column E that it is a nonprobate (N/P) asset. The balance on the date of death should be inserted in Column A. However, if community property was used to establish the trust, it is a community property asset, and only one-half of its value will be owned by the decedent because the other one-half belongs to the surviving spouse or domestic partner, no matter what it says on the trust document. Therefore, you would indicate in Column B that it is also community property (CP), and in Column C that the decedent owned one-half, and insert the value of the one-half interest in Column D.

Real Estate

Carefully review all deeds to real property (real estate) to verify how title is held. If there is any doubt about how title is held, contact a title company and request a title search. The title company will then provide you with a Record Owner Guarantee, which is a report of all property owned by the decedent in any California county. Fees vary, so ask in advance how much the title company will charge for the report. On the Schedule of Assets form list the common address of the property and the kind of property it is, such as "single family residence," "nine-unit apartment building," or "unimproved land." You do not need the legal description for our purposes here, although it may be required on later documents.

To determine the value of real property, consider the condition of the premises or property, the neighborhood, and recent sales prices of comparable property in the area. Assessed values shown on real property tax bills generally do not reflect the true value and should not be used. A private appraisal by a licensed real estate appraiser is good evidence of the value of real property, but it can be expensive. Real estate brokers in the area will also provide a letter of appraisal. (If a formal probate proceeding is required, you should not get a private appraisal. A court-appointed referee will perform the appraisal, so the fee for the private appraisal will be wasted. The probate referee will charge a fee for this service.) If a formal probate proceeding is required, the real property

	A Total Value of Asset on Date/Death	B How Is Asset Owned?	C Portion Owned by Decedent	D Value of Decedent's Interest	E Probate or Non-probate
2. Bank and Savings & Loan Accounts					
Trust savings account, No. 8903, Harbor Bank, San Pedro, in name of decedent as trustee for son, Jon	10,000	T/CP	1/2	5,000	N/P

will be appraised by a probate referee at a cost of one-tenth of 1% of the value of the property. If the decedent owned income property, you should obtain an appraisal from an expert in this field (unless, as mentioned above, there will be a formal probate court proceeding). The value of income property is based on such things as capitalization of income, the kind of financing, the quality of tenants, and the effects rent control may have on such property, as well as a number of other factors, and is probably not something you should try to figure out on your own. The yellow pages of your phone book will list the names of private real estate appraisers in your area.

An appraisal, whether by a private appraiser or a court-appointed referee, is good evidence of the date-of-death value for establishing a new "stepped-up" federal income tax basis of the property in the hands of the new owners when computing capital gains tax, if and when the property is sold. (We discuss tax considerations briefly in Chapter 7.)

Let's assume the decedent had a separate piece of land and owned a house with his or her spouse or domestic partner as community property. You would list the property like this:

	A Total Value of Asset on Date/Death	B How Is Asset Owned?	C Portion Owned by Decedent	D Value of Decedent's Interest	E Probate or Non-probate
3. Real Property (common address, brief description) 5 acres, unimproved grazing land,					
Alameda County	20,000	SP	all	20,000	P*
Single family residence,					
711 Hill St., Los Angeles, CA	300,000	CP	1/2	150,000	P*

*If this property was inherited by a surviving spouse or domestic partner, the simple community property transfer procedures set out in Chapter 15 can be used instead of formal probate.

Now assume the first piece of property was owned by decedent and his wife or partner as joint tenants and the second piece was decedent's separate property, which was passed to his son by use of a living (inter vivos) trust. The Schedule of Assets should be filled in like this:

	A Total Value of Asset on Date/Death	B How Is Asset Owned?	C Portion Owned by Decedent	D Value of Decedent's Interest	E Probate or Non-probate
3. Real Property (common address, brief description) 5 acres, unimproved grazing land,					
Alameda County	20,000	JT	1/2	10,000	N/P
Single family residence,					
711 Hill St., Los Angeles, CA	300,000	SP	all	300,000	N/P

Stocks and Bonds

Information on the type of securities the decedent owned and the way he or she held title can be obtained from examining the stock or bond certificates. Stocks should be listed by the number and type of shares (that is, common or preferred) and the name of the company issuing the shares. For preferred stock, put down the dividend rate. For bonds, put down the total gross face amount (usually in multiples of $1,000), name of the issuer, interest rate, and maturity date. For U.S. Treasury bills, list the total face amount and the maturity date. U.S. Treasury bills are issued either in a single name or in two names joined by "or." If issued in the decedent's name alone, they are included in the probate estate. If in co-ownership form, they pass to the surviving co-owner without probate; they are treated basically the same as joint tenancy assets and should be listed as such. For U.S. Series E savings bonds, list the issue date instead of the maturity date. The issue date is how the value is determined on Series E bonds. Securities that are registered in pay-on-death form may be transferred to the beneficiary on the death of the registered owner without probate.

Assume you have a decedent who owned some XYZ Telephone Company preferred stock and Series E savings bonds before his marriage as separate property. After marriage, he acquired some Transpacific Corporation stock in joint tenancy with his brother, a $5,000 Antioch Drainage System bond as community property with his wife, and a $10,000 U.S. Treasury bill in co-ownership (joint tenancy) form with his wife. Since the assets acquired after marriage are presumed to be community property (although the records don't reflect this), one-half of the decedent's interest in the Transpacific Corporation stock acquired in joint tenancy with the decedent's brother belongs to the surviving spouse. Therefore, the decedent's interest in the Transpacific stock is actually one-fourth (one-half of one-half). The surviving spouse would probably have to file a Spousal or Domestic Partner Property Petition (see Chapter 15) to claim her community property interest in this asset. The remaining two assets ($10,000 Treasury bill and Antioch Drainage System bond) are community property and are owned one-half by the decedent. In this case, your descriptions will look like this:

	A	B	C	D	E
	Total Value of Asset on Date/Death	How Is Asset Owned?	Portion Owned by Decedent	Value of Decedent's Interest	Probate or Non-probate
4. Securities					
Stock (name of company, type, and number of shares)					
50 shares, Transpacific common stock	16,000	JT	1/4	4,000	N/P
200 shares, XYZ Telephone Company 5%					
first preferred stock, par value $100	15,000	SP	all	15,000	P*
Bonds (face amount)					
Three U.S. Series E savings bonds, face					
amount $100 each, issued July 1967	300	SP	all	300	P*
$5,000 Antioch Drainage System,					
District of Contra Costa, 2000					
Drainage bond Series B, 4½% due					
June 1, 2010	5,000	CP	1/2	2,500	P*
$10,000 U.S. Treasury bill, due					
June 30, 2009	10,000	JT	1/2	5,000	N/P

*If decedent left a small estate or if these assets were left to his surviving spouse or registered domestic partner, they can be transferred outside of probate following the instructions in Chapters 11 and 15.

Information on stock and bond values at the date of death can be obtained from newspaper financial sections; however, it takes a little arithmetic to compute the valuations. The value per unit or share is the mean (midpoint) between the highest and lowest quoted selling prices on the date of death. For example, if the high was 15.8 and the low was 14.2, the mean would be determined by adding these two figures together, for a total of 30, and dividing by two (2) for a mean value of 15. Then, by multiplying the unit (mean) value by the number of shares owned for each kind of stock, you will have the total value of the shares. To determine the value of bonds, divide the total gross face amount (par value) by $100 and then multiply that figure by the mean value.

Stock sold on date of death

Description of stock:

100 shares, General Motors, common

Highest selling price on date of death:	84 =	84.00
Lowest selling price on date of death:	81.5 =	81.50
		165.50

165.50 ÷ 2 = 82.75 (mean selling price per share)

82.75 × 100 (shares) = $8,275.00 (date-of-death value)

If there were no sales on the date of death for the security you wish to value, but there were sales on the closest trading days before and after the date of death (for instance, if the decedent died on a Saturday or Sunday and the stock was traded on Friday and Monday), then take the average of the prices on the nearest trading dates before and after death.

No sales on date of death (decedent died on Sunday)

Description of stock:

20 shares, Natural Foods, common

Selling price on Friday (the nearest transaction date prior to death)

High:	12	
Low:	+ 10	
	22	÷ 2 = 11 (mean)

Selling price on Monday (the nearest transaction date after death)

High:	14	
Low:	+ 12	
	26	÷ 2 = 13 (mean)

The fair market value is obtained by averaging the Friday and Monday figures:

$$\frac{(11 + 13)}{2} = \$12.00$$

$12.00 × 20 (shares) = $240.00 (date-of-death value of the stock)

When the closest sales were made more than one trading day away from the date of death (that is, any day but a weekend or holiday), a slightly more complicated formula is used. The fair market value is determined by taking a weighted average of the mean price on the nearest date before the date of death and the mean price on the nearest date after the date of death. The average must be weighted inversely by the numbers of trading days between the selling dates and the valuation date, as in the following example.

Sales made two (2) trading days before date of death and three (3) trading days after date of death

Description of stock: 100 shares of AT&T, common

Selling price two (2) trading days before date of death:

High:	60	
Low:	+ 58	
	118	÷ 2 = 59 (mean)

Selling price three (3) trading days after date of death

High:	62	
Low:	+ 60	
	122	÷ 2 = 61 (mean)

The fair market value is obtained by the following computation (note that the number of trading days before date of death [2] are multiplied by the mean value of the stock on the selling date after date of death, and vice versa):

$$\frac{(3 × 59) + (2 × 61)}{5} = \$59.80 \text{ (unit value per share)}$$

$59.80 × 100 (shares) = $5,980 (value of shares)

Bond traded on date of death

Description of bond: $1,000 Sears Roebuck bond, 8 ⅝ %, due 2012

Highest selling price on date of death:	110 ⅞ =	110.875
Lowest selling price on date of death:	110 ½ =	+110.500
		221.375

Mean selling price = 221.375 ÷ 2	=	110.687
$1,000 (face value of bond) ÷ 100	=	10

110.687 (mean) 10 = $1,106.87 (value of bond at date of death)

Sometimes stock dividends are declared before death but not paid until after death, and these should be included in valuing the stock. For example, if a stock pays a quarterly dividend of $216 per share for the quarter ending June 30 and the decedent died on July 3 of the same year, the $216 dividend should be added to the value of the stock, even though the dividend has not been received as of the date of death.

For bonds, any accrued interest due and unpaid on the date of death should be included in the valuation. To calculate accrued interest, you compute the daily rate of interest and multiply it by the number of days since the last payment to the date of the decedent's death.

The decedent owned a $10,000 bond that pays 6% interest annually on January 1 and July 1 each year.

$10,000 bond
×   .06
$600.00 (interest paid annually) ÷ 365 days = $1.64
(daily interest)

Date of death: July 15

Date of last interest payment: July 1

Days since last interest payment: 14

Accrued interest: 14 × $1.64 = $22.96

If you are perplexed by newspaper financial pages (as many people are) and have problems in determining the values of securities, or if the decedent owned a large number of securities, contact a brokerage firm to obtain the valuations. Many stock brokerage firms have an estate security valuation service for this purpose, and they will provide you with a report of all the information you need at a very modest cost, based on the number of securities you want evaluated. Again, remember to insert the full value of the securities in Column A, and, if they were in co-ownership form, compute the value of the decedent's fractional interest for Column D.

For mutual funds, list the number of shares in the fund, the name of the particular fund, and the location of the fund management firm. Frequently, share certificates for mutual funds are actually held by the fund's custodian, not by the investor. Contact the fund management directly for information on the ownership and a description of the shares and the date-of-death value, or refer to the latest statement.

Assume a single person owned a major investment in a mutual fund as a joint tenant with her brother. You would list it like this:

	A	B	C	D	E
	Total Value of Asset on Date/Death	How Is Asset Owned?	Portion Owned by Decedent	Value of Decedent's Interest	Probate or Non-probate
Mutual Funds (name of fund, number of shares)					
35,000 shares, Dreyfus					
Special Income fund,					
State Street Bank and					
Trust Co., New York	16,000	JT	1/2	8,000	N/P

U.S. Savings Bonds in Co-Ownership or Beneficiary Form

U.S. savings bonds in co-ownership form will be shown registered to "John Jones or Sally Jones," as owners. Bonds registered in beneficiary form appear as "John Jones payable on death (or abbreviated "P.O.D.") Sally Jones." John Jones is the registered owner in this case, and Sally Jones is the beneficiary. Bonds registered in co-ownership with someone, or in beneficiary form, pass to the surviving co-owner or beneficiary on the death of the co-owner or registered owner, much like a joint tenancy asset, and are not subject to probate.

Most commercial banks have the forms for reissuing or redeeming U.S. savings bonds and will assist in these transactions. Only if the present decedent is the surviving co-owner, or survives the beneficiary in case of a beneficiary registration, will these bonds be subject to probate, because in such cases, the present decedent is the only owner of the bonds (there being no co-owner or designated beneficiary living). Savings bonds are tax-deferred assets and subject to income taxes when redeemed. To reissue or redeem savings bonds, the surviving co-owner should take the bonds, along with a certificate copy of the death certificate, to a local bank for assistance in preparing the forms.

Money Market Funds

A money market fund (as opposed to a bank money market account, which is simply another name for a bank account) is a mutual fund, much like a stock market mutual fund. Instead of investing in stocks or bonds, a money market fund lends money to various entities and the interest collected is paid out as "dividends" to the depositor, who is technically a "shareholder" in the fund. The fund's latest monthly statement will show the number of shares owned (normally, shares simply reflect the dollar amount invested; so 5,000 shares means a $5,000 investment) and the value of the decedent's interest in the fund, as well as the way she held title. If in doubt, call or write to the fund management at the address shown on the statement. Remember, even if the account is in the decedent's name alone it may very well be community property if the decedent was married or a registered domestic partner. These accounts can also be held in joint tenancy, like other assets.

Assume that the decedent left a separate property interest in a money market fund worth $3,175.

	A Total Value of Asset on Date/Death	B How Is Asset Owned?	C Portion Owned by Decedent	D Value of Decedent's Interest	E Probate or Non-probate
Mutual Funds (name of fund, number of shares)					
3,175 shares, Executive Money Fund, Account No. 57632, E. F. Hutton, Beverly Hills	3,175	SP	all	3,175	P*

* If the decedent's estate is small, these shares can be transferred outside of formal probate following the instructions in Chapter 11.

Now assume the decedent was married or a registered domestic partner and that the money market shares were community property.

	A Total Value of Asset on Date/Death	B How Is Asset Owned?	C Portion Owned by Decedent	D Value of Decedent's Interest	E Probate or Non-probate
Mutual Funds (name of fund, number of shares)					
Cash Reserve Management Fund, Inc., Paine Webber, Toluca Lake	30,000	CP	1/2	15,000	P*

* See above footnote.

Insurance

List on the schedule only insurance policies that are owned by the decedent. The policy itself does not always indicate the owner, and often insurance policies on the decedent's life are owned by another person, for example, a spouse or partner. (We discuss who owns insurance policies in more detail in "Federal Estate Tax Return," in Chapter 7.) If you write to the insurance company, it will provide you with a written record of the name of the owner. And remember, any insurance policy on the life of the decedent or a surviving spouse or domestic partner may be community property if, and to the extent, the premiums were paid with community funds.

Conversely, the decedent may have owned an insurance policy on a surviving spouse or partner (or someone else). Strange as it may seem, such a policy is considered an asset of the decedent's estate, and the cash value of the policy on the date of the decedent's death is included in the probate estate. Usually, the cash value—as opposed to the face value—of the policy is only a few thousand dollars. If the decedent had such a policy (on the life of someone else), you should write the insurance company to verify ownership and to get a statement of the cash value of the policy on the date of the decedent's death. Upon request, the insurance company will send you a *Life Insurance Statement* (Form 712) setting forth a computation of what is paid in connection with policies on the decedent's life, as well as the cash value of any policies the decedent owned on the life of another.

In describing insurance owned by the decedent on the Schedule of Assets, list the name of the insurance company, the policy number, and the name of the beneficiary. The value of an insurance policy on the decedent's life is the full amount of insurance proceeds paid, but the value of a policy the decedent owned on the life of another is the cash value provided by the insurance company.

Insurance proceeds on the decedent's life payable to named beneficiaries are nonprobate assets. In rare cases, the decedent's estate is the beneficiary, and in this case the insurance proceeds are included in the probate estate.

Suppose a decedent who was married or in a registered domestic partnership owned two life insurance policies as his separate property. One is a paid-up policy on the decedent's life purchased before his marriage or partnership registration and payable to his estate, and the other is on the life of his surviving spouse or partner. Here's how to list them:

	A Total Value of Asset on Date/Death	B How Is Asset Owned?	C Portion Owned by Decedent	D Value of Decedent's Interest	E Probate or Non-probate
5. Insurance (name of company, policy number, name of beneficiary, name of owner)					
Policies on decedent's life					
Proceeds, Acme Insurance Policy No. 23456, on decedent's life, payable to estate as beneficiary	10,000	SP	all	10,000	P*
Policies owned by decedent on another					
Decedent's interest as owner in Grand Insurance Co., Policy No. 654321, on life of decedent's spouse (or domestic partner)	1,500	SP	all	1,500	P*

* No formal probate will be necessary if decedent leaves a small estate or if this property is transferred to a surviving spouse or domestic partner.

What if the decedent purchased a policy on his life during his marriage or domestic partnership, without assigning ownership to anyone else and naming his daughter by a previous marriage as beneficiary? Here's how to list it:

	A Total Value of Asset on Date/Death	B How Is Asset Owned?	C Portion Owned by Decedent	D Value of Decedent's Interest	E Probate or Non-probate
5. Insurance (name of company, policy number, name of beneficiary, name of owner)					
Policies on decedent's life					
Proceeds, Beneficial Life Policy No. 45609, on decedent's life, payable to decedent's daughter, Mary	20,000	CP	1/2	10,000	N/P

Retirement and Death Benefits Through Decedent's Employment

If the decedent was employed, his or her employer should be asked whether there are any unpaid salary, pension, or survivors benefits payable. If so, list the name of the company paying the benefit, the name of the beneficiary, and the amount. Benefits payable to named beneficiaries are nonprobate assets. The value of each benefit is the actual amount paid in a lump sum. If the decedent was married, this is probably a community property asset.

Individual Retirement Accounts

If the decedent owned an individual retirement account (IRA), you should contact the institution where the investment was set up (bank, credit union, insurance company, or stock brokerage) and ask for instructions on how to transfer the asset to the beneficiary. In most cases, a certified copy of the decedent's death certificate is all that is required. An IRA is not subject to probate unless it is payable to the decedent's estate. When the IRA is opened, the owner designates a beneficiary to receive the investment on the death of the owner. Usually, if the beneficiary is the surviving spouse or partner, the IRA may be continued with the spouse or partner as the new owner. If a beneficiary has not been designated, or the named beneficiary dies before the owner, payment is usually made in the following order of priority: (1) the surviving spouse or domestic partner, (2) the decedent's surviving child, or (3) the decedent's estate.

Unlike most assets bequeathed at death, IRAs (except Roth IRAs) and other tax-deferred assets are subject to income taxes on withdrawal of funds because this income was not taxed before the death of the holder. If the decedent was over age 70½ and taking mandatory distributions, for the first year the heir must generally receive distributions at least as rapidly as the decedent received them. After that, minimum distributions are based on the beneficiary's life expectancy. If the decedent died before mandatory distributions began, the plan may allow the heir to withdraw the funds over his or her life expectancy.

	A	B	C	D	E
	Total Value of Asset on Date/Death	How Is Asset Owned?	Portion Owned by Decedent	Value of Decedent's Interest	Probate or Non-probate
6. Retirement and Death Benefits (description, beneficiary, amount) **Employee benefits**					
Death Benefit, Public Employees Retirement System, payable to decedent's spouse (or domestic partner)	50,000	CP	1/2	25,000	N/P

	A	B	C	D	E
	Total Value of Asset on Date/Death	How Is Asset Owned?	Portion Owned by Decedent	Value of Decedent's Interest	Probate or Non-probate
Individual Retirement Accounts					
IRA Account No. 13876-2, at Superior Savings and Loan, Kelso, California, payable to decedent's spouse (or domestic partner)	$2,500	CP	1/2	$1,250	N/P

RESOURCE

More information about retirement accounts.
IRAs, 401(k)s & Other Retirement Plans: Taking Your Money Out, by Twila Slesnick and John Suttle (Nolo), explains all the options of those who inherit a retirement account.

Amounts Due the Decedent

Any right the decedent had to receive money from another person or entity should be listed as an asset. List any personal loans, rents, dividends, unpaid fees, salary, or commissions owed to the decedent, with the name of the payor, the amount due, and a brief description of what it is for. The value of these items is the amount due, unless it is unlikely the debt will be collected, in which case it will have no value and should not be included. For instance, if the decedent made an unsecured loan to someone who refuses or is unable to pay it back, or the payments are extremely delinquent or the person cannot be located, then this is not regarded as an estate asset. If any note is secured by a deed of trust on real property, a brief description of the property should be noted.

The value of the notes will be the principal balance still owing and unpaid as of the date of death, plus the amount of any accrued but unpaid interest to that date.

Assume Robert Morgan, the decedent, had loaned $50,000 to his son, J.P., to purchase a house, and at the time of Robert's death, J.P. had repaid $15,000. Robert was married to Ellen, and the loan is considered to be community property.

	A Total Value of Asset on Date/Death	B How Is Asset Owned?	C Portion Owned by Decedent	D Value of Decedent's Interest	E Probate or Non-probate
7. Amounts Due the Decedent (name of payor, amount)					
$50,000 promissory note of J.P. Morgan, dated 3/1/xx, interest at 8%, payable $350 on the first of each month, secured by deed of trust on real property located at 515 Sutter Street, San Jose; principal balance on date of death $35,000	35,000	CP	1/2	17,500	P*
accrued interest	150			75	

* Formal probate would not be necessary if this note was left to Ellen. (See Chapter 15 for details on how to transfer property to a surviving spouse or domestic partner.)

The accrued interest is computed by determining the daily amount of interest on the principal balance due (that is, 0.08 × $35,000 ÷ 365 = $7.66), and multiplying this figure by the number of days from the date of the last note payment to the date of death. For instance, if the last note payment was May 1, 2011, and the decedent died on May 5, 2011, there would be five days' accrued and unpaid interest due on the date of death, or $38.30 (5 × $7.66).

Tangible Personal Property

This category is for miscellaneous items of personal property. Personal effects that are not particularly valuable can be grouped together under the general heading of "furniture, furnishings, and personal effects," and given a lump-sum value. Remember, you do not consider what these items cost, but what they are worth secondhand. This is generally a small fraction of their original purchase price. For example, the value of these items, except such things as valuable stereo equipment, pianos, home computers, and the like, for a five-room house would probably

be around $500 to $1,000. For valuable jewelry, furs, coins, paintings, antiques, electronic equipment, musical instruments, and so on, you should obtain a private appraisal from an expert in each field. (As mentioned earlier, if the assets will go through formal probate, a court-appointed referee will perform necessary appraisals, and you should not hire a private appraiser.) The yellow pages of your telephone book will list appraisers who specialize in various types of assets. Any appraisal fees should be paid from estate assets as discussed in Chapters 13 and 14. All items in this category are usually probate items.

For a decedent who is not married or in a registered domestic partnership, your descriptions will be in the following form:

	A Total Value of Asset on Date/Death	B How Is Asset Owned?	C Portion Owned by Decedent	D Value of Decedent's Interest	E Probate or Non-probate
9. Tangible Personal Property (household furniture, furnishings, personal effects, books, jewelry, artwork, valuable collections, antiques, etc.)					
One Tiffany blue diamond ring, 2 carats	2,500	SP	all	2,500	P*
Antique coin collection in decedent's residence	3,000	SP	all	3,000	P*
Household furniture, furnishings, and personal effects	750	SP	all	750	P*

* If you have a married or domestic partner decedent, the ring would probably be separate property, but the coin collection and personal effects would probably be community property and show a one-half interest.

Automobiles

Examine the ownership certificate (pink slip) to see how title to each vehicle is registered. Any automobile held in the name of "Mary Smith *or* Andy Smith" is considered by the Motor Vehicles Department to be in joint tenancy ownership, and it may be transferred to the surviving owner without probate. Similarly, California vehicles may be registered in TOD (transfer-on-death) form, which means that the TOD beneficiary inherits the vehicle without probate. (The procedures for transfer are given in Chapter 10.)

Describe automobiles by the year, make, and model. Automobiles are valued at the average between the wholesale and retail *Blue Book* price, unless the automobile is unusual (for example, antique, foreign, or classic), in which case an appraisal should be obtained. You can find a *Blue Book* at any car dealer or public library. *Kelley Blue Book* quotes are available online at www.kbb.com.

	A	B	C	D	E
	Total Value of Asset on Date/Death	How Is Asset Owned?	Portion Owned by Decedent	Value of Decedent's Interest	Probate or Non-probate
10. Automobiles (year, make, model)					
1998 Dodge Caravan, in name of John Doe and Mary Doe	10,000	CP	1/2	5,000	P*
1995 Cadillac Seville, 4-door sedan, in name of decedent	20,000	SP	all	20,000	P*

* If decedent left an estate of $100,000 or less (excluding joint tenancy property and property left to a surviving spouse or domestic partner), formal probate would not be necessary. (See Chapter 11.) Similarly, if he or she left an item of property to a surviving spouse or partner, that item would not have to go through formal probate. (See Chapter 15.)

Business Interests

If the decedent had any interest in a business as a sole proprietor or partner or owned an interest in a closely held (private) corporation, you should list it here with the name of the business, partnership, or corporation, and the decedent's percentage ownership and manner of holding title. You may need to contact the other parties involved to obtain this information. Assets like these are valued according to many technical rules and you will need to get an estimate of the value either from an accountant or a firm that is expert in business appraisals. Some CPA firms specialize in business appraisals; you can also ask a bank trust department to recommend an appraiser.

Other Assets

List here any other assets not included in the above categories. Here again, you will probably need an expert appraiser to determine the value of such things as copyrights or royalty interests, patents or future residuals if the amount involved is large. (Remember, don't hire a private appraiser if formal probate is required. Instead, contact the court-appointed probate referee and ask for an appraisal. Otherwise, you may have to pay both the referee's fee and the fee for the private appraisal.)

Assume the decedent owned an interest in a partnership as separate property, which she left to her daughter by use of a living (inter vivos) trust, and a community property interest in a business. These would be described like this:

	A Total Value of Asset on Date/Death	B How Is Asset Owned?	C Portion Owned by Decedent	D Value of Decedent's Interest	E Probate or Non-probate
11. Business Interests (names of partnerships or family corporations, brief descriptions)					
Eureka Mining Co., a general partnership,					
500 Unity Building, Banning, CA	15,000	SP	all	15,000	N/P
"The Rori Kennel," a sole proprietorship,					
111 Bunratty Rd., Kelso, CA	70,000	CP	1/2	35,000	P*

* If the decedent left her community property interest to her spouse or domestic partner, formal probate would be unnecessary and this asset could be transferred following the instructions in Chapter 15.

	A Total Value of Asset on Date/Death	B How Is Asset Owned?	C Portion Owned by Decedent	D Value of Decedent's Interest	E Probate or Non-probate
12. Other Assets (copyrights, royalty interests, any other property not listed above)					
Copyright on book *How to Play Tennis*,					
published 1982 by Harvest Pub. Co.,					
Los Angeles, annual royalties approx.					
$5,000 with three-year life					
expectancy. (Approx.)	15,000	CP	1/2	7,500	P*
Estimated future residuals due					
decedent from Screen Actors Guild					
for services prior to death	500	SP	all	500	P*

* These assets would not be subject to formal probate if decedent's entire estate is worth $100,000 or less, or were left to a surviving spouse or domestic partner. (See Chapters 11 and 15.)

Schedule of Assets for a Sample Estate

Let's look at a sample estate, the *Estate of Sybil Sample, Deceased*, and see how its Schedule of Assets would take form.

Sybil Sample married Cyrus Sample in San Jose, California, in 1974. They lived in California continuously during their marriage until Sybil's death. Sybil left all of her community and separate property to Cyrus, except for her savings bonds, which she left to her cousin Alice.

At the time of marriage, Sybil owned an unimproved lot in San Bernardino County; three $500 U.S. Series E savings bonds; a savings account at Union Bank in Arcadia held in Sybil's name as trustee for her mother, Anne; and a $40,000 promissory note secured by a deed of trust on real property. Sybil also owned a $15,000 Sun Life insurance policy on her life, naming her mother as beneficiary, on which one-third of the premiums were paid with her earnings during her marriage to Cyrus.

Cyrus, a newspaper columnist, owned a home in San Jose at the time of his marriage to Sybil, which he sold in 1976 for $120,000, receiving cash of $100,000 and a $20,000 promissory note secured by the real property. Using the $100,000 as a down payment, Cyrus purchased a new home in which Sybil and Cyrus took title in both their names as husband and wife. Cyrus and Sybil, who was a school librarian, both continued to work after marriage, depositing all of their excess earnings into a joint savings account at Pacific States Bank. During their marriage, Cyrus purchased 200 shares of AT&T stock and a 1999 Toyota Camry automobile with his earnings, taking title in his name alone. Sybil and Cyrus also invested money in Franklin Group Money Funds, a money market fund, and purchased a $10,000 Central High School District school bond, holding both of these assets as joint tenants. Cyrus also took out a $100,000 Aetna Life Insurance policy on his life during their marriage, and transferred complete ownership in the policy to Sybil. Sybil paid the premiums on the policy from her separate funds. For their anniversary in 1982, Cyrus gave Sybil a three-quarter carat diamond ring.

At her death Sybil also had an uncashed refund check from a hardware store and $3 in cash. She and Cyrus were owed $2,000 by Joe Swinger, to whom they had made an unsecured noninterest loan. At Sybil's death, a $5,000 pension plan death benefit became payable to Cyrus.

The Schedule of Assets for Sybil's estate is set out below. The information inserted on the schedule for each asset was determined by the following facts:

Item 1: Cash Items

The cash in Sybil's possession and the refund check are community property, having been acquired during her marriage. Thus, Sybil has a one-half vested interest in these items. These are technically part of her probate estate, but since Sybil left all of her community and separate property to Cyrus, they can be transferred without having to go through formal probate. (See Chapter 15.)

Item 2: Bank and Savings and Loan Accounts

The Pacific States Bank account, held in joint tenancy, passes to Cyrus outside of probate. Nevertheless, you should insert the full value of the account in Column A and the value of a one-half interest in Column D.

The savings account at Union Bank in Arcadia is a Totten trust account (sometimes called a pay-on-death account, or bank savings trust account), which passes to Sybil's mother as named beneficiary, without probate, on Sybil's death. The entire proceeds of the account are Sybil's separate property. She was the sole owner prior to death; she didn't transfer any percentage of ownership in the account to her mother when she made her a beneficiary, and didn't deposit any of her community property earnings in the account during marriage.

Item 3: Real Property

The residence is community property because title was acquired by Sybil and Cyrus during marriage as husband and wife, and one-half of the residence is included in Sybil's estate. The $100,000 that Cyrus received from the sale of his previous home was Cyrus's separate property, having been derived from a separate property asset he owned prior to his marriage. However, by using the $100,000 as a down payment on their new home during marriage and taking title as husband and wife, he made a $50,000 gift to Sybil from his separate property by converting it into community property. The $20,000 promissory note Cyrus received from the sale of his previous home (plus the income from the note) remains his

separate property, and no part of the note is included in Sybil's estate.

In the case of the residence, a formal probate court proceeding won't be necessary because it passes to Cyrus under Sybil's will. Cyrus can use the simplified procedure to transfer property to a surviving spouse. (See Chapter 15.)

The unimproved lot in San Bernardino is Sybil's separate property, since she owned it prior to marriage, and it is included 100% in her estate.

Item 4: Securities

Sybil owned the three U.S. Series E savings bonds prior to marriage, so they are her separate property and included 100% in her estate. They will be subject to probate because they were left to cousin Alice. The Franklin Group Money Fund shares and the $10,000 Central High School District school bond are held in joint tenancy and, therefore, are not subject to probate. Although it is held in Cyrus's name alone, the AT&T stock is community property, because they purchased it during their marriage with community property funds, and one-half of the stock is included in Sybil's estate. Because this property goes to Cyrus, no formal probate will be required. (See Chapter 15.)

Item 5: Insurance

The $15,000 Sun Life Policy that was owned by Sybil prior to her marriage was her separate property when she married Cyrus. However, because she paid one-third of the premiums during marriage with community property funds, she converted one-third of the policy proceeds into community property. Therefore, even though her mother is the named beneficiary, Cyrus owns a one-half vested interest in the community property portion of the proceeds, or one-sixth (one-half of one-third) of $15,000, which is $2,500. The policy proceeds are not subject to probate because there is a named beneficiary; however, since the premiums were paid from both separate and community property, the total value of the policy is apportioned between separate and community property, based on the portion of the total premiums paid from each. Thus, the amount included in

Sybil's gross estate is $12,500 ($15,000 less Cyrus's community interest of $2,500). In this case, you put the total value of the proceeds ($15,000) in Column A and the part owned by Sybil ($12,500) in Column D.

The $100,000 Aetna Life Policy on Cyrus's life is Sybil's separate property, and the total cash value of the policy on her date of death is included in her estate. It would be subject to formal probate except that Sybil left all of her property to Cyrus and, therefore, it qualifies for the simplified spousal transfer provisions discussed in Chapter 15. Sometimes you can transfer ownership of an insurance policy simply by furnishing the carrier with a copy of the will.

Item 6: Retirement and Death Benefits

The $5,000 pension plan death benefit, payable to Cyrus, is not subject to probate, but one-half is included in Sybil's estate as community property because it is payable by reason of her employment.

Item 7: Amounts Due the Decedent

The $2,000 loan due from Joe Swinger is community property and one-half is included in Sybil's estate. It would be subject to formal probate except that it qualifies for the simplified spousal transfer provisions discussed in Chapter 15.

Item 8: Promissory Notes

The $40,000 trust deed note owned by Sybil prior to marriage is her separate property and is included 100% in her estate. It would be subject to formal probate if it had been left to anyone but Cyrus.

Item 9: Tangible Personal Property

The household furniture and personal effects are included in Sybil's estate to the extent of her one-half community property interest. The gold diamond ring is Sybil's separate property, having been acquired as a gift, and is included 100% in her estate. Both of these would be subject to formal probate if they had not been left to a spouse.

Item 10: Automobiles

A one-half interest in the Camry is included in Sybil's estate as community property, even though Cyrus took title in his name alone. Since Cyrus inherits this vehicle anyway, nothing need be done to transfer ownership to him.

An example of the Schedule of Assets for Sybil's estate is shown below. After you review it, go on to the next chapter to see how to actually transfer the assets in Sybil's estate.

Sample Schedule of Assets

Schedule of Assets

Estate of _____ SYBIL SAMPLE _____, Deceased

Description of Assets	A Total Value of Asset on Date/Death	B How Is Asset Owned?	C Portion Owned by Decedent	D Value of Decedent's Interest	E Probate or Non-probate
1. Cash Items					
Cash in decedent's possession	3.00	CP	1/2	1.50	P
Uncashed checks payable to decedent:					
Refund from Abco Hardware	5.60	CP	1/2	2.80	P
2. Bank and Savings & Loan Accounts					
a. Sav. Acct. #1234, Pacific States	20,000	JT	1/2	10,000	NP
Bank, San Jose (acct. int.)	150	JT	1/2	75	NP
b. Sav. Acct. #0832, Union Bank	6,000	T (SP)	all	6,000	NP
Arcadia (in trust for Anne) (acct. int.)	70	T (SP)	all	70	NP
3. Real Property (common address, brief description)					
a. Single-family residence,					
930 Hill Street, San Jose	500,000	CP	1/2	250,000	P
b. Unimproved lot, San Bernardino					
County	15,000	SP	all	15,000	P
4. Securities					
Stock (name of company, type, and number of shares)					
200 shares AT&T common (in name of					
Cyrus Sample)	10,000	CP	1/2	5,000	P

Sample Schedule of Assets (cont'd)

	A	B	C	D	E
	Total Value of Asset on Date/Death	How Is Asset Owned?	Portion Owned by Decedent	Value of Decedent's Interest	Probate or Non-probate
Bonds (face amount)					
$10,000 Central High School Dist.	9,800	JT	1/2	4,900	NP
bond, Series C, 4%, 12-31-05 (acc. int.)	198	JT	1/2	99	NP
U.S. Savings Bonds/Treasury Bills (series, amount, date of issue)					
Three $500 U.S. Series E savings	1,500	SP	all	1,500	P
bonds, issued July 1975					
Mutual Funds (name of fund, number of shares)					
50,000 shares Franklin Group	50,000	JT	1/2	25,000	NP

5. Insurance (name of company, policy number, name of beneficiary, name of owner)

Policies on decedent's life

	A	B	C	D	E
$15,000 Sun Life Ins. Policy, No. 83792	15,000	1/3 CP	1/6 as CP	12,500	NP
(beneficiary: decedent's mother)		2/3 SP	2/3 as SP		

Policies owned by decedent on another

	A	B	C	D	E
$100,000 Aetna Life Policy, No. 24487	4,000	SP	all	4,000	P

6. Retirement and Death Benefits (description, beneficiary, amount)

Employee benefits

	A	B	C	D	E
$5,000 School employee's pension plan	5,000	CP	1/2	2,500	NP

Pension, profit-sharing, savings plans

Social Security/Railroad Retirement

Individual Retirement Accounts

Sample Schedule of Assets (cont'd)

	A Total Value of Asset on Date/Death	B How Is Asset Owned?	C Portion Owned by Decedent	D Value of Decedent's Interest	E Probate or Non-probate
7. Amounts Due the Decedent (name of payor, amount)					
$2,000 unsecured noninterest-bearing loan due from Joe Swinger	2,000	CP	1/2	1,000	P
8. Promissory Note (name of payor, date, amount, balance)					
$40,000 promissory note of Mynos cash, 5% int., dated 7-1-85, secured					
by trust deed on real property at	35,000	SP	all	35,000	P
123 Main St., Los Angeles (acc. int.)	123.50	SP	all	123.50	P
9. Tangible Personal Property (household furniture, furnishings, personal effects, books, jewelry, artwork, valuable collections, antiques, etc.)					
a. Household furnishings and personal effects	1,000	CP	1/2	500	P
b. Lady's gold ring, 3/4 carat diamond	1,500	SP	all	1,500	P
10. Automobiles (year, make, model)					
1999 Toyota Camry	4,000	CP	1/2	2,000	P
11. Business Interests (names of partnerships or family corporations, brief descriptions)					
12. Other Assets (copyrights, royalty interests, any other property not listed above)					
Total Value of Decedent's Gross Estate				$ 376,770.80	

Sample Schedule of Assets (cont'd)

Deductions (for federal estate tax purposes)

a. Personal debts owed by decedent at date of death

Clark's Department Store: $1,180 (CP) — $ 590

b. Mortgages/promissory notes due

Beneficial Sav. & Loan (house loan): $98,000 (CP) — 49,000

c. Expenses of estate administration

Appraisals, transfer fees, recording fees, court costs — 800

d. Last illness expenses

Richard Roe, M.D., medical services — 1,500

Mary Smith, nursing care — 600

e. Funeral expenses

Chapel Mortuary — 2,589

f. Sales contracts (automobiles, furniture, television)

C & D Financial (auto loan): $1,150 (CP) — 575

Total Deductions $ 55,654

Total Value of Decedent's Gross Estate (from previous page) $ 376,770.80

Total Deductions (from line above) 55,654.00

Value of Decedent's Net Estate $ 321,116.80

How to Identify the Best Transfer Procedure

After you've figured out what the decedent owned and who should get it, the next step is to determine the best method of actually transferring the property. This chapter does not actually deal with the "how-tos" of making transfers, but serves as a road map to the detailed transfer instructions contained in the chapters that follow. In other words, after reading this chapter carefully, you should be able to identify the most direct route to your property transfer goal.

On your Schedule of Assets (Chapter 5), you labeled each asset (in Column B) as separate property, community property, joint tenancy property, trust property, and so on. Let's briefly review the transfer rules for each.

Nonprobate Assets

Assets contained in estates where the decedent planned to avoid probate automatically avoid probate. It's important to realize, however, that the following list of nonprobate items does not include every kind of property that passes without formal probate proceedings. Because of several simplifications in California law in the last decade, some assets that used to have to be submitted to a probate court are now exempt from formal probate. Because a particular type of asset is not listed here does not mean that formal probate is required. It very well may not be. In the next section of this chapter we review all assets that are potentially subject to probate and help you to see if in fact you will have to file a formal probate proceeding or if you can use one of the simpler methods to transfer the property.

Joint Tenancy Assets

Joint tenancy assets are not subject to probate, and the decedent's interest in property held in this manner passes to the surviving joint tenant(s) by operation of law. Chapter 10 explains how to transfer title to the surviving joint tenant(s).

 SEE AN EXPERT

Note for surviving spouses and domestic partners. In most situations, property held in joint tenancy by spouses or domestic partners is community property. You may transfer it either as a joint tenancy asset or you may use a Spousal or Domestic Partner Property Order (discussed in Chapter 15) to officially establish the joint tenancy property as community property and obtain the favorable tax treatment that community property receives. We discuss these tax rules in Chapter 7. If after reading this discussion you are still confused, see an accountant.

Trustee Bank Accounts (Totten Trust Accounts or Pay-on-Death Accounts)

These accounts may be transferred outside of probate in the same manner as joint tenancy bank accounts by using the procedures explained in Chapter 10.

Living Trusts

Many people put their property in living (inter vivos) trusts to avoid probate. Any property held in a living trust created by the decedent is not subject to probate administration if the property was actually transferred to the trust, in which case title will be held in the name of the trustee. Occasionally, a decedent may have signed a trust document describing the assets to be held in the trust but for some reason failed to sign documents actually transferring title into his, her, or another's name as trustee. To check this, carefully examine all title documents, such as real property deeds, stock certificates, and motor vehicle pink slips. If the asset was transferred to the trust, the ownership document will show title held something like this: "I.M. Smart, trustee of the I.M. Smart Trust."

Miscellaneous items of personal property that don't have title documents can be included in a living trust without being formally transferred to the trust.

When the person who established a living trust dies, property held in the trust is transferred to the beneficiary (named in the trust document) by a successor trustee named in the trust. The procedure used to transfer property subject to a living trust is set out in Chapter 12.

U.S. Savings Bonds in Co-Ownership or Beneficiary Form

Bonds registered in this manner also avoid probate, and your local bank will assist in redeeming these bonds or reregistering them in the name of the new owner. The Federal Reserve Bank and many commercial banks have the required forms and will assist in preparing them. The original bond certificates and a certified copy of the decedent's death certificate are required to make the transfer.

Life Insurance and Death Benefits Payable to Named Beneficiaries

If life insurance and other death benefits payable to named beneficiaries have not already been collected, these benefits may be claimed by contacting the company or organization responsible for making payment. The company provides the necessary forms and will notify you of the other documents it requires (usually a certified copy of the decedent's death certificate and the policy). Instructions are in Chapter 2.

Insurance proceeds payable to the decedent's estate, as well as the cash value of any insurance policies the decedent owned on the life of another person, require probate unless the entire estate qualifies to avoid probate based on its small size (see Chapter 11) or unless the property is transferred to a surviving spouse (see Chapter 15).

Community Property With Right of Survivorship

If a married or partnered couple held title to property as "community property with right of survivorship," the survivor inherits the deceased person's half-interest automatically, without probate. The property must be clearly identified on the transfer document (a real estate deed, for example) as community property with the right of survivorship. (Civ. Code § 682.1.)

Life Estates

A life estate is created when a person transfers real property to someone else but keeps the right to use the property for the rest of his or her life. We define life estates in detail in Chapter 4 and discuss transfers of property held in life estates in Chapter 12.

Assets That May Be Subject to Formal Probate

The remaining assets on your schedule may have to go through formal probate. They will fall into one of the following three groups: (1) property held as community property, (2) property held in the decedent's name alone, or (3) property held in cotenancy form, usually expressed in a deed or title slip "as tenants in common." Broadly speaking, determining the size of the estate and whom the property is left to will tell you if formal probate is required.

Community Property or Separate Property That Passes Outright to the Decedent's Surviving Spouse or Domestic Partner

> **SKIP AHEAD**
> **Skip ahead.** If the decedent wasn't married or in a domestic partnership at death, you can skip this and go on to the next section.

Any property—community property or separate property—that goes outright (not subject to a life estate or in a trust) to the decedent's surviving spouse or domestic partner under the terms of the decedent's will or by intestate succession in the absence of a will does not require formal probate. (Prob. Code § 13500.) Nevertheless, a court order, called a Spousal or Domestic Partner Property Order, is often required to transfer title to certain types of assets, including real property or stocks and bonds. Chapter 15 describes the simple, informal court procedure for obtaining this court order. Procedures to transfer property to a surviving spouse or domestic partner can usually be commenced immediately after one spouse or partner dies, unless there is a survival period required in the will. There is no limitation on the amount or value of the assets transferred.

To find out if any of a decedent's assets fall into this category, examine the will carefully (if there is one) to see if the decedent left the property to the surviving spouse or partner. Then, verify that such property passes to the survivor without any limitations as to ownership. If the survivor is given a qualified ownership in the property, such as in a trust, it is not eligible to be transferred in this way.

If there is no will, then all community property, plus at least a part (and sometimes all) of the decedent's separate property, if any, will go outright to the surviving spouse or domestic partner under intestate succession laws. As you will know if you read Chapter 3, the amount of the separate property that a surviving spouse or partner is entitled to under intestate succession depends on whether the decedent left any surviving children or other close relatives entitled to receive a portion of the separate property. Refer to Chapter 3 to see how a decedent's separate property is divided in the absence of a will. Again, if a court order is necessary to transfer this property, as it probably is in the case of real property or securities, see Chapter 15.

If the decedent willed his or her interest in community property or separate property to someone other than the surviving spouse or partner, then you should use the procedures described below to transfer it.

Property in Estates Under $100,000

For many Californians of modest means, no formal probate is required. California Probate Code §§ 13000 to 13209 provide a simple way to transfer property in estates that don't exceed a total gross value of $100,000. All of the personal property may be transferred with a one-page affidavit. You may also use an affidavit procedure to transfer real property worth $20,000 or less, and title to real property up to $100,000 in value may be passed by a simple court

procedure. There is a waiting period, usually 40 days, before you can request the transfers.

These summary procedures may, in many instances, be used for estates over $100,000, because several kinds of assets aren't counted in computing the $100,000 limitation. For example, all joint tenancy property (both real and personal) is excluded, as well as all property that goes outright to a surviving spouse or domestic partner (community or separate), and certain other property. Chapter 11 explains this simple method of transferring assets in more detail. Even if the estate you are dealing with contains somewhat more than $100,000 of personal property (and real property held in joint tenancy), you will want to read Chapter 11 to see if the various exclusions allowed by law permit the estate to qualify anyway.

Remaining Assets

All remaining assets that do not fall into one of the above categories require a formal probate court proceeding before title may be transferred. Generally, this includes remaining assets that are:

- not held in trust
- not held in joint tenancy
- not community or separate property going outright to the surviving spouse or domestic partner, and
- not part of estates that are under $100,000 in value.

Fortunately, even if you find that an asset is subject to probate, you can still normally handle the necessary paperwork yourself. Probate court proceedings are not as cumbersome as they once were, and today a simple estate may normally be settled through court proceedings within nine months without the need to hire a lawyer. We tell you how to conduct a probate court proceeding in detail in Chapters 13 and 14.

Examples of How Assets Are Transferred in Typical Estates

Let's return now to the estate of Sybil Sample, which we introduced in the preceding chapter. Our idea here is to illustrate the process by which the assets of a typical estate are transferred. You may want to refresh your memory by reviewing the property in Sybil's estate before going on. If you analyze Sybil's Schedule of Assets in Chapter 5, you will find that the assets fall into the categories described above.

Joint Tenancy Assets

Sybil held three assets in joint tenancy with her husband, Cyrus: the savings account at Pacific States Bank, the $10,000 Central High School District school bond, and the 50,000 shares of Franklin Group Money Fund. These all go to Cyrus without the need for probate. Chapter 10 shows how to transfer joint tenancy assets.

Trustee Bank Account

The proceeds in the Totten trust account at Union Bank in Arcadia (Item 2) should be transferred to Sybil's mother, Anne, as beneficiary using the procedures outlined in Chapter 10. (This is the same as for a joint tenancy account.) Since Sybil established this account prior to her marriage, Cyrus has no community property interest in it.

Insurance Payable to Named Beneficiary

The proceeds of the Sun Life Insurance policy may be paid directly to the beneficiaries by contacting the company for the necessary claim forms and submitting a certified copy of the decedent's death certificate. Since Sybil's mother, Anne, is the named beneficiary of the policy, the insurance company will pay the proceeds to Anne unless it is advised otherwise. If Cyrus wants to collect his vested community interest in the proceeds, he must contact the insurance company and work out an arrangement with the company and Sybil's mother. If it cannot be done on this basis, Cyrus would have to see an attorney. Alternatively, Cyrus could obtain a Spousal or Domestic Partner Property Order (see Chapter 15) confirming that $2,500 of the proceeds belongs to him as his community property interest. Of course, because Cyrus gets most of the rest of the property, he might well conclude that for personal or family reasons he does not want to challenge Sybil's intent in naming Anne as beneficiary.

Pension Plan Death Benefit Payable to Named Beneficiary

The $5,000 school employee's pension plan death benefit, payable to Cyrus as named beneficiary, may be collected by submitting a certified copy of the death certificate to the pension plan office and asking for the necessary claim forms.

All Other Assets

The other assets on the schedule make up the part of Sybil's estate that is potentially subject to probate, unless they fall within one of the exceptions to probate discussed at the beginning of this chapter. The persons to whom these assets will pass and the method used to transfer such property depend on whether or not Sybil left a will naming who is to receive the property or whether she instead died intestate.

Sample Estates

In Chapter 5, we assumed that Sybil left a will, but here let's look at both possibilities and see what happens to the assets in each case. To make this easier, let's first divide Sybil's remaining assets into separate property and community property. Again, if you are not sure how to do this, please reread Chapter 4.

Community Property (Sybil's ½ interest)

Cash	$3.00
Abco Hardware refund	5.60
San Jose residence	250,000.00
AT&T stock	5,000.00
Loan due from Joe Swinger	1,000.00
Household furnishings, etc.	500.00
Toyota Camry	+ 2,000.00
	$258,508.60

Separate Property (Sybil's 100% interest)

San Bernardino lot	$15,000.00
Series E bonds	1,500.00
Aetna Life Insurance policy	4,000.00
Mynos cash T.D. note	35,123.00
Diamond ring	+ 1,500.00
	$57,123.00

Sybil Dies With a Will

Assume Sybil left a will leaving Cyrus all property except her savings bonds, which she left to her cousin Alice. All of the property (both community property and separate property) left to Cyrus may be transferred to him without formal probate administration using a Spousal or Domestic Partner Property Order, obtained by using the procedures outlined in Chapter 15.

A court order is not needed to transfer ownership of every asset to Cyrus. For instance, the AT&T stock and Camry are already in his name, and since most of the other assets have no title documents, they will pass to Cyrus automatically under Probate Code § 13500. Therefore, the only assets for which an official transfer document (the Spousal or Domestic Partner Property Order) will be required are the San Jose residence, the San Bernardino lot, and the Mynos cash trust deed note.

Because Sybil's will left some property to someone other than Cyrus (Cousin Alice), our next step is to see what the property consists of. If it is valued under $100,000, it may be transferred to the person(s) named in the will by using the affidavit procedure discussed in Chapter 11.

However, if Sybil willed property having a gross total value exceeding $100,000 to someone other than her surviving spouse, formal probate court proceedings are required before it can be transferred. Those proceedings are discussed in Chapter 14.

Sybil Dies Without a Will

If we assume Sybil died without a will, leaving Cyrus and her mother as her only heirs (there are no children), then intestate succession laws dictate that all of her community property would go outright to Cyrus and her separate property would be given one-half to Cyrus and one-half to her mother. (Remember, we show you how to figure out who inherits property in the absence of a will in Chapter 3.)

In this case, the community property and Cyrus's one-half interest in the separate property may be transferred to Cyrus without formal probate by use of a Spousal or Domestic Partner Property Order, as discussed in Chapter 15. The other one-half interest in the separate property must go through probate or, if it is valued at less than $100,000, may be transferred by the simplified procedures in Chapter 11. At the close of the probate proceeding, the court will make an order distributing a one-half interest in the separate property to Sybil's mother. If Cyrus and Sybil's mother do not wish to own a one-half interest in each separate property asset (which might not be practical in the case of the diamond ring or the Aetna Life Insurance policy), they may make an agreement for distribution after they obtain court orders.

Estate of Cyrus Sample, Deceased

Now for further illustration, let's see what happens to Cyrus's estate when he dies approximately two years later. Assume that Cyrus did not remarry after Sybil's death and was still a resident of San Jose, California, when he died. He had two children by a previous marriage, a daughter, Sally, and a son, Michael, who survived him. Prior to his death, Cyrus disposed of some of the assets he had received from Sybil's estate, and acquired others. To avoid probate of the bulk of his estate, Cyrus executed an inter vivos revocable living trust and transferred the family residence and a limited partnership interest into the trust. The trust named his brother Sam as successor trustee and Cyrus's children, Sally and Michael, as beneficiaries.

At the time of his death, Cyrus's estate consisted of the following property:

- savings Account No. 1234, Pacific States Bank, San Jose, California, having a principal balance of $20,000
- 200 shares, AT&T common stock, worth $10,000
- 10% interest in Westland Shopping Center, a limited partnership, in name of Cyrus Sample, as Trustee of the Cyrus Sample Revocable Trust, dated June 1, 20xx, valued at $200,000
- family residence, 930 Hill Street, San Jose, in the name of Cyrus Sample, as Trustee of the Cyrus Sample Revocable Trust, dated June 1, 20xx, having a value of $600,000
- $100,000 Aetna Life Insurance policy, on the life of Cyrus Sample, naming Sally and Michael as beneficiaries, and
- 2007 BMW, Model 320i, 2-door sedan, having a value of $22,000.

Since Cyrus wasn't married when he died, all of his property is his separate property. His will (executed at the same time as his inter vivos trust) leaves his entire estate to his two children. As we examine the transfer procedures available for the assets in Cyrus's estate, we will see that no formal probate proceedings are required to transfer the property.

First of all, the successor trustee of the Cyrus Sample Revocable Trust (Sam) can transfer the family residence and the partnership interest immediately without probate to Cyrus's two children as the beneficiaries. The real property will require the preparation of a deed, signed by Sam as successor trustee, transferring the residence to Sally and Michael. The limited partnership interest will require an assignment executed by Sam, as successor trustee, assigning Cyrus's interest to his children. As noted in Chapter 1, transfers of significant business interests should normally be handled through an attorney.

The proceeds of the Aetna Life policy will be paid to Sally and Michael, the named beneficiaries, without probate. The remaining personal property, consisting of the BMW automobile, AT&T stock, and the savings account at Pacific States Bank, all have a total gross value of $52,000. Thus, Sally and Michael, as the beneficiaries of Cyrus's will, may have each of these assets transferred to them without formal probate by using the affidavit procedure outlined in Chapter 11. ●

What About Taxes?

One of the first things estate beneficiaries want to know is whether or not they have to pay taxes on the property they inherit. Usually, the answer is "no." The only taxes that most estates have to be concerned about are income taxes. If, after the decedent's death, the estate assets produce enough income, they will generate an income tax bill, which will be paid either by filing an estate income tax return or by the beneficiaries who receive the income. Also, the estate representative must file the decedent's final income tax return and pay any taxes owed on income generated during the part of the tax year in which the decedent was alive.

Perhaps looming larger than income tax are the "death taxes" that most people have heard about, which are more accurately described as federal estate taxes and state inheritance taxes. These taxes are separate from income taxes but are not a threat to the average estate. The federal estate tax was abolished for 2010 and the first $5 million is exempt from tax for deaths in 2011 and 2012. California has no inheritance tax.

This chapter briefly reviews the various tax returns you may have to file in settling an estate. Tax laws pertaining to estates and to beneficiaries who inherit property can be complex, especially if the estate is large. If the estate you are settling has substantial assets or income to report, your best bet (absent a good self-help source) is to contact an accountant or attorney experienced in the area of estate taxes. An expert can advise you on how to minimize the impact of all taxes on the beneficiaries and the estate.

A detailed discussion of how to prepare a federal estate tax return would require another book. If an accountant or attorney prepares the return, the fee is ordinarily paid from the general assets of the estate or shared by the beneficiaries in proportion to their interests in the estate. Accounting fees are a deduction to the estate either on the estate's income tax returns or on the federal estate tax return, if one is required.

> **CAUTION**
>
> **Keep up with the rules.** Tax laws and regulations are bound to change in the years ahead. You should not rely on any of the dollar figures or detailed rules discussed here without checking recent IRS publications.

> **Tax Sites on the Internet**
>
> IRS publications, as well as tax forms and other information are available at www.irs.gov. California forms and publications are available at www.ftb.ca.gov.

Decedent's Final Income Tax Returns

If the decedent receives more than a small amount of income in the taxable year in which he or she died, final income tax returns may have to be filed for that year. The income levels at which returns must be filed may change from year to year.

For deaths in 2010, decedents who were not married at the time of death had to file a final federal income tax return if gross income exceeded $9,350 ($10,750 if the decedent was 65 or older) for the taxable year up to the date of death. Gross income includes all income received in the form of money from property (for example, interest, dividends, or rents) as well as income from employment, pension, and other public and private benefit programs unless they are exempt from tax. If a married decedent was living in the same household with his or her spouse at the time of death and was eligible to file a joint return, a final federal income tax return must be filed if the combined gross income of the decedent and spouse was $18,700 or more for the entire taxable year. The cutoff is $19,800 if one spouse was 65 or older and $20,900 if both spouses were 65 or older. (Domestic partners are not eligible to file joint returns. They must file as single taxpayers.)

A California income tax return must be filed for 2010 if an unmarried decedent under age 65 had a gross income of $14,754 or over ($29,508 for a married couple). If the decedent was 65 or older, the threshold is $19,704, or if one member of a married couple is 65 or older, $34,458. If both spouses were 65 or older, the threshold is $39,408.

EXAMPLE 1: Martha, an unmarried 68-year-old retired school teacher, earned gross income of $12,000 in the year of her death. Because

Martha is a single taxpayer over 65, final income tax returns (both federal and California) do not have to be filed for Martha.

EXAMPLE 2: Jack and his wife Jill are both over 65 and earned a combined gross income of $35,000 in the year of Jack's death. Jack and Jill were entitled to file joint income tax returns. Final income tax returns, both California and federal, must be filed for Jack because Jack and Jill's combined gross income for the entire taxable year exceeds the limit for federal purposes and the limit for California purposes.

If income tax has been withheld from the decedent's wages or he or she has paid any estimated tax, you should file a final return for the decedent even if it is not required. The purpose is to obtain a refund of the taxes paid or withheld. If a refund is due, you must file Form 1310, *Statement of Person Claiming Refund Due a Deceased Taxpayer*, with the return to claim the refund. Form 1310 isn't required if you are a surviving spouse filing a joint return with the decedent, or you are a court-appointed executor or administrator.

The due date for the decedent's final income tax returns (federal Form 1040 and California Form 540) is the same date as when the decedent was living—on or before the 15th day of the fourth month following the close of the decedent's regular tax year. This due date is usually April 15 of the year following death, unless the decedent had an accounting year different from a calendar year, which is rarely the case.

If the decedent died in the beginning of the year, before filing a return for the prior year, you may have to file two returns. For example, if the decedent died on March 1, 2011, before filing his or her return for 2010, a return must be filed for 2010 on or before April 15, 2011. The decedent's final return (if required), for the period from January 1, 2011, to March 1, 2011 (the date of death), would be due on April 15, 2012. If, for some reason, the tax returns cannot be filed on their due date, you may apply for an extension.

Ordinarily, it is the responsibility of the executor or administrator of the estate, assuming one has been formally appointed by the probate court, to file the final returns and any other returns still due for the decedent. Because the income tax returns are for the decedent, and not the estate, they are prepared and signed by the estate representative on behalf of the decedent. In this instance, the representative signs the return on the line indicated for the taxpayer. For example, "Joan Jones, Administrator of the Estate of Anne Rose, Deceased," or "Joan Jones, Executor of the Will of Anne Rose, Deceased."

If there is no court-appointed representative (as where the estate is not probated), the income tax returns should normally be filed by a surviving spouse. The spouse should sign the return and then write in the signature area "filing as surviving spouse." If the final income tax return is a joint return and a legal representative has been appointed (this will be the case only if a probate proceeding is required), both the legal representative and the surviving spouse must sign the return.

If there is no surviving spouse, administrator, or executor, it is extremely important that an accountant or the IRS be consulted before property is distributed. In this situation, the income tax return should be filed by a family member (usually one who stands to inherit) or a friend who assumes the responsibility of winding up the decedent's affairs. If this is not done, those who inherit the property, or have control of it, must jointly assume responsibility for filing or appoint one of their number to take charge of the estate for this purpose; if they do not, they may be subject to penalties for willful neglect or tax evasion. The income tax return should be signed by the heirs or beneficiaries jointly (or by one of them acting on behalf of all), followed by the words "Personal Representative(s) of the Estate of Joe Brown, Deceased."

In filling out the income tax return, the decedent's name should be put on the "name" line at the top of the return, followed by the word "deceased" and the date of death. If it is a joint return, both spouses' names should be included with "deceased" after the decedents' names, such as "John Smith and Mary Smith, deceased." Also write "Deceased" across the top of the form.

An excellent source of information on this subject is IRS Publication 559, *Tax Information for Survivors, Executors and Administrators*, available by calling 800-829-3676. You can also download this publication from the IRS website at www.irs.gov.

Fiduciary Income Tax Returns

Income received on assets in the decedent's estate after he or she has died is taxable, as is income received by an individual, and income tax returns must be filed if the estate has more than $600 in gross income in a taxable year for federal purposes, or gross income of $10,000 in one year for California purposes. The tax returns to report this income are called "fiduciary income tax returns" and are prepared on federal Form 1041 and California Form 541.

Fiduciary returns are normally required only if a formal probate court proceeding is opened and an estate representative is appointed by the court. The reason for this is that a probate proceeding usually takes from six to nine months to complete, and in many cases even longer. The legal representative of the estate must have a way to report the income received on the decedent's assets during the administration of the estate until the property is distributed to the new owners. If an asset is sold during probate administration, there may be a capital gain to report on these returns.

Fiduciary returns are due no later than the 15th day of the fourth month after the end of the estate's taxable year. The taxable year may be a fiscal year chosen by the accountant or estate representative, or a calendar year. Depending on the length of time it takes to close the estate, the first tax year may be less than 12 months. The estate is considered closed if all assets are distributed except for a reasonable amount set aside for closing expenses or unascertained liabilities.

If the probate proceeding takes less than a year, fiduciary returns are required for just the short time the estate is open, assuming the estate receives sufficient income during that period. In this case, the returns are treated as "final" returns and the beneficiaries (not the estate) pay the taxes due, if any, because all income and deductions are passed through to the beneficiaries on a "K-1" form. However, if the estate is open more than a year (or through the Christmas holidays into a new tax year, if a calendar year is being used), the first returns are called the "initial" returns, and subsequent returns must be filed for each year the estate is open. The same forms (federal Form 1041 and California Form 541) are used for all fiduciary returns, and the taxes due, other than on the final returns, are paid from the estate assets.

When a formal probate court proceeding is not required, fiduciary returns are not normally necessary. This is because property is usually transferred promptly, and the income it generates is taxed to and reported on the personal returns of the persons receiving it.

For example, income received on joint tenancy property would be reported by the surviving joint tenant(s), since they became the owner(s) of the property immediately on the death of the decedent.

How to Apply for a Taxpayer Identification Number

If a probate proceeding is opened and fiduciary returns are to be filed, you will need a federal identification number for the estate as soon as possible. Use Form SS-4 (*Application for Employer Identification Number*) to obtain an identification number (even though the estate has no employees). You can get the form at any IRS or Social Security office or the IRS website, or call the IRS at 800-829-3676 and ask them to mail one to you. It usually takes two to four weeks to obtain a tax identification number through the mail.

If you need the number sooner, you can apply for a number by phone, using the Tele-TIN program. Information about this is included in the Form SS-4 instructions. You may also apply for the number online at www.irs.gov/businesses/small.

When you get the number, notify all institutions reporting income paid on estate assets (banks, brokerage firms, etc.) and tell them to use the new number instead of the decedent's Social Security number.

Income received on community or separate property passing to a surviving spouse would, of course, be reported on the surviving spouse's income tax return. Similarly, others who receive property without probate under the simple affidavit procedure used for estates of $100,000 or less (see Chapter 11) would report income from such property on their personal income tax returns.

Other Income Tax Returns

If the decedent was engaged in a business, it is likely that there will be other returns required, such as business tax returns, employment tax returns, and sales and use tax returns. Also, if the decedent was a shareholder in a closely held (private) corporation or a partner in a partnership, tax returns will be due. Usually, in these situations, it is appropriate to employ an accountant—often, the accountant who prepared those returns during the decedent's lifetime.

Stepped-Up Tax Basis Rules for Inherited Property

Let's slow down for a moment to understand the tax status of property that is inherited. For example, what are the tax obligations of a person who inherits property and immediately turns around and sells it?

Normally, when either real or personal property is sold for more than its cost basis, the seller must pay a capital gains tax on the difference between the sales price and its cost basis. Cost basis is the dollar amount that was initially paid for an asset, plus or minus certain adjustments. Rules change, however, for inherited property. For both federal and California income tax purposes, when property is acquired by inheritance it gets a new stepped-up basis in the hands of the new owner equal to the fair market value at the date of the decedent's death (or six months later, if this "alternate valuation date" is chosen for federal tax purposes). In other words, the new owners do not have to pay tax on the difference between the original purchase price and the current value of the property.

EXAMPLE: Heidi buys a home in 1977 for $75,000. At her death, the fair market value of the property is $250,000. The property passes under Heidi's will to her daughter, Dessa. Dessa's basis for the property for reporting gain or loss when it is sold is $250,000.

During 2010, when the federal estate tax was repealed (see below), the stepped-up basis rule was limited to $1.3 million of appreciation, with an additional $3 million in appreciation available to a surviving spouse. This rule, called the "modified carryover basis rule," required the estate representative to allocate the allowable stepped-up basis to particular assets, such as a house or stocks, while valuing all other assets at their original cost basis. The modified carryover basis rule in effect for 2010 was eliminated by new laws passed in December of 2010 and it was replaced with the 100% stepped-up basis rule described above. This traditional stepped-up basis rule is currently available for all estates through 2012. For decedents dying in 2010, the estate representative may choose to use either the 2010 carryover basis rules or the revived stepped-up basis rules.

 SEE AN EXPERT

See a qualified expert if you need help with stepped-up basis.

In the case of community property, there is a substantial added tax benefit as a result of these stepped-up basis rules. This is because for state and federal income tax purposes the surviving spouse's one-half share of the community property is treated in the same manner as property the surviving spouse acquires from the deceased spouse. Thus, all community property (the decedent's and surviving spouse's shares) and all separate property included in the decedent's estate receives a new stepped-up basis equal to its fair market value as of the deceased spouse's death (or six months later, if the alternate valuation date is used on the federal estate tax return).

EXAMPLE: Paul and Margaret purchase $50,000 worth of stock with community property funds.

When Paul dies, his one-half community interest in the stock passes to Margaret. The fair market value of the stock at the time of Paul's death is $75,000. Therefore, Margaret's one-half interest, as well as Paul's one-half interest, receives a stepped-up basis for California and federal income tax purposes, meaning it will have a total tax basis of $75,000 if Margaret later sells the stock.

Many married couples hold title to their property as joint tenants to avoid probate. In the past, there has been some debate over whether property held in joint tenancy will be afforded a full step-up in its tax basis upon the death of one spouse. Usually, only the decedent's interest in joint tenancy property gets a stepped-up basis for both federal and California income tax purposes. But if joint tenancy property can be established as true community property held in joint tenancy for convenience, both the decedent's half and the surviving spouse's half will qualify for the stepped-up basis. One way to do this is to transfer the joint tenancy property to the surviving spouse as community property using a Spousal or Domestic Partner Property Petition, as described in Chapter 15.

Because federal tax laws do not recognize domestic partnerships or same-sex marriages, the benefits of the stepped-up basis are not currently available to domestic partners or same-sex couples who married in a state or country that legalized same-sex marriage.

Federal Estate Tax Return

A Federal Estate Tax Return (IRS Form 706) must be filed if the decedent's *gross* estate on the date of death exceeds a certain amount. Attorneys and accountants call this amount the "personal exemption" or "exclusion amount." Most estates don't need to file the return, because most estates aren't large enough. The exemption amount was gradually increased over a period of years until the federal estate tax was eliminated for decedents dying in 2010. However, the estate tax has been reinstated for decedents dying in 2011 and 2012 at an exemption amount of $5 million. For 2010 estates, the executor is given the option of using either the 2010 or 2011 tax rules.

The estate tax return is a long and detailed tax form with many schedules. If you are dealing with a very simple estate and are used to preparing your own tax returns, you may consider preparing the return yourself, but we recommend getting professional help.

Who Needs to File?

An estate tax return is required if the gross estate, on the date of death, exceeds the federal estate tax exemption (see the table below).

The Federal Estate Tax Exemption	
Year of Death	Estate tax return must be filed if gross value of the estate exceeds:
2009	$3.5 million
2010	estate tax repealed
2011–2012	$5 million
2013	$1 million unless Congress changes amount of exemption

The return must be filed if the gross estate is larger than the exempt amount, even if no tax will be due. For example, if all assets are left to the surviving spouse, they are exempt from federal estate tax, as long as the spouse is a United States citizen. So, if a person dies leaving $5 million to a surviving spouse, the gross value of the deceased spouse's estate requires the executor to file a return, but no tax will be due.

It is extremely important to understand that the gross value of an estate is used to determine whether or not a federal estate tax return is required. The actual tax, by contrast, is computed on the net value of all property owned by the decedent at death. The net estate value is arrived at by taking the total (gross) value of all of the decedent's property and subtracting such things as funeral expenses, expenses of settling the estate, and any debts owed by the decedent. (If you are hazy on the difference between the gross and net estate, please reread Chapter 1.)

Because the value of the gross estate is larger than the net estate, many estates still need to file a federal estate tax return (based on the gross estate), although no tax will be due based on the net estate.

EXAMPLE: Abel has a gross estate valued at $5.2 million when he dies in 2011. A federal estate tax return must be filed because the value of the estate is over the $5 million estate tax exemption for that year. However, Abel has deductions for debts (for example, a mortgage, car loan, or money owed to a family member), taxes due, last illness and funeral expenses, and administration expenses (for example, attorney and accountant fees, court costs, and certification and publication fees), that bring the value of his net estate below $5 million, so no tax is due.

Calculating the Value of the Estate for Tax Purposes

The amount of the gross estate is the total of Column D in the Schedule of Assets you prepared in Chapter 5.

The estate for federal estate tax purposes is usually not the same as the estate that goes through probate, called the probate estate. The difference is that the federal estate tax return must report all property in which the decedent had any interest. This includes property that passes outside of probate, such as joint tenancy property, pay-on-death accounts (also called Totten trusts), life insurance owned by the decedent, property held in living trusts, pensions, annuities, and profit-sharing and death benefits (whether payable to named beneficiaries or the decedent's estate). The probate estate, on the other hand, is only the property that must go through formal probate administration.

EXAMPLE: Ruth dies in 2011, leaving the bulk of her property to her brother. Most of the property is held in a living trust or owned in joint tenancy, so it can be transferred outside of probate. Only securities valued at $120,000 and miscellaneous personal property of little value are subject to probate. Ruth's estate has a gross value of $4 million. Because that amount is below the $5 million estate tax exemption amount, her executor does not need to file an estate tax return.

Joint Tenancy Property

Many people put their property (real estate or stocks, for example) in joint tenancy with someone else, to avoid probate. For example, an elderly parent may add a son or daughter to the deed to the family house as a joint tenant. In such cases, federal tax law requires that the entire joint tenancy property be included in the estate of the first owner, for estate tax purposes, if the others acquired their interests for less than full value.

Let's look at an example:

Margaret, a widow in her 80s, signs a deed transferring ownership of her house to herself and her grown daughter, Sarah, as joint tenants. This means Margaret and Sarah each own a half-interest in the property. But when Margaret dies, the value of the entire property (not just her half) is included in her estate for federal estate tax purposes, and will receive the full stepped-up income tax basis described above.

One asset that's easy to overlook when you're adding up the value of the gross estate are life insurance proceeds. The decedent's taxable estate will include the proceeds of life insurance on the decedent's life if:

- the proceeds are receivable by the estate
- the proceeds are receivable by another for the benefit of the estate, or
- the decedent possessed "incidents of ownership" in the policy.

Often a person who takes out an insurance policy will transfer ownership of the policy to someone else so the policy proceeds will not be included in his taxable estate when he or she dies. Married couples commonly do this. For instance, a husband may buy an insurance policy on his life, naming his wife as beneficiary, and then transfer ownership (including all incidents of ownership) of the policy to his wife to avoid having to pay taxes on the proceeds upon his death.

In order for the policy proceeds not to be included in the husband's taxable estate, he must have given away complete control over the policy—in other words, he must no longer be able to do anything with it at all. Put another way, incidents of ownership include not only the ownership of the policy in a technical, legal sense, but also the right of the insured person or the insured person's estate to the economic benefits of the policy. If the decedent had the power to change beneficiaries, revoke an assignment, obtain a loan against the cash value, pledge the policy for a loan, or surrender or cancel the policy, then he or she possessed incidents of ownership. The policy proceeds will be included in his or her taxable estate on his or her death even if the decedent thought he or she had transferred policy ownership to another. If you are confused about this, check with the insurance company (see Chapter 2), or an accountant or attorney experienced in estate tax matters.

The Filing Deadline

If you do need to file Form 706, it is due nine months after the date of death. The IRS, however, will automatically grant your request for a six-month extension if you make your request before the original due date. Use IRS Form 4768, *Application for Extension of Time to File a Return or Pay U.S. Estate (and Generation-Skipping Transfer) Taxes*. You'll have to include an estimate of the tax due—and a payment. The extension of time to file is not an extension of time to pay the tax.

RESOURCE

More information from the IRS. You can get the federal estate tax return (Form 706) online at www.irs.gov or from an IRS office that furnishes tax information and forms. The IRS booklet of instructions for completing the federal estate tax return, called simply *Instructions for Form 706*, is very helpful.

Estimating the Tax Due

Once you have calculated the value of the gross estate and determined that you need to file an estate tax return, you can go ahead and estimate how much, if any, tax will actually be due.

To estimate the amount of tax due, follow these steps:

1. Figure out the value of the taxable estate. To do that, subtract from the value of the gross estate the total amount of all deductions listed on the last page of the Schedule of Assets.

EXAMPLE: Oliver dies in 2011, leaving an estate worth $5.5 million. When a mortgage on the real estate and various expenses associated with his death and the winding up of his affairs are subtracted, the taxable estate is valued at $5.1 million.

2. Add to the taxable estate any taxable gifts made after December 31, 1976, that are not included in the gross estate. Don't count gifts that are exempt from tax—for example, gifts to tax-exempt charities or gifts of less than $13,000 made to one person in one year.

EXAMPLE CONTINUED: Oliver made taxable gifts of $50,000 in 2002 and another $50,000 in 2004. Adding these to the estate gives a total of $5.2 million.

3. Subtract the amount of the estate tax exemption from the taxable estate. For deaths in 2011, that amount is $5 million. (See "The Federal Estate Tax Exemption" chart, above.) This difference is the amount that will be subject to estate tax. If the taxable estate is less than the estate tax exemption, the estate will owe no tax.

EXAMPLE CONTINUED:

Oliver's taxable estate	$5,200,000
Estate tax exemption for 2011	− $5,000,000
Estimated amount subject to tax	$ 200,000

4. To estimate the amount of tax owed, multiply the amount subject to tax by the tax rate for the year of death. The tax rate for deaths in 2011 is 35%.

EXAMPLE CONTINUED:

Amount of Oliver's estate subject to tax	$ 200,000
Tax rate	× 0.35
Estimated tax	$ 70,000

Paying the Federal Tax

The federal estate tax, if any is due, must be paid in full when the return is filed. (If you apply for an extension, you'll need to pay an estimated amount of tax when you apply; the estate will still be charged interest on any unpaid tax from the due date until it is paid.)

If you don't file the return on the due date (or on the extension date), the estate will be charged a penalty, in addition to interest. The penalty is 5% of the amount of the tax for each month (or part of a month) that you're late, up to a maximum of 25%.

Most wills have a provision saying all taxes are to be paid from the residue of the estate. If there is no will, or the will makes no provision and there are two or more beneficiaries, then the taxes are charged to each of the beneficiaries, according to their percentage interests. Your accountant should be able to compute the amount chargeable to each beneficiary. If there isn't enough cash to pay the taxes, the executor must sell estate property or borrow money to raise the necessary funds.

California Inheritance Tax

The California inheritance tax applies only to decedents who died on or before June 8, 1982.

One common occurrence is to find that real estate, usually the family home, is still held in joint tenancy with the decedent's predeceased spouse. In most cases, all that is necessary is to record an Affidavit—Death of Joint Tenant (see Chapter 10) to remove the predeceased spouse's name from the title. But if the first spouse died on or before June 8, 1982, you must also file inheritance tax forms to determine whether or not there is any tax due and to obtain a release of the tax lien on the property.

For information, contact the State Controller's Office, Bureau of Tax Administration, Inheritance Tax, P.O. Box 942850, Sacramento, CA 94250-5880, 916-445-6321, and ask for an *Inheritance Tax Declaration* (Form IT-22) and *Marital Property Declaration* (Form IT-3), along with the instructions.

SEE AN EXPERT

Death taxes in other states. If the decedent owned real estate outside of California, estate or inheritance taxes may be owed to that state. Check with a lawyer there.

Tax Issues for Some Typical Estates

Let's look at some typical estates and see what tax returns must be filed for each.

Estate of Abigail Apple

Abigail died on October 11, 2011, at the age of 66. Her gross estate of $300,000 consisted of her one-half interest in community property owned by Abigail and her husband, Alfred, who is 68. Her estate did not require probate because all of her property passed outright to Alfred under Abigail's will.

Abigail and Alfred received interest and dividend income of $20,000 during the period of January 1, 2011, to October 11, 2011 (the date of Abigail's death), one half of which ($10,000) was attributable to Abigail.

Alfred is responsible for seeing that final income tax returns, both California and federal, are filed for Abigail for the period January 1, 2011, to October 11, 2011. They are due April 15, 2012. The returns for Abigail may or may not be joint returns with her husband, depending on which is the most advantageous way to file.

No federal estate tax return or California estate tax return is required, because Abigail's estate is not large enough to require the filing of these returns. Fiduciary income tax returns are also not required, because Abigail's estate did not require probate and no personal representative was appointed. Alfred will report any future income he receives from assets in Abigail's estate on his own personal income tax returns.

Estate of Joe Brown

Joe, a bachelor, died on March 12, 2010. The gross estate consisted of:

House	$ 800,000
Stock	550,000
Life insurance	700,000
Car	20,000
Bank account	+ 30,000
Total:	$2,100,000

The federal estate tax was repealed for decedents dying in 2010, so no federal estate tax return is due for Joes's estate. However, probate court proceedings were required, and the probate court appointed his brother Jack as executor of the will. Joe had received a total of $35,000 from his employment, along with dividends and interest, for the period January 1, 2010, to March 12, 2010 (the date of death). Joe hadn't yet filed his income tax returns for 2009 when he died. The tax returns that Jack must file as executor of Joe's estate are:

- Joe's 2009 personal income tax returns, both California and federal, due April 15, 2010.
- Joe's final income tax returns, both California and federal, for the period January 1, 2010, to March 12, 2010 (the date of Joe's death), due April 15, 2011.
- Fiduciary income tax returns (Form 1041), reporting income received during the period of probate administration on the estate assets from March 13, 2010 (the beginning of the estate's income tax year), until the estate is closed and the assets distributed to the beneficiaries.

Estate of Ralph Rambler

Reba and Ralph Rambler had been married for 25 years when Ralph died on April 20, 2011. His estate consisted of a one-half interest in the total community property he and Reba owned, as shown here:

Pacific Palisades home	$ 800,000
Santa Monica rental property	450,000
Boat	20,000
Stocks	200,000
Vacation home	300,000
Cadillac	20,000
Money market fund	+ 100,000
Total	$1,890,000

Ralph's will named Reba as executor and distributed his one-half interest in the house, car, and money market account to Reba, and the apartment building and stocks in trust to his three children. Therefore, his estate required probate. Reba and Ralph received income of $125,000 during the period from January 1, 2011, to April 20, 2011 (date of death), one-half of which was attributable to Ralph.

Reba is responsible for seeing that the following tax returns are filed:

- Ralph's final personal income tax returns for 2011, both California and federal. They're due April 15, 2012, and cover the period from January 1, 2011, to April 20, 2011. Reba can file a joint return for the entire year of 2011 even though Ralph died in April of that year. In the final return, Reba would include Ralph's income and deductions up to the date of his death, as well as her income and deductions for the entire year.
- Fiduciary income tax returns for Ralph's estate for the period beginning April 21, 2011, until the estate is closed.
- Ralph's gross estate is $1.89 million, which is under the $5 million exemption for the year 2011, so his executor will not have to file a federal estate tax return.

Transferring Title to Real Property

In California, beneficiaries legally acquire title to the decedent's real property on the date of death, however, they must take specific steps to officially document the transfer of title. In this chapter, we discuss how to transfer the title to real property to its new owners. This basic nuts-and-bolts information is relevant no matter whether the real property is left in a will, passes by intestate succession, or passes outside the will via one or another of the probate avoidance devices.

Ways to Transfer Real Estate After Death

To transfer real property belonging to a decedent, you will need to use a deed, affidavit, or court order, depending on how the decedent held title to the property and to whom it is left.

After you've obtained the appropriate document, it must be recorded in the office of the county recorder where the real property is located. (This is explained later in this chapter.)

To a Surviving Spouse or Domestic Partner

Generally, if the real property (whether community or separate) goes outright to the surviving spouse or domestic partner (either under the decedent's will or by intestate succession), you will need a Spousal or Domestic Partner Property Order, as explained in Chapter 15. If, however, the decedent's deed specifically shows title held "as community property" or "community property with right of survivorship" with the surviving spouse or partner, you may be able to clear title in the survivor's name with a simple affidavit, which is also explained in Chapter 15.

To a Surviving Joint Tenant

If title was held in joint tenancy, then an Affidavit—Death of Joint Tenant, which is explained in Chapter 10, may be used to remove the decedent's name from the title. However, for tax reasons discussed in Chapter 7, if spouses or domestic partners held community property in joint tenancy, the surviving spouse or partner may instead want to use the Spousal or Domestic Partner Property Order procedure explained in Chapter 15.

To Living Trust Beneficiaries

If title to the property is held in a living trust, a new deed must be prepared, usually by the successor trustee, transferring title to the beneficiaries named in the trust document. We show you how to accomplish this in Chapter 12.

Through Formal Probate

If the decedent's interest in the real property goes to his or her heirs or the beneficiaries in his or her will (other than a surviving spouse or partner), you must obtain an Order of Final Distribution through a formal probate court proceeding. The order transfers ownership to the heirs or beneficiaries, who take title as tenants in common when there is more than one person assuming ownership. Instructions for preparing an order are in Chapter 14, Step 18. However, see Chapter 11 for shortcut methods of transferring real property worth less than $100,000.

Basic Information on Recording Documents

Any document affecting title to real property (deed, court order, affidavit, or deed of trust) should be recorded in the office of the county recorder for the county in which the real property is located. This doesn't mean that an unrecorded document is null or void.

Of what significance, then, is recording? Recording a deed gives public notice of a person's rights in property, called "constructive notice" by lawyers. It informs the world of the ownership of the property and who has a mortgage on it. Once a deed is recorded, the law presumes that everyone (for example, banks, potential buyers, and title companies) has notice of this information. For example, if you buy a lot without a title search and do not check the public records yourself, you are nevertheless considered to have knowledge of whatever the records would have shown. If there is a judgment lien against the property, you are responsible for paying it even though no one ever told you about it. In other words, you had "constructive notice" of all information the recorder's office would have disclosed had you checked. This is why, when you buy a house or other real property, the title company always checks the records at the recorder's office to make sure the seller owns clear title to the property. Recording, then, is an orderly system of establishing ownership rights in, and lien rights against, property.

If a deed isn't recorded, the recorder's office will not have current property ownership information, and if someone relies on the out-of-date information in good faith, he or she will be protected. For example, if you have some ownership right in property and do not record it, it can be cut off by a competing right acquired by another person without knowledge of yours.

The recording of a document takes effect the moment it is received in the recorder's office. A deed, mortgage, or court order is stamped as received for recording at the hour and minute received and given a document or instrument number (sometimes a book and page number are used). A photocopy is then made for the recorder's records and bound with other similar documents in books of "Official Records" in the recorder's office, for the public to inspect. Using an alphabetical grantor-grantee index, one may find the proper page of these records to consult for a particular document. After a document is recorded, the original is returned to the person named on the deed to receive it—usually the one who requested the recording.

Change in Ownership Statements

Usually, a transfer of an interest in real property or a mobile home triggers a reassessment for local property tax purposes. For this reason, certain forms must be filed with local officials whenever there is a change in ownership of real property. In probate situations, the date of death is the date of transfer and the beneficiaries become the new owners on that date, subject to whatever administration procedures are required to transfer the title.

Preliminary Change of Ownership Report

Whenever a deed, court order, or other document affecting title to real property is recorded, it must be accompanied by a Preliminary Change of Ownership Report. A sample is shown below. You can get a copy by calling the county assessor's office or, most likely, by visiting the office's website. The form must be filed by the new owner (transferee) along with the transfer document when it is recorded. If the document is not recorded, the form must be filed with the county assessor within 45 days of the date of the change in ownership. (Rev. & Tax. Code § 480(a).)

Change in Ownership Statement— Death of Real Property Owner

The proper procedure to report the death of a real property owner is to file with the county assessor's office a form titled Change in Ownership Statement— Death of Real Property Owner, along with the Preliminary Change of Ownership Report. If there is an additional formal probate court proceeding, the forms must be filed with the assessor's office prior to, or at, the time the Inventory and Appraisal is filed with the court. (Rev. & Tax. Code § 480(b).) Each county has prepared its own form for this purpose, which is similar to the two-page form used in Los Angeles County, shown in Chapter 14. This form must be filed with each county assessor where the decedent owned real property at the time of death, accompanied by a copy of the death certificate.

The assessor's office treats the date of death as the date of the change in ownership, regardless of when title is actually transferred to the new owner, and will reassess the property as of that date unless it is excluded from reassessment (see below). In most cases, tax bills showing the date of death adjustments are sent within six months from the date of filing the Death of Real Property Owner form.

Preliminary Change of Ownership Report (front)

BOE-502-A (FRONT) REV. 10 (8-07)
PRELIMINARY CHANGE OF OWNERSHIP REPORT

	FOR RECORDER'S USE ONLY

[To be completed by transferee (buyer) prior to transfer of subject property in accordance with section 480.3 of the Revenue and Taxation Code.] A Preliminary Change of Ownership Report must be filed with each conveyance in the County Recorder's office for the county where the property is located; this particular form may be used in all 58 counties of California.

THIS REPORT IS NOT A PUBLIC DOCUMENT

SELLER/TRANSFEROR: Robert B. Demming, deceased
BUYER/TRANSFEREE: John Demming
ASSESSOR'S PARCEL NUMBER(S) 2346-019-014
PROPERTY ADDRESS OR LOCATION: 1506 Maple Street, Burbank, CA
MAIL TAX INFORMATION TO: Name John Demming
Address 7290 N. McDonald Ave., San Diego, CA 91775

NOTICE: A lien for property taxes applies to your property on January 1 of each year for the taxes owing in the following fiscal year, July 1 through June 30. One-half of these taxes is due November 1, and one-half is due February 1. The first installment becomes delinquent on December 10, and the second installment becomes delinquent on April 10. One tax bill is mailed before November 1 to the owner of record. **You may be responsible for the current or upcoming property taxes even if you do not receive the tax bill.**

The property which you acquired may be subject to a supplemental assessment in an amount to be determined by the _____

Assessor. For further information on your supplemental roll obligation, please call the _____ Assessor

at _____ .

PART I: TRANSFER INFORMATION *(please answer all questions)*

YES	NO	
☐	☒	A. Is this transfer solely between husband and wife (addition of a spouse, death of a spouse, divorce settlement, etc.)?
☐	☒	B. Is this transaction only a correction of the name(s) of the person(s) holding title to the property (for example, a name change upon marriage)? Please explain _____
☐	☒	C. Is this document recorded to create, terminate, or reconvey a lender's interest in the property?
☐	☒	D. Is this transaction recorded only as a requirement for financing purposes or to create, terminate, or reconvey a security interest (e.g., cosigner)? Please explain _____
☐	☒	E. Is this document recorded to substitute a trustee of a trust, mortgage, or other similar document?
☐	☒	F. Did this transfer result in the creation of a joint tenancy in which the seller (transferor) remains as one of the joint tenants?
☐	☒	G. Does this transfer return property to the person who created the joint tenancy (original transferor)?
		H. Is this a transfer of property:
☐	☒	1. to a revocable trust that may be revoked by the transferor and is for the benefit of the ☐ transferor ☐ transferor's spouse?
☐	☒	2. to a trust that may be revoked by the Creator/Grantor who is also a joint tenant, and which names the other joint tenant(s) as beneficiaries when the Creator/Grantor dies?
☐	☒	3. to an irrevocable trust for the benefit of the ☐ Creator/Grantor and/or ☐ Grantor's spouse?
☐	☒	4. to an irrevocable trust from which the property reverts to the Creator/Grantor within 12 years?
☐	☒	I. If this property is subject to a lease, is the remaining lease term 35 years or more including written options?
☒	☐	*J. Is this a transfer between ☒ parent(s) and child(ren)? ☐ or from grandparent(s) to grandchild(ren)?
☐	☒	*K. Is this transaction to replace a principal residence by a person 55 years of age or older? Within the same county? ☐ Yes ☐ No
☐	☒	*L. Is this transaction to replace a principal residence by a person who is severely disabled as defined by Revenue and Taxation Code section 69.5? Within the same county? ☐ Yes ☐ No
☐	☒	M. Is this transfer solely between domestic partners currently registered with the California Secretary of State?

*If you checked yes to J, K or L, you may qualify for a property tax reassessment exclusion, which may result in lower taxes on your property. **If you do not file a claim, your property will be reassessed.**

Please provide any other information that will help the Assessor to understand the nature of the transfer.

If the conveying document constitutes an exclusion from a change in ownership as defined in section 62 of the Revenue and Taxation Code for any reason other than those listed above, set forth the specific exclusions claimed: _____

Please answer all questions in each section. If a question does not apply, indicate with "N/A." Sign and date at bottom of second page.

PART II: OTHER TRANSFER INFORMATION

A. Date of transfer if other than recording date ___7-7-xx___

B. Type of transfer *(please check appropriate box)*:
  ☐ Purchase   ☐ Foreclosure   ☐ Gift   ☐ Trade or Exchange   ☐ Merger, Stock, or Partnership Acquisition
  ☐ Contract of Sale — Date of Contract _____
  ☒ Inheritance — Date of Death ___7-7-xx___   ☐ Other *(please explain)*: _____
  ☐ Creation of Lease   ☐ Assignment of a Lease   ☐ Termination of a Lease   ☐ Sale/Leaseback
  ☐ Date lease began
  ☐ Original term in years (including written options)
  ☐ Remaining term in years (including written options) _____
  Monthly Payment _____ Remaining Term _____

C. Was only a partial interest in the property transferred? ☐ Yes ☒ No
  If **yes**, indicate the percentage transferred _____%.

Preliminary Change of Ownership Report (back)

BOE-502-A (BACK) REV. 10 (8-07)

Please write Assessor's Parcel Number(s): _____ 2346-019-014

Please answer, to the best of your knowledge, all applicable questions, then sign and date. If a question does not apply, indicate with "N/A."

PART III: PURCHASE PRICE AND TERMS OF SALE

A. CASH DOWN PAYMENT OR value of trade or exchange *(excluding closing costs)*   Amount $_____

B. FIRST DEED OF TRUST @ _____ % interest for _____ years. Pymts./Mo. = $_____ (Prin. & Int. only)   Amount $_____
- ☐ FHA(_____ Discount Points)
- ☐ Conventional
- ☐ VA (_____ Discount Points)
- ☐ Cal-Vet
- ☐ Fixed rate
- ☐ Variable rate
- ☐ All inclusive D.T. ($_____ Wrapped)
- ☐ Loan carried by seller
- ☐ New loan
- ☐ Assumed existing loan balance
- ☐ Bank or savings & loan
- ☐ Finance company

Balloon payment   ☐ Yes   ☐ No   Due Date _____   Amount $_____

C. SECOND DEED OF TRUST @ _____ % interest for _____ years. Pymts./Mo. = $_____ (Prin. & Int. only)   Amount $_____
- ☐ Bank or savings & loan
- ☐ Loan carried by seller
- ☐ Fixed rate
- ☐ Variable rate
- ☐ New loan
- ☐ Assumed existing loan balance

Balloon payment   ☐ Yes   ☐ No   Due Date _____   Amount $_____

D. OTHER FINANCING: Is other financing involved not covered in (b) or (c) above?   ☐ Yes   ☐ No   Amount $_____

Type _____ @_____ % interest for _____ years. Pymts./Mo. = $_____ (Prin. & Int. only)
- ☐ Bank or savings & loan
- ☐ Loan carried by seller
- ☐ Fixed rate
- ☐ Variable rate
- ☐ New loan
- ☐ Assumed existing loan balance

Balloon payment   ☐ Yes   ☐ No   Due Date _____   Amount $_____

E. WAS AN IMPROVEMENT BOND ASSUMED BY THE BUYER?   ☐ Yes   ☐ No   Outstanding Balance: Amount $_____

F. TOTAL PURCHASE PRICE *(or acquisition price, if traded or exchanged, include real estate commission if paid)*

         TOTAL ITEMS A THROUGH E $_____

G. PROPERTY PURCHASED   ☐ Through a broker   ☐ Direct from seller   ☐ From a family member   ☐ Other *(please explain)*: _____.

If purchased through a broker, provide broker's name and phone number: _____

Please explain any special terms, seller concessions, or financing and any other information that would help the Assessor understand the purchase price and terms of sale: _____

PART IV: PROPERTY INFORMATION

A. TYPE OF PROPERTY TRANSFERRED:
- ☐ Single-family residence
- ☐ Multiple-family residence (no. of units: _____)
- ☐ Commercial/Industrial
- ☐ Other (Description: i.e., timber, mineral, water rights, etc. _____)
- ☐ Agricultural
- ☐ Co-op/Own-your-own
- ☐ Condominium
- ☐ Timeshare
- ☐ Manufactured home
- ☐ Unimproved lot

B. IS THIS PROPERTY INTENDED AS YOUR PRINCIPAL RESIDENCE?   ☐ Yes   ☐ No

If **yes**, enter date of occupancy _____ / _____ , 20 _____ or intended occupancy _____ / _____ , 20 _____ .
     (month)   (day)   (year)   (month)   (day)   (year)

C. IS PERSONAL/BUSINESS PROPERTY INCLUDED IN PURCHASE PRICE (i.e., furniture, farm equipment, machinery, etc.)
(other than a manufactured home subject to local property tax)?   ☐ Yes   ☐ No
If **yes**, enter the value of the personal/business property included in the purchase price $_____ *(Must attach itemized list.)*

D. IS A MANUFACTURED HOME INCLUDED IN PURCHASE PRICE?   ☐ Yes   ☐ No
If **yes**, how much of the purchase price is allocated to the manufactured home? _____
Is the manufactured home subject to local property tax?   ☐ Yes   ☐ No   What is the decal number?_____

E. DOES THE PROPERTY PRODUCE INCOME?   ☐ Yes   ☐ No   If **yes**, is the income from:
- ☐ Lease/Rent   ☐ Contract   ☐ Mineral rights   ☐ Other *(please explain)*: _____

F. WHAT WAS THE CONDITION OF THE PROPERTY AT THE TIME OF SALE?
- ☐ Good   ☐ Average   ☐ Fair   ☐ Poor

Please explain the physical condition of the property and provide any other information (such as restrictions, etc.) that would assist the Assessor in determining the value of the property:

CERTIFICATION

OWNERSHIP TYPE (☑)

Proprietorship   —
Partnership   —
Corporation   —
Other   —

I certify that the foregoing is true, correct and complete to the best of my knowledge and belief.
This declaration is binding on each and every co-owner and/or partner.

NAME OF NEW OWNER/CORPORATE OFFICER   TITLE

SIGNATURE OF NEW OWNER/CORPORATE OFFICER   DATE

▶ John Demming   3-31-xx

NAME OF ENTITY *(typed or printed)*   FEDERAL EMPLOYER ID NUMBER

John Demming

ADDRESS *(typed or printed)*   PHONE NUMBER (8 a.m. - 5 p.m.)   E-MAIL ADDRESS *(optional)*

7290 N. McDonald Ave., San Diego, CA 91775

(Note: The Assessor may contact you for additional information.)
If a document evidencing a change of ownership is presented to the recorder for recordation without the concurrent filing of a preliminary change of ownership report, the recorder may charge an additional recording fee of twenty dollars ($20).

Claim for Reassessment Exclusion

Some transfers are, or may be, excluded from reassessment, including transfers:

- to a surviving spouse or domestic partner
- to a revocable trust
- between parents and children, if the property is a residence or certain other qualifying property (children includes sons- and daughters-in-law, stepchildren, and children adopted before they turned 18), and
- from grandparents to grandchildren, if the property is a residence. To qualify, the parents of the grandchildren must be deceased and their death certificates must be provided. You must also complete a special claim form.

Even though these transfers are excluded from reassessment, a Preliminary Change of Ownership Report is still required. To claim the parent-child exclusion, you must file a Claim for Reassessment Exclusion for Transfer Between Parent and Child with the county assessor's office within three years after the date of transfer (date of death, in this case) or prior to the transfer of the real property to a third party, whichever is earlier (a transfer to the transferor's parent or child is not considered a transfer to a third party). This means, for example, that when children inherit property from parents and sell the property out of the estate to a third party, a claim must be filed before the sale. Otherwise, the right to the exclusion from reassessment is lost for the time they owned the property. There is one exception to this rule: A claim can be filed within six months after a supplemental tax assessment is mailed out by the tax assessor. The decedent's residence, plus an additional $1,000,000 of decedent's other real property, is excluded. The $1,000,000 applies to the assessed value, not the current market value.

Los Angeles County requires a copy of the will and death certificate with the form. If there is no will, submit a copy of your Letters of Administration (see Chapters 13 and 14) and a list of the heirs and their relationship to the decedent. (However, the transfer of a life estate to a nonspouse third party is treated as a change in ownership, triggering a reassessment even if the remainder interest passes to children of the transferor.)

How to Record Your Document Transferring Title

Recording a transfer document is not difficult; you can even do it by mail. Just follow these steps:

1. Select and prepare the appropriate document from the ones discussed at the beginning of this chapter.

2. Type or print the assessor's parcel number on the document. (You can find this number on the property tax bill.) Some printed forms of grant deeds and affidavits have a place to insert the number; if not (as in the case of a court order), type or print the number vertically in the margin on the side of the document preceded by the letters "A.P.N."

3. Type the name and address of the person to whom the document should be returned, and where the property tax bills are to be sent, in the upper left-hand corner. This person is usually the new owner. Printed documents have a place for this, as a rule. In the case of court orders, however, there is usually not enough room for all the required information. Most counties now require a cover page, which does have room, to be attached; a sample is shown below. You can get a cover page from the recorder's office. It is counted as a page in computing the recording fee. The name and address of either the surviving spouse or the estate representative should be typed in the upper left-hand corner as the person requesting recording. If this person is also the new owner of the real property, you may type below his or her name and address, "Mail tax statements same as above." However, if the person who requests the recording of the court order is not the new owner of the property, you should type at the bottom of the cover page of the court order the words, "Mail tax statements to: (name and address of new owner)," or the tax statements will continue to go to the old address.

4. The document you plan to record must normally be the original document. The signatures of the persons signing the document must be acknowledged by a notary public, except for

Claim for Reassessment Exclusion for Transfer Between Parent and Child (page 1)

BOE-58-AH (P1) REV. 13 (08-09) OWN-88 (REV. 8-09)

CLAIM FOR REASSESSMENT EXCLUSION FOR TRANSFER BETWEEN PARENT AND CHILD

RICK AUERBACH
ASSESSOR

COUNTY OF LOS ANGELES • OFFICE OF THE ASSESSOR
500 WEST TEMPLE STREET, ROOM 205
LOS ANGELES, CA 90012-2770 • Telephone 213.893.1239
Email: *helpdesk@assessor.lacounty.gov*
Website: *assessor.lacounty.gov*
Si desea ayuda en Español, llame al número 213.974.3211

NAME AND MAILING ADDRESS
(Make necessary corrections to the printed name and mailing address.)

A processing fee of no more than $175 may be charged for claims filed untimely. The fee will apply if a claim is filed more than 60 days after the date of a second notice of potential eligibility has been sent by the county assessor.

A. PROPERTY

ASSESSOR'S PARCEL NUMBER

PROPERTY ADDRESS	CITY

RECORDER'S DOCUMENT NUMBER	DATE OF PURCHASE OR TRANSFER

PROBATE NUMBER *(if applicable)*	DATE OF DEATH *(if applicable)*	DATE OF DECREE OF DISTRIBUTION *(if applicable)*

The disclosure of social security numbers is mandatory as required by Revenue and Taxation Code section 63.1. *[See Title 42 United States Code, section 405(c)(2)(C)(i) which authorizes the use of social security numbers for identification purposes in the administration of any tax.] A foreign national who cannot obtain a social security number may provide a tax identification number issued by the Internal Revenue Service. The numbers are used by the Assessor and the state to monitor the exclusion limit.*

B. TRANSFEROR(S)/SELLER(S) *(additional transferors please complete "B" on the reverse)*

1. Print full name(s) of transferor(s) _____

2. Social security number(s) _____

3. Family relationship(s) to transferee(s) _____

   If adopted, age at time of adoption _____

4. Was this property the transferor's principal residence? ☐ Yes ☐ No

   If **yes,** please check which of the following exemptions was granted or was eligible to be granted on this property:

   ☐ Homeowners' Exemption ☐ Disabled Veterans' Exemption

5. Have there been other properties that qualified for this exclusion? ☐ Yes ☐ No

   If **yes,** please attach a list of all previous transfers that qualified for this exclusion. (This list should include for each property: the County, Assessor's parcel number, address, date of transfer, names of all the transferees/buyers, and family relationship. Transferor's principal residence must be identified.)

6. Was only a partial interest in the property transferred? ☐ Yes ☐ No   If **yes,** percentage transferred _____ %

7. Was this property owned in joint tenancy? ☐ Yes ☐ No

8. If the transfer was through the medium of a trust, you **must** attach a copy of the trust.

CERTIFICATION

I certify (or declare) under penalty of perjury under the laws of the State of California that the foregoing and all information hereon, including any accompanying statements or documents, is true and correct to the best of my knowledge and that I am the parent or child (or transferor's legal representative) of the transferees listed in Section C. I knowingly am granting this exclusion and will not file a claim to transfer the base year value of my principal residence under Revenue and Taxation Code section 69.5.

SIGNATURE OF TRANSFEROR OR LEGAL REPRESENTATIVE	DATE
►	

SIGNATURE OF TRANSFEROR OR LEGAL REPRESENTATIVE	DATE
►	

MAILING ADDRESS	DAYTIME PHONE NUMBER ( )

CITY, STATE, ZIP	E-MAIL ADDRESS

(Please complete applicable information on reverse side.)

THIS DOCUMENT IS NOT SUBJECT TO PUBLIC INSPECTION

Claim for Reassessment Exclusion for Transfer Between Parent and Child (page 2)

BOE-58-AH (P2) REV. 13 (08-09) OWN-88 (REV. 8-09)

C. TRANSFEREE(S)/BUYER(S) *(additional transferees please complete "C" below)*

1. Print full name(s) of transferee(s) _____ _____

2. Family relationship(s) to transferor(s) _____ _____

   If adopted, age at time of adoption _____ _____

   If stepparent/stepchild relationship is involved, was parent still married to or in a registered domestic partnership *(registered means registered with the California Secretary of State)* with stepparent on the date of purchase or transfer? ☐ Yes ☐ No

   If **no,** was the marriage or registered domestic partnership terminated by: ☐ Death ☐ Divorce/Termination of partnership

   If terminated by death, had the surviving stepparent remarried or entered into a registered domestic partnership as of the date of purchase or transfer? ☐ Yes ☐ No

   If in-law relationship is involved, was the son-in-law or daughter-in-law still married to or in a registered domestic partnership with the daughter or son on the date of purchase or transfer? ☐ Yes ☐ No

   If **no,** was the marriage or registered domestic partnership terminated by: ☐ Death ☐ Divorce/Termination of partnership

   If terminated by death, had the surviving son-in-law or daughter-in-law remarried or entered into a registered domestic partnership as of the date of purchase or transfer? ☐ Yes ☐ No

3. ALLOCATION OF EXCLUSION (If the full cash value of the real property transferred exceeds the one million dollar value exclusion, the transferee must specify on an attachment to this claim the amount and allocation of the exclusion that is being sought.)

CERTIFICATION

I certify (or declare) under penalty of perjury under the laws of the State of California that the foregoing and all information hereon, including any accompanying statements or documents, is true and correct to the best of my knowledge and that I am the parent or child (or transferee's legal representative) of the transferors listed in Section B; and that all of the transferees are eligible transferees within the meaning of section 63.1 of the Revenue and Taxation Code.

SIGNATURE OF TRANSFEREE OR LEGAL REPRESENTATIVE	DATE
▶	
SIGNATURE OF TRANSFEREE OR LEGAL REPRESENTATIVE	DATE
▶	
MAILING ADDRESS	DAYTIME PHONE NUMBER ( )
CITY, STATE, ZIP	E-MAIL ADDRESS

Note: The Assessor may contact you for additional information.

B. ADDITIONAL TRANSFEROR(S)/SELLER(S) *(continued)*

NAME	SOCIAL SECURITY NUMBER	SIGNATURE	RELATIONSHIP

C. ADDITIONAL TRANSFEREE(S)/BUYER(S) *(continued)*

NAME	RELATIONSHIP

joint tenancy transfers, which only require a declaration under penalty of perjury. (See Chapter 10.) However, if you record a court order, it must be a copy certified by the court clerk.

5. A recording fee must accompany the document. This is usually around $9 for the first page and $3 for each additional page. Fees change, so call the recorder's office for the exact amount. If a clerk's certification of a court document is on the back of a page, it counts as an additional page. An additional $10 "monument" fee is collected on some property if it has a longer "metes and bounds" legal description.

6. When real property is sold, a documentary transfer tax is collected by the recorder's office on the recording of certain documents. Probate court orders are not subject to this tax. The following statement should appear on the cover page of the probate order: "This is a court-ordered conveyance or decree that is not pursuant to sale and is exempt from tax (Rev. & Tax. Code § 11911)." An Affidavit—Death of Joint Tenant is also exempt from tax when it is recorded, but no statement to this effect is needed when the affidavit is recorded.

7. Record the document along with a Preliminary Change of Ownership Report at the county recorder's office in which the property is located. If the real property is subject to a mortgage, the new owner should notify the person or company collecting the payments on the mortgage of the name and address of the new owner. Below is a sample letter that may be adapted for use when sending in documents for recording.

County Recorder
227 North Broadway
Los Angeles, CA 90012

April 10, 20xx

RE: Estate of John Doe, Deceased

Enclosed is a certified copy of the Court Order for Final Distribution made in the estate of the above-named decedent. Also enclosed is a Preliminary Change of Ownership Report.

Will you please record the order, and after it is recorded return it to the name and address of the person indicated in the upper left-hand corner of the first page. A check in the amount of $15.00 is enclosed to cover your recording fee.

Thank you for your assistance.

Very truly yours,

_____

(your signature)

Sample Cover Page

PLEASE COMPLETE THIS INFORMATION

RECORDING REQUESTED BY:
  Jon Taylor

AND WHEN RECORDED MAIL TO:
  Jon Taylor
  3311 — 22nd Street
  Santa Monica, CA 90405

  (Mail tax statements same as above)

THIS SPACE FOR RECORDER'S USE ONLY

TITLE:

<u>ORDER OF FINAL DISTRIBUTION</u>

This is a court-ordered conveyance or decree that is not pursuant to sale and is exempt from tax (Rev. & Tax. Code Sec. 11911).

THIS PAGE ADDED TO PROVIDE ADEQUATE SPACE FOR RECORDING INFORMATION
(Additional recording fee applies)

Mortgages

When someone dies and leaves real property subject to a mortgage or encumbrance, as a rule the real property passes to the new owner along with the encumbrance, unless the decedent's will provides otherwise. The new owner of the property then becomes responsible for making the payment on the mortgage, taxes, and so on. After the property is officially transferred, it is customary to notify the person or entity collecting the mortgage payments of the name and address of the new owner.

Most home loans contain due-on-sale clauses. That means if the property is sold, the mortgage lender can demand full payment. A mortgage lender cannot, however, call the loan when title is transferred by inheritance to a relative. (12 U.S.C. § 1701j-3(d).)

How to Transfer Securities

Securities, including stocks, bonds, debentures, or mutual fund shares owned by a decedent, must be reregistered in the name(s) of the new owners at some point during settlement of the decedent's estate. The actual transfers, except in the case of mutual fund shares, are made by a "transfer agent," whose name and address normally appear on the face of the stock or bond certificate. However, because transfer agents change frequently, it is a good idea to write or call in advance (or check with a stock brokerage firm) to verify the name and address of the current transfer agent before mailing any of the transfer documents. We provide a sample form letter below.

Shares in mutual funds are transferred by the company that manages the fund; you should contact the company to find out its requirements for selling, redeeming, or changing record ownership of the shares. You may get the name, address, and telephone number of the person to contact from the last monthly statement or from the brokerage company's website. Usually, the same documentation discussed in this chapter for other types of securities is required to transfer mutual funds.

Transferring title to securities involves a fair amount of detail work. Rather than tackle this project yourself, you might want to consider having a bank

Sample Letter to Transfer Agent

(Address of stock transfer agent)

Re: _____, deceased

Date of death: _____

To whom it may concern:

This is to notify you that the above-named decedent died on the date indicated.

The decedent's records indicate that at the time of death he/she was the owner of the following securities registered in the name(s) of:

Name of Security	Certificate Number	Par Value of Bond or Number of Shares	Type of Security

Please indicate on the enclosed copy of this letter whether or not this agrees with your records. If so, please let me know what documentation you will require to transfer title to the new owner(s). If you do not currently act as transfer agent for the company, please give me the name and address of the current transfer agent.

Thank you for your assistance.

Very truly yours,

_____
(your signature)

or stock brokerage firm handle the transfers for you. They are experienced in this area and will help with the documentation and process the transfers for a nominal charge.

Documents Required to Transfer Securities

Several documents are required to transfer securities after a death, depending on how the securities were originally owned (and sometimes depending on whom they are transferred to).

Through Formal Probate

You will normally need a probate court order to transfer securities if the estate exceeds $100,000 in value and the securities were either in the decedent's name alone or with another person as tenants in common. (The procedure for obtaining the court order is explained in Chapter 14.) Ownership as tenants in common normally occurs when an asset is owned by two or more people, unless title is specifically held as community property or in joint tenancy.

SKIP AHEAD

Skip ahead. If the securities pass outright to a surviving spouse or domestic partner, whether community property or separate property, go to "To a Surviving Spouse or Domestic Partner," below. If the estate is under $100,000, see "Through the Small Estate Procedure," below.

When a decedent owned securities as a tenant in common with a surviving person, the decedent's interest is subject to probate and the surviving person's is not. Although two new certificates must be issued, one in the name of the new owner of the decedent's interest and one in the name of the surviving tenant in common, a probate court order is required only for the transfer of the decedent's shares.

EXAMPLE: Marsha died owning 300 shares of stock as a tenant in common with her sister Clara. A new certificate for 150 shares must be issued in the name(s) of the person(s) who receive Marsha's one-half interest, and another certificate issued in the name of Clara as sole owner of the other 150 shares.

Documents to Be Submitted to the Transfer Agent

You'll need to submit the following:

- original stock certificate, bond, or debenture
- certified copy of Letters Testamentary or Letters of Administration ("letters"), certified within 60 days before they are sent to the transfer agent (we tell you how to get these in Chapter 13)
- stock power signed by the personal representative, with the signature guaranteed (see below)
- Affidavit of Domicile, signed by you as personal representative, with signature notarized (see below), and
- transmittal letter requesting the transfer, and giving the name(s), Social Security number(s), and address(es) of the new owner(s) (see below).

To a Surviving Joint Tenant

Securities registered in joint tenancy form will usually appear as "John Brown and/or Ruth Brown, as joint tenants" or, instead of "as joint tenants," it might say "JTRS" (Joint Tenants with Right of Survivorship) or "WROS" (With Right of Survivorship). All of these terms and abbreviations mean the same thing.

It is relatively easy to transfer securities held in joint tenancy, as no probate is required. This means transfer of joint tenancy property can be done almost immediately after death.

If there are no surviving joint tenants, the stocks belong to the last joint tenant to die and will be subject to probate in his or her estate. If it has not already been done, title must still be formally transferred to the last surviving joint tenant before it is then again transferred as part of her estate. To accomplish this, the transfer agent will need a certified copy of the death certificate of the first joint tenant to die, along with the other documents listed below.

Documents Required

You'll need the following:

- original stock certificate, bond, debenture, or other security
- stock power signed by surviving joint tenant(s) with signature guaranteed (see "The Stock or Bond Power," below)
- certified copy of death certificate (see Chapter 2)
- Affidavit of Domicile signed by surviving joint tenant(s), with signature(s) notarized (see "The Affidavit of Domicile," below), and
- transmittal letter signed by surviving joint tenant(s) (see "The Transmittal Letter," below).

To a Surviving Spouse or Domestic Partner

If the decedent was married or a registered domestic partner at the time of death, he or she may very likely have owned securities as community property. The decedent may also have owned other securities that were his or her separate property. Remember, however, that securities can be held in the name of one person alone and still be community property. If the securities are already held in the name of the surviving spouse or partner, no transfer is required. See Chapter 4 for a detailed discussion of community property and separate property.

If the securities have been left to a surviving spouse or domestic partner outright by a will or pass to a surviving spouse or partner by intestate succession, you may make the actual transfer easily with the following documents.

Documents Required

You'll need the following:

- original certificate, bond, or debenture
- stock power, signed by surviving spouse or partner, with signature guaranteed (see "The Stock or Bond Power," below)
- certified copy of Spousal or Domestic Partner Property Order (we discuss how to get this in Chapter 15)
- Affidavit of Domicile, signed by surviving spouse or partner, with signature notarized (see "The Affidavit of Domicile," below), and
- transmittal letter signed by the surviving spouse or partner (see "The Transmittal Letter," below).

Through the Small Estate Procedure

When the total value of the decedent's property in California is under $100,000, not counting certain property going to a surviving spouse or domestic partner, property owned in trust, or in joint tenancy (real or personal), the securities may be transferred by means of an affidavit signed by the person(s) entitled to receive the securities. This procedure, which is explained in detail in Chapter 11, usually applies when the securities are registered in the decedent's name alone or as a tenant in common with another. It can also be used as a simple way of transferring community property securities to a surviving spouse or partner, if the estate is small and meets the requirements for use of this procedure.

Documents Required

You'll need the following:

- affidavit given pursuant to California Probate Code § 13100, signed by person(s) entitled to receive the securities, with the signatures notarized (see Chapter 11)
- original stock certificate, bond, debenture, or mutual fund certificate
- certified copy of the decedent's death certificate (see Chapter 2)
- Affidavit of Domicile signed by person(s) entitled to the securities, with signature(s) notarized (see "The Affidavit of Domicile," below)
- transmittal letter signed by person(s) entitled to the securities (see "The Transmittal Letter," below), and
- stock or bond power, signed by persons entitled to receive securities (see "The Stock or Bond Power," below).

To Living Trust Beneficiaries

To transfer securities held by the decedent (or someone else as trustee) in a living trust, the best procedure is to write to the transfer agent for each security to make specific arrangements for the transfer. Usually, in this instance, the securities are held in the name of the decedent (or someone else) as trustee, and the living trust document names a successor trustee to take over on the death of the original trustee. The transfer agent will itemize the documents needed to make the transfer. Usually, a certified copy of the decedent's death certificate, a stock or bond power, and Affidavit of Domicile executed by the trustee or successor trustee are required. Sometimes a copy of the living trust document is requested, although the transfer agent should already have a copy, as it is normally needed to transfer the securities into the trust initially.

If a living trust was established but the securities in question were never formally transferred to it, you cannot use this procedure. You will probably need to transfer the securities under the terms of a formal probate unless they are part of a small estate or pass to the surviving spouse or domestic partner.

To "Transfer-on-Death" Beneficiaries

Ownership of stocks, bonds, and brokerage accounts can be registered as "transfer-on-death" to a beneficiary. Securities registered in this manner can be transferred to the beneficiary without going through probate. This is often referred to as stock registered "in beneficiary form."

A stock is registered in beneficiary form if the words "transfer on death" or "TOD" appear on the registration before the beneficiary's name and followed by the registered owner's name. Generally, an institution will allow you to transfer ownership to the beneficiary if you send a certified copy of the death certificate of the deceased owner and a stock power signed by the beneficiary. Send these two documents to the transfer agent along with a transmittal letter and the original stock ownership certificate.

CAUTION

Divorce reminder. If the decedent designated his or her spouse or partner as a transfer-on-death beneficiary and later divorced or terminated the partnership, the former spouse or partner does not inherit. (Prob. Code § 5600.)

The Stock or Bond Power

The "stock or bond power" authorizes the actual transfer of the securities. It must be executed by a person having the authority to sign on behalf of the decedent. In each of the foregoing transfer situations, we have indicated who should sign the stock or bond power.

Most stock, bond, and mutual fund certificates have the stock or bond power printed on the back. However, a separate but very similar form is normally used, called Stock or Bond Assignment Separate From Certificate, or Irrevocable Stock or Bond Power, which you can obtain from a bank, stockbroker, or office supply store (some brokerage websites allow you

Irrevocable Stock or Bond Power

IRREVOCABLE STOCK OR BOND POWER

Account Number _____

FOR VALUE RECEIVED, the undersigned does (do) hereby sell, assign, or transfer to:

_____ **Name(s) of new owner(s) of stock (i.e., surviving joint tenant(s), surviving spouse, surviving domestic partner, or beneficiary(ies))** _____

Social Security or Tax Identifying Number ____ **Insert Social Security number of new owner(s)** ____

IF STOCK, COMPLETE THIS PORTION

Number of shares
_____ shares of ____ **Type of stock (common, preferred, etc.)** ____

Name of company
stock of _____

represented by Certificate(s) No. ____ **Number of stock certificate** ____ inclusive,

standing in the name of the undersigned on the books of said company.

IF BONDS, COMPLETE THIS PORTION

Number of bonds
_____ bonds of ____ **Issuer of bond(s)** ____

_____ in the principal amount of $____ **Face value** ____

No(s).____ **Number(s) of bond certificate(s)** ____ inclusive, standing in

the name of the undersigned on the books of said company.

The undersigned does (do) hereby irrevocably constitute and appoint _____ **Leave this blank** _____

_____ attorney to transfer the said stock or bond(s), as

the case may be, on the books of said company, with full power of substitution in the premises.

IMPORTANT: The signature(s) to this power must correspond with the name(s) as written upon the face of the certificate(s) or bond(s) in every particular without alteration.

Dated: _____

Signed by surviving joint tenant; surviving spouse or domestic partner; executor or administrator of decedent's estate; or the beneficiary(ies) entitled in the case of small estates

_____

_____

Person(s) Executing This Power Sign(s) Here

_____

SIGNATURE GUARANTEED

to download this form from their sites). As you will notice in the sample just above, the form has a space to fill in the name of the person acting as attorney in fact. This person is normally an employee of the transfer agent who actually transfers the stock on the books of the corporation; leave this space blank.

Because transfer agents have no means of identifying the signature of the person who signs the stock power, they usually insist that the signature be "guaranteed." This may be done by a bank officer at the bank of the person executing the stock or bond power or by a broker handling the securities transfer. In either case, the bank or brokerage office stamps the stock or bond power "Signature Guaranteed," followed by the name of the bank, trust company, or brokerage firm. The person guaranteeing the signature signs just below the stamp.

The Affidavit of Domicile

The Affidavit of Domicile (sometimes called Affidavit of Residence) is required as proof that the decedent was a resident of California and not of the state in which the corporation is organized, in which case transfer taxes might be due. Many transfer agents require this affidavit as a matter of routine, so it is best to prepare it and send it along with the other documents to avoid delays. Banks and stockbrokers usually have these forms on hand, or you may type your own form by following the sample here. The person signing the affidavit must do so in front of a notary public.

The Transmittal Letter

A transmittal letter must accompany the original stock and bond certificates and other documents when they are sent to the transfer agent. Below we provide a sample letter that you can adapt to various situations. Note that you must provide the name or names of the new owners of the securities, along with their addresses and Social Security numbers. If the

securities are to be apportioned between two or more persons, be sure to indicate the number of shares going to each. Original certificates should be sent by registered mail, return receipt requested, and should be insured. Many attorneys also recommend that the original certificates be sent separately (but at the same time) from the transfer documents to guarantee that if the certificates are misdelivered no one will have the power to make a fraudulent transfer.

> **TIP**
>
> **Securities held by a custodian.** If the decedent owned securities held for him or her by a stockbroker or a bank as a custodian (meaning they were not registered in the decedent's name), you should contact the broker or custodian and arrange to have them put in the name(s) of the new owner(s).

How to Sell Securities

Sometimes beneficiaries may prefer to have securities sold or liquidated, rather than have them reregistered in their names as the new owners. When securities are sold, the transaction is handled by a stockbroker. The same documentation is required to sell securities as to have securities transferred, and the broker will help you with the forms. If the transfer agent insists on a court order, see Chapter 14, Step 13.

The Stock Transfer Tax

If the transfer agent is located in New York state, as is common, there will be a stock transfer tax to pay. The tax is presently 2.5 cents per share, and you must send a check payable to the transfer agent for the amount of the tax along with the transfer documents. It is a good idea to write or call the transfer agent in advance to verify the exact amount of tax. New York and Florida are the only states with a stock transfer tax. Select a transfer agent located in another state, if you have the option.

Affidavit of Domicile

AFFIDAVIT OF DOMICILE

STATE OF CALIFORNIA

COUNTY OF ___ County where affidavit will be signed

The undersigned, ___ Name of person who signs affidavit ___,

being duly sworn, deposes and says:

That he/she resides at ___ Address of person who signs affidavit ___

City of _____, County of _____,

State of _____, and is Executor/Administrator/Surviving   Cross out all titles except the one that applies to your case

Joint Tenant/Surviving Spouse/Surviving Domestic Partner of

___ Name of decedent ___, deceased, or sole beneficiary of the Will

or Estate of said decedent, who died on ___ Date of death ___, 20 ___.

That at the time of death, the decedent's residence or domicile (legal residence) was

___ Decedent's last address ___

in the State of California, and has been the same for the preceding ___ Years decedent was at this address

years, and that the decedent last voted in the State of California.

_____

Executor/Administrator/Surviving Joint Tenant/   Cross out all titles except the one that applies to your case
Surviving Spouse/Surviving Domestic Partner/
Beneficiary under decedent's will

Subscribed and sworn to (or affirmed) before me on this ___ day of _____, 20 ___,
by _____, proved to me on the basis of satisfactory evidence to be
the person(s) who appeared before me.

(seal)

Signature _____

Transmittal Letter

Name and address of transfer agent

Attention: Stock Transfer Department

Re: Estate of _____, Deceased

Enclosed are the following certificates registered in the names of _____

| Names shown on original certificates |

_____ :

Certificate Number	Type of Security	Number of Shares/ Face Amount of Bond	Name of Company or Government Entity

| Fill in information from original certificates |

Also enclosed are the following documents:

1. Separate Stock or Bond Power
2. Certified copy of Death Certificate
3. Affidavit of Domicile
4. Certified copy of letters (certified within 60 days)
5. Notarized Affidavit Under Prob. Code § 13100
6. Certified copy of Spousal or Domestic Partner Property Order

Use only items that apply to your case

Please cancel the enclosed certificates and issue new certificates as follows:

Name and Address	Social Security Number	Shares

| Fill in information about new shareholders |

Very truly yours,

Joint Tenancy Property

I t's not unusual to find many of a decedent's assets held in joint tenancy. Real estate brokers, bank officers, and stockbrokers often recommend joint tenancy ownership for married couples, and sometimes for other joint owners. Other people, aware that joint tenancy property avoids probate, use it for this reason. Sometimes elderly or ill persons place their bank accounts in joint tenancy with a younger relative or trusted friend so the relative or friend can conveniently cash checks, make deposits, and carry on business for the elderly or ill person.

For our purposes, the important characteristic of joint tenancy ownership is that it is one way to avoid probate. The moment one of the co-owners dies, her interest in the property shifts to the surviving joint tenant or tenants. (If there are two or more surviving joint tenants, the survivors remain joint tenants as far as that particular property is concerned.) A deceased joint tenant's creditors have no rights against property held in joint tenancy. Property held in joint tenancy doesn't pass under the provisions of the decedent's will, nor does it go to the decedent's heirs if the decedent died without a will.

Even though joint tenancy avoids probate, a few simple formalities must be completed to remove the decedent's name from the title, deed, certificate, or other record of ownership if the survivors wish to hold clear title to the property. We explain how to do this here.

When the last joint tenant dies, the property will be transferred as part of that person's estate. It will be subject to formal probate unless it passes to a surviving spouse or domestic partner (see Chapter 15) or as part of a small estate, as discussed in Chapter 11.

Where to Start

The first step is to verify that you are dealing with joint tenancy property. Examine deeds to real property and other ownership documents to make sure title is actually held in joint tenancy, and not in sole ownership, tenancy in common, or as community property. (It is also a good idea to check with a title company, because the decedent may have broken the joint tenancy prior to death without telling the other joint tenants.) Unless the title document (for example, deed, bank book, or stock certificate) says "as joint tenants" or "with right of survivorship" (sometimes this is abbreviated as "JTRS" or "WROS"), it is probably not joint tenancy. An exception to this is an automobile or other motor vehicle registered in the names of two people with the word "or" between their names, which is considered joint tenancy ownership as far as the Department of Motor Vehicles is concerned.

Bank accounts, stocks, bonds, and promissory notes, as well as real property, may be held in joint tenancy. A bank account held in the names of two persons connected by "or" without saying "as joint tenants" is treated as joint tenancy ownership by most banks, and the account will pass to the survivor when one of the owners dies.

Joint Tenancy and Estate Taxes: As discussed in Chapter 7, joint tenancy property does not avoid estate taxes, although many people mistakenly think it does. Even though property held in joint tenancy is excluded from probate, it is included in the decedent's taxable estate. In addition, for property that a decedent converted to joint tenancy while he or she was alive—for example, adding a joint tenant to his or her bank account for convenience or conveying his or her interest in real property to someone as a joint tenant to make it easier to transfer the property on his or her death—the decedent's original (whole) interest in the property is included in his or her taxable estate, unless he or she filed a gift tax return at the time of the transfer.

How to Clear Title to Real Property in Joint Tenancy

Real property, as we discussed in Chapter 4, is land or things permanently affixed to land, such as houses, trees, and fences. It includes condominiums and cooperatives (although some cooperatives in which the decedent's interest is a very limited one are treated as personal property), and may also include mobile homes permanently attached to land if the person who owns the mobile home also owns the land.

Step 1. Prepare an Affidavit— Death of Joint Tenant

This is the easiest way to clear joint tenancy title to real property, and the method most commonly used. All you need is a form called Affidavit—Death of Joint Tenant, which can be executed by anyone with knowledge of the facts. You will find a blank form in Appendix C. The affidavit, which is self-explanatory, states that the decedent named on the death certificate (which must be attached to the affidavit) is the same person named on the original deed to the property (quoting the decedent's name as it appears on the deed) as a joint tenant. Sometimes the names on the deed and on the death certificate may be different—initials might be used on one and a given name on the other. This isn't a problem unless the names are significantly different, in which case you will have to offer proof that the decedent and the joint tenant were the same person.

A sample affidavit is shown below. Much of the information needed to complete the affidavit is obtained from the original joint tenancy deed. The affidavit should be signed by the surviving joint tenant in the presence of a notary public.

As mentioned above, if you are dealing with the estate of the last joint tenant to die, but the interests of predeceased joint tenants were never formally ended, you must first terminate the interest of the first joint tenant(s) so that the record will show title held solely in the name of the last surviving joint tenant. The Affidavit—Death of Joint Tenant for the first joint tenant to die should be signed by the personal representative (executor or administrator) of the estate of the last surviving joint tenant, and recorded as discussed below.

Instructions for Filling in Affidavit— Death of Joint Tenant

In the top left-hand corner, fill in the name and address of the person to whom the document is to be returned. Usually, this is the person who signs the affidavit.

County: Fill in the county where the affidavit will be signed.

In the first blank in the next paragraph, fill in the name of the person who will sign the affidavit.

In the next blank, fill in the name of the decedent.

In the next two blanks, fill in the name of the decedent as it appears on the joint tenancy deed, and the date of the deed.

Next, fill in the names of the persons who signed the joint tenancy deed.

Next, fill in the names of the persons the deed transferred the property to.

Next, fill in information about where the deed is recorded: the number on the deed, the date it was recorded, the book and page where it was recorded, and the county. Deeds recorded before the mid-eighties may not have an instrument number. In this case, use the book and page number found near the recording date.

Then give the city and county where the property is located, and copy the legal description of the property from the deed. Be sure to copy the legal description carefully and accurately.

Sign the affidavit in front of a notary public.

Step 2. Attach a Certified Copy of the Death Certificate

Staple a certified copy of the decedent's death certificate to the affidavit. If you don't have one, see Chapter 2 for instructions on how to obtain one.

Step 3. Fill Out Preliminary Change of Ownership Report

The affidavit must be accompanied by a Preliminary Change of Ownership Report when it is recorded. You may also need to fill out a supplement to this form, if the property is being transferred from parent to child. (See Chapter 8.)

Step 4. Record the Affidavit With the County Recorder

The final step is to record the affidavit at the county recorder's office in the county where the real property is located. This should be done as soon as possible after the death. Mail it to the county recorder with a cover

Affidavit—Death of Joint Tenant

RECORDING REQUESTED BY:

Mary Doe

WHEN RECORDED MAIL TO:

Mary Doe
567 First Street
Los Angeles, CA 90017

SPACE ABOVE THIS LINE FOR RECORDER'S USE

AFFIDAVIT—DEATH OF JOINT TENANT

State of California)
) ss.
County of   Los Angeles   )

  Mary Doe   , of legal age, being first duly sworn, deposes and says:

That   Robert Doe   ,
the decedent mentioned in the attached certified copy of Certificate of Death, is the same person as
   Robert Doe   named as one of the parties in that certain deed
dated   June 20, 1985   , executed by   John Smith and Susan Smith   to
  Robert Doe and Mary Doe, husband and wife   ,
as joint tenants, recorded as instrument No. 85-58892   , on   June 24, 1985   ,
in Book/Reel D5100 , Page/Image 32 , of Official Records of Los Angeles
County, California, covering the following described property situated in the City of Los Angeles   ,
County of   Los Angeles   , State of California:

    Lot 101 of Tract 26834, as per map recorded in Book 691,
    Pages 3 to 8 of Maps, in the Office of the County Recorder of
    said county.

   Assessor's Parcel No.   567-892-003-1

Dated: September 26, 20xx   *Mary Doe*
               Signature

Subscribed and sworn to (or affirmed) before me on this 26 day of September , 20 xx ,
by Mary Doe , proved to me on the basis of satisfactory evidence to be the
person(s) who appeared before me.

(seal)   Signature *Nancy Notary*

letter requesting that it be recorded and returned to the address indicated in the upper left-hand corner of the document. Call the recorder's office to ascertain the amount of the recording fee. An affidavit with a death certificate attached is considered two pages for recording purposes. (Information on recording documents with the county recorder is in Chapter 8.) It isn't necessary to record a new deed when you record the affidavit. The purpose of the affidavit is to remove the deceased person's name from the title so ownership appears solely in the name of the survivor(s).

TIP

The Spousal or Domestic Partner Property Order alternative. Another way to transfer real property held in joint tenancy is through a Spousal or Domestic Partner Property Order. (See Chapter 15.) This method may be preferable if (1) the property is going to the surviving spouse or partner, and (2) the property is community property. As explained in Chapter 7, establishing (through the court order) that the joint tenancy property was, in fact, community property can have advantageous tax consequences when the property is later sold.

How to Clear Title to Securities Held in Joint Tenancy

Detailed information on how to transfer securities is in Chapter 9.

How to Clear Title to Motor Vehicles and Small Boats Held in Joint Tenancy

If the pink slip (ownership document) shows a vehicle or boat is registered in the names of two persons joined by "or" (for example, "Bob Smith or Sarah Lee"), this creates a joint tenancy under the Vehicle Code. If the pink slip names the decedent "and" another person (for example, "Bob Smith and Sarah Lee"), it is joint tenancy ownership only if it so states (for example, "Bob Smith and Sarah Lee, as joint tenants").

Vehicles may also be registered in a beneficiary or TOD form. In that case, the TOD beneficiary takes ownership of the vehicle, without probate. The transfer process is basically the same.

Automobile clubs will assist in transferring title to motor vehicles, or you may go in person to the Department of Motor Vehicles and submit the following items:

- the copy of the deceased joint tenant's death certificate (not necessarily a certified copy) (see Chapter 2)
- the vehicle or boat ownership certificate (pink slip) signed in the proper place on the back by the survivor
- the registration slip for the vehicle
- the $15 transfer fee, and
- a certificate of compliance with the smog pollution control law, unless the surviving joint tenant who is taking title is the spouse, domestic partner, child, grandparent, parent, sibling, or grandchild of the decedent.

Transfer of Ownership of Motor Vehicle Held in Joint Tenancy

STATE OF CALIFORNIA

CERTIFICATE OF TITLE

5555555555

AUTOMOBILE

VEHICLE ID NUMBER		YR MODEL MAKE		PLATE NUMBER
JH4DB1555MS555555		91 ACURA		5TTT555

BODY TYPE MODEL	AX	UNLADEN WEIGHT	FUEL	TRANSFER DATE	FEES PAID	REGISTRATION EXPIRATION DATE
SD			G		$302	01/22/92

YR 1ST SOLD	CLASS	YR	MO	EQUIPMT/TRUST NUMBER	ISSUE DATE
91	DT		WB		03/06/91

MOTORCYCLE ENGINE NUMBER   ODOMETER DATE   ODOMETER READING

REGISTERED OWNER(S)
JON DOE OR MARY DOE
1111 BERKELEY ST
OAKLEY CA 94444

FEDERAL LAW REQUIRES that you state the mileage upon transfer of ownership. Failure to complete or making a false statement may result in fines and/or imprisonment.

Odometer reading is |___|___|___| , |___|___|___| (no tenths) which is the actual mileage of the vehicle unless one of the following statements is checked. **WARNING** - Mileage ☐ is not the actual mileage.   ☐ Exceeds the odometer mechanical limits.

I **certify under penalty of perjury** under the laws of the State of California, that the signature(s) below releases interest in the vehicle **and** certifies to the truth and accuracy of the mileage information entered above.

1a. _____ X _____
      DATE   SIGNATURE OF REGISTERED OWNER

1b. _____ X _____
      DATE   SIGNATURE OF REGISTERED OWNER

IMPORTANT READ CAREFULLY

Any change of Lienholder (holder of security interest) must be reported to the Department of Motor Vehicles within 10 days.

LIENHOLDER(S)

2. X _____
   Signature releases interest in vehicle.

Release Date _____

014444   ET20220222
                REG. 17.30 (REV 9/90)

KEEP IN A SAFE PLACE — VOID IF ALTERED

Survivor dates and signs on Line 1a of front of "pink slip"

APPLICATION FOR TRANSFER BY NEW OWNER

(Please print or type.)

Any change of registered owner or lienholder must be recorded with the Department of Motor Vehicles (DMV) within ten (10) days. The title, transfer fee and in most instances, use tax and a smog certificate must be presented to DMV to record the ownership change.

NEW REGISTERED OWNER

3a. TRUE FULL NAME(S) OF NEW REGISTERED OWNER(S) (LAST, FIRST, MIDDLE) AS IT APPEARS ON DRIVER'S LICENSE OR I.D. CARD

3b. ☐ AND   (LAST, FIRST, MIDDLE)
    ☐ OR

4. STREET ADDRESS OR P.O. BOX NUMBER

5. CITY   STATE   ZIP CODE

6. MAILING ADDRESS STREET OR P.O. BOX NUMBER (DO NOT COMPLETE IF SAME AS RESIDENCE ABOVE)

7. CITY   STATE   ZIP CODE

8. FOR TRAILER COACHES ONLY — ADDRESS OR LOCATION WHERE KEPT

I certify under penalty of perjury under the laws of the State of California that the information entered by me on this document is true and correct and acknowledges the odometer mileage recorded by the seller. If there is a mailing address entered on this form, it is a valid, existing and accurate address. I consent to receive service of process at this mailing address pursuant to Civil Procedures Code Sections 415.20(b), 415.30(a) and 416.90.

9a. DATE   SIGNATURE OF NEW REGISTERED OWNER   PURCHASE DATE
                  X

9b. DATE   SIGNATURE OF NEW REGISTERED OWNER   PURCHASE PRICE OR IF GIFT, SO STATE
                  X

LEASED VEH.   10. ADDRESS OF NEW LESSEE IF DIFFERENT FROM LINE 4 ABOVE (WILL NOT BE PRINTED ON TITLE)

Survivor completes top portion (Lines 3a-9b) of back of "pink slip"

How to Clear Title to Joint Tenancy Bank Accounts (and Totten Trust Accounts)

Banks or savings and loan associations will transfer a joint account or Totten trust (pay-on-death) account to the survivor when presented with the following documents:

- a certified copy of the decedent's death certificate (see Chapter 2), and
- a savings account passbook or a check drawn for the balance of the checking account.

How to Clear Title to Money Market Funds and Mutual Funds

Mutual funds and money market funds are usually transferred by the fund management instead of a transfer agent, and, as a rule, the share certificates are held by the fund's custodian instead of by the owner of the shares. Consequently, transferring these types of assets is easier than with ordinary common stocks and bonds. The best procedure is to write or call the fund management directly and ask what they require to sell, redeem, or change the record ownership of the shares when the funds are held in joint tenancy. In almost all cases, a certified copy of the death certificate will be required.

How to Clear Title to U.S. Savings Bonds in Co-Ownership

Most local banks will help transfer jointly owned bonds to the surviving co-owner. If you take the bonds along with a certified copy of the death certificate to the bank, it will provide the forms and help you fill them out.

Transferring Small Estates Under $100,000

Overview of the Simplified Transfer Procedure for Small Estates

Small estates with assets worth $100,000 or less may be settled without formal probate proceedings, using relatively simple transfer procedures. This summary form of probate is available regardless of whether the assets are real property or personal property, as long as:

- No administration proceedings are pending or have been conducted for the decedent's estate; or, if they have, the personal representative has consented in writing to the summary procedure. (Prob. Code §§ 13101(a)(4), 13152(a)(5), and 13200(a)(7).)
- The gross value of all real and personal property owned by the decedent in California on the date of death is no more than $100,000. (This figure is the value of the property, not counting any money owed on the property.)

Actually, the $100,000 figure is a little misleading because, as we discuss in detail below, certain assets are not counted in computing whether or not the estate falls within the limitation. As a result, many apparently larger estates qualify to use these summary procedures to collect or transfer minor assets that would otherwise require a formal probate court proceeding.

No published notice is required with summary proceedings, and there are no special rules for notifying creditors as in a formal probate court proceeding. You usually do not have to file the original will with the court. In most cases, the procedure can be completed in just a few weeks, after a 40-day waiting period (six months for small-value real estate).

There are actually three separate procedures for small estates:

- for personal property (Prob. Code §§ 13100–13115)
- for real property not exceeding $20,000 in value (Prob. Code §§ 13200–13208), and
- for real or personal property not exceeding $100,000 in value (Prob. Code §§ 13150–13157).

If the estate qualifies, anyone entitled to inherit property from the decedent, whether as a beneficiary under the will or as an heir under intestate succession laws, may obtain title or possession of the property with these abbreviated transfer procedures. (Prob. Code § 13006.)

The trustee of a living trust created by the decedent during his or her lifetime may use the procedures if the trust is entitled to receive property under the decedent's will. In addition, a guardian, custodian, or conservator of the estate of a person who is entitled to receive property from the decedent may act on behalf of the person, and an attorney-in-fact authorized under a durable power of attorney may act on behalf of the beneficiary giving the power of attorney. (Prob. Code § 13051.)

The waiting period required by these transfer procedures is to allow creditors and legitimate claimants a chance to protect their interests in the property. Transferees who receive a decedent's property under these procedures are liable for the decedent's debts to the extent of the net value of the property received by the transferee and must also file any required tax returns and pay taxes due.

> **CAUTION**
>
> **Watch the clock.** Lawsuits against a transferee must be commenced within one year after the date of death. (Cal. Civ. Proc. Code § 366.2.)

Transferring personal property (household furniture, clothing, and keepsakes) is often handled independently by the family. When an asset has no title document and isn't worth much to begin with, it's reasonably safe and certainly efficient to simply hand it over to whomever is entitled to it under the decedent's will or under the laws of intestate succession.

Transfer Procedures for Small Estates		
Kind of Property	**Procedure**	**Waiting Period**
Personal property	Affidavit	40 days
Real property not exceeding $20,000 in value	Affidavit filed with probate court	6 months
Real property not exceeding $100,000 in value	Petition filed with probate court	40 days

How to Determine Whether You Can Use Summary Procedures

To find out if some or all of the decedent's assets may be transferred with these simplified procedures, you must first compute the gross value of all property the decedent owned when he or she died. We show you how to do this in Chapter 5. Summarized briefly, an estate's gross value is the fair market value on the date of death of all property owned by the decedent without subtracting any liens against the property, or debts or mortgages owed by the decedent.

> **EXAMPLE:** Lily died owning stocks worth $20,000, a car with a *Blue Book* value of $8,000, a $5,000 savings account, and an apartment full of furniture and antiques worth about $20,000. This comes to a total value of $53,000. Lily owes $6,000 on her car and $5,000 on her apartment furniture. The total gross value of Lily's estate is $53,000 because the money owed on her car and furniture is not considered in computing the gross value of her estate.

Fortunately, you can ignore several types of assets in computing whether the estate's gross value is under $100,000. (Prob. Code § 13050.) The following property isn't counted:
- real estate outside California
- joint tenancy property (real or personal)
- property (community, quasi-community, or separate) passing outright to a surviving spouse or registered domestic partner

- life insurance, death benefits, or other assets that pass to named beneficiaries outside of probate
- multiple-party accounts, IRAs or other assets that pass to named beneficiaries outside of probate, and pay-on-death accounts
- any manufactured home, mobile home, commercial coach, floating home, or truck camper registered under the Health and Safety Code
- any vessel numbered under the Vehicle Code
- any motor vehicle, mobile home, or commercial coach registered under the Vehicle Code
- amounts due the decedent for services in the armed forces
- salary or other compensation not exceeding $5,000 owed the decedent, and
- property held in trust, including a living (inter vivos) trust, or in which the decedent had a life or other estate that terminated on the decedent's death.

So, in the example above, Lily's heirs wouldn't count the value of her car when they're trying to determine whether or not her estate qualifies for small estate procedures.

As you can see from the above list, if an estate has substantial joint tenancy assets or other assets that are excluded from probate, or consists largely of property that passes outright to a surviving spouse or domestic partner, it may well qualify for summary probate proceedings. You can use the simplified procedure to transfer many items of personal property that might otherwise require probate, such as stocks, bonds, bank accounts, or property held in storage, or even real property up to $100,000 in value.

Before we look at how to transfer a small estate by summary administration, let's look at some examples of situations where it can be used.

> **EXAMPLE 1:** Curt, a young bachelor, was a California resident when he died, leaving an estate consisting of a $30,000 mountain cabin in Flagstaff, Arizona (real property), a $10,000 savings account in a Santa Barbara bank, and stocks worth $30,000, all in Curt's name

alone. Curt left no will, and his heirs under intestate succession laws are his parents. The mountain cabin in Arizona will not be included in computing the $100,000 limitation because it is real property located outside California. Therefore, his parents may use summary procedures to have the stocks and bank account transferred to them, because the total gross value of these two assets is under $100,000. The cabin would probably be subject to probate in Arizona, something not covered in this book.

EXAMPLE 2: Millie was a widow living in Pasadena when she died. Her will left all of her property to her three children, Marvin, Milton, and Mary, equally. Her estate consisted of an unimproved lot in San Bernardino County having a market value of $9,950, furniture and furnishings valued around $1,000, a $15,000 bank account, and 3,000 shares in a mutual fund valued at $20,000, all in her name alone. Millie also had some old furniture stored in Bekins Van and Storage Co. worth around $1,500. Since the gross value of Millie's probate estate is under $100,000 ($47,450, to be exact, including the real property), Marvin, Milton, and Mary can use the summary procedures to have all of these assets, including the real property, transferred to them as the new owners. To use this procedure, the children must all act together in signing the required affidavit, explained below.

EXAMPLE 3: Harry, a used car salesman in Long Beach, owned the following property at the time of his death: a $250,000 home, held as community property with his wife, Rita; a $20,000 joint tenancy savings account; and two automobiles worth $20,000 each. His estate also contained a mountain cabin in Harry's name alone, having a gross value of $39,500, and a $5,000 personal note from his brother, both of which were acquired before his marriage to Rita. Harry's will leaves the mountain cabin and the $5,000 note to his sister Pam, and everything else to Rita. Because the community property

home passes outright to Rita under Harry's will (see Chapter 8 for transfer information), and the joint savings account passes to Rita as surviving joint tenant (see Chapter 10 for transfer information), they are not included in computing the value of the estate for summary procedure purposes. The two automobiles are also not included because of the vehicle exemption (although, in this case, they could also be excluded as property passing outright to the surviving spouse). Harry's sister Pam may use summary procedures to have the mountain cabin and the $5,000 personal note transferred to her.

How to Transfer the Property

As mentioned, there are three different summary procedures for transferring or clearing title to property in small estates. The methods vary depending on whether you are dealing with:

- personal property
- real property not exceeding $20,000 in value, or
- real property not exceeding $100,000 in value.

In all cases, the gross value of the decedent's assets (excluding the property described above) must not exceed $100,000, and no probate proceedings may be conducted for the estate.

Personal Property

To receive property via this streamlined procedure, the person entitled to the property need only present an affidavit to the person, representative, corporation, or institution having custody or control of the property, or acting as a registrar or transfer agent of the property, requesting that the property be delivered or transferred to them. We include a tear-out affidavit in Appendix C.

When there are several assets to be transferred, they may all be included on one affidavit, or a separate affidavit may be used for each. A simple way to do this is to type one "master" copy of the affidavit of transfer, leaving out the description of the asset in Paragraph 6, and make as many photocopies as you will need. Then, simply insert the description of each asset to be transferred on one of the photocopies and have it signed by the person or persons entitled to receive the asset.

As a rule, if more than one person is entitled to inherit a particular asset, all beneficiaries must sign one affidavit.

> CAUTION
> **Minors cannot sign the affidavit.** If the decedent's will nominates a custodian under the Uniform Transfers to Minors Act, the custodian may sign the affidavit on behalf of the minor. If not, and the minor has no court-appointed guardian of her estate, and the amount to be distributed is not large, it may be possible for the parent having custody of the minor to sign the affidavit and receive the property on behalf of the minor if the person or entity holding the property is agreeable. Otherwise, an attorney would have to be consulted to arrange for a guardian or custodian of the minor to be appointed. (See Chapter 14.)

The form in Appendix C provides a place for the signatures to be acknowledged by a notary public. Although the Probate Code says a declaration under penalty of perjury is sufficient when dealing with personal property, a notarized affidavit is required by many institutions, especially when securities are involved. Check with the institution before you send in your request; it may save you the trouble of finding a notary to witness your signature.

These rules apply when using this affidavit procedure to collect or transfer personal property:

- At least 40 days must have elapsed since the death of the decedent before the affidavit or declaration is presented to the holder of the property.
- No administration proceedings may be pending or have been conducted for the decedent's estate.
- A certified copy of the decedent's death certificate must be attached to the affidavit.
- Evidence that the decedent owned the property—such as a stock certificate, promissory note, bank passbook, storage receipt, or bill of sale—must be presented with the affidavit. This requirement protects the holder or registrar of the property, who might be liable to another person who later makes a claim to the property.

If there is no evidence of ownership, the holder of the property may require an indemnity bond or some other method of indemnification before he or she hands over the property.

- Reasonable proof of identity must be furnished by the persons signing the affidavit. This requirement is satisfied if (1) the signatures on the affidavit are acknowledged by a notary public, (2) the person signing the affidavit is personally known to the holder of the property, or (3) the affidavit is signed in the presence of the holder of the property and the person who signs it presents a valid driver's license, passport, or other suitable identification.
- An Inventory and Appraisal of all real property owned by the decedent in California (excluding property in joint tenancy or in trust, etc.) must be obtained and attached to the affidavit. The appraiser must be a probate referee who has been appointed by the state controller to appraise property in the county where the property is located. The form and procedures for preparing the Inventory and Appraisal are generally the same as in a formal probate court proceeding. (See Chapter 14, Step 14.) However, in this case, you do not have to get a court order appointing the referee. Instead you may choose the referee (appraiser) yourself. Simply call the court clerk for a list of the names, addresses, and telephone numbers of the referees who qualify.

If these requirements are satisfied, the holder of the property is discharged from liability on delivery of the property to the successor. However, the person receiving the property is made personally liable for any unsecured debts of the decedent. The liability is limited to the fair market value of the property received, less the amount of any liens and encumbrances on the property.

EXAMPLE: Mary receives a living room set worth $500 under the terms of Sally's will. Mary is liable for up to $500 of Sally's unsecured debts (debts that don't have collateral pledged to guarantee their payment).

Anyone who falsifies information or uses the affidavit fraudulently is liable to the rightful owner in an amount three times the value of the property. The rightful owner may sue anytime within three years after the affidavit or declaration was presented to the holder of the property.

A sample affidavit is shown below with instructions on how to complete it.

Item 1: Insert name of decedent, and date and place of death.

Item 2: Attach certified copy of death certificate.

Item 5: If estate contains real property, check the first box, have property appraised by a probate referee, and attach the Inventory and Appraisal form to the affidavit. Otherwise, check the second box.

Item 6: Describe property with enough detail to be identifiable. If there is not enough space, put "See Attachment 6" and prepare a full-page attachment describing the property in detail.

Item 7: Insert name(s) of the person(s) entitled to the property. If a living trust is the beneficiary, list the name(s) of successor trustee(s) and the name of the trust (for example, "Jon Arnold, successor trustee of the Arnold Family Trust," or "Lois Taylor, successor trustee under trust agreement dated 7-20-89").

Item 8: Check the first box if the persons named in Item 7 will sign the affidavit. Check the second box if a guardian, conservator, or custodian will sign the affidavit on their behalf.

Here are instructions for collecting or transferring various types of personal property with an affidavit.

Securities (Stocks and Bonds)

A transfer agent of any security is required to change the registered ownership on the books of the corporation from the decedent to the successors upon being presented with the affidavit of transfer. (Prob. Code § 13105.) Chapter 9 tells you in detail how to transfer securities. In this type of transfer you should send the following documents (you will find most in the appendixes) to the transfer agent:

- affidavit (of transfer), signed by the persons entitled to receive the stock, with signatures notarized
- stock or bond power, signed by the persons entitled to receive the securities, with signatures guaranteed by a bank or stock brokerage firm (we discuss this in Chapter 9)
- Affidavit of Domicile, signed by the persons entitled to the securities, with signatures notarized (see Chapter 9)
- certified copy of the decedent's death certificate (see Chapter 2)
- original stock or bond certificates (see Chapter 9), and
- transmittal letter signed by the persons entitled to the securities (see Chapter 9).

Even though you send this information, some companies, especially if they are out of state, may ask for certified letters testamentary. Make it clear in your cover letter that no probate is being filed, and therefore no letters can be obtained. It may also be helpful to send a copy of California Probate Code § 13105 (see Appendix A), which authorizes recovery of attorney's fees from anyone who refuses to honor the affidavit and turn over assets.

Chapter 9 tells you where and how to send these documents.

Bank Accounts and Safe-Deposit Boxes

California banks are familiar with the procedures for transferring bank accounts and safe-deposit boxes under summary administration procedures, and many of the larger banks and savings and loans have their own form of affidavit. Call to find out if they do. If so, save yourself the time and use theirs. They prefer using forms they are familiar with. In any event, the following items will be required:

- affidavit (or declaration)
- certified copy of the decedent's death certificate
- bank passbook for savings accounts, bank money market accounts, or certificates of deposit, and
- safe-deposit box key, if applicable.

Money Market Funds

Mutual funds and money market funds are usually transferred by the fund management instead of a transfer agent, and, as a rule, the share certificates are held by the fund's custodian instead of by the owner of the shares. Consequently, transferring these types of assets is easier than with ordinary common stocks

Affidavit for Collection of Personal Property Under California Probate Code §§ 13100–13106

The undersigned state(s) as follows:

1. _____Curt Morris_____ died on ___June 10__, 20 xx ,

   in the County of _____Santa Barbara_____, State of California.

2. At least 40 days have elapsed since the death of the decedent, as shown by the attached certified copy of the decedent's death certificate.

3. No proceeding is now being or has been conducted in California for administration of the decedent's estate.

4. The gross value of the decedent's real and personal property in California, excluding the property described in Section 13050 of the California Probate Code, does not exceed $100,000.

5. ☐ An inventory and appraisal of the real property included in the decedent's estate is attached.
   ☒ There is no real property in the estate.

6. The following property is to be paid, transferred, or delivered to the undersigned under the provisions of California Probate Code Section 13100.

   a. Savings Account No. 321-51, Santa Barbara Savings Bank, 100 State Street, Santa Barbara, California;
   b. 500 shares, PDQ Corporation, common stock

7. The successor(s) of the decedent, as defined in Probate Code Section 13006, is/are:
   MARY MORRIS and MICHAEL MORRIS
   _____.

8. The undersigned ☒ is/are successor(s) of the decedent to the decedent's interest in the described property, or ☐ is/are authorized under California Probate Code Section 13051 to act on behalf of the successor(s) of the decedent with respect to the decedent's interest in the described property.

9. No other person has a right to the interest of the decedent in the described property.

10. The undersigned request(s) that the described property be paid, delivered, or transferred to the undersigned.

I/We declare under penalty of perjury under the laws of the State of California that the foregoing is true and correct.

Dated: _____July 20_____, 20 xx ___

_____Mary Morris_____

_____Michael Morris_____

_____

(See reverse side for Notarial Acknowledgments)

and bonds. The best procedure is to write or call the fund management directly and ask what it requires to sell, redeem, or change the record ownership of the shares. In almost all cases, a certified copy of the death certificate will be required, along with the affidavit or declaration.

Motor Vehicles, Small Boats, Mobile Homes, Etc.

Title to automobiles, trailers, and other vehicles registered under the Vehicle Code may be transferred after the 40-day waiting period by means of special forms available from the Department of Motor Vehicles verifying that the deceased owner "left no other property subject to probate." If more than one person has a right to the vehicle, they can agree that one person will take title and the others be reimbursed for the value of their interest. Any money owed on the vehicle is the responsibility of the new owner. To have title changed, the person entitled to the property should present the following items to the DMV:

- certificate of ownership and registration card, if available
- Affidavit for Transfer of Vehicle or Vessel Without Probate, and
- Miscellaneous Statement of Fact.

The DMV explains how to transfer a vehicle without probate at www.dmv.ca.gov/pubs/brochures/ howto/htvr2.htm.

A similar procedure is used for manufactured homes, mobile homes, floating homes, and commercial coaches or truck campers registered under the Health and Safety Code. The transfers are handled by the Department of Housing and Community Development, which has its own form for this purpose. There is a 40-day waiting period before the transfer can be made. For forms and information, contact the Department of Housing and Community Development, Registration and Titling section, 1800 Third Street, Sacramento, CA 95811-6942, 800-952-8356, or go to their website at www.hcd.ca.gov.

Miscellaneous Personal Property

The affidavit can be used to transfer other miscellaneous property, such as property held in storage under the decedent's name, promissory notes, or checks or money due the decedent for salary or retirement. All that is required is the affidavit describing the property and a certified copy of the decedent's death certificate. The documents should be presented to the persons holding the property, and the property should be released to the persons entitled to it.

For checks payable to the decedent received after the date of death, the affidavit should be sent to the company or person who issued the check requesting that it issue new checks made payable to the successors.

Trust Deed Notes

If the property transferred is an obligation secured by a lien on real property, such as a trust deed note, the affidavit must be recorded in the office of the county recorder where the real property is located. (Prob. Code § 13106.5.) Chapter 8 explains how to record documents. The description in the affidavit should include the recording reference of the deed of trust or other document creating the lien, or the legal description of the real property securing the debt, or both. After it has been recorded, a copy of the affidavit should be sent to the person or entity making payments on the obligation, with the request that future payments be sent to the new owner.

Real Property Not Exceeding $20,000 in Value

If the estate contains real property not exceeding $20,000 in value (such as an unimproved desert lot), the successors of the decedent may obtain title to the property by filing an Affidavit re Real Property of Small Value (DE-305) with the superior court and then recording a certified copy with the county recorder. Some special requirements apply to this procedure:

- The affidavit may not be filed until six months after the decedent's death.
- No probate proceedings may be pending or have been conducted in California for the estate.
- A complete legal description of the real property must be included in the affidavit.

- The signature of the person or persons signing the affidavit must be notarized.
- Funeral expenses, last illness expenses, and all unsecured debts of the decedent must have been paid before the affidavit is filed.
- A certified copy of the decedent's death certificate, and a copy of the will, if any, must be attached to the affidavit.
- An appraisal by a probate referee must be attached to the affidavit showing that the gross value of all real property the decedent owned in California (excluding real property held in joint tenancy or in a living trust, or that passes outright to a surviving spouse or domestic partner) does not exceed $20,000. See "Personal Property," above, for instructions on obtaining the Inventory and Appraisal.

When the affidavit and all attachments are complete, the original and one copy should be filed (in person or by mail) with the superior court of the county in which the decedent resided at the time of death, along with a filing fee (currently $20). If the decedent was not a California resident, the affidavit should be filed in the county in which the decedent owned real property. (See Chapter 13 on how to file court documents.) The court clerk will file the original affidavit and attachments and issue a certified copy without the attachments. To clear record title to the property in the name of the new owner, the certified copy should be recorded in the office of the county recorder of the county where the real property is located. See Chapter 8 for instructions on how to record documents. A tear-out affidavit is included in Appendix B. A sample is shown below with instructions on how to fill it in.

Instructions for Preparing Affidavit re Real Property of Small Value

Heading

First box: Insert the name, address, and telephone number (including area code) of the person who is entitled to the property and who will sign the affidavit. If there are more than one, list the one to whom the recorded affidavit will be mailed.

Second box: Insert the name of the county and address of the superior court where the affidavit will be filed.

Third box: Insert the name of the decedent exactly as it appears on the real property deed.

Items 1–4: Fill in the requested information.

Item 5a: Insert the legal description of the real property, taken exactly from the deed. If there is not enough room, check the box under 5a and copy the legal description on 8½" × 11" paper as Attachment 5a. Proofread the description carefully to make sure it is accurate.

Item 5b: Indicate what percentage interest of the property the decedent owned and whether he or she owned it as community property or separate property. For example, you might put "an undivided one-third interest as decedent's separate property" or "an undivided one-half community property interest."

Items 6a and 6b: If the decedent left a will, check Box 6a and attach a copy of the will to the affidavit. All beneficiaries entitled to an interest in the property under the will must sign the affidavit. If there is no will, check Box 6b, and have each heir entitled to receive a portion of the property under intestate succession laws (Chapter 3) sign the affidavit.

Item 7: If the decedent had a guardian or conservator at the time of death, fill in the requested information and mail or personally deliver a copy of the affidavit to the guardian or conservator. Otherwise, check "none."

When the affidavit has been completed and signed, and the signatures notarized, make sure the following documents are attached before you file it:

- certified copy of the decedent's death certificate
- copy of the decedent's will, if any, and
- Inventory and Appraisal of all California real property owned by decedent.

Property Not Exceeding $100,000 in Value

If the decedent owned property in California not exceeding $100,000 in value, the heirs or beneficiaries (successors of the decedent) may file a printed form petition with the superior court asking for an order determining their right to take the property without

Affidavit re Real Property of Small Value (page 1)

DE-305

ATTORNEY OR PARTY WITHOUT ATTORNEY *(Name, State Bar number, and address)*:
After recording return to:

Marvin Murdock
301 Green Street, Pasadena, CA 91000

TELEPHONE NO.: 560-918-7270
FAX NO. *(Optional)*:
E-MAIL ADDRESS *(Optional)*:
ATTORNEY FOR *(Name)*: In pro per

SUPERIOR COURT OF CALIFORNIA, COUNTY OF LOS ANGELES
STREET ADDRESS: 300 East Walnut
MAILING ADDRESS: 300 East Walnut
CITY AND ZIP CODE: Pasadena, CA 91101
BRANCH NAME: NORTHERN DISTRICT

MATTER OF *(Name)*:

MILLIE MURDOCK, DECEDENT

FOR RECORDER'S USE ONLY

CASE NUMBER:

FOR COURT USE ONLY

AFFIDAVIT RE REAL PROPERTY OF SMALL VALUE
($20,000 or Less)

1. Decedent *(name)*: Millie Murdock
   died on *(date)*: January 2, 20xx
2. Decedent died at *(city, state)*: Pasadena, California
3. At least **six months** have elapsed since the date of death of decedent as shown in the certified copy of decedent's death certificate attached to this affidavit. *(Attach a certified copy of decedent's death certificate.)*
4. a. [X] Decedent was domiciled in this county at the time of death.
   b. [ ] Decedent was **not** domiciled in California at the time of death. Decedent died owning real property in this county.
5. a. The following is a **legal description** of decedent's real property claimed by the declarants *(copy description from deed or other legal instrument)*:
   [ ] described in an attachment labeled Attachment 5a.

   Lot 5 of Tract 5721, as per Map recorded in Book 63 Page 31 of Maps in the Office of the County Recorder of said county.

   Assessor's Parcel No, 800-10-3000
   b. Decedent's interest in this real property is as follows *(specify)*: 100%

6. Each declarant is a successor of decedent (as defined in Probate Code section 13006) and a successor to decedent's interest in the real property described in item 5a, and no other person has a superior right, because each declarant is
   a. [X] **(will)** a beneficiary who succeeded to the property under decedent's will. *(Attach a copy of the will.)*
   b. [ ] **(no will)** a person who succeeded to the property under Probate Code sections 6401 and 6402.
7. Names and addresses of each guardian or conservator of decedent's estate at date of death
   [X] none   [ ] are as follows* *(specify)*:

8. The **gross value** of all real property in decedent's estate located in California as shown by the *Inventory and Appraisal*, excluding the real property described in Probate Code section 13050 (joint tenancy, property passing to decedent's spouse, etc.), does not exceed $20,000.

9. An *Inventory and Appraisal* of decedent's **real property** in California is attached. The *Inventory and Appraisal* was made by a probate referee appointed for the county in which the property is located. (You *may use Judicial Council form DE-160.)*

10. No proceeding is now being or has been conducted in California for administration of decedent's estate.

* You must have a copy of this affidavit with attachments personally served or mailed to each person named in item 7.

Page 1 of 2

Form Adopted for Mandatory Use
Judicial Council of California
DE-305 [Rev. July 1, 2008]

AFFIDAVIT RE REAL PROPERTY OF SMALL VALUE
(Probate—Decedents' Estates)

Probate Code, § 13200

Affidavit re Real Property of Small Value (page 2)

	DE-305
MATTER OF _(Name):_ MILLIE MURDOCK DECEDENT	CASE NUMBER:

11. Funeral expenses, expenses of last illness, and all known unsecured debts of the decedent have been paid. *[NOTE: You may be personally liable for decedent's unsecured debts up to the fair market value of the real property and any income you receive from it.]*

I declare under penalty of perjury under the laws of the State of California that the foregoing is true and correct.

Date: July 5, 20xx

   Marvin Murdock   ▶   *Marvin Murdock*

      (TYPE OR PRINT NAME)   (SIGNATURE OF DECLARANT)

Date: July 5, 20xx

   Milton Murdock   ▶   *Milton Murdock*

      (TYPE OR PRINT NAME)   (SIGNATURE OF DECLARANT)

☐ SIGNATURE OF ADDITIONAL DECLARANTS ATTACHED

NOTARY ACKNOWLEDGMENTS *(NOTE: No notary acknowledgment may be affixed as a rider (small strip) to this page. If additional notary acknowledgments are required, they must be attached as 8-1/2- by 11-inch pages.)*

STATE OF CALIFORNIA, COUNTY OF *(specify):*

On *(date):*   , before me *(name and title):*

personally appeared *(name(s)):*

who proved to me on the basis of satisfactory evidence to be the person(s) whose name(s) is/are subscribed to the within instrument and acknowledged to me that he/she/they executed the instrument in his/her/their authorized capacity(ies), and that by his/her/their signature(s) on the instrument the person(s), or the entity upon behalf of which the person(s) acted, executed the instrument.

I certify under PENALTY OF PERJURY under the laws of the State of California that the foregoing paragraph is true and correct.

WITNESS my hand and official seal.

(NOTARY SEAL)

      (SIGNATURE OF NOTARY PUBLIC)

STATE OF CALIFORNIA, COUNTY OF *(specify):*

On *(date):*   , before me *(name and title):*

personally appeared *(name(s)):*

who proved to me on the basis of satisfactory evidence to be the person(s) whose name(s) is/are subscribed to the within instrument and acknowledged to me that he/she/they executed the instrument in his/her/their authorized capacity(ies), and that by his/her/their signature(s) on the instrument the person(s), or the entity upon behalf of which the person(s) acted, executed the instrument.

I certify under PENALTY OF PERJURY under the laws of the State of California that the foregoing paragraph is true and correct.

WITNESS my hand and official seal.

(NOTARY SEAL)

      (SIGNATURE OF NOTARY PUBLIC)

(SEAL)	**CLERK'S CERTIFICATE**
	I certify that the foregoing, including any attached notary acknowledgments and any attached legal description of the property (but excluding other attachments), is a true and correct copy of the original affidavit on file in my office. *(Certified copies of this affidavit do not include the (1) death certificate, (2) will, or (3) inventory and appraisal. See Probate Code section 13202.)* Date: Clerk, by _____, Deputy

DE-305 [Rev. July 1, 2008]   **AFFIDAVIT RE REAL PROPERTY OF SMALL VALUE**   Page 2 of 2
           (Probate—Decedents' Estates)

probate administration. The petition is called a Petition to Determine Succession to Real Property (Prob. Code §§ 13151–13152). It is primarily for real property, but it may include a request that the court make an order determining that the petitioner has succeeded to personal property described in the petition as well. (If there is *only* personal property in the estate, the affidavit discussed above should be used.) The following requirements must be met:

- Forty days have elapsed since the decedent's death.
- No proceeding is being or has been conducted in California for administration of the decedent's estate.
- The gross value of the real and personal property in the estate does not exceed $100,000 (again, not counting property excluded by Probate Code § 13050, discussed above). You must attach an Inventory and Appraisal by a probate referee of the real and personal property showing the gross value. Do not list on the Inventory any property that is excluded in determining the $100,000 limitation.

This abbreviated proceeding can be used to transfer title to real property under $100,000 more quickly than is allowed under the affidavit procedure described above (which has a six-month waiting period), or if the unsecured creditors have not been paid.

The petition is filed in the superior court of the county where the decedent resided, or if the decedent was not a California resident, in the county where the decedent owned property.

The following steps show you how to obtain the court order:

1. Prepare and file with the court:
   - Petition to Determine Succession to Real Property (obtain Inventory and Appraisal of all real and personal property and attach to petition) (see Chapter 14, Step 14, for instructions)
   - Notice of Hearing, if required (see Chapter 15, Step 3, for instructions)
   - Certificate of Assignment, if required (see Chapter 14, Step 2)
   - filing fee (call court for amount), and
   - original will, if required (check local practice).
2. Before the hearing date on the petition:
   - mail Notice of Hearing
   - file original Notice of Hearing, showing date of mailing
   - prepare Order Determining Succession to Real Property (shown below)
   - file order, if required, and
   - check calendar notes at court (see Chapter 13).
3. After hearing:
   - file Order Determining Succession to Real Property
   - record certified copy of order in county where real property is located, and
   - file Preliminary Change of Ownership Report with the order (see Chapter 8).

Samples of the petition and order are given below. For other instructions (for example, Notice of Hearing) see Chapter 15.

Sample Attachment to Petition to Determine Succession to Real Property

---

Estate of Harry Reese, deceased

PETITION TO DETERMINE SUCCESSION TO REAL PROPERTY

Attachment 11--Legal Description of Real Property:

Decedent's 100% separate property interest in real property situated in the County of San Bernardino, State of California, improved with a single dwelling, commonly known as 85 Pine Street, Crestline, and legally described as:

Lot 23, block 289, in Tract XYZ, per Map recorded in Book 70, Pages 91 and 92 of maps, in the office of the County Recorder of said county.

Assessor's Parcel No. 234-56-7700

Instructions for Petition to Determine Succession to Real Property

Caption: Fill in the boxes at the top of the form just as you have filled them in on your other court forms. Leave the case number and hearing date boxes blank; when you file the petition, the clerk will give you this information.

Item 1: The petitioner (or his or her guardian or conservator) is the person who is entitled to succeed to the real property under the will or by intestate succession. If there is more than one such person, list all of them as petitioners. If there isn't enough room, type "See Attachment 1" and list them on a separate 8½" × 11" paper labeled Attachment 1 and attach it to the petition.

Items 2–4: Fill in the requested information.

Item 5: If the decedent left a will, check "testate" and attach a copy of the will, labeled Attachment 5. Otherwise, check "intestate." Some counties also want the original will filed with the petition, but most do not, so ask the court.

Item 7: Indicate whether or not probate proceedings have been begun for the decedent in another state.

Item 8: Before filing the petition, you must obtain an Inventory and Appraisal of all property required to be considered in determining whether the estate is within the $100,000 limitation. The procedure for obtaining the Inventory and Appraisal is the same as that used in a formal probate proceeding (see Chapter 14, Step 14), but in this case you may choose the referee yourself. Attach the Inventory and Appraisal form to the petition.

Items 9 and 10: For instructions, see Items 5, 6, and 7 of Step 1, Chapter 14, on how to prepare the Petition for Probate.

Item 11: Put the legal description and Assessor's Parcel Number of the property (from the deed to the property) on a plain 8½" × 11" paper and label it as Attachment 11. You may also include personal property here, if it passes to the petitioner. Indicate what interest the decedent owned and whether it was community or separate property.

Item 12: If the decedent left a will, check Box 12a and attach a copy of the will. Each beneficiary entitled to receive an interest in the real property under the will must sign the petition. If there is no will, check Box 12b and have each heir of the decedent who is entitled to a portion of the property sign the petition. (Some courts now require the *original* will to be filed separately with the petition—for "safekeeping"—so check with the court about this.)

Item 13: List the interest in the property claimed by each petitioner. For example, if there is only one petitioner, put "100% interest." If three successors are inheriting equally, put "John Doe, Jane Doe, and Robert Doe, each as to an undivided one-third interest."

Item 14: List persons potentially interested in the estate, to give them notice of the petition. If the decedent left a will, list the name, relationship, age, and residence or mailing address of everyone (whether living or deceased) mentioned in the will as a beneficiary. Also list this information for all persons listed in Items 9 and 10 (the decedent's heirs). Before completing this item, read the instructions for Attachment 8 to the Petition for Probate (Chapter 14, Step 1).

Item 15: Check the appropriate box and list the name(s) and addresses of all executors named in the will, if any, including alternate executors.

Item 16: If the petitioner is also the trustee of a trust that is entitled to receive property under the will, check this box and list in an attachment the names and addresses of all living persons who are potential beneficiaries of the trust.

Item 17: Check the first box only if the decedent had a guardian or conservator at the time of death. If so, list the guardian or conservator's name and address on a separate piece of paper labeled Attachment 17, and attach it to the petition.

Item 18: Enter the number of attachments.

All petitioners must sign the petition. If you need more lines, use the dotted lines as signature lines and type or print the names underneath each line. You can also add more lines in this space if you need to. Leave the signature line for the attorney blank, or put "not applicable."

When the petition is filed with the appropriate filing fee, the clerk will give it a hearing date, which

Petition to Determine Succession to Real Property (page 1)

DE-310

ATTORNEY OR PARTY WITHOUT ATTORNEY *(Name, state bar number, and address)*:	TELEPHONE AND FAX NOS.:	*FOR COURT USE ONLY*
Pam Reese 700 Harbor Way Long Beach, CA 91176	(213) 377-7794	

ATTORNEY FOR *(Name)*: In pro per

SUPERIOR COURT OF CALIFORNIA, COUNTY OF   LOS ANGELES
STREET ADDRESS: 825 Maple Avenue
MAILING ADDRESS: 825 Maple Avenue
CITY AND ZIP CODE: Torrance, CA 90503
BRANCH NAME: SOUTHEAST DISTRICT

MATTER OF *(Name)*:

HARRY REESE,
aka HARRY C. REESE, DECEDENT

PETITION TO DETERMINE SUCCESSION TO REAL PROPERTY (Estates $100,000 or Less) ☐ And Personal Property	CASE NUMBER:
	HEARING DATE:
	DEPT.: TIME:

1. Petitioner *(name of each person claiming an interest)*:   Pam Reese

     requests a determination that the real property ☐ and personal property   described in item 11 is property passing to petitioner and that no administration of decedent's estate is necessary.

2. Decedent *(name)*:   Harry Reese, aka Harry C. Reese
     a. Date of death: April 25,20xx
     b. Place of death *(city, state)*:   Long Beach, California   9:00 A.M.

3. At least 40 days have elapsed since the date of decedent's death.

4. a. ☒ Decedent was a resident of this county at the time of death.
     b. ☐ Decedent was **not** a resident of California at the time of death. Decedent died owning property in this county.

5. Decedent died ☐ intestate ☒ testate and a copy of the will and any codicil is affixed as Attachment 5 or 12a.

6. a. ☒ No proceeding for the administration of decedent's estate is being conducted or has been conducted in California.
     b. ☐ Decedent's personal representative's consent to use the procedure provided by Probate Code section 13150 et seq. is attached as Attachment 6b.

7. Proceedings for the administration of decedent's estate in another jurisdiction
     a. ☒ have **not** been commenced.
     b. ☐ have been commenced ☐ and completed.
     (Specify state, county, court, and case number):

8. The **gross value** of all real and personal property in decedent's estate located in California as shown by the *Inventory and Appraisal* attached to this petition, excluding the property described in Probate Code section 13050 (joint tenancy, property passing to decedent's spouse, etc.), does not exceed $100,000. *(Attach an* Inventory and Appraisal *(form DE-160) as Attachment 8.)*

9. a. The decedent is survived by *(check at least one box in each of items (1)-(3))*
     (1) ☒ spouse ☐ no spouse as follows: ☐ divorced or never married ☐ spouse deceased
     (2) ☐ child as follows: ☐ natural or adopted ☐ natural adopted by a third party ☒ no child
     (3) ☐ issue of a predeceased child ☒ no issue of a predeceased child
     b. Decedent ☐ is ☒ is not survived by a stepchild or foster child or children who would have been adopted by decedent but for a legal barrier. *(See Prob. Code, § 6454.)*

10. *(Complete if decedent was survived by (1) a spouse but no issue (only a or b apply); or (2) no spouse or issue. Check the* **first** *box that applies.)*
     a. ☐ Decedent is survived by a parent or parents who are listed in item 14.
     b. ☒ Decedent is survived by a brother, sister, or issue of a deceased brother or sister, all of whom are listed in item 14.
     c. ☐ Decedent is survived by other heirs under Probate Code section 6400 et seq., all of whom also listed in item 14.
     d. ☐ Decedent is survived by no known next of kin.

11. Attachment 11 contains (1) the **legal description** of decedent's real property and its Assessor's Parcel Number (APN)
     ☐ and personal property   in California passing to petitioner and (2) decedent's interest in the property. *(Attach the legal description of the real and personal property and state decedent's interest.)*

(Continued on reverse)

    **PETITION TO DETERMINE SUCCESSION
TO REAL PROPERTY**
(Probate)   Probate Code, § 13151

Petition to Determine Succession to Real Property (page 2)

MATTER OF *(Name)*:	CASE NUMBER:
HARRY REESE, DECEDENT	

12. Each petitioner is a successor of decedent (as defined in Probate Code section 13006) and a successor to decedent's interest in the real property ☐ and personal property described in item 11 because each petitioner is

    a. ☐ **(will)** a beneficiary who succeeded to the property under decedent's will.[1]

    b. ☒ **(no will)** a person who succeeded to the property under Probate Code sections 6401 and 6402.

13. The specific property interest claimed by each petitioner in the real property ☐ and personal property described in item 11 ☐ is stated in Attachment 13 ☒ is as follows *(specify)*: 100% interest

14. The names, relationships, ages, and residence or mailing addresses so far as known to or reasonably ascertainable by petitioner of (1) all persons named or checked in items 1, 9, and 10, (2) all other heirs of decedent, and (3) all devisees of decedent (persons designated in the will to receive any property)

    ☒ are listed below ☐ are listed in Attachment 14.

Name and relationship	Age	Residence or mailing address
Pam Reese, surviving spouse	Adult	700 Harbor Way Long Beach, CA 91176
James P. Reese, brother	Adult	2318 Avenita Rio Lobo San Clemente, CA 93344

15. The names and addresses of all persons named as executors in decedent's will

    ☒ are listed below ☐ are listed in Attachment 15 ☐ none named ☐ no will.

    Pam Reese (address listed above in Item 14)

16. ☐ Petitioner is the trustee of a trust that is a devisee under decedent's will. The names and addresses of all persons interested in the trust, as determined in cases of future interests under paragraphs (1), (2), or (3) of subdivision (a) of Probate Code section 15804 are listed in Attachment 16.

17. ☐ Decedent's estate was under a ☐ guardianship ☐ conservatorship at decedent's death. The names and addresses of all persons serving as guardian or conservator ☐ are listed below ☐ are listed in Attachment 17.

18. Number of pages attached: 4

Date:

* (Signature of all petitioners also required (Prob. Code, § 1020).)

▶ (not applicable)

(SIGNATURE OF ATTORNEY *)

I declare under penalty of perjury under the laws of the State of California that the foregoing is true and correct.

Date: June 20, 20xx

Pam Reese

(TYPE OR PRINT NAME)

▶ *Pam Reese*

(SIGNATURE OF PETITIONER[2])

▶

(TYPE OR PRINT NAME)

(SIGNATURE OF PETITIONER[2])

[1] See Probate Code section 13152(c) for the requirement that a copy of the will be attached in certain instances. If required, include as Attachment 5 or 12a.

[2] Each person named in item 1 must sign.

**PETITION TO DETERMINE SUCCESSION
TO REAL PROPERTY**
(Probate)

is usually four to five weeks later. You will not be required to appear at the hearing unless there is a problem. At least 15 days before the hearing, written notice of the hearing must be mailed or personally given to all persons listed in Items 14, 15, and 16 of the petition (heirs, devisees or trustees named in the will, and trust beneficiaries). The procedures for giving the Notice of Hearing are the same as for the Spousal or Domestic Partner Property Petition described in Chapter 15.

Before the hearing, you should also prepare the Order Determining Succession to Real Property for the judge to sign when he or she approves the petition. A sample is shown below. Some counties require the order to be submitted to the court several days *before* the hearing, so check your local court rules.

If the court approves the petition, the judge will sign the order at the hearing or shortly thereafter. When the order is signed, the successor of the decedent becomes personally liable for the unsecured debts of the decedent to the extent of the fair market value of the real property at the date of death, less liens and encumbrances. The new owner should record a certified copy of the order with the county recorder in the county where the real property is located. Chapter 8 gives instructions on how to record the order.

Instructions for Order Determining Succession to Real Property

Caption: Fill in the boxes at the top of the form just as you filled them in on the petition, except that you can now fill in the case number.

Item 1: Fill in date, time, and place of the hearing.

Item 3: Fill in the date of death and check the correct boxes.

Items 5 and 7: Check the correct boxes.

Item 9a: Fill in legal description of real property and describe personal property, if any. If there isn't enough room, check the box and put the description on a piece of paper labeled Attachment 9a.

Item 9b: Insert same information as in Item 13 of petition.

Item 10: Leave this box blank.

Item 11: Enter the number of pages attached, if any.

Box beneath judge's signature line: If you have attachments, check this box and, at the end of the last attachment page, type a place for the date and a signature line for the judge.

Order Determining Succession to Real Property

DE-315

ATTORNEY OR PARTY WITHOUT ATTORNEY *(Name, state bar number, and address):*

After recording return to:

Pam Reese
700 Harbor Way, Long Beach, CA 91176
TELEPHONE NO.: 213-377-7794
FAX NO. *(Optional):*
E-MAIL ADDRESS *(Optional):*
ATTORNEY FOR *(Name):* In pro per

SUPERIOR COURT OF CALIFORNIA, COUNTY OF LOS ANGELES
STREET ADDRESS: 825 Maple Avenue
MAILING ADDRESS: 825 Maple Avenue
CITY AND ZIP CODE: Torrance, CA 90503
BRANCH NAME: SOUTHEAST DISTRICT

MATTER OF *(Name):*

HARRY REESE,
aka HARRY C. REESE, DECEDENT

FOR RECORDER'S USE ONLY

CASE NUMBER:
SWP 12345

ORDER DETERMINING SUCCESSION TO REAL PROPERTY
(Estates $100,000 or Less)
☐ **And Personal Property**

FOR COURT USE ONLY

1. Date of hearing: 7/15/xx   Time: 9:00 A.M.
   Dept./Room: 3   Judge:

THE COURT FINDS

2. All notices required by law have been given.
3. Decedent died on *(date):* 4/25/xx
   a. ☒ a resident of the California county named above.
   b. ☐ a nonresident of California and left an estate in the county named above.
   c. ☐ intestate ☒ testate.
4. At least 40 days have elapsed since the date of decedent's death.
5. a. ☒ No proceeding for the administration of decedent's estate is being conducted
      or has been conducted in California.
   b. ☐ Decedent's personal representative has filed a consent to use the procedure
      provided in Probate Code section 13150 et seq.
6. The gross value of decedent's real and personal property in California, excluding
   property described in Probate Code section 13050, does not exceed $100,000.
7. Each petitioner is a successor of decedent (as defined in Probate Code section 13006) and a successor to decedent's interest in
   the real ☐ and personal property described in item 9a because each petitioner is
   a. ☒ **(will)** a beneficiary who succeeded to the property under decedent's will.
   b. ☐ **(no will)** a person who succeeded to the property under Probate Code sections 6401 and 6402.

THE COURT FURTHER FINDS AND ORDERS

8. No administration of decedent's estate is necessary in California.
9. a. The following described real ☐ and personal property is property of decedent passing to each petitioner *(give legal
      description of real property):* ☐ described in Attachment 9a.

   Real property in the County of San Bernardino, State of California,
   commonly known as 85 Pine Street, Crestline, and legally described as: Lot
   23, Block 789, in Tract XYZ, per Map recorded in Book 70, Pages 91 and 92
   of Maps, in the office of the County Recorder of said County.

   b. Each petitioner's **name** and specific property interest ☐ is stated in Attachment 9b ☒ is as follows *(specify):*

   Pam Reese — 100%

10. ☐ Other *(specify):*

Date:

_____
JUDGE OF THE SUPERIOR COURT

11. Number of pages attached: _____   ☐ SIGNATURE FOLLOWS LAST ATTACHMENT

Page 1 of 1

Form Adopted for Mandatory Use
Judicial Council of California
DE-315 [Rev. January 1, 2003]

**ORDER DETERMINING SUCCESSION
TO REAL PROPERTY**
(Probate)

Probate Code, § 13154

How to Transfer Trust Property and Property Subject to Life Estates

People seeking to avoid the delay and expense inherent in the probate process often adopt estate planning devices such as gifts, joint tenancy transfers, trusts, and, less often, life estates to transfer their assets without a will. Someone who sets up a living (or inter vivos) trust, called the "settlor" or "trustor," specifies in the trust document how, when, and to whom the property in trust is to be distributed. For example, Mary P. might set up a living trust with herself as trustee and her daughter Sue as beneficiary. She would then formally transfer items of property to the trust by putting the name of the trustee on the relevant deeds, title slips, etc. At Mary's death, whomever she designates as successor trustee on the living trust document simply transfers the proceeds of the trust to Sue, and no probate is required.

RESOURCE

More information about living trusts. You can learn about and make your own living trusts using Nolo's Online Living Trust or *Make Your Own Living Trust,* by Denis Clifford (Nolo).

A life estate can be used to accomplish much the same thing. In this instance, a person ensures that real property will pass without probate, upon his or her death, by deeding it to the intended beneficiary but retaining a life estate—that is, the right to use the property for the rest of his or her life.

Settling the estate of a person who had a living trust is much easier than completing a probate proceeding, which is one of the main reasons that people set up living trusts. The successor trustee just steps in and takes charge of the trust assets, pays final bills and taxes, and distributes the remaining trust property according to the instructions in the trust. The successor trustee needs only a certified copy of the death certificate and a copy of the living trust to do whatever is necessary on behalf of the trust. Once the trust property has been distributed, the trust ends. No formal termination document is required.

Nevertheless, certain steps should always be taken on the death of any individual. In Chapter 2, we discuss the initial responsibilities of an estate representative. The same procedures should be followed in the case of a living trust. The only difference is that you are dealing with a trust in place of a will, and a trustee instead of an executor or administrator.

Notifying Heirs and Beneficiaries

When the settlor of a revocable trust dies, the successor trustee must notify all of the trust beneficiaries and heirs of the settlor of the existence of the trust and of their right to receive a copy of the terms of the trust. (Prob. Code §§ 16060.5–16061.8.) An "heir" is any person, including the surviving spouse or registered domestic partner, who would be entitled to inherit property if there were no will. (See Chapter 3.)

The "terms of the trust" are broadly defined to include virtually anything that affects the administration or disposition of the trust. (Prob. Code § 16060.5.) The notice must also inform the recipients that there is a time limit (generally 120 days) in which to contest the trust. That warning must be in 10-point bold type.

A trustee who does not make a good faith effort to comply with the notice requirements can be held liable for damages, including attorney's fees and costs, caused by the failure to give the notice. A sample form that can be adapted for this purpose is shown below, titled Notification by Trustee. A tear-out copy is included in Appendix C.

Trust Property

Sometimes you may find that the decedent signed a trust document designating certain assets to be held in trust but for some reason failed to actually transfer title into the name of the trust. As a general rule, assets not transferred to the living trust are still subject to probate. Therefore, you should carefully examine all title documents (for example, real property deeds, stock certificates, and motor vehicle pink slips) to see if title was actually transferred to the trust. If the asset was transferred to the trust, the ownership document will show title held something like this: "The I.M. Smart Trust" or "I.M. Smart, Trustee Under Declaration of Trust dated June 1, 2000." Property that doesn't have formal title

Notification by Trustee (Probate Code Sec. 16061.7)

Name(s) of settlor(s) [person or persons who originally made the trust]

executed the _____ ,
          Name of trust

in his/her/their capacity(ies) as Settlor(s) on _____ , hereinafter referred to as the "Trust."
                                      Date of trust

1. The name, mailing address, and telephone number of each Trustee of the Trust is set forth below:

   _____

   _____

   _____

   _____

   _____

2. The address of the physical location where the principal place of administration of the Trust is located is:

   Insert the address where the usual day-to-day activity of the trust is carried on—
   ordinarily, the trustee's residence or usual place of business.

   _____

   _____

   _____

3. The terms of the Trust require disclosure of the following information:

   List any additional information that is required to be given to the beneficiaries under
   the trust instrument and any adjustments to the original trust document or disclaimers,
   directions, or instructions to the trustee that affect the administration or disposition of
   the trust.

   _____

   _____

   _____

4. You are entitled to receive from the Trustee a true and complete copy of the terms of the Trust by requesting it from the Trustee.

5. **YOU MAY NOT BRING AN ACTION TO CONTEST THE TRUST MORE THAN 120 DAYS FROM THE DATE THIS NOTIFICATION BY THE TRUSTEE IS SERVED UPON YOU OR 60 DAYS FROM THE DATE ON WHICH A COPY OF THE TERMS OF THE TRUST IS MAILED OR PERSONALLY DELIVERED TO YOU DURING THAT 120-DAY PERIOD, WHICHEVER IS LATER.**

_____   _____
Date   Trustee

documents, however, such as miscellaneous items of personal property, can be included in a living trust without being formally transferred to the trust. They need only be listed in the trust document.

Often it's hard for a person to inventory every little asset owned and place it in a trust. Therefore, a "pour-over will" is sometimes used along with a trust to cover assets that have been inadvertently overlooked or left outside the trust. The pour-over will simply states that such assets are to be transferred into a specified trust at the time of the testator's death. A pour-over will is treated the same as other wills, and formal probate is required if the assets covered by the will exceed $100,000. If such assets have a gross value under $100,000, the successor trustee can use the summary procedures in Chapter 11 to transfer them to the trust without formal probate.

Handling Debts and Expenses

The successor trustee should carefully examine the decedent's checkbooks, tax returns, and other financial records for evidence of any financial obligations the decedent may have had at death. Before distributing trust property, we recommend that sufficient money be withheld to pay any legitimate debts, such as personal loans, income taxes, credit card bills, accountant's fees, doctor bills and last illness expenses (over and above amounts paid by insurance or Medicare), and funeral expenses. A ledger should be kept of bills paid and any income received.

In a formal probate proceeding, creditors generally must file claims within four months or the claim is barred. In the case of a living trust, however, since no probate is required, creditors are not cut off at an early date, and each trust distributee is personally liable for any unpaid debts of the decedent to the extent of the value of the distribution received by that distributee. To avoid any such liability, the trustee can take advantage of a creditors' claim procedure for living trusts that operates in substantially the same way as the creditors' claim procedure for probate estates. (Prob. Code §§ 19000–19403.) The procedures are optional and would appear to be useful only in limited circumstances, such as in the case of large

disputed claims against the decedent or the estate. If you have such a situation, you should contact an attorney.

How to Transfer Property Held in Living Trusts

The procedures used to transfer property held in living trusts to the beneficiaries of the trust are similar to those used to transfer assets not held in trust.

Real Property

If real property is held in the trust, you will need to prepare some documents to show the transfer of title from the trustee to the trust beneficiaries. Ordinarily, when a trustee of a revocable living trust has died, this will not be known to the title companies or others dealing with trust property. Therefore, a successor trustee should first record an Affidavit— Death of Trustee for each piece of real property held in the name of the trust so public record will show that the original trustee has died. This gives the world notice that a successor trustee is now in place. A certified copy of the original trustee's death certificate must be attached to the affidavit. The form is similar to the Affidavit—Death of Joint Tenant, and a sample is shown below.

To transfer title to real property from the trust to the beneficiaries named in the trust, the successor trustee must also record a deed from himself or herself, as successor trustee, to the beneficiaries. A sample of such a deed is shown below. The transfer to the beneficiaries is exempt from the documentary transfer tax, and the statement shown on our sample should appear on the face of the deed. Instructions for recording the deed are given in Chapter 8. However, before a title company will insure title in the names of the beneficiaries, it will also require a certified copy of the death certificate of the trustee or creator of the trust and a copy of the trust document.

Affidavit—Death of Trustee

RECORDING REQUESTED BY:

Fred Fiduciary

WHEN RECORDED MAIL TO:

Fred Fiduciary
20800 Circle Drive
Anywhere, CA 90000-0000

SPACE ABOVE THIS LINE FOR RECORDER'S USE

AFFIDAVIT—DEATH OF TRUSTEE

State of California   )
) ss.
County of   )

The undersigned, being of legal age, being duly sworn, deposes and says:

That __I. M. Smart__, the decedent mentioned in the attached certified copy of Certificate of Death, is the same person as __I. M. Smart__ named as Trustee in that certain Declaration of Trust dated __5-1-95__, executed by __I. M. Smart__ as Trustor(s).

At the time of the demise of the decedent, the decedent was the record owner, as Trustee, of real property commonly known as __12345 Circle Terrace, San Bernardino, California__, which property is described in a Deed which was executed by __I.M. Smart__ as Grantor(s) on __May 1, 1995__ and recorded as Instrument No. __24023__ on __May 10,1995__ of Official Records of __San Bernardino__ County, State of California.

The legal description of said property is as follows:

Lot 22, Block 19 of Tract 7730 as designated on the map entitled "Ramona Acres, City and County of San Bernardino, State of California," filed in the office of said county on May 5, 1903, in Volume 4 of maps at page 9. Assessor's parcel No. 773-06-1996.

I, __Fred Fiduciary__, am the named Successor Trustee under the above-referenced Trust, which was in effect at the time of the death of the decedent mentioned in Paragraph 1 above, and which has not been revoked, and I hereby consent to act as such.

I declare under penalty of perjury, under the laws of the State of California, that the foregoing is true and correct.

Dated: __May 17, 20xx__   _Fred Fiduciary_
            Signature

Subscribed and sworn to (or affirmed) before me on this __17__ day of __May__, 20 __xx__, by __Fred Fiduciary__, proved to me on the basis of satisfactory evidence to be the person(s) who appeared before me.

(seal)   Signature _Nancy Notary_

Quitclaim Deed

RECORDING REQUESTED BY:

WHEN RECORDED MAIL TO:

    Betty Beneficiary
    12345 Circle Terrace
    San Bernardino, CA 90000

DOCUMENTARY TRANSFER TAX $ _____ None _____

_____ Computed on the consideration or value of property conveyed; OR

_____ Computed on the consideration or value less liens or encumbrances
        remaining at time of sale.

SPACE ABOVE THIS LINE FOR RECORDER'S USE

This conveyance transfers title to
the trust beneficiary; Grantor received
nothing in return. (R & T 11911)

Fred Fiduciary

Signature of Declarant or Agent determining tax – Firm Name

QUITCLAIM DEED

FOR NO CONSIDERATION, receipt of which is hereby acknowledged,

    Fred Fiduciary, Successor Trustee Under Declaration of Trust dated May 1, 1995,
    which acquired title as I. M. Smart, Trustee,

do(es) hereby REMISE, RELEASE, AND FOREVER QUITCLAIM to   Betty Beneficiary

the real property in the City of   San Bernardino

County of   San Bernardino   , State of California, described as

    Lot 22, Block 19 of Tract 7730 as designated on the map entitled "Ramona
    Acres, City and County of San Bernardino, State of California," filed in the
    office of the County Recorder of said county on May 5, 1903, in Volume 4 of
    Maps at page 9.

Assessor's Parcel No.   773-06-1996

Dated: June 10, 20xx   *Fred Fiduciary*

                         Signature

On June 10, 20xx , before me, Nancy Notary , a notary public, personally appeared
  Fred Fiduciary , who proved to me on the basis of satisfactory evidence to be the person(s)
whose name(s) is/are subscribed to the within instrument and acknowledged to me that he/she/they executed the same in his/her/
their authorized capacity(ies), and that by his/her/their signature(s) on the instrument the person(s), or the entity upon behalf of
which the person(s) acted, executed the instrument.

I certify under PENALTY OF PERJURY under the laws of the State of California that the foregoing is true and correct.

Witness my hand and official seal.

(Notary Signature) *Nancy Notary*

MAIL TAX STATEMENTS TO:
    Betty Beneficiary
    12345 Circle Terrace
    San Bernardino, CA 90000

Securities

For general information on how to transfer securities, see Chapter 9. The transfer agent for securities held in trust should be sent the following documents:

- certified copy of the death certificate
- copy of the trust document (if the transfer agent did not receive one when the securities were transferred into the trust)
- the original certificates for the securities
- a stock power signed by the trustee or successor trustee, with the signature guaranteed by an officer of a bank or brokerage firm
- an Affidavit of Domicile, and
- a letter of instructions for the transfer from the trustee to the beneficiaries. The letter should include the name, address, and Social Security number of each beneficiary receiving the securities.

Bank or Savings and Loan Accounts

Title to bank or savings and loan accounts can usually be transferred to the successor trustee and to a beneficiary on termination of the trust by submitting to the bank or savings and loan association a copy of the trust document and a certified copy of the death certificate.

Totten Trust Accounts

Totten trust accounts are accounts in the name of someone as trustee for one or more beneficiaries. (See Chapter 5.) The bank or savings institution will transfer funds in these kinds of accounts to the beneficiaries on the death of the account owner if it is presented with a certified copy of the trustee's death certificate.

These accounts are often set up for children or grandchildren. If the beneficiaries are minors, special requirements may apply to distribution of the funds. If the amount exceeds $5,000, either a guardianship, "blocked account," or a custodianship under the Uniform Transfers to Minors Act (Prob. Code §§ 3900–3925) will probably have to be established to hold and account for the money. (Prob. Code § 3413.) Amounts not exceeding $5,000, however, can be ordered paid to the minor's parents to be held for the benefit of the minor without a guardianship. (Prob. Code § 3413(d).) If you are dealing with minor beneficiaries, you may need to see an attorney.

Miscellaneous Trust Assets

For other assets held in trust, contact the principal parties involved to find out what is needed to have the assets transferred to the beneficiaries. In most cases, a copy of the trust document and a certified copy of the death certificate will be required. In addition, an assignment form may be needed for assets such as a trust deed note or partnership interest. The payor on the trust deed note or the general partner of a limited partnership interest should be able to assist you.

For automobiles and other motor vehicles held in trust, the successor trustee should contact the Department of Motor Vehicles. It will provide the forms and instructions to transfer the vehicle.

Life Tenancy (Life Estate)

A life tenancy (sometimes called a "life estate") is not a common form of ownership, but it deserves mention here. A life tenancy is ownership of property for the period of a lifetime only. Life tenancies, like trusts, are sometimes created to avoid the necessity of probate proceedings.

> **EXAMPLE:** Wanda is an elderly widow who owns a home that she wishes to go to her son Steven upon her death. Wanda may deed the property to Steven during her lifetime, with the deed saying that "Grantor (Wanda) reserves to herself a life estate in said property." This will transfer the ownership to Steve, but allow Wanda full use of the property during her lifetime. This will accomplish Wanda's objective of avoiding probate of the home upon her death because she will die without ownership of the property. Her life estate will terminate at the moment of her death, and the home will be owned by Steven.

Life estates are handled in much the same way as joint tenancy property on the death of the life tenant. To clear title to real property in which there was a life estate, you simply use the Affidavit—Death of Joint Tenant discussed in Chapter 10, and cross out the word "Joint" and replace it with the word "Life." Then your affidavit will say Affidavit—Death of Life Tenant. The affidavit is then recorded in the office of the county recorder in which the real property is located (discussed in Chapter 10), along with a certified copy of the death certificate. If other assets are subject to life estates, such as securities, the procedures discussed in Chapter 10 for clearing joint tenancy property should generally be followed. ●

An Overview of the Probate Court Process

This chapter provides an overview of what is involved in settling a simple estate through a superior (probate) court proceeding. (What constitutes a simple estate is discussed in more detail in Chapter 1.) Generally, this means there should be no complications such as large, disputed creditors' claims, disagreements among beneficiaries, questions of title to property, ambiguities in the will, or any other unusual or antagonistic situations—in short, nothing that requires special handling.

When you first read this material, probating an estate may seem difficult. Please don't be discouraged. If you follow our instructions carefully, you should have little difficulty in completing a court proceeding successfully. Before you start, we suggest you relax and read through this chapter one or two times to familiarize yourself with what is required. Then read Chapter 14, which describes what you must do step-by-step. When you feel comfortable, you can begin the paperwork.

Do You Really Need a Probate Court Proceeding?

Before you begin a probate court proceeding, you should study the decedent's assets to see if any, or even all, of them fall into categories that don't require probate. We discuss this in detail in Chapter 6.

Probate Checklist

The checklist below sets out all the steps in a simple probate court proceeding. Each step is explained in detail in the same order in the next chapter. You will probably want to refer to this checklist frequently as you proceed.

Dealing With the Probate Court

Here are the basics of what's involved in a probate court proceeding.

What Court Do You Use?

As you probably know, different courts in our legal system handle different matters. All probate cases are handled by the superior court of the county in which the decedent resided at the time of his or her death, no matter where he or she died. If the decedent was not a resident of California, the county in which the decedent owned real property is the proper venue.

When a superior court is dealing with a probate procedure, it is often called the "probate court." Some counties have branch courts whose locations can be determined by calling the main courthouse. If you live in one of the branch court districts, the probate proceeding may be commenced there.

Many superior courts now have websites, which may be able to answer your questions about where to file. To find your county's superior court website, check www.courtinfo.ca.gov/courts/find.htm.

If a decedent leaves real property in a state of which he or she isn't a resident, that property will be governed by the laws of that state, and proceedings to have title transferred must be commenced in the state where the property is located. When there are assets in more than one California county, the estate will be administered in the superior court of the county in which a petition to commence probate proceedings is first filed.

Although all superior (probate) courts follow the procedures outlined in the California Probate Code, each has a few special procedural rules of its own. Most counties have these court rules set out in pamphlets, often called "Probate Rules," or sometimes "Probate Policy Manual" or "Rules of Probate Practice." This booklet (or instruction sheet) tells you such things as when particular forms must be presented to the court, what must be included in court documents, and where to call for information. Call the probate department of the court where you will be filing your papers and arrange to obtain a copy.

Most county superior court websites have the local probate rules available for download from their sites. In some sites—for example, Los Angeles and Alameda Counties (www.lasuperiorcourt.org and

Formal Probate Court Proceeding Checklist		
	Basic Step	**Time Frame or Deadline**
First Month: Open Estate	1. File Petition for Probate; obtain hearing date (Steps 1 through 4)	Any time after death (no deadline or time limit)
	2. File original will and codicils, if any (Step 3)	Filed with Petition for Probate as separate filing
	3. Publish Notice of Petition to Administer Estate (Step 3)	Three times before hearing date; first publication must be at least 15 days prior to hearing
	4. Mail Notice of Petition to Administer Estate (Step 3)	At least 15 days prior to hearing date
	5. File proof of publication and proof of mailing Notice of Petition to Administer Estate (Step 3)	As early as possible before hearing date
	6. File proof of will, if required (Steps 5 and 6)	As early as possible before hearing date
	7. Check calendar notes (Step 9)	Two days or more before hearing
	8. File Order for Probate (and probate bond, if required (Step 8)	Time requirements vary between counties; check with court
Letters Issued	9. File letters and Duties and Liabilities of Personal Representative form (Steps 10 and 11)	At same time or after filing Order for Probate (Check local rules.)
Next 4 to 5 Months: Administer Estate	10. Apply for Taxpayer Identification Number (Chapter 7)	As early as possible after letters are issued
	11. Notify government agencies (Step 7)	Within 90days of death
	12. Open estate bank account (Chapter 13)	After letters are issued
	13. Arrange for preparation of income tax returns (Chapter 7)	As soon as possible after letters are issued
	14. Prepare Inventory and Appraisal and send to Referee (Step 14)	As soon as possible after letters are issued
	15. Mail Notice of Administration to creditors; pay debts without requiring formal claims (Step 15)	Within four months after letters are issued or within 30 days after first discovering a creditor
	16. File Approval or Rejection of formal Creditors' Claims (Step 15)	Any time before Petition for Final Distribution
	17. File Inventory and Appraisal with court (Step 14)	Within four months after letters are issued
	18. File Change in Ownership Statement with county assessor if Inventory lists real property (Step 14)	When Inventory and Appraisal is filed with court
	19. File federal estate tax return if necessary (Chapter 7)	Within nine months of date of death
Last Month: Close Estate	20. File Petition for Final Distribution (Step 16)	From four months to one year after letters are issued (within 18 months, if federal estate tax return is required)
	21. Mail Notice of Hearing to beneficiaries	Within 15 days of hearing date on petition
	22. File proof of mailing Notice of Hearing (Step 17)	As soon as possible before hearing date on petition
	23. File Order for Final Distribution (Step 18)	Procedures vary between counties; check with court
	24. Transfer assets and obtain receipts (Step 19)	Any time after Order for Final Distribution is signed
	25. File receipts and Petition for Final Discharge (Step 20)	After assets are distributed and all matters concluded

www.alameda.courts.ca.gov)—all the local rules (probate and others) are clumped together in the "Court Rules" or "Local Rules" link. To access the probate rules, go into the Local Rules link and scroll down until you see the chapter on probate.

Who Will Represent the Estate?

The estate representative (executor or administrator) represents the estate in the court proceeding. We discuss selection of the estate representative in detail in Chapter 2. To review very briefly:

- If there is a will that names an executor, that person is the estate representative.
- If there is no will (the decedent died intestate), the court will choose the estate representative, who is called an "administrator."
- If there is a will but no executor is named, or the person named is unable to serve, the court will choose the estate representative, who is called an "administrator with will annexed" (sometimes referred to as "administrator C.T.A.").

It is possible to have more than one person act as estate representative. If the will names two or more coexecutors and all are willing to serve, or if two or more persons wish to act as coadministrators, all must sign the Petition for Probate and the letters, as well as all other papers that require the signature of the estate representatives. The court will not issue separate letters. Additional signature lines may be added to the forms for this purpose. If two or more representatives are appointed by the court and one or more is unavailable or absent from the state, the remaining representatives cannot act alone without a court order.

Obtaining Court Forms

Virtually all documents used in a simple probate court proceeding are official printed forms, with the exception of the last petition and order. Below is a list of the main forms you will need, although some counties may require a few additional local forms.

You will find one copy of each statewide form in Appendix B. To obtain additional copies, you can photocopy the forms in the appendixes (be sure you get clear copies), buy them from the court, or download them from the Judicial Council website at www.courtinfo.ca.gov/forms.

When Judicial Council forms are reproduced on the front and back of a single sheet, the back sheet must be inverted ("tumbled") so that it can be read when clipped at the top in a file folder. However, if the forms are printed single-sided, then all pages should be right side up.

You can also order probate forms from the court by mail if you list the ones you want and enclose a check payable to the "Clerk of Superior Court" to cover the cost, plus tax and postage. The cost for forms varies from county to county, so your best bet is to call the court for the amount. In your cover letter, ask the clerk to also send you any additional local forms required, along with an explanation of what they are for. Some courts (for example, Los Angeles) refer to forms by a call number and want you to use their order forms. (See sample letter, below.)

Sample Letter Requesting Forms

(date)

Clerk of the Superior Court
111 N. Hill Street
Los Angeles, CA 90012

Please provide me with two copies of each of the following probate forms:

- Petition for Probate (DE-111)
- Certificate of Assignment
- Notice of Petition to Administer Estate (DE-121)
- Proof of Subscribing Witness (DE-131)
- Order for Probate (DE-140)
- Letters (DE-150)
- Duties and Liabilities of Personal Representative (DE-147)
- Application and Order Appointing Probate Referee
- Inventory and Appraisal (DE-160)
- Inventory and Appraisal (attachment) (DE-161)
- Allowance or Rejection of Creditor's Claim (DE-174)
- Notice of Hearing (Probate) (DE-120)
- Ex Parte Petition for Final Discharge and Order (DE-295).

Please also send me two copies of any additional local forms you require, along with an explanation of what they are used for. A check for $ _____ is enclosed to cover your fee.

Thank you for your assistance.

Very truly yours,

(name and address)

Commonly Used Probate Forms

Petition for Probate (DE-111)

Certificate of Assignment (for filing in branch courts)

Notice of Petition to Administer Estate (DE-121)

Proof of Subscribing Witness (used only when there is a will) (DE-131)

Proof of Holographic Instrument (used only for handwritten wills) (DE-135)

Order for Probate (DE-140)

Letters (DE-150)

Duties and Liabilities of Personal Representative (DE-147)

Notice of Administration to Creditors (DE-157)

Application and Order Appointing Probate Referee

Inventory and Appraisal (DE-160)

Inventory and Appraisal (attachment) (DE-161)

Allowance or Rejection of Creditor's Claim (DE-174)

Notice of Hearing (Probate) (DE-120)

Ex Parte Petition for Final Discharge and Order (DE-295).

Preparing Court Documents

Most of the forms you will need are the court-issued Judicial Council forms listed in the box above. You can get these forms in two places:

- in the appendix of this book, or
- online at www.courtinfo.ca.gov/forms.

On that website, the forms are "fillable," so that you can fill them out and print them using your computer. If you use a form in the back of the book, you'll need to fill it in using a typewriter or neat handwriting. If you do use a form from the back of the book, it's still a good idea to check the website to make sure that the court hasn't updated the form since the publication of this book.

In the few cases where a printed form is not available, you must type the entire document. Court documents must be created on 8½" × 11" white bond paper with lines numbered consecutively on the side. This is called pleading paper. You will find examples of documents on pleading paper in Chapter 14. Pleading paper is available at most office supply stores, and we recommend that you obtain a supply in advance so you will have it on hand if you need it.

You can also use your word processing program to create the document on pleading paper. Most word processing programs have a pleading paper function built in that lets you format your paper to look like pleading paper. The program will also help you enter the text in the right places. For instructions, use the help function on your word processing program and search for "pleading."

No matter how you get your pleading paper, don't forget to check the court's local rules for specific formatting requirements and always follow these general formatting rules:

- Documents must be double-spaced, using only one side of the paper, and each page must be numbered consecutively at the bottom.
- Each page, except for exhibits, must have a footer at the bottom containing the title of the paper, for example, Petition for Final Distribution or Order for Final Distribution.
- If attachments or exhibits are needed, they must be the same size (8½" × 11").
- All papers must be fastened together at the top.
- The first page of all documents must be in the following form:
  - Commencing with Line 1 in the upper left-hand corner, type the name of the petitioner, office or residence address, and telephone number.

- Leave the space blank between Lines 1 and 7 to the right of the center of the page for the use of the clerk.
- On or below Line 8, type the title of the court.
- Starting on Line 11, in the space left of the center, type the title of the case.
- To the right, opposite the title, put the case number.
- Immediately below the case number, put the nature of the document (for example, "Petition for … ," "Supplement to …").

Most of the documents that must be typed are simple forms that are easy to copy from examples in the next chapter. The only document of any length that must be completely typed in a probate court proceeding is the final petition requesting distribution of the estate. A detailed sample petition is shown in Chapter 14, Step 16.

In some counties, a stiff blue piece of paper, with the title of the document typed at the bottom, must be attached to any court documents typed on legal numbered paper when they are filed. The "blue backs" are not required for *printed* court forms nor on *copies* of documents—only on *original* typed documents. Other courts do not use these covers and may return documents if they are attached, so check local practice. You can get blue backs at most office supply stores. The blue back is attached by folding the top edge (about ¾") over your document and stapling it at the top in the center and at each side.

Some courts also require that all documents have two holes punched at the top with a standard two-hole punch. The holes should be centered.

Petitions and Orders

A petition is a document that asks the court to do something. In a simple probate proceeding, you are required to file two petitions. The first requests that the court admit the will to probate (if there is a will) and that a representative (executor) be appointed. If there is no will, it only requests the appointment of the representative (administrator). The second petition requests an order closing the estate and distributing the assets to the beneficiaries.

The person who prepares and files a petition is called the "petitioner." A petitioner who acts without an attorney is identified as "Petitioner In Pro Per." This is an abbreviation for "In Propria Persona," a Latin phrase meaning you're representing yourself without a lawyer.

If the court approves a petition, it will issue an order to that effect. Court orders are usually prepared by the petitioner and presented to the court for the judge's signature before or at the time of the hearing on the petition. Some courts allow the order to be submitted after the hearing date, so always check local rules.

Verifications

All statements in petitions should be verified at the end of the document by the petitioner. The verification paragraph is usually as follows:

> "I declare under penalty of perjury under the laws of the State of California that the foregoing, including any attachments, is true and correct. Executed this _____ day of _____, 20____, at _____, California."

The verification has the same effect as a sworn statement or an affidavit witnessed by a notary, so that a personal appearance in court is not necessary. All printed court forms have the verification printed on them, if one is required. If you have to type a document that needs to be verified, be sure to include the verification. For instance, a supplement to a petition must be verified in the same manner as the petition. Always be sure to insert the date when the verification is signed—it's easy to overlook this.

Filing Court Documents

To file court documents, either mail them or present them in person to the county clerk's office at the court-house. As a general rule, it is a good idea to include two copies of all documents in addition to the original, because some courts require them. The court always keeps the original document; any copies not needed will be returned to you. When you file your papers by mail, always keep a copy of each for your records in case the others get lost, and always include a stamped, self-addressed envelope so the court will return your conformed (stamped "filed" by the clerk) copies.

When you file the first petition, the court clerk stamps it with a case number, which you'll use on every other court document you prepare. In addition, each petition is given a hearing date. This is the time and date the court will decide whether or not it will approve the petition.

Filing Fees

The court charges a filing fee whenever a document is filed that requires a court hearing. In a simple probate proceeding, the filing fee is $395 for the Petition for Probate and another $395 for the Petition for Final Distribution. (San Francisco, San Bernardino, and Riverside may also charge a "construction surcharge," so be sure to call the clerk in these counties to ask for the correct amount.)

Certified Copies

A certified copy of a court document is one that has been certified by the clerk as a true and correct copy of the original document on file with the court. You may need certified copies during the administration process; you can order them from the court for a nominal fee. Call the court for the exact amount or ask for a copy of the fee schedule.

Beginning the Probate Process

A probate proceeding may begin at any time after someone dies. There is no time limit or deadline. In most cases, however, the process is initiated as soon as possible.

Filing the Probate Petition

You start the probate proceeding by filing a petition with the clerk of the superior court in the county where the decedent resided at the time of his or her death, no matter where he or she died. (Prob. Code § 7051.)

The person requesting to be appointed the estate representative (either the executor, administrator, or administrator with will annexed) files the probate petition. He or she is called "the petitioner." From now on, we will assume you are the petitioner and will be the estate representative.

If there's a will, the original is filed separately, at the same time, and a copy is attached to the petition. The petition asks the court to admit the will (if any) to probate and appoint someone to act as estate representative. The petition also gives the court certain information, such as the names of the decedent's heirs, the beneficiaries in the will, where the decedent lived, what kind of property he or she owned, and where and when he or she died.

The court clerk gives the petition a hearing date, which should be not less than 15 nor more than 30 days after it is filed. (Prob. Code § 8003(a).) In reality, the hearing date is usually five or more weeks from the filing date. In most situations there is no opposition to the petition. It is automatically approved, and the representative appointed, without anyone having to appear in court. If you appear at the hearing, dress appropriately—no shorts or tank tops. When your case is called, stand and state your name and that you are the "petitioner in pro per."

It is a good idea to file your first papers in person, especially if you're filing an original will. You may then pick up forms from that court for filing future documents and also obtain a copy of their probate court rules at the same time.

The Independent Administration of Estates Act

The probate petition will request that the court grant you permission to handle the estate under the Independent Administration of Estates Act. (Prob. Code §§ 10400–10600.)

> **CAUTION**
> **You cannot use the simplified procedures allowed by the Act if the decedent's will prohibits its use.** This almost never happens, but if the will prohibits the use of the Independent Administration of Estates Act, you can still do your own probate using the procedures outlined

in the next chapter. You will not, however, be able to pay creditors' claims or sell estate property without prior court approval. Obtaining court approval to pay formal creditors' claims is simple and merely requires mailing the original claim and a copy to the court asking that it be approved for payment and that a conformed copy be returned to you. Selling real property without the authority of the Independent Administration of Estates Act is more involved. It requires special documents and procedures not covered in this book. See "Sales of Estate Property," below.

This act is designed especially for simple estates (regardless of size) where there are no disputes among the beneficiaries. It allows the representative to do many things without having to obtain prior permission from the court. This is referred to as administering an estate "without court supervision." If all of the heirs and beneficiaries have a cooperative attitude toward the representative, settling the estate under the Act will save a lot of time and paperwork.

You may ask for either "full authority" or "limited authority" under the Act. "Full authority" means you have *all* of the powers granted by the Act. "Limited authority" means you have all of the powers *except* the power to (a) sell real property, (b) exchange real property, (c) grant an option to purchase real property, or (d) borrow money with the loan secured by an encumbrance upon real property. (Prob. Code § 10403.)

If you are granted either full or limited authority, you may do the following without court approval or notifying the beneficiaries:

- allow, pay, reject, or contest any claim against the estate
- sell listed securities
- make repairs or improvements to estate property
- sell perishable or depreciating property
- accept a deed in lieu of foreclosure, and
- pay taxes and expenses of administration.

Generally, however, you must obtain approval from the court to buy estate property, exchange estate property for your own property, or pay or compromise your own claims against the estate, unless you are also the sole beneficiary, or all known beneficiaries have consented to the transaction. (Prob. Code § 10501.)

Many other powers are granted to a personal representative who has authority to administer the estate without court supervision. (Prob. Code §§ 10550–10564.) However, the actions described above are usually the most helpful.

Other actions may be taken without court supervision by giving prior notice, called Notice of Proposed Action, to beneficiaries whose interests will be affected. The purpose of the notice is to give the beneficiaries a chance to object. Actions that require such notice are listed in Probate Code §§ 10510–10538. Those that may come up in simple estates are:

- selling or exchanging real estate (a bond may be required by the court when real estate is sold for cash under this procedure, unless the will waives bond)
- selling or exchanging nonperishable personal property
- leasing real estate for a term in excess of one year
- investing funds of the estate (other than in banks and savings and loan accounts, or direct obligations of the United States maturing in five years or less), or in direct obligations of the State of California maturing in one year or less
- completing a contract entered into by the decedent to convey real or personal property, and
- borrowing money, executing a mortgage or deed of trust, or giving other security. (Only a personal representative who has "full authority" under the Act may borrow money with the loan secured by an encumbrance on real property.)

A sample of the Notice of Proposed Action form is shown in Chapter 14. It includes a space for the recipient to object or consent to the proposed action. A person who fails to object to a proposed action gives up his or her right to have a court review the action later.

At least 15 days before the proposed action would be taken, a copy of the notice must be mailed to or personally served on all persons whose interest would be affected. The notice must be given by someone who is over 18 and does not have an interest in the estate, and proof of the mailing or personal service is filed with the court. A sample form is included in the next chapter, with instructions.

If the proposed action involves selling or granting an option to buy real estate, the notice must include the material terms of the sale and any payment that is to be made to a broker or agent.

Persons entitled to receive notice forms may waive, in writing, their right to notice. They must use a printed form, called Waiver of Notice of Proposed Action, which is available at the probate court. The waiver can apply to all actions taken by the personal representative or only certain actions specified on the form. Persons who should have received notice may also consent to an action that has already been taken.

The Notice of Petition to Administer Estate

When you file the probate petition, the court clerk assigns a hearing date. Notice of the time, date, and place of the hearing must then be given to all heirs, beneficiaries, creditors, and persons who may be interested in the estate. This gives them an opportunity to appear at the hearing and assert their rights, if they wish to do so.

Notice is given in two ways:

- publishing a Notice of Petition to Administer Estate in a newspaper in the city where the decedent lived at the time he or she died (or where he or she left property, if he or she is not a California resident), and
- mailing notice of the hearing date to all heirs, beneficiaries, and alternate executors, as well as any persons who are disinherited in the will or a codicil, within 15 days of the hearing date.

Procedures vary in different court districts as to who arranges for the preparation, publication, and mailing of the notice. In some counties, the petitioner does all the work, while in others the court clerk and the newspaper do everything. However, seeing that the notice is properly given is your responsibility, even if the job is delegated to a newspaper. We discuss this in more detail in Chapter 14.

The Notice of Petition to Administer Estate also advises interested persons that they may serve you with a written Request for Special Notice of the filing of certain documents, such as the Inventory and Appraisal or Petition for Distribution. The request is made on a printed court form. A person or business with a possible claim against the estate—a disgruntled heir or a funeral director, for example—may file such a request. Medi-Cal will file a request if it files a claim for reimbursement of the cost of health services that were provided to the decedent or his or her predeceased spouse. If one is filed, a copy will be sent to you, and you must notify the interested person in writing when a petition or the Inventory and Appraisal has been filed, and also when a Notice of Proposed Action is given, and send him or her a copy of the document. We explain how to do this in the next chapter.

Proving the Will

If there is a will, it must be "proven" in a probate court hearing (unless it is a "self-proving" will—see "Self-Proving Wills and Codicils," below). To prove a will, it must be shown either that (1) the decedent signed it in front of witnesses, declaring that it was his or her will, or (2) the witnesses understood it was his or her will. You do this by finding the witnesses and having them sign a declaration to this effect. The declaration is a simple printed court form with a photocopy of the will attached showing the signature of the witnesses and the filing stamp of the court clerk. We provide a sample in Step 5 of the next chapter.

If the decedent left a holographic will (an unwitnessed will in which the signature and material provisions are in the decedent's handwriting), you need a declaration from someone who knows the decedent's handwriting and who will verify that the will was written by the decedent. A commercially printed form will is a valid holographic will if a statement of testamentary intent is in the testator's own handwriting. (Prob. Code § 6111(c).) Any person having knowledge of the decedent's handwriting may sign the declaration, even if that person stands to inherit all or a part of the estate. This declaration is also a simple, printed court form, and is shown in Step 6 of the next chapter.

Self-Proving Wills and Codicils

Many formal wills and codicils are self-proving, meaning you won't need to get a declaration from the witnesses. A self-proving will or codicil is one signed by the witnesses under penalty of perjury declaring the document was executed according to law. (Prob. Code § 8220.) If the paragraph preceding the signature of the witnesses is in the following basic form, it is usually sufficient to prove the will or codicil, if no one appears to contest the probate.

If, however, someone questions the validity of the will during the probate proceeding, the court may require evidence beyond this clause. Some courts always require a written declaration by at least one witness, regardless of whether or not the original will is self-proving, so find out whether or not your court does.

Sample of Self-Proving Clause of Will

On the date written below, [name of decedent] declared to us, the undersigned, that this instrument, consisting of three (3) pages including the page signed by us as witnesses, was his will and requested us to act as witnesses to it. He thereupon signed his will in our presence (or acknowledged to us that he had signed it as his will), all of us being present at the same time, and we understand it to be his will. We now, at his request, in his presence, and in the presence of each other, subscribe our names as witnesses. We declare that at the time of signing this will the said testator appeared to be of sound and disposing mind and memory and not acting under duress, menace, fraud, or the undue influence of any person whomsoever.

Executed at _____, on _____, 20____. We declare under penalty of perjury under the laws of the State of California that the foregoing is true and correct.

_____

residing at _____

_____

residing at _____

Probate Calendar Notes or "Tentative Rulings"

In most of the larger counties, after a petition is filed, checkers, probate attorneys, or commissioners examine the petition before the hearing. They look to see if it conforms to certain requirements, such as whether notice of the probate proceeding has been given to the proper people (Chapter 14, Step 9), whether the petition is properly signed and verified, and whether all necessary information has been given. Each court keeps a calendar sheet of cases scheduled for hearing. Calendar notes, sometimes called "Tentative Rulings," are notations made by the probate examiner on the calendar sheets after the petition has been reviewed. If all is well, the probate examiner stamps on the calendar the letters "RFA," which means "Recommended for Approval." This means no one need show up in court, and the petition will be approved routinely. If, however, a problem exists, or more information is needed, the probate examiner notes on the calendar sheet what is required before approval can be granted.

Many superior courts allow you to access probate notes online. For example, Los Angeles County Superior Court probate notes are available on the court's website (go to www.lasuperiorcourt.org and click on the Probate Notes link).

In some counties, you may call the court's probate department two or three days before the hearing is scheduled and inquire if the petition has been approved. Some courts post calendar notes on their website or at the courthouse; others have a telephone number you call for a recording of all petitions that were approved.

If your petition isn't granted, talk to one of the "clearing attorneys," preferably in person, and find out what the problem is. Don't worry. Most problems, once they are explained, are easy to correct, and the worst thing that will happen is that your hearing will be postponed about three or four weeks to allow you time to correct the problem. Probate departments in larger counties are extremely busy, and the probate examiners do not have time to discuss the notes in detail nor advise what should be done. However, courts in smaller districts are usually very helpful.

Supplements to the Petition

If the calendar notes indicate that additional information is required, or corrections should be made, you may prepare a supplement to the petition providing the necessary information and file it before the hearing date. (See instructions in Chapter 14, Step 9.)

Correcting information on a petition that is already filed with the court is a lot of extra work. If you can't get the petition approved in time for the hearing, the court will continue it to a new date (usually about four or five weeks later) to give you time to do whatever is necessary to have it approved. Some courts have a rule that a matter may be continued only once, and others take the petition "off calendar" if it is continued three times. If a petition is marked "off calendar," rather than given a new date, this means the court has removed the petition from its calendar of cases and it has lost jurisdiction to act on the petition. However, this is not as bad as it sounds. All you need to do is request a new hearing date when you are ready and start over by giving notices of the hearing when the petition is reset.

Probate Bonds

Before being appointed by the court as executor or administrator, you must ordinarily post a bond (a sum of money or insurance policy) as insurance that you will faithfully perform your duties as representative, unless bond is waived in the decedent's will. Most wills include this waiver provision. To find out if a bond is required or waived, simply read the will.

If the will doesn't waive the bond, all beneficiaries under the will, or heirs if there is no will, may waive the bond as long as they are all adults and competent. The waivers must be in writing and attached to the Petition for Probate when it is filed with the court. The waivers can usually be obtained easily in a simple estate where the beneficiaries are all friendly. A waiver form is shown in Chapter 14, as Attachment 3d to the Petition for Probate.

Even if bond is waived in the will, the court may still impose a bond if it sees a need. Some courts require at least a minimum bond (around $10,000), even if written waivers are obtained. Following are some situations where a bond may be required:

- One of the beneficiaries is a minor and therefore not qualified to sign a waiver of bond.
- The will names two or more persons to serve as executors and all do not serve, and the will does not waive bond for fewer than the number specified.
- The executor or administrator resides outside of California.
- The executor named in a will that waives bond does not qualify, and an administrator with the will annexed is appointed instead.

When the estate is represented by an attorney, probate bonds are most often obtained from authorized surety companies. With "limited" independent administration authority, the amount of the bond is fixed at the value of all the personal property plus the probable value of the annual rents, issues, and profits from all property (including real property) in the estate. In contrast, if "full" independent administration authority is requested, the value of the decedent's interest in real property is included in fixing the amount of bond.

Most surety companies will not provide a bond for personal representatives who are acting in pro per without an attorney. If you cannot get a bond from a corporate surety, individuals may act as sureties instead, subject to the following limitations:

- At least two individual sureties must be used.
- The amount of the bond must be not less than twice the value of the personal property and twice the value of the probable annual income from the real and personal property.
- You may not be one of the sureties.
- The individuals must be California residents and either "householders" or owners of real property in California.
- Each individual's net worth must be at least the amount of the bond in real or personal property, or both, in California.

Abbreviations Used on Calendar Notes

Aff	affidavit (when used alone, means affidavit of mailing by the county clerk—applies to Notice of Hearing)	**N/D**	Notice of Death (refers to the published and mailed notice required to be given to the heirs and beneficiaries where the petition for probate is filed)
Appr	appraisement or appraisals (refers to an appraisal of the assets by the probate referee)		
		Off-Cal	off calendar (means the petition has been removed from the court's calendar and new notice will have to be given when a new hearing date is obtained)
Benef	beneficiary		
Bond w	bond waived		
Bond req	bond required		
Cert	certification	**O/W**	otherwise
Cod	codicil	**PC 8800(d) cert.**	No Property Tax Certification form on file
Cont	continuance	**PPM**	probate policy memoranda (refers to the court's pamphlet setting forth the rules of the court)
C/P	community property		
Cred	creditor		
Crt	court	**Pub**	publication (refers to published notice to persons interested in the estate of the filing of the petition for probate)
D/D	date of death		
Decd	decedent or deceased		
Dist	distribution	**RFA**	recommended for approval without a court appearance
FMV	fair market value		
Inc	no certificate from franchise tax board (applies to estates over $1 million)	**S/P**	separate property
		Supp	supplement or supplemental
		Verif	verification (statement at the end of a petition where the petitioner swears under penalty of perjury that the statements in the petition are true).
I&A	Inventory and Appraisal		
JTD	judge to determine (usually means an appearance in court is required for approval of an item)		

Blocked Accounts

In lieu of bond, alternate security can be provided by putting estate assets beyond your immediate control, to be released only on court order. (Prob. Code § 8483.) For instance, you may:

- Deposit estate money in an insured account in a financial institution in California (Prob. Code § 9700).
- Deposit estate securities (stocks and bonds) or other estate assets (for example, jewelry, fine art, and precious metals) with a trust company (Prob. Code § 9701). Most, but not all, banks are authorized trust companies.

Arrangements for the deposits may be made before or after the Petition for Probate is filed. The request that the blocked account be allowed is made by checking the appropriate box on the Petition for Probate (Item 2d). The money, securities or other assets deposited are then excluded from the computation of the amount of bond required. This task is easier if the securities or money are already on deposit with an authorized bank; otherwise it might be difficult to obtain possession of the assets before the representative is appointed by the court. Alternatively, you may allege in the petition that the money or other property will be deposited with an authorized institution promptly after you are appointed representative, subject to withdrawal only upon court order. In any event, a written receipt from the depository, including the statement that withdrawals will not be allowed except on court order, must be obtained and filed with the court.

To sum up, if bond is not waived in the will or if there is no will, you should obtain written waivers of bond from all adult heirs or beneficiaries and attach them to the petition for probate. In addition, you may request authorization in the petition to deposit some or all of the estate's personal property and funds not needed for estate expenses in blocked accounts with an authorized bank or trust company. If the court still imposes a bond, it should be minimal and individual sureties easily obtained.

Order for Probate and Letters

When the court approves the petition, you must prepare and send in an Order for Probate for the judge's signature. This is a simple printed form. The order appoints the estate representative, admits the will to probate, and usually appoints a probate referee to appraise the estate assets. After the order is signed, the court will issue "letters" to you. This document is your badge of office as estate representative. The original of the letters stays in the court file, and certified copies are supplied to you when you need evidence that you are authorized to act on behalf of the estate.

"Letters testamentary" are issued to an executor, "letters of administration" are issued to an administrator, and "letters of administration with will annexed" (or "letters of administration C.T.A.") are issued to an administrator with will annexed. They all amount to the same thing.

Probate Register/Case Summary

Every court keeps a journal page for each probate case, which carries information on everything that happens in the court proceeding, such as when a petition or order has been filed, the hearing date on a petition, whether the petition is approved, if bond is required, and when the estate inventory is filed. In most courts, you may call the probate department at the courthouse, give them the probate case number, and obtain the information over the phone. This information may also be available on the court's website.

If you are interested, you may go to the courthouse and examine the probate register as well as some probate files. These records are open to the public, and you may find the information helpful.

Taking Care of the Estate During Probate

One of your primary duties is to take good care of estate property while the probate process chugs along. This section discusses some of the tasks you'll run into. Any expense connected with protecting or preserving estate property during probate is an expense of administration and is payable out of estate assets.

Probate Referee/Inventory and Appraisal

The court will appoint a "probate referee" to appraise the non-cash assets in the estate as of date of the decedent's death.

Procedures vary between counties on how and when the referee is appointed. In some counties, the referee's name, address, and telephone number are stamped on your copy of the Petition for Probate when it is filed, or later on the Order for Probate. Some counties require you to file a special form requesting that a probate referee be appointed, so ask the court whether it follows this procedure. The referee is paid a fee of one-tenth of 1% of the total value of the non-cash assets appraised (minimum of $75), not to exceed $10,000. The referee is also allowed to be reimbursed for expenses such as mileage, mapping, and photos if real property is inspected. The referee does not appraise money or other cash assets where the value is clearly established.

The probate assets are described on a form titled "Inventory and Appraisal." You are responsible for preparing the form, which has two attachments. Cash items are described on Attachment No. 1, and non-cash assets are described on Attachment No. 2. Non-probate property, such as joint tenancy property, property held in trust, or insurance proceeds payable to a named beneficiary is not included. Also, property passing outright to a surviving spouse or domestic partner that may be transferred by means of a Spousal or Domestic Partner Property Petition (see Chapter 15) should not be included. When you have completed the form, send it to the probate referee who will insert the appraised values on Attachment No. 2 and return it to you for filing with the court. The Inventory and Appraisal, showing the referee's appraisals, must be filed with the court within four months after letters are issued. If not, some courts require the representative to appear and explain why it has not been filed, so you should start preparing the inventory as early as possible. Guidelines are in Chapter 14.

Change in Ownership Report (Prob. Code § 8800(d))

If the inventory includes real estate in California, a change of ownership report (death of real property owner) must be filed with the county assessor of each county in which real property is situated. (See Chapter 8.) To show that this requirement has been met, check the applicable box at Item 5 on the inventory form, stating that the change of ownership report has been filed, or that no filing is required because the decedent did not own real property in California.

Handling Debts and Creditors' Claims

Anyone who winds up a deceased person's affairs must see that all legitimate debts are paid. Claims are received in two ways. At the formal level, the Notice of Petition to Administer Estate published in the newspaper gives legal notice to all creditors to file their claims within four months after issuance of your letters. In some circumstances, a creditor may file a claim after the four-month period has expired. This is explained in more detail in the next chapter. Claims must be filed with the court and served upon the personal representative, or else the claims will be invalid. A Creditor's Claim form is available for this purpose. In uncomplicated estates, few formal claims are submitted.

In addition, you must give written notice within four months after the letters are issued to all known or reasonably ascertainable creditors and must continue to give notice as you become aware of new creditors. Although you must make reasonable efforts to identify all debts, the law does not require you to make an intensive search for creditors. The written notice advises the creditors that administration of the estate has been commenced and that claims must be filed with the court. (Prob. Code §§ 9050 and following.)

 CAUTION

If new creditors turn up. If you first acquire knowledge of the claim during the last 30 days of the period or after the four-month period has run, the notice must be mailed within 30 days after acquiring knowledge. This is explained in more detail in the next chapter.

The second level at which claims are made is the informal one, where bills keep coming to the decedent's last address. The usual ordinary expenses can be taken care of with a minimum of paperwork. Probate Code § 10552 allows you to pay debts at your discretion without court approval or without requiring a formal claim if you have independent administration authority. In addition, when there has been a written demand for payment, Probate Code § 9154 allows you to pay debts incurred by the decedent before death within 30 days after the claim period ends without requiring a formal claim, unless for some reason you dispute the amount or legitimacy of the debt.

SEE AN EXPERT

Complicated debts. If the decedent was heavily in debt or there are complicated or large disputed claims against the estate, you should probably seek help from an attorney.

How to Handle Assets During Administration

After letters are issued there is a four-month waiting period before the estate may be closed and distributed, during which the creditors are allowed to file their claims. Here are some suggestions on how to treat various types of assets during this period.

Bank Accounts

All accounts in the decedent's name (including out-of-state bank accounts) should be transferred to estate accounts in your name as the estate representative. Contrary to what many people believe, bank accounts in the name of a deceased person are not frozen for long periods of time, and banks will release the funds to you if you present a certified copy of your letters.

All money received during the administration of the estate (such as stock dividends) should be deposited into the estate checking account. The decedent's debts and expenses of administration (such

as court costs and publication fees) should be paid from the estate account. Keep an accurate record of each disbursement, indicating the reason for the payment and the date. For each deposit, keep a record of the source of the funds and the date received. This detailed information on receipts and disbursements will be needed to prepare the estate's income tax returns, if they are required.

If the estate checking account has more cash than you need to pay estate expenses, transfer the excess to insured interest-bearing accounts (Prob. Code § 9652) or invest it in government obligations maturing in five years or less or in direct obligations of the State of California maturing in one year or less. (Prob. Code § 9730.) Be sure not to mix any of your personal funds with the estate's funds. If it is necessary to pay estate expenses with your personal funds, you may later reimburse yourself from the estate. However, you should keep accurate records of such transactions.

Important: The estate is a separate taxpayer, and before opening the estate account most banks will require you to obtain a taxpayer identification number. Apply for the number as soon as possible on Form SS-4 (*Application for Employer Identification Number*), available from the Internal Revenue Service. The same number is used for state income tax purposes. See Chapter 7 for instructions on how to obtain the number.

Rent/Tangible Personal Property

If the decedent rented rather than owned his or her residence, you must decide whether or not to:

- pay additional rent on the decedent's apartment in order to safeguard the contents
- store the items at the estate's expense, or
- permit the beneficiaries to take possession of items to which they are presumptively entitled, pending administration. (Prob. Code § 9650(c).)

In most instances, the last alternative is preferable and usually not objectionable as long as the items are not of unusual value, no problems are anticipated, and you obtain a receipt. Keep in mind, however, that it is the duty of the estate representative to protect estate property, so exercise prudence.

If rented premises are to be vacated, you should immediately contact the landlord and give the required notice—usually 30 days—and arrange for a refund of any security deposit. If a long-term lease is involved, you should give prompt written notice and move out. The landlord has the duty to try to rerent the property. Assuming he or she accomplishes this at the same or a higher rent, or reasonably could have done so if he or she had tried, the estate is off the hook for additional rent from the day of the new rental. If you have more questions about mitigation of damages, see *California Tenants' Rights*, by Janet Portman and David Brown (Nolo).

Motor Vehicles

If the decedent owned a motor vehicle (auto, motor home, motorcycle, etc.) in his or her name alone, the identity of the person entitled to it is not in doubt (either under the will or by intestate succession), and it is clear there will be no objections, then the vehicle may be transferred to the new owner prior to the closing of the estate. (Vehicle Code § 5910.) However, you or the new owner should make sure there is adequate insurance coverage to eliminate any chance that a claim could be made against the estate based on a subsequent accident. Although the Vehicle Code does not specifically permit it, a transfer on the signature of the representative is normally honored by the Department of Motor Vehicles if submitted with a certified copy of your letters. Motor vehicles can be transferred only to licensed drivers.

If the vehicle is owned in joint tenancy with someone else, it may be transferred by the procedures outlined in Chapter 10. If money is owed on the vehicle, this obligation is normally assumed by the new owner, unless the decedent's will says otherwise.

If none of the beneficiaries wants the vehicle, it is probably wise to sell it quickly, as a depreciating asset, to avoid the expense of caring for it during administration of the estate.

Stocks and Bonds

The easiest way to handle stocks and bonds is to leave them in the decedent's name and transfer them to the beneficiaries on final distribution of the estate. Dividend checks and checks for interest on bonds or debentures will, of course, be made payable to the decedent, but you can endorse the checks and deposit them to the estate bank account. Usually, there is no problem with the checks being honored.

Sales of Estate Property

Sometimes it may be necessary or desirable to sell some estate assets before the estate is closed to raise cash to pay debts or to avoid the expense of caring for the property during probate. Selling property may also facilitate distribution of an asset, as when beneficiaries do not wish to own fractional interests in an asset, such as a one-third interest in a computer or a one-half interest in a stamp collection. Property may be sold during probate administration and distribution made in cash, if the beneficiaries agree.

If you have authority to administer the estate under the Independent Administration of Estates Act, you may sell estate property (real or personal) for cash or on credit, and for the price you determine, subject to the following rules.

Depreciating Personal Property

Personal property that will depreciate in value, or that will cause loss or expense to the estate if retained, may be sold without prior court approval and without prior notice to any person interested in the estate. Automobiles and furniture are frequently sold under this provision. In addition, if the cost of collecting, maintaining, and safeguarding tangible personal property would exceed its fair market value (for example, junk cars and garage sale leftovers), you may abandon or otherwise dispose of the property after giving written notice to the heirs. The minimum notice period is ten days by mail or five days by personal delivery. If an heir objects in writing within that period, you can demand that the objecting heir take the property into his or her possession at the heir's own expense. (Prob. Code § 9788.)

Securities, Stocks and Bonds

Securities listed on a stock or bond exchange may be sold for cash at the best price on the stock exchange without notifying the beneficiaries in advance or obtaining prior court approval. (Prob. Code §§ 10537 and 10200.) Despite this authority, some transfer agents may refuse to transfer title without a court order. In such case, we show you a simple way to obtain the order in the next chapter.

Other Personal Property

You may sell other personal property without prior court approval as well, but (except for property noted above) you must first give a Notice of Proposed Action to the beneficiaries whose interest will be affected by the sale. See "Beginning the Probate Process," above, regarding the Notice of Proposed Action procedure.

Real Estate

An estate representative who has full authority under the Act may also sell real estate without court supervision. In this case, the sale procedure is virtually the same as in other real estate sales. You just sign the required documents in the place of the decedent, upon furnishing a certified copy of your letters. The only special requirement is that a Notice of Proposed Action must be given 15 days before the sale date to all persons whose interests will be affected. The court is not involved in any other way. The usual requirements that apply to sales of real estate through a probate court proceeding, such as publication of notice of sale and court approval of the sale price and of agent's and broker's commissions, do not apply to sales under the Act. You may sell the property at a price and on terms you find acceptable. (Prob. Code § 10503.) The Notice of Proposed Action must, however, include the material terms of the transaction, including the sales price and commission paid an agent or broker. We recommend that the title company be notified in advance that the sale will be made without court supervision. Usually, the title company will want assurance that the notice has been given properly and will require a certified copy of the letters, as well as an executor's deed in the form shown in the next chapter.

If you don't have full independent administration authority, selling real property during probate is more complicated. The sale must be confirmed by the court, and you must file a Report of Sale and Petition for Order Confirming Sale of Real Property. The procedure is a cumbersome and detailed process that is not covered in this book. It is better to wait and sell the property after probate is closed, if possible. If you must sell the property during probate, consult Volume 2, Chapter 18, of *California Decedent Estate Practice* (CEB), a useful resource that is available in most law libraries.

Income Taxes

You should contact an accountant early in the proceedings to arrange for preparation of the decedent's final state and federal income tax returns. Of course, you can do the paperwork yourself, but the moderate fee you will pay to have an experienced person do the work is probably worth the trouble you save.

In addition, if the estate remains open long enough, it may receive enough income to require the filing of income tax returns for the estate. These are called fiduciary income tax returns. An accountant may advise you in this regard. (Income taxes are discussed in more detail in Chapter 7.)

Federal Estate Tax Return

If the value of all the decedent's property (this includes probate assets, joint tenancy property, insurance proceeds when the decedent owned the policy at death, death benefits, and property in trust) is high enough, a federal estate tax return will have to be prepared and filed within nine months of the date of death. (See Chapter 7.)

Real and Personal Property Taxes

Probate Code § 9650 requires the personal representative to pay all taxes on the property in his or her possession during administration of the estate.

California Income Tax Clearance

A California Income Tax Clearance must be obtained before the estate may be closed if the estate has a gross value exceeding $1 million on the date of death, and assets of $250,000 or more will be distributed to one or more beneficiaries who are not residents of California. This clearance takes the form of a California Franchise Tax Board certificate that says, in effect, that all income taxes of the estate or the decedent have been paid or adequately secured.

Preliminary Distributions

If the closing of the estate will be delayed for some reason, such as tax problems or delays in selling property, you may obtain a court order allowing distribution of a portion of the assets before the estate is ready to be finally closed. This allows the beneficiaries to enjoy all or a portion of their inheritance before final distribution.

To obtain the order, you must file a Petition for Preliminary Distribution with the court. You may request distribution of certain specific gifts or a pro rata distribution of a percentage of the estate. Generally, you must wait until the four-month claim period ends; however, the court will allow distribution two months after letters are issued if the distributees post a bond. Because most estates are ready to close after the claim period ends, we do not provide details on how to make preliminary distributions. Specific guidelines are given in the CEB publication *California Decedent Estate Practice*, Volume 2, Chapter 25, available in most law libraries.

Probate Code § 10520 permits limited preliminary distributions without a court order if the representative has authority under the Independent Administration of Estates Act and: (1) if the creditor's claim period has expired, and (2) the distribution can be made without loss to creditors or injury to the estate.

The following property can be distributed under this provision after giving a Notice of Proposed Action:

- estate income
- tangible personal property not exceeding $50,000 in value, and
- cash gifts under a will that do not exceed $10,000 to any one person.

Closing the Estate

When you've taken care of all the debts and claims made on the estate and filed all the right papers, you're ready to ask the court to wind up the probate and distribute the balance of the assets to the beneficiaries.

Petition for Final Distribution

The estate may be closed any time after the expiration of the creditor's claim period (four months from the date letters are issued) if:

- All debts and taxes have been paid or sufficiently secured.
- No problems prevent closing the estate.

If you've worked steadily on each of the steps described above, you should be ready to close the estate within six to seven months (nine months, if a federal estate tax return is required) from the time you filed the petition to open the estate.

To close the estate you must file a Petition for Final Distribution with the court, showing that the estate is in a condition to be closed and requesting that distribution be made to the beneficiaries. This final petition is not a printed form; it must be typed on numbered court paper according to special rules. (See Chapter 14, Step 16.) A sample of the petition, which may be adapted to your circumstances, is shown in Chapter 14 with instructions on how to prepare it. After the petition is filed and approved, the court will sign an Order for Final Distribution.

Representative's Commissions

As estate representative you are entitled to compensation for services, referred to as "commissions," which are paid out of the estate assets. (Prob. Code § 10800.) You may request or waive the commissions in the Petition for Final Distribution. The amount is based on the gross value of the probate estate (probate assets only, not joint tenancy or trust property or life insurance proceeds). Here is how it is computed:

4% of the first	$100,000
3% of the next	$100,000
2% of the next	$800,000
1% of the next	$9,000,000
0.5% of the next	$15,000,000
"reasonable amount" for everything above	$25,000,000

If you are the sole beneficiary, it is probably unimportant whether you claim the commissions or not, since you will receive all the estate anyway. However, if there are several beneficiaries and you have done all the work, you may want to discuss whether you will claim or waive the commissions to which you are entitled. You may also request less than the statutory amount. You can also obtain reimbursement from the estate for expenses such as travel, by listing the items on the Petition For Final Distribution. If commissions are paid to you, they are treated as taxable income and you must report them on your personal income tax return.

Waiver of Accounting

Ordinarily, when you file a Petition for Final Distribution, the court requires a detailed accounting of all monies or other items received, and all monies paid out, during administration. However, the accounting may be waived when all persons entitled to receive property from the estate have executed a written waiver of accounting. Probate Code § 10954 describes the conditions for obtaining the waivers. This simplifies the closing of the estate. When all beneficiaries are friendly, there is usually no problem in obtaining the waiver. The waivers may be signed by the following persons:

- any beneficiary who is an adult and competent
- if the distributee is a minor, by a person authorized to receive money or property belonging to the minor—parent, guardian (attach a certified copy of Letters of Guardianship), or custodian named in the will (see Chapter 14, Step 16)
- if the distributee is a conservatee, by the conservator (attach a certified copy of Letters of Conservatorship)
- if the distributee is a trust, by the trustee, but only after the trustee has first filed a written Consent to Act as Trustee
- if the distributee is an estate, by the personal representative (attach a certified copy of letters), or
- by an attorney-in-fact for the distributee.

We show you how to get the accounting waived in the next chapter in the instructions for Paragraph 13 of the Petition for Final Distribution.

A Waiver of Accounting is not required if adequate provision has been made for satisfaction in full of the person's interest. (Prob. Code § 10954(a)(2).) For example, if a will leaves each of the decedent's grandchildren a specified cash gift, and the estate has enough money to pay those gifts, a waiver is not required of the grandchildren. Similarly, if a will leaves only $1 to someone (possibly a disgruntled relative who might refuse to sign a waiver), and the estate can pay it, a waiver is not required.

Distributions to Minors

If there is a minor beneficiary who is entitled to receive noncash estate assets worth more than $10,000, a court-appointed guardian may be needed for the minor's estate, unless a custodian was named in the decedent's will to receive the property on behalf of the minor. Although minors can receive title to real estate, they cannot convey valid title if the property is sold. One alternative is to wait to sell until the minor becomes 18. If not, a guardian may be appointed for the minor's estate in a separate court proceeding.

Transferring the Assets

After the court signs the Order for Final Distribution (Chapter 14, Step 18), the property may be transferred to the beneficiaries. This is relatively easy with most assets. All beneficiaries must sign a receipt for the assets they receive, which you will file with the court along with another form requesting that you be discharged from your duties as estate representative. This concludes the court proceeding. See Chapter 14, Steps 19 and 20.

Conducting a Simple Probate Proceeding

Now that you have a general idea from Chapter 13 of what a probate court proceeding involves, this chapter will tell you exactly how to do it. It provides samples of all forms, with detailed explanations of how they should be prepared. You will find a complete set of tear-out printed court forms in Appendix B. You can make extra copies on a good photocopying machine or order them from the court. You can also download many of these forms from the California Judicial Council website at www.courtinfo.ca.gov. (See Chapter 13.) Remember, when you file documents with the court, always submit at least one extra copy and keep a copy for your files.

> **TIP**
>
> **Call the clerk first.** Before you head to the court (or the post office) to file your Petition for Probate, call the court clerk to find out if your court requires any additional forms to be filed along with DE-111. For example, some courts require you to submit Forms DE-147 and DE-147S (Duties and Liabilities of Personal Representatives with supplement) along with your Petition for Probate.
>
> If you're not sure what number to call, call the main number for the county's superior court and ask for the probate clerk or probate department. When you get the right number, write it in your files—you're likely to need it again at some point.

Step 1: Prepare the Petition for Probate

This is the document that initiates the probate proceeding. It requests that the will (if there is one) be admitted to probate and that a representative be appointed to administer the estate. Use this form whether or not there is a will. Be sure all attachments are full-sized sheets (8½" × 11").

Box 1 (Attorney or Party Without Attorney): Insert your name and address (as the petitioner and proposed personal representative of the estate) in the upper left-hand corner box. You will find this general format on all printed court forms. After the words "Attorney For," type "Petitioner in pro per," as in the sample form. This means you are acting as your own attorney.

Box 2 (Name and Address of Court): Type in the name of the county and the street address of the court. The county will be the one in which the decedent resided at the time of death. (See "What Court Do You Use?" in Chapter 13 for more on how to determine the correct county and court.)

Box 3 (Estate of): Type the name of the decedent, including all name variations under which he or she held property. All of these names should be carried forward to all probate documents filed with the court. If the decedent used more than one name, put the name used most often for legal purposes followed by "aka" ("also known as") and then the other names used for business purposes. For example, if John Doe held most of his property in that name but had several bank accounts and a car registration under Jack Doe and John L. Doe, you would insert "John Doe, aka Jack Doe, aka John L. Doe." If you are dealing with a female decedent who had prior marriages, you may find different last names, such as "Jane Storm, aka Jane Merryweather."

Box 4 (Petition for): Two boxes should be checked after the words "Petition for":

a. If there is a will and you are the executor named in the will, check the box that says "Probate of Will and for Letters Testamentary."

   If there is a will but no executor is named, or the named executor is unable or unwilling to act and no coexecutor or successor is named, you will be petitioning to serve as "administrator C.T.A." (See Chapter 13.) Check the box that says "Probate of Will and for Letters of Administration with Will Annexed."

   If there is no will, check the box that says "Letters of Administration."

   Leave the box saying "Letters of Special Administration" blank.

b. The second box to check is the next to last one, which says "Authorization to Administer Under the Independent Administration of Estates Act." Make sure the will doesn't prohibit this. (See Chapter 13.) Even if it does, you can probably still use the procedures outlined in this chapter, but you shouldn't check the box requesting authorization to use independent administration procedures.

Petition for Probate (page 1)

DE-111

	FOR COURT USE ONLY

ATTORNEY OR PARTY WITHOUT ATTORNEY *(Name, State Bar number, and address):*

Billy M. Kidd
1109 Sky Blue Mountain Trail
Billings, Montana 48906

TELEPHONE NO.: 715/555-6408   FAX NO. *(Optional):*
E-MAIL ADDRESS *(Optional):* billy@yahoo.com
ATTORNEY FOR *(Name):* Petitioner in pro per

SUPERIOR COURT OF CALIFORNIA, COUNTY OF LOS ANGELES
   STREET ADDRESS: 1725 Main Street
   MAILING ADDRESS: 1725 Main Street
   CITY AND ZIP CODE: Santa Monica, CA 90401
   BRANCH NAME: WEST DISTRICT

ESTATE OF *(Name):*   ANABELLE KIDD, aka
              ANABELLE O. KIDD,
                              DECEDENT

PETITION FOR [X] Probate of Will and for Letters Testamentary
          [ ] Probate of Will and for Letters of Administration with
              Will Annexed
          [ ] Letters of Administration
          [ ] Letters of Special Administration [ ] with general powers
          [X] Authorization to Administer Under the Independent
              Administration of Estates Act [ ] with limited authority

CASE NUMBER:

HEARING DATE:

DEPT.:   TIME:

1. Publication will be in *(specify name of newspaper):* Evening Outlook
   a. [ ] Publication requested.
   b. [X] Publication to be arranged.

2. **Petitioner** *(name each):* Billy M. Kidd   **requests that**
   a. [X] decedent's will and codicils, if any, be admitted to probate.
   b. [X] *(name):* Billy M. Kidd
          be appointed
          (1) [X] executor
          (2) [ ] administrator with will annexed
          (3) [ ] administrator
          (4) [ ] special administrator [ ] with general powers
          and Letters issue upon qualification.
   c. [X] full [ ] limited authority   be granted to administer under the Independent Administration of Estates Act.
   d. (1) [X] bond not be required for the reasons stated in item 3d.
      (2) [ ]   bond be fixed. The bond will be furnished by an admitted surety insurer or as
              ~wise provided by law. *(Specify reasons in Attachment 2 if the amount is different from the maximum
              ired by Prob. Code, § 8482.)*
      (3) [ ]   in deposits in a blocked account be allowed. Receipts will be filed.
          (Specify institution and location):

3. a. Decedent died on *(date):* 6-18-xx   at *(place):* Santa Monica, California
      (1) [X] a resident of the county named above.
      (2) [ ] a nonresident of California and left an estate in the county named above located at *(specify location
              permitting publication in the newspaper named in item 1):*

   b. Street address, city, and county of decedent's residence at time of death *(specify):*

      950 Euclid Street, Santa Monica, Los Angeles County, California 90403

Page 1 of 4

Form Adopted for Mandatory Use
Judicial Council of California
DE-111 [Rev. March 1, 2008]

PETITION FOR PROBATE
(Probate—Decedents Estates)

Probate Code, §§ 8002, 10450;

Petition for Probate (page 2)

	DE-111

ESTATE OF *(Name):*   ANABELLE KIDD, aka
            ANABELLE O. KIDD,
                                DECEDENT
	CASE NUMBER:

3. c. **Character and estimated value of the property of the estate** *(complete in all cases):*

   (1) Personal property: $ 48,500.00

   (2) Annual gross income from

       (a) real property: $ None

       (b) personal property: $ 3,400.00

   (3) **Subtotal** *(add (1) and (2)):* $ 51,900.00

   (4) Gross fair market value of real property: $ 400,000.00

   (5) (Less) Encumbrances: $ (95,000.00   )

   (6) Net value of real property: $ 305,000.00

   (7) **Total** *(add (3) and (6)):* $ 356,900.00

  d. (1) [X] Will waives bond.   [ ] Special administrator is the named executor, and the will waives bond.

     (2) [ ] All beneficiaries are adults and have waived bond, and the will does not require a bond.
         (Affix waiver as Attachment 3d(2).)

     (3) [ ] All heirs at law are adults and have waived bond. *(Affix waiver as Attachment 3d(3).)*

     (4) [ ] Sole personal representative is a corporate fiduciary or an exempt government agency.

  e. (1) [ ] Decedent died intestate.

     (2) [X] Copy of decedent's will dated: 7-1-xx   [ ] codicil dated *(specify for each):*

                                                       are affixed as Attachment 3e(2).

       (Include typed copies of handwritten documents and English translations of foreign-language documents.)

       [X] The will and all codicils are self-proving (Prob. Code, § 8220).

  f. **Appointment of personal representative** *(check all applicable boxes):*

   (1) Appointment of executor or administrator with will annexed:

     (a) [X] Proposed executor is named as executor in the will and consents to act.

     (b) [ ] No executor is named in the will.

     (c) [ ] Proposed personal representative is a nominee of a person entitled to Letters.
         (Affix nomination as Attachment 3f(1)(c).)

     (d) [ ] Other named executors will not act because of [ ] death [ ] declination
         [ ] other reasons *(specify):*

          [ ] Continued in Attachment 3f(1)(d).

   (2) Appointment of administrator:

     (a) [ ] Petitioner is a person entitled to Letters. *(If necessary, explain priority in Attachment 3f(2)(a).)*

     (b) [ ] Petitioner is a nominee of a person entitled to Letters. *(Affix nomination as Attachment 3f(2)(b).)*

     (c) [ ] Petitioner is related to the decedent as *(specify):*

   (3) [ ] Appointment of special administrator requested. *(Specify grounds and requested powers in Attachment 3f(3).)*

  g. Proposed personal representative is a

   (1) [ ] resident of California.

   (2) [X] nonresident of California *(specify permanent address):*

       1109 Sky Blue Mountain Trail, Billings, Montana 48906

   (3) [X] resident of the United States.

   (4) [ ] nonresident of the United States.

PETITION FOR PROBATE
(Probate—Decedents Estates)

Petition for Probate (page 3)

DE-111

ESTATE OF (Name): ANABELLE KIDD, aka ANABELLE O. KIDD, DECEDENT	CASE NUMBER:

4. [X] Decedent's will does not preclude administration of this estate under the Independent Administration of Estates Act.

5. a. Decedent is survived by *(check items (1) or (2), and (3) or (4), and (5) or (6), and (7) or (8))*

    (1) [ ] spouse.

    (2) [X] no spouse as follows:

        (a) [ ] divorced or never married.

        (b) [X] spouse deceased.

    (3) [ ] registered domestic partner.

    (4) [X] no registered domestic partner.

        (See Fam. Code, § 297.5(c); Prob. Code, §§ 37(b), 6401(c), and 6402.)

    (5) [X] child as follows:

        (a) [X] natural or adopted.

        (b) [ ] natural adopted by a third party.

    (6) [ ] no child.

    (7) [ ] issue of a predeceased child.

    (8) [X] no issue of a predeceased child.

  b. Decedent [ ] was [X] was not survived by a stepchild or foster child or children who would have been adopted by decedent but for a legal barrier. *(See Prob. Code, § 6454.)*

6. *(Complete if decedent was survived by (1) a spouse or registered domestic partner but no issue (only **a** or **b** apply), or (2) no spouse, registered domestic partner, or issue. (Check the **first** box that applies):*

  a. [ ] Decedent was survived by a parent or parents who are listed in item 8.

  b. [ ] Decedent was survived by issue of deceased parents, all of whom are listed in item 8.

  c. [ ] Decedent was survived by a grandparent or grandparents who are listed in item 8.

  d. [ ] Decedent was survived by issue of grandparents, all of whom are listed in item 8.

  e. [ ] Decedent was survived by issue of a predeceased spouse, all of whom are listed in item 8.

  f. [ ] Decedent was survived by next of kin, all of whom are listed in item 8.

  g. [ ] Decedent was survived by parents of a predeceased spouse or issue of those parents, if both are predeceased, all of whom are listed in item 8.

  h. [ ] Decedent was survived by no known next of kin.

7. *(Complete only if no spouse or issue survived decedent.)*

  a. [ ] Decedent had no predeceased spouse.

  b. [ ] Decedent had a predeceased spouse who

    (1) [ ] died not more than 15 years before decedent and who owned an interest in **real property** that passed to decedent,

    (2) [ ] died not more than five years before decedent and who owned **personal property** valued at $10,000 or more that passed to decedent,

    *(If you checked (1) or (2), check only the **first** box that applies):*

      (a) [ ] Decedent was survived by issue of a predeceased spouse, all of whom are listed in item 8.

      (b) [ ] Decedent was survived by a parent or parents of the predeceased spouse who are listed in item 8.

      (c) [ ] Decedent was survived by issue of a parent of the predeceased spouse, all of whom are listed in item 8.

      (d) [ ] Decedent was survived by next of kin of the decedent, all of whom are listed in item 8.

      (e) [ ] Decedent was survived by next of kin of the predeceased spouse, all of whom are listed in item 8.

    (3) [ ] neither (1) nor (2) apply.

8. Listed on the next page are the names, relationships to decedent, ages, and addresses, so far as known to or reasonably ascertainable by petitioner, of (1) all persons mentioned in decedent's will or any codicil, whether living or deceased; (2) all persons named or checked in items 2, 5, 6, and 7; and (3) all beneficiaries of a trust named in decedent's will or any codicil in which the trustee and personal representative are the same person.

DE-111 [Rev. March 1, 2008]

PETITION FOR PROBATE
(Probate—Decedents Estates)

Page 3 of 4

Petition for Probate (page 4)

ESTATE OF (Name): ANABELLE KIDD, aka ANABELLE O. KIDD,		DE-111
		CASE NUMBER:
	DECEDENT	

8. <u>Name and relationship to decedent</u>   <u>Age</u>   <u>Address</u>

     Mary Kidd Clark, daughter   Adult 789 Main Street, Venice, CA 90410

     Billy M. Kidd, son   Adult 1109 Sky Blue Mountain Trail
                                        Billings, Montana 48906

     Jon Kidd, son
     (predeceased decedent 4-5-82)

     Carson Kidd, grandson   Adult 711 Valley Road, Owens, CA 98455
     (son of Jon Kidd)

     Calvin Kidd, spouse
     (predeceased decedent 11-3-08)

     Pat Garret, alternate executor   Adult 25 So. Corral Street
                                        Santa Fe, New Mexico 57256

     Albertine Terreux, stranger   Adult 17 Rue Madeleine, Paris, France

     Consulate of France   n/a   8350 Wilshire Blvd., Los Angeles,
                                        CA 99035

        Continued on Attachment 8.

9. Number of pages attached: 3

Date:

_____
N/A
(TYPE OR PRINT NAME OF ATTORNEY)

▶ _____
(SIGNATURE OF ATTORNEY)*

* (Signatures of all petitioners are also required. All petitioners must sign, but the petition may be verified by any one of them (Prob. Code, §§ 1020, 1021; Cal. Rules of Court, rule 7.103).)

I declare under penalty of perjury under the laws of the State of California that the foregoing is true and correct.

Date: July 5, 20xx

_____
     Billy M. Kidd
(TYPE OR PRINT NAME OF PETITIONER)

▶ *Billy M. Kidd*
_____
(SIGNATURE OF PETITIONER)

_____
(TYPE OR PRINT NAME OF PETITIONER)

▶ _____
(SIGNATURE OF PETITIONER)

     Signatures of additional petitioners follow last attachment.

DE-111 [Rev. March 1, 2008]

PETITION FOR PROBATE
(Probate—Decedents Estates)

Page 4 of 4

Petition for Probate (Attachment 3d)

Estate of Anabelle Kidd, aka Anabelle D. Kidd, deceased

Petition for Probate
Attachment 3d - Waiver of Bond

Petitioner has personal knowledge of the decedent's financial affairs and alleges that the estate is but little indebted. The curent known liabilities of the estate consist of last illness expenses in the total amount of $4,300 and there are sufficient probate assets to guarantee payment of these expenses. There are no other unsecured creditors, contingent liabilities or tax liabilities, and the estate is solvent. Therefore, petitioner requests that no bond be required while he is serving as personal representative.

Also, you should be aware that some courts refuse to give full independent authority to estate representatives who are acting in pro per. Check local policy to avoid delays and extra work.

Unless real property of the estate will be sold during probate, we recommend you also check the last box, before the words "with limited authority." This means you are requesting all of the powers granted by the Independent Administration of Estates Act except the power to sell, or otherwise deal with, real property. If you do need to sell real property during probate, see Step 13.

If you request full authority and the estate contains real property, the court may require you to post a bond for the value of the cash that would be received on the sale of the real property, unless bond is waived in the decedent's will. Some courts require such a bond even if the heirs and beneficiaries have all filed written waivers.

Item 1: This item pertains to publication of the Notice of Petition to Administer Estate, which is discussed in Step 4, below. Selecting the proper newspaper is very important. The best way to handle this is to ask the court clerk for the names of newspapers of general circulation, if any, in the city where the decedent lived at the time of death and go in person to make arrangements for publication of the notice. Most newspapers are familiar with the requirements. Ask if they will prepare and file the required affidavit giving proof of the publication with the court. If not, you will have to do it yourself. (See Step 3.) As a rule, you must pay the newspaper publication fee in advance, which can be $200 or more. After you have determined the newspaper you will use, type its name in Item 1, and check Box 1b indicating that publication is being arranged for.

Item 2: Type in your name, as petitioner, on this line. If there are two petitioners, type both names.

Item 2a: If there is a will, check this box.

Item 2b: Check the first box and, on the same line, type in your name. Check Box (1), (2), or (3), whichever applies to your situation. (See Chapter 13 if you are in doubt.) Leave Box (4) blank.

Item 2c: If the estate contains real property that will be sold during probate, check the box requesting full authority under the Act. Otherwise, check the second box requesting limited authority.

Item 2d: Remember, you probably won't have to post a bond if all beneficiaries or all heirs waive the bond, or if the will waives the requirement of a bond, unless the court orders otherwise. (See Chapter 13.) Assuming you will be able to get waivers (if bond isn't waived by the will), check the first box that says "bond not be required." If it is preferable to deposit assets into a blocked account to avoid or reduce the amount of a bond, check the last box and fill in the name and address of the institution.

It is not always possible to obtain possession of the decedent's assets before being appointed representative and receiving letters. Arrangements can be made in advance by allowing a bank or trust company to retain on deposit money already in its possession. Or, the deposit may also be made after the Order

Receipt and Agreement by Depository

```
 1   Name:
     Address:
 2

 3

 4   Telephone No.:

 5   Petitioner in pro per

 6

 7

 8              SUPERIOR COURT OF CALIFORNIA

 9              COUNTY OF _____

10

11   Estate of              ) No._____
                            )
12      (name of decedent)  ) RECEIPT AND AGREEMENT BY
                            )
13              deceased.   ) DEPOSITORY (Prob. Code
                            )
14   _____)   § 541.1)

15

16      The undersigned acknowledges receipt from _____

17   _____, personal representative of the estate

18   of the above-named decedent, of the following items of personal

19   property:

20      a. 200 shares of Miracle Corporation common stock

21      b. Cash in sum of $12,000

22      The undersigned agrees that the foregoing cash and securities

23   will be held by the undersigned for the personal representative, and

24   will permit withdrawals only upon express order of the above-entitled

25   Court.

26      DATE: _____,20____

27              WESTERN STATES BANK

28              By:_____
                       (authorized officer)
```

RECEIPT AND AGREEMENT BY DEPOSITORY

for Probate is signed but before the letters are issued. Either alternative results in a bond in a reduced amount.

Practically speaking, the blocked account is most likely possible when the bank or trust company already is in possession of the decedent's assets. If the deposit is made before letters are issued, the depository is protected from liability to the same extent that it would have been if letters were issued before the deposit was made. (Prob. Code § 8401(c).) You must obtain a written receipt from the depository acknowledging its agreement that it will not allow any withdrawals except on court order. (Prob. Code § 8401(b).) The receipt should be filed with the court either with the petition or after the representative qualifies, depending on when the deposit is made. The sample receipt shown above is accepted in most courts.

Item 3a: Type in the date and city and state of the decedent's death, and check the appropriate box under Item 3a. The petition must be filed in the county of the decedent's residence, no matter where he or she died. (See Chapter 13.) If the decedent was not a resident of California, the petition must be filed in the county where he or she left real property or tangible personal property in California. If the decedent was a resident of the county in which you are filing your petition, check the first box. If he or she was not a resident of California but left real or tangible personal property here, check the second box and type in the address of the property.

Item 3b: Type in the street address, city, and county where the decedent lived at the time of death.

Item 3c: Type in, where indicated, the estimated gross fair market value of all the real property (less encumbrances) and all the personal property (taken from Schedule of Assets—see Chapter 5), plus the annual estimated income from any items of property that produce income. (Remember that personal property includes all assets that are not real property—for example, stocks, bank accounts, and household items.) Include only property that is being probated and, if any of the assets are community

Waiver of Bond: Attachment 3d

```
 1 ║  Estate of _____, Deceased
 2 ║
 3 ║              WAIVER OF BOND: ATTACHMENT 3d
 4 ║
 5 ║     The undersigned, as ____[an heir/a beneficiary]____
 6 ║  of the decedent, hereby waives the requirement of a bond by
 7 ║  _____[name of petitioner]_____, while serving
 8 ║  as estate representative.
 9 ║     DATED:_____, 20___.
10 ║
11 ║
12 ║              _____
13 ║                   [typed name]
```

property, include only the decedent's one-half interest. (See Chapter 4.) This information is used to determine the amount of bond, when one is required.

Special Requirement for Fresno County

In Fresno County, the waiver of bond must be in pleading format. This means it must be on pleading paper and it must contain a caption. A caption is the first half-page on most formal pleadings—it contains the name of the petitioner, the court, the county, the estate, the case number, and more. For more information on pleading format, see "Preparing Court Documents," in Chapter 13.

When submitting a Waiver of Bond to Fresno County Court, follow these steps:

1. Use the caption from Receipt and Agreement by Depository, above, as a model.
2. Reproduce lines 1–14 exactly—except replace the words "RECEIPT AND AGREEMENT BY DEPOSITORY (Prob. Code § 541.1)" with "WAIVER OF BOND: Attachment 3d."
3. Write the text of the Waiver of Bond (as shown in the example above) starting with "The undersigned...."
4. Have each beneficiary sign it, as described in Item 3d, and attach it to your Petition for Probate.

Item 3d: If the will waives the requirement of a bond, check the first box and leave the second one blank. If it doesn't waive bond, but does not specifically state that bond is required, check the box just below the first one and attach a Waiver of Bond as Attachment 3d (as shown above) signed by all beneficiaries named in the will. If there is no will, check the third box under Item 3d and attach a Waiver of Bond signed by all the heirs as Attachment 3d. Leave the fourth box blank. Each beneficiary may sign a separate waiver, or all may sign one (just add more signature lines).

In addition, when a waiver of bond is requested, some courts (for example, Los Angeles and San Diego) require a statement by the petitioner regarding knowledge of any creditors of the decedent and the

amount of any debts. The Attachment 3d shown in our sample petition, above, may be revised to conform to your situation. We recommend this information be included in all petitions requesting that bond be waived.

Item 3e: If the decedent did not leave a will, check the first box. If he or she died with a will, check the second box, type in the date of the will, and attach a copy of the will, labeled Attachment 3e(2), to your petition. If there are any codicils, the same information is needed plus a copy of the codicil. If the will is holographic (handwritten by the decedent), prepare an accurate typed copy and attach it along with a photocopy of the handwritten will as Attachment 3e(2).

If the typed and witnessed will and all codicils are self-proving (language in the will makes further verification by the witnesses unnecessary), check the box under Item 3e that indicates this. See Chapter 13 for an explanation of self-proving wills and codicils. Be sure to check if your county accepts self-proving wills. Otherwise, you must file a Proof of Subscribing Witness form (discussed in Step 5) before the hearing date on your petition.

Item 3f(1): The boxes under Section (1) of Item 3f apply only if the decedent left a will. If there is no will, skip Section (1) and go to Section (2) under Item 3f.

Complete Item 3f(1) as follows:

- If the proposed executor (you) is named as executor in the will, check the first box.
- If the will does not name an executor, check the second box.
- If the executor named in the will is unable or unwilling to act (he or she is dead, has disappeared, is too ill, or has declined to act), check Box (d), indicating the reason by checking one of the additional boxes that follow. Then prepare either a Declination to Act signed by the person who declines to serve (as shown below) or check the last box and provide the reason why the named executor cannot act. Attach the signed declination to the petition as Attachment 3f(1). (See Chapter 2 for the rules governing how an administrator with will annexed is chosen under these circumstances.) If

Nomination: Attachment 3f(2)(b)

```
 1   Estate of _____, deceased
 2   Attachment 3f(2)(b) to Petition for Probate
 3
 4                NOMINATION OF ADMINISTRATOR
 5      The undersigned, _____,
 6   surviving spouse of the above-named decedent, hereby nominates
 7   _____, a resident of the State
 8   of California and over the age of majority, to serve as
 9   administrator of the estate of the deceased.
10      DATED: _____, 20___
11                           _____
12                           _____
13
14
15
16
17
18
19
20
21
22
23
24
25
26
27
28
```

Attachment 3f(2)(b)

Nomination: Attachment 3f(1)(c)

```
1    Estate of _____, deceased

2    Attachment 3f(1)(c) to Petition for Probate

3

4             NOMINATION OF ADMINISTRATOR WITH WILL ANNEXED

5      The person named as executor in the decedent's will

6    predeceased the decedent, and the undersigned, being beneficiaries

7    of more than one-half of the estate, hereby nominate

     _____, a resident of the State of
8
     California and over the age of majority, as administrator of the
9
     decedent's estate with the will annexed.
10

11     DATED: _____, 20___

12                              _____

13                              _____

14

15

16

17

18

19

20

21

22

23

24

25

26

27

28
```

Declination: Attachment 3f(1)(d)

```
1    Estate of _____, deceased

2    Attachment 3f(1)(d) to Petition for Probate

3

4                    DECLINATION

5      The undersigned, named as executor in the decedent's will,

6    hereby declines to act and renounces all right to receive Letters

7    Testamentary herein.

8

9      DATED: _____, 20___

10                    _____

11                    _____

12

13

14

15

16

17

18

19

20

21

22

23

24

25

26

27

28
```

Declination

you are petitioning as the coexecutor or successor executor named in the will, you should check the first box in addition to the fourth box.

- If you are being nominated to be the personal representative, check the third box and attach a nomination as Attachment 3f(1)(c). The wording of the nomination should be the same as in the sample nomination (Attachment 3f(2)(b), for intestate situations) shown above.

Item 3f(2): Section (2) under Item 3f is for intestate estates (where the decedent died without a will). Review the discussion in "Who Will Represent the Estate?" in Chapter 13, before completing Section (2). If you are entitled by priority to be administrator, check the first box. If you are being nominated to be administrator by someone who would otherwise have priority to be administrator, check the second box and attach a nomination as Attachment 3f(2)(b), as shown in the sample above. If you, as the proposed administrator, are related to the decedent, check the third box and indicate the relationship.

Item 3f(3): Leave this box blank.

Item 3g: A person does not have to be a resident of California to be an administrator, but must be a resident of the United States. An executor named in the will may reside anywhere. However, any proposed personal representative (whether an executor, administrator, or administrator with will annexed) who is a nonresident of California must state his or her permanent address.

Item 4: Before checking this box, read the will to make sure it does not prohibit you from using the procedures of the Independent Administration of Estates Act. It is extremely rare for a will to prohibit this. See the comments in Chapter 13 regarding this situation.

Note on Items 5, 6, and 7: These items request information necessary to determine the decedent's heirs (people who inherit the estate in the absence of a will). Even if the decedent left a will, you must still list the heirs. Before completing these sections, carefully review Chapter 3, which gives detailed information on how to determine the heirs of a decedent. Chapter 3 also explains the meaning of certain common legal terminology, such as issue, predeceased spouse, and child.

Item 5a: For (1) under this item, check the first box if the decedent left a surviving spouse. If no spouse, check one of the next boxes indicating whether divorced, never married, or spouse deceased. For (3), check this box if the decedent is survived by a domestic partner. If not, check Box (4). For (5), if the decedent left surviving children, check this box and then indicate (by checking one of the boxes below) whether the child is natural or adopted, or natural adopted by a third party. "Natural" means biological. (See Chapter 3 for a definition of child as it pertains to each of these situations.) If there are no children, check the box under (6). If the decedent had a child who died before the decedent (a predeceased child), and the predeceased child left issue (child, grandchild, or great-grandchild) who are now living, check Box (7). If there are no issue of a predeceased child now living, check Box (8).

Item 5b: Check the first box only if you know of a parent-child relationship (as defined in Chapter 3) between a foster parent and foster child, or stepparent and stepchild, that might allow someone to inherit through the decedent's will or by intestate succession. You are required to give such persons notice of the probate proceeding. Otherwise, check the second box.

Many attorneys recommend that notice be served on all known stepchildren or foster children, whether or not you reasonably believe they might have had a parent-child relationship with the decedent, as described in Probate Code § 6454.

Item 6: If deceased is survived by any issue (children, grandchildren, and so on), skip Item 6. Otherwise, one box should be checked. To determine which one to check, follow these two steps:

1. If the decedent is survived by a spouse or domestic partner, then only Box a or b applies:

Box 6a: If the decedent is survived by a spouse or domestic partner and a parent or parents, check this box.

Box 6b: If there is a surviving spouse or domestic partner, no surviving parents, but surviving brothers or sisters or issue of deceased brothers or sisters, check this box.

2. If the decedent left no spouse or domestic partner and no children or issue of deceased

children (grandchildren, etc.), then check the first box under Item 6 that applies:

Box 6a: If there is a parent (or parents) surviving, check Box a and no other.

Box 6b: If no parents are living, but there are children of deceased parents living (brothers or sisters of the decedent), or if there are issue of deceased brothers or sisters living (nieces or nephews of the decedent), then check Box b only.

Box 6c: If the decedent is survived by a grandparent or grandparents, but none of the people listed for Boxes a and b, check this box.

Box 6d: If there are issue of the decedent's grandparents surviving (uncles, aunts, or cousins of the decedent), but none of the people listed in Boxes a through c, check Box d.

Box 6e: This box applies if the decedent had a predeceased spouse or domestic partner (a spouse or domestic partner who died before the decedent while married or partnered to the decedent) whose issue (children, grandchildren, etc.) are living. In this case (if Boxes a, b, c, and d do not apply), check Box e and list the issue of the predeceased spouse in Item 8, below.

Box 6f: If Boxes a through e do not apply, check Box f and then determine the next of kin by studying the charts shown in Chapter 3. List them in Item 8.

Box 6g: This box applies if a parent or parents of a predeceased spouse or domestic partner or their issue (brothers, sisters, nieces, nephews, and so on) are living.

Box 6h: Check this box if there is no known next of kin.

Item 7: This section is for determining distribution of real and personal property when there is a predeceased spouse or domestic partner. Complete Item 8 in all cases where the decedent left no surviving spouse, domestic partner, or issue. If the decedent had a predeceased spouse or domestic partner who died fewer than 15 years before the decedent owning an interest in real property that passed to the decedent, or died not more than five years before the decedent and owned personal property totaling $10,000 or more, and the property is still part of the present decedent's estate, Probate Code § 6402.5 provides that the property will pass by intestate succession (if there isn't a valid will) to the issue or next of kin of the predeceased spouse or domestic partner. The issue in this case would be from a prior marriage of the predeceased spouse or domestic partner, because the decedent left no issue. If this is your situation, check the applicable numbered boxes plus the first box (a, b, etc.) that apply and list the relatives of the predeceased spouse or domestic partner under Item 8, below. Generally, "property owned by the predeceased spouse" is property that was the predeceased spouse's or domestic partner's separate property (property the spouse or partner owned before marriage or received through gift or inheritance during the marriage) or a one-half interest in community property. The heirs determined under Probate Code § 6402.5 have priority over the heirs in Item 6.

> **EXAMPLE:** Joe and Ruth owned a home together as community property when they were married. Ruth died, leaving her half interest in the house to Joe. Joe never had children; Ruth had a child from a previous marriage. When Joe dies 14 years after Ruth without a will, leaving no spouse or issue, the one-half interest in the house that Ruth owned when she died goes to Ruth's child. (Even if Joe left a will, you would be required to list Ruth's child in the petition as a possible intestate heir along with the beneficiaries in the will. If Joe's will is later admitted to probate as his valid will and the will gives the property to someone else, Ruth's child does not inherit anything.)

Item 8: List the name, relationship, age, and residence or mailing address of everyone mentioned in the decedent's will and codicils (if any) as a beneficiary, whether living or deceased, plus all persons checked in Items 5, 6, and 7, above. If you list second-generation heirs, also list the deceased ancestor through whom they inherit, and state the deceased ancestor's relationship to the decedent. You are not required to make impractical and extended searches, but you must make reasonably diligent efforts to ascertain all heirs and beneficiaries of the decedent. (Prob. Code § 8002(a)(3).) You should also list alternate and second alternate executors named in the will, if any. Everyone listed in Item 8 will be mailed a notice of the hearing on the petition. Persons not related to the decedent by blood are designated as "strangers." You can show their ages as either "under 18" or "over 18." This alerts the court to the possible need of a guardian if assets will be distributed to a minor. Generally, don't use an "in care of" address. If more than one person in a household is listed, each should get a separate notice.

When listing persons named in the decedent's will and codicils, here are some things you should watch for to make sure you list everyone the court will require:

1. If any of the beneficiaries named in the will or codicil died before the decedent, list the deceased beneficiary's name, relationship to the decedent, and approximate date of death, if known. If the predeceased beneficiary was related to the decedent (kindred), then list the deceased beneficiary's issue, if any (that is, children, grandchildren, etc.), specifically identifying them as "daughter of …" The reason for this is that the issue of a predeceased beneficiary who was kindred of the decedent will inherit the predeceased beneficiary's share of the estate. (See Chapter 3.) If the predeceased beneficiary had no issue, state that. For example, "Robert Jones (predeceased decedent on 12-5-09; no surviving issue)."

2. If an heir or will beneficiary dies after the decedent, and a personal representative has been appointed for that person, list the name of the deceased heir or beneficiary with a notation that the person is deceased, followed by the name and address of the personal representative. For example, "John Doe (postdeceased decedent on March 17, 2010)/ Jack Smith, Executor, 123 Main Street, Sun City, CA 90000." If no personal representative has been appointed, list the beneficiary name as deceased and note that no personal representative has been appointed. When this is the case, notice should be sent to the last known address of the postdeceased heir or beneficiary.

When You Can't Locate an Heir or Beneficiary

If you can't find the address for an heir or beneficiary, you must prepare a "Declaration of Due Diligence" to let the court know what steps you have taken to locate the missing person. Type the declaration on plain paper and attach it to the petition. The petition should state the name of the missing person, last known address, approximate date when the person was last known to reside there, and the efforts you made to locate the person. "Due diligence" requires that you search for the person using obvious sources of information, such as:

- relatives
- friends
- employers
- telephone directories
- internet directories, and
- the real and personal property indexes at the assessor's office in the county of the person's last known address.

When the court receives the declaration, it will either decide that enough has been done to find the person, or it will tell you what else you need to do to give the person notice of the court proceeding.

---

3. If the will has a pour-over provision, meaning that property passes to a living trust, each trustee is listed as a beneficiary of the will. If the trustee and the personal representative are the same person, you must also list the names and addresses of all the beneficiaries of the trust so they will receive notice. In addition, you must state whether the trust was executed after, before, or concurrently with the execution of the will, and whether or not the trust was later revoked. (Prob. Code § 6300.)

4. If the decedent's will or codicil makes a gift to a nonrelative who died before the decedent, then the gift lapses. (See Chapter 3.) It is not necessary to list the deceased beneficiary's issue, because they will not inherit anything. However, be sure to list any alternate

beneficiaries named in the will. For instance, if the will contains this provision: "I give my stamp collection to my friend Sam. In the event Sam predeceases me, I give my stamp collection to my friend John," Sam should be listed as a deceased beneficiary (if he died before the decedent), and John should be listed as the alternate beneficiary.

5. If the will requires any beneficiary to survive the decedent for a certain period of time, list by name the persons who would receive any property if the beneficiary does not survive for the required period. For example: "I give all my jewelry to my sister Mary if she survives me for a period of six months. In the event my sister Mary does not survive me for a period of six months, I give all of my jewelry to my niece, Ellen." In this case, you should list Ellen as a contingent beneficiary who will inherit the jewelry in the event Mary does not survive for six months following the decedent's death. It isn't necessary to label Ellen as a contingent beneficiary; her name and address will merely be included with the other beneficiaries.

6. List any person named as a beneficiary in the will but subsequently deleted in a codicil. For example, if paragraph four of the will says, "I give $5,000 to my brother, Robert," and a later codicil says, "I delete paragraph four of my will in its entirety," then Robert should be listed in Item 9. The reason for this is that if the codicil is proven to be invalid, Robert would inherit the $5,000. Again, you don't have to explain why Robert is listed (that is, that he is a contingent beneficiary); the probate examiners will pick up his name from the codicil and recognize the reason he has been included.

7. You should list any executor named in the will who is not joining in the petition. For example, if the will names two persons to act as executors and only one signs the petition requesting to be appointed, then list the other person in Item 8 as a person interested in the estate. If the will lists alternate executors, list them as well. Executors who were named in any earlier wills should also be listed. Again, there is no need to

identify them as "non-petitioning coexecutor" or "alternate executor."

8. If the will refers to people only by category, such as "my children," "my issue," or "my brother's children," list the names of all people in this category in Item 8 and specify their relationship. For instance, if the will gives property to "my brother's children," then you would list them by name and specify their relationship as "son of decedent's brother Alfred," or "daughter of decedent's brother Alfred." See Chapter 3 for definitions of the more commonly used group terms, especially if your situation involves adopted children, stepchildren, or foster children.

9. If it appears that property may pass to a citizen of a foreign nation, the consul of that nation must be listed in Item 8 and given notice of the filing of the petition. For example, if the will leaves property to Françoise Terreux, a French citizen, you would list Françoise as the beneficiary, giving her address, and you would also list the French Consul and its local address. The local addresses of the consulate offices are listed in major metropolitan telephone books, usually under the heading "Consulate Generals." If an heir or beneficiary is a United States citizen merely residing in a foreign country, you do not have to list the foreign consul. In this latter case, you should indicate that the beneficiary is a United States citizen.

10. If any of the beneficiaries is a minor, list the child and the person (or persons) who has custody of him or her. Each must be given notice.

11. If the will names an organization as a beneficiary, it must also be listed and given notice.

Item 9: Fill in the number of pages of attachments.

Signature and Verification: The petitioner must sign the petition on page 4 near the bottom. Type or print the petitioner's name on the line at the left, and be sure to fill in the date above. If there are two petitioners, both must sign. Leave the signature line for the attorney blank or put "not applicable." All court forms should be signed in blue ink, not black, so the originals can be distinguished from copies.

Step 2: Prepare the Certificate of Assignment

This is a local form required in some counties that have branch courts. Branch courts are usually found in larger counties. They are smaller courts in outlying districts that serve the same function as the main court. The form requests that the court assign the probate matter to the main court or a particular branch court because the decedent resided within the district.

A completed sample of the form required in Los Angeles County (Probate Case Cover Sheet—Certificate of Grounds for Assignment to District) is shown below. The clerk will stamp in the case number. Call the court for the name of the district to insert in the last paragraph. If you file in another county that has branch courts, ask if there is a local form.

Step 3: Prepare the Notice of Petition to Administer Estate

As mentioned, when you file the Petition for Probate, the court clerk gives it a hearing date. Notice of the time and date of the hearing must then be given to certain persons. If the notice is not properly given, the petition will not be approved, so give careful attention to these procedures. The notice, on a printed form called Notice of Petition to Administer Estate, must be given in two ways.

Published Notice

The notice must be published in a newspaper of general circulation in the city where the decedent resided at the time of death (or, if the decedent was a nonresident of California, where he or she left property). If there is no such newspaper, or if the decedent did not reside in a city, the notice must be published in a newspaper of general circulation that is circulated in the area of the county in which the decedent lived. (Prob. Code § 8121.) The published notice gives a general notice to creditors and any other persons who may be interested in the estate. (Step

15 explains how to give individual written notice to certain known creditors.) To find the right newspaper, ask the court clerk if there are any newspapers published in the city or county where the decedent lived. If you have a choice, call to find out price and publication schedule. You may be surprised at the difference in cost among newspapers. Daily papers are usually the most expensive. As long as the newspaper has been approved by the county, you may pick the least expensive and still meet the legal requirement.

In some counties, including Los Angeles, the court clerk will deliver the notice to the newspaper for publication. If he does not, you will have to see that the newspaper gets a copy.

The notice must be published three times before the date of the court hearing, and the absolute deadline for the first publication is 15 days before the date of the hearing. Three publications in a newspaper published once a week or more often, with five days between the first and last publication dates, not counting those dates, is sufficient. Most newspapers are familiar with the publication rules. After the notice is published, a proof of publication must be filed with the court before the hearing date on the petition. Most newspapers have their own form. It must contain a copy of the notice and show the date of its first publication.

Find out if the newspaper will file the proof of publication directly with the court; otherwise, you will have to file it. Be sure to check the published notice for accuracy as to the case number, title of the notice, dates of publication, and wording. For example, a notice is defective and void if it does not show the name of the court. Also, be sure the notice states that the petition requests authority to administer the estate under the Independent Administration of Estates Act (unless, of course, you have not requested the authority).

Mailed Notice

The notice must be mailed by first class mail to all heirs and beneficiaries and other persons named in Item 8 of the petition (see Step 1, Item 8, above) at least 15 days before the hearing date. Some courts (for example, Riverside County) require that notice to

Certificate of Assignment (front)

NAME, ADDRESS AND TELEPHONE NUMBER OF ATTORNEY OR PARTY WITHOUT ATTORNEY: Billy M. Kidd 1109 Sky Blue Mountain Trail Billings, Montana 48906 Tel: 715-555-6408	STATE BAR NUMBER	Reserved for Clerk's File Stamp

ATTORNEY FOR (Name):   In pro per

SUPERIOR COURT OF CALIFORNIA, COUNTY OF LOS ANGELES

COURTHOUSE ADDRESS:
1725 Main Street, Santa Monica, CA 90401

Matter of:

ANABELLE KIDD, aka ANABELLE O. KIDD

☒ DECEDENT	☐ CONSERVATEE	☐ MINOR	☐ TRUST/OTHER

PROBATE CASE COVER SHEET - **CERTIFICATE OF GROUNDS FOR ASSIGNMENT TO DISTRICT**	CASE NUMBER:

This form is required for all new Probate cases filed in the Los Angeles Superior Court.

I. Select the correct district (3 steps):

1) Under Column **1** below, check the one type of action which best describes the nature of this case.

2) In Column **2** below, circle the reason for your choice of district that applies to the type of action you have checked.

— **Applicable Reason for Choosing District (See Column 2 below)** —

1. District where one or more of the parties reside.
2. District where minor/proposed conservatee reside.
3. District where petitioner resides.
4. District where decedent was domiciled.
5. Decedent/Ward/Conservatee was/is not domiciled in California, but held property at date of death/holds property in district.
6. Other: Statutory Authority _____.
7. May be filed in the appropriate district (Local Rule 2.0(c) states specific circumstances in which this may occur).

3) Fill in the information requested on Section II; complete section III; sign the certificate.

1	**TYPE OF ACTION** *(Check only one)*	**2**	**APPLICABLE REASONS** *(See above)*
Decedent Estates			
☒ A6210	Petition for Probate of Will - Letters Testamentary		④, 5., 7.
☐ A6211	Petition for Probate of Will - Letters of Administration with will annexed		4., 5., 7.
☐ A6212	Petition for Letters of Administration		4., 5., 7.
☐ A6213	Petition for Letters of Special Administration		4., 5., 7.
☐ A6214	Petition to Set Aside Small Estate (6602 Prob. Code)		4., 5., 7.
☐ A6215	Spousal Property Petition		4., 5., 7.
☐ A6216	Petition for Succession to Property		4., 5., 7.
☐ A6217	Summary Probate (7660 Prob. Code)		4., 5., 7.
☐ A6218	Petition re Real Property of Small Value (13200 Prob. Code)		4., 5., 7.
Conservatorship / Guardianship			
☐ A6230	Petition for Conservatorship of Person and Estate		2., 6., 7.
☐ A6231	Petition for Conservatorship of Person only		2., 6., 7.
☐ A6232	Petition for Conservatorship of Estate only		2., 5., 6., 7

PROBATE CASE COVER SHEET - CERTIFICATE OF GROUNDS FOR ASSIGNMENT TO DISTRICT

Certificate of Assignment (back)

Short Title Estate of Anabelle Kidd, aka Anabelle O. Kidd, deceased	CASE NUMBER:

1 TYPE OF ACTION *(Check only one)*	**2** APPLICABLE REASONS *(See above)*

Conservatorship / Guardianship

☐ A6240	Petition for Guardianship of Person and Estate	2., 6., 7.
☐ A6241	Petition for Guardianship of Person only	2., 6., 7.
☐ A6242	Petition for Guardianship of Estate only	2., 5., 6., 7.

Trust / Other Probate Court Matters

☐ A6254	Trust Proceedings	3., 6., 7.
☐ A6260	Petition for Compromise of Minor's Claim - no civil case filed (3500 Prob. Code)	1., 2., 6., 7.
☐ A6180	Petition to Establish Fact of Birth, Death or Marriage	1., 4., 7.
☐ A6200	Other Probate Matter (Specify): _____	6., 7.
☐ A6243	Proceeding for particular transaction where spouse lacks legal Capacity	2., 6., 7.
☐ A6233	Capacity determination and health care decision for adult without conservator	2., 6., 7.

II. Select the appropriate district: Enter the address of the party, decedent's residence, property, or other circumstance you have circled in column 2 as the proper reason for filing in the district you selected.

REASON: CHECK THE NUMBER YOU CIRCLED IN -2- WHICH APPLIES IN THIS CASE	ADDRESS OF SUBJECT PERSON / FIDUCIARY
☐ 1 ☐ 2 ☐ 3 ☑ 4 ☐ 5 ☐ 6 ☐ 7	950 Euclid Street
CITY: STATE ZIP CODE Santa Monica, CA 90402	

III. ☐ Another case (including Juvenile, Family Law, Adoptions, etc.) has been filed with Los Angeles Superior Court involving the same minor(s).

Case number: _____

IV. Certificate of Assignment: The undersigned hereby certifies that the above entitled matter is properly filed for assignment to the _____ District of the Los Angeles Superior Court pursuant to the California Probate Code and Rule 2.0 of this court for the reason checked above.

I declare under penalty of perjury under the laws of the State of California that the foregoing is true and correct and this declaration was executed on

July 5, 20xx .

Billy M. Kidd
_____
(SIGNATURE OF ATTORNEY/PARTY WITHOUT ATTORNEY)

New Probate Case Filing Instructions

This form is required so that the court can assign your case to the correct courthouse in the proper district for filing. It satisfies the requirement for a certificate as to reasons for authorizing filing in the courthouse location, as set forth in Los Angeles Superior Court Local Rule 2.0. It must be completed and submitted to the court along with the original Petition in ALL Probate cases filed in any district (including the Central District) of the Los Angeles County Superior Court.

THE FOLLOWING DOCUMENTS MUST BE COMPLETED AND READY TO BE FILED IN ORDER TO PROPERLY COMMENCE YOUR NEW COURT CASE:

1. Probate Case Cover Sheet (this form)

2. Original Petition

3. Other documents as required by statute, California Rules of Court, or Rules of this Court.

4. Payment in full of the filing fees or an Order of the Court waiving payment of the filing fees (fee waiver application forms available at the Forms Window).

Copies of original documents presented personally to the filing clerk will be conformed and returned to you.
If filed by mail, include a self-addressed-stamped-envelope for return of your conformed copies.

PROBATE CASE COVER SHEET - CERTIFICATE OF GROUNDS FOR ASSIGNMENT TO DISTRICT

> ### Checklist for Publication of Notice of Petition to Administer Estate
>
> ✓ The notice must be published in a newspaper of general circulation in the city where the decedent resided at the time of death (or where he or she left property, if nonresident). If there is no such newspaper or if the decedent didn't reside in a city or if the property isn't in a city, publication may be made in a newspaper of general circulation that is circulated in the area of the county in which the decedent lived.
>
> ✓ Notice must be published three times before the date of the court hearing, and first publication must be at least 15 days before the hearing date.
>
> ✓ There must be three publications in a newspaper published once a week or more often, with five days between the first and last publication dates, not counting those dates.
>
> ✓ Proof of the publication (by way of an affidavit from the newspaper) must be filed with the court before the hearing date on the petition.
>
> ✓ If the petition requests authority to administer the estate under the Independent Administration of Estates Act, the notice must specify this.

the Director of Health Services be given on this form prior to the hearing (see Step 7). The notice doesn't have to be mailed to the petitioner or anyone joining in the petition. You also don't have to mail this notice to known creditors—they are given mailed notice on a different form, discussed in Step 15.

The person doing the mailing (who cannot be you or any other person interested in the estate) must sign a declaration under penalty of perjury on the form, giving proof of the mailing which is filed with the court prior to the hearing.

Procedures vary in the different court districts as to who prepares the Notice of Petition to Administer Estate and who attends to the mailing and publication of the notice. In Los Angeles County, this is usually done by the legal newspaper, which prepares the notice, mails it, prepares and files proof of mailing, publishes the notice, and also prepares and files the proof of publication directly with the court. In other counties, the petitioner must do everything.

Call the court clerk and ask how it is handled in your county. To be safe, you may prepare the notice according to the instructions below, leaving the date of hearing blank, and submit the original and as many copies as you will need for mailing (plus an extra one to be stamped by the court and returned to you for your records) to the court clerk when you file your petition. He or she will either insert the date of hearing on the notices and return them to you, or notify you of the hearing date by stamping or writing it on your copy of the petition. In some counties, the petitioner is required to fill in the date of hearing according to certain days of the week when such matters are heard in that court. If this is the case, the clerk will advise you. If you pick a date, be sure you give yourself enough time to mail the notice 15 days prior to the hearing.

It is your responsibility to see that the notice is published and mailed, and that proof of the publication and mailing is filed with the court, no matter what procedure is followed.

Instructions for Preparing Notice of Petition to Administer Estate

Heading: Fill in same information as on Petition for Probate. In the last box of the heading (opposite the case number), be sure to type in all names by which decedent was known.

Item 1: Fill in decedent's name and all variations.

Item 2: Your name goes here. Insert the name of the county on the second line.

Item 3: Put in the name of the personal representative.

Item 4: If there is a will, check this box. If not, leave it blank.

Item 5: If you are requesting independent administration authority, check this box.

Item 6: Leave this blank until the court clerk gives you this information.

Item 10: Check the first box and type in your name, address, and telephone number where indicated.

Notice of Petition to Administer (front)

DE-121

ATTORNEY OR PARTY WITHOUT ATTORNEY *(Name, State Bar number, and address):*	FOR COURT USE ONLY
Billy M. Kidd 1109 Sky Blue Mountain Trail Billings, Montana 48906 TELEPHONE NO.: 715-555-6408 FAX NO. *(Optional):* E-MAIL ADDRESS *(Optional):* ATTORNEY FOR *(Name):* In pro per	

SUPERIOR COURT OF CALIFORNIA, COUNTY OF

STREET ADDRESS: 1725 Main Street

MAILING ADDRESS: 1725 Main Street

CITY AND ZIP CODE: Santa Monica, CA 90401

BRANCH NAME: WEST DISTRICT

ESTATE OF *(Name):*

ANABELLE KIDD, aka ANABELLE O. KIDD, DECEDENT

NOTICE OF PETITION TO ADMINISTER ESTATE OF *(Name):* Anabelle Kidd, aka Anabelle O. Kidd, deceased	CASE NUMBER: WEP 14813

1. To all heirs, beneficiaries, creditors, contingent creditors, and persons who may otherwise be interested in the will or estate, or both, of *(specify all names by which the decedent was known):*

   Anabelle Kidd, aka Anabelle O. Kidd, deceased

2. A **Petition for Probate** has been filed by *(name of petitioner):* Billy M. Kidd
   in the Superior Court of California, County of *(specify):* LOS ANGELES

3. The Petition for Probate requests that *(name):* Billy M. Kidd
   be appointed as personal representative to administer the estate of the decedent.

4. [X] The petition requests the decedent's will and codicils, if any, be admitted to probate. The will and any codicils are available for examination in the file kept by the court.

5. [X] The petition requests authority to administer the estate under the Independent Administration of Estates Act. (This authority will allow the personal representative to take many actions without obtaining court approval. Before taking certain very important actions, however, the personal representative will be required to give notice to interested persons unless they have waived notice or consented to the proposed action.) The independent administration authority will be granted unless an interested person files an objection to the petition and shows good cause why the court should not grant the authority.

6. **A hearing on the petition will be held in this court as follows:**

   a. Date: July 25, 20xx Time: 9:30 A.M. Dept.: A Room:

   b. Address of court: [X] same as noted above [ ] other *(specify):*

7. **If you object** to the granting of the petition, you should appear at the hearing and state your objections or file written objections with the court before the hearing. Your appearance may be in person or by your attorney.

8. **If you are a creditor or a contingent creditor of the decedent,** you must file your claim with the court and mail a copy to the personal representative appointed by the court within four months from the date of first issuance of letters as provided in Probate Code section 9100. The time for filing claims will not expire before four months from the hearing date noticed above.

9. **You may examine the file kept by the court.** If you are a person interested in the estate, you may file with the court a *Request for Special Notice* (form DE-154) of the filing of an inventory and appraisal of estate assets or of any petition or account as provided in Probate Code section 1250. A *Request for Special Notice* form is available from the court clerk.

10. [X] Petitioner [ ] Attorney for petitioner *(name):* Billy M. Kidd

    (Address): 1109 Sky Blue Mountain Trail
    Billings, Montana 48906

    (Telephone): 715-555-6408

NOTE: If this notice is published, print the caption, beginning with the words NOTICE OF PETITION TO ADMINISTER ESTATE, and do not print the information from the form above the caption. The caption and the decedent's name must be printed in at least 8-point type and the text in at least 7-point type. Print the case number as part of the caption. Print items preceded by a box only if the box is checked. Do not print the italicized instructions in parentheses, the paragraph numbers, the mailing information, or the material on page 2.

Page 1 of 2

Form Adopted for Mandatory Use Judicial Council of California DE-121 [Rev. January 1, 2006]	**NOTICE OF PETITION TO ADMINISTER ESTATE** **(Probate—Decedents' Estates)**	Probate Code, § 8100 www.courtinfo.ca.gov

Notice of Petition to Administer (back)

DE-121

ESTATE OF *(Name):*	CASE NUMBER:
Anabelle Kidd, aka Anabelle O. Kidd, deceased __DECEDENT__	WEP 14813

PROOF OF SERVICE BY MAIL

1. I am over the age of 18 and not a party to this cause. I am a resident of or employed in the county where the mailing occurred.
2. My residence or business address is *(specify):*

> 2328 – 20th Street, Santa Monica, California 90405

3. I served the foregoing *Notice of Petition to Administer Estate* on each person named below by enclosing a copy in an envelope addressed as shown below **AND**

    a. ☒ **depositing** the sealed envelope with the United States Postal Service on the date and at the place shown in item 4, with the postage fully prepaid.

    b. ☐ **placing** the envelope for collection and mailing on the date and at the place shown in item 4 following our ordinary business practices. I am readily familiar with this business's practice for collecting and processing correspondence for mailing. On the same day that correspondence is placed for collection and mailing, it is deposited in the ordinary course of business with the United States Postal Service, in a sealed envelope with postage fully prepaid.

4. a. Date mailed: July 8, 20xx   b. Place mailed *(city, state):* Santa Monica, California

5. ☐ I served, with the *Notice of Petition to Administer Estate,* a copy of the petition or other document referred to in the notice.

I declare under penalty of perjury under the laws of the State of California that the foregoing is true and correct.

Date: July 8, 20xx

Hilton Waller	▶ *Hilton Waller*
(TYPE OR PRINT NAME OF PERSON COMPLETING THIS FORM)	(SIGNATURE OF PERSON COMPLETING THIS FORM)

NAME AND ADDRESS OF EACH PERSON TO WHOM NOTICE WAS MAILED

	Name of person served	Address *(number, street, city, state, and zip code)*
1.	Mary Kidd Clark	789 Main Street Venice, California 90410
2.	Carson Kidd	711 Valley Road Owens, California 98455
3.	Pat Garret	25 So. Corral Street Santa Fe, New Mexico 57256
4.	Albertine Terreaux	17 Rue Madeleine Paris, France
5.	Consulate of France	8350 Wilshire Boulevard Los Angeles, California 90035
6.		

☐ Continued on an attachment. *(You may use form DE-121(MA) to show additional persons served.)*

Assistive listening systems, computer-assisted real-time captioning, or sign language interpreter services are available upon request if at least 5 days notice is provided. Contact the clerk's office for *Request for Accommodations by Persons With Disabilities and Order* (form MC-410). (Civil Code section 54.8.)

DE-121 [Rev. January 1, 2006]

NOTICE OF PETITION TO ADMINISTER ESTATE
(Probate—Decedents' Estates)

Page 2 of 2

Back of Form

Fill in the decedent's name and the case number at the top. Complete the Proof of Service by Mail as follows:

Item 2: Fill in the address of the person who mails the Notice.

Item 3: Check Box a if the notice was mailed directly by the individual. Box b pertains to businesses (usually law firms) where the Notice has been placed for mailing along with other business correspondence on the date and place shown.

Item 4: Fill in date of mailing, and the city and state where mailed.

Item 5: You don't have to check this box unless you prefer to mail a copy of the Petition for Probate along with the notice.

Type in the name of the person who mails the notice, and the date, where indicated. The person who mails the notice should sign the original after the copies of the notice have been mailed. In the space at the bottom of the form, type in the names and addresses of all persons to whom a copy of the notice was mailed. This will be everyone listed in Item 8 of the petition. When the notice is deposited in the mail mailing is complete and the period of notice is not extended. (Prob. Code § 1215(e)).

If you need additional space to show persons served, check the box near the bottom and use the attachment sheet provided in Appendix B.

Step 4: File Your Petition for Probate

After you've typed and signed the petition, you're ready to get it and some other documents ready for your first trip to the courthouse.

Check Petition for Probate for Accuracy and Make Copies

Review the petition carefully to make sure the appropriate schedules are attached and all the proper boxes are checked. If there is a will, attach a photocopy of it and any codicils to the petition as "Attachment 3e(2)." Make sure all other attachments are properly numbered. It is also important that the signatures on the photocopies be clear and legible. Make three photocopies of the petition.

Make Copies of Will and Codicils

Make about four photocopies of the will and each codicil, if any (and a typed transcript if either is handwritten), for your files. If the will is not self-proving, you must also obtain either (1) a photocopy made by the clerk's office *after* the original will is filed, showing the clerk's file stamp and the probate case number, or (2) a copy that has been certified by the court clerk. This is required to prove the will (Step 5).

Make Copies of Notice of Petition to Administer Estate

Make enough copies of the Notice of Petition to Administer Estate to mail to all persons listed in Item 8 of the petition, plus an extra copy for your file. (If the newspaper mails the notice, you don't have to do this.)

File the Petition and the Original Will and Codicils

Submit the original and two copies of the petition to the court by mail or in person. One copy will be stamped "filed" by the clerk and returned to you, and the other will be for the legal newspaper to pick up addresses for mailing Notices to the heirs and beneficiaries if the newspaper mails the notices. Keep one photocopy for your files. You can check with the court to see if it will fax the calendar notes to you for a small fee, which is usually added to the filing fee.

The original will and codicils, if any, are filed with the court at the same time you file the petition. These documents are presented separately, in their original form, and do not require any preparation for filing. You can file these documents in person or through the mail. If you mail them to the court, include a cover letter such as the one shown below. Send the original will by certified mail. Be sure to include a self-addressed, stamped envelope for the court to return your conformed copies, and be sure to keep a file copy of everything you send to the court for your records. You'll need to include a check for the filing fee (see below), so call the court clerk to find out the amount.

Pay the Filing Fee

You must pay an initial filing fee, currently $395, when you file the Petition for Probate. Some courts may charge more, so call the court to verify the amount. Make your check payable to the "Clerk of the Superior Court."

The filing fee should come out of the estate assets as an expense of administration. If it is necessary for you (or someone else) to advance the fee from personal funds, reimbursement may be made from the estate's assets as soon as an estate bank account is opened. (See Chapter 13.)

Sample Cover Letter

July 5, 20xx

CERTIFIED MAIL - RETURN RECEIPT REQUESTED

Clerk of the Superior Court
1735 Main Street
Santa Monica, California 90401

Re: Estate of Anabelle Kidd, Deceased

Dear Sir or Madam:

Enclosed are the following documents:
1. Petition for Probate
2. Notice of Petition to Administer Estate
3. Original Will, plus four copies
4. Probate Case Cover Sheet, and
5. Check in the amount of $_____.

Please file the original documents with the court and return the extra copies, conformed, in the enclosed stamped, self-addressed envelope, advising me of the time and date of the hearing.

Very truly yours,

Billy M. Kidd

Billy M. Kidd

Step 5: Complete the Proof of Subscribing Witness Form

If the will is a holographic one—that is, in the decedent's handwriting—go on to Step 6.

The Proof of Subscribing Witness form is required only if the decedent left a formal typed and witnessed will or codicil that does not have a self-proving clause. In other words, if a will or codicil has a self-proving clause, the Proof of Subscribing Witness is not required. A self-proving will contains language that makes verification by witnesses unnecessary. (See "Self-Proving Wills and Codicils" in Chapter 13.)

The Proof of Subscribing Witness form is a declaration by one of the witnesses to the will (or codicil) that it was signed and witnessed according to the requirements of the law.

Only one proof is required to prove a will or codicil if no one contests the validity of the documents. If there are any codicils, you must prepare a separate proof form for each. A conformed copy of the will (or codicil) showing the court clerk's filing stamp, or a certified copy, must be attached to the Proof of Subscribing Witness form. (You should have this as a result of filing the will in Step 4, above.) The signature on the copies of the will should be clear and legible.

When you have completed the proof form, mail it to the witness and ask that it be signed and returned to you. Enclose a self-addressed, stamped envelope for the convenience of the witness. After one Proof of Subscribing Witness form is signed, file it with the court. These documents should be on file as far in advance of the hearing date as possible, and in no event later than two days before the hearing. If you get more than one Proof of Subscribing Witness form, keep the extras as a reserve.

The following comments refer to certain items on the Proof of Subscribing Witness form that may need further explanation:

Item 1: Attach a conformed (or certified) copy of the will to the Proof of Subscribing Witness form, showing the filing stamp of the court clerk and the probate case number. Label it Attachment 1 at the

Proof of Subscribing Witness

DE-131

ATTORNEY OR PARTY WITHOUT ATTORNEY *(Name, state bar number, and address)* :	TELEPHONE AND FAX NOS.:	FOR COURT USE ONLY

ATTORNEY FOR *(Name)*:

SUPERIOR COURT OF CALIFORNIA, COUNTY OF

STREET ADDRESS:

MAILING ADDRESS:

CITY AND ZIP CODE:

BRANCH NAME:

ESTATE OF *(Name)*:

DECEDENT

CASE NUMBER:

PROOF OF SUBSCRIBING WITNESS

1. I am one of the attesting witnesses to the instrument of which Attachment 1 is a photographic copy. I have examined Attachment 1 and my signature is on it.
    a. ☐ The name of the decedent was signed in the presence of the attesting witnesses present at the same time by
        (1) ☐ the decedent personally.
        (2) ☐ another person in the decedent's presence and by the decedent's direction.
    b. ☐ The decedent acknowledged in the presence of the attesting witnesses present at the same time that the decedent's name was signed by
        (1) ☐ the decedent personally.
        (2) ☐ another person in the decedent's presence and by the decedent's direction.
    c. ☐ The decedent acknowledged in the presence of the attesting witnesses present at the same time that the instrument signed was decedent's
        (1) ☐ will.
        (2) ☐ codicil.

2. When I signed the instrument, I understood that it was decedent's ☐ will ☐ codicil.

3. I have no knowledge of any facts indicating that the instrument, or any part of it, was procured by duress, menace, fraud, or undue influence.

I declare under penalty of perjury under the laws of the State of California that the foregoing is true and correct.

Date:

▶

_____   _____
(TYPE OR PRINT NAME)   (SIGNATURE OF WITNESS)

_____
(ADDRESS)

ATTORNEY'S CERTIFICATION
(Check local court rules for requirements for certifying copies of wills and codicils)

I am an active member of The State Bar of California. I declare under penalty of perjury under the laws of the State of California that Attachment 1 is a photographic copy of every page of the ☐ will ☐ codicil presented for probate.

Date:

▶

_____   _____
(TYPE OR PRINT NAME)   (SIGNATURE OF ATTORNEY)

Form Approved by the
Judicial Council of California
DE-131 [Rev. January 1, 1998]
Mandatory Form [1/1/2000]

PROOF OF SUBSCRIBING WITNESS
(Probate)

Probate Code, § 8220

bottom of the first page. If there are any codicils, attach a separate Proof of Subscribing Witness form for each one, and attach a copy of the codicil, labeled Attachment 1, at the bottom of the first page of the codicil.

Item 1a: If the decedent signed the will or codicil personally in the presence of the witnesses, check Box 1a and the first box under Item 1a. In rare instances, wills are signed by someone else for the decedent because the decedent for some reason could not sign his or her own name (for instance, he or she was unable to write because of a stroke). If this is the case, check the second box under a.

Item 1b: If the decedent didn't sign in the presence of the witnesses, but acknowledged to the witnesses that he or she personally signed the will or codicil, check Box b and the first box under Item 1b. If the decedent acknowledged to the witnesses that another person signed for him or her at his direction and in his or her presence, then check the second box under Item 1b.

Item 1c: Check Box 1c and the additional box under Item 1c that indicates whether the document is the decedent's will or codicil.

Item 2: If the Proof of Subscribing Witness is for the decedent's will, check the first box. If it is for a codicil, check the second box.

The witness must sign the form. To the left of the signature line, type the witness's name and address. Leave the "Attorney's Certification" part of the form blank.

What happens if all the witnesses have died or can't be found? Don't worry; the will is still good. However, you must prepare a declaration like the one just below, which describes your efforts and inability to locate any of the witnesses (or which states that they are dead) and a statement "proving" the handwriting of the decedent. The wording in our sample is usually sufficient to prove handwriting in the absence of evidence to the contrary. Anyone having personal knowledge of the decedent's handwriting can make a sworn statement proving it is the decedent's handwriting. Since you (the petitioner) are probably a relative or close friend, you are a suitable person to do this.

The sample we have provided is self-explanatory and may be modified to suit your particular situation. For instance, Paragraph 4 may be reworded to add additional information showing your efforts to locate the witnesses, and you may add (or omit) from Paragraph 5 any facts that explain why you are qualified to prove the decedent's handwriting. Be sure to attach a certified or file-stamped copy of the will as Exhibit A.

Declaration re Execution of Will (front)

Name:
Address: Type your name, address, and
           telephone number

Telephone No.:

Petitioner in pro per

SUPERIOR COURT OF CALIFORNIA

COUNTY OF ___ Type name of county ___

Estate of   ) No. _____
)
)
_____   ) Hearing date:_____   Date, place, and
)   time of hearing
)
_____   ) Department:_____ Time:_____
          deceased.   )
) DECLARATION RE EXECUTION OF WILL
_____   )

    The undersigned, ___ Name of person who signs affidavit ___, hereby

declares:

    1. I am the petitioner in the above-entitled proceeding.

    2. The decedent's will, dated ___ Date of will ___, _____,

presented for probate herein, of which Exhibit "A" attached

hereto is a photographic copy, was signed at the end by

___ Names of all witnesses ___, _____ and

_____, as witnesses to its execution.

    3. After reasonable search and inquiry, I have been unable to

locate any of these witnesses to obtain evidence that the will was

executed in all particulars as required by law.

1.
Declaration re Execution of Will

Declaration re Execution of Will (back)

1   4. I mailed letters to each of the witnesses at the addresses

2   shown in the will, requesting that each sign and return to me an

3   affidavit of Proof of Subscribing Witness; however, the envelopes

4   were returned undeliverable with the notation that the witnesses

5   had moved and no forwarding addresses were given. I could find no

6   listing for anyone by the name of _____,

7   _____, or _____ in the

8   county telephone directory. I have no knowledge of any person who

9   knows any of these witnesses or their whereabouts.

10   5. I am _____ Relation to decedent of person signing affidavit (for example, "the son,"

11   "the daughter," or "a close friend") of the decedent and I have personal

12   knowledge of her handwriting and signature which I acquired

13   by having seen her write and having received letters in the

14   mail purporting to be from decedent. I have examined Exhibit

15   "A," which is a photographic copy of what purports to be the

16   decedent's will, and in my opinion the name subscribed on the

17   signature line was signed by the hand of the decedent personally.

18   I declare under penalty of perjury under the laws of the State

19   of California that the foregoing is true and correct and that

20   this declaration was executed on _____ Date signed _____,20__, at

21   Place signed _____, California.

22   Signature of person making declaration
                                          _____

23

24

25

26

27

28

Reword to explain efforts to locate the witnesses

2.

Declaration re Execution of Will

Step 6: Complete a Proof of Holographic Instrument

If the will is a holographic will—that is, in the decedent's handwriting—someone who can prove the decedent's handwriting must sign a Proof of Holographic Instrument form. Anyone, including you (the petitioner), who has personal knowledge of the decedent's handwriting can sign this form, even someone who will receive all or part of the estate by reason of the holographic will. Attach a clear photocopy of the handwritten will to the form, and label it Attachment 1 at the bottom of the first page. A sample of the form, with instructions for filling it in, is shown below.

This form is also used in cases where the decedent made handwritten changes on a typewritten or printed will.

Step 7: Notify Government Agencies

If the decedent was receiving health care under Medi-Cal, or was the surviving spouse or registered domestic partner of someone who did, you must send a notice within 90 days of the death to the Director of Health Services advising that office of the decedent's death. (Prob. Code § 9202(a).) Medi-Cal has four months after notice is given to file a claim for repayment of any benefits that should be returned.

If the personal representative knows or has reason to believe that an heir is confined in a prison or facility under the jurisdiction of the Department of Corrections or the Department of the Youth Authority or confined in any county or city jail, road camp, industrial camp, industrial farm, or other local correctional facility, the personal representative must give notice of the decedent's death and name and location of the decedent's heir to the Director of the California Victim Compensation and Government Claims Board within 90 days after letters are issued. (Prob. Code § 9202(b).) The director of the board has four months after notice is received to pursue collection of any outstanding restitution fines or orders. The notice should be addressed to the director at his Sacramento office and contain a copy of the death certificate.

In addition, in estates for which letters are first issued on or after July 1, 2008, you must give notice of the decedent's death to the Franchise Tax Board.

There is no special form for giving the notices. See Chapter 2 for a sample letter that may be used. Be sure to enclose a copy of the decedent's death certificate and an extra copy of the notice so that it can be endorsed and returned to you. Proof that the notice was given to the Franchise Tax Board will be needed later as an attachment to the Petition for Final Distribution.

Proof of Holographic Instrument

DE-135

ATTORNEY OR PARTY WITHOUT ATTORNEY *(Name, state bar number, and address)*:	TELEPHONE AND FAX NOS.:	FOR COURT USE ONLY

ATTORNEY FOR *(Name)*:

SUPERIOR COURT OF CALIFORNIA, COUNTY OF

STREET ADDRESS:

MAILING ADDRESS:

CITY AND ZIP CODE:

BRANCH NAME:

ESTATE OF *(Name)*:

Type same heading as on petition

DECEDENT

PROOF OF HOLOGRAPHIC INSTRUMENT	CASE NUMBER: **Fill in case number**

[Sidebar: Fill in all that apply]

1. I was acquainted with the decedent for the following number of years *(specify)*:

2. ☐ I was related to the decedent as *(specify)*:

3. I have personal knowledge of the decedent's handwriting which I acquired as follows:
   a. ☐ I saw the decedent write.
   b. ☐ I saw a writing purporting to be in the decedent's handwriting and upon which decedent acted or was charged. It was *(specify)*:

   c. ☐ I received letters in the due course of mail purporting to be from the decedent in response to letters I addressed and mailed to the decedent.
   d. ☐ Other *(specify other means of obtaining knowledge)*:

4. I have examined the attached copy of the instrument, and its handwritten provisions were written by and the instrument was signed by the hand of the decedent. *(Affix a copy of the instrument as Attachment 4.)*

[Sidebar: Attach photocopy of holographic will as Attachment 4]

I declare under penalty of perjury under the laws of the State of California that the foregoing is true and correct.

Date: **Date signed**

Type name of person who will sign proof

....
(TYPE OR PRINT NAME)

▶ _____
Signature of person who will sign proof

....
(ADDRESS)

ATTORNEY'S CERTIFICATION
(Check local court rules for requirements for certifying copies of wills and codicils)

[Sidebar: Leave this section blank]

I am an active member of The State Bar of California. I declare under penalty of perjury under the laws of the State of California that Attachment 4 is a photographic copy of every page of the holographic instrument presented for probate.

Date:

....
(TYPE OR PRINT NAME)

▶ _____
(SIGNATURE OF ATTORNEY)

Form Approved by the
Judicial Council of California
DE-135 [Rev. January 1, 1998]
Mandatory Form [1/1/2000]

PROOF OF HOLOGRAPHIC INSTRUMENT
(Probate)

Probate Code, § 8222

Step 8: Prepare Your Order for Probate

When the petition is approved, you must prepare an Order for Probate and submit it to the court for the signature of the judge. The purpose of the Order for Probate is to admit the will (if any) to probate and appoint an estate representative. Some counties require the order to be in the hands of the court three or more days prior to the hearing date so it may be examined before the judge signs it. In other counties, including Los Angeles, the order may be submitted on or after the date of the hearing. If you are unsure of the procedure followed by the court in your area, it is good practice to send it to the court several days ahead of the hearing date. You may mail your letters and, for those counties that require it, the Application for Appointment of Probate Referee at the same time. (See Steps 10, 11, and 12.)

How to Fill Out the Order for Probate

Caption: Fill in your name, address, the court's name, and case number, as you have on your other court papers.

Order for Probate: Indicate whether an executor or administrator is being appointed. Also indicate that you petitioned for authority (full or limited) under the Independent Administration of Estates Act.

Item 1: Fill in the date, time, location, and judge for the court hearing. Call the court for the name of the judge, or leave it blank.

Item 2: Fill in the date of death and check the correct box about residence. Indicate whether there was a will (testate) or not (intestate). If there is a will, fill in the date of the will and any codicils. For the date the will was admitted to probate, put the date of the court hearing.

Item 3: Fill in your name and check the appropriate box. Leave Item 3d blank.

Item 4: Check Box a if you petitioned for full authority to use the Independent Administration of Estates Act; check Box b if you asked for limited authority.

Item 5: Check Box a if bond is waived. If bond is required, check Box b and fill in the amount. If cash is to be deposited in a blocked account, check Box c and fill in the amount, and name and address of the depository. (You must file a receipt for the deposit with the court either before or shortly after letters are issued. Some banks and trust companies request a certified copy of the Order for Probate naming them as depository.)

Item 6: Check this box and the court will complete it.

Leave the rest of the form blank.

Step 9: Study and Respond to the Calendar Notes

As discussed in Chapter 13, calendar notes (sometimes called "tentative rulings") are shorthand terms used by the court's probate examiners to indicate whether a petition is approved or if there is a question or problem to be corrected. Many courts now list calendar notes on their websites. You can call the court to get the address. In some counties, the probate clerk will call you if there are any problems. In some counties, on the day before the hearing, you can call a number and listen to a taped announcement of all the petitions granted without requiring a court appearance. If your case is on the tape, go to the next step. If it is not, call the court to find out what the problem is and how to correct it.

If you need to provide additional information, you must either appear at the hearing personally or file a "supplement" to the petition. The supplement must be typed and verified (under penalty of perjury) by the petitioner in the same way as the original petition. The hearing date must be inserted on the right-hand side under the title of the document. It may be necessary to take the supplement to the court personally for it to be filed in time to have the petition approved on the hearing date. Delivering courtesy copies to the probate examiner can be helpful in getting matters approved. Be sure to tell the clerk at the court that the matter is set for hearing shortly, so the supplement will be placed in the case file in time for the hearing. Answering questions at the hearing is often an easier way to cure defects and, generally, is not intimidating.

Order for Probate

DE-140

ATTORNEY OR PARTY WITHOUT ATTORNEY *(Name, state bar number, and address):*	TELEPHONE AND FAX NOS.:	**FOR COURT USE ONLY**

Billy M. Kidd
1109 Sky Blue Mountain Trail
Billings, Montana 48906

TELEPHONE AND FAX NOS.: 715-555-6408

ATTORNEY FOR *(Name):* In pro per

SUPERIOR COURT OF CALIFORNIA, COUNTY OF LOS ANGELES
STREET ADDRESS: 1725 Main Street
MAILING ADDRESS: 1725 Main Street
CITY AND ZIP CODE: Santa Monica, CA 90401
BRANCH NAME: WEST DISTRICT

ESTATE OF *(Name):*

ANABELLE KIDD, aka
ANABELLE O. KIDD,   DECEDENT

ORDER FOR PROBATE

ORDER APPOINTING
[X] Executor
[ ] Administrator with Will Annexed
[ ] Administrator [ ] Special Administrator
[X] Order Authorizing Independent Administration of Estate
[X] with full authority [ ] with limited authority

CASE NUMBER: WEP 14813

WARNING: THIS APPOINTMENT IS NOT EFFECTIVE UNTIL LETTERS HAVE ISSUED.

1. Date of hearing: 7-25-xx   Time: 9:30 A.M.   Dept./Room: A   Judge:

THE COURT FINDS

2. a. All notices required by law have been given.
   b. Decedent died on *(date):* June 18, 20xx
      (1) [X] a resident of the California county named above.
      (2) [ ] a nonresident of California and left an estate in the county named above.
   c. Decedent died
      (1) [ ] intestate
      (2) [X] testate
      and decedent's will dated: July 1, 1980   and each codicil dated:
      was admitted to probate by Minute Order on *(date):* July 25, 20xx

THE COURT ORDERS

3. *(Name):* Billy M. Kidd
   is appointed **personal representative:**
   a. [X] executor of the decedent's will
   b. [ ] administrator with will annexed
   c. [ ] administrator

   d. [ ] special administrator
      (1) [ ] with general powers
      (2) [ ] with special powers as specified in Attachment 3d(2)
      (3) [ ] without notice of hearing
      (4) [ ] letters will expire on *(date):*

   and letters shall issue on qualification.

4. a. [X] **Full authority** is granted to administer the estate under the Independent Administration of Estates Act.
   b. [ ] **Limited authority** is granted to administer the estate under the Independent Administration of Estates Act (there is no authority, without court supervision, to (1) sell or exchange real property or (2) grant an option to purchase real property or (3) borrow money with the loan secured by an encumbrance upon real property).

5. a. [X] Bond is not required.
   b. [ ] Bond is fixed at: $ to be furnished by an authorized surety company or as otherwise provided by law.
   c. [ ] Deposits of: $ are ordered to be placed in a blocked account at *(specify institution and location):*
      and receipts shall be filed. No withdrawals shall be made without a court order. [ ] Additional orders in Attachment 5c.
   d. [ ] The personal representative is not authorized to take possession of money or any other property without a specific court order.

6. [X] *(Name):*   is appointed probate referee.

Date:

_____
JUDGE OF THE SUPERIOR COURT

7. Number of pages attached: [ ] SIGNATURE FOLLOWS LAST ATTACHMENT

Form Approved by the
Judicial Council of California
DE-140 [Rev. January 1, 1998]
Mandatory Form [1/1/2000]

ORDER FOR PROBATE

Probate Code, §§ 8006, 8400

Supplement to Petition for Probate of Will

John J. Smith
202 Park Street
Los Angeles, California 90087
Telephone: 213-555-8754

Petitioner in pro per

SUPERIOR COURT OF CALIFORNIA

FOR THE COUNTY OF LOS ANGELES

Estate of	) No. P 394860
	)
DOROTHY JANE SMITH	)
aka DOROTHY SMITH	) SUPPLEMENT TO PETITION FOR PROBATE
aka DOROTHY J. SMITH	) OF WILL AND FOR LETTERS TESTAMENTARY
	)
deceased.	) 5/30/xx, 9:15 A.M., Dept. 5
	)

The undersigned is the petitioner in the above-entitled proceeding. As a supplement to Paragraph 6 of the Petition for Probate of Will and for Letters Testamentary on file herein, the undersigned alleges as follows:

Carol Brown, daughter of the decedent, is the same person named as Carol Marie Smith in paragraph FIRST of the decedent's will.

I declare under penalty of perjury under the laws of the State of California that the foregoing is true and correct and that this declaration is executed on May 27, 20xx, at Los Angeles, California.

_____
John J. Smith

This supplement corrects the following problem: The decedent's daughter, Carol Brown, was married after the will was made, and was listed as an heir in the petition under her married name. Because she was named in the will under her maiden name, the court wanted proof that Carol Marie Smith was the same person and not someone else who was inadvertently omitted as an heir.

Bond (Personal) on Qualifying (page 1)

```
 1 │  Name:
   │  Address:
 2 │
   │
 3 │
   │  Telephone No.:
 4 │
 5 │  Petitioner in pro per
 6 │
 7 │
 8 │                    SUPERIOR COURT OF CALIFORNIA
   │                    COUNTY OF _____
 9 │
10 │  Estate of          ) NO.
   │   (name of decedent),  ) BOND (PERSONAL) ON QUALIFYING
11 │          deceased    )
12 │  _____ )
13 │
14 │      I, _(name of representative)_____, as principal and _(name of first surety)____,
15 │  and _(name of second surety)_____, as sureties, are bound to the State
16 │  of California in the sum of $_____. We bind ourselves, our
17 │  heirs, executors, and administrators, jointly and severally, to pay
18 │  in event of breach of this bond.
19 │      This bond is being executed under an order of the Superior
20 │  Court of California for _____ County,
21 │  made on _____, 20____, by which _(name of representative)____ was
22 │  appointed _(executor/administrator)_____ of the estate of the above-
23 │  named decedent, and letters _(testamentary/of administration)____ were directed
24 │  to be issued to _(name of representative)_____ on executing a bond under the
25 │  laws of California.
26 │
27 │
28 │
```

1.

Bond (Personal) on Qualifying

Bond (Personal) on Qualifying (page 2)

1 If _____, as _____, faithfully executes

2 the duties of the trust according to the law, this obligation shall

3 become void; otherwise, it will remain in effect.

4

5 DATED:_____   _____

6   (Name of Representative)

7 DATED:_____   _____

8   (Name of First Surety)

9 DATED:_____   _____

                            (Name of Second Surety)

10

11

12   DECLARATION OF SURETIES

13 _____ and _____, the sureties named in

14 the above bond state, each for himself/herself, declare that he/she

15 is a householder or property owner and resides within said state

16 and is worth the sum of

17 $_____ over and above all his debts and liabilities, exclusive

18 of property exempt from execution.

19   Signed and dated at _____, California, on

20 _____, 20__. I declare under penalty of perjury under the

21 laws of the State of California that the foregoing is true and

  correct.

22

23   _____

24   (First Surety)

25   _____

26   (Second Surety)

27

28

Bond (Personal) on Qualifying

If the calendar notes indicate bond is required, it must be filed before letters will be issued. See "Probate Bonds" in Chapter 13 for how to arrange for bond. A sample of a bond that may be used for personal sureties is shown above. Remember, when personal sureties are used, the bond must be in twice the amount required. The court should be contacted in advance to determine what evidence, if any, of net worth the sureties will have to show.

Step 10: Prepare the Letters

When the judge signs the order for probate appointing you as the estate representative, the court will issue to you the "letters" that confirm your appointment. However, you must prepare the letters that the court will issue to you.

Letters Testamentary or Letters of Administration are both prepared on the same form. Instructions and a sample form are shown below. You may sign the letters prior to the hearing date and send them to the court at the same time you mail the Order for Probate, as discussed in Step 8.

You should order at least two certified copies of the letters by enclosing a check payable to the "Clerk of Superior Court" in an amount sufficient to cover the court's certification fees, usually around $25 for each certified copy. You can call the court for the exact amount or look it up on the court's website. The certified copies are usually needed right away to transfer bank accounts from the decedent's name to that of the estate. You may order additional certified copies now, or later, if you need them. Be sure that your signature on the letters is not dated prior to the date you filed your petition.

How to Fill Out the Letters

Caption: Fill in your name, address, the court's name, and case number, as you have on your other court papers.

Letters: Check "testamentary" if there is a will, or the box under that if you are administrator with will annexed. Check "of administration" if there is no will.

Item 1: If there is no will, go to Item 2. If there is a will, check the first box and type the name of the representative below it. Then check either Box a or b, and go to Item 3.

Item 2: If there is no will, type in the name of the administrator and check Box a.

Item 3: Check this box and indicate whether you petitioned for full or limited authority under the Independent Administration of Estates Act.

Item 4: If possession of bank accounts or other assets has been blocked by the court, check this box.

Leave the rest of this half blank.

Affirmation: Check Box 2 and sign the form, and fill in the date and city.

Step 11: Prepare the Duties and Liabilities of Personal Representative Form

The Duties and Liabilities of Personal Representative form (DE-147) provides a summary of your responsibilities as personal representative. You must read it, fill out and sign the acknowledgment of receipt, and file it along with the letters. Check with your county's local probate rules to see if you are required to file the addendum to this form, the Confidential Supplement to Duties and Liabilities of Personal Representative form (DE-147S). This is a form where you list your date of birth and driver's license number. In courts where this form is required, the clerk will file it separately so that it does not become a public record. Samples of the Duties and Liabilities form and the Confidential Supplement are shown below, and tear-out copies are in Appendix B.

Letters

DE-150

ATTORNEY OR PARTY WITHOUT ATTORNEY (Name, state bar number, and address):	TELEPHONE AND FAX NOS.:	FOR COURT USE ONLY
Billy M. Kidd 1109 Sky Blue Mountain Trail Billings, Montana 48906	715-555-6408	

ATTORNEY FOR (Name): In pro per

SUPERIOR COURT OF CALIFORNIA, COUNTY OF LOS ANGELES

STREET ADDRESS: 1725 Main Street
MAILING ADDRESS: 1725 Main Street
CITY AND ZIP CODE: Santa Monica, CA 90401
BRANCH NAME: WEST DISTRICT

ESTATE OF (Name):

ANABELLE KIDD, aka
ANABELLE O. KIDD, DECEDENT

LETTERS

[X] **TESTAMENTARY**   [ ] **OF ADMINISTRATION**
[ ] **OF ADMINISTRATION WITH WILL ANNEXED**   [ ] **SPECIAL ADMINISTRATION**

CASE NUMBER:
WEP 14813

LETTERS

1. [X] The last will of the decedent named above having been proved, the court appoints (name):

   Billy M. Kidd
   a. [X] executor.
   b. [ ] administrator with will annexed.

2. [ ] The court appoints (name):

   a. [ ] administrator of the decedent's estate.
   b. [ ] special administrator of decedent's estate
       (1) [ ] with the special powers specified in the *Order for Probate*.
       (2) [ ] with the powers of a general administrator.
       (3) [ ] letters will expire on (date):

3. [X] The personal representative is authorized to administer the estate under the Independent Administration of Estates Act   [X] **with full authority**
      [ ] **with limited authority** (no authority, without court supervision, to (1) sell or exchange real property or (2) grant an option to purchase real property or (3) borrow money with the loan secured by an encumbrance upon real property).

4. [ ] The personal representative is not authorized to take possession of money or any other property without a specific court order.

WITNESS, clerk of the court, with seal of the court affixed.

(SEAL)   Date:

Clerk, by

_____
(DEPUTY)

AFFIRMATION

1. [ ] PUBLIC ADMINISTRATOR: No affirmation required (Prob. Code, § 7621(c)).

2. [X] INDIVIDUAL: **I solemnly affirm** that I will perform the duties of personal representative according to law.

3. [ ] INSTITUTIONAL FIDUCIARY (name):

   I solemnly affirm that the institution will perform the duties of personal representative according to law. I make this affirmation for myself as an individual and on behalf of the institution as an officer.
   (Name and title):

4. Executed on (date): July 20, 20xx
   at (place): Santa Monica , California.

▶ *Billy M. Kidd*
_____
(SIGNATURE)

CERTIFICATION

I certify that this document is a correct copy of the original on file in my office and the letters issued by the personal representative appointed above have not been revoked, annulled, or set aside, and are still in full force and effect.

(SEAL)   Date:

Clerk, by

_____
(DEPUTY)

Form Approved by the
Judicial Council of California
DE-150 [Rev. January 1, 1998]
Mandatory Form [1/1/2000]

LETTERS
(Probate)

Probate Code, §§ 1001, 8403,
8405, 8544, 8545;
Code of Civil Procedure, § 2015.6

Duties and Liabilities of Personal Representative (front)

DE-147

ATTORNEY OR PARTY WITHOUT ATTORNEY *(Name, state bar number, and address):*

Billy M. Kidd
1109 Sky Blue Mountain Trail
Billings, Montana 48906
TELEPHONE NO: 715-555-6408   FAX NO. *(Optional):*
E-MAIL ADDRESS *(Optional):*
ATTORNEY FOR *(Name):* In pro per

FOR COURT USE ONLY

SUPERIOR COURT OF CALIFORNIA, COUNTY OF   LOS ANGELES
STREET ADDRESS: 1725 Main Street
MAILING ADDRESS: 1725 Main Street
CITY AND ZIP CODE: Santa Monica, CA 90401
BRANCH NAME: WEST DISTRICT

ESTATE OF *(Name):*   ANABELLE KIDD, aka
ANABELLE O. KIDD,   DECEDENT

DUTIES AND LIABILITIES OF PERSONAL REPRESENTATIVE
and Acknowledgment of Receipt

CASE NUMBER:
WEP 14813

DUTIES AND LIABILITIES OF PERSONAL REPRESENTATIVE

When the court appoints you as personal representative of an estate, you become an officer of the court and assume certain duties and obligations. An attorney is best qualified to advise you about these matters. You should understand the following:

1. MANAGING THE ESTATE'S ASSETS

a. Prudent investments
You must manage the estate assets with the care of a prudent person dealing with someone else's property. This means that you must be cautious and may not make any speculative investments.

b. Keep estate assets separate
You must keep the money and property in this estate separate from anyone else's, including your own. When you open a bank account for the estate, the account name must indicate that it is an estate account and not your personal account. Never deposit estate funds in your personal account or otherwise mix them with your or anyone else's property. Securities in the estate must also be held in a name that shows they are estate property and not your personal property.

c. Interest-bearing accounts and other investments
Except for checking accounts intended for ordinary administration expenses, estate accounts must earn interest. You may deposit estate funds in insured accounts in financial institutions, but you should consult with an attorney before making other kinds of investments.

d. Other restrictions
There are many other restrictions on your authority to deal with estate property. You should not spend any of the estate's money unless you have received permission from the court or have been advised to do so by an attorney. You may reimburse yourself for official court costs paid by you to the county clerk and for the premium on your bond. Without prior order of the court, you may not pay fees to yourself or to your attorney, if you have one. If you do not obtain the court's permission when it is required, you may be removed as personal representative or you may be required to reimburse the estate from your own personal funds, or both. You should consult with an attorney concerning the legal requirements affecting sales, leases, mortgages, and investments of estate property.

2. INVENTORY OF ESTATE PROPERTY

a. Locate the estate's property
You must attempt to locate and take possession of all the decedent's property to be administered in the estate.

b. Determine the value of the property
You must arrange to have a court-appointed referee determine the value of the property unless the appointment is waived by the court. You, rather than the referee, must determine the value of certain "cash items." An attorney can advise you about how to do this.

c. File an inventory and appraisal
Within four months after Letters are first issued to you as personal representative, you must file with the court an inventory and appraisal of all the assets in the estate.

Page 1 of 2

Duties and Liabilities of Personal Representative (back)

ESTATE OF *(Name)*:		CASE NUMBER:
ANABELLE KIDD,	DECEDENT	WEP 14813

d. File a change of ownership
At the time you file the inventory and appraisal, you must also file a change of ownership statement with the county recorder or assessor in each county where the decedent owned real property at the time of death, as provided in section 480 of the California Revenue and Taxation Code.

3. NOTICE TO CREDITORS

You must mail a notice of administration to each known creditor of the decedent within four months after your appointment as personal representative. If the decedent received Medi-Cal assistance, you must notify the State Director of Health Services within 90 days after appointment.

4. INSURANCE

You should determine that there is appropriate and adequate insurance covering the assets and risks of the estate. Maintain the insurance in force during the entire period of the administration.

5. RECORD KEEPING

a. Keep accounts
You must keep complete and accurate records of each financial transaction affecting the estate. You will have to prepare an account of all money and property you have received, what you have spent, and the date of each transaction. You must describe in detail what you have left after the payment of expenses.

b. Court review
Your account will be reviewed by the court. Save your receipts because the court may ask to review them. If you do not file your accounts as required, the court will order you to do so. You may be removed as personal representative if you fail to comply.

6. CONSULTING AN ATTORNEY

If you have an attorney, you should cooperate with the attorney at all times. You and your attorney are responsible for completing the estate administration as promptly as possible. **When in doubt, contact your attorney.**

> **NOTICE:** 1. **This statement of duties and liabilities is a summary and is not a complete statement of the law. Your conduct as a personal representative is governed by the law itself and not by this summary.**
> 2. **If you fail to perform your duties or to meet the deadlines, the court may reduce your compensation, remove you from office, and impose other sanctions.**

ACKNOWLEDGMENT OF RECEIPT

1. I have petitioned the court to be appointed as a personal representative.

2. My address and telephone number are *(specify):*   1109 Sky Blue Mountain Trail
Billings, MT 48906
Tel # 715-555-6408

3. I acknowledge that I have received a copy of this statement of the duties and liabilities of the office of personal representative.

Date: JULY 20, 20xx

Billy M. Kidd   ▶ *Billy M. Kidd*
_____   _____
(TYPE OR PRINT NAME)   (SIGNATURE OF PETITIONER)

Date:

                                                                    ▶
_____   _____
(TYPE OR PRINT NAME)   (SIGNATURE OF PETITIONER)

> **CONFIDENTIAL INFORMATION:** If required to do so by local court rule, you must provide your date of birth and driver's license number on supplemental Form DE-147S. (Prob. Code, § 8404(b).)

DE-147 [Rev. January 1, 2002]   **DUTIES AND LIABILITIES OF PERSONAL REPRESENTATIVE**   Page 2 of 2
(Probate)

Confidential Supplement to Duties and Liabilities of Personal Representative

CONFIDENTIAL

DE-147S

ESTATE OF *(Name)*:

ANABELLE KIDD,   DECEDENT

CASE NUMBER:

WEP 14813

CONFIDENTIAL STATEMENT OF BIRTH DATE
AND DRIVER'S LICENSE NUMBER

(Supplement to *Duties and Liabilities of Personal Representative* (Form DE-147))

*(NOTE: This supplement is to be used if the court by local rule requires the personal representative to provide a birth date and driver's license number. Do **not** attach this supplement to Form DE-147.)*

This separate *Confidential Statement of Birth Date and Driver's License Number* contains confidential information relating to the personal representative in the case referenced above. This supplement shall be kept separate from the *Duties and Liabilities of Personal Representative* filed in this case and shall not be a public record.

INFORMATION ON THE PERSONAL REPRESENTATIVE:

1. Name: Billy M. Kidd

2. Date of birth: 7-11-54

3. Driver's license number: BO 8339025   State: Montana

TO COURT CLERK:
THIS STATEMENT IS **CONFIDENTIAL**. DO NOT FILE
THIS CONFIDENTIAL STATEMENT IN A PUBLIC COURT FILE.

Form Adopted for Mandatory Use
Judicial Council of California
DE-147S [New January 1, 2001]

**CONFIDENTIAL SUPPLEMENT TO DUTIES AND
LIABILITIES OF PERSONAL REPRESENTATIVE**
(Probate)

Probate Code, § 8404

Step 12: Prepare the Application Appointing Probate Referee

All noncash assets must be appraised by a probate referee appointed by the court. In most counties, and in the branch courts in Los Angeles, you don't have to request appointment of a referee; the court does it automatically. The sample form shown below is used only in the Central District in Los Angeles County. Some other counties also have their own forms—check with your local court to see if you must file a form to have a referee appointed.

As you'll see on the sample form below, you must set forth the approximate value of the cash, real estate, and other property in the estate. These figures need only be estimates. If you submit a duplicate copy of this form to the court with a self-addressed, stamped envelope, the clerk will return a conformed copy with the name, address, and telephone number of the referee. You can submit the application to the court with the Order for Probate or at a later date. A sample cover letter is shown below.

Step 13: Prepare Notice of Proposed Action, If Necessary

After letters are issued, you must wait four months before you may close the estate. This gives creditors time to file claims against the estate. During this period, you will take care of such things as estate bank accounts, tax returns, and the estate inventory.

You may also find it necessary to perform some of the acts allowed by the Independent Administration of Estates Act (discussed in Chapter 13). Some of these require a Notice of Proposed Action. It is usually required for the sale of estate property, with some exceptions as discussed in Chapter 13. Most courts want the original action notice, and any waiver or consent obtained, to be filed with the court with proof that it was given to all interested persons. Instructions for filling out the notice and a sample notice are shown below with a proof of service.

"Interested persons" are those whose interest in the estate would be affected by the proposed action. For example, if real property is to be sold, all persons entitled to inherit an interest in the property must be given the notice. A beneficiary receiving only a cash gift, or other specific property, is not entitled to notice. Anyone who has filed a Request for Special Notice with the court, however, must be given the notice, regardless of whether that person is entitled to any part of the property.

How to Fill Out a Notice of Proposed Action

Caption: Fill in your name, address, the court's name, and case number, as on other court papers.

Item 1: Type in name of executor or administrator.

Item 2: Check the box that indicates whether you petitioned for full or limited authority under the Independent Administration of Estates Act.

Item 3: Fill in the date of the proposed action, which must be at least 15 days after the date of this notice, unless all interested persons sign the consent on the back. Describe the action if there is room, or check the box if you describe it in an attachment.

Item 4: Check this box if the proposed action is a real estate transaction, and fill in the information.

Item 5: Fill in your name and address.

Item 7: Type in your name and phone number. Print or type your name, enter the date, and sign.

Leave the rest of the form blank; it is for the recipient.

Application and Order Appointing Probate Referee

NAME, ADDRESS, AND TELEPHONE NUMBER OF ATTORNEY OR PARTY WITHOUT ATTORNEY:	STATE BAR NUMBER	*Reserved for Clerk's File Stamp*
Fill in same heading as on petition		

ATTORNEY FOR (Name):

SUPERIOR COURT OF CALIFORNIA, COUNTY OF LOS ANGELES

COURTHOUSE ADDRESS:

Estate of:

Check this box

☐ DECEDENT   ☐ CONSERVATEE   ☐ MINOR

APPLICATION AND ORDER APPOINTING PROBATE REFEREE

CASE NUMBER:

It is requested that a Probate Referee be appointed to appraise the assets of the above-entitled estate consisting of the following approximate values:

1.   CASH $ __Approximate amount of cash in estate__

2.   REAL ESTATE $ __Approximate value of real property. If no real property, put "none."__

3.   PERSONAL PROPERTY $ __Approximate value of all other property__

REMARKS   __Leave this section blank__ _____

_____

Dated: ___**Date**_____   _____**Sign here**_____
                                                              Signature of Applicant

IT IS ORDERED that (name):

a disinterested person is appointed Probate Referee to appraise the above-entitled estate. The Probate Referee is authorized to establish the fair market value of the estate as of the date of death of the decedent, or as of the date of appointment of a conservator or guardian, under the laws of the State of California.

Dated: _____   _____
                                                              Judge of the Superior Court

_____

APPLICATION AND ORDER APPOINTING PROBATE REFEREE

PRO 001 01-02   Probate Code ☐ 8920

Letter to Court

July 12, 20xx

Clerk of the Superior Court
1725 Main Street
Santa Monica, California 90401

Re: Estate of ANABELLE KIDD, deceased
        Case No. WEP 14813
        Hearing Date: July 25, 20xx

Dear Sir or Madam:

Enclosed are the original and one copy of the following documents:

1.   Notice of Petition to Administer Estate (with proof of service by mail)

2.   Order for Probate

3.   Letters, and

4.   Duties and Liabilities of Personal Representative.

Please file the original documents with the court and return the extra copies, conformed, in the enclosed stamped, self-addressed envelope.

Please return two certified copies of letters. A check is enclosed to cover your certification fees.

Very truly yours,

Billy M. Kidd

Billy M. Kidd

Notice of Proposed Action (front)

DE-165

ATTORNEY OR PARTY WITHOUT ATTORNEY *(Name, state bar number, and address):*	TELEPHONE AND FAX NOS.:	FOR COURT USE ONLY
Billy M. Kidd 1109 Sky Blue Mountain Trail Billings, Montana 48906	715-555-6408	

ATTORNEY FOR *(Name):*   In pro per

SUPERIOR COURT OF CALIFORNIA, COUNTY OF LOS ANGELES

STREET ADDRESS: 1725 Main Street
MAILING ADDRESS: 1725 Main Street
CITY AND ZIP CODE: Santa Monica, CA 90401
BRANCH NAME: WEST DISTRICT

ESTATE OF *(Name):*

ANABELLE KIDD, aka
ANABELLE O. KIDD,   DECEDENT

NOTICE OF PROPOSED ACTION
Independent Administration of Estates Act
☐ Objection ☐ Consent

CASE NUMBER:

WEP 14813

> **NOTICE:** If you do not object in writing or obtain a court order preventing the action proposed below, you will be treated as if you consented to the proposed action and you may not object after the proposed action has been taken. If you object, the personal representative may take the proposed action only under court supervision. An objection form is on the reverse. If you wish to object, you may use the form or prepare your own written objection.

1. The personal representative (executor or administrator) of the estate of the deceased is *(names):*

   Billy M. Kidd

2. The personal representative has authority to administer the estate without court supervision under the Independent Administration of Estates Act (Prob. Code, § 10400 et seq.)
   a. ☒ with **full authority** under the act.
   b. ☐ with **limited authority** under the act (there is no authority, without court supervision, to (1) sell or exchange real property or (2) grant an option to purchase real property or (3) borrow money with the loan secured by an encumbrance upon real property).

3. **On or after** *(date):* ☐ August 20, 20xx ☐ , the personal representative will take the following action without court supervision *(describe in specific terms here or in Attachment 3):*
   ☐ The proposed action is described in an attachment labeled Attachment 3.

   The Executor will sell the real property located at 9560 Euclid Street, Santa Monica, California, for a total sales price of $129,000, all cash. Buyer to obtain own financing. Property to be sold as is, and seller will not make any repairs nor provide any warranty on house and other structures on lot. Sales price includes all built-in appliances. Seller to pay broker's commission of 6% of sales price, allocated as follows: 3% to Exceptional Real Estate and 3% to J. F. Realty. Seller to furnish buyer at seller's expense a California Land Title Association policy issued by Commonwealth Land Title Insurance. County transfer tax and documentary transfer fee to be paid by seller.

4. ☒ **Real property transaction** *(Check this box and complete item 4b if the proposed action involves a sale or exchange or a grant of an option to purchase real property.)*
   a. The material terms of the transaction are specified in item 3, including any sale price and the amount of or method of calculating any commission or compensation to an agent or broker.
   b. $ _____ is the value of the subject property in the probate inventory.   ☒ No inventory yet.

> **NOTICE:** A sale of real property without court supervision means that the sale will **NOT** be presented to the court for confirmation at a hearing at which higher bids for the property may be presented and the property sold to the highest bidder.

(Continued on reverse)

NOTICE OF PROPOSED ACTION
Objection—Consent
(Probate)

Probate Code, § 10580 et seq.

Notice of Proposed Action (back)

ESTATE OF *(Name)*:	CASE NUMBER:
ANABELLE KIDD, DECEDENT	WEP 14813

5. **If you OBJECT to the proposed action**
   a. **Sign** the objection form below and deliver or mail it to the personal representative at the following address *(specify name and address)*: Billy M. Kidd
      1109 Sky Blue Mountain Trail, Billings, Montana 48906
      OR
   b. **Send** your own written objection to the address in item 5a. *(Be sure to identify the proposed action and state that you object to it.)*
      OR
   c. **Apply** to the court for an order preventing the personal representative from taking the proposed action without court supervision.

   d. **NOTE:** Your written objection or the court order must be received by the personal representative before the date in the box in item 3, or before the proposed action is taken, whichever is later. If you object, the personal representative may take the proposed action only under court supervision.

6. **If you APPROVE the proposed action**, you may sign the consent form below and return it to the address in item 5a. If you do not object in writing or obtain a court order, you will be treated as if you consented to the proposed action.

7. **If you need more INFORMATION, call** *(name)*: Billy M. Kidd
   (telephone): 715-555-6408

Date: August 3, 20xx

.....Billy M. Kidd.....................
(TYPE OR PRINT NAME)

▶ *Billy M. Kidd*
(SIGNATURE OF PERSONAL REPRESENTATIVE OR ATTORNEY)

OBJECTION TO PROPOSED ACTION

[ ] **I OBJECT** to the action proposed in item 3.

> **NOTICE: Sign and return this form (both sides) to the address in item 5a. The form must be received before the date in the box in item 3, or before the proposed action is taken, whichever is later.** *(You may want to use certified mail, with return receipt requested. Make a copy of this form for your records.)*

Date:

. . . .
(TYPE OR PRINT NAME)

▶
(SIGNATURE OF OBJECTOR)

CONSENT TO PROPOSED ACTION

[ ] **I CONSENT** to the action proposed in item 3.

> **NOTICE: You may indicate your *consent* by signing and returning this form (both sides) to the address in item 5a. If you do not object in writing or obtain a court order, you will be treated as if you consented to the proposed action.**

Date:

. . . .
(TYPE OR PRINT NAME)

▶
(SIGNATURE OF CONSENTER)

DE-165 [Rev. January 1, 1998]

NOTICE OF PROPOSED ACTION
Objection—Consent
(Probate)

Page two

Proof of Service

BILLY M. KIDD
1109 Sky Blue Mountain Trail
Billings, Montana 48906

Telephone: 715-555-6408
Petitioner in pro per

SUPERIOR COURT OF CALIFORNIA

FOR THE COUNTY OF LOS ANGELES

Estate of	) CASE NO. WEP 14813
	)
ANABELLE KIDD, aka	) PROOF OF SERVICE BY MAIL OF
ANABELLE O. KIDD	) NOTICE OF PROPOSED ACTION
	)
deceased.	)
	)

STATE OF MONTANA, COUNTY OF BILLINGS;

   I am a resident of the county aforesaid; I am over the age of eighteen

years and not a party to the within entitled action; my business address is:

1809 - G Street, Billings, Montana.

   On August 3, 20xx, I served the attached NOTICE OF PROPOSED

ACTION on the interested parties by placing a true copy thereof enclosed in

a sealed envelope with postage thereon fully prepaid in the United States mail

at Billings, Montana, addressed as follows:

   Mary Kidd Clark, 789 Main Street, Venice, California 90410

   Carson Kidd, 711 Valley Road, Owens, California 98455

   I declare under penalty of perjury under the laws of the State of

California that the foregoing is true and correct.

DATED: August 10, 20xx   *Mary Smith*
                              Mary Smith

Proof of Service by Mail of Notice of Proposed Action

Sale of Real Property

When real property is sold under the Independent Administration of Estates Act, the title company will require the following documents:

- copy of the Notice of Proposed Action, with a proof of mailing showing that the Notice was given within the time period required
- certified copy of your Letters Testamentary, and
- a special deed, referred to as an Executor's Deed. A sample is shown below. You can find a blank form in Appendix C.

Sale of Securities

You may want to sell securities during probate to raise cash or to facilitate distribution when there are multiple beneficiaries. You should contact a stockbroker to handle the sale, which will take about 28 to 30 days to complete. See Chapter 9 on the documentation required. No prior court approval is necessary, and no Notice of Proposed Action is required to sell securities over the counter or when listed on an established stock or bond exchange when sold for cash. (Prob. Code §§ 10200(e)(2) and 10537(b)(1).) If a transfer agent nevertheless insists on a court order, you may file a short form with the court called Ex Parte Petition for Authority to Sell Securities and obtain the order without a court hearing. A sample is shown below. Here are instructions for preparing it.

If the will gives you, as executor, authority to sell property, check Box 2b. Otherwise, you must state the necessity for the sale in Item 2c. In many counties it is sufficient to allege that the sale is made to avoid distribution of undivided interests. Check Item 2d and indicate in Item 2e whether requests for special notice are on file. If so, a Waiver of Request for Special Notice must be attached. Use the Waiver of Bond form as a guide (see Petition for Probate). If the stock is specifically bequeathed, say so and attach the written consent of the beneficiaries.

On the reverse side of the form, list the correct name of each company, the precise number of shares or bonds to be sold, and the name of the exchange on which the security is traded, if so traded. Another column is provided for inserting recent "bid" and "asked" quotations for a security that is traded but not on an established exchange. If a security is traded on an exchange, the minimum selling price need not be stated. Otherwise, a minimum price should be provided that is approximately 10% below current trading prices to allow for fluctuations between the time the order is obtained and the time the stock is sold. If mutual fund shares are to be redeemed, insert in the minimum-selling-price column a statement that "the shares will be redeemed by the issuer for the net asset value per share on the date of redemption."

When the petition is ready to file, check with the court to find out its procedures for obtaining ex parte orders. It is usually advisable to file the petition in person to obtain the order quickly, rather than mail it to the court. Once the order has been signed, one certified copy must be obtained for each issuer listed in the petition.

Executor's Deed

RECORDING REQUESTED BY:

Billy M. Kidd

WHEN RECORDED MAIL TO:

1109 Sky Blue Mountain Trail
Billings, Montana 48906

SPACE ABOVE THIS LINE FOR RECORDER'S USE

DEED TO REAL PROPERTY

I, <u>Billy M. Kidd</u>, as <u>Executor</u>
of the Estate of <u>Anabelle Kidd, aka Anaabelle O. Kidd</u>, deceased, pursuant to authority
granted to me by Order of the Superior Court of California, for the County of <u>Los Angeles</u>,
on <u>July 25, 20xx</u>, in Case No. <u>WEP14813</u>, to administer the Estate of
<u>Anabelle Kidd, aka Anabelle O. Kidd</u>, deceased, under the Independent Administration
of Estates Act, and pursuant to Notice of Proposed Action duly given under the provisions of Probate Code Sections 10580,
et seq., do hereby convey to <u>John A. Buyer, an unmarried man</u>
as <u>his separate property</u>, without any representation, warranty,
or covenant of any kind, express or implied, all right, title, interest, and estate of the decedent at the time of death, and
all right, title, and interest that the estate may have subsequently acquired in the real property situated in the County of
<u>Los Angeles</u>, State of California, described as follows.

Lot 11 in Block 9 of Tract 5721, as per map recorded in Book 63, Page 31 of
Maps in the Office of the County Recorder of said county. Commonly known as
9560 Euclid Street, Santa Monica, Calif.

Assessor's Parcel No. <u>346-047-379</u>

Dated: <u>August 30, 20xx</u>   *Billy M. Kidd*
                          Signature

STATE OF CALIFORNIA   )
) ss.
COUNTY OF <u>Los Angeles</u>   )

   On <u>August 30, 20xx</u>, before me, the undersigned, a Notary Public in and for said State, personally
appeared <u>Billy M. Kidd</u>, as <u>Executor</u> of
the Estate of <u>Anabelle Kidd</u>, deceased, who proved to
me on the basis of satisfactory evidence to be the person(s) whose name(s) is/are subscribed to the within instrument and
acknowledged to me that he/she/they executed the same in his/her/their authorized capacity(ies), and that by his/her/their
signature(s) on the instrument the person(s) or entity upon behalf of which the person(s) acted, executed the instrument.

I certify under PENALTY OF PERJURY under the laws of the State of California that the foregoing paragraph is true and
correct.

WITNESS my hand and official seal.

   Nancy Notary
      (Notary Public)

Ex Parte Petition for Authority to Sell Securities and Order (page 1)

		DE-270, GC-070
ATTORNEY OR PARTY WITHOUT ATTORNEY *(Name, state bar number, and address):* TELEPHONE AND FAX NOS.:		FOR COURT USE ONLY

ATTORNEY OR PARTY WITHOUT ATTORNEY *(Name, state bar number, and address):*

Billy M. Kidd   715-555-6408
1109 Sky Blue Mountain Trail
Billings, Montana

ATTORNEY FOR *(Name):* In pro per

SUPERIOR COURT OF CALIFORNIA, COUNTY OF Los Angeles
   STREET ADDRESS: 1725 Main Street
   MAILING ADDRESS: 1725 Main Street
   CITY AND ZIP CODE: Santa Monica, CA 90401
   BRANCH NAME: WEST DISTRICT

ESTATE OF *(Name):*   ANABELLE KIDD, aka ANABELLE O. KIDD

[X] DECEDENT   [ ] CONSERVATEE   [ ] MINOR

EX PARTE PETITION FOR AUTHORITY TO SELL SECURITIES AND ORDER

CASE NUMBER:
WEP 14813

1. **Petitioner** *(name of each; see footnote¹ before completing):*   Billy M. Kidd

   is the [X] personal representative [ ] conservator [ ] guardian   of the estate and requests a court order authorizing sale of estate securities.

2. a. The estate's securities described on the reverse should be sold for cash at the market price at the time of sale on an established stock or bond exchange, or, if unlisted, the sale will be made for not less than the minimum price stated on the reverse.
   b. [ ] Authority is given in decedent's will to sell property; **or**
   c. [X] The sale is necessary to raise cash to pay
       (1) [ ] debts
       (2) [ ] legacies
       (3) [ ] family allowance
       (4) [ ] expenses
       (5) [ ] support of ward
       (6) [X] other *(specify):* To avoid distribution of undivided interests

   d. [x] The sale is for the advantage, benefit, and best interests of the estate, and those interested in the estate.
   e. Other facts pertinent to this petition are as follows:
       (1) [X] Special notice has not been requested.
       (2) [ ] Waivers of all special notices are presented with this petition.
       (3) [X] No security to be sold is specifically bequeathed.
       (4) [ ] Other *(specify):*

Date:

* (Signature of all petitioners also required (Prob. Code, § 1020).)

▶ (not applicable)
(SIGNATURE OF ATTORNEY *)

I declare under penalty of perjury under the laws of the State of California that the foregoing is true and correct.

Date: September 12, 20xx

. . . . Billy M. Kidd . . . .
(TYPE OR PRINT NAME)

▶ *Billy M. Kidd*
(SIGNATURE OF PETITIONER)

. . . .
(TYPE OR PRINT NAME)

▶
(SIGNATURE OF PETITIONER)

¹ Each personal representative, guardian, or conservator must sign the petition.

(Continued on reverse)

Form Approved by the
Judicial Council of California
DE-270, GC-070 [Rev. January 1, 1998]
Mandatory Form [1/1/2000]

**EX PARTE PETITION FOR AUTHORITY
TO SELL SECURITIES AND ORDER**

Probate Code, §§ 9630, 10000,
10200, 10201, 10252, 10261

Ex Parte Petition for Authority to Sell Securities and Order (page 2)

ESTATE OF *(Name):*	CASE NUMBER:
ANABELLE KIDD, deceased	WEP 14813

LIST OF SECURITIES

Number of shares or face value of bonds	Name of security	Name of exchange *(when required by local rule)*	Recent bid asked *(when required by local rule)*	Minimum selling price
250 shares	Federated Department Stores, Inc., common	NYSE		

ORDER AUTHORIZING SALE OF SECURITIES

THE COURT FINDS the sale is proper.

THE COURT ORDERS

The ☐ personal representative ☐ guardian ☐ conservator is authorized to sell the securities described above upon the terms and conditions specified. Notice of hearing on the petition is dispensed with.

Date:

_____
JUDGE OF THE SUPERIOR COURT
☐ SIGNATURE FOLLOWS LAST ATTACHMENT

**EX PARTE PETITION FOR AUTHORITY
TO SELL SECURITIES AND ORDER**

Step 14: Prepare the Inventory and Appraisal Form

On this important form, you list all of the decedent's property that is subject to probate in California. The noncash assets listed on the Inventory and Appraisal must be appraised by a probate referee who has been appointed by court order. (For information on the appointment of the probate referee, see Step 12.) All probate assets are appraised as of the date of death.

General Instructions

The inventory of the probate assets must be filed within four months after letters are issued. (Prob. Code § 8800.) Some courts (for example, Riverside County) strictly enforce this rule, so we recommend that the inventory be prepared as soon as possible on the form shown below. The description of the probate assets will follow the same general format as on the Schedule of Assets you prepared (Chapter 5), with these additional requirements:

1. If the decedent owned only a partial interest in an asset (for example, a one-half or one-third interest with others), indicate this in the beginning of your description. For example, a "one-half interest in promissory note secured by deed of trust …" or a "one-third interest in real property located at …." It must be made clear in the description that the decedent owned only a part interest; otherwise the referee will appraise the asset at its full value, which would be incorrect.

2. Be sure you list only assets subject to probate that were owned at the date of death.

3. The full *legal description* of all real property must be given. You must also include the assessor's parcel number, which you can find on the property tax bill.

4. For a mortgage or deed of trust secured by real property, include the recording reference or, if not recorded, a legal description of the real property. (Caution: If an encumbrance on real property is unrecorded, you should immediately see an attorney to take steps to make an estate's lien claim a matter of record.)

5. Indicate whether the property is community, quasi-community, or separate property of the decedent. If community property passes outright to the surviving spouse or domestic partner, it doesn't require probate (unless the surviving spouse or partner wishes the property to be probated) and is not listed on the inventory. (See Chapter 15.) If the decedent willed his or her one-half interest in community property to someone else, however, it is listed.

As you can see, the form itself is fairly short. This is because the assets are listed on separate attachment sheets stapled to the first page of the inventory. These attachments (the inventory of the assets) should list everything owned by the decedent at the time of death, except joint tenancy property, property held in trust (including living trusts), bank trust accounts (also called pay-on-death accounts), death benefits, and insurance proceeds payable to named beneficiaries. (You do, however, list insurance proceeds or death benefits payable to the estate.) Each asset must be numbered separately and fully described as shown in the samples below. Don't be afraid to call the referee and ask how to list a certain asset. If you have problems, obtain a pamphlet entitled *Probate Procedures Guide*, put out by the California Probate Referees Association. You can find it on the state controller's website at www.sco.ca.gov/eo_probate.html.

The first attachment (Attachment 1) is for assets for which the value is certain and which will be appraised by the personal representative. Under Probate Code § 8901, such assets include:

- money and checks, drafts, or money orders issued on or before the date of death that can be immediately converted to cash
- checks issued after the date of death for wages, or for refunds of tax and utility bills, medical insurance, and Medicare payments
- bank accounts and certificates of deposit
- money market funds or accounts, including a brokerage cash account, and
- insurance proceeds or retirement fund benefits payable in lump sum to the estate.

Each item should be specifically described and numbered consecutively, as in our example below.

Insert the value of each item in the column at the right, and show an overall total at the end.

All other property should be listed on Attachment 2, with the values left blank so the referee may fill in his or her appraisals. Our sample of Attachment 2 shows how to describe most noncash assets. The referee doesn't normally examine household items and personal effects, which means you should include an estimate of the value of these items in a cover letter when you forward the inventory to the referee. They are usually grouped together as one item and valued at what they would bring at a yard sale or if sold to someone who purchases household goods. In other words, they are not worth much. The referee will usually accept your suggested valuation, if it seems reasonable, and will insert it as the appraised value.

Instructions for the Inventory and Appraisal Form

Heading: In the large block titled "Inventory and Appraisal," check the box that says "Final." The other boxes are checked when a partial, supplemental, or corrected inventory is filed; however, in a simple estate, the initial inventory is usually the final inventory. In unusual circumstances, additional assets may be discovered after the filing of an inventory, in which case a supplemental inventory may be filed (checking the appropriate box) with separate attachments describing the additional assets. A supplemental inventory is sent to the referee and processed in the same way as the initial inventory.

Insert the date of death in the small box in the lower right corner of the heading.

Item 1: Fill in the total value of assets listed on Attachment 1.

Item 2: The total value of the assets appraised by the referee on Attachment 2 will be filled in by the referee.

Item 3: Check the first box, as indicated on the sample form, unless you are filing a partial or supplemental inventory, in which case you should check the next box.

Item 4: Check only if the assets are Attachment 1 assets that do not need to be appraised by a referee. The second box applies if the appointment of the referee has been waived and is usually left blank.

Item 5: If the inventory contains real property, you must file a Preliminary Change of Ownership Report with the county assessor's office when the inventory is filed with the court. The statement is filed in the county where the real property is located. (See Chapter 8.) Passage of title by inheritance is generally considered a change in ownership, requiring a reassessment for property tax purposes, unless the real property goes to a surviving spouse, surviving domestic partner, or decedent's children. Even if the property does go to a spouse, partner, or decedent's children, you must still file the statement.

Each county has its own form, which may be obtained by calling the county assessor's office. However, most accept forms furnished by other counties.

When the Inventory and Appraisal is filed, the personal representative must certify that either a Change in Ownership Statement has been filed or that the estate doesn't contain real property. (Prob. Code § 8800(d).) Do this by checking the applicable box in Item 5.

Items 6, 7, and 8 of Statement About the Bond: The statement about the bond must be completed in every Inventory and Appraisal. Check box 6 if bond was waived by the court.

If bond was required, check Box 7 and fill in the amount; when the appraised inventory is returned to you by the probate referee, check to make sure that the amount of the bond is sufficient. The two boxes in Item 7 that say "sufficient" or "insufficient" are for this purpose. To be sufficient, the amount of the bond should be equal to the value of all of the personal property plus the annual estimated income from real and personal property in the estate (or twice this amount if personal sureties are used), excluding cash or other personal property deposited in blocked accounts. If bond is insufficient, an additional bond will be required by the court. (See Chapter 13.) If blocked accounts were established, check Box 8 and fill in the information.

When the inventory is complete, it must be signed under oath by the estate representative (if more than one, each person must sign) at Items 5 and 8, and forwarded to the probate referee. The referee will fill in the reverse side of the form. In your cover letter,

Inventory and Appraisal (front)

DE-160/GC-040

ATTORNEY OR PARTY WITHOUT ATTORNEY *(Name, state bar number, and address):*

Billy M. Kidd
1109 Sky Blue Mountain Trail
Billings, Montana 48906

TELEPHONE NO.: 715-555-6408   FAX NO. *(Optional):*
E-MAIL ADDRESS *(Optional):*
ATTORNEY FOR *(Name):* In pro per

FOR COURT USE ONLY

SUPERIOR COURT OF CALIFORNIA, COUNTY OF   LOS ANGELES
STREET ADDRESS: 1725 Main Street
MAILING ADDRESS: 1725 Main Street
CITY AND ZIP CODE: Santa Monica, CA 90401
BRANCH NAME: WEST DISTRICT

ESTATE OF *(Name):*   ANABELLE KIDD, aka ANABELLE O. KIDD,

[X] DECEDENT   [ ] CONSERVATEE   [ ] MINOR

INVENTORY AND APPRAISAL

[ ] Partial No.:   [ ] Corrected
[X] Final   [ ] Reappraisal for Sale
[ ] Supplemental   [X] Property Tax Certificate

CASE NUMBER:
WEP 14813

~~Date of Death of Decedent or of Appointment of Guardian or Conservator:~~
6-18-xx

APPRAISALS

1. Total appraisal by representative, guardian, or conservator (Attachment 1): $ $38,590.38
2. Total appraisal by referee (Attachment 2): $
                                        TOTAL: $

DECLARATION OF REPRESENTATIVE, GUARDIAN, CONSERVATOR, OR SMALL ESTATE CLAIMANT

3. Attachments 1 and 2 together with all prior inventories filed contain a true statement of
   [X] all   [ ] a portion   of the estate that has come to my knowledge or possession, including particularly all money and all just claims the estate has against me. I have truly, honestly, and impartially appraised to the best of my ability each item set forth in Attachment 1.
4. [ ] No probate referee is required   [ ] by order of the court dated *(specify):*
5. **Property tax certificate.** I certify that the requirements of Revenue and Taxation Code section 480
   a. [ ] are not applicable because the decedent owned no real property in California at the time of death.
   b. [X] have been satisfied by the filing of a change of ownership statement with the county recorder or assessor of each county in California in which the decedent owned property at the time of death.

I declare under penalty of perjury under the laws of the State of California that the foregoing is true and correct.

Date: August 28, 20xx

Billy M. Kidd
(TYPE OR PRINT NAME; INCLUDE TITLE IF CORPORATE OFFICER)

▶ *Billy M. Kidd*
(SIGNATURE)

STATEMENT ABOUT THE BOND
(Complete in all cases. Must be signed by attorney for fiduciary, or by fiduciary without an attorney.)

6. [X] Bond is waived, or the sole fiduciary is a corporate fiduciary or an exempt government agency.
7. [ ] Bond filed in the amount of: $ [ ] Sufficient   [ ] Insufficient
8. [ ] Receipts for: $ have been filed with the court for deposits in a blocked account at *(specify institution and location):*

Date: August 28, 20xx
Billy M. Kidd
(TYPE OR PRINT NAME)

▶ *Billy M. Kidd*
(SIGNATURE OF ATTORNEY OR PARTY WITHOUT ATTORNEY)

Page 1 of 2

Form Adopted for Mandatory Use
Judicial Council of California
DE-160/GC-040 [Rev. January 1, 2007]

INVENTORY AND APPRAISAL

Probate Code, §§ 2610-2616, 8800-8980;
Cal. Rules of Court, rule 7.501
www.courtinfo.ca.gov

Attachment 1

DE-161, GC-041

ESTATE OF *(Name)*:	CASE NUMBER:
ANABELLE KIDD, deceased	WEP 14813

INVENTORY AND APPRAISAL
ATTACHMENT NO.: __1__

(In decedents' estates, attachments must conform to Probate Code section 8850(c) regarding community and separate property.)

Page: __1__ of: __2__ total pages.
(Add pages as required.)

Item No.	Description	Appraised value
1.	SEPARATE PROPERTY	$
	1. Cash in decedent's possession at time of death	26.39
	2. Checking Account No. 145 778, Westside National Bank, Los Angeles; balance at date of death	1,366.49
	3. Certificate of Deposit No. 3459, Central Savings and Loan Association, Santa Monica Branch Principal balance on date of death Accrued interest to date of death	20,000.00 143.00
	4. Uncashed check dated 6-12-xx from Jon Harrad payable to decedent	500.00
	5. Five $50 American Express traveler's checks, Nos. 13766 to 13770	250.00
	6. Magazine refund from Fortune Magazine	10.50
	7. Merrill Lynch Ready Assets Trust, Account No. 063-215-29235	6,294.00
	8. Proceeds at Acme Insurance, Policy No. 54377, payable to decedent's estate	10,000.00
	Total Attachment 1	$38,590.38

Form Approved by the Judicial Council of California DE-161, GC-041 [Rev. January 1, 1998] Mandatory Form [1/1/2000]	**INVENTORY AND APPRAISAL ATTACHMENT**	Probate Code, §§ 301, 2610-2613, 8800-8920, 10309

Attachment 2

	DE-161, GC-041
ESTATE OF *(Name)*: ANABELLE KIDD, deceased	CASE NUMBER: WEP 14813

INVENTORY AND APPRAISAL
ATTACHMENT NO.: 2

(In decedents' estates, attachments must conform to Probate Code section 8850(c) regarding community and separate property.)

Page: 2 of: 2 total pages.
(Add pages as required.)

Item No.	Description	Appraised value
1.	SEPARATE PROPERTY	$

9. Real property in the city of Santa Monica, County of Los Angeles, State of California, described as Lot 11 in Block 9 of Tract 5721, as per map recorded in Book 63, page 31 of Maps in the office of the County Recorder of said county. Commonly known as 9560 Euclid Street, Santa Monica, improved with a single dwelling. A.P.N. 3467-047-379 _____

10. One-third (1/3) interest as tenant in common with co-owners John and Mary Smith, in real property in the County of Contra Costa, described as Section 3, Township 20 North, Range 3 East (unimproved land) A.P.N. 4562-34-5770 _____

11. 250 shares, Federated Department Stores, Inc., common stock _____

12. 75 shares, BestCo, Inc., $3 Cumulative, convertible preferred stock _____

13. Five $100 U.S. Series E bonds, issued June 1975 _____

14. $22,000 promissory note dated June 1, 1998, to decedent by R. E. Jones, interest at 9%, secured by deed of trust recorded June 15, 1998, in Book 4879, Page 98 in Official Records of Los Angeles County
        Balance due at date of death _____
        Accrued interest from June 1, 20xx _____

15. $10,000 promissory note of June 1, 1999, to decedent by David Hudson, unsecured, payable interest only at 7% _____

16. Decedent's interest as owner in Great Life Insurance Co. Policy No. 365678 on life of decedent's daughter _____

17. Decedent's 50% interest in Valueless Mining Co., a limited partnership _____

18. Antique silver teapot, marked "Sheffield, 1893" _____

19. 1987 Chevrolet Camaro automobile _____

20. Household furniture, furnishings, and personal effects located at decedent's residence _____

        Total Attachment 2 _____

Form Approved by the
Judicial Council of California
DE-161, GC-041 [Rev. January 1, 1998]
Mandatory Form [1/1/2000]

INVENTORY AND APPRAISAL ATTACHMENT

Probate Code, §§ 301,
2610-2613, 8800-8920,
10309

Change in Ownership Statement—Death of Real Property Owner (Los Angeles County form) (page 1)

BOE-502-D (P1) REV. 03 (08-09) ASSR-176 (REV. 8-09)

CHANGE IN OWNERSHIP STATEMENT
DEATH OF REAL PROPERTY OWNER

This notice is a request for a completed Change in Ownership Statement. Failure to file this statement will result in the assessment of a penalty.

RICK AUERBACH
ASSESSOR

COUNTY OF LOS ANGELES • OFFICE OF THE ASSESSOR
500 WEST TEMPLE STREET, ROOM 225
LOS ANGELES, CA 90012-2770 • Telephone 213.974.3441
Email: *exempt@assessor.lacounty.gov*
Website: *assessor.lacounty.gov*
Si desea ayuda en Español, llame al número 213.974.3211

NAME AND MAILING ADDRESS
(Make necessary corrections to the printed name and mailing address)

Billy M. Kidd
1109 Sky Blue Mountain Trail
Billings, Montana 48906

Section 480(b) of the Revenue and Taxation Code requires that the personal representative file this statement with the Assessor in each county where the decedent owned property at the time of death. **File a separate statement for each parcel of real property owned by the decedent.**

NAME OF DECEDENT	DATE OF DEATH
Anabelle Kidd	June 18, 20xx

[✓] YES [ ] NO — Did the decedent have an interest in real property in this county? If **YES**, answer all questions. If **NO**, sign and complete the certification on page 2.

STREET ADDRESS OF REAL PROPERTY	CITY	ZIP CODE	ASSESSOR'S PARCEL NUMBER (APN)
9560 Euclid Street	Santa Monica	90404	3467-047-375

DESCRIPTIVE INFORMATION [✓] *(IF APN UNKNOWN)*

[ ] Copy of deed by which decedent acquired title is attached.
[ ] Copy of decedent's most recent tax bill is attached.
[ ] Deed or tax bill is not available; legal description is attached.

DISPOSITION OF REAL PROPERTY [✓]

[ ] Succession without a will
[ ] Probate Code 13650 distribution
[ ] Affidavit of death of joint tenant
[✓] Decree of distribution pursuant to will
[ ] Action of trustee pursuant to terms of a trust

TRANSFER INFORMATION [✓] Check all that apply and list details below.

[ ] Decedent's spouse   [ ] Decedent's registered domestic partner

[✓] Decedent's child(ren) or parent(s.) If qualified for exclusion from assessment, a *Claim for Reassessment Exclusion for Transfer Between Parent and Child* must be filed (see instructions.)

[✓] Decedent's grandchild(ren.) If qualified for exclusion from assessment, a *Claim for Reassessment Exclusion for Transfer from Grandparent to Grandchild* must be filed (see instructions.)

[ ] Other beneficiaries.

[ ] A trust.

NAME OF TRUSTEE	ADDRESS OF TRUSTEE

List names and percentage of ownership of all beneficiaries:

NAME OF BENEFICIARY	RELATIONSHIP TO DECEDENT	PERCENT OF OWNERSHIP RECEIVED
Mary Kidd Clark	Daughter	One-third
Billy M. Kidd	Son	One-third
Carson Kidd	Grandson	One-third

[ ] This property has been or will be sold prior to distribution. (Attach the conveyance document and/or court order.)

CONTINUED ON PAGE 2

THIS DOCUMENT IS NOT SUBJECT TO PUBLIC INSPECTION

Change in Ownership Statement—Death of Real Property Owner (Los Angeles County form) (page 2)

BOE-502-D (P2) REV. 03 (08-09) ASSR-176 (REV. 8-09)

[ ] YES [✓] NO   Will the decree of distribution include distribution of an ownership interest in any legal entity that owns real property in this county? If **YES**, will the distribution result in any person or legal entity obtaining control of more than 50% of the ownership of that legal entity? [ ] YES [ ] NO   If **YES**, complete the following section.

NAME AND ADDRESS OF LEGAL ENTITY	NAME OF PERSON OR ENTITY GAINING SUCH CONTROL

[ ] YES [✓] NO   Was the decedent the lessor or lessee in a lease that had an original term of 35 years or more, including renewal options? If **YES**, provide the names and addresses of all other parties to the lease.

NAME	MAILING ADDRESS	CITY	STATE	ZIP CODE

MAILING ADDRESS FOR FUTURE PROPERTY TAX STATEMENTS

ADDRESS	CITY	STATE	ZIP CODE
1109 Sky Blue Mountain Trail	Billings	MT	48906

CERTIFICATION

I certify (or declare) under penalty of perjury under the laws of the State of California that the information contained herein is true, correct and complete to the best of my knowledge and belief.

SIGNATURE OF PERSONAL REPRESENTATIVE ▶	PRINTED NAME OF PERSONAL REPRESENTATIVE Billy M. Kidd
TITLE Executor	DATE 9-10-20xx
E-MAIL ADDRESS	DAYTIME TELEPHONE ( )

INSTRUCTIONS

Failure to file a Change in Ownership Statement within the time prescribed by law may result in a penalty of either $100 or 10% of the taxes applicable to the new base year value of the real property or manufactured home, whichever is greater, but not to exceed $2,500 if that failure to file was not willful. This penalty will be added to the assessment roll and shall be collected like any other delinquent property taxes and subjected to the same penalties for nonpayment.

Section 480 of the Revenue and Taxation Code states, in part:

(a) Whenever there occurs any change in ownership of real property or of a manufactured home that is subject to local property taxation and is assessed by the county assessor, the transferee shall file a signed change in ownership statement in the county where the real property or manufactured home is located, as provided for in subdivision (c). In the case of a change in ownership where the transferee is not locally assessed, no change in ownership statement is required.

(b) The personal representative shall file a change in ownership statement with the county recorder or assessor in each county in which the decedent owned real property at the time of death that is subject to probate proceedings. The statement shall be filed prior to or at the time the inventory and appraisal is filed with the court clerk. In all other cases in which an interest in real property is transferred by reason of death, including a transfer through the medium of a trust, the change in ownership statement or statements shall be filed by the trustee (if the property was held in trust) or the transferee with the county recorder or assessor in each county in which the decedent owned an interest in real property within 150 days after the date of death.

The above requested information is required by law. Please reference the following:

* Passage of Decedent's Property: Beneficial interest passes to the decedent's heirs effectively on the decedent's date of death. However, a document must be recorded to vest title in the heirs. An attorney should be consulted to discuss the specific facts of your situation.

* Change in Ownership: California Code of Regulations, Title 18, Rule 462.260(c), states in part that "[i]nheritance (by will or intestate succession)" shall be "the date of death of decedent."

* Inventory and Appraisal: Probate Code, Section 8800, states in part, "Concurrent with the filing of the inventory and appraisal pursuant to this section, the personal representative shall also file a certification that the requirements of Section 480 of the Revenue and Taxation Code either:
  (1) Are not applicable because the decedent owned no real property in California at the time of death
  (2) Have been satisfied by the filing of a change in ownership statement with the county recorder or assessor of each county in California in which the decedent owned property at the time of death."

* Parent/Child and Grandparent/Grandchild Exclusions: A claim must be filed within three years after the date of death/transfer, but prior to the date of transfer to a third party; or within six months after the date of mailing of a Notice of Assessed Value Change, issued as a result of the transfer of property for which the claim is filed. An application may be obtained by calling 213.893.1239.

This statement will remain confidential as required by Revenue and Taxation Code Section 481, which states in part: "These statements are not public documents and are not open to inspection, except as provided by Section 408."

include additional information about unusual assets to help with the appraisals. For instance, in the case of income property or business interests, the referee will probably need operating statements for at least the last three years (usually the handiest source is the decedent's income tax returns). If the inventory contains real property that is subject to depreciation for income tax purposes, the referee will appraise the land and improvements separately, if requested to do so, so the new owner can later justify a new basis for depreciation.

After the referee completes his or her appraisals, he or she will insert the values of the assets appraised, sign it, and return it to you for filing with the court. In many counties, the inventory must be filed in duplicate. If the referee did not insert the total of Attachments 1 and 2, do this yourself.

! **CAUTION**

Sending copies to others. Under Probate Code § 8803, you must mail a copy of the Inventory and Appraisal to anyone who has requested special notice within 15 days after the inventory is filed with the court. See Step 3 for a sample "proof of mailing" form that may be adapted for this purpose. Title it Proof of Service by Mail of Notice of Filing Inventory and Appraisal, and indicate that a copy of the inventory was mailed.

Letter to Probate Referee

September 15, 20xx

Mr. Frank Adams
California Probate Referee
7856 Third Street
West Los Angeles, California 90410

Re: Estate of Anabelle Kidd, Deceased
     Los Angeles County Superior Court
     Case No. WEP 14813

Dear Mr. Adams:

I am advised that you have been appointed by the Court to appraise the assets in the above estate.

Enclosed are the original and one copy of the Inventory and Appraisal. Please appraise the assets listed on Attachment 2 and return to me for filing with the Court.

The approximate date-of-death value of the household furniture, furnishings, and personal effects was $350.

Should you require any addition information, please contact me at the address and phone number indicated below.

Very truly yours,

Billy M. Kidd

Billy M. Kidd
1109 Sky Blue Mountain Trail
Billings, Montana 48906
715-555-6408

Unique Assets

Appraisal of unique items, such as coin or art collections, usually requires expertise beyond that of most probate referees. If the decedent owned a unique, artistic, unusual, or special item of tangible personal property, you have the option of having it appraised by an independent expert instead of a probate referee. (Prob. Code §§ 8904 and 8905.)

If you want to do that, prepare another Attachment 1 that is separate from and additional to that prepared for the representative (if both the representative and independent expert are appraising items in the same inventory) listing all items to be appraised by the independent expert. At the end of this attachment, have the independent expert sign a declaration in the following form:

Declaration of Independent Expert

I have truly, honestly, and impartially appraised, to the best of my ability, each item set forth in this Attachment 1.

I declare under penalty of perjury under the laws of the State of California that the foregoing is true and correct.

Date: _____

_____
(Type or print name)

_____
(Signature of independent expert)

Step 15: Notify Creditors and Deal With Creditors' Claims and Other Debts

As estate representative, you must handle the decedent's debts. If you have authority to administer the estate under the Independent Administration of Estates Act, you may allow, pay, reject, contest, or compromise any claim against the estate without court supervision and without first giving a Notice of Proposed Action. (Prob. Code §§ 10552(a) and (b).)

Generally, creditors' claims are debts and obligations of the decedent that were due and unpaid as of the date of death and funeral expenses. Expenses and obligations incurred *after* the date of death, such as court filing fees, certification fees, and expenditures necessary to protect estate property, are administration expenses and don't require formal claims. Formal claims are also not required for tax bills, secured debts such as mortgages on real property, or judgments secured by recorded liens.

CAUTION

Notify all mortgage lenders. If the decedent owned a house or other real estate that was acquired with a "money purchase" loan (that is, a loan used to buy the real property), the loan is a "non-recourse" loan. That means the

lender has no recourse against the decedent's other assets. The lender can only go after the real estate that secures the loan. If, however, the decedent refinanced the loan, it is no longer a money purchase loan, and the lender can attach the decedent's other assets to pay off the debt. For this reason, many attorneys recommend giving a written Notice of Administration to Creditors (see below) to all lenders who hold mortgages on real property in the estate.

SEE AN EXPERT

Paying debts and claims is subject to many technical rules. If the estate you are settling involves large debts or claims other than the usual expenses, get the advice of an attorney.

Written Notice to Creditors

The personal representative must give actual written notice to all known or reasonably ascertainable creditors. (Prob. Code § 9050.) The written notice is in addition to the published notice discussed in Step 3. It is given on a printed form entitled Notice of Administration to Creditors, which advises the creditor how and where to file a claim. A sample is shown below.

Here are the rules on when claims may be filed (Prob. Code §§ 9051 and 9100):

- The notice must be given to all known or reasonably ascertainable creditors within four months after the date letters are first issued to the personal representative. All creditors so notified must file their claims within the four-month period.
- If a creditor is discovered only during the last 30 days of the four-month period, or *after* the four-month period has expired, notice must be given to that creditor within 30 days after discovery of the creditor. That creditor then has 60 days from the date notice is given to file a claim.
- If a creditor does not receive notice and only discovers that he has a claim after the four-month period has expired, he or she may petition the court to file a late claim under Probate Code § 9103. A late claim cannot be allowed after one year from the date of death.

Generally, claims are barred from payment if they are not filed within these time frames. In limited cases, a distributee of an estate may be liable for a claim if the creditor was known or reasonably ascertainable and the personal representative did not give the creditor written Notice of Administration. (Prob. Code § 9392.) Actions against a distributee must be commenced within one year of the date of death.

A personal representative is not liable to a creditor for failure to give written notice to that creditor unless the failure was in bad faith. The burden of proving bad faith is on the person seeking to impose liability. (Prob. Code § 9053.)

> **TIP**
>
> **Collect and examine all itemized bills and statements that have been sent to the decedent.** If they are legitimate, you may be able to save time and paperwork by paying them under the provisions of Probate Code § 10552 or § 9154, without giving written notice or requiring a formal claim, as discussed below.

There is no need to send the notice to creditors who have filed formal claims, or creditors who have submitted bills and will be paid without a formal claim under Probate Code § 9154, discussed below. Other than creditors who have already submitted bills or filed claims, written notice should be given to all creditors, or potential creditors, who can be identified through reasonably diligent efforts. For your protection, make a thorough search of the decedent's files and records for evidence of any obligation or potential liability the decedent may have had at death. Look for such things as outstanding loans, mortgages, promissory notes, disputed bills, pending or anticipated lawsuits where the decedent is or could be a defendant, and outstanding judgments against the decedent.

For each possible creditor, make a list of the name of the individual, corporation or other entity, the mailing address, the account number, and any other information relevant to the debt or obligation. Each creditor on this list should receive a written Notice of Administration of Estate of _____, Decedent, and should be required to file a formal Creditor's Claim. This task can be simplified by preparing a master copy of the notice, filling in all relevant information except the date in Item 3b, and making several photocopies.

When you're ready to mail the notice, fill in the date before sending it to the creditor, and have a disinterested person mail the copies of the notice and complete the proof of mailing on the back. The original notice(s) should be filed with the court.

How to Fill Out the Notice of Administration to Creditors

Caption: Fill in the decedent's name.

Item 1: Fill in the name, address, and phone number of the executor or administrator and the name of the decedent.

Item 2: Fill in the address and branch name of the court and the case number.

Item 3: In the first box, put the date letters were issued. In the second box, put the date you are mailing the notice.

Proof of Service: Have a disinterested person mail copies of the notice to creditors and fill out and sign the Proof of Service on the back of the original notice. Keep the original notice(s) until you are ready to close the estate and file them with the court when you file the Petition for Final Distribution.

Notice of Administration to Creditors (front)

DE-157

NOTICE OF ADMINISTRATION
OF THE ESTATE OF

ANABELLE KIDD, aka Anabelle O. Kidd
(NAME)

DECEDENT

NOTICE TO CREDITORS

1. *(Name)*: Billy M. Kidd
   (Address): 1109 Sky Blue Mountain Trail
   Billings, Montana 48906

   (Telephone): 715-555-6408
   is the **personal representative** of the ESTATE OF *(name)*: Anabelle Kidd , who is deceased.

2. The personal representative HAS BEGUN ADMINISTRATION of the decedent's estate in the
   a. **SUPERIOR COURT OF CALIFORNIA, COUNTY OF** *(specify)*:
      STREET ADDRESS: 1725 Main Street
      MAILING ADDRESS: 1725 Main Street
      CITY AND ZIP CODE: Santa Monica, California 90401
      BRANCH NAME: WEST DISTRICT

   b. Case number *(specify)*: WEP 14813

3. You must FILE YOUR CLAIM with the court clerk (address in item 2a) AND mail or deliver a copy to the personal representative before the **later** of the following times as provided in Probate Code section 9100:

   a. **four months** after *(date)*: July 25, 20xx , the date letters (authority to act for the estate) were first issued to the personal representative, OR

   b. **sixty days** after *(date)*: August 2, 20xx , the date this notice was mailed or personally delivered to you.

4. LATE CLAIMS: If you do not file your claim before it is due, you must file a petition with the court for permission to file a late claim as provided in Probate Code section 9103.

   WHERE TO GET A CREDITOR'S CLAIM FORM: If a *Creditor's Claim* (form DE-172) did not accompany this notice, you may obtain a copy from any superior court clerk or from the person who sent you this notice. A letter to the court stating your claim is *not* sufficient.

   FAILURE TO FILE A CLAIM: Failure to file a claim with the court and serve a copy of the claim on the personal representative will in most instances invalidate your claim.

   IF YOU MAIL YOUR CLAIM: If you use the mail to file your claim with the court, for your protection you should send your claim by certified mail, with return receipt requested. If you use the mail to serve a copy of your claim on the personal representative, you should also use certified mail.

   Note: To assist the creditor and the court, please send a copy of the *Creditor's Claim* form with this notice.

(Proof of Service on reverse)

Form Approved by the
Judicial Council of California
DE-157 [Rev. January 1, 1998]
Mandatory Form [1/1/2000]

NOTICE OF ADMINISTRATION TO CREDITORS
(Probate)

Probate Code. §§ 9050, 9052

Notice of Administration to Creditors (back)

[Optional]

PROOF OF SERVICE BY MAIL

1. I am over the age of 18 and not a party to this cause. I am a resident of or employed in the county where the mailing occurred.

2. My residence or business address is *(specify)*:

   25 Sutter Street, Billings, Montana 48906

3. I served the foregoing *Notice of Administration to Creditors* ☐ and a blank *Creditor's Claim* form* on each person named below by enclosing a copy in an envelope addressed as shown below AND

   a. ☒ **depositing** the sealed envelope with the United States Postal Service with the postage fully prepaid.

   b. ☐ **placing** the envelope for collection and mailing on the date and at the place shown in item 4 following our ordinary business practices. I am readily familiar with the business' practice for collecting and processing correspondence for mailing. On the same day that correspondence is placed for collection and mailing, it is deposited in the ordinary course of business with the United States Postal Service in a sealed envelope with postage fully prepaid.

4. a. Date of deposit: August 2, 20xx   b. Place of deposit *(city and state)*:

I declare under penalty of perjury under the laws of the State of California that the foregoing is true and correct.

Date: August 2, 20xx

Kitty Doyle   *Kitty Doyle*
(TYPE OR PRINT NAME)   (SIGNATURE OF DECLARANT)

NAME AND ADDRESS OF EACH PERSON TO WHOM NOTICE WAS MAILED

Bullocks Wilshire
P.O. Box 19807
Los Angeles, CA 90002

Jon Harrad
1206 - 19th Street
Santa Monica, CA 90047

Sullivan's Catering
11560 Lincoln Boulevard
Marina del Rey, CA 90408

Springs Ambulance Service
P.O. Box 2349
Santa Monica, CA 90405

Bankamericard Visa
P.O. Box 1848
Terminal Annex
Los Angeles, CA 90007

☐ List of names and addresses continued in attachment.

***NOTE:** To assist the creditor and the court, please send a copy of the Creditor's Claim (form DE-172) with the notice.*

DE-157 [Rev. January 1, 1998]   **NOTICE OF ADMINISTRATION TO CREDITORS**   Page two
                                              (Probate)

Bills You May Pay Without a Claim or Giving Written Notice

Under Probate Code § 9154, a written demand for payment, such as an itemized bill or statement, may be treated as an established claim if it's received within four months after letters are issued. You can pay these debts without giving written notice and without requiring a formal creditor's claim if they're bona fide debts and paid in good faith, and the estate is solvent. If the estate is insolvent, there is an order of priority for payment set by law in Probate Code § 11420. As you might guess, attorneys get paid first, before other creditors, except for priority debts due the U.S. government.

As a practical matter, in simple estates it's easier to pay ordinary expenses such as utility bills, charge account balances, doctor or other medical bills, funeral expenses, real estate and income taxes, and other clearly proper debts without giving written notice or requiring a formal claim as long as you're sure no one will object to the payment. Just remember these requirements: (1) You must have received a written demand for payment within four months after letters were issued, (2) the debt must be justly due, (3) the amount you pay must take into account any previous payments or offsets, (4) payment must be made within 30 days after the four-month period that begins with issuance of your letters, and (5) the estate must be solvent.

Formal Creditors' Claims

The published Notice of Petition to Administer Estate advises creditors how and when to file claims. Subject to the few exceptions discussed in "Written Notice to Creditors," above, a creditor must file a formal Creditor's Claim directly with the court and serve a copy on the personal representative within four months after letters are issued. Service on the personal representative must be made within the four-month period or within 30 days of the filing of the claim, whichever is later. Generally, you're not legally required to pay any claims not filed within this four-month period, so make note of this important cut-off date.

Few formal claims, if any, are filed in uncomplicated estates. Usually, you just receive bills addressed to the decedent at his or her last address, because most creditors don't know of the death.

A sample Creditor's Claim is shown below.

Claim by Personal Representative

If you, as personal representative, have paid any of the decedent's debts from your personal funds (funeral expenses or utility bills, for example), or have any other claim against the estate, you must file a formal Creditor's Claim with the court. Copies of canceled checks or other evidence of payment must be attached. A claims examiner will review the claim, and the court's approval or rejection will be endorsed on the Allowance or Rejection of Creditor's Claim form (discussed below), which you should submit with the claim when it is filed. After the court has approved the claim, you pay yourself the amount allowed out of estate funds.

As stated previously, payment of administrative expenses such as court filing fees don't require formal claims. You may be reimbursed for these expenses from the estate bank account immediately after your appointment.

Allowance or Rejection of Creditors' Claims

If formal claims are filed, you must allow, reject, or partially allow each one. You prepare an Allowance or Rejection of Creditor's Claim form to let the creditor and the court know what action you've taken on the claim. You file the original form with the court (with a copy of the claim attached) and send a copy to the creditor. The mailing or personal delivery to the creditor must be done by a disinterested adult, who afterwards must complete the proof of mailing or personal delivery on the back of the original form before it's filed. If you have independent powers, no further court action is required; however, if you don't have independent powers, the court must review your action and endorse its allowance or rejection on the original form.

Creditor's Claim (page 1)

DE-172

ATTORNEY OR PARTY WITHOUT ATTORNEY *(Name, state bar number, and address)*:	TELEPHONE AND FAX NOS.:	FOR COURT USE ONLY

Michael Sullivan   310-555-6632
11560 Lincoln Boulevard
Marina del Rey, California 90488

ATTORNEY FOR *(Name)*:   In pro per

SUPERIOR COURT OF CALIFORNIA, COUNTY OF Los Angeles
STREET ADDRESS: 1725 Main Street
MAILING ADDRESS: 1725 Main Street
CITY AND ZIP CODE: Santa Monica, CA 90401
BRANCH NAME: WEST DISTRICT

ESTATE OF *(Name)*:

ANABELLE KIDD, aka ANABELLE O. KIDD   DECEDENT

CREDITOR'S CLAIM	CASE NUMBER:
	WEP 14813

You must file this claim with the court clerk at the court address above before the LATER of (a) four months after the date letters (authority to act for the estate) were first issued to the personal representative, or (b) sixty days after the date the *Notice of Administration* was given to the creditor, if notice was given as provided in Probate Code section 9051. You must also mail or deliver a copy of this claim to the personal representative and his or her attorney. A proof of service is on the reverse.

WARNING: Your claim will in most instances be invalid if you do not properly complete this form, file it on time with the court, and mail or deliver a copy to the personal representative and his or her attorney.

1. Total amount of the claim: $ 347.00
2. Claimant *(name)*: Michael Sullivan
   a. [X] an individual
   b. [ ] an individual or entity doing business under the fictitious name of *(specify)*:

   c. [ ] a partnership. The person signing has authority to sign on behalf of the partnership.
   d. [ ] a corporation. The person signing has authority to sign on behalf of the corporation.
   e. [ ] other (specify):
3. Address of claimant *(specify)*:
   11560 Lincoln Boulevard, Marina del Rey, CA 90488
4. Claimant is [X] the creditor [ ] a person acting on behalf of creditor *(state reason)*:

5. [ ] Claimant is [ ] the personal representative [ ] the attorney for the personal representative.
6. I am authorized to make this claim which is just and due or may become due. All payments on or offsets to the claim have been credited. Facts supporting the claim are [ ] on reverse [ ] attached.

I declare under penalty of perjury under the laws of the State of California that the foregoing is true and correct.

Date: August 15, 20xx

Michael Sullivan
(TYPE OR PRINT NAME AND TITLE)

▶ *Michael Sullivan*
(SIGNATURE OF CLAIMANT)

INSTRUCTIONS TO CLAIMANT

A. On the reverse, itemize the claim and show the date the service was rendered or the debt incurred. Describe the item or service in detail, and indicate the amount claimed for each item. Do not include debts incurred after the date of death, except funeral claims.

B. If the claim is not due or contingent, or the amount is not yet ascertainable, state the facts supporting the claim.

C. If the claim is secured by a note or other written instrument, the original or a copy must be attached *(state why original is unavailable.* If secured by mortgage, deed of trust, or other lien on property that is of record, it is sufficient to describe the security and refer to the date or volume and page, and county where recorded. *(See Prob. Code, § 9152.)*

D. Mail or take this original claim to the court clerk's office for filing. If mailed, use certified mail, with return receipt requested.

E. Mail or deliver a copy to the personal representative and his or her attorney. Complete the *Proof of Mailing or Personal Delivery* on the reverse.

F. The personal representative or his or her attorney will notify you when your claim is allowed or rejected.

G. Claims against the estate by the personal representative and the attorney for the personal representative must be filed within the claim period allowed in Probate Code section 9100. See the notice box above.

(Continued on reverse)

Form Approved by the Judicial Council of California DE-172 [Rev. January 1, 1998] Mandatory Form [1/1/2000]	**CREDITOR'S CLAIM** **(Probate)**	Probate Code, §§ 9000 et seq., 9153 American LegalNet, Inc. www.USCourtForms.com

Creditor's Claim (page 2)

ESTATE OF *(Name):*	CASE NUMBER:
Annabelle Kidd, DECEDENT	WEP 14813

FACTS SUPPORTING THE CREDITOR'S CLAIM
☐ See attachment *(if space is insufficient)*

Date of item	Item and supporting facts	Amount claimed
6-10-xx	Food and service provided decedent per attached statement	$347.00
	TOTAL: $ 347.00	

PROOF OF   [X] **MAILING**   ☐ **PERSONAL DELIVERY**   **TO PERSONAL REPRESENTATIVE**
(Be sure to mail or take the original to the court clerk's office for filing)

1. I am the creditor or a person acting on behalf of the creditor. At the time of mailing or delivery I was at least 18 years of age.
2. My residence or business address is *(specify):*
       11560 Lincoln Blvd., Marina del Rey, Calif.
3. I mailed or personally delivered a copy of this *Creditor's Claim* to the personal representative as follows *(check either a or b below):*
   a. [X] **Mail**. I am a resident of or employed in the county where the mailing occurred.
       (1) I enclosed a copy in an envelope AND
          (a) [X] **deposited** the sealed envelope with the United States Postal Service with the postage fully prepaid.
          (b) ☐ **placed** the envelope for collection and mailing on the date and at the place shown in items below following our ordinary business practices. I am readily familiar with this business' practice for collecting and processing correspondence for mailing. On the same day that correspondence is placed for collection and mailing, it is deposited in the ordinary course of business with the United States Postal Service in a sealed envelope with postage fully prepaid.
       (2) The envelope was addressed and mailed first-class as follows: Billy M. Kidd
          (a) Name of personal representative served:
          (b) Address on envelope: 1109 Sky Blue Mountain Trail
                              Billings, Montana 48906
          (c) Date of mailing: August 15, 20xx
          (d) Place of mailing *(city and state):*   Marina del Rey, CA 90488
   b. ☐ **Personal delivery**. I personally delivered a copy of the claim to the personal representative as follows:
       (1) Name of personal representative served:
       (2) Address where delivered:

       (3) Date delivered:
       (4) Time delivered:

I declare under penalty of perjury under the laws of the State of California that the foregoing is true and correct.

Date: August 15, 20xx

     Michael Sullivan   ▶   *Michael Sullivan*
      (TYPE OR PRINT NAME OF CLAIMANT)   (SIGNATURE OF CLAIMANT)

DE-172 [Rev. January 1,1998]   **CREDITOR'S CLAIM**   Page two
                                     (Probate)

You should examine each Creditor's Claim form carefully to make sure (1) it's signed and dated, (2) the debt was incurred or the service was rendered before the date of death, and (3) the claim was filed within the four-month claim period or within 60 days after written notice was given. Otherwise, it may be defective and not be an allowable claim.

If you receive a Creditor's Claim for a debt you question for some reason (for example, the amount is too high or the service rendered wasn't satisfactory), you may reject the claim in whole or in part. A creditor who refuses to accept the amount you allow has 90 days from the date of the rejection within which to file suit against the estate. If the suit is not filed within such time, the claim is barred forever. If the creditor files suit, you'll need an attorney. Whenever a claim is rejected, you must wait three months from the date of rejection before filing a petition to close the estate.

Payment of Claims

Claims for funeral expenses, last illness expenses, and wage claims that have been allowed and approved should be paid promptly as soon as there are sufficient funds in the estate, after retaining enough to pay administration expenses and debts owed to the United States or California. (Prob. Code § 11421.)

Strictly speaking, you're not required to pay any other claims without a court order. However, this rule isn't strictly observed. You may safely pay other allowed and approved claims as long as (1) the time for filing or presenting claims has not expired, (2) the estate is solvent and there is cash available for payment, and (3) no one having an interest in the estate is going to challenge the payment. If the claim is based on a written contract, interest accrues at the rate and in accordance with the contract. (Prob. Code § 11423.)

If the Department of Health Services has filed a claim for the cost of Medi-Cal services, you must ordinarily pay the full claim before probate closes. If the estate doesn't have enough cash, but does contain real estate, the Department may agree to let property be distributed, but with a lien against the estate. Contact the Department if you run into difficulty paying the debt.

How to Fill Out the Allowance or Rejection of Creditor's Claim

Caption: Fill in your name, address, the court's name, and case number, as you have on your other court papers.

Items 1-7: Fill in the requested information (most of it is on the Creditor's Claim). Leave Item 2 blank if you don't know when the claim was filed with the court.

Items 8 and 9: Fill in the amount you are approving or rejecting.

Item 10: Enter the date you mail this form to the creditor.

Item 11: Check the box if you are authorized to administer the estate under the Independent Administration of Estates Act.

Print your name, and date and sign the form. Leave the rest of the front page blank.

Proof of Service: Whoever mails or gives the form to the creditor should fill out and sign the Proof of Service on the back of the original of the form, after a copy is sent to the creditor. Then you should file the original with the court.

Allowance or Rejection of Creditor's Claim (page 1)

DE-174

ATTORNEY OR PARTY WITHOUT ATTORNEY (Name, State Bar number, and address):	FOR COURT USE ONLY
Billy M. Kidd 1109 Sky Blue Mountain Trail Billings, Montana 48906 TELEPHONE NO.: 715-555-6408 FAX NO. (Optional): E-MAIL ADDRESS (Optional): ATTORNEY FOR (Name): In pro per	

SUPERIOR COURT OF CALIFORNIA, COUNTY OF Los Angeles
STREET ADDRESS: 1725 Main Street
MAILING ADDRESS: 1725 Main Street
CITY AND ZIP CODE: Santa Monica, CA 90401
BRANCH NAME: WEST DISTRICT

ESTATE OF   ANABELLE KIDD, aka
(Name):   ANABELLE O. KIDD,
                                                    DECEDENT

ALLOWANCE OR REJECTION OF CREDITOR'S CLAIM	CASE NUMBER: WEP 14813

NOTE TO PERSONAL REPRESENTATIVE

Attach a copy of the creditor's claim to this form. If approval or rejection by the court is not required, do not include any pages attached to the creditor's claim.

PERSONAL REPRESENTATIVE'S ALLOWANCE OR REJECTION

1. Name of creditor (specify):   Michael Sullivan
2. The claim was filed on (date):
3. Date of first issuance of letters: July 25, 20xx
4. Date of Notice of Administration: August 2, 20xx
5. Date of decedent's death: June 18, 20xx
6. Estimated value of estate: $250,000.00
7. Total amount of the claim: $347.00
8. [x] Claim is allowed for: $347.00   (The court must approve certain claims before they are paid.)
9. [ ] Claim is rejected for: $ (A creditor has 90 days to act on a rejected claim.* See box below.)
10. Notice of allowance or rejection given on (date):
11. [x] The personal representative is authorized to administer the estate under the Independent Administration of Estates Act.

Date: August 20, 20xx

_____   ▶   Billy M. Kidd
Billy M. Kidd   _____
(TYPE OR PRINT NAME OF PERSONAL REPRESENTATIVE)   (SIGNATURE OF PERSONAL REPRESENTATIVE)

NOTICE TO CREDITOR ON REJECTED CLAIM

From the date that notice of rejection is given, you must act on the rejected claim (e.g., file a lawsuit) as follows:

1. **Claim due:** within 90 days* after the notice of rejection.
2. **Claim not due:** within 90 days* after the claim becomes due.

*The 90-day period mentioned above may not apply to your claim because some claims are not treated as creditors' claims or are subject to special statutes of limitations, or for other legal reasons. You should consult with an attorney if you have any questions about or are unsure of your rights and obligations concerning your claim.

COURT'S APPROVAL OR REJECTION

12. [ ] Approved for: $
13. [ ] Rejected for: $

Date:

_____
SIGNATURE OF JUDICIAL OFFICER

14. Number of pages attached: _____   [ ] SIGNATURE FOLLOWS LAST ATTACHMENT

(Proof of Mailing or Personal Delivery on reverse)

		Page 1 of 2
Form Adopted for Mandatory Use Judicial Council of California DE-174 [Rev. January 1, 2009]	ALLOWANCE OR REJECTION OF CREDITOR'S CLAIM (Probate—Decedents' Estates)	Probate Code, § 9000 et seq., 9250-9256, 9353

Allowance or Rejection of Creditor's Claim (page 2)

DE-174

ESTATE OF *(Name):*	ANABELLE KIDD, aka ANABELLE O. KIDD,	CASE NUMBER:
	DECEDENT	WEP 14813

PROOF OF [x] MAILING [ ] PERSONAL DELIVERY TO CREDITOR

1. At the time of mailing or personal delivery I was at least 18 years of age and **not a party** to this proceeding.

2. My residence or business address is *(specify):* 25 Sutter Street, Billings, MT 48906

3. I mailed or personally delivered a copy of the *Allowance or Rejection of Creditor's Claim* as follows *(complete either a or b)*:

   a. [x] **Mail.** I am a resident of or employed in the county where the mailing occurred.

      (1) I enclosed a copy in an envelope AND

         (a) [x] **deposited** the sealed envelope with the United States Postal Service with the postage fully prepaid.

         (b) [ ] **placed** the envelope for collection and mailing on the date and at the place shown in items below following our ordinary business practices. I am readily familiar with this business's practice for collecting and processing correspondence for mailing. On the same day that correspondence is placed for collection and mailing, it is deposited in the ordinary course of business with the United States Postal Service in a sealed envelope with postage fully prepaid.

      (2) The envelope was addressed and mailed first-class as follows:

         (a) Name of creditor served: Michael Sullivan

         (b) Address on envelope: 11560 Lincoln Boulevard Marina del Rey, CA 90488

         (c) Date of mailing:

         (d) Place of mailing *(city and state):*

   b. [ ] **Personal delivery.** I personally delivered a copy to the creditor as follows:

      (1) Name of creditor served:

      (2) Address where delivered:

      (3) Date delivered:

      (4) Time delivered:

I declare under penalty of perjury under the laws of the State of California that the foregoing is true and correct.

Date: August 20, 20xx

_____	▶ *Samantha Long* _____
Samatha Long	
(TYPE OR PRINT NAME OF DECLARANT)	(SIGNATURE OF DECLARANT)

DE-174 [Rev. January 1, 2009]	**ALLOWANCE OR REJECTION OF CREDITOR'S CLAIM** (Probate—Decedents' Estates)	Page 2 of 2

Step 16: Prepare the Petition for Final Distribution

After the creditor's claim period has expired (four months from the issuance of letters), you may file a petition with the court requesting an order distributing the assets to the beneficiaries—if the estate is in a condition to be closed. Following is a checklist of the requirements to help you determine whether or not the estate is ready to be closed:

1. The creditor's claim period must have expired.
2. All creditor's claims must have been allowed and approved and paid or sufficiently secured. If any were rejected, the time to file suit on the rejected claims must have expired. (See Step 15, above.)
3. All expenses of administration, including charges for legal advertising, bond premiums, and probate referee's fees, have been paid.
4. All personal property taxes and income taxes must be paid, or payment secured.
5. A California Income Tax Clearance certificate must be obtained if the estate's gross value exceeds $1 million, and assets of $250,000 or more will be distributed to beneficiaries in other states or countries. (See Chapter 13.)

To apply for the certificate, use Form FTB-3571, called *Request for Estate Income Tax Clearance Certificate* (as required under Revenue & Taxation Code § 19513), which you can obtain by contacting the Franchise Tax Board at 916-845-6500 or at www.ftb.ca.gov. The form is self-explanatory and should be filled in and mailed to the Franchise Tax Board, Fiduciary Audit, Attn: Tax Certificate Unit, P.O. Box 1468, Sacramento, CA 95812-1468. The tax board has 30 days within which to issue the certificate, so the hearing on the Petition for Final Distribution should be set far enough in advance so that the certificate will be obtained by the hearing date. When you get the certificate, file it with the court right away.

If you do not have enough information to complete all tax returns but the estate is otherwise ready to close, you may request a cash reserve to cover payment of any taxes that may be due. For example, if the decedent died early in the year and received enough income for that year to require a final income tax return, you have the option of either filing the decedent's final income tax return before filing the petition for final distribution and paying the tax (assuming you have the required information), or you may wait and file the return after the end of the calendar year and request a sufficient reserve from distribution to pay the estimated taxes.

Federal *estate* taxes may also be paid from a cash reserve, if the estate is large enough to require a federal estate tax return and it has not yet been finalized. The estate's final fiduciary income tax returns are always filed *after* the estate is closed and distributed. You do not have to request a tax reserve for the final fiduciary returns, because the income and deductions are passed through to the beneficiaries. Tax matters are discussed in Chapter 7.

Besides taxes that may be paid after distribution, the petition should also request a reserve for miscellaneous closing expenses such as the cost of transferring securities, certifying and recording copies of the Order for Final Distribution, fees for preparation of income tax returns, and reasonable storage, delivery, and shipping costs for distribution of tangible personal property to a distributee.

There is no printed form for the Petition for Final Distribution, but you should have no trouble typing it if you carefully follow the sample shown here.

Note that alternative paragraphs are listed to take care of different situations. Use only the provisions that fit your situation, which you can determine after reading the notes below that are keyed to each numbered provision. If you omit any of the paragraphs in the example (which may be likely, depending on your situation) be sure to renumber the paragraphs. Also, all exhibits should be lettered consecutively, without skipping any letters.

CAUTION

Special local requirements. Our sample forms should be acceptable for most counties. However, some courts have requirements of their own for the preparation of petitions and orders, so be sure to carefully read their printed probate rules. You might even examine some probate files at the courthouse for specific examples of these forms.

Petition for Final Distribution (page 1)

1　BILLY M. KIDD
　　1109 Sky Blue Mountain Trail
2　Billings, Montana 48906

3　Telephone: 715-555-6408
　　Petitioner in pro per
4

5

6

7

　　　　　　　　SUPERIOR COURT OF CALIFORNIA
8
　　　　　　　FOR THE COUNTY OF LOS ANGELES
9

10　Estate of　　　　　　　　) CASE NO. WEP 14813
　　　　　　　　　　　　　　　)
11　　ANABELLE KIDD, aka　　　) PETITION FOR FINAL DISTRIBUTION
　　　ANABELLE O. KIDD　　　　) ON WAIVER OF ACCOUNTING (AND FOR
12　　　　　　　　　　　　　　) ALLOWANCE OF STATUTORY COMMISSIONS)
　　　　　　　　　　　　　　　)
13　　　　　　　　　　　　　　) (Prob. Code §§ 10400-10406,
　　　　　　　　　　　　　　　) 10954, 11600-11642)
　　　　　　　　　　　　　　　)
14　　　　　　deceased.　　　　) Hearing Date:
　　　　　　　　　　　　　　　) Time:
15　_____) Department:
　　_____) Judge:
16

17

18　Petitioner, BILLY M. KIDD, as personal representative of the estate of

19　the above-named decedent, states:

20　　1. ANABELLE KIDD, aka ANABELLE O. KIDD, died testate (or

21　intestate) on June 18, 20xx, a resident of the county named above.

22　Petitioner was appointed personal representative of decedent's estate

23　and letters were issued to petitioner on August 20, 20xx.

24　　2. Notice of death was timely published. Petitioner made a thorough

25　search of decedent's files and records for evidence of any obligation or

26　potential liability the decedent may have had at death. No reasonably

27　ascertainable creditors were found beyond those who submitted bills

28

　　　　　　　　　　　　　　　1
　　　PETITION FOR FINAL DISTRIBUTION ON WAIVER OF ACCOUNTING

Petition for Final Distribution (page 2)

in the ordinary course, all of which were paid within the four-month claim period, and therefore specific notice of administration under Probate Code Section 9050 was not required. (Or, if applicable: Actual notice of administration under Probate Code Section 9050 was given to each known or reasonably ascertainable creditor, except those within the class described in Probate Code Section 9054, and the notices are on file herein with proof of service. Attached as Exhibit "A" is a list of all creditors who were given notice, including the date notice was mailed.) More than four (4) months have elapsed since letters were first issued (Add, if applicable: and more than 60 days have elapsed since the last notice of administration was given.) The time for filing claims has expired.

3. The decedent did not receive Medi-Cal benefits, nor was the decedent the surviving spouse or registered domestic partner of a person who received such health care, and notice to the Director of Health Services is not required.

(or)

3. Notice of this proceeding with a copy of the decedent's death certificate was mailed to the Director of Health Services on _____, 20____.

4. No heir is known to be or reasonably believed to be in a correctional facility and notice to the Director of California Victim Compensation and Government Claims Board is not required.

(or)

4. Notice of this proceeding with a copy of the decedent's death certificate was mailed to the Director of California Victim Compensation and Government Claims Board on _____, 20__.

2

PETITION FOR FINAL DISTRIBUTION ON WAIVER OF ACCOUNTING

Petition for Final Distribution (page 3)

5. Notice to the Franchise Tax Board was given on

_____, 20__.

6. No claims were filed against the estate.

(or)

6. Exhibit "B" to this petition lists all claims filed against the estate, including the name of the claimant, amount of the claim, the date filed, and the action taken. (Add, if applicable: The date of service of notice of rejection of each rejected claim is also stated. Petitioner has no knowledge of any suit having been filed on any rejected claim and no service of process has been served upon petitioner. The time to file suit has expired.) All debts paid were legally enforceable claims against the estate.

7. Certain debts were paid under the provisions of Probate Code Section 9154, without formal claims having been filed. All such creditors made a written demand for payment within four months after letters were issued. The debts were justly due, were paid in good faith within 30 days after expiration of the four-month claim period, the amounts paid were net payments or setoffs. The estate is solvent.

8. All debts of the decedent and of the estate and all administration expenses, including charges for legal advertising, probate referee's fees, and bond premiums, if any, have been paid and the estate is in a condition to be closed.

9. An Inventory and Appraisal of the estate assets was filed, showing the value of the estate to be $ _____.

10. The estate was administered under the Independent Administration of Estates Act. No independent acts were performed that required a Notice of Proposed Action.

(or)

3

PETITION FOR FINAL DISTRIBUTION ON WAIVER OF ACCOUNTING

Petition for Final Distribution (page 4)

10. The estate was administered under the Independent Administration of Estates Act. Petitioner performed the following actions without court supervision, after having given a Notice of Proposed Action if required:

a. Petitioner sold the decedent's residence at 9560 Euclid Street, Santa Monica, to John A. Buyer for the sales price of $129,900. Notice of Proposed Action was given to all persons whose interest was affected by the sale, and no objections were received. The original notice is on file herein, with proof of service.

b. Petitioner sold the decedent's Chevrolet automobile to Willy Worthy, without notice, for cash in the sum of $8,000. Said automobile would have depreciated in value and caused expense to the estate by being kept.

c. To avoid the expense of storing the decedent's household furniture, furnishings, and personal effects, petitioner allowed the beneficiaries to take possession of the items they were presumptively entitled to, as authorized by Probate Code Section 9650(c), and the remaining items were sold without notice at public sales, for cash. Said property would have caused expense to the estate by being kept and it was in the best interests of the estate that it be disposed of promptly.

11. No personal property taxes are due or payable by the estate. (or, All personal property taxes have been paid.)

12. All income tax returns due by the decedent or the estate as of the date of this petition have been filed and the taxes paid. (Note: If all income taxes not paid, add: except returns for the tax year(s) of

PETITION FOR FINAL DISTRIBUTION ON WAIVER OF ACCOUNTING

Petition for Final Distribution (page 5)

(describe). Petitioner will request a reserve from distribution to pay all taxes in full.) (Also add, if applicable: The value of the estate assets at the date of decedent's death exceeded $1 million, and assets of at least $250,000 are distributable to nonresident beneficiaries. The certificate of the California Franchise Tax Board required by Revenue and Taxation Code Section 19513 is on file herein.)

    13. No California or federal estate taxes are due.

(or)

    13. California and federal estate taxes will be owed by the estate and have not yet been paid. Petitioner believes that estate taxes will not exceed $_____, and petitioner will request a sufficient reserve from distribution to pay all estate taxes in full.

    14. The assets on hand, including their community or separate character, are set forth in Exhibit "C."

    15. The names, present addresses, ages, and relationship to decedent of all persons entitled to receive property of the estate and the plan of distribution are set forth in Exhibit "D."

    16. Petitioner waives the filing of a final account. (Add, if appropriate: Waivers of Account by the remaining beneficiaries are attached as Exhibits "E," etc.)

    17. Petitioner waives any right to statutory commissions.

(or)

    17. Petitioner's statutory commissions are computed as follows:

Amount of Inventory and Appraisal	$ 211,480.38	
4% on first	$100,000.00 =	$4,000.00
3% on next	$100,000.00 =	3,000.00
2% on next	$ 11,480.38 =	229.61
Total commissions	=	$7,229.61

PETITION FOR FINAL DISTRIBUTION ON WAIVER OF ACCOUNTING

Petition for Final Distribution (page 6)

1   18. Petitioner requests authorization to withhold $_____ for

2   closing expenses (Add, if applicable: and as a reserve for payment of

3   income taxes or other liabilities that may hereafter be determined to

4   be due from the estate.)

5   19. No compensation has been paid from estate assets to the

6   representative or to an attorney for the representative.

7   20. There is no family or affiliate relationship between the

8   representative and any agent hired by the representative during the

9   administration of the estate.

10   Add, if estate contains cash

11   21. Petitioner has kept all cash invested in interest-bearing

12   accounts or other investments authorized by law, except what was

13   needed to administer estate.

14   Add, if applicable

15   22. The estate contained real property and a change of ownership

16   report was filed with the county assessor in the county where the real

17   property is located.

18   WHEREFORE, petitioner prays that the administration of the estate

19   be brought to a close without the requirement of an accounting; that

20   all reported acts and proceedings of petitioner as herein set forth be

21   confirmed and approved; that petitioner be authorized to retain

22   $_____ for closing expenses and to pay liabilities, and to

23   deliver the unused part to the beneficiaries of the estate without

24   further Court Order after the closing expenses have been paid;

25   (Add, if applicable: that petitioner be allowed $7,229.61 as statutory

26   commissions; that distribution of the estate in petitioner's hands

27   and any other property of decedent or the estate not now known or

28

PETITION FOR FINAL DISTRIBUTION ON WAIVER OF ACCOUNTING

Petition for Final Distribution (page 7)

1   discovered be made to the persons entitled to it, as set forth in the

2   petition, and the Court make such further Orders as may be proper.

3   DATED: December 10, 20xx

4   *Billy M. Kidd*

5   BILLY M. KIDD, Petitioner

6

             Attach verification page as last page after exhibits

7

8

9

10

11

12

13

14

15

16

17

18

19

20

21

22

23

24

25

26

27

28

PETITION FOR FINAL DISTRIBUTION ON WAIVER OF ACCOUNTING

1
2
3   Verification
4

5   I, the undersigned, the petitioner and personal representative

6   of the estate of the above-named decedent, declare that I have

7   read the foregoing Petition for Final Distribution on Waiver

8   of Accounting and the requests designated therein and know its

9   contents. I declare that the petition, including all attachments,

10 is true to my knowledge, except as to matters in it stated on my

11 own information and belief, and as to those matters I believe it

12 to be true.

13   I declare under penalty of perjury under the laws of the State

14 of California that the foregoing is true and correct and that

    this declaration was executed on _____Date signed_____, 20_____,

15 at _____Place signed_____, California.

16
                                    _____You sign here_____
17   Petitioner

18
19
20
21
22
23
24
25
26
27
28

Petition for Final Distribution Exhibit "A"

ESTATE OF ANABELLE KIDD, DECEASED

EXHIBIT "A"

Creditors Given Notice of Administration

(Probate Code Sec. 9050)

Creditor	Nature of Debt	Date of Service of Notice
Springs Ambulance Service	Last illness expense	8-2-xx
Sullivan's Catering Service	Food and services provided decedent	8-2-xx
Bankamericard Visa	Credit card balance	8-2-xx
Bullock's Wilshire	Account balance	8-2-xx
John Harrad	Personal loan	8-2-xx

Petition for Final Distribution Exhibit "B"

ESTATE OF ANABELLE KIDD, DECEASED

EXHIBIT "B"

Creditors' Claims

Claimant	Amount of Claim	Date Filed	Date of Service of Notice of Rejection or Date Paid
Wilshire Medical Center	$237.50	9-4-xx	Paid 10-15-xx
Sullivan's Catering Service	347.00	9-5-xx	Paid 10-15-xx
Harry's Auto Shop	150.00	8-23-xx	Rejected on 8-31-xx
Bankamericard Visa	789.56	8-23-xx	Paid 8-31-xx

To prepare the Petition for Final Distribution, you will need the numbered court paper that we discussed in Chapter 13. Review the instructions in that section before you begin. Here are a few key points:

- The title of the court must start on or below Line 8.
- The title of the estate usually starts on Line 11 on the left side of the paper, as shown.
- On the right side, type in the case number assigned to you when you filed your first petition, as shown in our sample.
- Double-space the body of the petition so each typewritten line is opposite one of the numbers on the left side of the paper. Also, be sure to keep within the margins.

Here are some guidelines for preparing the petition:

Heading: Under the case number, type in the title of the petition as shown. Add the words in parentheses if you will request commissions. (If distribution will be made to a trust, add "AND DISTRIBUTION TO TESTAMENTARY TRUST.") Some courts (for example, Riverside County) require that the applicable Probate Code sections be shown under the title. Under that, type in a space for the time and place of the hearing.

The body of the petition starts on the next numbered line after your heading—in our sample, this happens to be Line 19.

Paragraph 1: Indicate whether the decedent died testate (with a will) or intestate (without a will). It's good practice to include the date letters were issued.

Paragraph 2: If you gave written Notice of Administration to any creditor (see Step 15), use the alternate language in parentheses and attach a schedule of all creditors who were given notice, and the date of the notice. (Remember, if the notice was given during the last 30 days of the four-month period, the claims period doesn't expire until 60 days after that last notice was given.)

Paragraphs 3 and 4: Use whichever language applies.

Paragraph 5: Insert the date notice was given to the Franchise Tax Board. This notice is required in all probate cases for which letters are first issued on or after July 1, 2008.

Paragraph 6: If no formal claims were filed, use the first Paragraph 6. If formal claims were filed with the court, use the second Paragraph 6 and list them in an exhibit. (If the accounting is waived, you do not have to list debts paid without formal claims under Probate Code § 9154.)

If there were rejected claims, add the wording in parentheses.

Paragraph 7: When debts are paid without formal claims, as in most estates, we recommend you include this paragraph. Such debts usually do not have to be listed if an accounting is waived, but some courts may require it.

Paragraph 9: Fill in the total appraised value of the estate inventory. You can get this figure from the Inventory and Appraisal form. (See Step 14.)

Paragraph 10: If you performed any actions without court supervision under the Independent Administration of Estates Act, especially those that require a Notice of Proposed Action, list and describe them here. Ordinary steps taken in administering the estate and in caring for and preserving the estate assets, such as making ordinary repairs, paying taxes and other expenses, terminating a lease, or storing personal property, need not be listed. However, describe major transactions that substantially affect or alter the property in the estate and the assets that remain on hand for distribution. For instance, if property was sold or additional assets were acquired, describe these actions. Some examples are shown in our sample petition. Others might be:

"Sold 100 shares of General Oil Corp. common stock, for cash on an established stock exchange."

"Invested funds of the estate in a $10,000 U.S. Treasury Bond, series 2000, due August 15, 20xx."

"Continued the operation of the decedent's business known as "John's Auto Repair Shop," to preserve the interest of the estate and those persons interested in the business."

"Executed a $5,000 promissory note, dated January 7, 20xx, interest at 10%, all due and payable January 7, 20xx, secured by deed of trust on real property of the estate located at 1801 Cove Street, Seaside, California."

If a Notice of Proposed Action was given, most counties require that the original be filed with the court (before or at the same time as the Petition for Final Distribution) with a proof of mailing attached, or the consent of the parties shown on the form. A proof of mailing may be typed separately, as shown in Step 13.

Paragraphs 11, 12, and 13: These allegations are required to show the condition of the estate.

In **Paragraph 12,** add the last two sentences shown in parentheses, if this applies to your situation. (See Chapter 13.)

Paragraph 14: The petition must have a schedule attached to it describing in detail all property in the probate estate that is to be distributed, showing the appraised value and total balance on hand. See Exhibit "C," below. There is no need to explain the difference between property included in the Inventory and Appraisal and the property on hand if an account is waived. If there is real property, the legal description, common address, and assessor's parcel number must be given. With the exception of the cash remaining on hand, the value of the assets will be the same as the appraised value shown on the Inventory and Appraisal form (Step 14, above). This is called the "carry value." If any of the assets have been sold, they will not be listed on this schedule because they are not "on hand" for distribution. Instead, the cash received from the sale will be in the estate's bank account. The amount of cash on hand will be whatever is left in the estate account (both checking and savings) reasonably close to the date you prepare the petition. Any assets that have been acquired since the estate was opened will also be included in the schedule. Cash or other personal property held in blocked accounts should be so indicated, with the name of the depository given. The court order will then direct the depository to distribute the property to the beneficiaries on the closing of the estate.

Paragraph 15: Another schedule must be attached naming all persons who are entitled to receive property from the estate, showing their addresses, ages, relationship to the decedent, and the amount of property each will receive. The schedule will vary somewhat, depending on whether or not there is a will.

- **When there is no will:** The schedule must list all the heirs who are entitled to the estate according to the laws of intestate succession (as explained in Chapter 3), and the share (fraction) each will receive. Usually, you don't have to itemize the property going to each heir, because each will merely receive his or her proportionate share of each and every asset. However, some counties (for example, San Diego) require a separate distribution schedule specifically describing the assets going to each distributee. If any heir is deceased, be sure to indicate this and show the date of death, and then list the issue of the deceased heir. A sample of a schedule for an intestate estate is shown below (Example 2).

- **When there is a will:** The decedent's will determines how the property is to be distributed. Therefore, you must set out the will provisions and list all of the beneficiaries and the property they receive. The easiest way to do this is to simply quote the paragraphs in the will that say how the property is to go. After that, list the beneficiaries' names, addresses, ages ("over 18" or "under 18"), and relationship to the decedent, and what they are to get. Persons who are not related to the decedent are listed as "strangers." See Example 1, below.

As we discussed in Chapter 3, occasionally it is difficult to determine how the property is to be distributed, and you may have some doubt as to how to proceed. This might be the case if the will gives away a lot more than the decedent had, or if a beneficiary under a will predeceased the decedent (or didn't survive him by the number of days required by the will) and there is no alternate beneficiary. In this situation, your best bet is to consult a lawyer. Once your questions are answered, you can complete the probate of the estate on your own. See Chapter 16 for material on how to hire and compensate lawyers.

If the will directs that all of the property is to go to one person, or to several persons in equal shares, this schedule will be much like the one in an intestate estate where each beneficiary receives a percentage, or fraction.

Many wills direct that specific gifts be given to certain persons, such as, "I give $1,000 to John, and I give my antique blue china dishes to Mary, and the remainder of my estate to my daughter, Jane." Unless the will provides otherwise, the specific gifts must normally be paid or distributed first. Whatever property is left is called the "remainder" or "residue" of the estate. If it should so happen that no residue is left after the specific gifts are distributed or paid, then the person or persons entitled to the residue are simply out of luck, *unless there is a provision in the will to prevent this from happening.*

Examples 1 and 3, below, show how this schedule might be prepared for a testate estate (one having a will).

A specific gift (for example, "I give my 200 shares of IBM stock to Jane") carries with it income on the property from the date of death, less taxes and other expenses attributable to the property during administration. (Prob. Code § 12002.) Also, unless a will provides otherwise, gifts for a specific amount of money receive interest one year after the date of death if not paid within that time. (Prob. Code § 12003.) To compute the interest, see Probate Code § 12001. Most estates are closed within a year and don't have to deal with this problem.

Example 4, below, shows how you would prepare the distribution schedule if you encounter a will that makes only specific gifts of property and does not contain a provision disposing of the residue of the estate. The property not disposed of by the will passes to the decedent's heirs under intestate succession laws (discussed in Chapter 3). Therefore, it passes one-third to each of the two brothers, and the children of the deceased sister share the one-third their mother would have inherited, or one-sixth each. Poor Albert, the decedent's nephew, doesn't receive anything because the decedent disposed of the Pontiac automobile before his death.

- **When the will contains a trust:** If the will distributes property in trust for one or more of the beneficiaries, the proposed distribution schedule will list the trustee as a beneficiary, showing the amount distributed to the trust. You do not have to list the trust beneficiaries, nor the property they each receive from the trust. The distribution schedule must also quote the language in the will providing for the trust and the trust provisions. Wills containing trusts are usually many pages long, which in turn makes this exhibit longer. Example 5 shows you an abridged sample of a distribution schedule for a will that contains a simple trust. A Consent to Act as Trustee and Waiver of Accounting signed by the trustee must be attached to the petition or filed separately before the hearing date.

    If the trustee (as well as the successor trustee, if the will named one) cannot serve or declines to act, you will have to see an attorney to have a trustee appointed by the court before distribution will be ordered. You will also have to file a Declination to Act as Trustee in addition to the successor trustee's Consent to Act. Samples of these forms are shown below.

Petition for Final Distribution Exhibit "C"

Estate of Anabelle Kidd, Deceased

Exhibit "C"

Assets on Hand

<u>SEPARATE PROPERTY</u>   <u>Carry Value</u>

1. One-third (1/3) interest as tenant in common
   with co-owers John and Mary Smith, in real
   property in the County of Contra Costa,
   described in Section 3, Township 20 North,
   Range 3 East; unimproved land, Assessor's
   Parcel No. 4562-34-5770 $5,000.00

2. 250 shares, Federated Stores, Inc. common stock   6,000.00

3. 75 shares, Bestco, Inc. $3 Cumulative,
   convertible preferred stock   1,500.00

4. Five $100 U.S. Series E bonds, issued June 1975   500.00

5. $22,000 promissory note dated June 1, 1998, to
   decedent by R.E. Jones, interest at 9%, secured
   by deed of trust recorded June 15, 1998, in
   Book 4879, Page 98, in Official Records of Los
   Angeles County

   Balance at date of death   20,000.00
   Accrued interest   150.00

6. $10,000 promissory note of June 1, 1999, to
   decedent by David Hudson, unsecured, interest
   at 7%, payable interest only   10,000.00

7. Decedent's interest as owner in Great Life
   Insurance Company Policy No. 36678   1,300.00

8. Decedent's 50% interest in Valueless Mining Co.,
   a Limited Partnership   250.00

9. Antique silver teapot, marked "Sheffield, 1893"   90.00

10. Household furniture, furnishings, and personal
    effects located at decedent's residence   350.00

11. Cash on deposit in checking Account No. 345 778,
    Westside National Bank, Los Angeles   40,000.00

12. Certificate of Deposit No. 3459, Central Savings
    and Loan Association, Santa Monica Branch   <u>100,000.00</u>
                                                $185,140.00

Petition for Final Distribution Exhibit "D" (example 1)

Estate of Anabelle Kidd, Deceased

Exhibit "D"

Beneficiaries Under Decedent's Will and
Proposed Distribution

1. The decendent's will disposes of her estate as follows:

   "I give to my friend, ALBERTINE TERREUX, that certain silver teapot marked 'Sheffield, 1893.'

   "I give, devise, and bequeath all the rest, residue, and remainder of my property, of whatsoever kind and character and wheresoever situated, to my husband, CALVIN KIDD. If my husband should predecease me, then in that event I give the residue of my estate to my three children, MARY KIDD CLARK, BILLY M. KIDD, and JON KIDD, in equal shares. If any of my children should predecease me, then that child's share shall go to his or her then living lawful issue, by right of representation."

2. The decedent's husband, CALVIN KIDD, predeceased the decedent. The decedent's son JON KIDD, also predeceased the decedent, and under the terms of the decedent's will his share of the estate passes to his son, CARSON KIDD.

3. Petitioner proposes to distribute the estate on hand as follows:

Name and Address	Age	Relationship	Share
Albertine Terreux 17 Rue Madeleine Paris, France	Adult	Stranger	Silver teapot marked "Sheffield, 1893"
Mary Kidd Clark 789 Main Street Venice, California 90410	Adult	Daughter	1/3 Residue
Billy M. Kidd 1109 Sky Blue Mountain Trail Billings, Montana 48906	Adult	Son	1/3 Residue
Carson Kidd 711 Valley Road Owens, California 98455	Adult	Grandson	1/3 Residue

Petition for Final Distribution Exhibit "D" (example 2)

```
          Estate of Bonnie Doe, Deceased
                   Exhibit "D"
       Heirs of Decedent and Proposed Distribution


   Decedent's heirs at law and the respective shares to which they
are entitled are:
```

Name and Address	Age	Relationship	Share
Robert Doe 100 Ocean Avenue Santa Monica, CA 90000	Over 18	Son	1/2
Mary Smith (Deceased January 10, 1986)		Daughter	
Margaret Smith 1022 - 10th Street Culver City, CA 90000	Over 18	Granddaughter (daughter of Mary Smith)	1/4
William Smith 123 Main Street Los Angeles, CA 90000	Over 18	Grandson (son of Mary Smith)	1/4

Petition for Final Distribution Exhibit "D" (example 3)

Estate of John Doe, Deceased

Exhibit "D"

<u>Beneficiaries Under Decedent's Will</u>
<u>And</u>
<u>Proposed Distribution</u>

1. The decedent's will disposes of this estate as follows:

"I hereby give, devise, and bequeath all of my estate, of every kind and character, to my wife, JANE DOE.

"Should my wife, JANE DOE, predecease me or fail to survive a period of six months following my death, then and in that event, I give, devise, and bequeath the sum of
$1,000 to my daughter, MARY CLARK, I hereby give, devise, and bequeath all the rest, residue, and remainder of my estate, both real and personal of whatsoever kind and character and wheresoever situated to my son, ROBERT DOE.

"In the event either of my said two children shall predecease me, or fail to survive a period of six months following my death, then I direct that the share which would otherwise have been paid to him or her be distributed to my surviving child."

2. The decedent's wife, JANE DOE, predeceased the decedent. The decedent's daughter, MARY CLARK, and the decedent's son, ROBERT DOE, survived the decedent for six months and are now living.

<u>Name and Address</u>	<u>Age</u>	<u>Relationship</u>	<u>Share</u>
Mary Clark 789 Main Street Venice, California 90000	Over 18	Daughter	$1,000
Robert Doe 21 Kelley Court Santa Ana, CA 90000	Over 18	Son	100% Residue

Petition for Final Distribution Exhibit "D" (example 4) (page 1)

Estate of Susan Jones, Deceased

Exhibit "D"
<u>Beneficiaries Under Decedent's Will</u>
<u>And</u>
<u>Proposed Distribution</u>

1. The decedent's Will disposes of her estate as follows:

"FIRST, I give my collection of tennis trophies to my niece, Eileen.

SECOND, I give my 1984 Pontiac automobile to my nephew, Albert.

THIRD, I give my household furniture, furnishings, and personal effects, and artwork to my brother Mark.

FOURTH, I give my condominium located at 2009 Sagebrush Circle in Palm Springs, to my brother Ron.

FIFTH, I give the sum of $10,000 to my sister, Mary."

2. Petitioner, as personal representative of the estate, did not come into possession of the 1984 Pontiac automobile referred to in Article Second of the decedent's Will, and said property was not among the assets of the decedent's estate.

3. The decedent's sister, Mary Smith, predeceased the decedent on January 3, 1996. Accordingly the gift of $10,000 given to Mary Smith in Article Fifth of the Will should be distributed to Mary Smith's surviving issue, her daughter Betty Smith and her son James Smith, in equal shares.

4. Included among the assets of the decedent's estate were 200 shares of Miracle Corporation stock and a 1994 Buick automobile. The decedent's Will does not dispose of these assets, and under the laws of intestate succession such property should be distributed to the decedent's heirs at law whose names, ages, and relationships are set forth below.

5. Proposed Distribution:

<u>Name and Address</u>	<u>Age</u>	<u>Relationship</u>	<u>Share</u>
Mark Jones 21 Paseo St. Cathedral City, CA 90000	Over 18	Brother	Household furniture, furnishings, personal effects, and artwork, plus 1/3 interest as an heir at law in 200 shares of Miracle Corporation stock and 1994 Buick automobile

Petition for Final Distribution Exhibit "D" (example 4) (page 2)

Estate of Susan Jones, Deceased

Ron Jones 89 Thermal Dr. Apt. 8 Needles, CA 90000	Over 18	Brother	Condominium at 2009 Sagebrush Circle, Palm Springs, plus 1/3 interest as an heir at law in 200 shares of Miracle Corporation stock and 1994 Buick automobile

Mary Smith, deceased Sister

Eileen Jones 1835 Navajo Circle Palm Springs, CA 90000	Under 18	Niece	Trophies
Betty Smith 10 Acorn St. Sun City, CA 90000 (daughter of Mary Smith)	Over 18	Niece	$5,000 plus 1/6 interest as an heir at law in 200 shares of Miracle Corporation stock and 1994 Buick automobile
James Smith 10 Acorn St. Sun City, CA 90000 (son of Mary Smith)	Over 18	Nephew	$5,000 plus 1/6 interest as an heir at law in 200 shares of Miracle Corporation stock and 1994 Buick automobile

Petition for Final Distribution Exhibit "D" (example 5) (page 1)

Estate of Laura Smith, Deceased

Exhibit "D"

Beneficiaries Under Decedent's Will
and Proposed Distribution

1. The decedent's Will disposes of her estate as follows:
"THIRD, I hereby give:

A. My nephew, ARTHUR JONES, the sum of $5,000. If he should predecease me, this gift shall lapse and become part of the residue of my estate.

B. My niece, FRIEDA JONES, the sum of $5,000. If she should predecease me, this gift shall lapse and become part of the residue of my estate.

C. I give, devise, bequeath all the rest, residue, and remainder of my estate, both real and personal and wherever situated, to my children, SHARON SMITH, SALLY SMITH, and LINDA SMITH, in equal shares. All of my children are over the age of twenty-one (21) as of the date of this will, with the exception of LINDA. It is my wish that the portion of my estate bequeathed and devised to LINDA be held in trust by ALEXANDER BROWN, as Trustee, to be held, administered, and distributed in accordance with the following provisions.

1. I direct that my Trustee provide for the health, education, welfare, and support, and other needs of LINDA, so long as she is living and is under age thirty-five (35). The Trustee shall pay to or apply for her benefit, as much of the
net income and principal of the trust as in the Trustee's discretion he deems necessary, after taking into consideration to the extent the Trustee deems advisable any other income or resources she may possess. Any unexpended income shall be added to the principal.

2. When LINDA for whom a share has been so allocated in trust attains the age of twenty-five (25), the Trustee shall distribute to the said child one-half (1/2) of the principal of such child's trust as then constituted; when said child attains age thirty-five (35) the Trustee shall distribute to said child the undistributed balance of her trust.

3. To carry out the purpose of the trust created for LINDA and subject to any limitations stated elsewhere in this will, the Trustee is vested with the following powers with respect to

Petition for Final Distribution Exhibit "D" (example 5) (page 2)

```
                    Estate of Laura Smith, Deceased
EXHIBIT "D" - PAGE 2
```

the trust estate and any part of it, in addition to those powers now or hereafter conferred by law:

    a. To continue to hold any property including shares of the Trustee's own stock, and to operate at the risk of the trust estate any business that the Trustee receives or acquires under the trust as long as the Trustee deems advisable;

    b. To manage, control, grant options on, sell (for cash or on deferred payments), convey, exchange, partition, divide, improve, and repair trust property;

    c. To borrow money, and to encumber or hypothecate trust property by mortgage, deed of trust, pledge, or otherwise;

    4. If LINDA dies before becoming entitled to receive distribution of her share of the estate, the undistributed balance of her portion shall be distributed to her issue, if any, by right of representation, and if none then to my surviving children in equal shares."

2. Proposed Distribution:

Name and Address	Age	Relationship	Share
Arthur Jones 35 Berkeley Square, No. 6 Newhall, California	Adult	Nephew	$5,000
Frieda Jones 3885 Overlook Drive Ojai, California	Adult	Niece	$5,000
Sharon Smith 2332 - 20th Street Santa Monica, California	Adult	Daughter	1/3 residue
Sally Smith 1139 Oak Avenue Ocean Park, California	Adult	Daughter	1/3 residue
Alexander Brown 477 Palisades Park Drive Brentwood Park, California	Adult	Trustee	1/3 residue

3. Alexander Brown has consented to act as Trustee, and a Consent to Act as Trustee and Waiver of Accounting by Alexander Brown is attached to this petition.

Distribution to Minors (Under 18)

Usually, you cannot safely distribute property to a minor unless a guardian has been appointed for the minor's estate. However, there are exceptions if the amount to be distributed is small, the decedent's will names a custodian to receive the minor's property, or the minor has a court-appointed guardian. Here are some guidelines.

Minor Has a Court-Appointed Guardian

If a guardian is appointed for the minor's estate, you may distribute the minor's property to the guardian. In this case, add a paragraph to the body of the petition in Paragraph 15 in the following basic form:

> _(Name of minor)_ , one of the beneficiaries, is a minor, and petitioner proposes to distribute the property belonging to the minor to _(name of guardian)_ as guardian of the minor's estate. A copy of Letters of Guardianship issued to the guardian is attached to petition as Exhibit __.

> ⓘ **CAUTION**
> **More information about guardianships.** If you need to have a court appoint a guardian for a minor, refer to *The Guardianship Book for California: How to Become a Child's Legal Guardian*, by David Brown and Emily Doskow (Nolo).

Decedent's Will Names a Custodian to Receive Minor's Property

If there is no guardian for the minor's estate, but the decedent nominated a custodian in his or her will (or in some other document) to receive the minor's property, then the personal representative may transfer the property to that person. The property will be held for the benefit of the minor under the California Uniform Gifts to Minors Act or the California Uniform Transfers to Minors Act.

Specific language must be used when transferring title to the property to the custodian, for example, "John Doe, as Custodian for Mary Doe, under the California Uniform Transfers to Minors Act." Any type of property may be transferred under the California Uniform Transfers to Minors Act.

The custodian has certain duties with respect to the custodial property, such as keeping records of all transactions regarding the property, including information necessary for the minor's tax return, and making them available for inspection. The custodian also has certain powers with respect to the management of the custodial property. The regulations governing transfers under the Uniform Transfers to Minors Act are set out in Probate Code §§ 3900 to 3925.

When making a distribution to a custodian nominated by the decedent to receive a minor's property, add the following paragraph to Paragraph 15 of the petition:

> Petitioner proposes to distribute the property belonging to _(name of minor)_ , a minor, to _(name of custodian)_ as custodian for the minor under the California Uniform Transfers to Minors Act, as authorized by the decedent's will. A consent to act as custodian, signed by _(name of custodian)_ , is attached hereto as Exhibit __ .

Attach as an exhibit the consent document. The consent should be a simple statement, signed and dated by the custodian, such as:

> I hereby consent to act as custodian for _(name of minor)_ , under the California Uniform Transfers to Minors Act.

Minor's Estate Does Not Exceed $5,000

If there is no appointed guardian, and the decedent did not nominate a custodian to receive the minor's property but the total estate of the minor (that is, what he or she already owns plus what he or she is inheriting) does not exceed $5,000, then money or other personal property belonging to the minor may be delivered to a parent of the minor. They can hold it in trust for him or her until she reaches age 18.

To accomplish this, a declaration signed by the parent under oath (under penalty of perjury) should be attached to the petition attesting to the fact that the total estate of the minor, including the money or other property delivered to the parent, does not exceed $5,000 in value. A sample declaration is shown below. In this situation, add the following paragraph to Paragraph 15 of the petition:

Consent to Act as Trustee and Waiver of Accounting

```
Name:
Address:



Telephone No.:

Petitioner in pro per


            SUPERIOR COURT OF CALIFORNIA
            COUNTY OF _____


Estate of          ) NO. _____
                   )
   MARY BROWN,     ) CONSENT TO ACT AS TRUSTEE AND
                   )
      deceased     ) WAIVER OF ACCOUNTING
_____)


   The undersigned, named in the Will of the above-named

decedent to act as Trustee of the testamentary trust provided

for therein, hereby consents to act as Trustee and waives

the filing and settlement of a final account by the estate

representative.

   DATED:_____,20__


                    _____
```

Declination to Act as Trustee

```
1    Name:
     Address:
2

3

4    Telephone No.:

5    Petitioner in pro per

6

7                    SUPERIOR COURT OF CALIFORNIA
8                    COUNTY OF _____

9
     Estate of          ) NO. _____
10                       )
11   _____, aka ) DECLINATION TO ACT AS TRUSTEE
                         )
12   _____,       )
                         )
13        deceased       )
     _____)
14

15      The undersigned, being nominated by name to act as Trustee of the

16   trust created under the decedent's will, does hereby decline to act

17   as Trustee.

18      DATED:_____,20__

19

20                        _____

21

22

23

24

25

26

27

28
```

(Name of minor) , one of the beneficiaries entitled to receive property of the estate, is a minor. The total estate of the minor does not exceed $5,000, and petitioner proposes to distribute the property belonging to the minor to the minor's parent, ___ _(name of parent)_ , to be held in trust for the benefit of the minor until he/she reaches age 18, pursuant to Probate Code §§ 3400–3401. A declaration signed by _(name of parent)_ attesting to the fact that the total estate of the minor, including the money or other property to be paid or delivered to the parent, does not exceed $5,000 in value, is attached hereto as Exhibit ___.

Property to Be Distributed Does Not Exceed $10,000

If the minor has no guardian of the estate and the decedent did not nominate a custodian, but the property to be transferred does not exceed $10,000 in value, the personal representative may, under certain conditions, designate another adult as custodian under the California Uniform Transfers to Minors Act. This is true even if the will contains no express authorization for such a distribution or if the decedent died intestate. (Prob. Code § 3906.) The conditions are:

- The personal representative must consider the transfer to be in the best interests of the minor; and
- The will must not prohibit the transfer or contain provisions inconsistent with such a transfer.

If you wish to make this type of transfer, we suggest adding a paragraph in substantially the following form to Paragraph 15 of the petition:

(Name of minor) , one of the beneficiaries entitled to receive property of the estate, is a minor. The minor does not have a guardian appointed for his/her estate, nor did the decedent designate a guardian or custodian to receive property belonging to the minor. The property to be distributed to _(name of minor)_ does not exceed a value of $10,000, and petitioner, in his/her capacity as personal representative of the decedent's estate, believes it will be in the best interest of the minor to transfer the property belonging to the minor to _(name of custodian)_ , the minor's

(state relationship , for example, parent, adult sister) , as custodian for _(name of minor)_ under the California Uniform Transfers to Minors Act to hold without bond until the minor attains the age of 18 years, pursuant to the provision of Probate Code § 3906. [Add, if the decedent left a will: The custodianship is not prohibited by or inconsistent with the terms of the decedent's will or any other governing instrument.] _(Name of custodian)_ has consented to act as custodian and her written consent is attached hereto as Exhibit ___.

Prepare a consent as described in Item 2, above.

Property to Be Distributed Consists of Money

If the minor has no guardian of the estate and money is to be distributed to the minor, the court may order that the money be deposited in a bank in California or in a trust company authorized to transact a trust business in this state, or invested in an account in an insured savings and loan association, subject to withdrawal only upon authorization of the court. (Prob. Code § 3413.) In this situation, you may add the following paragraph to Paragraph 15 of the petition:

The cash distribution to _(name of minor)_ should be deposited in an account at _(name of institution)_ , subject to withdrawal only on order of the court.

You should contact the bank or trust company in advance to make arrangements for the deposit. A form of receipt and agreement to be signed by the depository is shown under Item 2d of the instructions for preparing the Petition for Probate.

Other Types of Property Distributed to a Minor

In the absence of a guardian or designated custodian for the minor's estate, transfer of other types of property to a minor must normally be authorized by the court. However, transfer to a custodian under the California Uniform Transfers to Minors Act may still be made if the court approves the transfer. If you are faced with this situation, we suggest you see an attorney to handle the transfer for you.

Paragraph 16: This paragraph waives the requirement of an accounting. (See Chapter 13.) When the accounting is waived, the representative does not have to prepare a detailed list of receipts and disbursements during probate administration, which makes the closing of the estate much easier. All beneficiaries or heirs receiving property from the estate must sign waivers before the court will allow the accounting to be waived. The form, called Waiver of Accounting, is shown as Exhibit "E" to the sample petition. If you are the sole beneficiary, you may waive the accounting by a statement in the petition as shown in Paragraph 16. If there are other beneficiaries, a separate waiver may be attached for each one, or all of the beneficiaries may sign one waiver.

Persons who receive property as surviving joint tenants, as named beneficiaries under the decedent's life insurance policies or from living trusts, do not have to sign waivers.

If all beneficiaries or heirs will not sign the waiver, contact a lawyer to find out how the courts in your county want the accounting prepared.

Paragraph 17: This paragraph refers to the commissions to which you are entitled as estate representative. (See Chapter 13.) If you waive your commissions, type the first paragraph. If you claim them, type the second paragraph and fill in the computation.

Paragraph 18: This paragraph is recommended when there are other beneficiaries besides the estate representative and there is cash available for distribution. The court will authorize funds to be withheld to cover closing expenses and other liabilities that may be due after the estate is closed. This saves the representative from the chore of collecting expenses from the distributees after distribution. If the estate contains no cash, do not include this paragraph.

Paragraphs 19, 20, 21, and 22: These paragraphs contain allegations required under Probate Code § 1064. Include any of them that apply. In Paragraph 20, "family" means a relationship by blood or marriage, and "affiliate" generally means an entity that directly or indirectly controls the estate representative. (Prob. Code § 1064(c).) If the estate contains no cash, omit Paragraph 21 or revise it to state that there was no cash to invest. If the estate did not contain real property, omit Paragraph 22.

Final Paragraph: The final paragraph in the Petition for Final Distribution is called the "prayer" which requests that the petition be approved and distribution be made as set forth therein. The last sentence is called the "omnibus clause," which should always be included to provide for after-discovered property. An omnibus clause may avoid the necessity of reopening the proceeding when property is discovered after the representative's discharge.

Declaration re Distribution to a Minor

Name:
Address:

Telephone Number:
Petitioner in pro per

SUPERIOR COURT OF CALIFORNIA

FOR THE COUNTY OF _____

Estate of   ) NO. _____
)
_____   ) DECLARATION UNDER SECTION 3401 OF
            deceased.   ) THE CALIFORNIA PROBATE CODE
_____   )

The undersigned declares:

I am one of the parents of _____, a minor, who

is a distributee of the estate of the above-named decedent, and as

such I am entitled to said minor's custody; no guardian has been

appointed for said minor's estate, nor has said minor an estate in

excess of $5,000; the said minor has due from the above estate money

or personal property not exceeding $5,000; I agree to account to

said minor for all of the said property that I may receive from the

above estate on behalf of said minor, upon said minor reaching the

age of majority; I further agree to receipt for the said property

due to the minor, and to fully release and hold harmless the personal

representative of the above estate upon payment or delivery of the

said money or personal property.

I declare under penalty of perjury under the laws of the State

of California that the foregoing is true and correct. Executed this

_____ day of _____, 20___.

                                   _____

DECLARATION

Petition for Final Distribution—Exhibit "E"

```
 1   Name:
     Address:
 2

 3
     Telephone Number:
 4   Petitioner in pro per

 5

 6

 7

 8                    SUPERIOR COURT OF CALIFORNIA
 9           FOR THE COUNTY OF ___Name of county_____

10   Estate of              )  NO. ___Case number_____
11                          )
                            )  WAIVER OF ACCOUNTING
     Name of estate as it
12   appears on petition     )
                            )
13           deceased.      )
14   _____

15

16      The undersigned, ___Name of beneficiary who will sign waiver____, beneficiary

17   of the Estate of the above-named decedent, hereby waives the filing

18   and settlement of a final account.

19   DATED: ___Date signed_____

20                           _____Name of beneficiary_____

21

22

23

24

25

26

27

28
```

EXHIBIT E

Filing the Petition for Final Distribution

When you have completed the Petition for Final Distribution, this is how you get it ready to file:

1. Staple it together at the top in at least two places. Some courts may require a blue document backer to be attached to all documents (except printed Judicial Council forms) with the name of the document typed at the bottom. Other courts require that all documents be two-hole punched at the top, so check with the court before you file.

2. Sign and date it at the end and don't forget to sign the verification page. (This is very important.)

3. Staple a self-addressed, stamped envelope to the petition so a conformed (file-stamped) copy can be returned to you. In some counties the probate examiner may mail you a copy of the calendar notes if you attach another self-addressed, stamped envelope marked "calendar notes."

4. Make two copies of the petition, one for your file and one to send to the court with the original to be conformed and returned to you for your file.

5. Enclose a transmittal letter (a sample is shown below). In some court districts (San Bernardino, for example), you are required to send in the Order for Final Distribution at the same time you file the petition. In some other courts, you will also have to enclose a Notice of Hearing (Probate), which is discussed in Step 17, below.

6. A fee, currently $395, is required by some courts when the petition is filed. Make the check payable to "Clerk of Superior Court."

Transmittal Letter

County Clerk

(Address)

RE: Estate of _____
     Case No. _____

Dear Sir or Madam:

Enclosed are the following items:

1. Original and two copies of the Petition for Final Distribution in the above estate. Please file the original petition and return the extra copies to me, conformed, in the enclosed stamped, self-addressed envelope.

2. Original and _____ copies of Notice of Hearing. Please fill in the date, time, and place of the hearing and return all copies to me for processing.

3. Check payable to your order in the amount of $395, as the filing fee.

Very truly yours,

_____

Step 17: Prepare Notice of Hearing (Probate)

The Notice of Hearing on the Petition for Final Distribution must be mailed at least 15 days before the date of hearing to the following persons:

- if there is a will, to all the beneficiaries affected
- if there is no will, to all heirs who succeed to the estate
- if any portion of the estate escheats to the State of California, to the Attorney General at Sacramento
- to anyone who has requested special notice (send a copy of the petition, too)
- if a distributee is a trustee of a trust, to the trustee
- if the trustee is also the personal representative, to certain trust beneficiaries (Prob. Code § 1208), and
- if a court has appointed a guardian or conservator for a distributee, the guardian or conservator, as well as the distributee.

If you are the sole beneficiary, a Notice of Hearing is unnecessary; you don't have to send notice to yourself. Alternate beneficiaries named in the will also aren't given notice unless they receive property from the estate.

The notice is given on the printed form shown below. In many counties the notice must be prepared ahead of time and sent to the court at the time you file the petition so the court clerk may insert the date of the hearing on the notice and return it to you. In some counties (Los Angeles, for example), you don't have to send in the notice form when you file the petition. Instead, the date of the hearing is stamped or written on the petition form by the court clerk. You then must fill in this date on the Notice of Hearing form. Some counties require the notice to be submitted with the petition even though notice is not required, such as when the petitioner is also the sole distributee. Inquire locally as to the required procedure. Make a copy of the notice for each beneficiary, plus an extra one to be stamped and returned to you for your file. Some courts keep the original and return the copies only.

Caption: Fill in your name, address, the court's name, and case number, as you have on your other court papers.

Item 1: Fill in your name and title (executor, administrator), and that you have filed "A Petition for Final Distribution on Waiver of Accounting." If the petition requests statutory commissions, be sure to add this to the title.

Item 3: Fill in the requested information about the hearing. If the street address of the court is not shown in the caption, check the second box and type in the street address.

On the back of the form, fill in the name of the estate at the top, and the case number. Leave the top section (Clerk's Certificate of Posting/Mailing) blank. Complete the Proof of Service by Mail the same way as on the back of the Notice of Administration of Estate (explained in Step 3). In the space at the bottom, type in the name and address of everyone who is entitled to notice. A copy should be mailed to each of these persons. The person who mails the notice should fill in and sign the Proof of Service on the original notice (or one of the copies, if the court kept the original), after all copies are sent. The original proof of mailing must be filed with the court before the hearing.

Step 18: Prepare Order of Final Distribution

You will have to type the Order of Final Distribution form and mail it to the court for the judge's signature. When you send the order, enclose a transmittal letter modeled on the one in Step 16, above. If real estate is being transferred, ask the court to return a certified copy of the order so you can record it, and include a check for the certification fee (call the court to find out the amount). Some courts require the order to be submitted a number of days before the hearing date. Ask about local rules.

The sample order shown below should fulfill the requirements of most courts, and may be modified to conform to your particular situation. The first paragraph must include the date, time of hearing,

Notice of Hearing (Probate) (page 1)

DE-120

ATTORNEY OR PARTY WITHOUT ATTORNEY *(Name, State Bar number, and address):*	FOR COURT USE ONLY

Billy M. Kidd
1109 Sky Blue Mountain Trail
Billings, Montana 48906

TELEPHONE NO.: 715-555-6408 FAX NO. *(Optional):*

E-MAIL ADDRESS *(Optional):*

ATTORNEY FOR *(Name):* In pro per

SUPERIOR COURT OF CALIFORNIA, COUNTY OF LOS ANGELES

STREET ADDRESS: 1725 Main Street
MAILING ADDRESS: 1725 Main Street
CITY AND ZIP CODE: Santa Monica, CA 90401
BRANCH NAME: WEST DISTRICT

[X] ESTATE OF *(Name):* [ ] IN THE MATTER OF *(Name):*

Anabelle Kidd, aka Anabelle O. Kidd,

[X] DECEDENT [ ] TRUST [ ] OTHER

NOTICE OF HEARING—DECEDENT'S ESTATE OR TRUST	CASE NUMBER: WEP14813

This notice is required by law.
This notice does not require you to appear in court, but you may attend the hearing if you wish.

---

1. NOTICE is given that *(name):* Billy M. Kidd
   (representative capacity, if any): Executor
   has filed *(specify):** A Petition for Final Distribution on Waiver of Accounting

2. You may refer to the filed documents for more information. *(Some documents filed with the court are confidential.)*

3. A HEARING on the matter will be held as follows:

   a.   Date: December 30, 20xx Time: 9:30 A.M. Dept.: A   Room:

   b.   Address of court [X] shown above [ ] is *(specify):*

Assistive listening systems, computer-assisted real-time captioning, or sign language interpreter services are available upon request if at least 5 days notice is provided. Contact the clerk's office for *Request for Accommodations by Persons With Disabilities and Order* (form MC-410). (Civil Code section 54.8.)

---

* Do **not** use this form to give notice of a petition to administer estate (see Prob. Code, § 8100 and form DE-121) or notice of a hearing in a guardianship or conservatorship (see Prob. Code, §§ 1511 and 1822 and form GC-020).

Page 1 of 2

Form Adopted for Mandatory Use Judicial Council of California DE-120 [Rev. July 1, 2005]	**NOTICE OF HEARING—DECEDENT'S ESTATE OR TRUST** (Probate—Decedents' Estates)	Probate Code §§ 851, 1211, 1215, 1216, 1230, 17100 *www.courtinfo.ca.gov*
		American LegalNet, Inc. www.USCourtForms.com

Notice of Hearing (Probate) (page 2)

[X] ESTATE OF *(Name):* [ ] IN THE MATTER OF *(Name):*	CASE NUMBER:
Anabelle Kidd, aka Anabelle O. Kidd,	
[X] DECEDENT [ ] TRUST [ ] OTHER	WEP14813

CLERK'S CERTIFICATE OF POSTING

1. I certify that I am not a party to this cause.
2. A copy of the foregoing *Notice of Hearing—Decedent's Estate or Trust*
   a. was posted at *(address):*

   b. was posted on *(date):*

Date: _____   Clerk, by _____ , Deputy

PROOF OF SERVICE BY MAIL *

1. I am over the age of 18 and not a party to this cause. I am a resident of or employed in the county where the mailing occurred.
2. My residence or business address is *(specify):*   1809 - G Street, Billings, Montana 30400

3. I served the foregoing *Notice of Hearing—Decedent's Estate or Trust* on each person named below by enclosing a copy in an envelope addressed as shown below AND
   a. [X] **depositing** the sealed envelope on the date and at the place shown in item 4 with the United States Postal Service with the postage fully prepaid.
   b. [ ] **placing** the envelope for collection and mailing on the date and at the place shown in item 4 following our ordinary business practices. I am readily familiar with this business's practice for collecting and processing correspondence for mailing. On the same day that correspondence is placed for collection and mailing, it is deposited in the ordinary course of business with the United States Postal Service in a sealed envelope with postage fully prepaid.

4. a. Date mailed: December 14, 20xx   b. Place mailed *(city, state):* Billings, Montana

5. [ ] I served with the *Notice of Hearing—Decedent's Estate or Trust* a copy of the petition or other document referred to in the Notice.

I declare under penalty of perjury under the laws of the State of California that the foregoing is true and correct.

Date: December 14, 20xx

Mary Smith	*Mary Smith*
(TYPE OR PRINT NAME OF PERSON COMPLETING THIS FORM)	(SIGNATURE OF PERSON COMPLETING THIS FORM)

NAME AND ADDRESS OF EACH PERSON TO WHOM NOTICE WAS MAILED

	Name of person served	Address *(number, street, city, state, and zip code)*
1.	Mary Kidd Clark	789 Main Street, Venice, California 90410
2.	Carson Kidd	711 Valley Road, Owens, California 98455
3.	Albertine Terreux	17 Rue Madeleine, Paris, France
4.	Consulate of France	8350 Wilshire Blvd., Los Angeles, CA 90035

[ ] Continued on an attachment. *(You may use* Attachment to Notice of Hearing Proof of Service by Mail, *form DE-120(MA)/GC-020(MA), for this purpose.)*

* Do not use this form for proof of personal service. You may use form DE-120(P) to prove personal service of this Notice.

DE-120 [Rev. July 1, 2005]	**NOTICE OF HEARING—DECEDENT'S ESTATE OR TRUST** (Probate—Decedents' Estates)	Page 2 of 2

department number, and the judge's name. If you don't know the judge's name, you can leave a blank space and the court will fill it in. The order must always list in detail the property to be distributed to each person and its appraisal value—that is, the value on the Inventory and Appraisal, also called the "carry value." Some counties (for example, San Bernardino) require that you include in the order the address of any beneficiaries receiving real property. In the case of real property, the legal description and assessor's parcel number must be given. Be sure to proofread the legal description with the deed to the property to make sure it is accurate, since the order will be recorded with the county recorder's office as evidence of the transfer of ownership. We suggest one person read aloud from the deed while another reads the description in the order carefully. Or, if you have a legible copy of the legal description on a deed, title insurance report, or homestead declaration, you can photocopy the document, cut out the legal description, tape it onto the order, and photocopy the whole document.

The persons receiving specific gifts of property are always listed first, and those receiving the assets making up the balance of the estate (residue) are described after that. Make sure you don't include any of the specific gifts in the residue. No riders or exhibits may be attached to any court order, and nothing should appear after the signature of the judge.

If property will be distributed to a trust, you must set out the terms of the trust in full, again, in the Order of Final Distribution, changing the wording to the present tense and the third person. For example, "my daughter" should be changed to "decedent's daughter," or "I direct that my Trustee provide …" should be changed to "The Trustee shall provide …." Based on Example 5 of the exhibit for Paragraph 13 of the Petition for Final Distribution, this is what the order would recite:

IT IS FURTHER ORDERED that the following property shall be and the same is hereby distributed as follows:

To ARTHUR JONES, the sum of $5,000;

To FRIEDA JONES, the sum of $5,000;

All the rest, residue, and remainder of the estate, hereinafter more particularly described, together with any and all other property not now known or discovered which may belong to the decedent or her estate, or in which the decedent or her estate may have an interest, is hereby distributed as follows:

To SHARON SMITH, one-third (1/3) thereof;

To SALLY SMITH, one-third (1/3) thereof;

To ALEXANDER BROWN, as Trustee, one-third (1/3) thereof in trust for decedent's daughter, LINDA SMITH, to be held, administered, and distributed in accordance with the following provisions:

The Trustee shall provide for the health, education, welfare, and support, and other needs of LINDA, so long as she is living and is under age thirty-five (35). The Trustee shall pay to or apply for her benefit, as much of the net income and principal of the trust as in the Trustee's discretion … (etc.).

If property will be distributed to a minor, here are some examples of the wording that may be used:

To _____, the parent of _____, a minor, the sum of $5,000 to hold in trust for the minor until the minor's majority.

To _____, as Custodian for _____, a minor, under the California Uniform Transfers to Minors Act, the following property: (describe property).

You will also need to record a Preliminary Change in Ownership Report if real property has been transferred. (See Chapter 8.)

Order of Final Distribution (page 1)

1	BILLY M. KIDD 1109 Sky Blue Mountain Trail
2	Billings, Montana 48906
3	Telephone: 715-555-6408
	Petitioner in pro per
4	
5	
6	
7	SUPERIOR COURT OF CALIFORNIA
8	FOR THE COUNTY OF LOS ANGELES
9	
10	Estate of) CASE NO. WEP 14813)
11	ANABELLE KIDD, aka) ORDER OF FINAL DISTRIBUTION) ON WAIVER OF ACCOUNTING
12	ANABELLE O. KIDD,)) Hearing Date: 12-30-xx
13	deceased.) Time: 9:30 A.M. ――――――――――――――――――) Department A
14	
15	
16	BILLY M. KIDD, as personal representative of the estate of the
17	above-named decedent, having filed a Petition for Final
18	Distribution without rendering account, and the report and petition
19	coming on this day, December 30, 20xx, regularly for hearing at
20	9:30 A.M. in Dept. A of the above-entitled Court, the Honorable
21	Herbert Wise, Judge presiding, petitioner, Billy M. Kidd appearing
22	in propria persona and there being no opposition, the Court, after
23	examining the petition and hearing the evidence, finds that due
24	notice of the hearing of the petition has been regularly given as
25	prescribed by law; that all of the allegations of the petition are
26	true; that the assets described in this decree of distribution
27	comprise the entire estate on hand for distribution; that no federal
28	estate taxes were due from the estate; that all personal property

1.

ORDER OF FINAL DISTRIBUTION

Order of Final Distribution (page 2)

1 taxes due and payable by said estate have been paid; and that said

2 report and petition should be approved and distribution ordered as

3 prayed for.

4   IT IS THEREFORE ORDERED by the Court that notice to creditors has

5 been given as required by law; that the personal representative has in

6 his possession belonging to said estate the assets described herein;

7 that said report and petition are approved; (Add, if applicable: that the

8 personal representative is authorized to retain $_____ as a reserve

9 for closing expenses and to pay liabilities and to deliver the unused

10 portion to the beneficiaries of the estate without further Court Order;

11 and that the personal representative is hereby authorized to pay to

12 himself the sum of $5,370.61, hereby allowed as statutory commissions.

13   IT IS FURTHER ORDERED that the decedent's will disposes of his

14 estate as follows:

15   Quote dispositive provisions of the will verbatim. If there is no will, leave paragraph out.

16   IT IS FURTHER ORDERED that the following property shall be and the

17 same is hereby distributed as follows:

18   To ALBERTINE TERREUX, the decedent's antique silver teapot, marked

19 "Sheffield, 1893"; Appraised Value: $90.00

20   All the rest, residue, and remainder of the estate, hereinafter more

21 particularly described, together with any other property of the estate

22 not now known or discovered which may belong to the estate, or in which

23 the decedent or the estate may have an interest, is hereby distributed

24 to MARY KIDD CLARK, BILLY M. KIDD, and CARSON KIDD, in equal shares.

25   The residue of the estate, insofar as is now known, consists of

26 the following property:

27

28

2.

ORDER OF FINAL DISTRIBUTION

Order of Final Distribution (page 3)

1. One-third (1/3) interest as tenant in common   Carry Value
   with co-owners John and Mary Smith, in real
   property in the County of Contra Costa,
   described as Section 3 Township 20 North,
   Range 3 East. Unimproved land. Assessor's
   Parcel No. 4562-34-5770. $ 5,000.00

2. 250 shares, Federated Stores, Inc. Common
   stock $ 6,000.00

3. 75 shares, Bestco, Inc., $3 Cumulative,
   convertible preferred stock $ 1,500.00

4. Five $100 U.S. Series E bonds, issued
   June 1975 $ 500.00

5. $22,000 promissory note dated June 1, 1998,
   to decedent by R. E. Jones, interest at 9%,
   secured by deed of trust recorded June 15,
   1998, in Book 4879, Page 98, in Official
   Records of Los Angeles County

                      Balance at date of death $ 20,000.00
                      Accrued interest $ 150.00

6. $10,000 promissory note of June 1, 1999, to
   decedent by David Hudson, unsecured,
   interest at 7%, payable interest only $ 10,000

7. Decedent's interest as owner in Great Life
   Insurance Company Policy No. 36678 $ 1,300.00

8. Decedent's 50% interest in Valueless Mining
   Co., a Limited Partnership $ 250.00

9. Household furniture, furnishings, and personal
   effects located at decedent's residence $ 350.00

3.

ORDER OF FINAL DISTRIBUTION

Order of Final Distribution (page 4)

10. Cash on deposit in checking Account

    No. 345 778, Westside National Bank,

    Los Angeles $ 40,000.00

11. Certificate of Deposit No. 3459, Central

    Savings and Loan Association, Santa Monica

    Branch $100,000.00

DATED:_____, 20____

                       _____

                       JUDGE OF THE SUPERIOR COURT

4.

ORDER OF FINAL DISTRIBUTION

Step 19: Transfer the Assets and Obtain Court Receipts

Although the Order for Final Distribution is proof in itself of a beneficiary's right to property from an estate, the estate representative must still see that title is transferred in the case of certain types of assets.

A formal receipt, typed on numbered court paper, should be prepared and signed by each person who receives property in the Order of Final Distribution. The receipt should list the property received by the distributee, as shown below. If real property is being distributed, the personal representative must file a statement that identifies the date and place or location of the recording of the Order of Final Distribution. (Prob. Code § 11753.) This can usually be typed on the Affidavit for Final Discharge, shown below.

Cost Basis Data: As discussed in Chapter 7, assets passing to beneficiaries usually carry a new, stepped-up income tax basis, which is the appraised value on the date of death (inventory value), not the date when the assets are distributed. Beneficiaries should be advised of the income tax basis of each asset they receive. The cost basis data can be shown on the court receipt as the "Carry Value," or provided in a separate letter.

Missing Beneficiaries: If you can't locate a beneficiary who is entitled to receive a cash gift, you may deposit the money, in the name of the beneficiary, with the county treasurer. (Prob. Code § 11850.) If the beneficiary turns up, he or she can claim the money by petitioning the probate court. If the gift is other personal property and remains unclaimed for a year, the court will order that it be sold and the proceeds paid to the county. (Prob. Code § 11851.)

Real Property

Real property is transferred by recording a certified copy of the Order for Final Distribution, containing a legal description of the property, in each county in which any part of the property lies. (See Chapter 8 on how to record documents with the recorder's office.) The new owner(s) should tell the county tax collector where to mail tax bills. Fire insurance policies should also be changed to show the new ownership.

Promissory Notes

You should endorse over and deliver promissory notes to the distributee together with any deed of trust, pledge, or other security, and a copy of the Order for Final Distribution. The endorsement may be typed on the note in substantially the following form:

> ___*(Name of city)*___, California, ___*(date)*___, 20___.
> For value received, I hereby transfer and assign to ___
> *(name of beneficiary)*___ all right, title, and interest of ___
> *(name of decedent)*___ at the time of his/her death in the
> within note [*add, if applicable:* and the deed of trust
> securing the same, so far as the same pertains to said
> note, without recourse].
>
>
> Executor/Administrator of the Estate of
> _____, deceased.

Trust Deed Notes

If there are trust deed notes to be transferred, this is also handled by recording a certified copy of the Order for Final Distribution in the county in which the property described in the deed of trust is located. This will establish a record of the transfer from the name of the decedent to the name of the new owner. There is no need to prepare and record a separate Assignment of Deed of Trust for this purpose. If the note itself is being held by a bank, the new owner should send a copy of the order to the bank with directions on where to send future statements and payment requests.

Stocks and Bonds

Stocks and bonds should be transferred as discussed in Chapter 9. When stock shares must be divided among two or more persons and the shares do not come out even, an extra share may be taken by one person and the others given cash to make up the difference, if the distributees agree. For instance, if 25 shares of stock were to be divided among three beneficiaries, each would take eight shares (24 total). Then the extra share could be given to one beneficiary, who would give cash to the other beneficiaries equal to the value of their interest in the extra share so everyone would receive assets of the same value.

Mutual Funds and Money Market Funds

Transferring record ownership of mutual funds and money market funds is usually handled by the fund custodian. Therefore, the easiest way to deal with these assets is to contact the fund management directly (the monthly statement should tell you the address) and ask what is required to transfer or redeem the shares.

Tangible Personal Property

Items of tangible personal property, such as household furnishings, and other personal effects, usually have no record of title and require only physical delivery. Reasonable storage, delivery, and shipping costs for distribution of such items are chargeable to the estate.

Automobiles, Motor Vehicles, and Small Boats

The Department of Motor Vehicles will help in the transfer of title to these assets. Usually, this requires the representative to endorse the certificate of title (pink slip) as "owner" and present a certified copy of letters and pay a transfer fee. The new owner must apply for the transfer using the endorsed Certificate of Ownership and completing the Application for Transfer by New Owner on the reverse side. The insurance company should be notified of the change in ownership as well.

Cash in Blocked Accounts

Cash or other assets that were placed in blocked accounts to reduce bond will be released if you present the bank or institution holding the assets, with a certified copy of the Order of Final Distribution. The assets can then be distributed to the beneficiaries.

Step 20: Request Discharge From Your Duties

After you've delivered all property to the persons who are entitled to it, you may request that the court discharge you from your duties as the estate representative. The printed form for this purpose is titled "Ex Parte Petition for Final Discharge and Order." "Ex Parte" means without a hearing.

Instructions and a sample form are shown below. You'll find a blank copy in Appendix B.

Some courts require all receipts to be filed at the same time and some courts also require a copy of the court order. This is to make it easier for the probate examiners to make sure there is a receipt from everybody.

If everything is in order, the judge will sign the order on the bottom of the form, discharging you as the representative, and this concludes the court proceeding. If you had to post a bond while serving as representative, be sure to send a copy of the Order of Final Discharge to the bonding company to terminate the bond.

In most instances, you will wait at least a year after distribution before filing for discharge because you will have winding-up duties to fulfill—for example, signing fiduciary income tax returns, handling tax reserves, and transferring assets. If there is a surety bond, however, every effort should be made to get the Order for Final Discharge signed before the next premium is due. When a signed copy of the discharge comes back from the court, you should send a copy to the bonding company with a request that the bond be canceled and any unearned premium be refunded to the representative. (Surety bond premiums are not refundable for the first year. After the first year, a pro rata portion is refundable.) If there is a refund, it should be divided among the residuary beneficiaries.

Caption: Fill in your name, address, and court's name, and case number, as on your other court forms.

Item 1: Check the first box and insert the date the Order for Final Distribution was signed by the court.

Item 2a: If personal property was distributed, check this box and provide receipts as noted.

Item 2b: If no personal property was distributed, check this box.

Item 2c: If real property was distributed, check this box and insert the recording information. If you do not have the recording information, call the recorder's office and obtain the information over the phone. Be sure to have a copy of the order in front of you when you call.

Item 2d: If no real property was distributed, check this box.

Item 2e: If the estate representative is the sole distributee, check this box, indicating no receipt is required.

Item 2f: Leave this box blank.

Item 3: Sign and date the form.

Complete the section at the bottom, under "Order for Final Discharge," by inserting the name of the personal representative where indicated and checking the appropriate box below.

Court Receipt

1 Name:
   Address:
2
3 Telephone Number:
   Petitioner in pro per
4
5
6
                SUPERIOR COURT OF THE STATE OF CALIFORNIA
7
                    FOR THE COUNTY OF LOS ANGELES
8
9 Estate of   ) NO. _____
10   )
   _____) RECEIPT OF DISTRIBUTEE
11 _____)
            deceased.   )
12 _____)
13   The undersigned hereby acknowledges receipt from _____
14 _____, as personal representative of the estate of the
15 above-named decedent, of the following listed property:
16   Cash in the sum of $_____;
17   1/3 interest in 200 shares of Miracle Corporation stock;
18   1994 Buick automobile; and
19   Household furniture, furnishings, personal effects, and artwork.
20   The undersigned acknowledges that the above property
21 constitutes all of the property to which the undersigned is
22 entitled pursuant to the Order of Final Distribution made in the
23 above estate on _____, 20___.
24
25   Dated: _____, 20___
26
27   _____
28

_____
                      RECEIPT ON DISTRIBUTION

Ex Parte Petition for Final Discharge and Order

DE-295/GC-395

ATTORNEY OR PARTY WITHOUT ATTORNEY *(Name, State Bar number, and address):*	FOR COURT USE ONLY
Billy M. Kidd 1109 Sky Blue Mountain Trail Billings, Montana 48906	

TELEPHONE NO.: 715-555-6408   FAX NO. *(Optional):*

E-MAIL ADDRESS *(Optional):*

ATTORNEY FOR *(Name):*   In pro per

SUPERIOR COURT OF CALIFORNIA, COUNTY OF   LOS ANGELES

STREET ADDRESS: 1725 Main Street

MAILING ADDRESS: 1725 Main Street

CITY AND ZIP CODE: Santa Monica, CA 90401

BRANCH NAME: WEST DISTRICT

[X] ESTATE [ ] CONSERVATORSHIP [ ] GUARDIANSHIP OF

(Name):   ANABELLE KIDD, aka ANABELLE O. KIDD,

[X] DECEDENT [ ] CONSERVATEE [ ] MINOR

EX PARTE PETITION FOR FINAL DISCHARGE AND ORDER

CASE NUMBER:
WEP 14813

1. Petitioner is the [X] personal representative [ ] conservator [ ] guardian of the estate of the above-named decedent, conservatee, or minor. Petitioner has distributed or transferred all property of the estate as required by the final order [ ] and all preliminary orders for distribution or liquidation filed in this proceeding on *(specify date each order was filed):*   December 30, 20xx

2. All required acts of distribution or liquidation have been performed as follows *(check all that apply):*
   a. [X] All personal property, including money, stocks, bonds, and other securities, has been delivered or transferred to the distributees or transferees as ordered by the court. The receipts of all distributees or transferees are now on file or are filed with this petition. Conformed copies of all receipts previously filed are attached on Attachment 2.
   b. [ ] No personal property is on hand for distribution or transfer.
   c. [X] Real property was distributed or transferred. The order for distribution or transfer of the real property; the personal representative's, conservator's, or guardian's deed; or both, were recorded as follows *(specify documents recorded, dates and locations of recording, and document numbers or other appropriate recording information):*

      The Order of Final Distribution was recorded January 10, 20xx, in Contra Costa County as Document NO. 05-123456.

   d. [ ] No real property is on hand for distribution or transfer.
   e. [ ] No receipts are required because Petitioner is the sole distributee.
   f. [ ] The minor named above attained the age of majority on *(date):*

3. Petitioner requests discharge as personal representative, conservator, or guardian of the estate.

I declare under penalty of perjury under the laws of the State of California that the foregoing is true and correct.

Date: 3-5-20xx

Billy M. Kidd   *Billy M. Kidd*

_____   ▶ _____
(TYPE OR PRINT NAME OF PETITIONER)   (SIGNATURE OF PETITIONER)

ORDER FOR FINAL DISCHARGE

THE COURT FINDS that the facts stated in the foregoing *Ex Parte Petition for Final Discharge* are true.

THE COURT ORDERS that *(name):*   Billy M. Kidd

is discharged as [X] personal representative [ ] conservator [ ] guardian of the estate of the above-named decedent, conservatee, or minor, and sureties are discharged and released from liability for all acts subsequent hereto.

Date: 3-20-20xx

Billy M. Kidd   JUDICIAL OFFICER
_____   [ ] SIGNATURE FOLLOWS LAST ATTACHMENT.

Page 1 of 1

Form Adopted for Mandatory Use Judicial Council of California DE-295/GC-395 [New January 1, 2006]	**EX PARTE PETITION FOR FINAL DISCHARGE AND ORDER** **(Probate—Decedents' Estates and Conservatorships and Guardianships)**	Probate Code, §§ 2100, 2627, 2631, 11753, 12250; *www.courtinfo.ca.gov*

CHAPTER

15

Handling Property That Passes Outright to the Surviving Spouse or Domestic Partner

All property that a surviving spouse or registered domestic partner is entitled to receive outright from a deceased spouse or partner may be "set aside" to the survivor without formal probate. (Prob. Code § 13500.) There is no limitation on the amount or value of the assets transferred. This includes community property, separate property, and quasi-community property. Quasi-community property is property acquired by couples outside California that would have been community property if acquired in California. It is treated just like community property. (See Chapter 4.)

An Overview of These Simplified Procedures

A surviving spouse or domestic partner will normally have no problem acquiring assets that don't have official title documents, such as household furniture and personal effects. However, title companies, stock transfer agents, and others won't turn over property to the survivor without some kind of official document establishing that the property really belongs to the survivor. Not surprisingly, they want assurance that the survivor's position is valid.

Different documents are used, depending on the type of property involved. For community real property, a simple form affidavit can usually be used. For other property, the surviving spouse or partner can obtain a Spousal or Domestic Partner Property Order from the superior court. This chapter shows you how to use each method.

When to Use These Procedures

The simplified procedures outlined in this chapter should not be used in complex property situations. They apply only to simple estates with assets such as houses, cars, household goods, bank accounts, stocks, bonds, mutual funds, promissory notes, personal belongings, and antiques. If there are complex investments, large or complex claims by creditors, or strained family relations, or if the decedent owned an interest in a good-sized business, the surviving spouse or partner should consult an attorney.

To qualify as a surviving spouse or surviving domestic partner, the survivor must have been either legally married to the decedent or in a registered domestic partnership at the time of death. The procedures discussed in this chapter apply only to property that goes *outright* to a surviving spouse or partner, either under the deceased's will or by intestate succession. If any of the decedent's property passes to the surviving spouse or partner under a "qualified" form of ownership, formal probate is usually required. Qualified ownership means there is some sort of limitation on the ownership—for example, if property is willed to the surviving spouse or partner and someone else as joint tenants or tenants in common, or under a trust that gives the surviving spouse or partner the right to use the property only during his or her lifetime, or the survivor's use of the property is restricted in some way.

If the will says, "I leave my entire estate to my wife, providing she survives me for 30 days," this is not considered a qualified interest. If the surviving spouse or domestic partner survives for the required period, the property may be transferred to the surviving spouse or partner without probate by the procedures described in this chapter.

These shortcut procedures to transfer property to a surviving spouse or domestic partner will not work if the decedent willed all or part of his or her interest in the community property or separate property to someone else. Here are a couple of examples of will provisions that necessitate probate:

> I leave my husband a life estate in my interest in our home in Montebello. Upon my husband's death, I leave my interest in said property to my two granddaughters, Holly and Celeste.

The husband is given a life estate (a qualified ownership) in the home; because it doesn't pass outright to him as surviving spouse, it will require probate.

> I leave my residence at 18865 Navajo Circle, Indio, to my son, Raymond. I leave the sum of $50,000 to my daughter, Elsa. I leave the residue of my estate to my husband, Anthony.

Because the decedent's interest in the residence in Indio and the $50,000 do not pass to the decedent's surviving spouse, these assets will require probate. However, the assets contained in the residue of the estate, which pass outright to the decedent's husband, Anthony, can be transferred without formal probate administration using the "abbreviated" procedures described here.

TIP

Small estate note. Remember, if the total gross value of the decedent's real and personal property that is willed to someone else (or passes to someone else under intestate succession) is less than $100,000, it may be possible to use the transfer procedures outlined in Chapter 11.

Creditors' Claims

The surviving spouse or partner is responsible for any debts chargeable against community or separate property he or she receives using these procedures, no matter when claims are made to him or her. When formal probate proceedings are used, however, most creditors' claims are cut off four months after probate is begun (exceptions to this rule are discussed in Chapter 14). In most estates, because no (or a very few) creditors even present claims in the first place, using the spousal set-aside procedures outlined in this chapter will cause no problems. If, however, after examining the decedent's affairs you anticipate the possibility of substantial creditors' claims against the estate, consider putting the property through formal probate. It will give you peace of mind knowing that creditors cannot bring any claims after the deadlines have passed.

If the deceased spouse's or partner's estate goes through a formal probate proceeding, under Probate Code § 11444, the debts are characterized as separate or community property and are allocated to the separate or community property of the parties accordingly. More detailed rules apply in particular situations. When there is an issue as to whether a debt should be paid from community property or a decedent's separate property, you should consult an attorney.

Community vs. Separate Property

If a will gives a decedent's entire estate to a spouse or partner, it is not crucial to know the character of the property. However, in most instances, before going ahead with these unsupervised transfer procedures in the estate you are settling, you must know whether the decedent's property is community property or separate property, and of course, you must be sure the survivor is entitled to inherit it. In the absence of a will, it is essential that you know whether the property is community or separate in order to determine who will inherit it. How to classify property as community or separate is discussed in detail in Chapter 4. If you are not absolutely sure as to the community and separate property ownership of the property you are dealing with, read that chapter before continuing. How to identify who will inherit property, whether or not there is a will, is covered in Chapter 3.

Collecting Compensation Owed the Decedent

A surviving spouse or partner (or the guardian or conservator of the estate of the surviving spouse or partner) may collect salary or other compensation owed by an employer for personal services of the decedent, including compensation for unused vacation, by presenting the employer with a declaration in the form shown below. The procedure may be used immediately, regardless of the size of the estate; however, the amount collected cannot exceed $5,000, and the surviving spouse or partner must be entitled to the compensation under the decedent's will or by intestate succession. (Prob. Code § 13600). If a guardian or conservator presents the declaration, he or she must also provide proof of appointment to that position.

Affidavit for Transferring Community Real Property

There is a 40-day waiting period before the surviving spouse or partner may sell or otherwise dispose of any community real property—a provision that allows others (creditors, or anyone else who claims an interest in the property) to file their claims against it. If someone does claim an interest in the real property, you should see a lawyer.

For community real property, most title insurance companies will accept a simple form affidavit to clear title in the name of the surviving spouse or partner. To use the affidavit, the deed to the property must clearly show that title was held as community property; that is, the deed must show ownership in the names of the parties as "community property," as "domestic partners," or as "husband and wife." The affidavit cannot be used for community property held in joint tenancy, or in the decedent's name alone; instead, the Death of Joint Tenant affidavit (see Chapter 10) or Spousal or Domestic Partner Property Petition (see "The Spousal or Domestic Partner Property Petition," below) is required.

To complete the community property affidavit, insert the legal description of the property and other recording information, which can be taken from the original deed. The surviving spouse or partner signs the affidavit in the presence of a notary public and then records it in the county where the real property is located, along with a certified copy of the decedent's death certificate. (See Chapter 8 on how to record documents.) Samples are shown below. It is a good idea to check with the title company before using the affidavit, since the title company may have specific requirements.

Form Letter for Recording Affidavit by Mail

July 30, 20xx

County Recorder
P.O. Box 53115
Los Angeles, California 90053-0115

Re: John Doe, Deceased

To Whom It May Concern:

Enclosed is [choose one: an Affidavit—Death of Spouse or an Affidavit—Death of Domestic Partner]. Please record the affidavit, and after it is recorded return it to me at the address indicated in the upper left-hand corner of the affidavit. A certified copy of the decedent's death certificate is attached to the affidavit.

Also enclosed is a Preliminary Change of Ownership Report.

A check in the amount of $7.00 is enclosed to cover your recording fee.

Very truly yours,

Mary Doe

Mary Doe

Declaration for Collection of Compensation Owed to Deceased Spouse or Domestic Partner

---

Declaration for Collection of Compensation Owed to Deceased Spouse or Domestic Partner
(California Probate Code Section 13600)

STATE OF CALIFORNIA

COUNTY OF _____ } ss.

I, _____, being duly sworn, state:

1. _____

   died on _____, 20_____, and at the time of death was a resident of California.

2. ☐ I am the surviving spouse of the decedent.
   ☐ I am the guardian or conservator of the estate of the surviving spouse.
   ☐ I am the surviving domestic partner of the decedent.
   ☐ I am the guardian or conservator of the estate of the surviving domestic partner.

3. The surviving spouse or domestic partner of the decedent is entitled to the earnings of the decedent under the decedent's will or by intestate succession and no one else has a superior right to the earnings.

4. No proceeding is now being or has been conducted in California for administration of the decedent's estate.

5. Sections 13600 to 13605 of the California Probate Code require that the earnings of the decedent, including compensation for unused vacation, not in excess of five thousand dollars ($5,000) net, be paid promptly to me.

6. Neither the surviving spouse nor domestic partner, nor anyone acting on behalf of either the surviving spouse or partner, has a pending request to collect compensation owed by another employer for personal services of the decedent under Sections 13600 to 13650 of the California Probate Code.

7. Neither the surviving spouse nor domestic partner, nor anyone acting on behalf of either the surviving spouse or partner, has collected any compensation owed by an employer for personal services of the decedent under Sections 13600 to 13650 of the California Probate Code except the sum of _____ dollars ($_____).

8. I request that I be paid the salary or other compensation owed by you for personal services of the decedent, including compensation for unused vacation, not to exceed five thousand dollars ($5,000) net, less the _____ dollars ($_____), which was previously collected.

I declare under penalty of perjury that the foregoing is true and correct.

_____   _____
Date   Signature

Affidavit—Death of Spouse

RECORDING REQUESTED BY:

Name of surviving spouse

WHEN RECORDED MAIL TO:

Name and address of surviving spouse

`Mail tax statements same as above`

SPACE ABOVE THIS LINE FOR RECORDER'S USE

AFFIDAVIT—DEATH OF SPOUSE

State of California   )

) ss.

County of   )

_____ **Name of surviving spouse** _____, of legal age, being first duly sworn, deposes and says:

That affiant was validly married to _____ **Name of decedent** _____ immediately prior to the latter named party's death, and the affiant in conjunction with the decedent held title as "husband and wife" or as "husband and wife as community property" to the following described property:

Insert legal description. If not enough room, put "See Exhibit A," and attach a full page showing legal description.

That the affiant and the above-named decedent were married on _____ **Date of marriage** _____ and affiant is the widow/widower of decedent; and that _____ **Name of decedent** _____ died on _____ **Date of death** _____, as evidenced by a certified copy of the Certificate of Death attached hereto, and that the affiant has carefully examined all of the decedent's personal possessions, letters, papers, effects, and belongings, and is certain that either (1) no will was executed by the decedent based not only on affiant's failure to discover a will, but because affiant was never informed of decedent having executed or declared a will, and affiant is certain that he/she would have been consulted, or would at least have had knowledge of that fact if a testamentary disposition were attempted, or (2) if a will is present that it is the last complete will (with codicils and/or other amendments) and that this will devised the subject property to the affiant; and that the above-described property has been at all times since acquisition considered the community property of decedent and affiant and that any and all contributions to said property from whatever source were also considered by decedent and affiant to be community in nature; and that with respect to the above-described property, there has not been nor will there be an election filed pursuant to Probate Code Sections 13502 or 13503 in any probate proceedings in any court of competent jurisdiction; and that this affidavit is made for the protection and benefit of the grantee or grantees of the subject property, in conjunction with the successors, assigns, and personal representatives of the grantee or grantees and all other parties hereafter dealing with or who may acquire an interest in the property herein described.

Dated: _____ _____
               Signature

Subscribed and sworn to (or affirmed) before me on this _____ day of _____, 20_____, by_____, proved to me on the basis of satisfactory evidence to be the person(s) who appeared before me.

(seal)   Signature _____

Affidavit—Death of Domestic Partner

RECORDING REQUESTED BY:

Name of surviving partner

WHEN RECORDED MAIL TO:

Name and address of surviving partner

```
Mail tax statements same as above
```

SPACE ABOVE THIS LINE FOR RECORDER'S USE

AFFIDAVIT—DEATH OF DOMESTIC PARTNER

State of California   )

)   ss.

County of   )

_____ **Name of surviving domestic partner** _____, of legal age, being first duly sworn, deposes and says:

That affiant was the registered domestic partner of _____ **Name of decedent** _____ immediately prior to the latter named party's death, and the affiant in conjunction with the decedent held title as "community property" to the following described property:

Insert legal description. If not enough room, put "See Exhibit A," and attach a full page showing legal description.

That the affiant and the above-named decedent filed a Declaration of Domestic Partnership with the California Secretary of State on _ **Date of registration** _____ and affiant is the surviving domestic partner of decedent; and that _____ **Name of decedent** _____ died on ___ **Date of death** ___, as evidenced by a certified copy of the Certificate of Death attached hereto, and that the affiant has carefully examined all of the decedent's personal possessions, letters, papers, effects, and belongings, and is certain that either (1) no will was executed by the decedent based not only on affiant's failure to discover a will, but because affiant was never informed of decedent having executed or declared a will, and affiant is certain that he/she would have been consulted, or would at least have had knowledge of that fact if a testamentary disposition were attempted, or (2) if a will is present that it is the last complete will (with codicils and/or other amendments) and that this will devised the subject property to the affiant; and that the above-described property has been at all times since acquisition considered the community property of decedent and affiant and that any and all contributions to said property from whatever source were also considered by decedent and affiant to be community in nature; and that with respect to the above-described property, there has not been nor will there be an election filed pursuant to Probate Code Sections 13502 or 13503 in any probate proceedings in any court of competent jurisdiction; and that this affidavit is made for the protection and benefit of the grantee or grantees of the subject property, in conjunction with the successors, assigns, and personal representatives of the grantee or grantees and all other parties hereafter dealing with or who may acquire an interest in the property herein described.

Dated: _____   _____
                                    Signature

Subscribed and sworn to (or affirmed) before me on this _____ day of _____, 20_____, by_____, proved to me on the basis of satisfactory evidence to be the person(s) who appeared before me.

(seal)   Signature _____

Survivorship Community Property

If the spouses or partners held title to real estate as "community property with right of survivorship," the property automatically passes to the survivor, without probate court involvement. To change title to the survivor's name, the survivor should prepare and file an affidavit called Affidavit—Death of Spouse or Domestic Partner—Survivorship Community Property. A sample is shown below, and a blank form is in Appendix C.

Complete the Affidavit

You can get much of the information you need to complete the affidavit from the original deed—the one that transferred the property to the parties as community property with the right of survivorship.

In the top left-hand corner, fill in the name and address of the person to whom the document is to be returned. Usually, this is the survivor, who signs the affidavit.

Just below the title of the affidavit, fill in the state (California) and the county where the affidavit will be signed.

In the first blank in the next paragraph, fill in the name of the surviving spouse or partner, who will sign the affidavit.

In the next blank, fill in the name of the deceased spouse or partner.

In the next two blanks, fill in the name of the deceased spouse or partner as it appears on the deed, and the date of the deed.

After "executed by," fill in the names of the persons who signed the deed.

Next, fill in the names of the spouses or partners.

Next, fill in information about where the deed is recorded: the number on the deed, the date it was recorded, the book and page where it was recorded, and the county.

Then give the city and county where the property is located, and copy—carefully and exactly—the legal description of the property from the deed. Also fill in the Assessor's Parcel Number (APN).

Sign the affidavit in front of a notary public.

Possible Complications

Names don't match. The affidavit states that the decedent named on the death certificate (which must be attached to the affidavit) is the same person named on the deed that transferred the property to the parties as survivorship community property. If the names on the deed and on the death certificate are different—for example, initials are used on one and a given name on the other—it isn't a problem unless the names are significantly different. In that case, you will have to show that the two names identified the same person.

Both spouses or partners have died. If you are dealing with the estate of the second spouse or partner to die, but the interest of the first spouse or partner was never formally ended, you must first terminate the interest of the first spouse or partner so that the record will show title held solely in the name of the last surviving owner. The survivorship community property affidavit for the first to die should be signed by the executor or administrator of the estate of the last surviving spouse or partner, and recorded as discussed below.

Affidavit—Death of Spouse or Domestic Partner —Survivorship Community Property

RECORDING REQUESTED BY:

    Mary Doe

WHEN RECORDED MAIL TO:

    Mary Doe
    567 First St
    Los Angeles, CA 90017

SPACE ABOVE THIS LINE FOR RECORDER'S USE

AFFIDAVIT—DEATH OF SPOUSE OR DOMESTIC PARTNER—
SURVIVORSHIP COMMUNITY PROPERTY

State of California   )
) ss.
County of   Los Angeles   )

_____ Mary Doe _____, of legal age, being first duly sworn, deposes and says:

That ____ Robert Doe ____,

the decedent mentioned in the attached certified copy of Certificate of Death, is the same person as _____

_____ Robert Doe _____ named as one of the parties in the deed dated

____ July 20, 20xx ____, executed by ____ John Smith and Susan Smith ____ to

Mary Doe and Robert Doe ,

as community property with right of survivorship, recorded as instrument No. ____ 01-59237 ____, on

____ July 21, 20xx ____, in Book/Reel __ D 7261 __, Page/Image __ 104 __, of Official Records of

Los Angeles County, California, covering the following described property

situated in the City of ____ Los Angeles ____, County of ____ Los Angeles ____,

State of California:

    Lot 101 of Tract 26834, as per map recorded in
    Book 691, pages 3 to 8 of Maps, in the Office of
    the County Recorder of said county.

    Assessor's Parcel No. __ 567-892-003-1 __

Dated: ____ February 3, 20xx ____   *Mary Doe*
                                          Signature

Subscribed and sworn to (or affirmed) before me on this ____ 3 ____ day of ____ February ____, 20 __ xx __,

by _____ Mary Doe _____, proved to me on the basis of satisfactory evidence to be the

person(s) who appeared before me.

(seal)   Signature *Nancy Notary*

Attach a Death Certificate

Attach a certified copy of the decedent's death certificate to the affidavit. If you don't have a certified copy of the certificate, see Chapter 2 for instructions on how to get one.

Fill Out Preliminary Change of Ownership Report

All documents that transfer real property must be accompanied by a Preliminary Change of Ownership Report when they are recorded. See Chapter 8.

Record the Affidavit With the County Recorder

The final step is to record the affidavit at the county recorder's office in the county where the real property is located. Do this as soon as possible after the death. Mail it to the county recorder with a cover letter requesting that it be recorded and returned to the address indicated in the upper left-hand corner of the document. Call the recorder's office to find out the amount of the recording fee. An affidavit with a death certificate attached is considered two pages for recording purposes.

It isn't necessary to record a new deed when you record the affidavit. The purpose of the affidavit is to remove the deceased spouse's or partner's name from the title so ownership appears solely in the name of the survivor.

The Spousal or Domestic Partner Property Petition

In other situations, a slightly more involved procedure is required for real property and certain other assets. This involves the surviving spouse or partner (or the personal representative if the surviving spouse or partner is deceased, or conservator if either one is incapacitated) filing a Spousal or Domestic Partner Property Petition with the superior court in the county of the decedent's residence (or in the county where the property is located, if the decedent was not a California resident). This petition is appropriate for the following types of property:

- Real property held in the names of the parties in joint tenancy or where the deed does not indicate the manner in which title is held, or real property held in the name of the decedent alone, or in the name of the decedent with a third party. Absent a court order in a formal probate proceeding, the title company will want a Spousal or Domestic Partner Property Order specifying that the property belongs to the surviving spouse or partner before it will insure title, unless the deed says title is held by the parties as community property, in which case the affidavit discussed above may be used instead.

- Securities, stocks, and bonds that are in the names of the parties as "community property" or as "tenants in common," or are held in the name of the decedent alone. The stock transfer agent will require a Spousal or Domestic Partner Property Order before transferring title to the securities.

- Trust deed notes or promissory notes payable to the decedent alone, or to the decedent and the surviving spouse or partner. The person or entity making payment on the notes will normally require evidence in the form of a court order before making payments to the new owner. In the case of a trust deed note, a certified copy of the Spousal or Domestic Partner Property Order should be recorded in the county where the real property securing the note is located as evidence of the transfer of ownership.

- Motor vehicles held in the name of the decedent alone, or in the names of the decedent and the surviving spouse or partner if their names are not joined by "or." The DMV has many simple transfer documents for motor vehicles and it is worthwhile to check with them before applying for a court order authorizing the transfer. However, if you have to file a Spousal or Domestic Partner Property Petition for other assets anyway, it is no more trouble to add the motor vehicle to the petition.

- Bank accounts in the name of the decedent alone, or in the name of the decedent and spouse or partner as community property or as tenants in common. Since banks sometimes follow different procedures, you should check with the bank first to see if the transfer can be made without a court order. If so, you may be able to avoid having to obtain the court order to transfer a bank account.

> ! **CAUTION**
> **If you claim that property held in joint tenancy is community property.** When you do this, the petition must explain the way in which the property was converted to community property and give the date. If the decedent and the surviving spouse or partner changed joint tenancy property to community property after December 31, 1984, it must be based on an agreement signed by both spouses or partners (Civil Code §§ 5110.710–5110.740, now Family Code §§ 850–853), and the court will require that a photocopy of the document, showing signatures, be attached to the petition. If the joint tenancy property was acquired before January 1, 1985, it may be proved that it is community property either by a writing or other supporting facts (for example, that there was an oral agreement between the spouses or partners) which must be set forth in the petition. (See example of Attachment 7b to petition below.)

The Spousal or Domestic Partner Property Petition is a printed court form with schedules attached that describe the property and give facts to support the surviving spouse's or partner's claim. One schedule describes the survivor's one-half interest in community property (the half already owned by the survivor), which the court is requested to "confirm" as belonging to the surviving spouse or partner. Another schedule describes the decedent's one-half interest in community property and his or her 100% interest in any separate property that the court is requested to transfer to the surviving spouse or partner.

If probate court proceedings are required to transfer other assets (meaning if a Petition for Probate has been or will be filed), the Spousal or Domestic Partner Property Petition must be filed in the probate proceeding using the same case number.

Once filed, the court will set the Petition for hearing. A notice of the hearing must then be mailed to a number of people established by law (close relatives, others interested in the estate, etc., as explained in Step 3, below) at least 15 days prior to the hearing. An appearance in court is not usually required, unless someone objects to the petition.

If everything is in order, and there are no objections, the court will routinely approve the petition and grant an order declaring that the property "passes to" and "belongs to" the surviving spouse or partner. If the decedent's will requires the surviving spouse or partner to survive for a specified period of time (for example, 30 days, 90 days, or 180 days), you must wait to file the petition because the court will not order property transferred until the expiration of the required survivorship period. Once obtained, the court order is used as the official document to transfer or clear title to the property, and no further proceedings are required. The entire procedure takes about a month.

Property Petition Checklist

Each item in the checklist is discussed below. Most forms needed for this procedure are included in the appendixes at the back of this book. If you need extra copies you may obtain them from the court where you file your papers, or make photocopies. We recommend that you review Chapter 13 on court procedures before you begin.

Prepare and file with the court:

- ☐ Spousal or Domestic Partner Property Petition.
- ☐ Notice of Hearing, if required.
- ☐ Certificate of Assignment, if required (see Chapter 14, Step 2).
- ☐ Filing fee.
- ☐ Original will (filed for safekeeping).

Before the hearing date on the petition:

- ☐ Mail Notice of Hearing.
- ☐ File original Notice of Hearing that shows date of mailing.
- ☐ Prepare Spousal or Domestic Partner Property Order.
- ☐ File Spousal or Domestic Partner Property Order, if required.
- ☐ Check calendar notes (see Chapter 13).

After hearing:

- ☐ File Spousal or Domestic Partner Property Order.
- ☐ Record Spousal or Domestic Partner Property Order in counties where real property (or real property securing trust deed notes) is located.
- ☐ Transfer assets to surviving spouse or partner.

Step 1: Prepare the Spousal or Domestic Partner Property Petition

Caption boxes: In the first box, type the petitioner's name, address, and telephone number. After "Attorney for," type "In pro per." In the second box, fill in the court's address (including county) and branch name, if any. In the "Estate of" box, type the decedent's name, including all variations used. Under that, check either the "Spousal" or "Domestic Partner" box, depending on your situation. Leave the case number and hearing date boxes blank; the court clerk will give you a case number when you file the petition.

Item 1: Usually the surviving spouse or partner is the petitioner. However, the personal representative of the survivor's estate (executor or administrator in a formal probate proceeding), may be the petitioner if the spouse or partner survived the decedent but then died, or a conservator acting on behalf of the surviving spouse or partner may be the petitioner if the survivor is incapacitated. In this case, a copy of letters evidencing the appointment must be attached to the petition.

Items 1a and 1b: Box 1a, which should always be checked, refers to the decedent's one-half interest in community property or quasi-community property, or the decedent's 100% interest in separate property, that the surviving spouse or partner contends should be transferred to him or her without probate administration. Box 1b refers only to the one-half interest in community property that is already owned by the surviving spouse or partner. This box is usually checked to request that the one-half interest in the community property be "confirmed" as belonging to the survivor. If the decedent didn't own any community property, don't check Box 1b.

Item 1c: Although it is usually not required for these proceedings, this item gives you the option of requesting that the court appoint a probate referee to appraise the noncash assets listed in the petition. The referee charges a fee of one-tenth of 1% of the value of

Spousal or Domestic Partner Property Petition (front)

DE-221

ATTORNEY OR PARTY WITHOUT ATTORNEY *(Name, State Bar number, and address):*	FOR COURT USE ONLY

Mary Doe
1022 Ninth Street
Santa Monica, CA 90403

TELEPHONE NO.: (213) 365-4084 FAX NO. *(Optional):*

E-MAIL ADDRESS *(Optional):*

ATTORNEY FOR *(Name):* In pro per

SUPERIOR COURT OF CALIFORNIA, COUNTY OF LOS ANGELES
STREET ADDRESS: 1725 Main Street
MAILING ADDRESS: 1725 Main Street
CITY AND ZIP CODE: Santa Monica 90401
BRANCH NAME: West District

ESTATE OF *(Name):*

JOHN DOE, aka JOHN C. DOE   DECEDENT

CASE NUMBER:

HEARING DATE:

☐ **SPOUSAL** ☐ **DOMESTIC PARTNER** **PROPERTY PETITION**

DEPT.:   TIME:

1. **Petitioner** *(name):* Mary Doe   **requests**
   a. ☒ determination of property passing to the surviving spouse or surviving registered domestic partner without administration (Fam. Code, § 297.5, Prob. Code, § 13500).
   b. ☒ confirmation of property belonging to the surviving spouse or surviving registered domestic partner (Fam. Code, § 297.5, Prob. Code, §§ 100, 101).
   c. ☐ immediate appointment of a probate referee.

2. Petitioner is
   a. ☒ surviving spouse of the decedent.
   b. ☐ personal representative of *(name):*   , surviving spouse.
   c. ☐ guardian or conservator of the estate of *(name):*   , surviving spouse.
   d. ☐ surviving registered domestic partner of the decedent.
   e. ☐ personal representative of *(name):*   , surviving registered domestic partner.
   f. ☐ conservator of the estate of *(name):*   , surviving registered domestic partner.

3. Decedent died on *(date):* July 14, 20xx

4. Decedent was
   a. ☒ a resident of the California county named above.
   b. ☐ a nonresident of California and left an estate in the county named above.
   c. ☐ intestate ☒ testate and a copy of the will and any codicil is affixed as Attachment 4c.
      (Attach copies of will and any codicil, a typewritten copy of any handwritten document, and an English translation of any foreign-language document.)

5. a. *(Complete in all cases)* The decedent is survived by
      (1) ☐ no child. ☒ child as follows: ☒ natural or adopted ☐ natural, adopted by a third party.
      (2) ☒ no issue of a predeceased child. ☐ issue of a predeceased child.
   b. Decedent ☐ is ☒ is not survived by a stepchild or foster child or children who would have been adopted by decedent but for a legal barrier. *(See Prob. Code, § 6454.)*

6. *(Complete only if no issue survived the decedent. Check **only** the **first** box that applies.)*
   a. ☐ The decedent is survived by a parent or parents who are listed in item 9.
   b. ☐ The decedent is survived by a brother, sister, or issue of a deceased brother or sister, all of whom are listed in item 9.

7. Administration of all or part of the estate is not necessary for the reason that all or a part of the estate is property passing to the surviving spouse or surviving registered domestic partner. The facts upon which petitioner bases the allegation that the property described in Attachments 7a and 7b is property that should pass or be confirmed to the surviving spouse or surviving registered domestic partner are stated in Attachment 7.
   a. ☒ Attachment 7a[1] contains the legal description *(if real property add Assessor's Parcel Number)* of the deceased spouse's or registered domestic partner's property that petitioner requests to be determined as having passed to the surviving spouse or partner from the deceased spouse or partner. This includes any interest in a trade or business name of any unincorporated business or an interest in any unincorporated business that the deceased spouse or partner was operating or managing at the time of death, subject to any written agreement between the deceased spouse or partner and the surviving spouse or partner providing for a non pro rata division of the aggregate value of the community property assets or quasi-community assets, or both.

   [1] See Prob. Code, § 13658 for required filing of a list of known creditors of a business and other information in certain instances. If required, include in Attachment 7a.

Page 1 of 2

Form Adopted for Mandatory Use
Judicial Council of California DE-221
[Rev. January 1, 2005]

SPOUSAL OR DOMESTIC PARTNER PROPERTY PETITION
(Probate—Decedents Estates)

Family Code, § 297.5;
Probate Code, § 13650

Spousal or Domestic Partner Property Petition (back)

ESTATE OF (Name):	CASE NUMBER:
John Doe, aka John C. Doe DECEDENT	

7. b. [X] Attachment 7b contains the legal description (if real property add Assessor's Parcel Number) of the community or quasi-community property petitioner requests to be determined as having belonged under Probate Code sections 100 and 101 and Family Code section 297.5 to the surviving spouse or surviving registered domestic partner upon the deceased spouse's or partner's death, subject to any written agreement between the deceased spouse or partner and the surviving spouse or partner providing for a non pro rata division of the aggregate value of the community property assets or quasi-community assets, or both.

8. There [ ] exists [X] does not exist   a written agreement between the deceased spouse or deceased registered domestic partner and the surviving spouse or surviving registered domestic partner providing for a non pro rata division of the aggregate value of the community property assets or quasi-community assets, or both. (If petitioner bases the description of the property of the deceased spouse or partner passing to the surviving spouse or partner or the property to be confirmed to the surviving spouse or partner, or both, on a written agreement, a copy of the agreement must be attached to this petition as Attachment 8.)

9. The names, relationships, ages, and residence or mailing addresses so far as known to or reasonably ascertainable by petitioner of (1) all persons named in decedent's will and codicils, whether living or deceased, and (2) all persons checked in items 5 and 6
   [X] are listed below [ ] are listed in Attachment 9.

Name and relationship	Age	Residence or mailing address
Jane Doe, Daughter	Adult	1022 Ninth Street Santa Monica, CA 90403

10. The names and addresses of all persons named as executors in the decedent's will and any codicil or appointed as personal representatives of the decedent's estate [X] are listed below [ ] are listed in Attachment 10 [ ] none

   Mary Doe, 1022 Ninth Street, Santa Monica, CA 90405
   (Petitioner herein)

11. [ ] The petitioner is the trustee of a trust that is a devisee under decedent's will. The names and addresses of all persons interested in the trust who are entitled to notice under Probate Code section 13655(b)(2) are listed in Attachment 11.

12. A petition for probate or for administration of the decedent's estate
    a. [ ] is being filed with this petition.
    b. [ ] was filed on (date):
    c. [X] has not been filed and is not being filed with this petition.

13. Number of pages attached: ___3___

Date:

_____(not applicable)_____	► _____
(TYPE OR PRINT NAME)	(SIGNATURE OF ATTORNEY)

I declare under penalty of perjury under the laws of the State of California that the foregoing is true and correct.

Date: July 28, 20xx

_____Mary Doe_____	► *Mary Doe* _____
(TYPE OR PRINT NAME)	(SIGNATURE OF PETITIONER)

DE-221 [Rev. January 1, 2005]   **SPOUSAL OR DOMESTIC PARTNER PROPERTY PETITION**   Page 2 of 2
(Probate—Decedents Estates)

all noncash assets. Some counties require the filing of an Inventory and Appraisal before hearing a Spousal or Domestic Partner Property Petition, so check local practice. Unless the court requires it, however, it shouldn't be necessary to have a referee appointed unless you are dealing with property that has appreciated in value, such as stocks or real property. You should have an official record of the date-of-death value of appreciated property, because all of the decedent's separate property and both halves of the community property receive a new stepped-up federal income tax basis equal to the date-of-death value of the asset. This substantially reduces the amount of capital gains tax paid, if and when the property is sold. (See Chapter 7.) The stepped-up basis rules are not available to domestic partners, because federal tax laws do not recognize domestic partnerships as marriages.

The value of stocks and bonds can usually be established by contacting a stockbroker or by referring to newspaper financial pages which provide an official date-of-death record. However, in the case of real property, you should obtain an appraisal documenting the date-of-death value of the property. The appraisal should be obtained as soon as possible after the death because it may be more difficult to establish value later if much time has elapsed. Some people rely on a letter from a real estate broker, supported by a list of recent comparable sales in the area, to establish fair market value. Private appraisers may charge from $300 to $400 to appraise a piece of real property, while many probate referees will appraise assets outside of a court proceeding for the same fee charged in a probate matter (for example, one-tenth of 1% of the value of the asset). Call the probate department of the courthouse for the names of referees in the county where the real property is located.

If you request the appointment of a probate referee in the court proceeding, the referee's name, address, and telephone number are stamped on the conformed copy of the petition when it is filed. You must then prepare an Inventory and Appraisal with the attachments describing the property, following the procedures outlined in Chapter 14 for formal probate court proceedings, and forward it to the referee, who will appraise the assets and return it to you for filing

with the court prior to the hearing. Ordinarily, if you have a probate referee appraise the assets, you will not get the appraised Inventory back in time to file it with the court prior to the hearing date (usually four or five weeks from the day you file your petition), which means you will have to request that the court continue the hearing to a later date. A simple phone call to the court can accomplish this. The appraised value of each asset will be shown in the Spousal or Domestic Partner Property Order, thereby providing an official record for future use.

Item 2: Check Box 2a if the surviving spouse is the petitioner, which is usually the case. However, if the petitioner is the personal representative of the surviving spouse's estate, check Box 2b. Box 2c is to be checked if the petition is filed by a conservator or guardian of the surviving spouse.

Check Box 2d if the decedent's domestic partner is the petitioner. If the petitioner is the personal representative of the surviving partner's estate, check Box 2e. Check Box 2f only if the petition is filed by a conservator of the estate of the domestic partner.

> ! CAUTION
>
> **Powers of Attorney.** If the surviving spouse or partner signed a Durable Power of Attorney to cover his or her other financial affairs, the person acting as agent under such a power *cannot* file a Spousal or Domestic Partner Property Petition on behalf of the surviving spouse or partner.

Item 3: Fill in the date of death.

Item 4c: If the decedent died without a will, check the first box. If the decedent left a will, check the second box and be sure to attach a copy of the will (and any codicils) to the petition as Attachment 4c. If the will (or codicil) is handwritten, also attach an exact typewritten version. You must also file the original will for "safekeeping" when you submit the petition, unless it has been filed in another case.

Item 5a: If the decedent is survived by a child or children, check the second box under (1) and then check one or more of the additional boxes on the same line indicating whether the child is natural, adopted, or adopted by a third party.

If there are no surviving children, check the first box under (1).

If the decedent had a child or children who died before the decedent (predeceased child) leaving a child or children or grandchildren (issue) living, check the second box under (2). If not, check the first box.

Item 5b: Check the first box in Item 5b if the decedent had a foster child or stepchild he or she would have adopted but for a legal barrier. If he or she did not, check the second box. See Chapter 3 for a discussion of parent and child relationships.

Item 6: Complete this section only if the deceased spouse or partner left no children, grandchildren, or great-grandchildren (issue) surviving. Only one of the two boxes should be checked. If there are surviving parents, check Box 6a, and list them in Item 9, below. If there are no parents, but a surviving brother, sister, or children of a predeceased brother or sister, check Box 6b and list their names, addresses, and ages under Item 9, below.

Items 7a and 7b: Prepare two separate attachments on plain white bond paper the same size as the Petition. Attachment 7a should list and describe the decedent's interest in community or separate property that passes outright to the surviving spouse or partner. The decedent's interest in community property should be shown as one-half, and in separate property 100%. (See sample below.) Attachment 7b is practically the same, except that it should list only the surviving spouse's or partner's one-half interest in community property. Be sure to describe the property fully, as shown in the sample below, indicating whether it is community property or separate property. Pay particular attention to the legal description for real estate; identify the property exactly as it is shown on the real property deed. A copy of the deed showing vesting at the decedent's death must also be attached.

Community property held in joint tenancy may be included in the attachments if you wish to have a court order finding the joint tenancy property to be community property. As we mentioned earlier, the court order may help establish a new stepped-up income tax basis for both halves of community property that joint tenancy property would not otherwise receive. (See Chapter 7.)

If the decedent owned an interest in a going trade or business, additional information, including a list of creditors, is required, and the surviving spouse or partner should have the help of an attorney.

Attachment 7: Here the court requires an attachment giving information to support the surviving spouse's or partner's contention that the property listed in Attachments 7a and 7b is community property or separate property and why it should pass to, or be confirmed as belonging to, the surviving spouse or partner. A sample of Attachment 7 that may be adapted to your particular situation is shown below. Normally, to establish that property is community property, most courts require the following information:

- Date and place of marriage or registration of the domestic partnership
- Description and approximate value of any real or personal property owned by decedent on the date of marriage or registration. (This tells the court whether the decedent owned a substantial amount of separate property when he or she married the surviving spouse or prior to the registration of the domestic partnership. Property acquired after the date of marriage or registration through the combined efforts of the parties will be presumed to be community property, absent evidence to the contrary.)
- Decedent's occupation at time of marriage or registration
- Decedent's net worth at time of marriage or registration
- Description, approximate value, and date of receipt of any property received by decedent after date of marriage or registration by gift, bequest, devise, descent, proceeds of life insurance, or joint tenancy survivorship. These assets are the decedent's separate property (unless they have been commingled with other assets or converted to community property by an agreement between the parties).
- Identification of any property received by decedent under any of the devices listed directly above that is still a part of this estate

Attachment 7a

Estate of John Doe, Deceased

Spousal or Domestic Partner Property Petition

Attachment 7a

Legal description of the deceased spouse's or deceased partner's property passing to the surviving spouse or partner:

Community Property:

Decedent's undivided one-half (1/2) interest in the following community property assets:

1. Real property, improved with a single dwelling and separate garage, commonly known as 1022 Ninth Street, Santa Monica, California, standing in the name of John Doe and Mary Doe, husband and wife as joint tenants, legally described as Lot 23, Block 789, in Tract ZYZ, per map recorded in Book 73, Pages 91-94 of Maps, records of Los Angeles County. Assessor's I.D. No. 435-22-477.

2. $25,000 trust deed note of Robert Smith, dated October 1, 1997, payable to John Doe and Mary Doe, interest at 6%, payable $400 per month, principal and interest, secured by deed of trust dated October 1, 1997, recorded October 25, 1997, as Instrument No. 3645 in Book T5553, Page 578, covering real property in the City of Santa Monica, County of Los Angeles, State of California, described as:

> Lot 231 of Tract No. 1234, in the City of Santa Monica, County of Los Angeles, State of California, as per map recorded in Book 29, Pages 33 to 37 inclusive of Maps, in the office of the County Recorder of said County. Assessor's I.D. No. 345-35-588.

3. 454 shares of W.R. Grace Company common stock (held in the name of the decedent, acquired as community property).

Separate property:

A 100% interest in the following separate property assets:

4. 200 shares of XYX Corporation common stock.

5. 50% interest in Desert Sands West, a limited partnership.

Attachment 7b

Estate of John Doe, Deceased

Spousal or Domestic Partner Property Petition

Attachment 7b

Legal description of the community or quasi-community property to be confirmed to the surviving spouse or partner:

Community Property:

Petitioner's undivided one-half (1/2) interest in the following community property assets:

1. Real property, improved with a single dwelling and separate garage, commonly known as 1022 Ninth Street, Santa Monica, California, standing in the name of John Doe and Mary Doe, husband and wife as joint tenants, legally described as Lot 23, Block 789, in Tract ZYZ, per map recorded in Book 73, Pages 91-94 of Maps, records of Los Angeles County. Assessor's I.D. No. 435-22-477.

2. $25,000 trust deed note of Robert Smith, dated October 1, 1997, payable to John Doe and Mary Doe, interest at 6%, payable $400 per month, principal and interest, secured by deed of trust dated October 1, 1997, recorded October 25, 1997, as Instrument No. 3645 in Book T5553, Page 578, covering real property in the City of Santa Monica, County of Los Angles, State of California, described as:

   Lot 231 of Tract No. 1234, in the City of Santa Monica, County of Los Angeles, State of California, as per map recorded in Book 29, Pages 33 to 37 inclusive of Maps, in the office of the County Recorder of said County. Assessor's I.D. No. 345-35-588.

3. 454 shares of W.R. Grace Company common stock (held in the name of the decedent, acquired as community property).

Attachment 7

Estate of John Doe, Deceased

Spousal or Domestic Partner Property Petition

Attachment 7

The facts in support of allegation that property listed as Items 1, 2, and 3 of Attachments 7a and 7b is community property that should pass or be confirmed to the surviving spouse or partner are:

1. Petitioner and decedent were married on July 10, 1960, in New York City. They remained married and continuously lived together as husband and wife from 1960 to the date of decedent's death.

2. At the time of the marriage decedent owned no real property and the value of the personal property then owned by the decedent was no more than Five Hundred Dollars ($500.00). Decedent was not indebted at the time to any significant extent, and his net worth was approximately Five Hundred Dollars ($500.00).

3. Decedent's occupation at the time of marriage was that of a bookkeeper.

4. Decedent and his surviving spouse first came to California in 1965, and their net worth at the time was no more than a few thousand dollars.

5. During the marriage, the decedent inherited 200 shares of XYZ Corporation common stock and a 50% interest in Desert Sands West, a Limited Partnership, from his mother, Jane Doe, who died in Los Angeles County in 1963. Said stock and partnership interest, described as Items 4 and 5 of Attachment 7a are the decedent's separate property. Decedent did not receive any other property by inheritance nor any property of significant value by way of gift.

6. The real property described in Item 1 of Attachments 7a and 7b was acquired in 1969 by the decedent and his surviving spouse as joint tenants. Decedent and his surviving spouse had no written agreement concerning their property, but at all times it was understood and orally agreed between them that all property they acquired during their marriage, notwithstanding the form of conveyance by which the property was taken or acquired, including all property held in the name of either spouse alone or in their names as joint tenants, would be and remain their community property.

Under the terms of Article Fourth of the decedent's Will, a copy of which is attached hereto as Attachment 4c, the decedent devised his entire estate outright to his wife. Accordingly, the separate property listed as Items 4 and 5 of Attachment 7a passes to decedent's surviving spouse, Mary Doe, petitioner herein.

- If claim is based on any document, a photocopy showing signatures. (Normally, these would be the decedent's will, a deed to real property showing title held as community property or a written agreement between the parties.)
- Date decedent first came to California, and
- Any additional facts upon which claim of community property is based. (Here you may add anything of significance that would support a claim by the surviving spouse or partner to community property, such as a commingling of community and separate property, or actions by the parties showing an intention to treat property either as community property or separate property.)

For separate property, you should provide the following information:

- If the separate property passes outright to the surviving spouse or partner under the decedent's will, the paragraph number in the will. (See example of Attachment 7.)
- If there is no will, how the surviving spouse's or partner's share of the separate property is computed under intestate succession law. (See Chapter 3.) For example, if the decedent is survived by two children as well as the surviving spouse or partner, put:

> The decedent died without a will, and is survived by a son and daughter in addition to the surviving spouse. Under the laws of intestate succession, the surviving spouse is entitled to receive one-third of the decedent's separate property.

Item 8: Under Probate Code § 13651(a), you must disclose whether or not there was a written agreement between the decedent and the surviving spouse or partner that provides for a "non pro rata" division of the aggregate value of the community or quasi-community property. These agreements are rare; if one exists it was probably prepared by an attorney. If the decedent had one of these agreements, check the first box and attach a copy. Otherwise check the second box. Note: If the decedent and his or her surviving spouse or partner signed a written agreement concerning the character of their property (that is, describing it as community or separate), attach that agreement to the Petition as Attachment 8.

Item 9: This section is for listing all persons potentially interested in the estate so they may be given notice of the filing of the petition. If the decedent left a will, you must list here the name, relationship, age, and residence or mailing address of everyone mentioned in the decedent's will or codicil as a beneficiary, whether living or deceased. In addition, the name, relationship, age, and residence of all persons checked in Items 5 and 6 of the petition should be listed (these are the decedent's heirs under intestate succession laws). Even if the surviving spouse or partner claims the entire estate, the heirs must be given notice so they may present any adverse claims. Often, the heirs are the same as the beneficiaries named in the will; if so, you need list each person only once. Persons not related to the decedent by blood are described as "strangers." Ages may be shown as either "under eighteen" or "over eighteen." For a detailed explanation of the persons who should be included in this listing, see Item 8 of the instructions for preparing the Petition for Probate in Chapter 14, Step 1. If you don't have enough room for all the names, prepare an attachment in the same format and attach it to the petition as Attachment 9.

Item 10: List here the names and addresses of all persons named as executors in the decedent's will (or appointed as executors or administrators, if a probate proceeding is pending). If there is enough space on the petition to list them, check the first box. Otherwise, check the second box and prepare a separate schedule and attach it to the petition as Attachment 10. If the surviving spouse or partner is the executor or administrator, you should also enter his or her name here. If none, check the last box.

Item 11: Check this box if the decedent left a will and the executor or administrator CTA is the trustee of a trust that is entitled to receive property under the will, and prepare a list of the names and addresses of all persons who are potential beneficiaries of the trust (now or in the future) so far as known to any petitioner and attach it as Attachment 11.

Item 12: If a Petition for Probate or administration of the decedent's estate is required, check the appropriate box and fill in the filing date, if any.

Item 13: Check Box 11 and enter the number of attachments.

Signatures: Sign the petition as petitioner where indicated, and be sure to fill in the date. Leave the signature line for the attorney blank, or type "Not applicable."

Step 2: File the Petition

Make one photocopy for your files, and another photocopy if local court rules require the petition to be filed in duplicate. Read the petition over carefully to make sure all the required boxes are checked. If there is a will, don't forget to attach a copy to the petition.

The petition, along with the other required documents and filing fee, should be filed with the court clerk's office in the superior court of the county in which the decedent resided (or in the county where the property is located, if the decedent was not a resident of California), in person or by mail.

Prepare a Certificate of Assignment, if necessary. This form is normally required if you file your papers in a county that has branch courts. (See Chapter 14 on probate court procedures for instructions on how to fill it in.)

The fee for filing the petition varies from county to county, and you should call the court for the amount of the fee. The check should be made payable to the county clerk of the county in which you file your papers. Most courts accept personal checks, but verify this before you mail your papers.

The sample form letter shown below may be adapted to your particular situation when mailing the petition and other documents to the court for filing. Not all items listed in the form letter will apply in all situations, so include only those that apply to your particular estate. Be sure to include a self-addressed, stamped envelope so the court clerk will return conformed (file stamped) copies of your documents to you.

Letter to Court

August 16, 20xx

Clerk of Superior Court
Probate Department
1725 Main Street
Santa Monica, CA 90402

RE: Estate of John Doe, Deceased

Enclosed are the following documents:

1. Original and two copies of Spousal or Domestic Partner Property Petition

2. Original and four copies of Notice of Hearing

3. Original and one copy of Certificate of Assignment

4. Filing fee of $_____.

Please file the original documents with the Court and return the extra copies to me, conformed with your filing stamp, indicating the case number and time and date of the hearing on the Petition. A stamped, self-addressed envelope is enclosed for your convenience.

Very truly yours,

Mary Doe

Mary Doe
1022 Ninth Street
Santa Monica, CA 90403

RELATED TOPIC

Probate note. When the Spousal or Domestic Partner Property Petition is joined with a Petition for Probate, notice of the hearing is combined with the Notice of Petition to Administer Estate given in the probate proceedings. In this case, wording is added to the Notice of Petition to Administer Estate to indicate that the hearing is on the Spousal or Domestic Partner Property Petition as well as the Petition for Probate, and that a copy of the Spousal or Domestic Partner Property Petition (if required) was mailed with the notice. (We show you how to do this in Chapter 14.)

Notice of Hearing (front)

DE-120

ATTORNEY OR PARTY WITHOUT ATTORNEY *(Name, State Bar number, and address)*:	FOR COURT USE ONLY
Mary Doe 1022 Ninth Street Santa Monica, CA 90403 TELEPHONE NO.: 213-365-4084 FAX NO. *(Optional)*: E-MAIL ADDRESS *(Optional)*: ATTORNEY FOR *(Name)*: In pro per	

SUPERIOR COURT OF CALIFORNIA, COUNTY OF   LOS ANGELES
STREET ADDRESS: 1725 Main Street
MAILING ADDRESS: 1725 Main Street
CITY AND ZIP CODE: Santa Monica, CA 90401
BRANCH NAME: WEST DISTRICT

[X] ESTATE OF *(Name)*:   [ ] IN THE MATTER OF *(Name)*:
John Doe, aka, John C. Doe,
           [X] DECEDENT   [ ] TRUST   [ ] OTHER

NOTICE OF HEARING—DECEDENT'S ESTATE OR TRUST	CASE NUMBER: WEP 4084

This notice is required by law.
This notice does not require you to appear in court, but you may attend the hearing if you wish.

1. NOTICE is given that *(name)*:   Mary Doe
   (representative capacity, if any): Surviving Spouse
   has filed *(specify)*:*   Spousal or Domestic Partner Property Petition

2. You may refer to the filed documents for more information. *(Some documents filed with the court are confidential.)*

3. A HEARING on the matter will be held as follows:

   a.   Date: August 24, 20xx   Time: 9:30 A.M.   Dept.: A   Room:

   b.   Address of court   [X] shown above   [ ] is *(specify)*:

   Assistive listening systems, computer-assisted real-time captioning, or sign language interpreter services are available upon request if at least 5 days notice is provided. Contact the clerk's office for *Request for Accommodations by Persons With Disabilities and Order* (form MC-410). (Civil Code section 54.8.)

   * Do **not** use this form to give notice of a petition to administer estate (see Prob. Code, § 8100 and form DE-121) or notice of a hearing in a guardianship or conservatorship (see Prob. Code, §§ 1511 and 1822 and form GC-020).

Page 1 of 2

Form Adopted for Mandatory Use Judicial Council of California DE-120 [Rev. July 1, 2005]	**NOTICE OF HEARING—DECEDENT'S ESTATE OR TRUST** (Probate—Decedents' Estates)	Probate Code §§ 851, 1211, 1215, 1216, 1230, 17100 www.courtinfo.ca.gov

American LegalNet, Inc.
www.USCourtForms.com

Notice of Hearing (back)

		CASE NUMBER:
[X] ESTATE OF *(Name):* [ ] IN THE MATTER OF *(Name):*		
John Doe, aka, John C. Doe,		
[X] DECEDENT [ ] TRUST [ ] OTHER		WEP 4084

CLERK'S CERTIFICATE OF POSTING

1. I certify that I am not a party to this cause.
2. A copy of the foregoing *Notice of Hearing—Decedent's Estate or Trust*
   a. was posted at *(address):*

   b. was posted on *(date):*

Date: Clerk, by _____ , Deputy

PROOF OF SERVICE BY MAIL *

1. I am over the age of 18 and not a party to this cause. I am a resident of or employed in the county where the mailing occurred.
2. My residence or business address is *(specify):*

   2332-20th Street, Santa Monica, California 90405

3. I served the foregoing *Notice of Hearing—Decedent's Estate or Trust* on each person named below by enclosing a copy in an envelope addressed as shown below AND

   a. [X] **depositing** the sealed envelope on the date and at the place shown in item 4 with the United States Postal Service with the postage fully prepaid.

   b. [ ] **placing** the envelope for collection and mailing on the date and at the place shown in item 4 following our ordinary business practices. I am readily familiar with this business's practice for collecting and processing correspondence for mailing. On the same day that correspondence is placed for collection and mailing, it is deposited in the ordinary course of business with the United States Postal Service in a sealed envelope with postage fully prepaid.

4. a. Date mailed: August 7, 20xx   b. Place mailed *(city, state):* Santa Monica, California

5. [ ] I served with the *Notice of Hearing—Decedent's Estate or Trust* a copy of the petition or other document referred to in the Notice.

I declare under penalty of perjury under the laws of the State of California that the foregoing is true and correct.

Date: August 7, 20xx

Laura Jones   *Laura Jones*
_____   _____
(TYPE OR PRINT NAME OF PERSON COMPLETING THIS FORM)   (SIGNATURE OF PERSON COMPLETING THIS FORM)

NAME AND ADDRESS OF EACH PERSON TO WHOM NOTICE WAS MAILED

	Name of person served	Address *(number, street, city, state, and zip code)*
1.	Jane Doe	1022 Ninth Street, Santa Monica, California 90403
2.		
3.		
4.		

[ ] Continued on an attachment. *(You may use Attachment to Notice of Hearing Proof of Service by Mail, form DE-120(MA)/GC-020(MA), for this purpose.)*

* Do not use this form for proof of personal service. You may use form DE-120(P) to prove personal service of this Notice.

DE-120 [Rev. July 1, 2005]   **NOTICE OF HEARING—DECEDENT'S ESTATE OR TRUST**   Page 2 of 2
                                 (Probate—Decedents' Estates)

Step 3: Mail and File a Notice of Hearing

When you file the petition, the court clerk will establish a hearing date, and all persons listed in Items 7 and 8 of the petition (except the petitioner) must be given notice of the time, date, and place of the hearing. You provide this notice on a printed form called Notice of Hearing. The person filing the petition is responsible for preparing the notice and seeing that it is properly given. A copy of the notice is shown above, with instructions on how to fill it in. You will find a blank Notice of Hearing form in Appendix B.

In some counties, the Notice of Hearing must be presented or mailed to the court when you file the petition. The court clerk fills in the time and date of the hearing on the original copy, plus any extra copies, and returns them with your conformed copy of the petition in the stamped, self-addressed envelope you provided. Some courts keep the original and return only the copies. In other counties, the petitioner must choose a hearing date according to when such matters are heard on the court calendar. Check with the court where you file your papers for the procedures it follows. If you pick a date, be sure to allow enough time to give the 15 days' notice to the people it must be served on.

When the Notice of Hearing is completed, with the time, date, and place of the hearing, mail a copy (not the original) 15 days prior to the hearing date to all the persons, other than the petitioner, named in Item 9 and Item 10 of the petition. The mailing must be done by someone over 18 years of age who is not a person interested in the estate. Thus, the notice cannot be mailed by the surviving spouse or partner, any of the heirs or beneficiaries, or others named in Item 9 or 10 of the petition. After the notice is mailed, the person giving the notice must complete the affidavit on the reverse side of the original copy of the notice, giving proof of the mailing.

File the original notice (or a copy, if the court kept the original) with the Proof of Service by Mail, with the court prior to the hearing date.

Front

Heading: Fill in the same information as on the Spousal or Domestic Partner Property Petition, and insert the case number.

Item 1: Type your name on the first line. On the second line, type representative capacity (for example, "Surviving Spouse"). On the third line type "a Spousal or Domestic Partner Property Petition."

Item 3: Fill in the date and place of the hearing and address of the court.

Back

Heading: Fill in name of estate and case number. Leave the next section (Clerk's Certificate of Posting/Mailing) blank.

Proof of Service by Mail: Complete this section the same as on the back of the Notice of Administration (explained in Chapter 14, Step 3). In the space at the bottom, list the name and address of each person to whom a copy of the notice was mailed. (This must be everyone listed in Items 9 and 10 of the petition, except the petitioner.)

Step 4: Prepare Your Spousal or Domestic Partner Property Order

The point of filing a Spousal or Domestic Partner Property Petition is to obtain an official document from the court stating that the property described in the petition belongs to the surviving spouse or partner. It is the responsibility of the petitioner to prepare the Spousal or Domestic Partner Property Order for the judge's signature by following the instructions outlined below.

A sample order is shown below.

Instructions for Filling Out the Spousal or Domestic Partner Property Order

Caption boxes: Fill in as you did on the Spousal or Domestic Partner Property Petition, except that now you can add the case number.

Item 1: Fill in date, time, and department (courtroom) of hearing as it appears on your Notice of Hearing.

Spousal or Domestic Partner Property Order

DE-226

ATTORNEY OR PARTY WITHOUT ATTORNEY *(Name, State Bar number, and address):*
After recording return to:

Mary Doe
1022 Ninth Street
Santa Monica, CA 90403
TELEPHONE NO.: 213-365-4084
FAX NO. *(Optional):*
E-MAIL ADDRESS *(Optional):*
      In pro per
ATTORNEY FOR *(Name):*

FOR RECORDER'S USE ONLY

SUPERIOR COURT OF CALIFORNIA, COUNTY OF LOS ANGELES
STREET ADDRESS: 1725 Main Street
MAILING ADDRESS: 1725 Main Street
CITY AND ZIP CODE: Santa Monica 90401
BRANCH NAME: West District

ESTATE OF *(Name):*
JOHN DOE, aka JOHN C. DOE,
DECEDENT

CASE NUMBER:
WEP 4084

FOR COURT USE ONLY

[X] **SPOUSAL** [ ] **DOMESTIC PARTNER**   **PROPERTY ORDER**

1. Date of hearing: 8-24-xx   Time: 9:30 A.M.
   Dept.: A   Room:

THE COURT FINDS

2. All notices required by law have been given.

3. Decedent died on *(date):* July 14, 20xx
   a. [X] a resident of the California county named above.
   b. [ ] a nonresident of California and left an estate in the county named above.
   c. [ ] intestate. [X] testate.

4. Decedent's [X] surviving spouse [ ] surviving registered domestic partner
   is *(name):* Mary Doe

THE COURT FURTHER FINDS AND ORDERS

5. a. [X] The property described in Attachment 5a is property passing to the surviving spouse or surviving registered domestic partner named in item 4, and no administration of it is necessary.
   b. [ ] See Attachment 5b for further order(s) respecting transfer of the property to the surviving spouse or surviving registered domestic partner named in item 4.

6. [ ] To protect the interests of the creditors of *(business name):*
   an unincorporated trade or business, a list of all its known creditors and the amount owed each is on file.
   a. [ ] Within *(specify):*   days from this date, the surviving spouse or surviving registered domestic partner named in item 4 shall file an undertaking in the amount of $
   b. [ ] See Attachment 6b for further order(s) protecting the interests of creditors of the business.

7. a. [X] The property described in Attachment 7a is property that belonged to the surviving spouse or surviving registered domestic partner under Family Code section 297.5 and Probate Code sections 100 and 101, and the surviving spouse's or surviving domestic partner's ownership upon decedent's death is confirmed.
   b. [ ] See Attachment 7b for further order(s) respecting transfer of the property to the surviving spouse or surviving domestic partner.

8. [ ] All property described in the *Spousal or Domestic Partner Property Petition* that is not determined to be property passing to the surviving spouse or surviving registered domestic partner under Probate Code section 13500, or confirmed as belonging to the surviving spouse or surviving registered domestic partner under Probate Code sections 100 and 101, shall be subject to administration in the estate of decedent. [ ] All of such property is described in Attachment 8.

9. [ ] Other *(specify):*

[ ] Continued in Attachment 9.

10. Number of pages attached: __2__

Date:

_____
JUDICIAL OFFICER
[X] SIGNATURE FOLLOWS LAST ATTACHMENT

Page 1 of 1

Form Adopted for Mandatory Use
Judicial Council of California
DE-226 [Rev. January 1, 2005]

SPOUSAL OR DOMESTIC PARTNER PROPERTY ORDER
(Probate—Decedents Estates)

Family Code, § 297.5;
Probate Code, § 13656

Attachment 7a

Estate of John Doe, Deceased

Spousal or Domestic Partner Property Order

Attachment 7a

Legal description of property confirmed as belonging to surviving spouse:

Community Property:

Undivided one-half (1/2) interest in the following community property assets:

1. Real property, improved with a single dwelling and separate garage, commonly known as 1022 Ninth Street, Santa Monica, California, standing in the name of John Doe and Mary Doe, husband and wife as joint tenants, legally described as Lot 23, Block 789, in Tract ZYZ, per map recorded in Book 73, Pages 91-94 of Maps, records of Los Angeles County. Assessor's I.D. No. 435-22-477.

2. $25,000 trust deed note of Robert Smith, dated October 1, 1997, payable to John Doe and Mary Doe, interest at 6%, payable $400 per month, principal and interest, secured by deed of trust dated October 1, 1997, recorded October 25, 1997, as Instrument No. 3645 in Book T5553, Page 578, covering real property in the City of Santa Monica, County of Los Angeles, State of California, described as:

   Lot 231 of Tract No. 1234, in the City of Santa Monica, County of Los Angeles, State of California, as per map recorded in Book 29, Pages 33 to 37 inclusive of Maps, in the office of the County Recorder of said County. Assessor's I.D. No. 345-35-588.

3. 454 shares of W.R. Grace Company common stock (held in the name of the decedent, acquired as community property).

Dated: _____, 20_____

_____

Judge of the Superior Court

Item 3: Fill in date of death.

Item 3a or 3b: Check correct box.

Item 3c: Indicate whether decedent died intestate (without a will) or testate (with a will).

Item 4: Fill in the name of the surviving spouse or domestic partner and check the appropriate box.

Items 5a and 7a: Check Box 5a and prepare an Attachment 5a describing the decedent's one-half interest in the community property and any separate property that passes outright to the surviving spouse or domestic partner. To do this, you can resubmit Attachment 7a of your petition; just change the title to "Spousal or Domestic Partner Property Order" and "Attachment 5a." For Item 7a, prepare Attachment 7a, which will describe only the surviving spouse's or partner's one-half interest in the community property. You can resubmit Attachment 7b of your petition. Just be sure to:

- change the title to "Spousal or Domestic Partner Property Order"
- change the name of the attachment to "Attachment 7a," and
- add a line for the date and signature of the judge, as shown in our example.

The attachments should be on plain white bond paper, the same size as the petition, and the property described the same way as in the petition.

Items 6b and 7b: These items refer to attachments "for further order respecting transfer of the property to the surviving spouse or surviving domestic partner." Such orders are required only in unusual circumstances. In most estates you can leave this blank.

Item 6: This section applies only to a trade or business owned by a decedent.

Item 8: If during the proceedings it has been ascertained that some part of the property described in the petition does not pass to or belong to the surviving spouse or partner, check this box. (This means the property will be subjected to probate administration, unless the entire estate is worth less than $100,000. See Chapter 11.)

Item 9: Leave this box blank.

Item 10: Check the box, add up pages of attachments, and fill in.

Some counties, such as Los Angeles, do not permit attachments to a court order after the judge's signature. Because you will have at least one or two attachments, this means you should check the box at the bottom of the Spousal or Domestic Partner Property Order and then type lines at the bottom of the last page attached to the order for the judge's signature and the date, as shown in our example of Attachment 7a. (We do not show an example of Attachment 5a to the order, inasmuch as it is the same as Attachment 7a to the petition, except for the title.)

In most counties, if the petition is unopposed, the Spousal or Domestic Partner Property Order will be signed without an appearance in court by anyone. Because of this, some counties require the order to be submitted to the court for review a certain number of days prior to the hearing date. In other counties, the order may be sent in after the hearing date for the judge's signature, so you should check local practice.

In either case, once the Spousal or Domestic Partner Property Order is signed, you will need one certified copy for each issue of security to be transferred, and one certified copy to record in each county in which any item of real property is located. A sample form letter for mailing the order and requesting certified copies is shown below.

Letter to Court

September 1, 20xx

Clerk of the Superior Court
1500 Main Street
Santa Monica, CA 90402

RE: Estate of John Doe, Deceased
    Case No. : _____

Enclosed is a Spousal or Domestic Partner Property Order in the above-entitled matter.

Please have the order signed and filed with the Court, returning one certified copy to me in the enclosed stamped, self-addressed envelope. A check in the amount of $3.50, made payable to the Los Angeles County Clerk, is enclosed to cover your certification fees.

Very truly yours,

Mary Doe
Mary Doe
1022 Ninth Street
Santa Monica, CA 90403

How to Transfer the Assets to the Surviving Spouse or Partner

Assuming you have now obtained a copy of the Spousal or Domestic Partner Property Order (as well as a number of certified copies), you are ready to actually transfer the property. Here is how you do it.

Real Property

Title to real property is transferred by recording a certified copy of the Spousal or Domestic Partner Property Order in the office of the county recorder for each county where the real property is located. If there are several items of real property in one county, you need record only one certified copy of the order in that county. See Chapter 8 on how to record documents with the county recorder.

Securities

Send the transfer agent the following items by registered mail, insured, for each issue:

- certified copy of Spousal or Domestic Partner Property Order
- stock power signed by the surviving spouse or partner, with signature guaranteed
- original stock or bond certificates
- Affidavit of Domicile
- stock transfer tax (if transfer agent is located in New York or Florida), and
- transmittal letter, giving instructions.

See Chapter 9 on how to transfer securities, where to get the forms, and how to fill them in.

Promissory Notes and Trust Deed Notes

Usually, if the surviving spouse or partner notifies the person making payments on the note that the note is now the sole property of the surviving spouse or partner (or owned by the surviving spouse or partner with another), and furnishes the payor with a certified copy of the Spousal or Domestic Partner Property Order, the payor will adjust his or her records and make future checks payable to the new owner. The surviving spouse or partner should keep a certified copy of the order with his or her other important papers as evidence of ownership of any promissory notes. If the note is secured by a deed of trust on real property, recording a certified copy of the order in the county in which the property described in the deed of trust is located will establish a record of transfer to the new owner.

Automobiles

The surviving spouse or partner should go in person to the Department of Motor Vehicles to transfer title to any community property automobiles or other motor vehicles. Upon being presented with the Certificate of Ownership (pink slip) and a copy of the Spousal or Domestic Partner Property Order, the DMV will provide the survivor with the required forms to complete the transfer of title.

Bank Accounts

Bank accounts usually can be transferred into the name of the surviving spouse or partner without loss of interest simply by submitting the passbook or Certificate of Deposit together with a certified copy of the Spousal or Domestic Partner Property Order to the bank or savings and loan association with a request that the account or accounts be transferred.

Money Market Funds and Mutual Funds

Transferring record ownership in these types of assets is handled by the fund management, which will transfer title to the surviving spouse or partner when presented with a certified copy of the Spousal or Domestic Partner Property Order.

Miscellaneous Assets

Any tangible personal property held by third parties, as well as other property interests such as partnership and joint venture interests, usually can be transferred by presenting a certified copy of the court order to the persons having possession or control over the property.

If You Need Expert Help

Even simple estates sometimes have quirks that can't be resolved by a layperson. An estate that appears to be straightforward and uncomplicated at the outset may suddenly turn out to be neither if someone challenges the will or otherwise intervenes in the probate court proceedings.

You should seek the advice or assistance of a professional if you find yourself in any of the following situations:

- Separate and community property of a married couple are commingled, and you don't know how to distribute the decedent's property.
- A creditor files a large disputed claim against the estate.
- The will gives away property that is no longer owned by the decedent.
- An heir or beneficiary can't be located.
- Someone challenges your right to settle the estate.
- The will is ambiguous.
- A would-be beneficiary contests the will or otherwise interferes with settlement of the estate.

The most sensible approach to settling an estate without professional help is to be pragmatic. Do as much of the routine estate work by yourself as you are able to, and be prepared to seek help if you need it.

What Kind of Expert Do You Need?

Don't assume that every time you have a probate question, you need to hire a probate lawyer. You may be able to get the help you need more quickly and cheaply from another kind of expert. For example, a tax accountant will be able to assist you with estate tax or income tax problems. And a nonlawyer who specializes in probate paperwork can help you fill out and file your probate forms.

Using a Legal Document Assistant

California law authorizes nonlawyers called "legal document assistants" to prepare forms for consumers who wish to handle their own legal work. Legal document assistants are experienced paralegals who charge much less than lawyers. Many of them now operate independent offices, so customers can go to them directly instead of hiring a lawyer (who, often as not, gives the actual paperwork to a paralegal the law firm employs).

Legal document assistants don't offer legal advice. You are responsible for making decisions about how to proceed and for providing the information to fill out the papers. They can prepare your papers and file them with the court for you.

Most legal document assistants specialize in one or two areas; for example, some handle only divorce paperwork, and others just do bankruptcy or eviction papers. Be sure to use one who is experienced in probate paperwork.

Finding a Probate Paralegal

The author of this book, Julia Nissley, is a legal document assistant and operates a probate form preparation service. You can write to her at Probate Direct, LLC, 25852 McBean Parkway, #192, Valencia, CA 91355, or call 800-664-4869. Her email address is jpnissley@probatedirect.com.

You can also look on the Internet or in the yellow pages under "Paralegal Services" or "Attorney Services."

Using a Lawyer

If you do need a lawyer, find one who does not object to your doing most of your own legal work and who will charge a reasonable hourly rate for occasional help and advice. While this isn't impossible, it may be difficult, because some lawyers may not want to accept piecemeal work in a field where much higher fees are available for handling an entire probate.

Finding a Lawyer

Finding a lawyer who charges reasonable rates and whom you feel you can trust is not always easy. Picking a name out of the telephone book may get you the right attorney the first time, but you might end up with an attorney who is unsympathetic, one who charges too much, or one who isn't really knowledgeable about probate matters. This sorry result is not necessarily inevitable. Just as you can competently handle much of your own probate work by taking the time to inform yourself on how to do it, you can also find the right attorney for help if you need it.

TIP

Let Nolo take the guesswork out of finding a lawyer. Nolo's Lawyer Directory provides detailed profiles of attorney advertisers, including information about the lawyer's education, experience, practice areas, and fee schedule. Go to www.lawyers.nolo.com or Nolo's main website at www.nolo.com.

As a general rule, you will be better off using a lawyer who specializes to some extent in probate matters. Many attorneys devote a large part of their practice to probate and will do a competent job while charging fairly for their services. However, because this area is so specialized, you simply can't expect much creative help from someone who doesn't work regularly with these matters.

If your employer or union offers a prepaid legal services plan that offers you a free or low-cost consultation with a lawyer, take advantage of it. But remember that you need to talk to someone who is familiar with probate law and practice. And if the lawyer starts telling you that you need to turn everything over to him or her, you may want to get a second opinion.

The best way to find a suitable attorney is through a friend or some trusted person who has had a satisfactory experience with one. Ask small business owners and others you know who deal with their own investments or business decisions who they use and what it usually costs.

Use caution when dealing with high-profile legal clinics that advertise heavily. Do some comparison shopping. You can often get better service from a specialist who doesn't buy television time at thousands of dollars per minute. If you do deal with a legal clinic, make sure the price you are quoted includes all the services you need. It is not unusual for legal clinics to advertise a very low basic price and then add to it considerably, based on the assertion that your particular problem costs more.

Also beware of referral panels set up by local bar associations. Although some lawyers are given minimal screening as to their expertise in certain areas of the law before they qualify to be listed, the emphasis more often than not is on the word "minimal." You might get a good referral from these panels, but sometimes they just serve as havens for inexperienced practitioners who do not have enough clients.

Once you get a few referrals that sound good, call those law offices and state your problem. If you want advice on a particular problem, find out if the lawyer is willing to see you to discuss it.

When you find an attorney you like, make an appointment to discuss your situation personally. Be ready to pay for this consultation. It is not always wise to accept a free initial consultation, as you put the attorney in a position of profiting only if he or she sells you some service, whether you need it or not. Be sure to bring all the relevant documents and information with you when you go, so your time and money will be well spent.

Lawyers' Fees

Standard fees for handling a probate start to finish are set by California statute as a percentage of the gross value of the property subject to probate. (See Chapter 1.)

You can, however, negotiate a different lump sum or an hourly rate with a lawyer. If you hire a lawyer just for occasional advice, or to review some of your paperwork, you'll probably want to pay the lawyer by the hour. Lawyers who work for individuals and small businesses charge anywhere from about $150 to $400 an hour; $200 to $300 is a common range.

It's always a good idea to get your fee agreement with the lawyer in writing, to avoid misunderstandings. If it is reasonably foreseeable that you will end up paying more than $1,000 for legal fees and costs, the law requires that the agreement between you and the lawyer be in writing. (This law doesn't apply if you have hired the lawyer for similar services before.) The contract must state the hourly rate and other standard fees that may apply, the general nature of the services to be provided, and the responsibilities of both you and the attorney—for example, you may be responsible for paying out-of-pocket court fees as the case progresses. (Bus. & Prof. Code § 6148(a).)

Bills sent by the attorney can't contain just a bare amount due; they must state the rate or other method of arriving at the total. If you are billed for costs and expenses, the bill must clearly identify them. If you haven't gotten a bill in a month, you may ask for one, and the lawyer must provide it within ten days. (Bus. & Prof. Code § 6148(b).)

Glossary

Abatement. Cutting back certain gifts under a will when necessary to create a fund to meet expenses, pay taxes, satisfy debts, or to have enough to take care of other bequests which are given priority under law or under the will.

Ademption. The failure of a specific bequest of property because the property is no longer owned by the testator at the time of his death.

Administrator. The title given to the person who is appointed by the probate court, when there is no will, to collect assets of the estate, pay its debts, and distribute the rest to the appropriate beneficiaries.

Administrator With Will Annexed. Sometimes termed "Administrator CTA," this title is given to the administrator when there is a will but the will either fails to nominate an executor or the named executor is unable to serve.

Adopted Child. Any person, whether an adult or a minor, who is legally adopted as the child of another in a court proceeding.

Affidavit. A voluntary written or printed statement of facts that is signed under oath before a notary public (or other officer having authority to administer oaths) by any person having personal knowledge of the facts. Affidavits are used in lieu of live testimony to support the facts contained in a petition or other document submitted in the course of the probate process.

Antilapse Statute. A statute that prevents dispositions in a will from failing in the event the beneficiary predeceases the testator. See "Lapse."

Appraiser. A person possessing expertise in determining the market or fair value of real or personal property. The probate court appoints an appraiser to place a value on the estate for tax purposes.

Attestation. The act of witnessing the signing of a document by another, and the signing of the document as a witness. Thus, a will requires both the signature by the person making the will and attestation by at least two witnesses.

Beneficiary. A person (or organization) receiving benefits under a legal instrument such as a will, trust, or life insurance policy. Except when very small estates are involved, beneficiaries of wills only receive their benefits after the will is examined and approved by the probate court. Beneficiaries of trusts receive their benefits directly as provided in the trust instrument.

Bequeath. The first-person legal term used to leave someone personal property in the will, for example, "I bequeath my antique car collection to my brother Jody."

Bequest. The legal term used to describe personal property left in a will.

Bond. A document guaranteeing that a certain amount of money will be paid to the victim if a person occupying a position of trust does not carry out his or her legal and ethical responsibilities. Thus, if an executor, trustee, or guardian who is bonded (covered by a bond) wrongfully deprives a beneficiary of his or her property (say, by taking it on a one-way trip to Las Vegas), the bonding company will replace it, up to the limits of the bond. Bonding companies, which are normally divisions of insurance companies, issue a bond in exchange for a premium (usually about 10% of the face amount of the bond). Because the cost of any required bond is paid out of the estate, most wills provide that no bond shall be required.

Children. Children are: (1) the biological offspring of the person making the will (the testator), unless they have been legally adopted by another, (2) persons who were legally adopted by the testator, (3) children born outside of marriage if the testator is the mother, (4) children born outside of marriage if the testator is the father and has acknowledged the child as being his under

California law (this can be done in writing or by the conduct of the father—for more information see *Living Together: A Legal Guide for Unmarried Couples*, by Ralph Warner, Toni Ihara, and Frederick Hertz (Nolo)), and (5) stepchildren and foster children if the relationship began during the person's minority, continued throughout the parties' joint lifetimes, and it is established by clear and convincing evidence that the decedent would have adopted the person but for a legal barrier.

Class. A group of beneficiaries or heirs that is designated only by status—for example, "children" or "issue." A class member is simply anyone who fits in the category.

Codicil. A supplement or addition to a will. It may explain, modify, add to, subtract from, qualify, alter, restrain, or revoke provisions in the will. Because a codicil changes a will, it must be executed with the same formalities as a will. When admitted to probate, it forms a part of the will.

Collateral. Property pledged as security for a debt.

Community Property. Very generally, all property acquired by a couple after marriage and before permanent separation, except for gifts to and inheritances by one spouse or partner only, or unless the nature of property has been changed by agreement between the spouses or partners. Assets purchased during the marriage or partnership with the income earned by either spouse or partner during the marriage or partnership are usually community property, unless the spouses or partners have entered into an agreement to the contrary. Property purchased with the separate property of a spouse or partner is separate property, unless it has been given to the community by gift or agreement. If separate property and community property are mixed together (commingled) in a bank account and expenditures are made from this bank account, the goods purchased will usually be treated as community property.

Community Property With Right of Survivorship. Property owned by a married couple that is clearly identified, on the title document, as "community property with right of survivorship." When one spouse or partner dies, the surviving spouse or partner inherits the deceased's half-interest automatically, without probate.

Conditional Bequest. A bequest that passes only under certain specified conditions or upon the occurrence of a specific event. For example, if you leave property to Aunt Millie provided she is living in Cincinnati when you die, and otherwise to Uncle Fred, you have made a conditional bequest.

Conformed Copy. A copy of a document filed with the court that has been stamped with the filing date by the court clerk.

Consanguinity. An old-fashioned term referring to the relationship enjoyed by people who have a common ancestor. Thus, consanguinity exists between brothers and sisters but not between husbands and wives.

Contingent Beneficiary. Any person entitled to property under a will in the event one or more prior conditions are satisfied. For example, if Fred is entitled to take property under a will on the condition that Harry does not survive the testator, Fred is a contingent beneficiary. Similarly, if Ellen is named to receive a house only in the event her mother, who has been named to receive the house, moves out of it, Ellen is a contingent beneficiary.

Creditor. For probate purposes, a creditor is any person or entity to whom the decedent was liable for money at the time of his or her death, and any person or entity to whom the estate owes money (say a taxing authority, funeral home, etc.).

CTA. An abbreviation for the Latin phrase "cum testamento annexo," meaning "with the will annexed." Thus, an administrator who is appointed to serve in a context where a will exists but no executor was either named or able to serve is termed an administrator CTA or administrator with will annexed.

Decedent. For probate purposes, the person who died, either testate or intestate, and left the estate.

Decree. A court order.

Deductions. Items that cause the value of the estate to be reduced. They include the decedent's debts, any expenses associated with a last illness, funeral expenses, taxes, and costs of administration (for example, court filing fees, certification fees, bond premiums, fees for public notices, etc.).

Deed. A document that describes a transfer of ownership in respect to a particular parcel of real property, a description of which is also set out in the document. There are many types of deeds, including quitclaim deeds (a naked transfer of the property ownership without any guarantees), grant deeds (a transfer of ownership accompanied by a number of standard guarantees or warranties, including the fact that the person making the transfer has the power to do so), as well as joint tenancy deeds, gift deeds, and so on.

Deed of Trust. A special type of deed (similar to a mortgage) that places legal title to real property in the hands of one or more trustees as security for repayment of a loan. Thus, if Ida borrows $100,000 to buy a house, she will be required as a condition of the loan to sign a deed of trust in favor of the designated trustees, who will retain the deed of trust until the loan has been paid off. It is not uncommon for homes to carry two deeds of trust—one executed as security for a loan to buy the house and another (termed the "second deed of trust") executed at a later time as security for another loan (for example, for home improvement, purchase of another parcel, cash to buy stocks, etc.).

Devise. A legal term that now means any real or personal property that is transferred under the terms of a will. Previously, the term referred only to real property.

Devisee. A person or entity who receives real or personal property under the terms of a will.

Discharge. The term used to describe the court order releasing the administrator or executor from any further duties regarding the estate being subjected to probate proceedings. This typically occurs when the duties have been completed but can also happen in the middle of the probate proceedings when the executor or administrator wishes to withdraw.

Distributee. Someone who receives property from an estate.

Domestic Partner. One of two persons who have filed a Declaration of Domestic Partnership with the secretary of state. See the introduction to this book for more information about domestic partner benefits.

Donee. One who receives a gift. Thus, the beneficiary of a trust is generally referred to as the donee.

Donor. One who, while alive, gives property to another, usually in the form of a trust.

Encumbrances. Debts (for example, taxes, mechanic's liens, and judgment liens) and loans (for example, mortgages, deeds of trust, and security interests) that use property as collateral for payment of the debt or loan are considered to encumber the property because they must be paid off before title to the property can pass from one owner to the next. Generally, the value of a person's ownership in such property (called the "equity") is measured by the market value of the property less the sum of all encumbrances.

Equity. The difference between the fair market value of your real and personal property and the amount you still owe on it, if any.

Escheat. A legal doctrine under which property belonging to a deceased person with no heirs passes to the state.

Estate. Generally, the property you own when you die. There are different ways to measure your estate, depending on whether you are concerned with tax reduction (taxable estate), probate avoidance (probate estate), net worth (net estate), or attorney fees for probate (gross estate).

Estate Planning. The art of dying with the smallest taxable estate and probate estate possible while continuing to prosper when you're alive and yet passing your property to your loved ones with a minimum of fuss and expense.

Estate Taxes. See "Federal Estate Taxes."

Executor/Executrix. The person specified in a will to manage the estate, deal with the probate court, collect the assets, and distribute them as the will has specified. If there is no will, or no executor nominated under the will, the probate court will appoint such a person, who is then called the administrator of the estate.

Expenses of Administration. The expenses incurred by an executor or administrator in carrying out the terms of a will or in administering an estate in accordance with the law applicable to persons dying intestate. These include probate court fees, and fees charged by the executor or administrator, attorney, accountant, and appraiser.

Fair Market Value. That price for which an item of property would be purchased by a willing buyer, and sold by a willing seller, both knowing all the facts and neither being under any compulsion to buy or sell. All estates are appraised for their fair market value, and taxes are computed on the basis of the estate's net fair market value.

Federal Estate Taxes. Taxes imposed by the federal government on property as it passes from the dead to the living. For deaths in 2011 and 2012, the first $5 million of property is exempt from tax. Also, all property left to a surviving spouse who is a U.S. citizen is exempt. (This exemption does not apply to domestic partners.)

Gift. Property passed to others for no return or substantially less than its actual market value is considered a gift when the giver (donor) is still alive, and a bequest, legacy, or devise when left by a will.

Gross Estate. For federal estate tax filing purposes, the total of all property a decedent owned at the time of death, without regard to any debts or liens against such property or the expenses of administration of the estate. However, taxes are due only on the value of the property the decedent actually owned. The gross estate is also used when computing attorney's fees for probating estates. These are established by statute as a percentage of the gross estate, the percentage varying with the size of the estate.

Heir. Any person who is entitled by law to inherit in the event an estate is not completely disposed of under a will, and any person or institution named in a will.

Heir at Law. A person entitled to inherit under intestate succession laws.

Holographic Will. A will in which the signature and material provisions are in the handwriting of the person making it. Any statement of testamentary intent contained in a holographic will may be either in the testator's own handwriting or as part of a commercially printed form will. Holographic wills are valid in California.

Inheritance Tax. California no longer has a state inheritance tax. But if federal estate tax is owed, some of the amount is paid to the state and allowed as a credit on the amount of federal tax owed. See Chapter 7.

Intangible Personal Property. Personal property that does not assume a physical form but which derives its value from the rights and powers that it gives to its owner. Thus, stock in a corporation, the right to receive a pension, and a patent or copyright are all examples of intangible personal property. Intangible personal property is, as a matter of law, deemed to be located where the decedent resides at the time of his or her death, even if, in fact, a title slip (for example, a stock or bond certificate) is physically located elsewhere.

Inter Vivos Trusts. See "Living Trust."

Intestate. When a person dies without having made a will he or she is said to die "intestate." In that event, the estate is distributed according to the laws governing intestate succession.

Intestate Succession. The method by which property is distributed when a person fails to leave a will. In such cases, California law provides that the property be distributed in certain shares to the closest surviving relatives. Generally, property goes to the surviving spouse or registered domestic partner, children, parents, siblings, nieces and nephews, and next of kin, in that order. In California, intestate succession rules can be different depending on whether separate or community property is involved (see Chapter 3). The intestate succession laws are also used in the event children are unintentionally overlooked in the will or if the beneficiary named to inherit the residuary estate predeceases the testator and there is no alternate.

Inventory. A complete listing of all property owned by the decedent at death that is filed with the probate court in the event a probate petition is filed.

Issue. A term generally meaning all natural children and their children down through the generations. Thus, a person's issue includes his or her children, grandchildren, great-grandchildren, and so on. Adopted children are considered the issue of their adopting parents and the children of the adopted children (and so on) are also considered issue. A term often used in place of issue is "lineal descendants."

Joint Tenancy. A way to hold title to jointly owned real or personal property. When two or more people own property as joint tenants, and one of the owners dies, the others automatically become owners of the deceased owner's share. Thus, if a parent and child own a house as joint tenants, and the parent dies, the child automatically becomes full owner. Because of this "right of survivorship," a joint tenancy interest in property does not go through probate, or, put another way, is not part of the probate estate. Instead it goes directly to the surviving joint tenant(s) once some tax and transfer forms are completed.

Kindred. All persons described as relatives of the decedent under the California Probate Code.

Lapse. The failure of a gift of property left in a will because when the testator dies the beneficiary is deceased and no alternate has been named. California has a statute (termed an "antilapse" statute) that prevents gifts to relatives from lapsing unless the relative has no heirs of his or her own.

Lawful Issue. The phrase was once used to distinguish between legitimate and illegitimate children (and their issue). Now, the phrase means the same as "issue" and "lineal descendant."

Legacy. An old legal word meaning a transfer of personal property by will. The more common term for this type of transfer is "bequest" or "devise."

Letters of Administration. A document issued by the court that designates an administrator of an estate and authorizes him or her to carry out his or her proper duties.

Letters Testamentary. The formal instrument of authority given to an executor by the probate court, empowering him or her to carry out his or her duties as executor. If an administrator has been appointed, letters of administration are granted.

Life Estate. The type of ownership a person possesses in real estate when he or she has only the right of possession for his or her life, and the ownership passes to someone else after his or her death.

Lineal Descendants. Persons who are in the direct line of descent from an ancestor, such as children, grandchildren, and great-grandchildren. The term does not include nondescendant relatives such as siblings, nieces and nephews, and cousins.

Living Trust. A trust set up while a person is alive and that remains under the control of that person during the remainder of his or her life. Also referred to as "inter vivos trusts," living trusts can minimize the value of property passing through probate. This is because they enable people (called "trustors") to specify that money or other property (called the "trust corpus") will pass directly to their beneficiaries at the time of their death, free of probate.

Marital Exemption. A deduction allowed by the federal estate tax laws for all property passed to a surviving spouse, if the surviving spouse is a U.S. citizen. This deduction (which really acts like an exemption) allows anyone, even a billionaire, to pass his or her entire estate to a surviving spouse without any tax at all. (This federal exemption does not apply to domestic partners.)

Marriage. A specific status conferred on a couple by the state. In California, it is necessary to file papers with a county clerk and have a marriage ceremony conducted by authorized individuals in order to be married, unless there is a valid marriage in another state.

Minor. In California, any person under 18 years of age.

Net Estate. The value of all property owned at death less liabilities.

Next of Kin. The closest living relatives of a decedent, under the California law governing intestate succession.

Personal Effects. Belongings of a personal nature, such as clothes and jewelry.

Personal Property. All items, both tangible and intangible, that are considered susceptible to ownership and that are not real property (e.g., house, land, crops, cabin, etc.) are termed personal property. Property in an estate may be treated differently depending on whether it is considered personal or "real."

Personal Representative. The generic title applied to the person who is authorized to act on behalf of the decedent's estate. Almost always, this person is either the administrator or executor.

Per Stirpes. A Latin term meaning that a beneficiary inherits through a deceased ancestor by right of representation. In real life, the term is normally used in wills to control the way property should be divided when one or more joint beneficiaries of a gift has died before the testator, leaving living children of his or her own. See Chapter 3.

Petition. Any document filed with a court requesting a court order. In the probate context, the term is normally used to describe the initial document filed with the probate court requesting that the estate be probated, subsequent requests by the executor for court permission to take certain actions in respect to the estate, and a final request to discharge the executor or administrator from his or her duties.

Predeceased Domestic Partner. The term applied to a domestic partner who has died before the decedent while in a registered domestic partnership with him or her.

Predeceased Spouse. The term applied to a spouse who has died before the decedent while married to him or her.

Pretermitted Heir. A child, spouse, or domestic partner who, under certain circumstances, is not mentioned in the will and who the court believes was accidentally overlooked by the testator when making his or her will. This typically occurs when a child has been born or adopted after the will was made. Because state law presumes that persons want their children to inherit, the failure to provide for them in a will is considered unintentional unless there is evidence of an intent to disinherit. Mentioning them in the will and then not providing for them is considered sufficient evidence of intent to disinherit in California. If the court determines that an heir was pretermitted, that heir is entitled to receive the same share of the estate as he or she would have had the testator died intestate.

Probate. Generally, the process by which: (1) the authenticity of your will (if any) is established, (2) your executor or administrator is appointed, (3) your debts and taxes are paid, (4) your heirs are identified, and (5) property in your probate estate is distributed according to your will or intestate succession laws. Many people feel that formal, court-supervised probate is a costly, time-consuming process that is best avoided if possible. Accordingly, instead of leaving their property in a will, they use probate avoidance devices, such as joint tenancy, trusts (including savings bank, living, insurance, and testamentary trusts), or life insurance.

Probate Estate. All the assets owned at death that require some form of legal proceeding before title may be transferred to the proper heirs. Accordingly property that passes automatically at death (property in a trust, life insurance proceeds, property in a "pay-on-death" account, or property held in joint tenancy) is not in the probate estate.

Public Administrator. A publicly appointed person who handles the administration of an estate when no other person has been appointed as executor or administrator. This usually occurs when there are no known heirs.

Quasi-Community Property. Property acquired by a husband and wife or registered domestic partners during their marriage or registered partnership while residing outside California that would have been community property had it been acquired in California. California law treats it the same as community property. In essence, this means that in assessing whether or not a decedent's property is community property, the residence of the decedent when the property was acquired is irrelevant. An important exception: Real property located outside California is not considered quasi-community property.

Real Property. Land, things affixed to the land such as trees and crops, buildings, stationary mobile homes, cabins, and camps are all termed real property. All property that is not real property is termed personal property. See "Personal Property."

Residence. The physical location that a person considers and treats as his or her home, both presently and for the indefinite future. For example, although members of Congress typically spend most of their time in Washington, DC, they generally consider the states they come from as their residences. With rare exceptions, a person may have only one residence. The concept of residence is important to the subject of probate since a decedent's estate, with the exception of certain property located in other states, is subject to the laws of the state where the decedent was residing.

Residuary Estate. All the property contained in the probate estate except for property that has been specifically and effectively left to designated beneficiaries.

Right of Representation. When the descendants of a deceased person take the same share collectively that the deceased person would have taken if living at the time of a decedent's death. See "Per Stirpes."

Self-Proving Will. A will that is executed in a way that allows the court to accept it as the true will of the decedent without further proof. In California, a will is self-proving when two witnesses to the will sign under penalty of perjury that they observed the testator sign it and that the testator told them it was his or her will.

Separate Property. In the probate context, all property owned by a California decedent that is not considered community or quasi-community property. Separate property generally includes all property acquired by the decedent before marriage or domestic partnerhip and after a legal separation or dissolution, property acquired by separate gift or inheritance at any time, property acquired from separate property funds, and property that has been designated separate property by agreement of the spouses or partners.

Specific Bequest. A specific item, distinguished from all others of the same kind belonging to the testator, that is designated in the will as going to a specific beneficiary. If the specific item is no longer in the estate when the decedent dies, the bequest fails and resort cannot be made to other property of the decedent. Thus, if John leaves his 1954 Mercedes to Patti, and when John dies the 1954 Mercedes is long gone, Patti doesn't receive John's current car or the cash equivalent of the Mercedes.

Succession. The act of acquiring title to property when it has not been disposed of by will. Thus, when Abbie receives her mother's coin collection through "succession," she gets it under the intestate laws rather than as a beneficiary under a will.

Surviving Domestic Partner. The surviving member of a couple who, while both were alive, filed a Declaration of Domestic Partnership with the California Secretary of State. (Prob. Code § 37.)

Tangible Personal Property. Personal property that takes a tangible form, such as automobiles, furniture, and heirlooms. Although such items as stock ownership and copyrights may be represented in the form of paper certificates, the actual property is not in physical form and is therefore considered intangible personal property. See "Intangible Personal Property."

Taxable Estate. The fair market value of all assets owned by a decedent at date of death (gross estate) less certain allowable deductions, such as debts of the decedent, last illness and funeral expenses, and expenses of administering the decedent's estate (attorney's fees, court costs, and newspaper publication fees).

Tenancy in Common. The ownership of property by two or more persons in such a manner that each has an undivided interest in the whole and each can pass his or her interest upon death to his or her own heirs/beneficiaries instead of to the other owners (as is the case with joint tenancy). Also, unlike joint tenancies, the ownership shares need not be equal.

Testamentary Disposition. A disposition of property in a will.

Testate. Having left a will. For example, if Elmer dies having made a will, he is said to have died testate.

Testator. One who has made a will; one who dies leaving a will.

Transfer Agent. A representative of a corporation who is authorized to transfer ownership of a corporation's stock from one person to another. An executor or administrator must use a transfer agent when passing title to a decedent's stock to an heir or beneficiary.

Trust. A legal arrangement under which one person or institution (called a "trustee") controls property given by another person (termed a "trustor," "grantor," or "settlor") for the benefit of a third person (called a "beneficiary"). The property itself is sometimes termed the "corpus" of the trust. See "Living Trust."

Uniform Transfer-on-Death Securities Registration Act. A law adopted by the State of California that allows you to name someone to inherit your stocks, bonds, or brokerage accounts without probate. When you register your ownership, you make a request to take ownership in what's called "beneficiary form." The beneficiary has no rights to the stock while you are alive, but on your death, the beneficiaries can claim the securities without probate.

Uniform Transfers to Minors Act. A set of statutes adopted by the California legislature which provides a way for someone to give or leave property to a minor by appointing a "custodian" to manage the property for the minor. It is common for wills to appoint a custodian for property left to minors in the will.

Will. A written document, signed and witnessed as required by law, in which a person expresses what he or she wants to happen in respect to his or her property, children, pets, and so on, after his or her death.

California Probate Code §§ 13100–13106

Affidavit Procedure for Collection or Transfer of Personal Property

§ 13100. Collection or transfer of personal property without probate

Excluding the property described in Section 13050, if the gross value of the decedent's real and personal property in this state does not exceed one hundred thousand dollars ($100,000) and if 40 days have elapsed since the death of the decedent, the successor of the decedent may, without procuring letters of administration or awaiting probate of the will, do any of the following with respect to one or more particular items of property:

(a) Collect any particular item of property that is money due the decedent.

(b) Receive any particular item of property that is tangible personal property of the decedent.

(c) Have any particular item of property that is evidence of a debt, obligation, interest, right, security, or chose in action belonging to the decedent transferred, whether or not secured by a lien on real property.

(Enacted Stats 1990 ch 79 § 14 (AB 759), operative July 1, 1991. Amended Stats 1996 ch 862 § 34 (AB 2751), operative Jan. 1, 1997.)

§ 13101. Furnishing affidavit or declaration

(a) To collect money, receive tangible personal property, or have evidences of a debt, obligation, interest, right, security, or chose in action transferred under this chapter, an affidavit or a declaration under penalty of perjury under the laws of this state shall be furnished to the holder of the decedent's property stating all of the following:

(1) The decedent's name.

(2) The date and place of the decedent's death.

(3) "At least 40 days have elapsed since the death of the decedent, as shown in a certified copy of the decedent's death certificate attached to this affidavit or declaration."

(4) Either of the following, as appropriate:

(A) "No proceeding is now being or has been conducted in California for administration of the decedent's estate."

(B) "The decedent's personal representative has consented in writing to the payment, transfer, or delivery to the affiant or declarant of the property described in the affidavit or declaration."

(5) "The current gross fair market value of the decedent's real and personal property in California, excluding the property described in Section 13050 of the California Probate Code, does not exceed one hundred thousand dollars ($100,000)."

(6) A description of the property of the decedent that is to be paid, transferred, or delivered to the affiant or declarant.

(7) The name of the successor of the decedent (as defined in Section 13006 of the California Probate Code) to the described property.

(8) Either of the following, as appropriate:

(A) "The affiant or declarant is the successor of the decedent (as defined in Section 13006 of the California Probate Code) to the decedent's interest in the described property."

(B) "The affiant or declarant is authorized under Section 13051 of the California Probate Code to act on behalf of the successor of the decedent (as defined in Section 13006 of the California Probate Code) with respect to the decedent's interest in the described property."

(9) "No other person has a superior right to the interest of the decedent in the described property."

(10) "The affiant or declarant requests that the described property be paid, delivered, or transferred to the affiant or declarant."

(11) "The affiant or declarant affirms or declares under penalty of perjury under the laws of the State of California that the foregoing is true and correct."

(b) Where more than one person executes the affidavit or declaration under this section, the statements required by subdivision (a) shall be modified as appropriate to reflect that fact.

(c) If the particular item of property to be transferred under this chapter is a debt or other obligation secured by a lien on real property and the instrument creating the lien has been recorded in the office of the county recorder of the county where the real property is located, the affidavit or declaration shall satisfy the requirements both of this section and of Section 13106.5.

(d) A certified copy of the decedent's death certificate shall be attached to the affidavit or declaration.

(e) If the decedent's personal representative has consented to the payment, transfer, or delivery of the described property to the affiant or declarant, a copy of the consent and of the personal representative's letters shall be attached to the affidavit or declaration.

(Enacted Stats 1990 ch 79 § 14 (AB 759), operative July 1, 1991. Amended Stats 1996 ch 862 § 35 (AB 2751), operative Jan. 1, 1997.)

§ 13102. Presenting decedent's evidence of ownership

(a) If the decedent had evidence of ownership of the property described in the affidavit or declaration and the holder of the property would have had the right to require presentation of the evidence of ownership before the duty of the holder to pay, deliver, or transfer the property to the decedent would have arisen, the evidence of ownership, if available, shall be presented with the affidavit or declaration to the holder of the decedent's property.

(b) If the evidence of ownership is not presented to the holder pursuant to subdivision (a), the holder may require, as a condition for the payment, delivery, or transfer of the property, that the person presenting the affidavit or declaration provide the holder with a bond or undertaking in a reasonable amount determined by the holder to be sufficient to indemnify the holder against all liability, claims, demands, loss, damages, costs, and expenses that the holder may incur or suffer by reason of the payment, delivery, or transfer of the property. Nothing in this subdivision precludes the holder and the person presenting the affidavit or declaration from dispensing with the requirement that a bond or undertaking be provided and instead entering into an agreement satisfactory to the holder concerning the duty of the person presenting the affidavit or declaration to indemnify the holder.

(Enacted Stats 1990 ch 79 § 14 (AB 759), operative July 1, 1991.)

§ 13103. Inventory and appraisal of real property

If the estate of the decedent includes any real property in this state, the affidavit or declaration shall be accompanied by an inventory and appraisal of the real property. The inventory and appraisal of the real property shall be made as provided in Part 3 (commencing with Section 8800) of Division 7. The appraisal shall be made by a probate referee selected by the affiant or declarant from those probate referees appointed by the Controller under Section 400 to appraise property in the county where the real property is located.

(Enacted Stats 1990 ch 79 § 14 (AB 759), operative July 1, 1991.)

§ 13104. Proof of identity

(a) Reasonable proof of the identity of each person executing the affidavit or declaration shall be provided to the holder of the decedent's property.

(b) Reasonable proof of identity is provided for the purposes of this section if both of the following requirements are satisfied:

   (1) The person executing the affidavit or declaration is personally known to the holder.

   (2) The person executes the affidavit or declaration in the presence of the holder.

(c) If the affidavit or declaration is executed in the presence of the holder, a written statement under penalty of perjury by a person personally known to the holder affirming the identity of the person executing the affidavit or declaration is reasonable proof of identity for the purposes of this section.

(d) If the affidavit or declaration is executed in the presence of the holder, the holder may reasonably rely on any of the following as reasonable proof of identity for the purposes of this section:

   (1) An identification card or driver's license issued by the Department of Motor Vehicles of this state that is current or was issued during the preceding five years.

   (2) A passport issued by the Department of State of the United States that is current or was issued during the preceding five years.

   (3) Any of the following documents if the document is current or was issued during the preceding five years and contains a photograph and description of the person named on it, is signed by the person, and bears a serial or other identifying number:

      (A) A passport issued by a foreign government that has been stamped by the United States Immigration and Naturalization Service.

      (B) A driver's license issued by a state other than California.

      (C) An identification card issued by a state other than California.

      (D) An identification card issued by any branch of the armed forces of the United States.

(e) For the purposes of this section, a notary public's certificate of acknowledgment identifying the person executing the affidavit or declaration is reasonable proof of identity of the person executing the affidavit or declaration.

(f) Unless the affidavit or declaration contains a notary public's certificate of acknowledgment of the identity of the person, the holder shall note on the affidavit or declaration either that the person executing the affidavit or declaration is personally known or a description of the identification provided by the person executing the affidavit or declaration.

(Enacted Stats 1990 ch 79 § 14 (AB 759), operative July 1, 1991.)

§ 13105. Transfer of property to successor

(a) If the requirements of Sections 13100 to 13104, inclusive, are satisfied:

   (1) The person or persons executing the affidavit or declaration as successor of the decedent are entitled to have the property described in the affidavit or declaration paid, delivered, or transferred to them.

   (2) A transfer agent of a security described in the affidavit or declaration shall change the registered ownership on the books of the corporation from the decedent to the person or persons executing the affidavit or declaration as successor of the decedent.

(b) If the holder of the decedent's property refuses to pay, deliver, or transfer any personal property or evidence thereof to the successor of the decedent within a reasonable time, the successor may recover the property or compel its payment, delivery, or transfer in an action brought for that purpose against the holder of the property. If an action is brought against the holder under this section, the court shall award reasonable attorney's fees to the person or persons bringing the action if the court finds that the holder of the decedent's property acted unreasonably in refusing to pay, deliver, or transfer the property to them as required by subdivision (a).

(Enacted Stats 1990 ch 79 § 14 (AB 759), operative July 1, 1991.)

§ 13106. Protection of transferor from liability

(a) If the requirements of Sections 13100 to 13104, inclusive, are satisfied, receipt by the holder of the decedent's property of the affidavit or declaration constitutes sufficient acquittance for the payment of money, delivery of property, or changing registered ownership of property pursuant to this chapter and discharges the holder from any further liability with respect to the money or property. The holder may rely in good faith on the statements in the affidavit or declaration and has no duty to inquire into the truth of any statement in the affidavit or declaration.

(b) If the requirements of Sections 13100 to 13104, inclusive, are satisfied, the holder of the decedent's property is not liable for any taxes due to this state by reason of paying money, delivering property, or changing registered ownership of property pursuant to this chapter.

(Enacted Stats 1990 ch 79 § 14 (AB 759), operative July 1, 1991.)

Judicial Council Forms

You can download all Judicial Council forms at www.courtinfo.ca.gov/forms.

DE-111	Petition for Probate
DE-120	Notice of Hearing
DE-121	Notice of Petition to Administer Estate
DE-121(MA)	Attachment to Notice of Petition to Administer Estate
DE-131	Proof of Subscribing Witness
DE-135	Proof of Holographic Instrument
DE-140	Order for Probate
DE-147	Duties and Liabilities of Personal Representative
DE-147S	Confidential Supplement to Duties and Liabilities of Personal Representative
DE-150	Letters
DE-157	Notice of Administration to Creditors
DE-160	Inventory and Appraisal
DE-161	Inventory and Appraisal Attachment
DE-165	Notice of Proposed Action
DE-174	Allowance or Rejection of Creditor's Claim
DE-221	Spousal or Domestic Partner Property Petition
DE-226	Spousal or Domestic Partner Property Order
DE-270	Ex Parte Petition for Authority to Sell Securities and Order
DE-295	Ex Parte Petition for Final Discharge and Order
DE-305	Affidavit re Real Property of Small Value ($20,000 or Less)
DE-310	Petition to Determine Succession to Real Property (Estates $100,000 or Less)
DE-315	Order Determining Succession to Real Property (Estates $100,000 or Less)

ATTORNEY OR PARTY WITHOUT ATTORNEY *(Name, State Bar number, and address)*:	*FOR COURT USE ONLY*
TELEPHONE NO.: FAX NO. *(Optional)*: E-MAIL ADDRESS *(Optional)*: ATTORNEY FOR *(Name)*:	

SUPERIOR COURT OF CALIFORNIA, COUNTY OF
STREET ADDRESS:
MAILING ADDRESS:
CITY AND ZIP CODE:
BRANCH NAME:

ESTATE OF *(Name)*:

DECEDENT

PETITION FOR ☐ Probate of Will and for Letters Testamentary ☐ Probate of Will and for Letters of Administration with Will Annexed ☐ Letters of Administration ☐ Letters of Special Administration ☐ with general powers ☐ Authorization to Administer Under the Independent Administration of Estates Act ☐ with limited authority	CASE NUMBER: HEARING DATE: DEPT.: TIME:

1. Publication will be in *(specify name of newspaper)*:
    a. ☐ Publication requested.
    b. ☐ Publication to be arranged.

2. **Petitioner** *(name each)*:   **requests that**
    a. ☐ decedent's will and codicils, if any, be admitted to probate.
    b. ☐ *(name)*:
        be appointed
        (1) ☐ executor
        (2) ☐ administrator with will annexed
        (3) ☐ administrator
        (4) ☐ special administrator ☐ with general powers
        and Letters issue upon qualification.
    c. ☐ full ☐ limited authority   be granted to administer under the Independent Administration of Estates Act.
    d. (1) ☐ bond not be required for the reasons stated in item 3d.
        (2) ☐ $ bond be fixed. The bond will be furnished by an admitted surety insurer or as otherwise provided by law. *(Specify reasons in Attachment 2 if the amount is different from the maximum required by Prob. Code, § 8482.)*
        (3) ☐ $ in deposits in a blocked account be allowed. Receipts will be filed. *(Specify institution and location)*:

3. a. Decedent died on *(date)*:   at *(place)*:
        (1) ☐ a resident of the county named above.
        (2) ☐ a nonresident of California and left an estate in the county named above located at *(specify location permitting publication in the newspaper named in item 1)*:

    b. Street address, city, and county of decedent's residence at time of death *(specify)*:

Form Adopted for Mandatory Use Judicial Council of California DE-111 [Rev. March 1, 2008]	**PETITION FOR PROBATE** **(Probate—Decedents Estates)**	Probate Code, §§ 8002, 10450; *www.courtinfo.ca.gov*

ESTATE OF *(Name):*	CASE NUMBER:
DECEDENT	

3. c. **Character and estimated value of the property of the estate** *(complete in all cases):*

    (1)   Personal property: $

    (2) Annual gross income from

        (a) real property: $

        (b) personal property: $ _____

    (3) **Subtotal** *(add (1) and (2)):* $ _____

    (4) Gross fair market value of real property: $

    (5) (Less) Encumbrances: $(_____)

    (6) Net value of real property: $ _____

    (7) **Total** *(add (3) and (6)):* $ _____

  d. (1) ☐ Will waives bond. ☐ Special administrator is the named executor, and the will waives bond.

      (2) ☐ All beneficiaries are adults and have waived bond, and the will does not require a bond.
                (Affix waiver as Attachment 3d(2).)

      (3) ☐ All heirs at law are adults and have waived bond. *(Affix waiver as Attachment 3d(3).)*

      (4) ☐ Sole personal representative is a corporate fiduciary or an exempt government agency.

  e. (1) ☐ Decedent died intestate.

      (2) ☐ Copy of decedent's will dated: ☐ codicil dated *(specify for each):*

                               are affixed as Attachment 3e(2).

           (Include typed copies of handwritten documents and English translations of foreign-language documents.)
              ☐ The will and all codicils are self-proving (Prob. Code, § 8220).

  f. **Appointment of personal representative** *(check all applicable boxes):*

    (1) Appointment of executor or administrator with will annexed:

        (a) ☐ Proposed executor is named as executor in the will and consents to act.

        (b) ☐ No executor is named in the will.

        (c) ☐ Proposed personal representative is a nominee of a person entitled to Letters.
                  (Affix nomination as Attachment 3f(1)(c).)

        (d) ☐ Other named executors will not act because of ☐ death ☐ declination
                ☐ other reasons *(specify):*

                ☐ Continued in Attachment 3f(1)(d).

    (2) Appointment of administrator:

        (a) ☐ Petitioner is a person entitled to Letters. *(If necessary, explain priority in Attachment 3f(2)(a).)*

        (b) ☐ Petitioner is a nominee of a person entitled to Letters. *(Affix nomination as Attachment 3f(2)(b).)*

        (c) ☐ Petitioner is related to the decedent as *(specify):*

    (3) ☐ Appointment of special administrator requested. *(Specify grounds and requested powers in Attachment 3f(3).)*

  g. Proposed personal representative is a

    (1) ☐ resident of California.

    (2) ☐ nonresident of California *(specify permanent address):*

    (3) ☐ resident of the United States.

    (4) ☐ nonresident of the United States.

PETITION FOR PROBATE
(Probate—Decedents Estates)

ESTATE OF (Name):	CASE NUMBER:
DECEDENT	

4. ☐ Decedent's will does not preclude administration of this estate under the Independent Administration of Estates Act.

5. a. Decedent was survived by *(check items (1) or (2), and (3) or (4), and (5) or (6), and (7) or (8))*

    (1) ☐ spouse.

    (2) ☐ no spouse as follows:

        (a) ☐ divorced or never married.

        (b) ☐ spouse deceased.

    (3) ☐ registered domestic partner.

    (4) ☐ no registered domestic partner.

        (See Fam. Code, § 297.5(c); Prob. Code, §§ 37(b), 6401(c), and 6402.)

    (5) ☐ child as follows:

        (a) ☐ natural or adopted.

        (b) ☐ natural adopted by a third party.

    (6) ☐ no child.

    (7) ☐ issue of a predeceased child.

    (8) ☐ no issue of a predeceased child.

   b. Decedent ☐ was ☐ was not survived by a stepchild or foster child or children who would have been adopted by decedent but for a legal barrier. *(See Prob. Code, § 6454.)*

6. *(Complete if decedent was survived by (1) a spouse or registered domestic partner but no issue (only **a** or **b** apply), or (2) no spouse, registered domestic partner, or issue. (Check the **first** box that applies):*

   a. ☐ Decedent was survived by a parent or parents who are listed in item 8.

   b. ☐ Decedent was survived by issue of deceased parents, all of whom are listed in item 8.

   c. ☐ Decedent was survived by a grandparent or grandparents who are listed in item 8.

   d. ☐ Decedent was survived by issue of grandparents, all of whom are listed in item 8.

   e. ☐ Decedent was survived by issue of a predeceased spouse, all of whom are listed in item 8.

   f. ☐ Decedent was survived by next of kin, all of whom are listed in item 8.

   g. ☐ Decedent was survived by parents of a predeceased spouse or issue of those parents, if both are predeceased, all of whom are listed in item 8.

   h. ☐ Decedent was survived by no known next of kin.

7. *(Complete only if no spouse or issue survived decedent.)*

   a. ☐ Decedent had no predeceased spouse.

   b. ☐ Decedent had a predeceased spouse who

        (1) ☐ died not more than 15 years before decedent and who owned an interest in **real property** that passed to decedent,

        (2) ☐ died not more than five years before decedent and who owned **personal property** valued at $10,000 or more that passed to decedent,

        *(If you checked (1) or (2), check only the **first** box that applies):*

        (a) ☐ Decedent was survived by issue of a predeceased spouse, all of whom are listed in item 8.

        (b) ☐ Decedent was survived by a parent or parents of the predeceased spouse who are listed in item 8.

        (c) ☐ Decedent was survived by issue of a parent of the predeceased spouse, all of whom are listed in item 8.

        (d) ☐ Decedent was survived by next of kin of the decedent, all of whom are listed in item 8.

        (e) ☐ Decedent was survived by next of kin of the predeceased spouse, all of whom are listed in item 8.

        (3) ☐ neither (1) nor (2) apply.

8. Listed on the next page are the names, relationships to decedent, ages, and addresses, so far as known to or reasonably ascertainable by petitioner, of (1) all persons mentioned in decedent's will or any codicil, whether living or deceased; (2) all persons named or checked in items 2, 5, 6, and 7; and (3) all beneficiaries of a trust named in decedent's will or any codicil in which the trustee and personal representative are the same person.

PETITION FOR PROBATE
(Probate—Decedents Estates)

ESTATE OF (Name):		
	DECEDENT	CASE NUMBER:

8. Name and relationship to decedent   Age   Address

[ ] Continued on Attachment 8.

9. Number of pages attached: _____

Date:

(TYPE OR PRINT NAME OF ATTORNEY)   ▶   (SIGNATURE OF ATTORNEY)*

* (Signatures of all petitioners are also required. All petitioners may sign, but the petition may be verified by any one of them (Prob. Code, §§ 1020, 1021; Cal. Rules of Court, rule 7.103).)

I declare under penalty of perjury under the laws of the State of California that the foregoing is true and correct.

Date:

(TYPE OR PRINT NAME OF PETITIONER)   ▶   (SIGNATURE OF PETITIONER)

(TYPE OR PRINT NAME OF PETITIONER)   ▶   (SIGNATURE OF PETITIONER)

[ ] Signatures of additional petitioners follow last attachment.

DE-111 [Rev. March 1, 2008]

PETITION FOR PROBATE
(Probate—Decedents Estates)

ATTORNEY OR PARTY WITHOUT ATTORNEY *(Name, State Bar number, and address):*	*FOR COURT USE ONLY*
TELEPHONE NO.: FAX NO. *(Optional):*	
E-MAIL ADDRESS *(Optional):*	
ATTORNEY FOR *(Name):*	

SUPERIOR COURT OF CALIFORNIA, COUNTY OF

STREET ADDRESS:

MAILING ADDRESS:

CITY AND ZIP CODE:

BRANCH NAME:

☐ ESTATE OF *(Name):*   ☐ IN THE MATTER OF *(Name):*

☐ DECEDENT   ☐ TRUST   ☐ OTHER

NOTICE OF HEARING—DECEDENT'S ESTATE OR TRUST	CASE NUMBER:

This notice is required by law.
This notice does not require you to appear in court, but you may attend the hearing if you wish.

---

1. NOTICE is given that *(name):*
   (representative capacity, if any):

   has filed *(specify):**

2. You may refer to the filed documents for more information. *(Some documents filed with the court are confidential.)*

3. A HEARING on the matter will be held as follows:

   a.   Date: Time: Dept.:   Room:

   b.   Address of court   ☐ shown above   ☐ is *(specify):*

Assistive listening systems, computer-assisted real-time captioning, or sign language interpreter services are available upon request if at least 5 days notice is provided. Contact the clerk's office for *Request for Accommodations by Persons With Disabilities and Order* (form MC-410). (Civil Code section 54.8.)

* Do **not** use this form to give notice of a petition to administer estate (see Prob. Code, § 8100 and form DE-121) or notice of a hearing in a guardianship or conservatorship (see Prob. Code, §§ 1511 and 1822 and form GC-020).

Page 1 of 2

Form Adopted for Mandatory Use Judicial Council of California DE-120 [Rev. July 1, 2005]	**NOTICE OF HEARING—DECEDENT'S ESTATE OR TRUST** **(Probate—Decedents' Estates)**	Probate Code §§ 851, 1211, 1215, 1216, 1230, 17100 *www.courtinfo.ca.gov*

ESTATE OF (Name): ☐ IN THE MATTER OF (Name):	CASE NUMBER:
☐ DECEDENT ☐ TRUST ☐ OTHER	

CLERK'S CERTIFICATE OF POSTING

1. I certify that I am not a party to this cause.
2. A copy of the foregoing *Notice of Hearing—Decedent's Estate or Trust*
   a. was posted at *(address):*

   b. was posted on *(date):*

Date: Clerk, by _____ , Deputy

PROOF OF SERVICE BY MAIL *

1. I am over the age of 18 and not a party to this cause. I am a resident of or employed in the county where the mailing occurred.
2. My residence or business address is *(specify):*

3. I served the foregoing *Notice of Hearing—Decedent's Estate or Trust* on each person named below by enclosing a copy in an envelope addressed as shown below AND

   a. ☐ **depositing** the sealed envelope on the date and at the place shown in item 4 with the United States Postal Service with the postage fully prepaid.

   b. ☐ **placing** the envelope for collection and mailing on the date and at the place shown in item 4 following our ordinary business practices. I am readily familiar with this business's practice for collecting and processing correspondence for mailing. On the same day that correspondence is placed for collection and mailing, it is deposited in the ordinary course of business with the United States Postal Service in a sealed envelope with postage fully prepaid.

4. a. Date mailed: b. Place mailed *(city, state):*

5. ☐ I served with the *Notice of Hearing—Decedent's Estate or Trust* a copy of the petition or other document referred to in the Notice.

I declare under penalty of perjury under the laws of the State of California that the foregoing is true and correct.

Date:

_____   _____
(TYPE OR PRINT NAME OF PERSON COMPLETING THIS FORM)   (SIGNATURE OF PERSON COMPLETING THIS FORM)

NAME AND ADDRESS OF EACH PERSON TO WHOM NOTICE WAS MAILED

	Name of person served	Address *(number, street, city, state, and zip code)*
1.		
2.		
3.		
4.		

☐ Continued on an attachment. *(You may use Attachment to Notice of Hearing Proof of Service by Mail, form DE-120(MA)/GC-020(MA), for this purpose.)*

* Do not use this form for proof of personal service. You may use form DE-120(P) to prove personal service of this Notice.

ATTORNEY OR PARTY WITHOUT ATTORNEY *(Name, State Bar number, and address):*

FOR COURT USE ONLY

TELEPHONE NO.:   FAX NO. *(Optional):*

E-MAIL ADDRESS *(Optional):*

ATTORNEY FOR *(Name):*

SUPERIOR COURT OF CALIFORNIA, COUNTY OF

    STREET ADDRESS:

    MAILING ADDRESS:

    CITY AND ZIP CODE:

    BRANCH NAME:

ESTATE OF *(Name):*

                                               DECEDENT

NOTICE OF PETITION TO ADMINISTER ESTATE OF
(Name):

CASE NUMBER:

To all heirs, beneficiaries, creditors, contingent creditors, and persons who may otherwise be interested in the will or estate, or both, of *(specify all names by which the decedent was known):*

A **Petition for Probate** has been filed by *(name of petitioner):*
in the Superior Court of California, County of *(specify):*

The Petition for Probate requests that *(name):*
be appointed as personal representative to administer the estate of the decedent.

☐ The petition requests the decedent's will and codicils, if any, be admitted to probate. The will and any codicils are available for examination in the file kept by the court.

☐ The petition requests authority to administer the estate under the Independent Administration of Estates Act. (This authority will allow the personal representative to take many actions without obtaining court approval. Before taking certain very important actions, however, the personal representative will be required to give notice to interested persons unless they have waived notice or consented to the proposed action.) The independent administration authority will be granted unless an interested person files an objection to the petition and shows good cause why the court should not grant the authority.

A hearing on the petition will be held in this court as follows:

a. Date: Time: Dept.:   Room:

b. Address of court: ☐ same as noted above ☐ other *(specify):*

If you object to the granting of the petition, you should appear at the hearing and state your objections or file written objections with the court before the hearing. Your appearance may be in person or by your attorney.

If you are a creditor or a contingent creditor of the decedent, you must file your claim with the court and mail a copy to the personal representative appointed by the court within four months from the date of first issuance of letters as provided in Probate Code section 9100. The time for filing claims will not expire before four months from the hearing date noticed above.

You may examine the file kept by the court. If you are a person interested in the estate, you may file with the court a *Request for Special Notice* (form DE-154) of the filing of an inventory and appraisal of estate assets or of any petition or account as provided in Probate Code section 1250. A *Request for Special Notice* form is available from the court clerk.

☐ Petitioner   ☐ Attorney for petitioner *(name):*

(Address):

(Telephone):

NOTE: If this notice is published, print the caption, beginning with the words NOTICE OF PETITION TO ADMINISTER ESTATE, and do not print the information from the form above the caption. The caption and the decedent's name must be printed in at least 8-point type and the text in at least 7-point type. Print the case number as part of the caption. Print items preceded by a box only if the box is checked. Do not print the italicized instructions in parentheses, the paragraph numbers, the mailing information, or the material on page 2.

Page 1 of 2

Form Adopted for Mandatory Use
Judicial Council of California
DE-121 [Rev. January 1, 2006]

NOTICE OF PETITION TO ADMINISTER ESTATE
(Probate—Decedents' Estates)

Probate Code, § 8100
www.courtinfo.ca.gov

ESTATE OF (Name):	CASE NUMBER:

DECEDENT

PROOF OF SERVICE BY MAIL

- I am over the age of 18 and not a party to this cause. I am a resident of or employed in the county where the mailing occurred.

  My residence or business address is (specify):

- I served the foregoing Notice of Petition to Administer Estate on each person named below by enclosing a copy in an envelope addressed as shown below **AND**

  - a. ☐ **depositing** the sealed envelope with the United States Postal Service on the date and at the place shown in item 4, with the postage fully prepaid.
  - b. ☐ **placing** the envelope for collection and mailing on the date and at the place shown in item 4 following our ordinary business practices. I am readily familiar with this business's practice for collecting and processing correspondence for mailing. On the same day that correspondence is placed for collection and mailing, it is deposited in the ordinary course of business with the United States Postal Service, in a sealed envelope with postage fully prepaid.

- a. Date mailed:
- b. Place mailed (city, state):

- ☐ I served, with the Notice of Petition to Administer Estate, a copy of the petition or other document referred to in the notice.

I declare under penalty of perjury under the laws of the State of California that the foregoing is true and correct.

Date:

_____ ►
(TYPE OR PRINT NAME OF PERSON COMPLETING THIS FORM)

_____
(SIGNATURE OF PERSON COMPLETING THIS FORM)

NAME AND ADDRESS OF EACH PERSON TO WHOM NOTICE WAS MAILED

Name of person served	Address (number, street, city, state, and zip code)

☐ Continued on an attachment. (You may use form DE-121(MA) to show additional persons served.)

Assistive listening systems, computer-assisted real-time captioning, or sign language interpreter services are available upon request if at least 5 days notice is provided. Contact the clerk's office for *Request for Accommodations by Persons With Disabilities and Order* (form MC-410). (Civil Code section 54.8.)

NOTICE OF PETITION TO ADMINISTER ESTATE
(Probate—Decedents' Estates)

ESTATE OF *(Name):*

—

DECEDENT

CASE NUMBER:

ATTACHMENT TO NOTICE OF PETITION TO ADMINISTER ESTATE—PROOF OF SERVICE BY MAIL

(This attachment is for use with form DE-121.)

NAME AND ADDRESS OF EACH PERSON TO WHOM NOTICE WAS MAILED

No.	Name of person served	Address *(number, street, city, state, and zip code)*

Form Approved for Optional Use
Judicial Council of California
DE-121(MA) [New January 1, 2006]

**ATTACHMENT TO NOTICE OF PETITION TO ADMINISTER ESTATE—
PROOF OF SERVICE BY MAIL
(Probate—Decedents' Estates)**

ORNEY OR PARTY WITHOUT ATTORNEY *(Name, state bar number, and address)* : TELEPHONE AND FAX NOS.: **FOR COURT USE ONLY**

TORNEY FOR *(Name)*:

UPERIOR COURT OF CALIFORNIA, COUNTY OF

STREET ADDRESS:

MAILING ADDRESS:

CITY AND ZIP CODE:

BRANCH NAME:

STATE OF *(Name)*:

DECEDENT

PROOF OF SUBSCRIBING WITNESS

CASE NUMBER:

I am one of the attesting witnesses to the instrument of which Attachment 1 is a photographic copy. I have examined Attachment 1 and my signature is on it.

a. ☐ The name of the decedent was signed in the presence of the attesting witnesses present at the same time by

    (1) ☐ the decedent personally.

    (2) ☐ another person in the decedent's presence and by the decedent's direction.

b. ☐ The decedent acknowledged in the presence of the attesting witnesses present at the same time that the decedent's name was signed by

    (1) ☐ the decedent personally.

    (2) ☐ another person in the decedent's presence and by the decedent's direction.

c. ☐ The decedent acknowledged in the presence of the attesting witnesses present at the same time that the instrument signed was decedent's

    (1) ☐ will.

    (2) ☐ codicil.

When I signed the instrument, I understood that it was decedent's   ☐ will   ☐ codicil.

I have no knowledge of any facts indicating that the instrument, or any part of it, was procured by duress, menace, fraud, or undue influence.

eclare under penalty of perjury under the laws of the State of California that the foregoing is true and correct.

ate:

▶

....
     (TYPE OR PRINT NAME)

(SIGNATURE OF WITNESS)

....
     (ADDRESS)

ATTORNEY'S CERTIFICATION

(Check local court rules for requirements for certifying copies of wills and codicils)

am an active member of The State Bar of California. I declare under penalty of perjury under the laws of the State of California that tachment 1 is a photographic copy of every page of the ☐ will ☐ codicil presented for probate.

ate:

▶

....
     (TYPE OR PRINT NAME)

(SIGNATURE OF ATTORNEY)

Form Approved by the
ludicial Council of California
E-131 [Rev. January 1, 1998]
Mandatory Form [1/1/2000]

PROOF OF SUBSCRIBING WITNESS
(Probate)

Probate Code, § 8220

ATTORNEY OR PARTY WITHOUT ATTORNEY *(Name, state bar number, and address)*:

TELEPHONE AND FAX NOS.:

FOR COURT USE ONLY

ATTORNEY FOR *(Name)*:

SUPERIOR COURT OF CALIFORNIA, COUNTY OF

STREET ADDRESS:

MAILING ADDRESS:

CITY AND ZIP CODE:

BRANCH NAME:

ESTATE OF *(Name)*:

DECEDENT

CASE NUMBER:

PROOF OF HOLOGRAPHIC INSTRUMENT

I was acquainted with the decedent for the following number of years *(specify)*:

☐ I was related to the decedent as *(specify)*:

I have personal knowledge of the decedent's handwriting which I acquired as follows:

a. ☐ I saw the decedent write.

b. ☐ I saw a writing purporting to be in the decedent's handwriting and upon which decedent acted or was charged. It was *(specify)*:

c. ☐ I received letters in the due course of mail purporting to be from the decedent in response to letters I addressed and mailed to the decedent.

d. ☐ Other *(specify other means of obtaining knowledge)*:

I have examined the attached copy of the instrument, and its handwritten provisions were written by and the instrument was signed by the hand of the decedent. *(Affix a copy of the instrument as Attachment 4.)*

I declare under penalty of perjury under the laws of the State of California that the foregoing is true and correct.

Date:

▶

. . . .
(TYPE OR PRINT NAME)

(SIGNATURE)

. . . .
(ADDRESS)

ATTORNEY'S CERTIFICATION

(Check local court rules for requirements for certifying copies of wills and codicils)

I am an active member of The State Bar of California. I declare under penalty of perjury under the laws of the State of California that Attachment 4 is a photographic copy of every page of the holographic instrument presented for probate.

Date:

▶

. . . .
(TYPE OR PRINT NAME)

(SIGNATURE OF ATTORNEY)

Form Approved by the
Judicial Council of California
DE-135 [Rev. January 1, 1998]
Mandatory Form [1/1/2000]

PROOF OF HOLOGRAPHIC INSTRUMENT
(Probate)

Probate Code, § 8222

ATTORNEY OR PARTY WITHOUT ATTORNEY *(Name, state bar number, and address)*:	TELEPHONE AND FAX NOS.:	*FOR COURT USE ONLY*
ATTORNEY FOR *(Name)*:		

SUPERIOR COURT OF CALIFORNIA, COUNTY OF

STREET ADDRESS:

MAILING ADDRESS:

CITY AND ZIP CODE:

BRANCH NAME:

ESTATE OF *(Name)*:

DECEDENT

ORDER FOR PROBATE	CASE NUMBER:

ORDER APPOINTING
- [ ] **Executor**
- [ ] **Administrator with Will Annexed**
- [ ] **Administrator** [ ] **Special Administrator**

[ ] **Order Authorizing Independent Administration of Estate**
- [ ] **with full authority** [ ] **with limited authority**

WARNING: THIS APPOINTMENT IS NOT EFFECTIVE UNTIL LETTERS HAVE ISSUED.

1. Date of hearing: Time: Dept./Room: Judge:

THE COURT FINDS

a. All notices required by law have been given.

b. Decedent died on *(date)*:
  - (1) [ ] a resident of the California county named above.
  - (2) [ ] a nonresident of California and left an estate in the county named above.

c. Decedent died
  - (1) [ ] intestate
  - (2) [ ] testate

  and decedent's will dated: and each codicil dated:

  was admitted to probate by Minute Order on *(date)*:

THE COURT ORDERS

(Name):

is appointed **personal representative**:

a. [ ] executor of the decedent's will   d. [ ] special administrator

b. [ ] administrator with will annexed   (1) [ ] with general powers

c. [ ] administrator   (2) [ ] with special powers as specified in Attachment 3d(2)

          (3) [ ] without notice of hearing

          (4) [ ] letters will expire on *(date)*:

and letters shall issue on qualification.

a. [ ] **Full authority** is granted to administer the estate under the Independent Administration of Estates Act.

b. [ ] **Limited authority** is granted to administer the estate under the Independent Administration of Estates Act (there is no authority, without court supervision, to (1) sell or exchange real property or (2) grant an option to purchase real property or (3) borrow money with the loan secured by an encumbrance upon real property).

a. [ ] Bond is not required.

b. [ ] Bond is fixed at: $ to be furnished by an authorized surety company or as otherwise provided by law.

c. [ ] Deposits of: $ are ordered to be placed in a blocked account at *(specify institution and location)*:

and receipts shall be filed. No withdrawals shall be made without a court order. [ ] Additional orders in Attachment 5c.

d. [ ] The personal representative is not authorized to take possession of money or any other property without a specific court order.

[ ] *(Name)*:   is appointed probate referee.

Date:

_____
JUDGE OF THE SUPERIOR COURT

Number of pages attached: _____   [ ] SIGNATURE FOLLOWS LAST ATTACHMENT

Form Approved by the
Judicial Council of California
DE-140 [Rev. January 1, 1998]
Mandatory Form [1/1/2000]

ORDER FOR PROBATE

Probate Code, §§ 8006, 8400

<table>
<tr><td>

ATTORNEY OR PARTY WITHOUT ATTORNEY *(Name, state bar number, and address):*

—

TELEPHONE NO.:   FAX NO. *(Optional):*

E–MAIL ADDRESS *(Optional):*

ATTORNEY FOR *(Name):*

</td><td>

FOR COURT USE ONLY

</td></tr>
</table>

SUPERIOR COURT OF CALIFORNIA, COUNTY OF

   STREET ADDRESS:

   MAILING ADDRESS:

   CITY AND ZIP CODE:

   BRANCH NAME:

ESTATE OF *(Name):*

                                          DECEDENT

DUTIES AND LIABILITIES OF PERSONAL REPRESENTATIVE and Acknowledgment of Receipt	CASE NUMBER:

DUTIES AND LIABILITIES OF PERSONAL REPRESENTATIVE

When the court appoints you as personal representative of an estate, you become an officer of the court and assume certain duties and obligations. An attorney is best qualified to advise you about these matters. You should understand the following:

1. MANAGING THE ESTATE'S ASSETS

a. Prudent investments

You must manage the estate assets with the care of a prudent person dealing with someone else's property. This means that you must be cautious and may not make any speculative investments.

b. Keep estate assets separate

You must keep the money and property in this estate separate from anyone else's, including your own. When you open a bank account for the estate, the account name must indicate that it is an estate account and not your personal account. Never deposit estate funds in your personal account or otherwise mix them with your or anyone else's property. Securities in the estate must also be held in a name that shows they are estate property and not your personal property.

c. Interest-bearing accounts and other investments

Except for checking accounts intended for ordinary administration expenses, estate accounts must earn interest. You may deposit estate funds in insured accounts in financial institutions, but you should consult with an attorney before making other kinds of investments.

d. Other restrictions

There are many other restrictions on your authority to deal with estate property. You should not spend any of the estate's money unless you have received permission from the court or have been advised to do so by an attorney. You may reimburse yourself for official court costs paid by you to the county clerk and for the premium on your bond. Without prior order of the court, you may not pay fees to yourself or to your attorney, if you have one. If you do not obtain the court's permission when it is required, you may be removed as personal representative or you may be required to reimburse the estate from your own personal funds, or both. You should consult with an attorney concerning the legal requirements affecting sales, leases, mortgages, and investments of estate property.

2. INVENTORY OF ESTATE PROPERTY

a. Locate the estate's property

You must attempt to locate and take possession of all the decedent's property to be administered in the estate.

b. Determine the value of the property

You must arrange to have a court-appointed referee determine the value of the property unless the appointment is waived by the court. You, rather than the referee, must determine the value of certain "cash items." An attorney can advise you about how to do this.

c. File an inventory and appraisal

Within four months after Letters are first issued to you as personal representative, you must file with the court an inventory and appraisal of all the assets in the estate.

Page 1 of 2

Form Adopted for Mandatory Use
Judicial Council of California
DE-147 [Rev. January 1, 2002]

DUTIES AND LIABILITIES OF PERSONAL REPRESENTATIVE
(Probate)

Probate Code, § 8404

ESTATE OF (Name):		
	DECEDENT	CASE NUMBER:

1. File a change of ownership

At the time you file the inventory and appraisal, you must also file a change of ownership statement with the county recorder or assessor in each county where the decedent owned real property at the time of death, as provided in section 480 of the California Revenue and Taxation Code.

3. NOTICE TO CREDITORS

You must mail a notice of administration to each known creditor of the decedent within four months after your appointment as personal representative. If the decedent received Medi-Cal assistance, you must notify the State Director of Health Services within 90 days after appointment.

4. INSURANCE

You should determine that there is appropriate and adequate insurance covering the assets and risks of the estate. Maintain the insurance in force during the entire period of the administration.

5. RECORD KEEPING

a. Keep accounts

You must keep complete and accurate records of each financial transaction affecting the estate. You will have to prepare an account of all money and property you have received, what you have spent, and the date of each transaction. You must describe in detail what you have left after the payment of expenses.

b. Court review

Your account will be reviewed by the court. Save your receipts because the court may ask to review them. If you do not file your accounts as required, the court will order you to do so. You may be removed as personal representative if you fail to comply.

6. CONSULTING AN ATTORNEY

If you have an attorney, you should cooperate with the attorney at all times. You and your attorney are responsible for completing the estate administration as promptly as possible. **When in doubt, contact your attorney.**

NOTICE: 1. This statement of duties and liabilities is a summary and is not a complete statement of the law. Your conduct as a personal representative is governed by the law itself and not by this summary.
2. If you fail to perform your duties or to meet the deadlines, the court may reduce your compensation, remove you from office, and impose other sanctions.

ACKNOWLEDGMENT OF RECEIPT

1. I have petitioned the court to be appointed as a personal representative.

2. My address and telephone number are (specify):

3. I acknowledge that I have received a copy of this statement of the duties and liabilities of the office of personal representative.

Date:

_____   ►   _____
(TYPE OR PRINT NAME)   (SIGNATURE OF PETITIONER)

Date:

_____   ►   _____
(TYPE OR PRINT NAME)   (SIGNATURE OF PETITIONER)

CONFIDENTIAL INFORMATION: If required to do so by local court rule, you must provide your date of birth and driver's license number on supplemental Form DE-147S. (Prob. Code, § 8404(b).)

ESTATE OF *(Name)*:	CASE NUMBER:
DECEDENT	

CONFIDENTIAL STATEMENT OF BIRTH DATE
AND DRIVER'S LICENSE NUMBER

(Supplement to *Duties and Liabilities of Personal Representative* (Form DE-147))

*(NOTE: This supplement is to be used if the court by local rule requires the personal representative to provide a birth date and driver's license number. Do **not** attach this supplement to Form DE-147.)*

This separate *Confidential Statement of Birth Date and Driver's License Number* contains confidential information relating to the personal representative in the case referenced above. This supplement shall be kept separate from the *Duties and Liabilities of Personal Representative* filed in this case and shall not be a public record.

INFORMATION ON THE PERSONAL REPRESENTATIVE:

1. Name:

2. Date of birth:

3. Driver's license number: State:

TO COURT CLERK:
THIS STATEMENT IS **CONFIDENTIAL**. DO NOT FILE
THIS CONFIDENTIAL STATEMENT IN A PUBLIC COURT FILE.

Form Adopted for Mandatory Use
Judicial Council of California
DE-147S [New January 1, 2001]

**CONFIDENTIAL SUPPLEMENT TO DUTIES AND
LIABILITIES OF PERSONAL REPRESENTATIVE**
(Probate)

Probate Code, § 8404

DE-150

ATTORNEY OR PARTY WITHOUT ATTORNEY (Name, state bar number, and address):	TELEPHONE AND FAX NOS.:	FOR COURT USE ONLY

ATTORNEY FOR (Name):

SUPERIOR COURT OF CALIFORNIA, COUNTY OF

STREET ADDRESS:

MAILING ADDRESS:

CITY AND ZIP CODE:

BRANCH NAME:

ESTATE OF (Name):

DECEDENT

LETTERS		CASE NUMBER:
☐ **TESTAMENTARY** ☐ **OF ADMINISTRATION WITH WILL ANNEXED**	☐ **OF ADMINISTRATION** ☐ **SPECIAL ADMINISTRATION**	

LETTERS

☐ The last will of the decedent named above having been proved, the court appoints (name):

  a. ☐ executor.

  b. ☐ administrator with will annexed.

☐ The court appoints (name):

  a. ☐ administrator of the decedent's estate.

  b. ☐ special administrator of decedent's estate

    (1) ☐ with the special powers specified in the *Order for Probate.*

    (2) ☐ with the powers of a general administrator.

    (3) ☐ letters will expire on (date):

☐ The personal representative is authorized to administer the estate under the Independent Administration of Estates Act ☐ **with full authority**

☐ **with limited authority** (no authority, without court supervision, to (1) sell or exchange real property or (2) grant an option to purchase real property or (3) borrow money with the loan secured by an encumbrance upon real property).

☐ The personal representative is not authorized to take possession of money or any other property without a specific court order.

WITNESS, clerk of the court, with seal of the court affixed.

(SEAL)	Date:
	Clerk, by
	_____ (DEPUTY)

AFFIRMATION

1. ☐ PUBLIC ADMINISTRATOR: No affirmation required (Prob. Code, § 7621(c)).

2. ☐ INDIVIDUAL: **I solemnly affirm** that I will perform the duties of personal representative according to law.

3. ☐ INSTITUTIONAL FIDUCIARY (name):

  I solemnly affirm that the institution will perform the duties of personal representative according to law. I make this affirmation for myself as an individual and on behalf of the institution as an officer. *(Name and title):*

4. Executed on (date):

  at (place):   , California.

▶ _____
(SIGNATURE)

CERTIFICATION

I certify that this document is a correct copy of the original on file in my office and the letters issued by the personal representative appointed above have not been revoked, annulled, or set aside, and are still in full force and effect.

(SEAL)	Date:
	Clerk, by
	_____ (DEPUTY)

Form Approved by the
Judicial Council of California
DE-150 [Rev. January 1, 1998]
Mandatory Form [1/1/2000]

LETTERS
(Probate)

Probate Code, §§ 1001, 8403,
8405, 8544, 8545;
Code of Civil Procedure, § 2015.6

NOTICE OF ADMINISTRATION
OF THE ESTATE OF

_____

(NAME)

DECEDENT

NOTICE TO CREDITORS

1. *(Name)*:
   (Address):

   (Telephone):
   is the **personal representative** of the **ESTATE OF** *(name)*: , who is deceased.

2. The personal representative HAS BEGUN ADMINISTRATION of the decedent's estate in the
   a. **SUPERIOR COURT OF CALIFORNIA, COUNTY OF *(specify)*:**

   STREET ADDRESS:
   MAILING ADDRESS:
   CITY AND ZIP CODE:
   BRANCH NAME:

   b. Case number *(specify)*:

3. You must FILE YOUR CLAIM with the court clerk (address in item 2a) AND mail or deliver a copy to the personal representative before the **later** of the following times as provided in Probate Code section 9100:

   a. **four months** after *(date)*: [_____] , the date letters (authority to act for the estate) were first issued to the personal representative, OR

   b. **sixty days** after *(date)*: [_____] , the date this notice was mailed or personally delivered to you.

4. LATE CLAIMS: If you do not file your claim before it is due, you must file a petition with the court for permission to file a late claim as provided in Probate Code section 9103.

WHERE TO GET A CREDITOR'S CLAIM FORM: If a *Creditor's Claim* (form DE-172) did not accompany this notice, you may obtain a copy from any superior court clerk or from the person who sent you this notice. A letter to the court stating your claim is *not* sufficient.

FAILURE TO FILE A CLAIM: Failure to file a claim with the court and serve a copy of the claim on the personal representative will in most instances invalidate your claim.

IF YOU MAIL YOUR CLAIM: If you use the mail to file your claim with the court, for your protection you should send your claim by certified mail, with return receipt requested. If you use the mail to serve a copy of your claim on the personal representative, you should also use certified mail.

Note: To assist the creditor and the court, please send a copy of the *Creditor's Claim* form with this notice.

(Proof of Service on reverse)

Form Approved by the
Judicial Council of California
DE-157 [Rev. January 1, 1998]
Mandatory Form [1/1/2000]
NOTICE OF ADMINISTRATION TO CREDITORS
(Probate)
Probate Code, §§ 9050,
9052

PROOF OF SERVICE BY MAIL

1. I am over the age of 18 and not a party to this cause. I am a resident of or employed in the county where the mailing occurred.
2. My residence or business address is *(specify)*:

3. I served the foregoing *Notice of Administration to Creditors* ☐ and a blank *Creditor's Claim* form* on each person named below by enclosing a copy in an envelope addressed as shown below AND
   a. ☐ **depositing** the sealed envelope with the United States Postal Service with the postage fully prepaid.
   b. ☐ **placing** the envelope for collection and mailing on the date and at the place shown in item 4 following our ordinary business practices. I am readily familiar with the business' practice for collecting and processing correspondence for mailing. On the same day that correspondence is placed for collection and mailing, it is deposited in the ordinary course of business with the United States Postal Service in a sealed envelope with postage fully prepaid.

4. a. Date of deposit: b. Place of deposit *(city and state)*:

I declare under penalty of perjury under the laws of the State of California that the foregoing is true and correct.

Date:

▶

. . . .
(TYPE OR PRINT NAME)   (SIGNATURE OF DECLARANT)

NAME AND ADDRESS OF EACH PERSON TO WHOM NOTICE WAS MAILED

☐ List of names and addresses continued in attachment.

NOTE: *To assist the creditor and the court, please send a copy of the* Creditor's Claim *(form DE-172) with the notice.*

NOTICE OF ADMINISTRATION TO CREDITORS
(Probate)

ATTORNEY OR PARTY WITHOUT ATTORNEY (Name, state bar number, and address):	FOR COURT USE ONLY
TELEPHONE NO.: FAX NO. (Optional): E-MAIL ADDRESS (Optional): ATTORNEY FOR (Name):	

SUPERIOR COURT OF CALIFORNIA, COUNTY OF

STREET ADDRESS:

MAILING ADDRESS:

CITY AND ZIP CODE:

BRANCH NAME:

ESTATE OF (Name):

☐ DECEDENT   ☐ CONSERVATEE   ☐ MINOR

INVENTORY AND APPRAISAL	CASE NUMBER:
☐ **Partial No.:** ☐ **Corrected** ☐ **Final** ☐ **Reappraisal for Sale** ☐ **Supplemental** ☐ **Property Tax Certificate**	Date of Death of Decedent or of Appointment of Guardian or Conservator:

APPRAISALS

Total appraisal by representative, guardian, or conservator (Attachment 1): $

Total appraisal by referee (Attachment 2): $

                               TOTAL: $

DECLARATION OF REPRESENTATIVE, GUARDIAN, CONSERVATOR, OR SMALL ESTATE CLAIMANT

Attachments 1 and 2 together with all prior inventories filed contain a true statement of

☐ all   ☐ a portion   of the estate that has come to my knowledge or possession, including particularly all money and all just claims the estate has against me. I have truly, honestly, and impartially appraised to the best of my ability each item set forth in Attachment 1.

☐ No probate referee is required   ☐ by order of the court dated (specify):

Property tax certificate. I certify that the requirements of Revenue and Taxation Code section 480

a. ☐ are not applicable because the decedent owned no real property in California at the time of death.

b. ☐ have been satisfied by the filing of a change of ownership statement with the county recorder or assessor of each county in California in which the decedent owned property at the time of death.

I declare under penalty of perjury under the laws of the State of California that the foregoing is true and correct.

Date:

▶

_____   _____
(TYPE OR PRINT NAME; INCLUDE TITLE IF CORPORATE OFFICER)   (SIGNATURE)

STATEMENT ABOUT THE BOND

(Complete in all cases. Must be signed by attorney for fiduciary, or by fiduciary without an attorney.)

☐ Bond is waived, or the sole fiduciary is a corporate fiduciary or an exempt government agency.

☐ Bond filed in the amount of: $ ☐ Sufficient   ☐ Insufficient

☐ Receipts for: $ have been filed with the court for deposits in a blocked account at (specify institution and location):

Date:

▶

_____   _____
(TYPE OR PRINT NAME)   (SIGNATURE OF ATTORNEY OR PARTY WITHOUT ATTORNEY)

Page 1 of 2

ESTATE OF *(Name):*		
	CASE NUMBER:	

☐ DECEDENT ☐ CONSERVATEE ☐ MINOR

DECLARATION OF PROBATE REFEREE

1. I have truly, honestly, and impartially appraised to the best of my ability each item set forth in Attachment 2.

10. A true account of my commission and expenses actually and necessarily incurred pursuant to my appointment is:

Statutory commission: $ ____

Expenses *(specify):* $ ____

TOTAL: $ ____

I declare under penalty of perjury under the laws of the State of California that the foregoing is true and correct.

Date:

▶

_____ _____
(TYPE OR PRINT NAME)   (SIGNATURE OF REFEREE)

INSTRUCTIONS

(See Probate Code sections 2610-2616, 8801, 8804, 8852, 8905, 8960, 8961, and 8963 for additional instructions.)

1. See Probate Code section 8850 for items to be included in the inventory.

2. If the minor or conservatee is or has been during the guardianship or conservatorship confined in a state hospital under the jurisdiction of the State Department of Mental Health or the State Department of Developmental Services, mail a copy to the director of the appropriate department in Sacramento. (Prob. Code, § 2611.)

3. The representative, guardian, conservator, or small estate claimant shall list on Attachment 1 and appraise as of the date of death of the decedent or the date of appointment of the guardian or conservator, at fair market value, moneys, currency, cash items, bank accounts and amounts on deposit with each financial institution (as defined in Probate Code section 40), and the proceeds of life and accident insurance policies and retirement plans payable upon death in lump sum amounts to the estate, except items whose fair market value is, in the opinion of the representative, an amount different from the ostensible value or specified amount.

4. The representative, guardian, conservator, or small estate claimant shall list in Attachment 2 all other assets of the estate which shall be appraised by the referee.

5. If joint tenancy and other assets are listed for appraisal purposes only and not as part of the probate estate, they must be separately listed on additional attachments and their value excluded from the total valuation of Attachments 1 and 2.

6. Each attachment should conform to the format approved by the Judicial Council. *(See Inventory and Appraisal Attachment (form DE-161/GC-041) and Cal. Rules of Court, rules 2.100—2.119.)*

ESTATE OF *(Name)*:

___

INVENTORY AND APPRAISAL
ATTACHMENT NO.: _____

*(In decedents' estates, attachments must conform to Probate
Code section 8850(c) regarding community and separate property.)*

Page: _____ of: _____ total pages.
(Add pages as required.)

Item No.   Description   Appraised value

1. $

Form Approved by the
Judicial Council of California
DE-161, GC-041 [Rev. January 1, 1998]
Mandatory Form [1/1/2000]

INVENTORY AND APPRAISAL ATTACHMENT

Probate Code, §§ 301,
2610-2613, 8800-8920,
10309

ATTORNEY OR PARTY WITHOUT ATTORNEY *(Name, state bar number, and address)*: TELEPHONE AND FAX NOS.:	*FOR COURT USE ONLY*

ATTORNEY FOR *(Name)*:

SUPERIOR COURT OF CALIFORNIA, COUNTY OF
   STREET ADDRESS:
   MAILING ADDRESS:
   CITY AND ZIP CODE:
   BRANCH NAME:

ESTATE OF *(Name)*:

                                                  DECEDENT

NOTICE OF PROPOSED ACTION **Independent Administration of Estates Act** ☐ Objection ☐ Consent	CASE NUMBER:

NOTICE: If you do not object in writing or obtain a court order preventing the action proposed below, you will be treated as if you consented to the proposed action and you may not object after the proposed action has been taken. If you object, the personal representative may take the proposed action only under court supervision. An objection form is on the reverse. If you wish to object, you may use the form or prepare your own written objection.

---

1. The personal representative (executor or administrator) of the estate of the deceased is *(names)*:

2. The personal representative has authority to administer the estate without court supervision under the Independent Administration of Estates Act (Prob. Code, § 10400 et seq.)
   a. ☐ with **full authority** under the act.
   b. ☐ with **limited authority** under the act (there is no authority, without court supervision, to (1) sell or exchange real property or (2) grant an option to purchase real property or (3) borrow money with the loan secured by an encumbrance upon real property).

3. **On or after** *(date)*: [_____] , the personal representative will take the following action without court supervision *(describe in specific terms here or in Attachment 3)*:
   ☐ The proposed action is described in an attachment labeled Attachment 3.

4. ☐ **Real property transaction** *(Check this box and complete item 4b if the proposed action involves a sale or exchange or a grant of an option to purchase real property.)*
   a. The material terms of the transaction are specified in item 3, including any sale price and the amount of or method of calculating any commission or compensation to an agent or broker.
   b. $ _____ is the value of the subject property in the probate inventory.   ☐ No inventory yet.

NOTICE: A sale of real property without court supervision means that the sale will NOT be presented to the court for confirmation at a hearing at which higher bids for the property may be presented and the property sold to the highest bidder.

(Continued on reverse)

NOTICE OF PROPOSED ACTION
Objection—Consent
(Probate)

Probate Code, § 10580 et seq.

If you OBJECT to the proposed action

  a. **Sign** the objection form below and deliver or mail it to the personal representative at the following address *(specify name and address)*:

    OR

  b. **Send** your own written objection to the address in item 5a. *(Be sure to identify the proposed action and state that you object to it.)*

    OR

  c. **Apply** to the court for an order preventing the personal representative from taking the proposed action without court supervision.

  d. **NOTE:** Your written objection or the court order must be received by the personal representative before the date in the box in item 3, or before the proposed action is taken, whichever is later. If you object, the personal representative may take the proposed action only under court supervision.

If you APPROVE the proposed action, you may sign the consent form below and return it to the address in item 5a. If you do not object in writing or obtain a court order, you will be treated as if you consented to the proposed action.

If you need more INFORMATION, call *(name)*:

                     (telephone):

Date:

. . . .   ▶ _____

            (TYPE OR PRINT NAME)   (SIGNATURE OF PERSONAL REPRESENTATIVE OR ATTORNEY)

OBJECTION TO PROPOSED ACTION

☐ **I OBJECT** to the action proposed in item 3.

NOTICE: Sign and return this form (both sides) to the address in item 5a. The form must be received before the date in the box in item 3, or before the proposed action is taken, whichever is later. *(You may want to use certified mail, with return receipt requested. Make a copy of this form for your records.)*

Date:

. . . .   ▶ _____

            (TYPE OR PRINT NAME)   (SIGNATURE OF OBJECTOR)

CONSENT TO PROPOSED ACTION

☐ **I CONSENT** to the action proposed in item 3.

NOTICE: You may indicate your *consent* by signing and returning this form (both sides) to the address in item 5a. If you do not object in writing or obtain a court order, you will be treated as if you consented to the proposed action.

Date:

. . . .   ▶ _____

            (TYPE OR PRINT NAME)   (SIGNATURE OF CONSENTER)

ATTORNEY OR PARTY WITHOUT ATTORNEY *(Name, State Bar number, and address)*:	FOR COURT USE ONLY
TELEPHONE NO.: FAX NO. *(Optional)*:	
E-MAIL ADDRESS *(Optional)*:	
ATTORNEY FOR *(Name)*:	

SUPERIOR COURT OF CALIFORNIA, COUNTY OF

STREET ADDRESS:

MAILING ADDRESS:

CITY AND ZIP CODE:

BRANCH NAME:

ESTATE OF

(Name):

DECEDENT

ALLOWANCE OR REJECTION OF CREDITOR'S CLAIM	CASE NUMBER:

NOTE TO PERSONAL REPRESENTATIVE

Attach a copy of the creditor's claim to this form. If approval or rejection by the court is not required, do not include any pages attached to the creditor's claim.

PERSONAL REPRESENTATIVE'S ALLOWANCE OR REJECTION

1. Name of creditor *(specify)*:
2. The claim was filed on *(date)*:
3. Date of first issuance of letters:
4. Date of *Notice of Administration*:
5. Date of decedent's death:
6. Estimated value of estate: $
7. Total amount of the claim: $
8. ☐ Claim is allowed for: $ *(The court must approve certain claims before they are paid.)*
9. ☐ Claim is rejected for: $ *(A creditor has 90 days to act on a rejected claim.* See box below.)*
10. Notice of allowance or rejection given on *(date)*:
11. ☐ The personal representative is authorized to administer the estate under the Independent Administration of Estates Act.

Date:

▶

_____   _____
(TYPE OR PRINT NAME OF PERSONAL REPRESENTATIVE)   (SIGNATURE OF PERSONAL REPRESENTATIVE)

NOTICE TO CREDITOR ON REJECTED CLAIM

From the date that notice of rejection is given, you must act on the rejected claim (e.g., file a lawsuit) as follows:

1. **Claim due:** within 90 days* after the notice of rejection.
2. **Claim not due:** within 90 days* after the claim becomes due.

*The 90-day period mentioned above may not apply to your claim because some claims are not treated as creditors' claims or are subject to special statutes of limitations, or for other legal reasons. You should consult with an attorney if you have any questions about or are unsure of your rights and obligations concerning your claim.

COURT'S APPROVAL OR REJECTION

12. ☐ Approved for: $
13. ☐ Rejected for: $

Date:

_____
SIGNATURE OF JUDICIAL OFFICER

14. Number of pages attached: _____   ☐ SIGNATURE FOLLOWS LAST ATTACHMENT

(Proof of Mailing or Personal Delivery on reverse)   Page 1 of 2

Form Adopted for Mandatory Use
Judicial Council of California
DE-174 [Rev. January 1, 2009]

**ALLOWANCE OR REJECTION OF CREDITOR'S CLAIM
(Probate—Decedents' Estates)**

Probate Code § 9000 et seq.,
9250–9256, 9353
www.courtinfo.ca.gov

ESTATE OF		
(Name):		
	DECEDENT	
		CASE NUMBER:

PROOF OF ☐ **MAILING**   ☐ **PERSONAL DELIVERY**   **TO CREDITOR**

1. At the time of mailing or personal delivery I was at least 18 years of age and **not a party** to this proceeding.

2. My residence or business address is (specify):

3. I mailed or personally delivered a copy of the *Allowance or Rejection of Creditor's Claim* as follows (complete either a or b):

   a. ☐ **Mail.** I am a resident of or employed in the county where the mailing occurred.

      (1) I enclosed a copy in an envelope AND

         (a) ☐ **deposited** the sealed envelope with the United States Postal Service with the postage fully prepaid.

         (b) ☐ **placed** the envelope for collection and mailing on the date and at the place shown in items below
            following our ordinary business practices. I am readily familiar with this business's practice for collecting
            and processing correspondence for mailing. On the same day that correspondence is placed for
            collection and mailing, it is deposited in the ordinary course of business with the United States Postal
            Service in a sealed envelope with postage fully prepaid.

      (2) The envelope was addressed and mailed first-class as follows:

         (a) Name of creditor served:

         (b) Address on envelope:

         (c) Date of mailing:

         (d) Place of mailing (city and state):

   b. ☐ **Personal delivery.** I personally delivered a copy to the creditor as follows:

      (1) Name of creditor served:

      (2) Address where delivered:

      (3) Date delivered:

      (4) Time delivered:

I declare under penalty of perjury under the laws of the State of California that the foregoing is true and correct.

Date:

           ▶

_____   _____
(TYPE OR PRINT NAME OF DECLARANT)   (SIGNATURE OF DECLARANT)

ATTORNEY OR PARTY WITHOUT ATTORNEY *(Name, State Bar number, and address):*	FOR COURT USE ONLY
TELEPHONE NO.: FAX NO. *(Optional):*	
E-MAIL ADDRESS *(Optional):*	
ATTORNEY FOR *(Name):*	

SUPERIOR COURT OF CALIFORNIA, COUNTY OF
STREET ADDRESS:
MAILING ADDRESS:
CITY AND ZIP CODE:
BRANCH NAME:

ESTATE OF *(Name):*	CASE NUMBER:
DECEDENT	HEARING DATE:

☐ **SPOUSAL** ☐ **DOMESTIC PARTNER** **PROPERTY PETITION**	DEPT.:	TIME:

Petitioner *(name):*   **requests**

a. ☐ determination of property passing to the surviving spouse or surviving registered domestic partner without administration (Fam. Code, § 297.5, Prob. Code, § 13500).

b. ☐ confirmation of property belonging to the surviving spouse or surviving registered domestic partner (Fam. Code, § 297.5, Prob. Code, §§ 100, 101).

c. ☐ immediate appointment of a probate referee.

Petitioner is

a. ☐ surviving spouse of the decedent.

b. ☐ personal representative of *(name):*   , surviving spouse.

c. ☐ guardian or conservator of the estate of *(name):*   , surviving spouse.

d. ☐ surviving registered domestic partner of the decedent.

e. ☐ personal representative of *(name):*   , surviving registered domestic partner.

f. ☐ conservator of the estate of *(name):*   , surviving registered domestic partner.

Decedent died on *(date):*

Decedent was

a. ☐ a resident of the California county named above.

b. ☐ a nonresident of California and left an estate in the county named above.

c. ☐ intestate ☐ testate and a copy of the will and any codicil is affixed as Attachment 4c.
(*Attach copies of will and any codicil, a typewritten copy of any handwritten document, and an English translation of any foreign-language document.*)

a. *(Complete in all cases)* The decedent is survived by

(1) ☐ no child. ☐ child as follows: ☐ natural or adopted ☐ natural, adopted by a third party.

(2) ☐ no issue of a predeceased child. ☐ issue of a predeceased child.

b. Decedent ☐ is ☐ is not survived by a stepchild or foster child or children who would have been adopted by decedent but for a legal barrier. *(See Prob. Code, § 6454.)*

*(Complete only if no issue survived the decedent. Check **only** the **first** box that applies.)*

a. ☐ The decedent is survived by a parent or parents who are listed in item 9.

b. ☐ The decedent is survived by a brother, sister, or issue of a deceased brother or sister, all of whom are listed in item 9.

Administration of all or part of the estate is not necessary for the reason that all or a part of the estate is property passing to the surviving spouse or surviving registered domestic partner. The facts upon which petitioner bases the allegation that the property described in Attachments 7a and 7b is property that should pass or be confirmed to the surviving spouse or surviving registered domestic partner are stated in Attachment 7.

a. ☐ Attachment 7a[1] contains the legal description *(if real property add Assessor's Parcel Number)* of the deceased spouse's or registered domestic partner's property that petitioner requests to be determined as having passed to the surviving spouse or partner from the deceased spouse or partner. This includes any interest in a trade or business name of any unincorporated business or an interest in any unincorporated business that the deceased spouse or partner was operating or managing at the time of death, subject to any written agreement between the deceased spouse or partner and the surviving spouse or partner providing for a non pro rata division of the aggregate value of the community property assets or quasi-community assets, or both.

[1] See Prob. Code, § 13658 for required filing of a list of known creditors of a business and other information in certain instances. If required, include in Attachment 7a.

Form Adopted for Mandatory Use
Judicial Council of California DE-221
[Rev. January 1, 2005]

SPOUSAL OR DOMESTIC PARTNER PROPERTY PETITION
(Probate—Decedents Estates)

Family Code, § 297.5;
Probate Code, § 13650

b. ☐ Attachment 7b contains the legal description *(if real property add Assessor's Parcel Number)* of the community or quasi-community property petitioner requests to be determined as having belonged under Probate Code sections 100 and 101 and Family Code section 297.5 to the surviving spouse or surviving registered domestic partner upon the deceased spouse's or partner's death, subject to any written agreement between the deceased spouse or partner and the surviving spouse or partner providing for a non pro rata division of the aggregate value of the community property assets or quasi-community assets, or both.

There ☐ exists ☐ does not exist a written agreement between the deceased spouse or deceased registered domestic partner and the surviving spouse or surviving registered domestic partner providing for a non pro rata division of the aggregate value of the community property assets or quasi-community assets, or both. *(If petitioner bases the description of the property of the deceased spouse or partner passing to the surviving spouse or partner or the property to be confirmed to the surviving spouse or partner, or both, on a written agreement, a copy of the agreement must be attached to this petition as Attachment 8.)*

The names, relationships, ages, and residence or mailing addresses so far as known to or reasonably ascertainable by petitioner of (1) all persons named in decedent's will and codicils, whether living or deceased, and (2) all persons checked in items 5 and 6

☐ are listed below ☐ are listed in Attachment 9.

Name and relationship	Age	Residence or mailing address

0. The names and addresses of all persons named as executors in the decedent's will and any codicil or appointed as personal representatives of the decedent's estate ☐ are listed below ☐ are listed in Attachment 10 ☐ none

1. ☐ The petitioner is the trustee of a trust that is a devisee under decedent's will. The names and addresses of all persons interested in the trust who are entitled to notice under Probate Code section 13655(b)(2) are listed in Attachment 11.

2. A petition for probate or for administration of the decedent's estate
   a. ☐ is being filed with this petition.
   b. ☐ was filed on *(date)*:
   c. ☐ has not been filed and is not being filed with this petition.

3. Number of pages attached: _____

Date:

▶

_____
(TYPE OR PRINT NAME)

_____
(SIGNATURE OF ATTORNEY)

declare under penalty of perjury under the laws of the State of California that the foregoing is true and correct.

Date:

▶

_____
(TYPE OR PRINT NAME)

_____
(SIGNATURE OF PETITIONER)

SPOUSAL OR DOMESTIC PARTNER PROPERTY PETITION
(Probate—Decedents Estates)

DE-226

ATTORNEY OR PARTY WITHOUT ATTORNEY *(Name, State Bar number, and address):*
After recording return to:

TELEPHONE NO.:

FAX NO. *(Optional):*

E-MAIL ADDRESS *(Optional):*

ATTORNEY FOR *(Name):*

SUPERIOR COURT OF CALIFORNIA, COUNTY OF

STREET ADDRESS:

MAILING ADDRESS:

CITY AND ZIP CODE:

BRANCH NAME:

FOR RECORDER'S USE ONLY

ESTATE OF *(Name):*

CASE NUMBER:

DECEDENT

☐ **SPOUSAL** ☐ **DOMESTIC PARTNER** **PROPERTY ORDER**

FOR COURT USE ONLY

Date of hearing: Time:

Dept.: Room:

THE COURT FINDS

All notices required by law have been given.

Decedent died on *(date):*

a. ☐ a resident of the California county named above.

b. ☐ a nonresident of California and left an estate in the county named above.

c. ☐ intestate. ☐ testate.

Decedent's ☐ surviving spouse ☐ surviving registered domestic partner is *(name):*

THE COURT FURTHER FINDS AND ORDERS

a. ☐ The property described in Attachment 5a is property passing to the surviving spouse or surviving registered domestic partner named in item 4, and no administration of it is necessary.

b. ☐ See Attachment 5b for further order(s) respecting transfer of the property to the surviving spouse or surviving registered domestic partner named in item 4.

☐ To protect the interests of the creditors of *(business name):*

an unincorporated trade or business, a list of all its known creditors and the amount owed each is on file.

a. ☐ Within *(specify):* days from this date, the surviving spouse or surviving registered domestic partner named in item 4 shall file an undertaking in the amount of $

b. ☐ See Attachment 6b for further order(s) protecting the interests of creditors of the business.

a. ☐ The property described in Attachment 7a is property that belonged to the surviving spouse or surviving registered domestic partner under Family Code section 297.5 and Probate Code sections 100 and 101, and the surviving spouse's or surviving domestic partner's ownership upon decedent's death is confirmed.

b. ☐ See Attachment 7b for further order(s) respecting transfer of the property to the surviving spouse or surviving domestic partner.

☐ All property described in the *Spousal or Domestic Partner Property Petition* that is not determined to be property passing to the surviving spouse or surviving registered domestic partner under Probate Code section 13500, or confirmed as belonging to the surviving spouse or surviving registered domestic partner under Probate Code sections 100 and 101, shall be subject to administration in the estate of decedent. ☐ All of such property is described in Attachment 8.

☐ Other *(specify):*

☐ Continued in Attachment 9.

). Number of pages attached: _____

ate:

JUDICIAL OFFICER

☐ SIGNATURE FOLLOWS LAST ATTACHMENT

Page 1 of 1

rm Adopted for Mandatory Use
Judicial Council of California
DE-226 [Rev. January 1, 2005]

SPOUSAL OR DOMESTIC PARTNER PROPERTY ORDER
(Probate—Decedents Estates)

Family Code, § 297.5;
Probate Code, § 13656

ATTORNEY OR PARTY WITHOUT ATTORNEY *(Name, state bar number, and address)*:	TELEPHONE AND FAX NOS.:	*FOR COURT USE ONLY*

ATTORNEY FOR *(Name)*:

SUPERIOR COURT OF CALIFORNIA, COUNTY OF

STREET ADDRESS:

MAILING ADDRESS:

CITY AND ZIP CODE:

BRANCH NAME:

ESTATE OF *(Name)*:

☐ DECEDENT ☐ CONSERVATEE ☐ MINOR

EX PARTE PETITION FOR AUTHORITY TO SELL SECURITIES AND ORDER	CASE NUMBER:

Petitioner *(name of each; see footnote[1] before completing)*:

is the ☐ personal representative ☐ conservator ☐ guardian of the estate and requests a court order authorizing sale of estate securities.

a. The estate's securities described on the reverse should be sold for cash at the market price at the time of sale on an established stock or bond exchange, or, if unlisted, the sale will be made for not less than the minimum price stated on the reverse.

b. ☐ Authority is given in decedent's will to sell property; **or**

c. ☐ The sale is necessary to raise cash to pay

    (1) ☐ debts

    (2) ☐ legacies

    (3) ☐ family allowance

    (4) ☐ expenses

    (5) ☐ support of ward

    (6) ☐ other *(specify)*:

d. ☐ The sale is for the advantage, benefit, and best interests of the estate, and those interested in the estate.

e. Other facts pertinent to this petition are as follows:

    (1) ☐ Special notice has not been requested.

    (2) ☐ Waivers of all special notices are presented with this petition.

    (3) ☐ No security to be sold is specifically bequeathed.

    (4) ☐ Other *(specify)*:

Date:

Signature of all petitioners also required (Prob. Code, § 1020).)

▶ _____

(SIGNATURE OF ATTORNEY *)

I declare under penalty of perjury under the laws of the State of California that the foregoing is true and correct.

Date:

. . . .

(TYPE OR PRINT NAME)

▶ _____

(SIGNATURE OF PETITIONER)

. . . .

(TYPE OR PRINT NAME)

▶ _____

(SIGNATURE OF PETITIONER)

*Each personal representative, guardian, or conservator must sign the petition.

(Continued on reverse)

Form Approved by the
Judicial Council of California
DE-270, GC-070 [Rev. January 1, 1998]
Mandatory Form [1/1/2000]

EX PARTE PETITION FOR AUTHORITY TO SELL SECURITIES AND ORDER

Probate Code, §§ 9630, 10000, 10200, 10201, 10252, 10261

ESTATE OF *(Name)*:	CASE NUMBER:
—	

LIST OF SECURITIES

Number of shares or face value of bonds	Name of security	Name of exchange *(when required by local rule)*	Recent bid asked *(when required by local rule)*	Minimum selling price

ORDER AUTHORIZING SALE OF SECURITIES

THE COURT FINDS the sale is proper.

THE COURT ORDERS

The ☐ personal representative ☐ guardian ☐ conservator   is authorized to sell the securities described above upon the terms and conditions specified. Notice of hearing on the petition is dispensed with.

Date:

_____
JUDGE OF THE SUPERIOR COURT

☐ SIGNATURE FOLLOWS LAST ATTACHMENT

**EX PARTE PETITION FOR AUTHORITY
TO SELL SECURITIES AND ORDER**

ATTORNEY OR PARTY WITHOUT ATTORNEY *(Name, State Bar number, and address):*

FOR COURT USE ONLY

TELEPHONE NO.: FAX NO. *(Optional):*

E-MAIL ADDRESS *(Optional):*

ATTORNEY FOR *(Name):*

SUPERIOR COURT OF CALIFORNIA, COUNTY OF

STREET ADDRESS:

MAILING ADDRESS:

CITY AND ZIP CODE:

BRANCH NAME:

☐ ESTATE ☐ CONSERVATORSHIP ☐ GUARDIANSHIP OF

(Name):

☐ DECEDENT ☐ CONSERVATEE ☐ MINOR

EX PARTE PETITION FOR FINAL DISCHARGE AND ORDER

CASE NUMBER:

Petitioner is the ☐ personal representative ☐ conservator ☐ guardian of the estate of the above-named decedent, conservatee, or minor. Petitioner has distributed or transferred all property of the estate as required by the final order ☐ and all preliminary orders for distribution or liquidation filed in this proceeding on *(specify date each order was filed):*

All required acts of distribution or liquidation have been performed as follows *(check all that apply):*

a. ☐ All personal property, including money, stocks, bonds, and other securities, has been delivered or transferred to the distributees or transferees as ordered by the court. The receipts of all distributees or transferees are now on file or are filed with this petition. Conformed copies of all receipts previously filed are attached on Attachment 2.

b. ☐ No personal property is on hand for distribution or transfer.

c. ☐ Real property was distributed or transferred. The order for distribution or transfer of the real property; the personal representative's, conservator's, or guardian's deed; or both, were recorded as follows *(specify documents recorded, dates and locations of recording, and document numbers or other appropriate recording information):*

d. ☐ No real property is on hand for distribution or transfer.

e. ☐ No receipts are required because Petitioner is the sole distributee.

f. ☐ The minor named above attained the age of majority on *(date):*

Petitioner requests discharge as personal representative, conservator, or guardian of the estate.

I declare under penalty of perjury under the laws of the State of California that the foregoing is true and correct.

Date:

▶

_____ _____
(TYPE OR PRINT NAME OF PETITIONER) (SIGNATURE OF PETITIONER)

ORDER FOR FINAL DISCHARGE

THE COURT FINDS that the facts stated in the foregoing *Ex Parte Petition for Final Discharge* are true.

THE COURT ORDERS that *(name):*

is discharged as ☐ personal representative ☐ conservator ☐ guardian of the estate of the above-named decedent, conservatee, or minor, and sureties are discharged and released from liability for all acts subsequent hereto.

Date:

_____
JUDICIAL OFFICER
☐ SIGNATURE FOLLOWS LAST ATTACHMENT.

Page 1 of 1

Form Adopted for Mandatory Use
Judicial Council of California
DE-295/GC-395
[New January 1, 2006]

EX PARTE PETITION FOR FINAL DISCHARGE AND ORDER
(Probate—Decedents' Estates and Conservatorships and Guardianships)

Probate Code, §§ 2100, 2627,
2631, 11753, 12250;
www.courtinfo.ca.gov

ATTORNEY OR PARTY WITHOUT ATTORNEY *(Name, State Bar number, and address):*
After recording return to:

TELEPHONE NO.:
FAX NO. *(Optional):*
E-MAIL ADDRESS *(Optional):*
ATTORNEY FOR *(Name):*

SUPERIOR COURT OF CALIFORNIA, COUNTY OF

STREET ADDRESS:
MAILING ADDRESS:
CITY AND ZIP CODE:
BRANCH NAME:

MATTER OF *(Name):*

DECEDENT

FOR RECORDER'S USE ONLY

CASE NUMBER:

FOR COURT USE ONLY

AFFIDAVIT RE REAL PROPERTY OF SMALL VALUE
($20,000 or Less)

1. Decedent *(name):*
   died on *(date):*
2. Decedent died at *(city, state):*
3. At least **six months** have elapsed since the date of death of decedent as shown in the certified copy of decedent's death certificate attached to this affidavit. *(Attach a certified copy of decedent's death certificate.)*
4. a. ☐ Decedent was domiciled in this county at the time of death.
   b. ☐ Decedent was **not** domiciled in California at the time of death. Decedent died owning real property in this county.
5. a. The following is a **legal description** of decedent's real property claimed by the declarants *(copy description from deed or other legal instrument):*
   ☐ described in an attachment labeled Attachment 5a.

   b. Decedent's interest in this real property is as follows *(specify):*

6. Each declarant is a successor of decedent (as defined in Probate Code section 13006) and a successor to decedent's interest in the real property described in item 5a, and no other person has a superior right, because each declarant is
   a. ☐ **(will)** a beneficiary who succeeded to the property under decedent's will. *(Attach a copy of the will.)*
   b. ☐ **(no will)** a person who succeeded to the property under Probate Code sections 6401 and 6402.
7. Names and addresses of each guardian or conservator of decedent's estate at date of death
   ☐ none ☐ are as follows* *(specify):*

8. The **gross value** of all real property in decedent's estate located in California as shown by the *Inventory and Appraisal,* excluding the real property described in Probate Code section 13050 (joint tenancy, property passing to decedent's spouse, etc.), does not exceed $20,000.

9. An *Inventory and Appraisal* of decedent's **real property** in California is attached. The *Inventory and Appraisal* was made by a probate referee appointed for the county in which the property is located. (You *may use Judicial Council form DE-160.)*

10. No proceeding is now being or has been conducted in California for administration of decedent's estate.

* You must have a copy of this affidavit with attachments personally served or mailed to each person named in item 7.

Form Adopted for Mandatory Use
Judicial Council of California
DE-305 [Rev. July 1, 2008]

AFFIDAVIT RE REAL PROPERTY OF SMALL VALUE
(Probate—Decedents' Estates)

Probate Code, § 13200

MATTER OF	CASE NUMBER:
_(Name):	
	DECEDENT

11. Funeral expenses, expenses of last illness, and all known unsecured debts of the decedent have been paid. *[NOTE: You may be personally liable for decedent's unsecured debts up to the fair market value of the real property and any income you receive from it.]*

I declare under penalty of perjury under the laws of the State of California that the foregoing is true and correct.

Date:

▶

_____   _____
(TYPE OR PRINT NAME)   (SIGNATURE OF DECLARANT)

Date:

▶

_____   _____
(TYPE OR PRINT NAME)   (SIGNATURE OF DECLARANT)

☐ SIGNATURE OF ADDITIONAL DECLARANTS ATTACHED

NOTARY ACKNOWLEDGMENTS *(NOTE: No notary acknowledgment may be affixed as a rider (small strip) to this page. If additional notary acknowledgments are required, they must be attached as 8-1/2- by 11-inch pages.)*

STATE OF CALIFORNIA, COUNTY OF *(specify):*

On *(date):* , before me *(name and title):*

personally appeared *(name(s)):*

who proved to me on the basis of satisfactory evidence to be the person(s) whose name(s) is/are subscribed to the within instrument and acknowledged to me that he/she/they executed the instrument in his/her/their authorized capacity(ies), and that by his/her/their signature(s) on the instrument the person(s), or the entity upon behalf of which the person(s) acted, executed the instrument.

I certify under PENALTY OF PERJURY under the laws of the State of California that the foregoing paragraph is true and correct.

WITNESS my hand and official seal.

(NOTARY SEAL)

_____
(SIGNATURE OF NOTARY PUBLIC)

STATE OF CALIFORNIA, COUNTY OF *(specify):*

On *(date):* , before me *(name and title):*

personally appeared *(name(s)):*

who proved to me on the basis of satisfactory evidence to be the person(s) whose name(s) is/are subscribed to the within instrument and acknowledged to me that he/she/they executed the instrument in his/her/their authorized capacity(ies), and that by his/her/their signature(s) on the instrument the person(s), or the entity upon behalf of which the person(s) acted, executed the instrument.

I certify under PENALTY OF PERJURY under the laws of the State of California that the foregoing paragraph is true and correct.

WITNESS my hand and official seal.

(NOTARY SEAL)

_____
(SIGNATURE OF NOTARY PUBLIC)

(SEAL)	**CLERK'S CERTIFICATE**
	I certify that the foregoing, including any attached notary acknowledgments and any attached legal description of the property (but excluding other attachments), is a true and correct copy of the original affidavit on file in my office. *(Certified copies of this affidavit do not include the (1) death certificate, (2) will, or (3) inventory and appraisal. See Probate Code section 13202.)*
	Date: Clerk, by _____ , Deputy

ATTORNEY OR PARTY WITHOUT ATTORNEY *(Name, state bar number, and address)*:	TELEPHONE AND FAX NOS.:	FOR COURT USE ONLY
ATTORNEY FOR *(Name)*:		

SUPERIOR COURT OF CALIFORNIA, COUNTY OF

STREET ADDRESS:

MAILING ADDRESS:

CITY AND ZIP CODE:

BRANCH NAME:

MATTER OF *(Name)*:

DECEDENT

PETITION TO DETERMINE SUCCESSION TO REAL PROPERTY (Estates $100,000 or Less) ☐ **And Personal Property**	CASE NUMBER:
	HEARING DATE:
	DEPT.: TIME:

Petitioner *(name of each person claiming an interest)*:

requests a determination that the real property ☐ and personal property described in item 11 is property passing to petitioner and that no administration of decedent's estate is necessary.

Decedent *(name)*:

a. Date of death:

b. Place of death *(city, state)*:

At least 40 days have elapsed since the date of decedent's death.

a. ☐ Decedent was a resident of this county at the time of death.

b. ☐ Decedent was **not** a resident of California at the time of death. Decedent died owning property in this county.

Decedent died ☐ intestate ☐ testate and a copy of the will and any codicil is affixed as Attachment 5 or 12a.

a. ☐ No proceeding for the administration of decedent's estate is being conducted or has been conducted in California.

b. ☐ Decedent's personal representative's consent to use the procedure provided by Probate Code section 13150 et seq. is attached as Attachment 6b.

Proceedings for the administration of decedent's estate in another jurisdiction

a. ☐ have **not** been commenced.

b. ☐ have been commenced ☐ and completed.
(Specify state, county, court, and case number):

The **gross value** of all real and personal property in decedent's estate located in California as shown by the *Inventory and Appraisal* attached to this petition, excluding the property described in Probate Code section 13050 (joint tenancy, property passing to decedent's spouse, etc.), does not exceed $100,000. *(Attach an* Inventory and Appraisal *(form DE-160) as Attachment 8.)*

a. The decedent is survived by *(check at least one box in each of items (1)-(3))*

(1) ☐ spouse ☐ no spouse as follows: ☐ divorced or never married ☐ spouse deceased

(2) ☐ child as follows: ☐ natural or adopted ☐ natural adopted by a third party ☐ no child

(3) ☐ issue of a predeceased child ☐ no issue of a predeceased child

b. Decedent ☐ is ☐ is not survived by a stepchild or foster child or children who would have been adopted by decedent but for a legal barrier. *(See Prob. Code, § 6454.)*

*(Complete if decedent was survived by (1) a spouse but no issue (only a or b apply); or (2) no spouse or issue. Check the **first** box that applies.)*

a. ☐ Decedent is survived by a parent or parents who are listed in item 14.

b. ☐ Decedent is survived by a brother, sister, or issue of a deceased brother or sister, all of whom are listed in item 14.

c. ☐ Decedent is survived by other heirs under Probate Code section 6400 et seq., all of whom also listed in item 14.

d. ☐ Decedent is survived by no known next of kin.

Attachment 11 contains (1) the **legal description** of decedent's real property and its Assessor's Parcel Number (APN) ☐ and personal property in California passing to petitioner and (2) decedent's interest in the property. *(Attach the legal description of the real and personal property and state decedent's interest.)*

(Continued on reverse)

Form Approved by the Judicial Council of California
DE-310 [Rev. January 1, 1998]
Mandatory Form [1/1/2000]

PETITION TO DETERMINE SUCCESSION TO REAL PROPERTY
(Probate)

Probate Code, § 13151

2. Each petitioner is a successor of decedent (as defined in Probate Code section 13006) and a successor to decedent's interest
   in the real property ☐ and personal property ☐ described in item 11 because each petitioner is
   a. ☐ **(will)** a beneficiary who succeeded to the property under decedent's will. [1]
   b. ☐ **(no will)** a person who succeeded to the property under Probate Code sections 6401 and 6402.
3. The specific property interest claimed by each petitioner in the real property ☐ and personal property ☐ described in item 11
   ☐ is stated in Attachment 13 ☐ is as follows *(specify)*:
4. The names, relationships, ages, and residence or mailing addresses so far as known to or reasonably ascertainable by petitioner
   of (1) all persons named or checked in items 1, 9, and 10, (2) all other heirs of decedent, and (3) all devisees of decedent (persons
   designated in the will to receive any property)
   ☐ are listed below ☐ are listed in Attachment 14.

Name and relationship	Age	Residence or mailing address

5. The names and addresses of all persons named as executors in decedent's will
   ☐ are listed below ☐ are listed in Attachment 15 ☐ none named ☐ no will.

6. ☐ Petitioner is the trustee of a trust that is a devisee under decedent's will. The names and addresses of all persons
   interested in the trust, as determined in cases of future interests under paragraphs (1), (2), or (3) of subdivision (a) of
   Probate Code section 15804 are listed in Attachment 16.
7. ☐ Decedent's estate was under a ☐ guardianship ☐ conservatorship at decedent's death. The names and
   addresses of all persons serving as guardian or conservator ☐ are listed below ☐ are listed in Attachment 17.

8. Number of pages attached: _____

Date: _____

(Signature of all petitioners also required (Prob. Code, § 1020).)

▶ _____
(SIGNATURE OF ATTORNEY *)

declare under penalty of perjury under the laws of the State of California that the foregoing is true and correct.

Date: _____

▶ _____
(SIGNATURE OF PETITIONER[2])

. . . .
(TYPE OR PRINT NAME)

▶ _____
(SIGNATURE OF PETITIONER[2])

. . . .
(TYPE OR PRINT NAME)

See Probate Code section 13152(c) for the requirement that a copy of the will be attached in certain instances. If required, include as Attachment 5 or 12a.

Each person named in item 1 must sign.

DE-310 [Rev. January 1, 1998]

**PETITION TO DETERMINE SUCCESSION
TO REAL PROPERTY**
(Probate)

Page two

ATTORNEY OR PARTY WITHOUT ATTORNEY *(Name, state bar number, and address):*

After recording return to:

TELEPHONE NO.:
FAX NO. *(Optional):*
E-MAIL ADDRESS *(Optional):*
ATTORNEY FOR *(Name):*

SUPERIOR COURT OF CALIFORNIA, COUNTY OF

STREET ADDRESS:
MAILING ADDRESS:
CITY AND ZIP CODE:
BRANCH NAME:

MATTER OF *(Name):*

FOR RECORDER'S USE ONLY

DECEDENT

CASE NUMBER:

ORDER DETERMINING SUCCESSION TO REAL PROPERTY
(Estates $100,000 or Less)
☐ **And Personal Property**

FOR COURT USE ONLY

Date of hearing: _____ Time: _____
Dept./Room: _____ Judge: _____

THE COURT FINDS

1. All notices required by law have been given.
2. Decedent died on *(date):*
   a. ☐ a resident of the California county named above.
   b. ☐ a nonresident of California and left an estate in the county named above.
   c. ☐ intestate ☐ testate.
3. At least 40 days have elapsed since the date of decedent's death.
   a. ☐ No proceeding for the administration of decedent's estate is being conducted or has been conducted in California.
   b. ☐ Decedent's personal representative has filed a consent to use the procedure provided in Probate Code section 13150 et seq.
4. The gross value of decedent's real and personal property in California, excluding property described in Probate Code section 13050, does not exceed $100,000.
5. Each petitioner is a successor of decedent (as defined in Probate Code section 13006) and a successor to decedent's interest in the real ☐ and personal property described in item 9a because each petitioner is
   a. ☐ **(will)** a beneficiary who succeeded to the property under decedent's will.
   b. ☐ **(no will)** a person who succeeded to the property under Probate Code sections 6401 and 6402.

THE COURT FURTHER FINDS AND ORDERS

6. No administration of decedent's estate is necessary in California.
   a. The following described real ☐ and personal property is property of decedent passing to each petitioner *(give legal description of real property):* ☐ described in Attachment 9a.

   b. Each petitioner's **name** and specific property interest ☐ is stated in Attachment 9b ☐ is as follows *(specify):*

10. ☐ Other *(specify):*

Date: _____

_____
JUDGE OF THE SUPERIOR COURT

11. Number of pages attached: _____

☐ SIGNATURE FOLLOWS LAST ATTACHMENT

Page 1 of 1

Form Adopted for Mandatory Use
Judicial Council of California
DE-315 [Rev. January 1, 2003]

**ORDER DETERMINING SUCCESSION
TO REAL PROPERTY**
(Probate)

Probate Code, § 13154

Non-Judicial-Council Forms

Declaration Regarding Property Passing to Decedent's Surviving Spouse or
   Registered Domestic Partner Under Probate Code § 13500

Who Inherits Under the Will?

Schedule of Assets

Notification by Trustee

Affidavit—Death of Joint Tenant

Affidavit—Death of Trustee

Affidavit—Death of Spouse

Affidavit—Death of Domestic Partner

Affidavit—Death of Spouse or Domestic Partner—Survivorship Community Property

Affidavit for Collection of Personal Property Under California Probate Code
   §§ 13100–13106

Deed to Real Property

Probate Case Cover Sheet—Certificate of Grounds for Assignment to District (L.A. County)

Application and Order Appointing Probate Referee (L.A. County)

Change in Ownership Statement (Death of Real Property Owner) (L.A. County)

Preliminary Change of Ownership Report

Declaration Regarding Property Passing to Decedent's
Surviving Spouse or Registered Domestic Partner Under Probate Code § 13500

The undersigned declares:

1. _____ died

   on _____, 20_____, and on the date of death was a resident of California.

2. On the date of death, decedent was married to or was a registered domestic partner of

   _____ , who survives the decedent.

3. Among the decedent's assets was _____

   _____

   _____

4. The decedent's interest in the described property passed to decedent's surviving spouse or partner upon

   decedent's death by the terms of decedent's will and any codicils to it.

   or

4. The decedent died intestate and the above-described property is the community property of the decedent

   and the decedent's surviving spouse or partner, having been acquired during the parties' marriage or domestic

   partnership while domiciled in California, and not having been acquired by gift or inheritance, and passes to the

   decedent's surviving spouse or partner by the laws of inheritance governing passage of title from decedent in the

   absence of a will.

5. Decedent's surviving spouse or domestic partner therefore is entitled to have the described property delivered to

   that spouse or partner without probate administration, pursuant to California Probate Code § 13500.

The undersigned declares under penalty of perjury that the foregoing is true and correct and that this declaration

was executed on _____, 20_____, at _____

_____ California.

_____
(Signature)

Declaration Regarding Property Passing to Decedent's Surviving Spouse or
Registered Domestic Partner Under Probate Code § 13500

©nolo   www.nolo.com   Page 1 of 1

Who Inherits Under the Will?

Beneficiaries Named in Will	Property Inherited

Schedule of Assets

Estate of _____, Deceased

Description of Assets	A Total Value of Asset on Date/Death	B How Is Asset Owned?	C Portion Owned by Decedent	D Value of Decedent's Interest	E Probate or Non-probate
1. Cash Items					
Cash in decedent's possession	_____	_____	_____	_____	_____
Uncashed checks payable to decedent:					
_____	_____	_____	_____	_____	_____
_____	_____	_____	_____	_____	_____
_____	_____	_____	_____	_____	_____
_____	_____	_____	_____	_____	_____
2. Bank and Savings & Loan Accounts					
_____	_____	_____	_____	_____	_____
_____	_____	_____	_____	_____	_____
_____	_____	_____	_____	_____	_____
_____	_____	_____	_____	_____	_____
_____	_____	_____	_____	_____	_____
3. Real Property (common address, brief description)					
_____	_____	_____	_____	_____	_____
_____	_____	_____	_____	_____	_____
_____	_____	_____	_____	_____	_____
_____	_____	_____	_____	_____	_____
_____	_____	_____	_____	_____	_____
4. Securities					
Stock (name of company, type, and number of shares)					
_____	_____	_____	_____	_____	_____
_____	_____	_____	_____	_____	_____
_____	_____	_____	_____	_____	_____
_____	_____	_____	_____	_____	_____
_____	_____	_____	_____	_____	_____
_____	_____	_____	_____	_____	_____
_____	_____	_____	_____	_____	_____
_____	_____	_____	_____	_____	_____
_____	_____	_____	_____	_____	_____

	A	B	C	D	E
	Total Value of Asset on Date/Death	How Is Asset Owned?	Portion Owned by Decedent	Value of Decedent's Interest	Probate or Non-probate

Bonds (face amount)

_____

_____

_____

U.S. Savings Bonds/Treasury Bills (series, amount, date of issue)

_____

_____

_____

_____

Mutual Funds (name of fund, number of shares)

_____

_____

_____

5. **Insurance** (name of company, policy number, name of beneficiary, name of owner)
   Policies on decedent's life

   _____

   _____

   _____

   Policies owned by decedent on another

   _____

   _____

6. **Retirement and Death Benefits** (description, beneficiary, amount)
   Employee benefits

   _____

   _____

   Pension, profit-sharing, savings plans

   _____

   _____

   Social Security/Railroad Retirement

   _____

   Individual Retirement Accounts

   _____

   _____

	A	B	C	D	E
	Total Value of Asset on Date/Death	How Is Asset Owned?	Portion Owned by Decedent	Value of Decedent's Interest	Probate or Non-probate

7. Amounts Due the Decedent (name of payor, amount)

8. Promissory Note (name of payor, date, amount, balance)

9. Tangible Personal Property (household furniture, furnishings, personal effects, books, jewelry, artwork, valuable collections, antiques, etc.)

10. Automobiles (year, make, model)

11. Business Interests (names of partnerships or family corporations, brief descriptions)

12. Other Assets (copyrights, royalty interests, any other property not listed above)

Total Value of Decedent's Gross Estate _____

Deductions (for federal estate tax purposes)

a. Personal debts owed by decedent at date of death

$ _____

_____

_____

_____

b. Mortgages/promissory notes due

_____

_____

_____

_____

_____

c. Expenses of estate administration

_____

_____

_____

_____

_____

d. Last illness expenses

_____

_____

_____

_____

_____

_____

_____

e. Funeral expenses

_____

_____

_____

f. Sales contracts (automobiles, furniture, television)

_____

_____

_____

Total Deductions $ _____

Total Value of Decedent's Gross Estate (from previous page) $ _____

Total Deductions (from line above)   _____

Value of Decedent's Net Estate $ _____

Notification by Trustee
(Probate Code Sec. 16061.7)

_____

executed the _____ ,

in his/her/their capacity(ies) as Settlor(s) on _____ , hereinafter referred to as the "Trust."

1. The name, mailing address, and telephone number of each Trustee of the Trust is set forth below:

_____

_____

_____

_____

_____

2. The address of the physical location where the principal place of administration of the Trust is located is:

_____

_____

_____

_____

_____

3. The terms of the Trust require disclosure of the following information:

_____

_____

_____

_____

_____

4. You are entitled to receive from the Trustee a true and complete copy of the terms of the Trust by requesting it from the Trustee.

5. **YOU MAY NOT BRING AN ACTION TO CONTEST THE TRUST MORE THAN 120 DAYS FROM THE DATE THIS NOTIFICATION BY THE TRUSTEE IS SERVED UPON YOU OR 60 DAYS FROM THE DATE ON WHICH A COPY OF THE TERMS OF THE TRUST IS MAILED OR PERSONALLY DELIVERED TO YOU DURING THAT 120-DAY PERIOD, WHICHEVER IS LATER.**

_____   _____

Date   Trustee

SPACE ABOVE THIS LINE FOR RECORDER'S USE

AFFIDAVIT—DEATH OF JOINT TENANT

State of California   )

)   ss.

County of _____)

_____, of legal age, being first duly sworn, deposes and says:

That _____,

the decedent mentioned in the attached certified copy of Certificate of Death, is the same person as _____

_____ named as one of the parties in that certain deed

dated _____, executed by _____ to

_____,

as joint tenants, recorded as instrument No._____, on _____,

in Book/Reel _____, Page/Image_____, of Official Records of _____

County, California, covering the following described property situated in the City of _____,

County of _____, State of California:

Assessor's Parcel No. _____

Dated: _____   _____

                                        Signature

Subscribed and sworn to (or affirmed) before me on this _____ day of _____, 20_____,

by_____, proved to me on the basis of satisfactory evidence to be the

person(s) who appeared before me.

(seal)   Signature _____

RECORDING REQUESTED BY:

WHEN RECORDED MAIL TO:

SPACE ABOVE THIS LINE FOR RECORDER'S USE

AFFIDAVIT—DEATH OF TRUSTEE

State of California ⟩

⟩ ss.

County of ⟩

The undersigned, being of legal age, being duly sworn, deposes and says:

That _____, the decedent mentioned in the attached certified copy of Certificate of Death, is the same person as _____ named as Trustee in that certain Declaration of Trust dated _____, executed by _____ as Trustor(s).

At the time of the demise of the decedent, the decedent was the record owner, as Trustee, of real property commonly known as _____, which property is described in a Deed which was executed by _____ as Grantor(s) on _____ and recorded as Instrument No. _____ on _____ of Official Records of _____ County, State of California.

The legal description of said property is as follows:

I, _____, am the named Successor Trustee under the above-referenced Trust, which was in effect at the time of the death of the decedent mentioned in Paragraph 1 above, and which has not been revoked, and I hereby consent to act as such.

I declare under penalty of perjury, under the laws of the State of California, that the foregoing is true and correct.

Dated: _____   _____
                                    Signature

Subscribed and sworn to (or affirmed) before me on this _____ day of _____, 20_____, by _____, proved to me on the basis of satisfactory evidence to be the person(s) who appeared before me.

(seal)   Signature _____

RECORDING REQUESTED BY:

WHEN RECORDED MAIL TO:

SPACE ABOVE THIS LINE FOR RECORDER'S USE

AFFIDAVIT—DEATH OF SPOUSE

State of California   )

)   ss.

County of   )

_____, of legal age, being first duly sworn, deposes and says:

That affiant was validly married to _____ immediately prior to the latter named party's death, and the affiant in conjunction with the decedent held title as "husband and wife" or as "husband and wife as community property" to the following described property:

That the affiant and the above-named decedent were married on _____ and affiant is the widow/widower of decedent; and that _____

died on _____, as evidenced by a certified copy of the Certificate of Death attached hereto, and that the affiant has carefully examined all of the decedent's personal possessions, letters, papers, effects, and belongings, and is certain that either (1) no will was executed by the decedent based not only on affiant's failure to discover a will, but because affiant was never informed of decedent having executed or declared a will, and affiant is certain that he/she would have been consulted, or would at least have had knowledge of that fact if a testamentary disposition were attempted, or (2) if a will is present that it is the last complete will (with codicils and/or other amendments) and that this will devised the subject property to the affiant; and that the above-described property has been at all times since acquisition considered the community property of decedent and affiant and that any and all contributions to said property from whatever source were also considered by decedent and affiant to be community in nature; and that with respect to the above-described property, there has not been nor will there be an election filed pursuant to Probate Code Sections 13502 or 13503 in any probate proceedings in any court of competent jurisdiction; and that this affidavit is made for the protection and benefit of the grantee or grantees of the subject property, in conjunction with the successors, assigns, and personal representatives of the grantee or grantees and all other parties hereafter dealing with or who may acquire an interest in the property herein described.

Dated: _____   _____
                                Signature

Subscribed and sworn to (or affirmed) before me on this _____ day of _____, 20_____, by_____, proved to me on the basis of satisfactory evidence to be the person(s) who appeared before me.

(seal)   Signature _____

RECORDING REQUESTED BY:

WHEN RECORDED MAIL TO:

AFFIDAVIT—DEATH OF DOMESTIC PARTNER

State of California   )
) ss.

County of _____)

_____, of legal age, being first duly sworn, deposes and says:

That affiant was the registered domestic partner of _____ immediately prior to the latter named party's death, and the affiant in conjunction with the decedent held title as "community property" to the following described property:

That the affiant and the above-named decedent filed a Declaration of Domestic Partnership with the California Secretary of State on _____ and affiant is the surviving domestic partner of decedent; and that _____ died on _____, as evidenced by a certified copy of the Certificate of Death attached hereto, and that the affiant has carefully examined all of the decedent's personal possessions, letters, papers, effects, and belongings, and is certain that either (1) no will was executed by the decedent based not only on affiant's failure to discover a will, but because affiant was never informed of decedent having executed or declared a will, and affiant is certain that he/she would have been consulted, or would at least have had knowledge of that fact if a testamentary disposition were attempted, or (2) if a will is present that it is the last complete will (with codicils and/or other amendments) and that this will devised the subject property to the affiant; and that the above-described property has been at all times since acquisition considered the community property of decedent and affiant and that any and all contributions to said property from whatever source were also considered by decedent and affiant to be community in nature; and that with respect to the above-described property, there has not been nor will there be an election filed pursuant to Probate Code Sections 13502 or 13503 in any probate proceedings in any court of competent jurisdiction; and that this affidavit is made for the protection and benefit of the grantee or grantees of the subject property, in conjunction with the successors, assigns, and personal representatives of the grantee or grantees and all other parties hereafter dealing with or who may acquire an interest in the property herein described.

Dated: _____   _____
                                      Signature

Subscribed and sworn to (or affirmed) before me on this _____ day of _____, 20_____, by_____, proved to me on the basis of satisfactory evidence to be the person(s) who appeared before me.

(seal)   Signature _____

RECORDING REQUESTED BY:

WHEN RECORDED MAIL TO:

SPACE ABOVE THIS LINE FOR RECORDER'S USE

AFFIDAVIT—DEATH OF SPOUSE OR DOMESTIC PARTNER— SURVIVORSHIP COMMUNITY PROPERTY

State of California   )

) ss.

County of _____)

_____, of legal age, being first duly sworn, deposes and says:

That _____,

the decedent mentioned in the attached certified copy of Certificate of Death, is the same person as _____

_____ named as one of the parties in the deed dated

_____, executed by _____ to

_____,

as community property with right of survivorship, recorded as instrument No._____, on

_____, in Book/Reel _____, Page/Image_____, of Official Records of

_____ County, California, covering the following described property

situated in the City of _____, County of _____,

State of California:

Assessor's Parcel No. _____

Dated: _____   _____

                                 Signature

Subscribed and sworn to (or affirmed) before me on this _____ day of _____, 20_____,

by_____, proved to me on the basis of satisfactory evidence to be the

person(s) who appeared before me.

(seal)   Signature _____

Affidavit for Collection of Personal Property
Under California Probate Code §§ 13100–13106

The undersigned state(s) as follows:

1. _____ died on _____, 20____,

   in the County of _____, State of California.

2. At least 40 days have elapsed since the death of the decedent, as shown by the attached certified copy of the decedent's death certificate.

3. No proceeding is now being or has been conducted in California for administration of the decedent's estate.

4. The gross value of the decedent's real and personal property in California, excluding the property described in Section 13050 of the California Probate Code, does not exceed $100,000.

5. ☐ An inventory and appraisal of the real property included in the decedent's estate is attached.
   ☐ There is no real property in the estate.

6. The following property is to be paid, transferred, or delivered to the undersigned under the provisions of California Probate Code Section 13100.

7. The successor(s) of the decedent, as defined in Probate Code Section 13006, is/are:

   _____.

8. The undersigned ☐ is/are successor(s) of the decedent to the decedent's interest in the described property, or ☐ is/are authorized under California Probate Code Section 13051 to act on behalf of the successor(s) of the decedent with respect to the decedent's interest in the described property.

9. No other person has a right to the interest of the decedent in the described property.

10. The undersigned request(s) that the described property be paid, delivered, or transferred to the undersigned.

I/We declare under penalty of perjury under the laws of the State of California that the foregoing is true and correct.

Dated: _____, 20_____

_____

_____

_____

(See reverse side for Notarial Acknowledgments)

STATE OF CALIFORNIA   )
) ss.
COUNTY OF _____)

On _____, before me, a Notary Public in and for said State, personally appeared _____, who proved to me on the basis of satisfactory evidence to be the person(s) whose name(s) is/are subscribed to the within instrument and acknowledged to me that he/she/they executed the same in his/her/their authorized capacity(ies) and that by his/her/their signature(s) on the instrument the person(s) or the entity upon behalf of which the person(s) acted, executed the instrument.

I certify under PENALTY OF PERJURY under the laws of the State of California that the foregoing is true and correct.

WITNESS my hand and official seal.

_____
(Notary Public)

STATE OF CALIFORNIA   )
) ss.
COUNTY OF _____)

On _____, before me, a Notary Public in and for said State, personally appeared _____, who proved to me on the basis of satisfactory evidence to be the person(s) whose name(s) is/are subscribed to the within instrument and acknowledged to me that he/she/they executed the same in his/her/their authorized capacity(ies) and that by his/her/their signature(s) on the instrument the person(s) or the entity upon behalf of which the person(s) acted, executed the instrument.

I certify under PENALTY OF PERJURY under the laws of the State of California that the foregoing is true and correct.

WITNESS my hand and official seal.

_____
(Notary Public)

STATE OF CALIFORNIA   )
) ss.
COUNTY OF _____)

On _____, before me, a Notary Public in and for said State, personally appeared _____, who proved to me on the basis of satisfactory evidence to be the person(s) whose name(s) is/are subscribed to the within instrument and acknowledged to me that he/she/they executed the same in his/her/their authorized capacity(ies) and that by his/her/their signature(s) on the instrument the person(s) or the entity upon behalf of which the person(s) acted, executed the instrument.

I certify under PENALTY OF PERJURY under the laws of the State of California that the foregoing is true and correct.

WITNESS my hand and official seal.

_____
(Notary Public)

nolo
www.nolo.com   **Affadavit for Collection of Personal Property**
Under California Probate Code §§ 13100–13106   Page 2 of 2

RECORDING REQUESTED BY:

WHEN RECORDED MAIL TO:

SPACE ABOVE THIS LINE FOR RECORDER'S USE

DEED TO REAL PROPERTY

I, _____, as _____

of the Estate of _____, deceased, pursuant to authority

granted to me by Order of the Superior Court of California, for the County of _____,

on _____, in Case No. _____, to administer the Estate of

_____, deceased, under the Independent Administration

of Estates Act, and pursuant to Notice of Proposed Action duly given under the provisions of Probate Code Sections 10580,

et seq., do hereby convey to _____,

as _____, without any representation, warranty,

or covenant of any kind, express or implied, all right, title, interest, and estate of the decedent at the time of death, and

all right, title, and interest that the estate may have subsequently acquired in the real property situated in the County of

_____, _____ State of California, described as follows.

Assessor's Parcel No. _____

Dated: _____   _____
                                         Signature

STATE OF CALIFORNIA   )
) ss.
COUNTY OF _____   )

    On _____, before me, the undersigned, a Notary Public in and for said State, personally

appeared _____, as _____ of

the Estate of _____, deceased, who proved to

me on the basis of satisfactory evidence to be the person(s) whose name(s) is/are subscribed to the within instrument and

acknowledged to me that he/she/they executed the same in his/her/their authorized capacity(ies), and that by his/her/their

signature(s) on the instrument the person(s) or entity upon behalf of which the person(s) acted, executed the instrument.

I certify under PENALTY OF PERJURY under the laws of the State of California that the foregoing is true and correct.

WITNESS my hand and official seal.

_____
(Notary Public)

NAME, ADDRESS AND TELEPHONE NUMBER OF ATTORNEY OR PARTY WITHOUT ATTORNEY:	STATE BAR NUMBER	Reserved for Clerk's File Stamp

ATTORNEY FOR (Name):

SUPERIOR COURT OF CALIFORNIA, COUNTY OF LOS ANGELES

COURTHOUSE ADDRESS:

Matter of:

☐ DECEDENT   ☐ CONSERVATEE   ☐ MINOR   ☐ TRUST/OTHER

PROBATE CASE COVER SHEET - CERTIFICATE OF GROUNDS FOR ASSIGNMENT TO DISTRICT	CASE NUMBER:

This form is required for all new Probate cases filed in the Los Angeles Superior Court.

Select the correct district (3 steps):

1) Under Column **1** below, check the one type of action which best describes the nature of this case.

2) In Column **2** below, circle the reason for your choice of district that applies to the type of action you have checked.

─── **Applicable Reason for Choosing District (See Column 2 below)** ───

1. District where one or more of the parties reside.
2. District where minor/proposed conservatee reside.
3. District where petitioner resides.
4. District where decedent was domiciled.
5. Decedent/Ward/Conservatee was/is not domiciled in California, but held property at date of death/holds property in district.
6. Other: Statutory Authority _____.
7. May be filed in the appropriate district (Local Rule 2.0(c) states specific circumstances in which this may occur).

3) Fill in the information requested on Section II; complete section III; sign the certificate.

1 TYPE OF ACTION *(Check only one)*	**2** APPLICABLE REASONS *(See above)*
Decedent Estates	
☐ A6210 Petition for Probate of Will - Letters Testamentary	4., 5., 7.
☐ A6211 Petition for Probate of Will - Letters of Administration with will annexed	4., 5., 7.
☐ A6212 Petition for Letters of Administration	4., 5., 7.
☐ A6213 Petition for Letters of Special Administration	4., 5., 7.
☐ A6214 Petition to Set Aside Small Estate (6602 Prob. Code)	4., 5., 7.
☐ A6215 Spousal Property Petition	4., 5., 7.
☐ A6216 Petition for Succession to Property	4., 5., 7.
☐ A6217 Summary Probate (7660 Prob. Code)	4., 5., 7.
☐ A6218 Petition re Real Property of Small Value (13200 Prob. Code)	4., 5., 7.
Conservatorship / Guardianship	
☐ A6230 Petition for Conservatorship of Person and Estate	2., 6., 7.
☐ A6231 Petition for Conservatorship of Person only	2., 6., 7.
☐ A6232 Petition for Conservatorship of Estate only	2., 5., 6., 7

PROBATE CASE COVER SHEET - CERTIFICATE OF GROUNDS FOR ASSIGNMENT TO DISTRICT

Short Title	CASE NUMBER:

1 TYPE OF ACTION *(Check only one)*	**2** APPLICABLE REASONS *(See above)*
Conservatorship / Guardianship	
☐ A6240 Petition for Guardianship of Person and Estate	2., 6., 7.
☐ A6241 Petition for Guardianship of Person only	2., 6., 7.
☐ A6242 Petition for Guardianship of Estate only	2., 5., 6., 7.
Trust / Other Probate Court Matters	
☐ A6254 Trust Proceedings	3., 6., 7.
☐ A6260 Petition for Compromise of Minor's Claim - no civil case filed (3500 Prob. Code)	1., 2., 6., 7.
☐ A6180 Petition to Establish Fact of Birth, Death or Marriage	1., 4., 7.
☐ A6200 Other Probate Matter (Specify): _____	6., 7.
☐ A6243 Proceeding for particular transaction where spouse lacks legal Capacity	2., 6., 7.
☐ A6233 Capacity determination and health care decision for adult without conservator	2., 6., 7.

II. Select the appropriate district: Enter the address of the party, decedent's residence, property, or other circumstance you have circled in column 2 as the proper reason for filing in the district you selected.

REASON: CHECK THE NUMBER YOU CIRCLED IN -2- WHICH APPLIES IN THIS CASE	ADDRESS OF SUBJECT PERSON / FIDUCIARY
☐ 1 ☐ 2 ☐ 3 ☐ 4 ☐ 5 ☐ 6 ☐ 7	
CITY: STATE ZIP CODE	

III. ☐ Another case (including Juvenile, Family Law, Adoptions, etc.) has been filed with Los Angeles Superior Court involving the same minor(s).

   Case number: _____

IV. Certificate of Assignment: The undersigned hereby certifies that the above entitled matter is properly filed for assignment to the _____
   District of the Los Angeles Superior Court pursuant to the California Probate Code and Rule 2.0 of this court for the reason checked above.

   I declare under penalty of perjury under the laws of the State of California that the foregoing is true and correct and this declaration was executed on

   _____.

   _____
   (SIGNATURE OF ATTORNEY/PARTY WITHOUT ATTORNEY)

New Probate Case Filing Instructions

This form is required so that the court can assign your case to the correct courthouse in the proper district for filing. It satisfies the requirement for a certificate as to reasons for authorizing filing in the courthouse location, as set forth in Los Angeles Superior Court Local Rule 2.0. It must be completed and submitted to the court along with the original Petition in ALL Probate cases filed in any district (including the Central District) of the Los Angeles County Superior Court.

**THE FOLLOWING DOCUMENTS MUST BE COMPLETED AND READY TO BE FILED IN ORDER TO
PROPERLY COMMENCE YOUR NEW COURT CASE:**

1. Probate Case Cover Sheet (this form)

2. Original Petition

3. Other documents as required by statute, California Rules of Court, or Rules of this Court.

4. Payment in full of the filing fees or an Order of the Court waiving payment of the filing fees (fee waiver application forms available at the Forms Window).

*Copies of original documents presented personally to the filing clerk will be conformed and returned to you.
If filed by mail, include a self-addressed-stamped-envelope for return of your conformed copies.*

PROBATE CASE COVER SHEET - CERTIFICATE OF GROUNDS FOR ASSIGNMENT TO DISTRICT

PRO 010 05-03   Page 2 of 2

ATTORNEY FOR (Name):

SUPERIOR COURT OF CALIFORNIA, COUNTY OF LOS ANGELES

COURTHOUSE ADDRESS:

Estate of:

☐ DECEDENT   ☐ CONSERVATEE   ☐ MINOR

CASE NUMBER:

APPLICATION AND ORDER APPOINTING PROBATE REFEREE

It is requested that a Probate Referee be appointed to appraise the assets of the above-entitled estate consisting of the following approximate values:

1.   CASH $ _____

2.   REAL ESTATE $ _____

3.   PERSONAL PROPERTY $ _____

REMARKS   _____

_____

Dated: _____   _____
                                                            Signature of Applicant

IT IS ORDERED that (name):

a disinterested person is appointed Probate Referee to appraise the above-entitled estate. The Probate Referee is authorized to establish the fair market value of the estate as of the date of death of the decedent, or as of the date of appointment of a conservator or guardian, under the laws of the State of California.

Dated: _____   _____
                                                            Judge of the Superior Court

---

APPLICATION AND ORDER APPOINTING PROBATE REFEREE

BOE-502-D (P1) REV. 03 (08-09) ASSR-176 (REV. 8-09)

CHANGE IN OWNERSHIP STATEMENT
DEATH OF REAL PROPERTY OWNER

This notice is a request for a completed Change in Ownership Statement. Failure to file this statement will result in the assessment of a penalty.

RICK AUERBACH
ASSESSOR

COUNTY OF LOS ANGELES • OFFICE OF THE ASSESSOR
500 WEST TEMPLE STREET, ROOM 225
LOS ANGELES, CA 90012-2770 • Telephone 213.974.3441
Email: *exempt@assessor.lacounty.gov*
Website: *assessor.lacounty.gov*
Si desea ayuda en Español, llame al número 213.974.3211

NAME AND MAILING ADDRESS
(Make necessary corrections to the printed name and mailing address)

Section 480(b) of the Revenue and Taxation Code requires that the personal representative file this statement with the Assessor in each county where the decedent owned property at the time of death. **File a separate statement for each parcel of real property owned by the decedent.**

NAME OF DECEDENT	DATE OF DEATH

☐ YES ☐ NO Did the decedent have an interest in real property in this county? If **YES**, answer all questions. If **NO**, sign and complete the certification on page 2.

STREET ADDRESS OF REAL PROPERTY	CITY	ZIP CODE	ASSESSOR'S PARCEL NUMBER (APN)

DESCRIPTIVE INFORMATION ☑ *(IF APN UNKNOWN)*

☐ Copy of deed by which decedent acquired title is attached.

☐ Copy of decedent's most recent tax bill is attached.

☐ Deed or tax bill is not available; legal description is attached.

DISPOSITION OF REAL PROPERTY ☑

☐ Succession without a will

☐ Probate Code 13650 distribution

☐ Affidavit of death of joint tenant

☐ Decree of distribution pursuant to will

☐ Action of trustee pursuant to terms of a trust

TRANSFER INFORMATION ☑ Check all that apply and list details below.

☐ Decedent's spouse   ☐ Decedent's registered domestic partner

☐ Decedent's child(ren) or parent(s). If qualified for exclusion from assessment, a *Claim for Reassessment Exclusion for Transfer Between Parent and Child* must be filed (see instructions.)

☐ Decedent's grandchild(ren.) If qualified for exclusion from assessment, a *Claim for Reassessment Exclusion for Transfer from Grandparent to Grandchild* must be filed (see instructions.)

☐ Other beneficiaries.

☐ A trust.

NAME OF TRUSTEE	ADDRESS OF TRUSTEE

List names and percentage of ownership of all beneficiaries:

NAME OF BENEFICIARY	RELATIONSHIP TO DECEDENT	PERCENT OF OWNERSHIP RECEIVED

☐ This property has been or will be sold prior to distribution. (Attach the conveyance document and/or court order.)

CONTINUED ON PAGE 2

THIS DOCUMENT IS NOT SUBJECT TO PUBLIC INSPECTION

| | YES | | NO | Will the decree of distribution include distribution of an ownership interest in any legal entity that owns real property in this county? If **YES**, will the distribution result in any person or legal entity obtaining control of more than 50% of the ownership of that legal entity? ☐ YES ☐ NO If **YES**, complete the following section. |

NAME AND ADDRESS OF LEGAL ENTITY	NAME OF PERSON OR ENTITY GAINING SUCH CONTROL

| | YES | | NO | Was the decedent the lessor or lessee in a lease that had an original term of 35 years or more, including renewal options? If **YES**, provide the names and addresses of all other parties to the lease. |

NAME	MAILING ADDRESS	CITY	STATE	ZIP CODE

MAILING ADDRESS FOR FUTURE PROPERTY TAX STATEMENTS

ADDRESS	CITY	STATE	ZIP CODE

CERTIFICATION

I certify (or declare) under penalty of perjury under the laws of the State of California that the information contained herein is true, correct and complete to the best of my knowledge and belief.

SIGNATURE OF PERSONAL REPRESENTATIVE	PRINTED NAME OF PERSONAL REPRESENTATIVE

TITLE	DATE

E-MAIL ADDRESS	DAYTIME TELEPHONE ( )

INSTRUCTIONS

IMPORTANT

Failure to file a Change in Ownership Statement within the time prescribed by law may result in a penalty of either $100 or 10% of the taxes applicable to the new base year value of the real property or manufactured home, whichever is greater, but not to exceed $2,500 if that failure to file was not willful. This penalty will be added to the assessment roll and shall be collected like any other delinquent property taxes and subjected to the same penalties for nonpayment.

Section 480 of the Revenue and Taxation Code states, in part:

a) Whenever there occurs any change in ownership of real property or of a manufactured home that is subject to local property taxation and is assessed by the county assessor, the transferee shall file a signed change in ownership statement in the county where the real property or manufactured home is located, as provided for in subdivision (c). In the case of a change in ownership where the transferee is not locally assessed, no change in ownership statement is required.

b) The personal representative shall file a change in ownership statement with the county recorder or assessor in each county in which the decedent owned real property at the time of death that is subject to probate proceedings. The statement shall be filed prior to or at the time the inventory and appraisal is filed with the court clerk. In all other cases in which an interest in real property is transferred by reason of death, including a transfer through the medium of a trust, the change in ownership statement or statements shall be filed by the trustee (if the property was held in trust) or the transferee with the county recorder or assessor in each county in which the decedent owned an interest in real property within 150 days after the date of death.

The above requested information is required by law. Please reference the following:

Passage of Decedent's Property: Beneficial interest passes to the decedent's heirs effectively on the decedent's date of death. However, a document must be recorded to vest title in the heirs. An attorney should be consulted to discuss the specific facts of your situation.

Change in Ownership: California Code of Regulations, Title 18, Rule 462.260(c), states in part that "[i]nheritance (by will or intestate succession)" shall be "the date of death of decedent."

Inventory and Appraisal: Probate Code, Section 8800, states in part, "Concurrent with the filing of the inventory and appraisal pursuant to this section, the personal representative shall also file a certification that the requirements of Section 480 of the Revenue and Taxation Code either:
(1) Are not applicable because the decedent owned no real property in California at the time of death
(2) Have been satisfied by the filing of a change in ownership statement with the county recorder or assessor of each county in California in which the decedent owned property at the time of death."

Parent/Child and Grandparent/Grandchild Exclusions: A claim must be filed within three years after the date of death/transfer, but prior to the date of transfer to a third party; or within six months after the date of mailing of a Notice of Assessed Value Change, issued as a result of the transfer of property for which the claim is filed. An application may be obtained by calling 213.893.1239.

This statement will remain confidential as required by Revenue and Taxation Code Section 481, which states in part: "These statements are not public documents and are not open to inspection, except as provided by Section 408."

ELIMINARY CHANGE OF OWNERSHIP REPORT

be completed by transferee (buyer) prior to transfer of subject property in accordance with section 480.3 of the enue and Taxation Code.] A Preliminary Change of Ownership Report must be filed with each conveyance in County Recorder's office for the county where the property is located; this particular form may be used in all ounties of California.

FOR RECORDER'S USE ONLY

THIS REPORT IS NOT A PUBLIC DOCUMENT

LER/TRANSFEROR:

YER/TRANSFEREE:

SESSOR'S PARCEL NUMBER(S)

OPERTY ADDRESS OR LOCATION:

L TAX INFORMATION TO: Name
                          Address

TICE: A lien for property taxes applies to your property on January 1 of each year for the taxes owing in the following fiscal year, July 1 through June One-half of these taxes is due November 1, and one-half is due February 1. The first installment becomes delinquent on December 10, and the second allment becomes delinquent on April 10. One tax bill is mailed before November 1 to the owner of record. **You may be responsible for the current or oming property taxes even if you do not receive the tax bill.**

property which you acquired may be subject to a supplemental assessment in an amount to be determined by the _____ essor. For further information on your supplemental roll obligation, please call the _____ Assessor

PART I: TRANSFER INFORMATION (please answer all questions)

NO

☐ A. Is this transfer solely between husband and wife (addition of a spouse, death of a spouse, divorce settlement, etc.)?

☐ B. Is this transaction only a correction of the name(s) of the person(s) holding title to the property (for example, a name change upon marriage)? Please explain _____

☐ C. Is this document recorded to create, terminate, or reconvey a lender's interest in the property?

☐ D. Is this transaction recorded only as a requirement for financing purposes or to create, terminate, or reconvey a security interest (e.g., cosigner)? Please explain _____

☐ E. Is this document recorded to substitute a trustee of a trust, mortgage, or other similar document?

☐ F. Did this transfer result in the creation of a joint tenancy in which the seller (transferor) remains as one of the joint tenants?

☐ G. Does this transfer return property to the person who created the joint tenancy (original transferor)?

  H. Is this a transfer of property:

☐   1. to a revocable trust that may be revoked by the transferor and is for the benefit of the ☐ transferor ☐ transferor's spouse?

☐   2. to a trust that may be revoked by the Creator/Grantor who is also a joint tenant, and which names the other joint tenant(s) as beneficiaries when the Creator/Grantor dies?

☐   3. to an irrevocable trust for the benefit of the ☐ Creator/Grantor and/or ☐ Grantor's spouse?

☐   4. to an irrevocable trust from which the property reverts to the Creator/Grantor within 12 years?

☐ I. If this property is subject to a lease, is the remaining lease term 35 years or more including written options?

☐ *J. Is this a transfer between ☐ parent(s) and child(ren)?   ☐ or from grandparent(s) to grandchild(ren)?

☐ *K. Is this transaction to replace a principal residence by a person 55 years of age or older? Within the same county? ☐ Yes ☐ No

☐ *L. Is this transaction to replace a principal residence by a person who is severely disabled as defined by Revenue and Taxation Code section 69.5? Within the same county? ☐ Yes ☐ No

☐ M. Is this transfer solely between domestic partners currently registered with the California Secretary of State?

ou checked yes to J, K or L, you may qualify for a property tax reassessment exclusion, which may result in lower taxes on your property. **If you not file a claim, your property will be reassessed.**

se provide any other information that will help the Assessor to understand the nature of the transfer.

e conveying document constitutes an exclusion from a change in ownership as defined in section 62 of the Revenue and Taxation Code for any on other than those listed above, set forth the specific exclusions claimed: _____.

se answer all questions in each section. If a question does not apply, indicate with "N/A." Sign and date at bottom of second page.

PART II: OTHER TRANSFER INFORMATION

Date of transfer if other than recording date _____

Type of transfer (please check appropriate box):

☐ Purchase   ☐ Foreclosure   ☐ Gift   ☐ Trade or Exchange   ☐ Merger, Stock, or Partnership Acquisition

☐ Contract of Sale — Date of Contract _____

☐ Inheritance — Date of Death _____   ☐ Other (please explain): _____

☐ Creation of Lease   ☐ Assignment of a Lease   ☐ Termination of a Lease   ☐ Sale/Leaseback

☐ Date lease began

☐ Original term in years (including written options)

☐ Remaining term in years (including written options) _____

Monthly Payment _____   Remaining Term _____

Was only a partial interest in the property transferred? ☐ Yes ☐ No

If **yes**, indicate the percentage transferred _____%.

Please write Assessor's Parcel Number(s): _____

Please answer, to the best of your knowledge, all applicable questions, then sign and date. If a question does not apply, indicate with "N/A."

PART III: PURCHASE PRICE AND TERMS OF SALE

A. CASH DOWN PAYMENT OR value of trade or exchange *(excluding closing costs)*   Amount $ _____

B. FIRST DEED OF TRUST @ _____ % interest for _____ years. Pymts./Mo. = $ _____ (Prin. & Int. only)   Amount $ _____
- ☐ FHA (_____ Discount Points)
- ☐ Conventional
- ☐ VA (_____ Discount Points)
- ☐ Cal-Vet
- Balloon payment   ☐ Yes
- ☐ Fixed rate
- ☐ Variable rate
- ☐ All inclusive D.T. ($ _____ Wrapped)
- ☐ Loan carried by seller
- ☐ No   Due Date _____
- ☐ New loan
- ☐ Assumed existing loan balance
- ☐ Bank or savings & loan
- ☐ Finance company
- Amount $ _____

C. SECOND DEED OF TRUST @ _____ % interest for _____ years. Pymts./Mo. = $ _____ (Prin. & Int. only)   Amount $ _____
- ☐ Bank or savings & loan
- ☐ Loan carried by seller
- Balloon payment   ☐ Yes
- ☐ Fixed rate
- ☐ Variable rate
- ☐ No   Due Date _____
- ☐ New loan
- ☐ Assumed existing loan balance
- Amount $ _____

D. OTHER FINANCING: Is other financing involved not covered in (b) or (c) above?   ☐ Yes   ☐ No   Amount $ _____

Type _____ @ _____ % interest for _____ years. Pymts./Mo. = $ _____ (Prin. & Int. only)
- ☐ Bank or savings & loan
- ☐ Loan carried by seller
- Balloon payment   ☐ Yes
- ☐ Fixed rate
- ☐ Variable rate
- ☐ No   Due Date _____
- ☐ New loan
- ☐ Assumed existing loan balance
- Amount $ _____

E. WAS AN IMPROVEMENT BOND ASSUMED BY THE BUYER?   ☐ Yes   ☐ No   Outstanding Balance: Amount $ _____

F. TOTAL PURCHASE PRICE *(or acquisition price, if traded or exchanged, include real estate commission if paid)*

                              TOTAL ITEMS A THROUGH E $ _____

G. PROPERTY PURCHASED   ☐ Through a broker   ☐ Direct from seller   ☐ From a family member   ☐ Other *(please explain)*: _____

If purchased through a broker, provide broker's name and phone number: _____

Please explain any special terms, seller concessions, or financing and any other information that would help the Assessor understand the purchase price and terms of sale: _____

PART IV: PROPERTY INFORMATION

A. TYPE OF PROPERTY TRANSFERRED:
- ☐ Single-family residence
- ☐ Multiple-family residence (no. of units: _____)
- ☐ Commercial/Industrial
- ☐ Other (Description: i.e., timber, mineral, water rights, etc. _____)
- ☐ Agricultural
- ☐ Co-op/Own-your-own
- ☐ Condominium
- ☐ Timeshare
- ☐ Manufactured home
- ☐ Unimproved lot

B. IS THIS PROPERTY INTENDED AS YOUR PRINCIPAL RESIDENCE?   ☐ Yes   ☐ No

If **yes**, enter date of occupancy _____ / _____ , 20 _____ or intended occupancy _____ / _____ , 20 _____
                        (month)   *(day)*   *(year)*   *(month)*   *(day)*   *(year)*

C. IS PERSONAL/BUSINESS PROPERTY INCLUDED IN PURCHASE PRICE (i.e., furniture, farm equipment, machinery, etc.) (other than a manufactured home subject to local property tax)?   ☐ Yes   ☐ No

If **yes**, enter the value of the personal/business property included in the purchase price $ _____ *(Must attach itemized l*

D. IS A MANUFACTURED HOME INCLUDED IN PURCHASE PRICE?   ☐ Yes   ☐ No

If **yes**, how much of the purchase price is allocated to the manufactured home? _____

Is the manufactured home subject to local property tax?   ☐ Yes   ☐ No   What is the decal number? _____

E. DOES THE PROPERTY PRODUCE INCOME?   ☐ Yes   ☐ No   If **yes**, is the income from:
- ☐ Lease/Rent
- ☐ Contract
- ☐ Mineral rights
- ☐ Other *(please explain)*: _____

F. WHAT WAS THE CONDITION OF THE PROPERTY AT THE TIME OF SALE?
- ☐ Good
- ☐ Average
- ☐ Fair
- ☐ Poor

Please explain the physical condition of the property and provide any other information (such as restrictions, etc.) that would assist the Assessor in determin the value of the property: _____

CERTIFICATION

OWNERSHIP TYPE (☑)
- Proprietorship   —
- Partnership   —
- Corporation   —
- Other   —

I certify that the foregoing is true, correct and complete to the best of my knowledge and belief. This declaration is binding on each and every co-owner and/or partner.

NAME OF NEW OWNER/CORPORATE OFFICER   TITLE

SIGNATURE OF NEW OWNER/CORPORATE OFFICER   DATE
▶

NAME OF ENTITY *(typed or printed)*   FEDERAL EMPLOYER ID NUMBER

ADDRESS *(typed or printed)*   PHONE NUMBER (8 a.m. - 5 p.m.)   E-MAIL ADDRESS *(optional)*

(Note: The Assessor may contact you for additional information.)
If a document evidencing a change of ownership is presented to the recorder for recordation without the concurrent filing of a preliminary change of ownership report, the recorder may charge an additional recording fee of twenty dollars ($20).

Index

 **Keep Up to Date**

 Go to Nolo.com/newsletters to sign up for free newsletters and discounts on Nolo products.

- **Nolo Briefs.** Our monthly email newsletter with great deals and free information.

- **Nolo's Special Offer.** A monthly newsletter with the biggest Nolo discounts around.

- **BizBriefs.** Tips and discounts on Nolo products for business owners and managers.

- **Landlord's Quarterly.** Deals and free tips just for landlords and property managers, too.

 Don't forget to check for updates at **Nolo.com.** Under "Products," find this book and click "Legal Updates."

Let Us Hear From You

 Register your Nolo product and give us your feedback at Nolo.com/book-registration.

- Once you've registered, you qualify for technical support if you have any trouble with a download or CD (though most folks don't).

- We'll also drop you an email when a new edition of your book is released—and we'll send you a coupon for 15% off your next Nolo.com order!

PAE21

BUSINESS

Bankruptcy for Small Business Owners $39.99
Business Buyout Agreements (book with CD) $49.99
Business Loans From Family & Friends: How to Ask, Make It Legal & Make It Work $29.99
The California Nonprofit Corporation Kit (Binder w/CD) $69.99
California Workers' Comp $39.99
The Complete Guide to Buying a Business (book with CD) $24.99
The Complete Guide to Selling a Business (book with CD) $34.99
Consultant & Independent Contractor Agreements (book with CD) $34.99
Contracts: The Essential Business Desk Reference $39.99
The Corporate Records Handbook (book with CD) $69.99
The Craft Artist's Legal Guide (book with CD) $39.99
Create Your Own Employee Handbook (book with CD) $49.99
Dealing With Problem Employees $49.99
Deduct It! Lower Your Small Business Taxes $34.99
The eBay Business Start-Up Kit (book with CD) $24.99
Effective Fundraising for Nonprofits $24.99
The Employer's Legal Handbook $49.99
The Essential Guide to Family & Medical Leave (book with CD) $49.99
The Essential Guide to Federal Employment Laws $44.99
The Essential Guide to Handling Workplace Discrimination & Harassment $39.99
The Essential Guide to Workplace Investigations (book with CD) $44.99
Every Nonprofit's Guide to Publishing $29.99
Every Nonprofit's Tax Guide $34.99
Form a Partnership (book with CD) $39.99
Form Your Own Limited Liability Company (book with CD) $44.99
Healthy Employees, Healthy Business $29.99
Hiring Your First Employee: A Step-by-Step Guide $24.99
Home Business Tax Deductions: Keep What You Earn $34.99
How to Form a Nonprofit Corporation (book with CD)—National Edition $49.99
How to Form a Nonprofit Corporation in California (book with CD) $49.99
How to Form Your Own California Corporation (Binder w/CD) $39.99
How to Form Your Own California Corporation (book with CD) $39.99
How to Run a Thriving Business: Strategies for Success & Satisfaction $19.99
How to Write a Business Plan (book with CD) $34.99
Incorporate Your Business (book with CD)—National Edition $49.99
The Job Description Handbook (book with CD) $29.99
Legal Guide for Starting & Running a Small Business $39.99
Legal Forms for Starting & Running a Small Business (book with CD) $29.99

ORDER ANYTIME AT NOLO.COM
call 800-728-3555 or mail or fax the order form in this book

Prices subject to change.

Estate Planning for Blended Families.. $34.99
The Executor's Guide: Settling a Loved One's Estate or Trust................................. $39.99
Get It Together: Organize Your Records (book with CD) $21.99
How to Probate an Estate in California $49.99
Living Wills & Powers of Attorney for California.. $29.99
Make Your Own Living Trust (book with CD).. $39.99
The Mom's Guide to Wills & Estate Planning $21.99
Plan Your Estate $44.99
Quick & Legal Will Book (book with CD) $21.99
Quicken Willmaker Book & Software Kit.. $49.99
Special Needs Trusts: Protect Your Child's Financial Future (book with CD).......... $34.99
The Trustee's Legal Companion $39.99

FAMILY MATTERS

Building a Parenting Agreement That Works.. $24.99
The Complete IEP Guide: How to Advocate for Your Special Ed Child $34.99
Divorce After 50.. $29.99
Divorce & Money: How to Make the Best Financial Decisions During Divorce $34.99
Divorce Without Court: A Guide to Mediation & Collaborative Divorce $34.99
Every Dog's Legal Guide: A Must-Have for Your Owner $19.99
Get It Together: Organize Your Records So Your Family Won't Have To (book with CD) $21.99
The Guardianship Book for California $44.99
A Judge's Guide to Divorce (book with CD) $24.99
A Legal Guide for Lesbian & Gay Couples (book with CD) $34.99
Living Together: A Legal Guide for Unmarried Couples (book with CD)............... $34.99
Making It Legal: A Guide to Same-Sex Marriage, Domestic Partnerships & Civil Unions....... $29.99
Nannies & Au Pairs: Hiring In-Home Childcare.. $19.99
Nolo's Essential Guide to Divorce $24.99
Nolo's IEP Guide: Learning Disabilities $34.99
Parent Savvy.. $19.99
Prenuptial Agreements (book with CD) $34.99

GOING TO COURT

Beat Your Ticket: Go to Court & Win—National Edition $21.99
The Criminal Law Handbook: Know Your Rights, Survive the System.................... $39.99
Everybody's Guide to Small Claims Court—National Edition.................................. $29.99
Everybody's Guide to Small Claims Court in California $29.99
Fight Your Ticket & Win in California.. $29.99
How to Change Your Name in California (book with CD) $34.99
How to Win Your Personal Injury Claim.. $34.99
Legal Research: How to Find & Understand the Law.. $49.99
Nolo's Deposition Handbook... $34.99
Represent Yourself in Court: How to Prepare & Try a Winning Case $39.99
Win Your Lawsuit: A Judge's Guide to Representing Yourself in California Superior Court $39.99

HOMEOWNERS, LANDLORDS & TENANTS

IMMIGRATION

MONEY MATTERS

RETIREMENT & SENIORS

PATENTS AND COPYRIGHTS

SOFTWARE

CALL OR CHECK NOLO.COM FOR SPECIAL DISCOUNTS ON SOFTWARE!

Order Form

		Our "No-Hassle" Guarantee
Name	Name	Return anything you buy directly from Nolo for any reason and we'll cheerfully refund your purchase price. No ifs, ands or buts.
Billing Address	**Shipping** address	
City	City	
State, Zip	State, Zip	☐ Check here if you do not wish to receive mailings from other companies
Daytime Phone		
Email		

Item Code	Quantity	Item	Unit Price	Total Price

Method of payment		
	Subtotal	
☐ Check ☐ VISA	Add your local sales tax (California only)	
☐ American Express	Shipping: RUSH $13, Basic $7 (See below)	
☐ MasterCard	*"I bought 3, ship it to me FREE!"* (Ground shipping only)	
☐ Discover Card	TOTAL	

Account Number

Expiration Date

Signature

Shipping and Handling

Rush Delivery—Only $13

We'll ship any order to any street address in the U.S. by UPS 2nd Day Air* for only $13!

* Order by 9:30 AM Pacific Time and get your order in 2 business days. Orders placed after 9:30 AM Pacific Time will arrive in 3 business days. P.O. boxes and S.F. Bay Area use basic shipping. Alaska and Hawaii use 2nd Day Air or Priority Mail.

Basic Shipping—$7

Use for P.O. Boxes, Northern California and Ground Service.

Allow 1-2 weeks for delivery.

U.S. addresses only.

For faster service, use your credit card and our toll-free numbers

Call our customer service group Monday thru Friday 9am to 5pm PST

 Phone
1-800-728-3555

 Fax
1-800-645-0895

 Mail
Nolo
950 Parker Street
Berkeley, CA 94710

...OR ORDER 24 HOURS A DAY @ NOLO.COM

 **NOLO** *Online Legal Forms*

Nolo offers a large library of legal solutions and forms, created by Nolo's in-house legal staff. These reliable documents can be prepared in minutes.

Create a Document

- **Incorporation.** Incorporate your business in any state.
- **LLC Formations.** Gain asset protection and pass-through tax status in any state.
- **Wills.** Nolo has helped people make over 2 million wills. Is it time to make or revise yours?
- **Living Trust (avoid probate).** Plan now to save your family the cost, delays, and hassle of probate.
- **Trademark.** Protect the name of your business or product.
- **Provisional Patent.** Preserve your rights under patent law and claim "patent pending" status.

Download a Legal Form

Nolo.com has hundreds of top quality legal forms available for download—bills of sale, promissory notes, nondisclosure agreements, LLC operating agreements, corporate minutes, commercial lease and sublease, motor vehicle bill of sale, consignment agreements and many, many more.

Review Your Documents

Many lawyers in Nolo's consumer-friendly lawyer directory will review Nolo documents for a very reasonable fee. Check their detailed profiles at **Nolo.com/lawyers**.

Nolo's Bestselling Books

Plan Your Estate
$44.99

The Trustee's Legal Companion
A Step-by-Step Guide to Administering a Living Trust
$39.99

The Executor's Guide
Settling a Loved One's Estate or Trust
$39.99

Get It Together
Organize Your Records So Your Family Won't Have To
$24.99

Make Your Own Living Trust
$39.99

Every Nolo title is available in print and for download at Nolo.com.